THE ANUBIEION AT SAQQARA III

POTTERY FROM THE ARCHAIC TO THE THIRD INTERMEDIATE PERIOD

Dedicated to all who helped both during and after the excavation; to those whose expert advice I have sought over the years; and especially to David Aston, who did so much more work than most editors would undertake and my wife Janine Bourriau for her expertise and her support.

ONE HUNDRED AND THIRD EXCAVATION MEMOIR
EDITED BY DAVID ASTON

THE ANUBIEION AT SAQQARA III

POTTERY FROM THE ARCHAIC TO THE THIRD INTERMEDIATE PERIOD

BY

PETER FRENCH

ASSISTED BY JANINE BOURRIAU

EGYPT EXPLORATION SOCIETY
3 DOUGHTY MEWS, LONDON WC1N 2PG
2013

LONDON
SOLD AT
THE OFFICES OF THE EGYPT EXPLORATION SOCIETY
3 Doughty Mews, London WC1N 2PG
www.ees-shop.com

British Library Cataloguing-in-Publication Data
A catalogue for this book is available from the British Library
ISBN: 978-0-85698-214-9

PRINTED IN GREAT BRITAIN
Typeset by Julia Thorne, www.tetisheri.co.uk
Printed by Short Run Press, 25 Bittern Road, Sowton Industrial Estate, Exeter, Devon, EX2 7LW

Contents

List of Figures

Scale 1:3 except Fig. 80 inset (1:6) and Fig. 82 (1:4).

Abbreviations

General Abbreviations

To save space, the usual point (.) is omitted from the abbreviations OK/FIP/MK/SIP/NK/TIP, dia, max, min, qty and veg in the catalogue texts and tables.

Abb. Abbildung(en)
c. circa
cm centimetre(s)
dia, dias diameter(s)
ed., eds editor(s)
EES Egypt Exploration Society
e.g. for example (exempli gratia)
Fig., Figs Figure(s)
FIP First Intermediate Period
Grid ref Grid reference
max maximum
MK Middle Kingdom
min minimum
NK New Kingdom
No. Number
OK Old Kingdom
pers. comm. personal communication
Pl., pl., Pls, pls Plate(s)
Pt Ptolemy
qty quantity
ref reference
SCA Supreme Council for Antiquities
SIP Second Intermediate Period
Taf. Tafel(n)
TIP Third Intermediate Period
UP Unregistered Pottery
veg vegetable matter
Vol., Vols Volume(s)

Bibliographical Abbreviations

Ä&L Ägypten und Levante. Internationale Zeitschrift für ägyptische Archäologie und deren Nachbargebiete
ÄA Ägyptologische Abhandlungen
ACE The Australian Centre for Egyptology
AERA Ancient Egypt Research Associates, Inc.
ARCE American Research Center in Egypt
AV Archäologische Veröffentlichungen, Deutsches Archäologisches Institut, Abteilung Kairo
BAR British Archaeological Reports
BCÉ Bulletin de Liaison du Groupe International d'Étude de la Céramique Égyptienne
BIFAO Bulletin de l'Institut Français d'Archéologie Orientale
BSAE British School of Archaeology in Egypt
CdÉ Chronique d'Égypte

CCÉ Cahiers de la Céramique Égyptienne
CChEM Contributions to the Chronology of the Eastern Mediterranean
DAIK Deutsches Archäologisches Institut, Abteilung Kairo
DÖAW Denkschriften der Österreichischen Akademie der Wissenschaften
EEF Egypt Exploration Fund
EES Egypt Exploration Society
JEA The Journal of Egyptian Archaeology
MDAIK Mitteilungen des Deutschen Archäologischen Instituts, Abteilung Kairo
MMA Metropolitan Museum of Art
ÖAW Österreichische Akademie der Wissenschaften
OUP Oxford University Press
pers. comm. Personal communication
SAGA Studien zur Archäologie und Geschichte Altägyptens
SCA Supreme Council of Antiquities
SJE Scandinavian Joint Expedition to Sudanese Nubia
SMA Studies in Mediterranean Archaeology
UZK Untersuchungen der Zweigstelle Kairo des Österreichischen Archäologischen Institutes

Preface and Acknowledgements

By kind permission of the Supreme Council for Antiquities and its predecessor organisations, the pottery from the Egypt Exploration Society's Anubieion excavations was stored at the nearby excavation house. Until 1996, at times when the house was open and staffed for the use of members of the Memphis expedition, study of the material was financed by the EES. When this work was resumed in 2006 the first three seasons were financed by the EES, but thereafter the withdrawal of their annual grant from The British Academy made this impossible. Work from autumn 2007 to spring 2009 was financed by a direct grant from The British Academy and grants from The McDonald Institute for Archaeological Research, The Thomas Mulvey Egyptology Fund, The Foreign Travel Fund and Darwin College, all of the University of Cambridge, and from The Seven Pillars of Wisdom Trust Fund. To all these donors we owe a deep debt of gratitude. The spring season 2009 was partly, and autumn season 2009 wholly, financed by the participants.

Pamela Rose worked with the author during excavation seasons 1978 and 1979, and members of the Anubieion excavation team helped in the tedious task of marking sherds in all three seasons. Janine Bourriau identified the pottery fabrics and, from 2006, assisted in the sherd cataloguing. Elizabeth Bettles, Silke Grallert and Andrea Klug participated in the study work in 1994, Afaf Wahba Abd el-Salam in 2007 and Naglaa Ahmed Ali in 2008. Illustrators Andrew Boyce, Sabine Laemmel and William Schenck were responsible for the drawings for all three volumes; for the present volume most of the drawing is the work of Andrew Boyce. Most of the inking of the illustrations is similarly by Andrew Boyce, the remainder by William Schenck.

Many specialists were consulted in conjunction with the work on the present volume: for the Archaic Period, Renée Friedman and Christiana Köhler; for the Old Kingdom and First Intermediate Period, Bettina Bader, Mary Ownby, Dietrich Raue, Teodozja Rzeuska and Anna Wodzińska; for the Middle Kingdom, Susan Allen, Dorothea Arnold, David Aston, Bettina Bader and Carla Gallorini; for the New Kingdom, David Aston, Kathryn Eriksson, Vronwy Hankey(†), Colin Hope, Sabine Laemmel and Anne Seiler. To all of these we are most grateful for their helpful suggestions, in some cases made many years ago, and to Susan Allen and Dorothea Arnold for kind permission to refer to unpublished material from Lisht North and Dahshur. Thanks are due also to Jason Quinlan and Hilary McDonald for cover photographs of sherds from the Anubieion, and to Ancient Egypt Research Associates for facilitating this.

Much is owed to editor David Aston, who not only vetted the final text with its numerous parallels from other sites but, beyond the call of duty, took on the task of scanning the inked drawings and laying out the figures in accordance with the author's mock-ups. How much the catalogue leans upon his numerous Middle Kingdom and New Kingdom publications will also be evident.

The successive Directors for Saqqara and the Antiquities Inspectors assigned to the expedition have been unfailingly helpful, and we are grateful to our colleagues Usama el-Shimy and Sabry Farag for their patience and understanding during the final seasons. In the EES's Cairo office, Rawya Ismail and Faten Salah handled the necessary paperwork, and for the SCA Magdi el-Ghandour, and for the final season Mohammed Ismail, organised the work permits with great efficiency and friendliness.

Cover illustrations

Front cover, photographs courtesy of Ancient Egypt Research Associates:

- Upper left **644** (Fig 77a) Jason Quinlan
- Upper right **4** (Fig 1d) Hilary McDonald

- Centre — <u>**371**</u> Top, BPD/BHR/BPV **19** (Fig 49n) — Hilary McDonald
  Left, BCB **117** (Fig 49m)
  Right, ARP=ARS/AYY **2** (Not illustrated)

- Lower left — <u>**651**</u> (BGL **118**) (Fig 79a) — Jason Quinlan

- Lower right — <u>**774**</u> (UP 998 **9+10+11+34**) (Fig 94a) — Jason Quinlan

Back cover, photograph by the author:

- Area 14, looking west

CHAPTER 1

Introduction

Following a short season of survey in 1976, excavations by the Egypt Exploration Society in the temple of Anubis, known as the Anubieion, took place over three seasons in 1977–79, directed by Professor H. S. Smith. Two volumes have been published, dealing with the settlement and temple precinct and with the underlying cemeteries respectively (Jeffreys and Smith, 1988; Giddy, 1992). Architectural fragments and small finds were included in these volumes. One short chapter by the present author in the second volume attempted to use some of the pottery to date burials in the sand which (with one exception) were not themselves accompanied by any pottery vessels, but otherwise the study and publication of the ceramics and skeletal material were left for further volumes.

In 1977, in the expectation that a large quantity of sand would have to be moved in order to uncover the Ptolemaic temple buildings, the excavation employed some 100 workmen. The work started simultaneously in two unconnected parts of the site, designated Area 5 and Areas 12–14, supervised by a small number of staff. Areas 12–14 answered to the original expectations in that substantial stone structures, and some smaller ones of brick, were found buried under layers of sand containing brick rubble and dust, stone fragments and only a relatively small amount of pottery. Area 5, on the other hand, proved to contain multi-roomed buildings of brick and small stones, showing evidence of occupation and reconstruction over several centuries: in other words, a complex stratified domestic site built on sand.

In anticipation of a modest amount of pottery, only one ceramicist then of limited experience (the present author) was included in the excavation team, and would have sufficed had all work been in Areas 12–14. However Area 5 was, from the first, yielding some 10,000 sherds a day, 6 days a week. This material consisted not only of Ptolemaic and Roman pottery from the temple phase, but also of displaced sherds from previous use of the site, dating to all earlier periods from the Archaic onwards. Areas 12–14 produced fewer pre-Ptolemaic sherds but added Coptic re-occupation pottery for good measure. In these circumstances it was only possible to extract a small number of representative diagnostic sherds from each context. In practice certain easily recognised pieces such as 'Meidum' bowls, blue-painted sherds, torch stems and spindle-shaped Ptolemaic unguentaria were always among those saved, in the hope that they might provide fixed points from which the pottery sequence could be constructed. Some other forms, in particular sherds of large coarse vessels, are under-represented because storage space was limited. With the much-appreciated help of some other team members, the sherds retained were marked with their contexts and each was individually numbered.

In 1978 the number of workmen was reduced and a second ceramicist (Pamela Rose) shared the workload. However, since it was in the low-yielding Areas 12–14 that work was stopped, the flow of ceramics was less affected than might have been hoped, and it was only in 1979, when a further reduction in the number of workmen took place, that it was possible to make a more judicious selection of material. Over the three seasons some 32,000 sherds were retained for study, from a total of at least a million excavated. No statistically valid sample was produced as there was no time to count or weigh the sherds.

After the Anubieion excavations ceased, the focus of attention shifted to Memphis, where following seasons of survey (1981–83), excavations took place (1984–88/90) in an area of Middle and New Kingdom occupation. During these seasons, the author divided his time between participation in this work and study of the Anubieion pottery, though the principal ceramicist at Memphis from 1984 was Janine Bourriau and (the lessons of the Anubieion having been learnt) the work was on a more limited scale and more generously staffed. When the Memphis excavations came to an end and only study work was being undertaken there, it was possible to step up efforts on the Anubieion; thousands of sherds were catalogued and many hundreds drawn by illustrator Andrew Boyce. Then in 1996, when the present volume was approaching completion and considerable progress had been made on the two succeeding ones, the EES required all Anubieion work to be completed for publication in one further season. Since this was impossible, their permission to continue the work was withheld until, in

2005, the SCA advised that the Saqqara excavation house and pottery store were shortly to be demolished. Permission was then granted for work to be resumed. From 2006 to 2009 two study seasons by the present writer and Janine Bourriau took place each year, in some seasons aided by illustrators Sabine Laemmel and William Schenck. In 2009, with the kind permission of Dr Zahi Hawass, the SCA and Dr Mark Lehner, a selection of the material was transferred to the Giza laboratory of the Ancient Egypt Research Associates for use in field school teaching. Here the last of the Anubieion pottery, of the Coptic re-occupation, is currently being prepared for publication by the present author. The other pottery to be published was appropriately deposited for safe keeping in the Anubieion 'Dog Galleries', to be available for re-evaluation by others; the unpublished retained sherds, mostly non-diagnostics, were disposed of locally.

The present volume is now ready for press. Vols IV and V, on the ceramics of the Late Period cemetery and the temple phase, should follow shortly.

CHAPTER 2

Methodology

The Pottery Volumes

Due to the number of sherds excavated and their almost unparalleled date range, the Anubieion pottery will be published in three volumes. After much deliberation it was decided not to repeat detailed information already presented in Vols I and II, nor to reprint the site plans and matrices given there. To do so would make the present volume larger and more expensive and further delay its appearance.

This present volume deals with the pottery from the Archaic Period to the late New Kingdom/Third Intermediate Period. Most was out of its primary context, having been disturbed in ancient or modern times, so could not be dated from the site stratigraphy. The dating is therefore typologically based, i.e. it depends upon better stratified or more closely associated pottery from other sites, so the volume necessarily devotes much space to this parallel material. In these circumstances some mis-identifications are almost inevitable and are apologised for in advance. As far as possible the local Memphis/Saqqara area is referred to, but material from further afield is quoted where local parallels are scarce, and in particular the invaluable well recorded series from the eastern Delta site of Tell el-Dab'a/Qantir. At Memphis, references are for the most part to the EES excavations on Kom Rabia.

Of the participants in the preparation of the present volume, Janine Bourriau had extensive experience of the pottery of the Middle and New Kingdoms, but neither she nor the author had much knowledge of the earlier material; it was therefore a boon that in 2006 Teodozja Rzeuska published her invaluable work on Late Old Kingdom pottery from another part of the Saqqara necropolis. The typology she proposed paralleled in almost every respect the one already devised for the Anubieion, with the advantage that her sherds, which had evidently been less disturbed, were usually better preserved. (Conversely, many more of the Anubieion sherds are recorded as polished, so may have suffered less from weathering.) For the Old Kingdom–First Intermediate Period, as far as possible the present volume follows Rzeuska's order of presentation from restricted to unrestricted forms, ending with bread-moulds, stands, ringstands and miniature vessels, and the summary description at the head of each entry duplicates Rzeuska's, so that the two volumes can be used in tandem. However the various fabric classes, which Rzeuska subordinated to her shape typology, have been kept separate so that the order Niles, marls, mixed clay, imports and 'uncertain' could be applied consistently throughout the volume.

It is not possible for all descriptive terms to be consistent with those used in other publications, since these are themselves inconsistent. Thus in the Old Kingdom chapter the term 'high stand' is employed to be consistent with Rzeuska's volume, but the more commonly found 'offering stand' is preferred in the other chapters. 'Ringstand' has been used throughout in preference to 'potstand' for the ceramic rings used to support vessels which would not stand unaided; it is perhaps fortunate that none was published by Rzeuska.

The Middle and New Kingdom pottery is arranged otherwise, with the unrestricted forms before the restricted, so that it can more easily be compared with the Memphis volumes (Bourriau 2010; Bourriau and Gallorini in preparation; for the latter at the time of writing it was sometimes possible to provide detailed parallels, sometimes not) and most other recent publications. During the Middle Kingdom, within the Nile group and the marl group a number of forms were produced in more than one fabric, so the forms have been arranged in order and individual fabrics could not be kept together. During the New Kingdom, most forms were produced in only one fabric, so it has been possible to keep individual fabrics together and list them in numerical order, as was done for Memphis (Bourriau 2010).

A problem specific to the present volume concerns the divisions between the late Old Kingdom and the First Intermediate Period, and between the First Intermediate Period and the Middle Kingdom. In the Memphite area, in ceramic terms there is really no clear-cut division: many forms evolve gradually and when only rim-sherds are available it can be impossible to assign them to either one of the two eras. The problem is particularly acute in respect of the offering ('high') stands, but some other forms are almost equally difficult, and doubtless there will be anomalies. Almost as difficult to deal with is the status of the Second Intermediate Period, an era less easily identifiable in the Memphis/Saqqara region than in the Delta. The problem is summarised by Bourriau (2010, 33–35) but is basically one of dating the (gradual?) replacement of ceramics in the Middle Kingdom style by those derived from Upper and Middle Egyptian practice. Finally, there is some difficulty in differentiating the pottery of the later Ramessides from that of the Third Intermediate Period; fortunately there appears to be little pottery from the Anubieion at this time.

The Arrangement of the Pottery Catalogue

Each sherd or group of sherds is assigned a consecutive 'series' number in underlined bold, for ease of reference. These should not be thought of as 'Type' numbers, since many are no more than sub-types at best. At upper left there appears a number between 1 and 3500, with many gaps. These numbers do not constitute a meaningful series, i.e. sherds with adjacent numbers are not necessarily similar; they equate to the original field notes, and are included so that future researchers may check with the original notebooks and the boxes of sherds stored at Saqqara. Where two or more entries have later been amalgamated all the numbers appear, separated by a slash /. There follow a brief physical description where necessary, a ware description and a table of the sherds constituting the group. Unless specified otherwise, details of form and ware refer to all examples under that heading.

It is seldom the case that two sherds are completely identical in form, unless they derive from the same vessel (and not always then!). Nevertheless, it is not feasible to draw even every diagnostic sherd and the ceramicist must decide which are so similar as to be to all intents and purposes the same; it is then the better preserved example which will normally be illustrated. In the present volume, the second and subsequent sherds are described in the Figure column of a table as 'As' an illustrated one when they are effectively identical to it, or 'Similar to' it if there are differences too small to justify separate illustration. Where there is no entry in this column it may be assumed that the sherd is effectively identical to the sole illustration, or that the series (e.g. those of some miniature vessels) is so variable in minor respects that it is impracticable to specify an exact parallel. This method of description provides a guide to the frequency of occurrence and the distribution of sherds of a specific form. On occasion, a footnote beneath the table adds minor details or refers to an illustration in another part of the catalogue.

The table sets out the phase attributed by the excavators to the context in which the sherd(s) occurred, the context and in bold the individual running number of the sherd, the grid reference in Area 5 (or the Area if other than Area 5), one or more major dimension, occasionally an additional attribute, and reference to a figure if the sherd was drawn. Where there is more than one sherd in a table, the entries are as far as possible in phase and sub-phase order. The sub-phases are written as e.g. iva, not iv.a as in Vols I and II, to avoid widening the columns in the tables.

Where two or more sherds from the same context join, this is indicated by '+'. To save space, it has occasionally been possible to put two or more non-joining entries on a single line separated by commas. Grid references are abbreviated to two figures instead of the four employed in Vols I and II, since the last two would always be 00; very occasionally a level was also measured in by the excavators. The major dimension is most commonly the rim diameter, specified as 'top' or 'max(imum)' according to which was measured, as appropriate to the vessel form. In the final column, where not every sherd was drawn, it is usual but not invariable to specify which drawing the undrawn piece most closely resembles.

With rare exceptions, all pencil drawings were made and inked at full size. In the present volume all except Fig. 82 and the inset on Fig. 80 are reproduced at scale 1:3. Where the diameter could be determined only approximately, this is indicated by a small break either side of the central vertical line.

Collecting, Marking and Numbering the Sherds

The Anubieion excavation was organised along traditional lines. The Egyptian work force was divided into a relatively skilled minority, who removed sand and other material with *turiyas* (a type of mattock) and unskilled or junior workmen who carried this spoil away in baskets and deposited it nearby. They were organised by a *rais* (foreman) and supervised by members of the excavation team. Each deposit exposed was allocated a three-letter context code, commencing with AAA. When a change of context was recognised, the next code in the series was introduced. The workmen were instructed to remove the contexts one at a time, but the level of skill and degree of attention varied considerably and in practice much mixing took place, as was in any case inevitable in the mobile desert sands. When a structure or other feature appeared, a team member or the *rais* would intervene with a trowel, and as the excavation proceeded some of the most skilled and careful workmen were also entrusted with trowels. Sherds were placed in a basket labelled with the context code, a new basket being started when the previous one was full or a new context appeared. In theory every sherd was to be saved, but this involved a workman's bending down to pick it up, so in practice many were removed with the spoil, especially towards the end of the working day. Since pit voids and their fills were separately coded and features such as stone walls and coffins were included in the context series, not every coded context contained pottery.

Area 5 was laid out on a grid system, with pegs every 10 metres, and areas rather than trenches were excavated. Individual metre squares were measured in for small finds, but for the baskets of pottery larger areas, which were sometimes being excavated simultaneously by many workmen, were considered sufficiently distinctive provided the context was judged to be the same throughout. This explains why most entries cover more than one grid square. Four-figure grid numbers were to be measured in, to locate each object to the nearest centimetre, and are quoted in Vols I and II, but it proved impracticable to take the time to measure so accurately and in practice even the small finds were located only to a two-figure (100 × 100 cm) square, even though 00 was always appended. In the present volume only two-figure numbers are quoted; where two or three squares are involved the numbers are separated by 'slashes' (e.g. 02/03/04), but to save space longer series are designated by 'to' (e.g. 02 to 05). East–west measurements precede north–south. Grid extensions to the west and south, adjoining Area 5, are prefixed W and S respectively. In Areas 1 and 2, a theoretical extension of the Area 5 grid was sometimes quoted, sometimes not. In Areas 12–14 a separate grid was at first laid out but soon abandoned and is not quoted. No grid was applied in Area 26, a sondage in the adjacent Bubastieion enclosure.

The pottery retained from each newly-designated context or context-group was boxed or bagged separately and the context given the next number in a UP (Unregistered Pottery) series. In Areas 1, 2, 5 and 26 these UP numbers are not normally given in the present publication, since they would serve no purpose. Exceptions are the 'Surface' AAA groups, because new series of individual numbers were started for new areas of the site, and a few other necessary cases including UP 805, a box originated for important sherds from two unlabelled baskets, and AAD and BDP where a second series was originated in error. The UP numbers are more frequently required in Areas 12–14. This came about because many contexts in these Areas were described during excavation but the context designations were added only later, when several contexts differently described were amalgamated by the excavators.

Within each UP series, the individual sherds were numbered starting from 1. If sherds from a single context had already been individually numbered but were later found to join they are recorded here with a '+' sign. If joining sherds are from different contexts the fact is spelled out. Only a fraction of the approximately one million sherds excavated and by no means all the 32,000 set aside for study will be published; in general, body sherds will not be, unless of a distinctive or unusual ware or with some noteworthy characteristic.

A few complete vessels and some sherds were removed for 'registration' and could not be fully recorded; in at least one case the ceramicists did not see the vessel concerned at all. If it proves possible to examine these in the Saqqara magazines at a later date, they will be included in a subsequent volume.

A few sherds published in the present volume were included in Chapter 6 of Vol. II, in an attempt to date the New Kingdom and Late Dynastic burials before the bulk of the pottery had been studied. These sherds have been examined and re-described, and in some cases re-dated; details will be found in entries **198**, **491**, **513/44/87/89**, **639/65/68/69**.

Colour conventions

Painted decoration was a characteristic of Egyptian pottery only at certain periods, and in the present volume is almost entirely restricted to the New Kingdom. In the figures, black is represented by dark solid shading, red by diagonal hatching and blue by pale grey shading.

CHAPTER 3

The Predecessors of the Anubieion

A detailed history of the Anubieion, and of the previous use of the site, can be found in *The Anubieion at Saqqara*, Vol. I (Jeffreys and Smith 1988) and Vol. II (Giddy 1992) and will not be repeated here. Nevertheless, the reader without ready access to these volumes will need a brief explanation of the history illuminated, it is to be hoped, by the ceramic studies in the present volume and its intended successors.

The desert on the west side of the Nile at the apex of the Delta seems to have been little used prior to the foundation of the city of Memphis (*c*.3000 BC), the inhabitants of the valley preferring to bury their dead on the edge of the eastern desert, and in particular in the stretch from Maadi to Helwan. Soon after the unification of the country and the establishment of its new capital, however, the western desert began to be used for this purpose, large mastaba tombs of the First Dynasty being constructed on the cliff-top overlooking the valley (Emery 1961). Thus was inaugurated the intensive use of Saqqara and the adjacent desert strip to north and south as one enormous cemetery, a use which continued for more than three thousand years.

The area of desert eventually chosen for the site of the temple of the god Anubis lies only about one hundred metres south of the most southerly of Emery's 'Great Tombs'. Emery was obliged to excavate northwards from this point, because of the presence of the modern Inspectorate buildings astride the Anubieion's northern enclosure wall. That further tombs of this period, though perhaps on a more modest scale, lie (or lay) beneath the Anubieion is hinted at by the presence of a handful of sherds of the Archaic period (First and Second Dynasties, 2920–2649 BC).

A large stone mastaba tomb, uninscribed and therefore not closely dated but thought to be of the Third or early Fourth Dynasty (2649–*c*.2500 BC) (Vol. II, 2) stands beneath the Anubieion's southern enclosure wall as witness to a continued interest in this part of the necropolis, even if the spectacular complexes of Netjerykhet Djoser and Sekhemkhet were constructed some distance away to the south-west in an area already host to major royal tombs of the Second Dynasty. A modest representative series of contemporary pottery derives from the Anubieion excavations. Yet it was in the first years of the Sixth Dynasty that the major building activity on the site was undertaken, with the construction of the pyramid complex of Teti (2323–2291 BC). With the pyramid came the usual extensive mortuary temple and causeway down to the valley, and at the same time or shortly thereafter, subsidiary pyramids and, on the north side, the spectacular mastaba tombs of the great officials of his reign, among them the much-visited tombs of Mereruka and Kagemni. As was usual, a cult of the dead king continued for many years after his death, in the case of Teti throughout the remaining years of the Sixth Dynasty (2291–2152 BC) and on into the less well-regulated First Intermediate Period (2152–2040 BC). It is to these two-and-a-half centuries following the death of Teti that we ascribe most of the early sherds from the Anubieion, though they were out of their primary contexts so the find-spots cannot establish a sequence. We may speculate that enthusiasm for the cult would have been at a higher pitch in the earlier part of the period than the later, when more recent royal burials would have provided competition, and it may have ceased altogether in the turbulent later years. Furthermore, the majority of the Anubieion sherds are from fine vessels requiring both time and skill to make and to fire, and therefore calm and settled times. Most such vessels would be equally suitable to accompany burials and for cult use, to say nothing of possible appropriation for daily use by priests of the cult appreciative of the finer things of life.

The next indication of activity in the area consists of a pyramid perhaps of the Tenth Dynasty and burials of the Middle Kingdom (*c*.2100–after 1640 BC) (Vol. II, 2). Two tombs, of Sek-Weskhet and Sa-Hathor-Ipi, actually lie beneath the area under excavation (Vol. I, Fig. 28), with other Middle Kingdom tombs nearby. Many, probably all, are of nobles connected with the cult of Teti, which should have been either continued or revived in this period. Between them they represent both the early and the later Twelfth Dynasty (Silverman 2009, 47). To the time of these men, and probable successors in the service of the cult, belongs the relatively modest assemblage of pottery of known Middle Kingdom types, most notably the well-known marl clay storage jars and Nile clay hemispherical cups of the period, but including also a sprinkling of cult stand fragments and other forms. It has to be said, however, that not all of these sherds can be dated exactly, and some may really belong to the immediately preceding years. Be that as it may, there is sufficient evidence among the best-known types for activity at least during the settled and prosperous times of the Twelfth and early Thirteenth Dynasties. In the later years of the Middle Kingdom and during the Second Intermediate Period (1783–after 1640 BC) Egypt was again divided, though for most, if not all, of this time Saqqara and the Memphite area in general were under the reasonably stable rule of the Thirteenth Dynasty.

We are on firmer ground, figuratively speaking, with the establishment of the New Kingdom (*c.*1550–1070 BC). But if the figurative ground is firmer, the actual ground had become much less so. The Teti pyramid complex was founded on the bedrock, which alone would support its great weight. To reach this, the Sixth Dynasty workmen may have needed to shift a great deal of wind-blown sand, which they would have dumped somewhere close by and which the wind would at once have set about dispersing again. Then, in the years preceding the New Kingdom, it is clear that robbing of stone from the Teti pyramid complex was carried out on a considerable scale (Vol. II, 4), leading to the displacement of blocks, fragments and chippings in great quantities. One way and another, by the time of the New Kingdom a depth of deposit of up to four metres had accumulated above the level of the Old Kingdom surfaces. Through this unstable material and down into the bedrock were sunk New Kingdom tomb-shafts, five of which were seen to survive within the excavated area. Two further shafts may be surmised from the remains of two tomb chapels discovered within the same area (Vol. II, 3). These formed part of an extensive necropolis which appears to have continued in use until the Third Intermediate Period, though the latest burials may merely have utilised pre-existing tombs. Finally, and outside the scope of the present volume, further burials were deposited in the sand during the Late Dynastic Period. It was on top of all this evidence of previous activity that the Anubieion was founded.

CHAPTER 4

The Phases of the Anubieion and their Dating

The history of the Anubieion site was divided by the excavators into Phases o–vii, the complex Phase iv being sub-divided iv.a–d. The pre-temple phases were based on stratigraphy, inscriptions, reliefs and small finds, and for Phase ii a preliminary examination of the pottery (Vol. II, 2–7, 80–81, 88):

- Phase o: Old and Middle Kingdoms (and by implication First and Second Intermediate Periods)
- Phase i: New Kingdom and Third Intermediate Period
- Phase ii: Late Dynastic Period, probably 5th–4th century BC (6th–5th now preferred, see Aston, D. A. 2010, 107–15)

The temple and post-temple phases were based primarily upon stratigraphy and coins (Vol. 1, 24):

- Phase iii: mid-4th century BC: initial constructions
- Interlude
- Phase iv.a: 300/270 to 230 BC, beginning 'in the time of Ptolemy II' (*ibid.*, 50): stone rectangle
- Phase iv.a: 230 to 200 or 180 BC: compound wall
- Phase iv.b: 200 or 180 to 150 or 130 BC
- Phase ivc–d: 150 or 130 BC to AD 50 or later
- Abandonment
- Phase v: before AD 130 to before AD 347
- Phase vi: after AD 423 to before AD 774
- Phase vii: before AD 774 to present

Matrix N (Vol. I, Fig. 47), summarising the sequence in Areas 12–14, departs from this scheme, dividing Phase iv into early ('Ptol II?'), middle ('Ptol V') and late ('1st C AD') sub-phases. The subsequent phases are also not entirely in accord, Phase v being summarised as 4th–5th C (AD) and Phase vi as 6th–7th C, followed by a 'Mamluk' phase (on the strength of a coin of the early 15th century) and finally Phase vii 'Modern'. These descriptions are all adhered to, and for the present volume the discrepancies are not significant.

For the most part, the evidence of the pottery typology confirms in a very satisfactory manner the phases attributed to the hundreds of individual contexts in the matrices. Where this is not the case, however, a dilemma presents itself, which is found in every excavation but is acute at the Anubieion because of the nature of the ground. It is the difficult problem of distinguishing between residuality, the effect of natural forces, and over- or under-digging.

Residuality results from human or animal activity in the past. In cemeteries, tombs were frequently reused for later burials by those wishing to spare themselves the labour of constructing new ones. As a consequence, sherds from vessels which had held food offerings for the deceased of more than one generation are found jumbled inside or outside the tomb, more-or-less as the last robber left them. On settlement sites, people dig holes — little holes to stand a small pot in or to amuse a child; bigger holes to bury a dog or sink a water-jar; and enormous holes to seek stone blocks with which to build a house. That same dog may well have hollowed out a shelter as protection from the elements. Sherds thrown up are thereby mixed with the rubbish of later times, or may be incorporated intentionally or accidentally into mud bricks. All of this brings earlier sherds into later contexts. Some joining pairs have even been identified from widely-separated parts of the site and in contexts of differing date: instances in the present volume are **14** of the Archaic Period (where the two sherds are also very differently weathered), **118** of the Old Kingdom, and **627** and **737** of the New Kingdom. Perhaps it is not only today's young people who like to throw small objects about.

As for the natural forces, during the excavation season it could be observed that on windy days (of which there were many), sand was being blown along the surface from one area to another and, more significantly, was falling from the sides of the excavated squares into lower levels in a continuous rain, bringing with it sherds as these were progressively exposed and loosened. This brought later sherds into earlier contexts.

In the third case, where large numbers of workmen are employed and close supervision is not always possible, the distinction between one context and the next may not be accurately made; when those contexts consist of unstable layers of sand, the problem becomes acute. Sherds are then attributed to contexts which may be either too early or too late.

When a context is known to be of much earlier date, the attribution to it of some later sherds can be accounted for by under-digging or recent mixing, but when sherds of a given vessel type occur in contexts of adjacent date it can be impossible to tell whether such vessels were made over a long period or have been subject to one of the effects described.

In the great majority of cases the pottery confirms the dating based upon the stratigraphy and the non-ceramic inclusions, or its presence can be otherwise explained. There remain, however, contexts where the pottery typology is at odds with the suggested dating, which may be due to misinterpretation of the stratigraphy or a result of over- or under-digging. Examples from later phases will be discussed in the relevant volumes. In the present volume, some significant cases in Area 5 concern contexts dated to the Old and Middle Kingdom Phase o but which contain pottery of the New Kingdom and later. The number of sherds is best shown in tabulated form (omitting mixed contexts except where both are dated to Phase o):

Context (Matrix)	Archaic–FIP	Middle Kingdom	New Kingdom	Late Dynastic**	Ptolemaic–Early Roman**
AIL (A)	1	–	–	2	1
AMN (A)*	–	–	–	–	–
AQG (D)	11	10	37	46	3
BDY (A,B,F)	2	5	4	3	–
BEN (D)	1	2	9	5	–
BEO (D)	5	3	14	1	–
AQG/BEO	1	–	9	–	–

* One sherd recorded as retained but not catalogued at the time of compilation

** Some Late Dynastic and Ptolemaic–Early Roman sherds not yet catalogued at the time of compilation

This pattern requires explanation. The exceptional number of Late Dynastic sherds from AQG is mainly due to a group consisting of a small jar and a number of cups (for some of them, see Vol. II, 81–82 and Pl. 61). It seems evident that these vessels were in holes cut down into AQG; contexts dated to Phase ii should have been assigned for the voids and fills of these holes, but were not. In fact, the part of the site concerned (principally GR 11/12–S01/S02) shows mixing of AQG, AJY of Phase ii and AVB of Phase ivb, a matter to be dealt with at greater length in a subsequent volume. A larger jar of Phase ii, AQG **303**, was probably in another hole dug down into AQG in a different part of the site. The other Late Dynastic sherds, in AQG and elsewhere, can probably be interpreted as contamination due to under-digging, i.e. to the overlying contexts not being completely removed.

The predominance of New Kingdom sherds in Phase o, however, cannot be explained unless much of the sand interpreted as of Phase o must really have been from Phase i. Beyond this, it is not possible to tell for certain whether the excavations really impinged upon the Phase o levels at all. The evidence for genuine Middle Kingdom levels appears to be stronger than for levels of the Archaic–Old Kingdom, though the Marl C body sherds (three from AQG and one each from BDY and BEO) included in the Middle Kingdom figures might be earlier, when this fabric occurs but is much less common. The evidence is ultimately inconclusive, but serves as a salutary reminder that at this difficult site all contextual information, and especially that from the more extensive lower levels, has to be treated with caution.

Although many contexts in Area 5 were attributed in the matrices to the New Kingdom Phase i, none contained recorded sherds; unsurprisingly, since most were walls and shaft voids.

A few context designations include an = sign. This came about in two slightly different ways: in Area 5 extensive sand layers in two parts of the site, designated respectively ACE of Phase iii–iva and AJH of Phase iva, were excavated independently but eventually met up and at this point the layer was designated ACE=AJH; in Area 13 a number of contexts initially given individual designations were later considered to be identical, giving rise to contexts called ADS/ARP=ARS, ARP=ARS, ARP=ARS/AYY and ARU=ARZ, all of Phase iv (Pt II?).

In Areas 1 and 2, none of the contexts attributed to phases earlier than the Late Dynastic Phase ii contained pottery. Everything from these Areas in the present volume is therefore in secondary contexts.

In Areas 12–14, the only pottery-bearing context earlier than Phase ii is ADU of Area 13, attributed to Phase o and specified (Matrix N) as being of the Old Kingdom. The pottery from this context is discussed in Chapter 6.

Among later contexts one appears to be in error. A stone rubble wall AWG of Phase ivc in Area 5, from which are recorded three NK sherds of **513** and one of **648**, but at the time of writing nothing of later date, was labelled with GR 20/21/22–S03 to S06. However, Matrix C shows this wall as belonging to Rooms 3–4, which are too far north. Possibly compound wall AME/AMF was intended, or more probably the widespread early context AQG.

In the present volume at least, a piecemeal re-interpretation of the relatively few dubious contexts will not be otherwise attempted and the previously-assigned phases are retained in the tables.

CHAPTER 5

Fabrics and Wares from the Archaic Period to the Third Intermediate Period

Egyptian pottery fabrics are divided in a general way into marl clays and Nile clays. Marls are derived from ancient limestone rocks, while Niles are sedimentary alluvial deposits carried by the river and deposited by flooding in more recent times (Nordström and Bourriau 1993, 157–61). Marls and Niles can usually be distinguished with the naked eye or with a ×10 hand lens. Potters sometimes, but fortunately not commonly, mixed clays of both types; these mixtures are more difficult to classify because they are much more variable.

Sherds were classified and described from a fresh break parallel to the rim, as far as possible in bright sunlight, with the aid of a ×10 hand lens. In cases of difficulty or ambiguity a binocular microscope was employed at ×10, ×20 or ×30 magnification.

Wherever possible, the present volume employs the well-known and widely quoted 'Vienna System' of pottery fabric classification (Nordström and Bourriau 1993, 168–82). Both marl and Nile clay fabrics are catered for in this system and the same classification is applied uniformly irrespective of date, but mixed clay and imported vessels are not included, nor are some fabrics of the Archaic Period and a few others; the Ptolemaic and Roman Periods are also not catered for.

A parallel but more detailed system devised by Janine Bourriau in 1975 for the fabrics of vessels found at Saqqara, and developed subsequently by herself and others, is the 'Saqqara System'. For the Archaic Period and the Old Kingdom, Niles were given the prefix A and marls the prefix B; for the Middle Kingdom, they were respectively D and E; for the New Kingdom, respectively G and H. Vessels of later date have prefixes later in the alphabet, outside the scope of the present volume. Oasis and imported fabrics of every period received the prefix P. For the Vienna System it is necessary to specify Nile or marl clay, since each has its own alphabetical series A, B, C etc; no such prefix is needed for the Saqqara System, since each classification is unique.

In the present publication, for the Archaic Period and Old Kingdom only the Vienna System classification is used. Although these periods were catered for by the Saqqara System, it has seldom been applied and requires further work. For the Middle and New Kingdoms the Saqqara System classification is given first, followed in brackets by the Vienna System, e.g. H1 (Marl D). The Saqqara System 'P' series of oasis and imported fabrics has no Vienna System counterpart.

One series outside either system is a mixed clay(?) fabric of the Archaic Period and Old Kingdom, probably of local manufacture, classified by Teodozja Rzeuska (Rzeuska 2006, 35; Rzeuska 2009, 141–48) as P.60 (with a point after the P, which here stands for 'sample' in Polish). Samples of Rzeuska's material subjected to petrographic analysis proved (*ibid.*, 530–34) somewhat variable in their inclusions, but were originally reported as having a matrix of Nile silt, from which Rzeuska (*ibid.*, 43) considered them to be a natural mixture of Nile and marl clays from a secondary deposit so far unidentified. Re-examination confirmed the probable presence of both Nile and marl clays, but tended to stress the marl component, allowing the possibility that some Nile clay was added to the marl paste (Ownby 2009, 151). Among the Anubieion sherds a number of Archaic and Old Kingdom–First Intermediate Period sherds were originally classified as P.60, though recognised to be rather heterogeneous. Subsequent petrographic analysis of four of these Anubieion sherds (Ownby, unpublished) has shown that they might be more appropriately classified as Nile D (Nile clay with many limestone inclusions), a fabric not included in Rzeuska's catalogue. In these circumstances, the four Anubieion sherds analysed (**357/59/61/63**) have been catalogued in the present volume as Mixed Clay P.60/Nile D and the remainder (**14–20/358/60/63/65–71**) as Mixed Clay P.60/(Nile D?). There is much less consistency in the preparation and firing of fabrics in the Archaic Period and Old Kingdom, and analysis of more samples of this complex fabric or group of fabrics is greatly to be desired.

The fabrics of the Middle and New Kingdoms are described in detail in a recent volume on the pottery from

Memphis (Bourriau 2010, 17–32); previous publications (Bourriau and Nicholson 1992; Nordström and Bourriau 1993; Bourriau, Smith and Nicholson 2000; Bourriau, Smith and Serpico 2001) include colour plates of sherd sections. A summary description of all fabrics in the present volume follows, provided by Janine Bourriau; where relevant, the Vienna System classification for the Middle and New Kingdoms is followed by that of the Saqqara System. Fabrics not recorded at the Anubieion are omitted from the table, as are minor variations among the fabric headings such as 'coarse', and 'sandy', and borderline cases, specified in the catalogue as 'near' (e.g. B1 near B2).

Vienna System	Saqqara System (MK)	Saqqara System (NK)
Nile A	-	-
Nile B1	D1	G2
Nile B2	D4	G1
Nile C	D3	G4
Nile D	D7	G5
-	-	G6a
Marl A1	-	-
Marl A2	E7	H10
Marl A3	E4	-
Marl A4	-	H2, H4
Marl B	-	H8
Marl C1	E1A	-
Marl C2	E1C	-
Marl C Compact	E1B	-
Marl D	-	H1, H14
-	-	Mixed Clay Fabric 1

Nile Valley Fabrics

- Nile A (–/–) Texture very fine. Any naturally occurring coarse inclusions have been removed by soaking the clay and no plant remains are visible.
- Nile B1 (D1/G2) Texture fine. Vessel wall thin. Firing soft and even. Abundant well sorted fine sand. Plant remains seldom exceed 0.5 or mineral inclusions 0.05.
- Nile B2 (D4/G1) Texture medium. Much more varied in all respects than the preceding. More and larger plant remains, with voids on the surface. Can be similar to D3/G4 but technology usually less rough. The commonest fabric in both the Middle and New Kingdoms.
- Nile C (D3/G4) Texture coarse. Vessel wall thickness usually 1.0+. Sand, plant and mineral inclusions larger and more abundant than preceding. Plant and mineral voids on the surface. Some MK examples hand made, with irregular orientation of plant and other inclusions.
- Nile D (D7/G5) Texture medium. Limestone tempered. Always highly fired. Differs from Nile B2 and Nile C only in the many fine to coarse limestone particles dominating the break, which are often decomposed in the Middle and New Kingdoms but not in the Old Kingdom, when less highly fired. Can be difficult to distinguish from P.60.
- –/(–/G6a) Nile with marl slip (Bourriau, Smith and Nicholson 2000, 17–18). Texture medium. Break usually has a grey or black core. Clay carefully processed to be very dense and hard. Abundant sand inclusions but sparse plant remains and limestone.
- Marl A1 (–/–) Texture fine. Hard fabric dominated by abundant fine to medium limestone inclusions but not highly fired enough for these to decompose. Break usually pale red or red-brown but can have a pale grey core. Moderate quantity of fine sand and small quantity of plant remains.

- Marl A2 (E7/H10) Texture fine. Similar to preceding but limestone inclusions do not dominate. Dense and very hard, and more highly fired than Marl A1. All inclusions fine and evenly distributed.
- Marl A3 (E4/–) Texture very fine. Break usually greenish grey. Dense and hard, with conspicuous air pockets. Sparse fine sand and mineral inclusions.
- Marl A4 (–/H2 and H4) Texture fine. H2 has abundant poorly sorted sand, often a moderate quantity of plant remains, and some limestone. H4 has finer and better sorted inclusions.
- Marl B (–/H8) Texture medium. At highest firing, surface becomes white. It is gritty to the touch, due to abundant poorly sorted, angular sand and conspicuous red-brown and black, fine to medium rock inclusions.
- Marl C Compact (E1B/–) Texture fine. Conspicuous limestone. Distinct zones in the break. More carefully prepared and appears finer and denser than Marl C1 or C2, with less sand and finer inclusions.
- Marl C1 (E1A/–) Texture coarse. Conspicuous abundant decomposing limestone. Surfaces cream/white. Old Kingdom examples often have plant remains, suggesting some Nile clay was added. Used mainly for large vessels made by coiling or by shaping on a turntable. Manufacture may be local to Memphis/Fayum region.
- Marl C2 (E1C/–) Texture coarse. Differs from Marl C1 by having more sand temper.
- Marl D (–/H1 and H14) Texture coarse. Extremely hard. H14 has more abundant and poorly sorted sand and mineral inclusions than H1; both have abundant fine, medium and coarse limestone inclusions.
- Mixed Clay Fabric 1 (–/–) Previously H5 and G6b (Aston D.A. 1998, 68; Bourriau, Smith and Nicholson 2000, 17/19–24; Aston D.A. and B.G. Aston 2001, 52). Usually has a burnished marl slip. Specialised fabric for amphorae, storage jars and large shallow bowls but found used for other forms at the Anubieion. Differs from G6a in having more and poorly sorted mineral inclusions, especially limestone.
- Mixed Clay(?) P.60 Not in either system. See this chapter, page 19.

Oasis and Imported Fabrics

Classified according to the Saqqara System only, and at the Anubieion occur only in the New Kingdom.

- Oasis or Canaanite Fabric P23 Derived from a marl clay (Bourriau 2002, 114). Poorly mixed, dense and hard. Abundant, poorly sorted limestone and some mineral inclusions. Visual matches from Amarna and Thebes (Bourriau 2002, 114), suggest a wide distribution. For a note on the origin of this fabric, see the New Kingdom catalogue, entry **780–82**.
- Oasis Fabric P25 Derived from a clay containing kaolin (Bourriau 2002, 113–14). Dense and hard. The break shows distinctive cream, pink and brown or grey zones, though varying somewhat according to the firing. Poorly sorted sand and mineral inclusions. Abundant particles of decomposed limestone.
- Oasis Fabric P44 Derived from a marl clay (Bourriau 2002, 114). Dense and hard. The break often has a distinctive grey core. Sparse, poorly sorted sand. Abundant, poorly sorted mineral inclusions but fewer than in P23 and dominated by particles of decomposed limestone.
- 'Canaanite' Fabric P16 (Bourriau, Smith and Serpico 2001, 125–27.) Dense and extremely hard. Dominated by abundant, poorly sorted black and red-brown rock particles and decomposed limestone.
- 'Canaanite' Fabric P30 (Bourriau, Smith and Serpico 2001, 116–21.) Dense, but crumbly due to abundant fine sand and other mineral inclusions such as limestone and shell, all well sorted.
- 'Canaanite' Fabric P31 (Bourriau, Smith and Serpico 2001, 121–25.) Medium hard. Poorly sorted sand, limestone and shell inclusions. Can also contain sandstone cemented into a calcium/quartz mix ('kurkar').
- 'Canaanite' Fabric P33 (Bourriau, Smith and Serpico 2001, 132–38.) Dense and hard. Dominated by abundant, poorly sorted limestone inclusions and fragments of shell and microfossils. Distinctive abundant particles of unmixed red-brown clay.
- 'Canaanite' Fabric P40 (Bourriau, Smith and Serpico 2001, 127–32.) Dense and medium hard. Moderate quantity of fine to medium sand, limestone and red and black rock.
- Cypriot(e) Fabric P7 (Nordström and Bourriau 1993, 184.) Base Ring I and II. Dense and hard. Inclusions distinctly less fine than P32 (and P4), with sand, plant remains and limestone; these are more frequent and coarser in Base Ring II than I.
- Cypriot(e) Fabric P32 (Nordström and Bourriau 1993, 184.) Red Lustrous. Extremely fine and hard, distinguishing it from all other Egyptian and imported fabrics except P4 (below). Surfaces and break uniform pink/red. The only identifiable inclusions are very fine sand and tiny rock and mineral particles.

Described as Cypriot(e) (Eriksson 2007, 51–52) but may also have been made elsewhere.

- Mycenaean Fabric P4 (Nordström and Bourriau 1993, 184.) Texture very fine. Dense and hard. Sparse, very fine mineral inclusions and plant remains; often difficult to identify any inclusions at all. Mycenaean in this context is a blanket term for Late Helladic wares which may derive from other manufacturing centres, in addition to Mycenae itself.

Fabric classifications take into account only the clay mass and the inclusions within it, whether natural or added by the potter, so in the present volume as full a description as practicable of each sherd or group of sherds follows, adding details of surface treatment to arrive at a full ware description: *fabric* + *surface treatment* = *ware*. The details are usually given in the order: hardness, surface colour, break colour ('zones' are the strips of colour between the colours near the surface and the core); then frequency and size of sand, vegetable (plant) remains, limestone and other inclusions; finally slip, polish or burnish, and painted or other decoration. Hardness was judged by resistance to the making of a fresh break. Colours are described in general terms only: Munsell numbers are not given, as colours can vary greatly around or up and down a single pot and are also susceptible to different interpretation by different persons or even by the same person in different lights, as well as to changes due to preservation conditions. The *sorting* of the sand refers to the uniformity of grain size, well sorted being very uniform, poorly sorted very variable. Vegetable (plant) matter, usually grass or straw, is described on a scale of fine to coarse according to stem diameter and maximum length. Measurements of limestone and other inclusions are almost always in two dimensions only, the third not being visible in the break. Presence or absence of a slip is judged by eye, with or without magnification; usually this is unambiguous (a clearly demarcated slip edge is a great help) but on more severely weathered sherds it can be difficult to see. *Burnish* is used when separate strokes can be clearly distinguished, *polish* when they cannot, though in other publications the distinction is not always made; preservation in desert conditions can erode the surface but wind-blown sand can add a misleading sheen.

In respect of individual sherds, users of the present volume may notice some inconsistencies between the Vienna/Saqqara System classification and the detailed description which follows it. This is due to differences in perception on the part of Janine Bourriau, who classified the sherds by fabric, and the author, who described them, over a period of several years. It can come about because a different break was used, or the examination was carried out under different natural light conditions due to the season, weather or time of day, or even from so small a matter as the angle at which the sherd was held. Fabric and ware classification has greatly advanced in the last 30 or 40 years; its practitioners are well aware that more remains to be done, but that with such, almost infinitely variable, material a perfect solution is unlikely to be achieved.

It must be emphasised that sherds which show no surface treatment now may originally have had it; the vagaries of preservation in desert conditions are evident when two sherds of quite different appearance prove to join, as occasionally in the present volume.

CHAPTER 6

The Archaic to Third Intermediate Period Pottery in its Contexts

Surface contexts

The term 'topsoil' is inappropriate for an excavation carried out in desert sand. The uppermost deposits are therefore described as 'surface' contexts, though not all the sherds were visible before excavation and the excavators judged just where the underlying deposits began. In the early days of the first season, the author's wish to save some surface sherds for study was accepted and it was agreed to treat these contexts like all others; this was a fortunate decision, because in parts of the site wind erosion had removed most of the evidence for the final occupation but the sherds remained *in situ*.

The original pottery documentation employed the abbreviation 'TS' (for 'topsoil'), but in Areas 1 and 5 and most of Area 2 the surface contexts were later designated AAA, the form adopted in the present volume. Otherwise, BAA is the top level in the excavated tomb shaft AQT. CAA is the surface contexts in the Bubastieion Area 26. In part of Area 2 the surface was designated DAA (Matrix H) but in any case yielded no pottery. In Areas 12–14 the situation is more complicated, ARD being applied in Area 12, ABA in Area 13 and AKI and ANJ in different parts of Area 14. These designations are followed in the present volume.

It was often necessary to use more than one UP number for the surface contexts in an Area. In Area 1, the excavations largely took place along the inner face of the south enclosure wall (UP 484), but also east of the modern road (UP 608 'AAA East'). In Area 2, in addition to the general series (UP 445) a separate series (UP 998) was used for the excavations outside the south-west corner of the Anubieion, and two further series, 'Upper debris' (UP 582) and 'Lower debris' (UP 585), for deposits within the Anubieion precinct, close to the enclosure wall. Four further short series relate to specific spots: 'Test Pit' (UP 583), 'Topsoil West' (UP 587), 'Test trench in corner of lane wall and western north–south wall' (UP 589) and 'North of lane wall' (UP 734).

The extensive excavations in Area 5 benefited from the grid system laid down across the entire area (see Chapter 2), though as the work proceeded the original baselines for the southern and western edges came within the excavated area and the grid had to be extended into south (S) and west (W) squares. As the excavations were extended it became necessary to initiate new UP numbers for surface contexts in order to avoid the creation of a single enormously long run of sherd numbers. Each UP number was intended to relate to a restricted set of grid squares without overlapping any adjacent series, and on the whole this was achieved, though occasional minor overlaps do occur. A few errors will also be observed, where small numbers of sherds were added to the wrong series, but since the tables always specify the grid square(s) and surface material is always concerned, this is of little importance. It should be mentioned that the original set of squares 00 to 10-00 to 10 was not at first extended when the excavation was, the new work being referred to only as east, west, south-east etc of the grid, so when this was eventually extended the entire relevant set of squares had to be applied to pottery already recovered, resulting in rather imprecise locations. There are also several combinations of an immediately sub-surface context and one from the surface, e.g. BHM/AAA.

In Areas 12–14 the situation was somewhat different. The first few contexts excavated were allocated three-letter codes, but thereafter contexts were merely described as e.g. 'sand with brick rubble', so a new UP series had to be started whenever the description changed. After the excavation was completed, three-letter codes were retrospectively applied and frequently several series were seen to belong to the same code. Surface contexts ANJ, AKI (in combination with AKJ) and ABA (in various combinations) therefore occur several times and the UP numbers have to be given in brackets after the code. Some stratified contexts were similarly combined (see below, page 29).

Area 1 'East of the Modern Road'. Not described in Vols I and II

A small sounding, not shown on any matrix, was made on the east side of the unsurfaced modern road which led to the SCA inspectorate buildings and the modern village and separated Areas 12 to 14 from Area 5. No structures were located and the pottery was recorded as derived from surface context AAA East. Sherds of several phases were recovered; those in the present volume (four Old Kingdom/First Intermediate Period, three Middle Kingdom and four New Kingdom) are in secondary context, attesting only to pre-temple activity in the area. It may be observed that no fewer than three of the fourteen shabtis attributed to the Third Intermediate Period are from the surface context in this small area, described as Area 1, East or Area 1, East Trench; four more came from the surface elsewhere in Area 1 (Vol. II, 30–32).

Area 1 'Area of loose stones'. Vol. I, 19, 98

A short series of contexts BFA–BFD was recorded at grid 30-S25, i.e. a few metres to the north of the 'South Postern' series, which follows. It is referred to (Vol. I, 98) as belonging to Matrix J but does not actually appear there. Only BFB and BFD yielded pottery (BFD, one sherd only). BFB is said (*ibid.*, 19) to be an area of large loose stones perhaps from demolished buildings, and similarly (*ibid.*, 98) to be limestone rubble (no other contexts are described). The sherds are considered as probably from a surface deposit. The majority are from the temple phase, but no fewer than 11 are slipped and polished open forms of the Old Kingdom/First Intermediate Period, perhaps indicative of a specialised activity close by, whereas the Middle and New Kingdoms produced only one and three respectively. Even allowing for a biased selection process, this pattern is unusual.

Areas 1 and 2 'South Postern'. Vol. I, 18–19, 98; Figs 22 (Matrix J)–23/43–44

Matrix J shows the sequence connected with brick magazines a little to the north of the South Enclosure Wall, in the vicinity of the South Postern. Unlike much of Areas 1 and 2, it was treated as an outlier of the Area 5 grid. Apart from the surface context AAA, only DBC/E/N/U/X/W of Area 1 produced retained pottery, all from the small area 28 to 30-S30 to S32. The excavators dated most of the sequence to the temple phase, albeit with some uncertainty about its detailed chronology, so the sherds in the present volume were in secondary contexts. Nevertheless, the two beer jars and one bread mould of the Old Kingdom/First Intermediate Period, one Marl C body sherd of the same time or the Middle Kingdom and three sundry New Kingdom sherds (including one from a Canaanite jar) bear witness to use of this part of the cemetery in the 2000 years prior to the construction of the temples.

Area 2. 'SW Corner of Enclosure Wall'. Vol. I, 18, 98; Figs 20 (Matrix H)–21/45–46.

A small excavation was undertaken immediately outside the south-west corner of the Anubieion, to establish whether or not the Anubieion south enclosure wall and the north wall of the adjacent Bubastieion were joined at that point. It was rapidly established that this was not the case and the work was discontinued. Like the South Postern excavation but unlike much of Areas 1 and 2, the work was included in the Area 5 grid, almost all the pottery deriving from W06 to W11-S50 to S63.

The only pre-temple context containing sherds (five were retained) was the sand layer DAM, sealed in part by an avenue or platform of bricks but otherwise only by other loose fills. It is attributed to Phase ii; the two sherds in the present volume are of the Middle and New Kingdoms. The remaining contexts with pottery were DAG/H/J/Y of Phase iv, DAC/F of Phase v, and DAW, not on Matrix H but of Phase iv or later. The numerous sherds from the New Kingdom and earlier in these later deposits were probably thrown up when the foundation trench for the south wall was dug, and bear witness to intensive use of this part of the cemetery prior to the construction of the temples. A number are also of considerable interest in their own right, especially the blue-painted New Kingdom sherds, clearly from one or more disturbed burials of some distinction.

Area 2. 'Within South Enclosure Wall'. Vol. I, 19–20, 40–41, 98–100; Figs 24 (Matrix K)–26, 43–44

An excavation of limited scope was carried out alongside the South Enclosure Wall, following a *sondage* in 1976. No grid references were supplied with the pottery, but the excavated area can be seen on the plan (Vol. I, Figs 43–44) to lie within 06 to 26-S39 to S43. Although the level of the breakup of the Teti pyramid buildings was attained in 1976, no pottery from that season had been kept for study and the earliest levels reached in the 1977 season belonged to the temple phase. Many contexts of this phase, from the BQ- and BS- series, yielded sherds of the Archaic Period and the Old Kingdom/First Intermediate Period, as well as two Marl C body sherds from Old or Middle Kingdom vessels. There were fewer sherds than expected from the New Kingdom, considering that the (previously excavated) New Kingdom tomb of 'Akhpet was within the excavated area. Everything in the present volume must be held to be from secondary contexts. The number of Archaic–First Intermediate Period sherds indicates use of the area at that time; in particular, the presence of miniature vessels may point to the presence of one or more tombs. Shaft DCT, referred to (Vol. I, 19) as belonging to an Old or Middle Kingdom tomb, is thus probably of the Old Kingdom or the First Intermediate Period, perhaps one of several in the vicinity.

Although of little relevance to the pottery presented here, a number of contexts attributed to Phase ivc are, in the light of sherds they contained, more probably of Phase ivd. Pending completion of work on this material, the original Phase attributions have been retained for the present volume.

Area 5. New Kingdom Shaft Tomb. Vol. I, 100, Figs 6 (Matrix B) (shaft only), 30. Vol. II, 7–15 (including Figs 2–5), (finds, 25, 29, 31)

The one-and-only shaft tomb excavated is described in detail elsewhere (Vol. II, 7–15) and only a summary is given here. The shaft itself, designated AQT, led to five interconnecting chambers, three of which had originally formed a second tomb with its own shaft at the west end. Shaft and chambers had been robbed in ancient and/or modern times, and contained pottery of all the major periods from the Old Kingdom to the early Roman. The upper fill BAA of the shaft is assigned to Phases vi–vii, its lower fill (from which most of the pottery was derived) and all the chamber fills to Phase v, but it is possible to identify some of the pottery as probably part of the original tomb equipment, and thus of Phase i. The deposits are:

- Shaft fills BAA, BAC, BEI.
- Chamber 1 fills BJG, BJO
- Chamber 2 fill BNR
- Chamber 3 fills BNN, BNR
- Chamber 5 fills BNN, BNR, BNS.

The fills of the chambers were sub-divided into Sections A–K; these sub-divisions are duly specified, but the material had been so scattered within each chamber that they are of little significance.

Only three sherds of Old Kingdom/First Intermediate Period date were recorded from the chambers, all from fills BNN/BNR, i.e from the most westerly chambers 3 and 5, and specifically the west end (W06/W07) so they very probably entered through the shaft at that end. A Marl C body sherd (Old or Middle Kingdom) and a bread mould body sherd (Middle or New Kingdom) were found in Chamber 1 and may have entered via the eastern shaft AQT. There is thus almost no ceramic evidence for a date earlier than the New Kingdom for the tomb(s), and this is in accord with the other evidence (Vol. II, 11–12).

In contrast to the paucity of earlier material, many sherds of the New Kingdom are recorded from the chambers, almost all from the most easterly (and largest), Chamber 1. **590** 'beer jars' are very well represented, as are **525/36** bowls and **513** cups, consistent with a funerary assemblage. (A complete pot said (Vol. II, 10) to have been 'lying' in Chamber 3 seems not to have been shown to the ceramicists; the two concentric circles (Fig. 3) appear to represent a standing jar with a diameter of *c.*25 cm.)

As to the fills of shaft AQT, the upper ones (BAA, BAC) contained large numbers of Ptolemaic sherds derived from the temple phases and have nothing to say about the origin of the tomb: the Old Kingdom/First Intermediate Period and New Kingdom sherds from here (there are no Middle Kingdom) could have come from quite other contexts and fallen in at a much later date. The lowest fill (BEI) and the mixed fill (BAC/BEI) just above it are more helpful: of the Old Kingdom/First Intermediate Period there is only one **335** tiny plate (from BAC/BEI) and of the Middle Kingdom again nothing, confirming the evidence of the chambers. The 'pure' fill BEI at the bottom of the shaft contained another **590** 'beer jar', which could be restored with the aid of sherds from BAC/BEI to yield a good Ramesside profile; most of the other sherds from BAC/BEI were from further **590** 'beer jars' and **525/36** bowls.

There are three pairs of joining New Kingdom sherds, from each of which one sherd was found in a shaft fill and one in a tomb chamber. These are in **525** (two pairs) and **611**. They could have fallen from the surface while the shaft was partially open, or the one in the shaft may have been carried up to the surface and later fallen back in.

Although it cannot be proved, it is likely that the New Kingdom sherds from the chambers and lower shaft fills derive from burials in Chambers 1–5. The **590** 'beer jars' have been dated (Aston B.G. 2011, 217–21) as a series from the late Eighteenth Dynasty to the Twentieth, with the majority in the Nineteenth, though unfortunately the rims from the tomb were not individually drawn or described so cannot be more closely dated. A blue-painted sherd from shaft fill BAC/BEI **650** is probably Ramesside (Colin Hope, pers. comm.). The **513** cups should also not be earlier than Ramesside, and although the **525/36** bowls are difficult to date closely, they include a few with red rims, of which the same is true. It should also be borne in mind that none of the distinctive **483** black-rimmed bowls, which continue until about the reign of Tuthmosis III, was recorded from the tomb, the shaft, or anywhere else in Area 5, the sole example coming from Area 1 'East of the Modern Road'. Furthermore, the numerous blue-painted sherds from Area 5 are unlikely to be earlier than Amenhotep III and many are specifically Ramesside. The implication is either that the original burials in Chambers 1–5 were of the (later?) Eighteenth Dynasty and the tomb was reused (or continued in use) in the Ramesside period, or that the tomb was Ramesside from the outset. The only shabti from the tomb (Vol. II, 29) is dated only to the Eighteenth–Nineteenth Dynasty, which is in accord with these findings but adds nothing to them. Other tombs in the area lend weight to a Ramesside date (Vol. II, 4–5) but there is so much ceramic evidence of the Eighteenth Dynasty from Area 5 that their construction and original use was probably earlier.

The hypothesis that the chambers were reused in the Twenty-second or Twenty-third Dynasty (Vol. II, 13), perhaps based on a single shabti from the shaft fill (*ibid.*, 31), is difficult to prove or disprove on the ceramic evidence, since the pottery of this period differs little from its Ramesside predecessors and the material is so fragmentary.

Area 5 Other contexts. Vols I and II, *passim*

The excavation of this Area was the expedition's main concern in all three seasons, and eventually extended to more than 700 square metres. Phase o, ascribed to the Old and Middle Kingdoms (but see Chapter 4 and below), was reached in some parts of the site; Phase i, of the New Kingdom and Third Intermediate Period, was exposed much more widely. The stratigraphy is described in detail in Vols I and II and will not be repeated here.

Most of the Archaic sherds derive from Area 5, but only one is from a Phase o context, the others being from Late Dynastic and temple levels. All are thus in secondary contexts and most are likely to have been moved at least twice. Nor can any pattern be identified in the horizontal distribution, a fact emphasised by the wide separation of the two joining sherds in **14**. The Archaic sherds could have arrived as components in mud bricks, but since they are mostly of the First Dynasty and large mastaba tombs of that time are strung out in a north–south direction only a little further to the north, it is more likely that this early cemetery continued into the area later occupied by the Anubieion (see Areas 12–14, below).

Several contexts ascribed to Phase o yielded pottery, but because they belonged to a time when the structures built by Teti were being broken up, none of the sherds was in a primary context. Furthermore, the sherds included many of the New Kingdom and even a small number from later vessels. In the difficult excavation conditions at the Anubieion this is understandable but the reason needs to be considered. The contexts may really have been of the New Kingdom and were incorrectly dated, or they may have been 'under-dug', i.e. the workmen had not completely cleared the overlying contexts, or sherds may have fallen into the excavation from the trench sides: in most cases it is not possible to arrive at the reason. In any case, most of the Old Kingdom/First Intermediate Period pottery lay in later levels, so all in all it is best considered typologically, regardless of context. There is then seen to be little of the pre-Teti period in relation to the area excavated, and certainly proportionately less than in Areas 12–14 (see below). This may indicate that the cemetery of the Third and/or Fourth Dynasty followed the cliff edge and did not extend far to the west. In its turn, this may have influenced the positioning of the Teti pyramid.

The great majority of the Old Kingdom/First Intermediate Period sherds correspond to the material published by Teodozja Rzeuska, which she dates (2006, 383) from the reign of Teti onwards through the Seventh and Eighth

Dynasties. This span matches closely the history of the Anubieion site, where the pyramid of Teti himself and to its north the tombs of the great men of his time (Mereruka, Kagemni, Seshemnefer etc.) would not only have been lavishly provided with funerary pottery but were the centre of a funerary cult continuing for several centuries (Silverman 2000, 260), or if discontinued, revived in the late Eleventh or early Twelfth Dynasty (Willems 2008, 174–78). Here, among many tombs of the First Intermediate Period, stand those of the officials Ihy and Hetep, who served Teti's cult in the early years of the Twelfth Dynasty. Then, whether or not the builder of an unfinished pyramid on the east side was Merykare of the Tenth Dynasty (Vol. II, 2), with its own cult, there are certainly tombs of the Middle Kingdom beneath the causeway of Teti's pyramid. These belonged to Sekweskhet and Sahathoripy (Vol. II, Pl. 2; Silverman 2000, Fig. 10) and, with later modifications and extensions (Silverman 2000, 269–72), should attest to activity in the late Twelfth Dynasty and probably into the Thirteenth.

Although there is less pottery of the Middle Kingdom than of the preceding and succeeding periods, there is quite enough to confirm activity in both the Twelfth and Thirteenth Dynasties. However, little of it came from contexts of Phase o, and that little was mostly bread moulds. These might be thought to have been used by the priests rather than deposited in the tombs, but their presence in contexts associated with the destruction of the very monuments the priests were serving is difficult to explain and would require further excavation of these lower levels. Otherwise, Middle Kingdom pottery is liberally distributed in later contexts, with a good deal in those of Phase ii, and is clearly in secondary deposition throughout.

Many contexts were ascribed to the New Kingdom/Third Intermediate Period Phase i, but most were walls or shaft voids and even the four floors produced no ceramics. Much of the New Kingdom pottery lay, with much of the Middle Kingdom, in contexts ascribed to Phase ii of the Late Dynastic period, meaning one of three things: the contexts were really of the New Kingdom and were incorrectly dated; they were 'over-dug', i.e. the excavations had penetrated underlying contexts; or sherds from Middle and New Kingdom levels were redeposited in these contexts in the Late Dynastic period. Since most of these Late Dynastic contexts also produced Late Dynastic pottery (to be published in Vol. IV), the first explanation is excluded. Some 'over-digging' may have taken place, but what we appear to have is a major refurbishment of the area during the Late Dynastic period. This will be discussed at greater length in Vol. IV, but must have followed a time when pottery of the Middle and New Kingdoms was thrown out of the underground burial chambers of shaft tombs, and possibly in part from their above-ground tomb chapels, in the course of tomb-robbing and/or the demolition of the latter. The accompanying Late Dynastic pottery may then have derived from burials of that period deposited in the earlier burial chambers and shafts and soon to be disturbed in their turn.

Although the New Kingdom pottery must be regarded as in secondary contexts, it is nevertheless informative. The Anubieion did not produce any pottery indisputably of the Second Intermediate Period but this is difficult to identify in the Memphis region because of the continuing influence of the Middle Kingdom style until the conquest by the first Eighteenth Dynasty kings (Bourriau 2010, 4–5). There is then sufficient ceramic evidence to establish use of Area 5 in the early Eighteenth Dynasty. After this we have ceramics demonstrating intensive use of the area throughout the Eighteenth and Nineteenth Dynasties and probably into the later Ramesside period. The expedition uncovered shaft tombs and their chapels packed into the available space, probably as tightly as was practicable having regard to the likely spread of the underground chambers. Without further excavation they cannot be dated with confidence though the excavators believed many to be Ramesside (Vol. II, 7). It is certain that many burials of the Eighteenth Dynasty took place; these might, in theory, have reused Middle Kingdom tombs and their shafts, allowing the new construction to be wholly Ramesside, but it is at least equally likely that the first tombs were dug in the Eighteenth Dynasty and either Ramesside burials were made in their burial chambers and shafts or the digging of new tombs continued into the Ramesside period (see Chapter 10).

For the Third Intermediate Period there is little ceramic evidence and that inconclusive, due in part to the slow pace of stylistic development at this time. Fourteen shabtis are attributed to this period but half of them came from late contexts in the small Area 1 and only five from the whole of Area 5. It was common practice at this time to deposit coffins in earlier tombs and tomb shafts. Such unceremonious burials may never have had much, if any, accompanying pottery, though it is also possible that earlier excavators have failed to distinguish it from similar Ramesside material and not recorded it adequately (Aston D.A. 2009b, 317–48).

Areas 12–14. Vol. I, 43–51, Figs 47 (Matrix N)–58/62; Vol. II, 1–2, (finds, 17–22, 26–32)

These Areas lay to the east of the major excavation in Area 5, and at a slightly lower level as the ground slopes away towards the cliff edge. Area 12 was at the northern end of the excavation and was crossed by the

Serapieion (Serapeum) Way; Area 13 was the Lower and Area 14 the Upper Terrace. A grid was established in Area 13 in the first days of the excavation but soon abandoned and is not referred to in the present publication. Most of the deposits defined by the excavators consisted of sand with varying quantities of naturally occurring pebbles and of mud brick dust and rubble, so distinctions between them are less clear-cut and less significant than in other Areas. Areas 12–14 were the site of the main temple buildings, on which construction apparently began in the Twenty-sixth Dynasty or shortly thereafter (Vol I, 50), and of a village built on the temple ruins in the Christian (Coptic) period. The pottery associated with the construction and occupation phases lies outside the scope of the present volume and will be discussed subsequently.

Area 12 and the Serapieion (Serapeum) Way

The east–west route from the valley to the Serapieion lay through the Anubieion enclosure, and may already have existed in its original form when Phase iii of the temple was planned (Vol I, 53 and Fig. 52). It had to climb the steep scarp, which it achieved in Phase iii by means of a brick pavement. In Phase iv this was replaced by a set of stone staircases. The excavators recognised four phases of the Serapieion Way, of which the first, Way 1, was a brick ramp BWJ laid on clean sand. Way 2 appears to have been similar. Ways 3 and 4, constructed on top of Ways 1 and 2, proceeded by staircases with landings at each terrace (*ibid.*, 58 and Fig. 52).

Diagnostic sherds from the excavation of the Way were given group numbers from UP 1025 to UP 1048, but no contexts were designated until later and it was not always possible to reconcile the excavators' descriptions with these. It has thus often been necessary to retain the UP series numbers in the sherd tables, and for these no phase dating is available. For present purposes the matter is not important, since none of the sherds listed will have been in primary context, and their significance lies in their occurrence at this specific location rather than whether they lay under, in or above the various phases of the Way. Only a very few sherds from Area 12 were not from the Way.

The series numbers with the excavators' descriptions, and the context designations where known, are as follows:

UP	1025	**BWK**	Way 4.	Sand level underlying dark Level 3
	1026	**BWZ**		Level 1c. Brown-grey debris below chippings
	1027	**BWY**	Way 4	Level 3. Brown-grey debris and included chippings
	1028	**BWX**		Under steps 2 and 3. Mud rubble layer
	1029	**BWW**	Way 4	(Level) 3. Lower brown level
	1030	**BWR**		Level 1a. Brown brick debris under mortar
	1031	**Modern**	Way 3	Sand level over N(orth) spur wall
	1032	**BWQ**	Way 4	Level 4. In sand under mortar pavement of Way 3, Step 1, not sealed by it
	1033		Way 4	Level 1, Step 8
	1034			Structure 4. Within and immediately under top mortar bedding of Step 3
	1035		Way 3	Brown debris below mortar
	1036		Way 4	Level 1b. Chipping spread within Level 1, brown brick debris
	1037			Top 20 cm of Step 4
	1038			Among mud brick work N. of Ser Way stonework, N. of stone removed
	1039			Rubble 2
	1040	**BWL?**		From brickwork N. (of) and above Ser Way stonework
	1041	**BWZ?**		Brown debris under Way iii paving
	1042	**BXD?**		From surface of Lower Serapeum Way
	1043			Brick rubble overlying mortar bed on rising stone steps of Way 3
	1044		Way 4	(Level) 1. Brown level immediately below mortar bedding
	1045		Way 3	Level 1c
	1046			Sand level 1
	1047			Between Ser Way stone block and underlying brickwork
	1048		Way 4	(Level) 1. Brown level under mortar bedding

Although none of the construction work associated with the temple or the Way should be earlier than the Late Dynastic period, and no contexts in Area 12 were dated by the excavators as prior to the Late Dynastic Phase ii, the ceramic record points unambiguously to much earlier activity in the area. The sherds from Way contexts retained for study prove to be overwhelmingly of the Old Kingdom/First Intermediate Period. Of the diagnostic sherds (mostly rims), 36 are attributed to this period, with two of the Middle Kingdom and one of the New Kingdom; the Late Dynastic and Ptolemaic–early Roman periods are not represented at all. Of the 201 retained body sherds (not all of which are published), where there is a greater degree of uncertainty in the dating, 152 are certainly or probably Old Kingdom/First Intermediate Period, one probably Middle Kingdom, 22 certainly or probably New Kingdom and 11 certainly or probably Late Dynastic. The other 15 are of uncertain date. There is a similar pattern among the few Area 12 sherds not from Way contexts.

There are no Archaic sherds from Area 12 but this may be due to chance. About half of the Old Kingdom/First Intermediate Period sherds are from beer jars, some pre-dating the Teti pyramid, whereas most of the non-beer jar sherds are of the Sixth Dynasty and later. Activity in this part of the site throughout the Old Kingdom and First Intermediate Period is therefore certain. There is little evidence of the Middle Kingdom and not much more of the New Kingdom, when most is Ramesside; Area 12 is probably not a focus of funerary activity in these periods.

Areas 13 and 14

The only contexts in Areas 13 and 14 dated by the excavators as prior to the Late Dynastic Phase ii were ADI, ADO and ADU, all in Area 13 and all specified as of the Old Kingdom. ADO consisted of limestone blocks so had no ceramic content; sand level ADI featured only as the mixed context ADI/ADK, with a single sherd and that from a Koan amphora clearly from the Phase ii context ADK. Thus only ADU is both pottery-bearing and earlier than the Late Dynastic period, even though limestone and plaster fragments from tombs of the Old Kingdom or First Intermediate Period were recovered from later contexts in Areas 13 and (mostly) 14 (Vol. II, 17–20).

The ADU pottery kept for study was listed in three series; only later was it ascribed to a single context. These series were UP 122 (46 sherds), UP 330 (20 sherds) and UP 335 (seven sherds). The first two were reported as from the walls and fills of a brick mastaba tomb, most sherds from UP 122 being specified as from the NW, NE and SW segments; the divisions are retained in the present volume but it became clear that they had little significance. UP 335 was described only as being 'from low levels', so is less precisely located. The suggestion (Vol. I, 43) that the brick mastaba was an element in two rows of these continuing the line of the Early Dynastic cemetery to the north cannot be substantiated from the pottery but is to be taken seriously. Three of the small number of Anubieion Archaic Period sherds come from Areas 13/14, albeit from later contexts. Most of the pottery from ADU is authentically Old Kingdom/First Intermediate Period, little if any of it pre-Teti, with only a few contaminating sherds of later date (including Late Dynastic and Coptic). The brickwork does indeed appear to belong to a mastaba tomb, which the pottery indicates should belong to the reign of Teti or a little later.

There is also a great deal of Old Kingdom pottery from sand and brick-rubble layers ascribed to the Late Dynastic and (especially) to the temple period. It includes many beer jar fragments, a clear indication of Old Kingdom burials in the vicinity, and among the 'Meidum' bowls both Second to Fourth Dynasty examples with angular (carinated) shoulder and the later, round-shouldered type. The earlier material comes as no surprise, since a large stone mastaba tomb of this period lies under the south enclosure wall of the temple (Vol I, Fig. 59).

Although no contexts were ascribed to the Middle Kingdom, there was a good deal of pottery of this period in later deposits, almost all of it in Area 13. The sherds include several from characteristic Middle Kingdom Marl C jars, and Nile fabric beer jars and hemispherical bowls. The pottery supports the evidence of limestone relief fragments (Vol. II, 18–20) that Middle Kingdom tombs are to be expected in the vicinity, and extends the date of these, or of cults connected with them, through the second half of the Twelfth Dynasty and well into the Thirteenth.

Similarly, no contexts were ascribed to the New Kingdom but there were many sherds, again mostly from Area 13. They duplicate much of the repertoire found in Area 5 and add a few forms not represented there. Elite burials are indicated by three Canaanite jar fragments and sherds of small Mycenaean vessels. Although it is possible that the material derives from shaft tombs further to the west, it is more likely that there were New Kingdom tombs nearby, either shafts (new or reused) or possibly tombs cut horizontally into the rock face or vertically alongside it and now concealed by sand. Many limestone relief fragments were recovered (Vol. II, 20–27), almost all from Area 14, in unexplained contrast to the predominance of sherds from Area 13.

Area 26. Bubastieion. Vol I, 78–79.

Shallow soundings were made in 1976 and 1978 in the adjacent enclosure south of the Anubieion, designated Area 26 and almost certainly the Bubastieion. In 1978 contexts were assigned in a series from CAA onwards. Diagnostic sherds were recovered only from the surface contexts CAA and CAA North and from context CAL, the date of which is unknown. Ten sherds of the Old Kingdom/First Intermediate Period and four of the New Kingdom are catalogued, one of each from CAL, all others from CAA and CAA North. Although nothing useful can be deduced in detail, the pottery indicates that the area was in use at the same time as the Anubieion site, long before the construction of either temple.

CHAPTER 7

The Pottery of the Archaic Period

As Christiana Köhler points out (Köhler 1998, 15) in relation to a much larger body of material, at this time there is great variability between one vessel and another, and when only sherds are present it is difficult to find even two identical examples. Parallels with published material are therefore bound to be approximate, and the valued opinions of Christiana Köhler (CK) and Renée Friedman (RF) have been given the most weight. However, both stressed the problems inherent in the identification of single small sherds of this period and the provisional nature of their conclusions.

The Anubieion ceramic record includes nothing which need be attributed to the Predynastic Period. A few sherds could be of Naqada II or III but also of the early First Dynasty, and since mastaba tombs of high officials of that Dynasty are nearby, this date is to be preferred. Where the Anubieion sherds can be dated with a degree of precision, it is to the First Dynasty that they belong, and some specifically to the first half of that Dynasty. The Second Dynasty is not reliably attested.

Wheel-throwing using centrifugal force was not practised at this time. The sherds are usually too small to show whether the vessel was handmade or wheel assisted, though in some cases a wheel-assisted rim appears likely.

NILE CLAY FABRICS, 1–7

1 Jar with undercut rim

First Dynasty, probably first half (RF). There is a similar fragment, albeit in a marl fabric, from Buto (Köhler 1998, Taf. 53 [11]) though the context cannot be precisely dated.

657 **1** Fig. 1a

Handmade.

Unclassified Nile Clay. Fired hard. Surfaces dark brown, perhaps a slip. Break pale brown with thick grey core. Fairly plentiful fine well-sorted sand. Sparse fine veg to 0.2. More limestone than usual, to 0.1 and one piece 0.2. Possible slip on exterior, but weathered. Surfaces apparently polished, but perhaps sand-blasted.

Phase	Context & No.	Grid ref	Dia rim (top)	Fig
ii	AIY under Room 10 **157**	09 to 12-03/04	14	1a

2 Medium-sized to large globular jar

For a similar form of about the same size, though again made of marl clay, see another example from Buto (Köhler 1998, Taf. 52 [11]]). This is from a series of contexts extending up to the end of Naqada III; on this basis and bearing in mind its Saqqara provenance, **2** is perhaps most plausibly dated to the mid to late First Dynasty.

1434 **2** Fig. 1b

Possibly wheel assisted at the rim.

Nile C. Fired fairly hard. Surfaces weathered. Break pale brown with red zones and grey core. Plentiful poorly sorted sand including rounded grains. Plentiful fine and coarse veg to 1.3. Sparse limestone to 0.1. Small areas of thick red-brown slip survive on exterior and on top of rim. Polished where slip survives.

Phase	Context & No.	Grid ref	Dia rim (top)	Fig
ivd/v	ATY/AEK **3**	22/23-01/02	10.5	1b

3 Large jars

This rim form originates on large imported Predynastic jars (Hartung 2001, *inter alia* Taf. 31 [191]; Taf. 62 [407–11]), but the wares appear to be Egyptian. Although the sherds could have been brought in mud bricks, the most likely explanation is derivation from burials of the (early?) First Dynasty in the area.

645 3 Fig. 1c

Nile B1. Fired fairly hard. Surfaces concealed by slip. Break red-brown with red zones and grey core. Fairly plentiful fine well-sorted sand. Sparse fine veg to 0.2. Sparse limestone to 0.05. Pinkish red slip on both surfaces, thick except on interior below the minimum diameter. Both surfaces polished, except interior below this point.

Nile B2. Fired fairly hard, BHY **29** misfired and beginning to sinter. ASZ/ATB **23** surfaces red-brown where slip lost, BHY **29** grey where uncoated. Break, ASZ/ATB **23** red-brown with thin pink zones and grey core, BHY **29** grey all through. Fairly plentiful poorly sorted sand. ASZ/ATB **23** fairly plentiful fine veg to 0.2, BHY **29** none visible. Sparse limestone to 0.05. Slip on both surfaces, ASZ/ATB **23** exterior red, interior black from stacking in the kiln, BHY **29** partly red and partly grey. Both surfaces polished where slip survives.

Phase	Context & No.	Grid ref	Dia rim (top)	Fabric	Fig
iv (Pt II?)/iv (Pt II?)	ARP=ARS/AYY 5	Area 13	c.14	B1	1c
ivd/ivd	ASZ/ATB 23	06/07-05/06/07	c.13?	B2	As 1c
?	BHY 29	W01-21	?	B2	As 1c

4 Radial-burnished bowl

First Dynasty, probably first half (RF)

1408 4 Fig. 1d

Rim sherd of bowl, with only short length of surviving rim. Handmade.

Nile B2. Fired fairly soft. Surfaces brown where slip lost. Break brown with thick red core. Fairly plentiful poorly sorted sand. Fairly plentiful fine and coarse veg to 0.2. Sparse limestone to 0.05. Red-brown slip on both surfaces, though mostly weathered off exterior. Traces of burnish on exterior, probably but not certainly parallel to rim. On interior, strokes parallel to rim, each *c.*0.25 wide and close together; then strokes at an angle below them, as if radiating from centre of base. Surfaces visibly well smoothed where slip lost.

Phase	Context & No.	Grid ref	Dia rim (top)	Fig
vi/vi/vi	AEP/AEQ/AER **78**	02-04 to 07	*c.*20–25	1d

5 Bowl (or base of stand?)

The probable manufacture by hand indicates an early date. No parallel, as either bowl or stand, has been found in the OK or MK, but an Archaic bowl from Buto (Köhler 1998, Taf. 25 [6]) is similar in form and diameter (30), is coarsely tempered with both sand and straw, and is significantly recorded as orange-brown in the break; it differs chiefly in being uncoated.

1458 5 Fig. 1e

The profile is not the same all round, and it may be handmade.

Nile B2. Fired medium. Surfaces orange-brown where slip lost. Break orange-brown with pink zones and grey core. Fairly plentiful poorly sorted sand. Fairly plentiful fine and coarse veg to 0.6. Sparse limestone to 0.1. Red slip on both surfaces, thick on exterior. Not polished or burnished.

Phase	Context & No.	Grid ref	Max dia rim	Fig
iii/iva/ivb	BPU/BHR/BKN **5**	02/03-21/22	*c*.24	1e

6 Straight-walled plate or shallow bowl

Possibly as early as Naqada II (CK) though the simple direct rim is similar to that of many types, including a slipped and polished Fourth Dynasty form from Dahshur (Faltings 1989, Abb. 9e [A 52]).

2826 6 Fig. 1f

Handmade, with veg inclusions at various angles. The black colour appears to be intentional.

Nile B2. Fired fairly soft. Surfaces brown where slip lost. Break brown all through. Fairly plentiful poorly sorted sand. Fairly plentiful fine and coarse veg to 0.8. No visible limestone. Three orange mineral inclusions, each less than 0.1. Areas of slip survive on both surfaces, fired black. Polished or burnished where slip survives.

Phase	Context & No.	Grid ref	Dia rim (top)	Fig
ivc	BQF **6**	Area 2	? (20–30?)	1f

7 Body sherd from large jar with potmark

Not from the Anubieion, but found on the surface about 100 metres to the north, near the most southerly of the First Dynasty mastabas. Probably mid First Dynasty. The combination of a square, triangle or circle and another sign is common (e.g. Petrie 1953, Fig. XXII, Type 76F; Fig. XXIII Types 76L, 76N). It is very frequent in the Saqqara tomb of Hemaka (Emery 1938, Pls 38–41, *passim*), from which 7 may have come. The more complex sign is a combination of upright and inverted 'ka' hieroglyphs, sometimes used thus, or upright only, to contain a single hieroglyph (Kaplony 1963, Taf. 32 [99A, 101]; Taf. 66 [233/34], etc); it may be the name of Hemaka himself (Emery 1938, 63, Fig. 23; 64, Fig. 25).

The square is noted on a poorly contexted bread-mould from Buto (Köhler 1998, Taf. 46 [2]) and on a First Dynasty jar at Tarkhan (Petrie *et al.* 1913, Pl. XXX [30]). It recurs in the MK, at Kahun (Gallorini 2009, 134, Type 3.11.3 and Fig. 6 [6]) and at the Anubieion on **453**.

For a summary of all the potmarks in the present volume, see Appendix 1.

2895 7 Fig. 1l

Body sherd from a large jar, with incised pre-firing potmark consisting of a rectangle and a composite hieroglyph. No wheel-ribbing, but wipe-marks on both surfaces, horizontal if the hieroglyphs are upright. Curvature indicates the potmark was added just above the greatest diameter. Handmade.

Nile B2. Fired fairly hard. Exterior red-brown, interior pink. Break pinkish brown with grey core. Moderate qty poorly sorted sand. Moderate qty fine and coarse veg to 0.3. Sparse limestone, but pieces to 0.3. Uncoated. Not polished or burnished.

Phase.	Context & No.	Grid ref	Fig
vii	AAA (UP 8) **9**	Archaic Necropolis	11

MARL CLAY FABRICS, 8–13

Marl A1 is common from Naqada II to the OK. Marl A4 was originally recognised as occurring in the MK but more commonly in the NK (Nordström and Bourriau, 1993, 178). Marl C was also seen at first as a fabric of the MK (Arnold Do., 1981, 167) but occurrences in the Fourth Dynasty were soon suspected (Nordström and Bourriau, 1993, 180) and may occur at Buto in the Archaic Period (author, personal observation).

8 Pattern-burnished hole-mouth jar or incurved bowl

Probably First Dynasty (RF).

755 8 Fig. 1g

Handmade, but with an even thickness and fairly thin wall.

Unclassified fine marl. Fired fairly soft. Surfaces pink, exterior where slip lost. Break pale pink all through. Two accidental inclusions of identical purple stone, 0.2 and 0.2 × 0.3, and a very small third similar, project from interior surface, as does one piece of limestone 0.1. Otherwise, the only inclusions are extremely fine well-sorted sand and tiny particles of limestone, visible at ×40 magnification, and many tiny sparkling inclusions of an unknown material, not flat mica and probably not salt. Red slip on exterior and splash on interior. Pattern-burnished, in lattice pattern, on exterior only.

Phase	Context & No.	Grid ref	Dia rim (top)	Fig
o	BDY **32**	01/02/03-S07/S08	*c.*10–12	1g

9 Wide-mouthed jar

Early First Dynasty; perhaps Upper Egyptian (CK).

2214 9 Fig. 1h

Rim sherd, with changing profile even along the 5 cm preserved length. Horizontal ridges on exterior and interior, but shallow and irregular, and probably wholly handmade.

Marl A4. Fired fairly soft. White firing surfaces. Break pale pinkish brown with faint, diffuse, greenish core. Plentiful poorly sorted sand. Moderate qty fine and some coarse veg to 0.3. A few red and orange particles to 0.1, probably naturally occurring ochre. Sparse limestone to 0.05, and some tiny black rock particles. Surfaces smoothed but uncoated. Not polished or burnished. Partly discoloured grey, possibly from bad firing, more probably post-firing.

Phase	Context & No.	Grid ref	Dia rim (top)	Fig
ivc	BQI **157**	Area 2	*c.*14	1h

10–11 Jars with undercut rim

There is a reasonably close parallel to **10** from Elephantine (Raue 1999, Abb. 34 [6]), described as 'partly dry polished', which accords with the traces on **10**. This is also similar to **11**, but an even better match to this is another (*ibid.*, Abb. 36 [5]) described as 'wet-smoothed'. Both are in Marl A4, and dated to the later First Dynasty. However, a similar example to **11** from Giza (Nazlet el-Samman) in slipped and burnished Marl A1 (Hawass and Senussi 2008, 180 [H27]) is not very different and attributed to the Fourth Dynasty. See also **42**.

936 **10** Fig. 1i

Undercut, slightly irregular, rim. If the proposed date is correct it should be handmade, but this cannot be confirmed. Areas of brown staining (oil?) on the surfaces and in the break.

Marl A1. Fired medium. Surfaces red-brown. Break red-brown all through. Fairly plentiful fine well-sorted sand with a few larger grains. Small qty fine veg to 0.2. Fairly plentiful tiny limestone flecks, sparse to 0.1 and one piece 0.2. Possible traces of reddish (perhaps self-?) slip on rim, and of polish or burnish where slipped.

Phase	Context & No.	Grid ref	Dia rim (top)	Fig
ivd	ASY **30**	03 to 05-S04 to S06	11	1i

697 **11** Fig. 1j

Lower edge of rim not parallel to top: rim height varies from 1.4 to 1.8 along the preserved length of only 4.1. This may be from re-use of the neck as a ringstand after breaking, with which the pattern of wear just inside the rim would be consistent. Too worn to show whether handmade or wheel assisted.

Marl C1 (E1a). Misfired, brittle. Surfaces grey. Break grey with reddish-brown core. Plentiful poorly sorted sand. No visible veg. Very plentiful tiny limestone flecks, and sparse to 0.05. Exterior discoloured and weathered, interior uncoated, with very pale brown firing surface probably originally white. Not polished or burnished as preserved.

Phase	Context & No.	Grid ref	Dia rim (top)	Fig
ivb	AVB **40**	09-S01/S02/S03	*c* 10–12	1j

12 Base of small globular jar

First Dynasty (CK).

880 **12** Fig. 1k

Small flat base. Smoothed interior, scraping facets on exterior.

Marl A1. Fired medium. Surfaces pinkish orange, exterior where slip lost. Break pinkish orange with dark brown patches, which occur also on exterior and may be oil staining. Fairly plentiful fine well-sorted sand. No visible veg. Many tiny limestone flecks and sparse to 0.1, also one piece 0.2. Small areas of surviving red slip on exterior but not under base; interior smoothed, with wipe marks at various angles, and uncoated (but weathered). Polished where slip survives.

Phase	Context & No.	Grid ref	Dia base	Fig
vii	AAA (UP 23) **398**	10-06	2.5	1k

13 Slipped bowl with widely spaced horizontal burnish

Probably Archaic Period (CK) but cannot be dated more precisely. The unusually thin rim is seen again on a marl bowl with polished red slip from Buto (Köhler 1998, Taf. 55 [1]), of similar size though drawn with a shallower stance; this is attributed to Naqada III so may best be interpreted as a forerunner of **13**.

2022 **13** Fig. 1m

Little evidence of vertical curvature but widening towards the break. Probably handmade.

Marl A4. Fired fairly soft to medium. Exterior concealed by slip; interior greenish white. Break pale green all through. Fairly plentiful poorly sorted sand. Moderate qty fine veg to 0.3. Sparse red mineral inclusions to 0.1, and some tiny black rock particles. Red-brown slip on exterior, taken just over the rim to a straight edge 0.2 down; interior uncoated. Two shallow horizontal lines of burnish on exterior.

Phase	Context & No.	Grid ref	Dia rim (top)	Fig
ivd	BCR **2**	17/18-07/08	*c.*15 (?)	1m

MIXED CLAY FABRIC, 14–20

For discussion of this fabric, see page 19.

14 Small dish or lid

First or Second Dynasty (CK).

2216 **14** Fig. 1n

Two joining fragments of a small, crudely made dish (or lid) from widely separated contexts; the two are very differently weathered, so the object was anciently broken. The rim appears to be wheel assisted. AGD **29** has some blotchy discolouration of the surfaces from an adhesion subsequently lost.

Mixed Clay P.60/(Nile D?). Fired fairly soft. Surfaces (of AVZ **10**) are firing surfaces, white near the rim, otherwise pale red-brown where another object was stacked on top in the kiln. Break pale red-brown all through. Fairly plentiful poorly sorted sand. Sparse fine veg to 0.3. Many tiny limestone flecks to 0.1, white rather than the usual yellow, due to a low firing temperature. Surfaces wet-smoothed, uncoated. Not polished or burnished.

Phase	Context & No.	Grid ref	Dia rim (top)	Fig
ivb–c	AVZ **10***	19-01/02	10	1n
ivd	AGD **29***	05/06-01/02/03	10	1n

* Join

15 Small shallow bowl

Appears to be a version of the small bowl of the Archaic Period, similar to one from Tarkhan (Petrie 1914, Fig. XXVIII [14t,u]. An example (dia 16) from Buto, with a thinner rim and no string-marks (Faltings 2000, Abb. 7 [17]), is in Nile clay (as usual in the Delta) but again red slipped and polished.

2892 **15** Fig. 1o

Upper part of a small bowl, preserved just far enough down to show the in-turn to a (probably flat) base. The wall is quite thick for the size of vessel. The sharpness of the rim may indicate wheel-assistance there, but the jumbled inclusions show it was probably otherwise handmade.

Mixed Clay P.60/(Nile D?). Fired fairly soft. Surfaces greenish cream where slip lost. Break pale brown with thin greenish cream zones near surfaces. Fairly plentiful poorly sorted sand. Small qty fine only veg to 0.3. Moderate qty tiny limestone flecks, and sparse to 0.05 with one piece 0.1. Traces of red slip on all surfaces: probable on exterior, almost certain on interior and top of rim. Traces of polish or burnish where slip survives.

Phase	Context & No.	Grid ref	Dia rim (top)	Fig
iva	BGD **5**	06/07/08-01/02	11–14	1o

16–18 Radial-burnished bowls

'Tableware' of the First Dynasty (RF). The clay is well mixed, in spite of the nodules in **16**, which is slightly coarser and more highly fired than **18**. A similar series of bowls (dias up to 32) with direct rim as **16** and **18**, including some described as in marl clay, is published from Buto (Faltings 2000, Abb. 6); most have horizontal burnish near the rim and radial burnish below. The five bases included are all flat, as **17**, and of about the same diameter. See also a rim (dia 16) from Mendes (Friedman 1992, Fig. 1d).

The small Anubieion rims may have been drawn too upright.

2044 **16** Fig. 2a

Mixed Clay P.60/(Nile D?). Fired medium, rather misfired, brittle. Surfaces pale brown where slip lost. Break pale brown with thick dark brown core. Fairly plentiful fine well-sorted sand with a few larger grains. Moderate qty fine veg to 0.2. Plentiful tiny limestone flecks and sparse to 0.1, some pieces exploded due to the firing temperature. A few reddish brown mineral inclusions to 0.05. Some nodules of poorly mixed clay to 0.05. Brown slip, fired dark on exterior, reddish brown on interior. Both surfaces burnished with narrow horizontal bands, so close as sometimes to run together.

Phase	Context & No.	Grid ref	Dia rim (top)	Fig
iva	BHR **165**	01-22/23	*c.*30–35	2a

2822 **17** Fig. 2b

Part of the base of a bowl, lacking the centre. Smoothing marks on the underside follow the rounded edge.

Mixed Clay P.60/(Nile D?). Fired fairly hard. Surfaces pale red-brown where slip lost. Break pale brown shading to an ill-defined greenish grey core. Small qty very fine sand and a few larger smooth translucent grains. Small qty fine veg to 0.2. Sparse limestone to 0.05 but no flecks visible. Tiny red and dark mineral fragments visible at ×40 magnification. Red slip on all surfaces, thicker on interior than exterior. Radiating burnish on interior, the strokes continuous between wall and base. Traces of lighter overall polish on exterior, including underside.

Phase	Context & No.	Grid ref	Dia base	Fig
ii	BDX **47**	03/04-07	*c.*8	2b

2042 **18** Fig. 2c

Mixed Clay P.60/(Nile D?). Fired fairly soft. Surfaces concealed by slip. Break pale brown all through. Clay very dense. Fairly plentiful fine and medium well-sorted sand. Moderate qty fine veg to 0.2. At ×40 magnification, a small number of tiny black mineral inclusions not visible at ×10. Sparse limestone to 0.05. Slipped: exterior red-brown, interior brown; areas compacted by burnish show darkest. On exterior, thin, perfunctory horizontal burnish strokes On interior, more strokes but some areas are not covered. Strokes are wide (to 0.3) but shallow: contrast **16**.

Phase	Context & No.	Grid ref	Dia rim (top)	Fig
vi/vi	AHC/AMJ **3**	22 to 26-08/09/10	*c*.30(?)	2c

19 Deep bowl

Archaic Period(?). An example (dia top 17) from Buto, with the rim divided even more deeply almost into rim and flange (Faltings 2000, Abb.7 [11]), is in Nile clay (as usual in the Delta), again red slipped but only smoothed.

1424 **19** Fig. 2d

The groove in the flange may be from string-tying before firing. Crisp modelling indicates wheel-assistance.

Mixed Clay P.60/(Nile D?). Fired fairly soft to medium. Surfaces pale orange-brown where uncoated or slip lost. Break pale red-brown with thick, diffuse pale pink core. Fairly plentiful fine sand with a few larger grains. Moderate qty fine veg to 0.3. Many tiny limestone flecks, and sparse to 0.1. Traces of red slip on exterior, near top of rim. Polished or burnished where slip survives.

Phase	Context & No.	Grid ref	Dia rim (top)	Fig
vii	AAA (UP 588) **568**	W01/01-28/29/30	*c*.19	2d

20 Ledge-rim bowl (or ringstand?)

Naqada II to first half of First Dynasty (RF). Fabric rather coarse for a bowl, but for one (max dia 20) of similar Type in coarse, white coated Nile clay, see an example from Buto (Faltings 2000, Abb. 7 [10]).

2112 **20** Fig. 2e

Rim variable in form along its 3.5 cm length. Faint scraping marks on exterior, at 45 degrees to rim. Surfaces uneven; clearly handmade.

Mixed Clay P.60/(Nile D?). Fired fairly soft. Surfaces brown, but burnt grey except lower part of exterior. Break brown all through. Fairly plentiful poorly sorted sand. Moderate qty mostly fine veg to 0.3. Several voids to 0.4 × 0.2, from seeds or exploded limestone. Surfaces fairly smooth. Probably uncoated. Not polished or burnished.

Phase	Context & No.	Grid ref	Dia rim (top)	Fig
?	ANS (UP 1009) **11**	Area 14	*c*.17	2e

IMPORTED FABRIC—CANAANITE/PALESTINIAN, 21

21 Canaanite/Palestinian jar with short, curved neck.

Archaic Period(?). There is a similar but not identical imported jar from Buto dated to Naqada IIc–IId1 (Köhler 1992, Fig. 6 [2]), and some similarity may be observed to Egyptian-made jars of about the same time from Hierakonpolis (Adams and Friedman 1992, Fig. 8a/c).

828 <u>21</u> Fig. 2f

Jar rim. Smooth, tightly angled curve to interior of very short neck, broken only by a shallow groove near the rim. Sharp angle at edge of rim and low ridge at base of neck suggest wheel-assistance, although latter is discontinuous. Traces of black adhesions on interior, but above as well as below narrowest point, so more probably mummification material than contents (unless the same).

<u>Import.</u> Surfaces pale yellowish brown. Break pale yellowish brown all through. Plentiful angular grey and white inclusions, and some smoother red, mostly to 0.05 but a few to 0.1. No visible veg. No visible limestone. Probable self-slip on exterior, and interior down to narrowest point only. Not polished or burnished.

Phase	Context & No.	Grid ref	Max dia rim	Fig
iv (Pt V)	AZO (UP 318) **11**	Area 13	14	2f

UNCERTAIN FABRIC, 22

<u>22</u> Deep bowl of uncertain (imported?) fabric

Probably a deep bowl of the Archaic Period or early OK. Weathering and string-tying(?) have blurred the outline, but it somewhat resembles an example (dia top also 12) from Buto (Faltings 2000, Abb. 7 [12]) with a concave exterior to the rim, uncoated and only smoothed, as well as a slightly larger bowl from Buto (Köhler 1998, Taf. 29 [5]) from a pit context of around the end of the Archaic Period.

1410 <u>22</u> Fig. 2g

Weathered rim sherd from a thick-walled vessel. The deep grooves are probably from string-tying.

<u>Import(?).</u> Firing not recorded. Firing(?) surfaces yellow-brown. Break yellow-brown all through. Plentiful fine well-sorted sand with a few larger grains. No visible veg. Sparse angular grey rock particles. Sparse limestone to 0.1 and one streak 0.3 × 0.1. Possibly self-slipped but no coloured slip. Not polished or burnished.

Phase	Context & No.	Grid ref	Dia rim (top)	Fig
ivb–c	BGW **354**	15 to 18-03/04/05	12	2g

CHAPTER 8

The Pottery of the Old Kingdom and the First Intermediate Period

For Old Kingdom activity prior to the construction of the pyramid of Teti, which dominates the site, there is meagre but sufficient evidence. It consists principally of beer jars, 'Meidum' bowls in Nile clay, marl clay and mixed clay, and lids or shallow bowls with an internal ledge. Both the Third and the Fourth Dynasty may be represented. It can be argued that such sherds could derive from the dissolution of mud bricks manufactured much later; while impossible to refute, this explanation is unnecessary, since a large stone mastaba tomb of the period underlies the south enclosure wall of the temple.

That most of the early pottery from the Anubieion was in some way related to the early Sixth Dynasty pyramid of Teti was recognised from the outset, and the parallel series published by Teodozja Rzeuska (2006), from another part of the Saqqara necropolis but of the same period, served only as welcome confirmation. How much was originally in the king's pyramid and its subsidiaries, how much in the large mastaba tombs of his major officials or in the smaller tombs that clustered around them, and how much came originally from his cult, which probably continued to be practised until the late First Intermediate Period if not later, it is impossible to know.

Wheel-throwing using centrifugal force was still not normally practised at this time, though wheel assistance is sometimes in evidence. The division between the First Intermediate Period and Middle Kingdom material is to some extent artificial. Although some forms may belong specifically to the Twelfth or Thirteenth Dynasty, others, most particularly the stands, are difficult to place. That polished slips become rare in the Middle Kingdom serves as a guide, but they are unlikely to have fallen out of favour overnight. Similarly, although the Marl C fabric flourishes in the Middle Kingdom, earlier examples are known from the Anubieion (this volume, **<u>337/47/52</u>**) and elsewhere. There is no evidence of a hiatus in the pottery record: continuity and gradual development are the order of the day.

NILE CLAY FABRICS, 23–335

<u>23–34</u> Beer Jars (Rzeuska 2006, Forms 1–12, Pls 9–34)

These crude handmade vessels are very common on OK–FIP sites. The Anubieion series includes no complete or nearly complete forms, the porous and lightly fired material breaking up very easily. Even the long series published by Rzeuska, consisting entirely of complete or almost complete vessels, and the even longer one from Giza (Hawass and Senussi, 218–21), exhibit such variability that it is seldom practicable to match individual examples.

An exception is **<u>23</u>**, with deep, clearly marked grooves. The Anubieion example illustrated is a close match to one of the Fourth Dynasty from Dahshur (Faltings 1989, Abb. 3b [91]), corresponding to Petrie's $68F_3/F_4$ (reproduced in Hendricks *et al.*, 2002, Fig. 4). There is a similar jar from the Japanese excavations at north-west Saqqara, dated to the Third to early Fourth Dynasty (Yoshimura, Kawai and Kashiwagi, 2005, 374, Fig. 10.3). At Elephantine, the form is said to begin in the Second Dynasty or perhaps as early as the First (Raue 1999, 176–77 with n. 406, Abb. 36 [7]), and continues into at least the late Second (*ibid.*, Abb. 37 [8]) and the first half of the Third (*ibid.*, Abb. 38 [3]). At Buto, an almost identical (and identically preserved) jar (Köhler 1998, Taf. 14 [2]) is derived from a pit of the transition from the Second to the Third Dynasty.

According to Dietrich Raue (pers. comm.), **<u>27</u>** occurs at Dahshur (so its currency should include the Third or early Fourth Dynasty) but **<u>24/31/32</u>** do not, while of **<u>29</u>** only the deep groove in AJH under AVH **16** has counterparts there, and in beer jars made of marl clay. **<u>27</u>** matches fairly well a jar of the early Fourth Dynasty from Elephantine (Raue 1999, Abb. 40 [9]).

Other forms, including **24/27/31/32**, are approximately paralleled in the Mendes Phase IVb and III series (Adams 2009, Figs 42 and 51), dated to about the Fourth Dynasty, but were not necessarily confined to that Dynasty. Judging by a photograph (Bárta 1996, Fig. 2), the early Fifth Dynasty jars from Abusir correspond approximately to **24/28/30**.

Anna Wodzińska, who examined large numbers of Fourth Dynasty beer jars at Giza, records (Wodzińska 2007, 296 and Fig. 11.10 [AB4]) 284 examples with white and 65 with red 'coat', but does not state the size of the full sample. Only a few vessels in the Anubieion series show a red slip, and in Rzeuska's material this is confined to her Forms 3 and 6 (Pls 13–14 and 19–20). Unfortunately, the Anubieion examples cannot be of her Form 6 and do not match her Form 3 except in a general way. In fact, the Anubieion series as recorded includes only one example of Rzeuska's small wide-mouthed Form 6 (Pls 19–20), so her Phase II, Pepi I–Merenre (Rzeuska 383), is not well represented. The Anubieion series is a better match to Phase I (Teti–Userkare) and the later Phases III and IV (Pepi II–the Eighth Dynasty).

The distribution within the excavated area may have significance. In particular, an unusually large number derive from Areas 12–14 (including the site of the Serapeum Way), and here OK mastaba tombs should be expected; some others, and especially **26**, are from Area 5.

The white washed Anubieion rims (AJY **18** of **27** and the small beer jar **35**) find counterparts in six of Rzeuska's pieces: [12] of her Form 2 (Phase I), [52] and [59] of her Form 7, [65] and [72] of her Form 8, and [82] of her Form 10 (all Phase III). **35** is a good match for [46] of her Form 6, and although AJY **18** is too undistinguished to find a close parallel, a white wash on several Anubieion body sherds confirms the practice was fairly common.

The clay lining inside AJY **18** (which is also white washed) would be more familiar in a bread mould but may not have been unique, as AIW **7** of **24** was originally so recorded, though later examination revealed no traces. Clay linings are not specified by Rzeuska.

On the whole, it is safer to date most of the Anubieion beer jars generally to the OK–FIP, noting that some may be Third or Fourth Dynasty while most could be accommodated comfortably within the reign of Teti, and taking note of the heavy concentration in Areas 12–14.

For a particularly fine OK relief of a man about to drink from a beer jar, see Harpur and Scremin 2008, 149 [212], and for various scenes depicting such jars, Harpur 2011, 462–64 (Figs 6–22) and 467–68 (Pls 4, 5, 7).

2270 **23** Fig. 2h

Deep, clearly marked groove near the rim. Some variability, but compared with the other beer jars, within quite narrow limits. Surfaces wiped but uneven.

Nile B2 near C. ABC/D/A **5** and ABV/Y/Z **7** fired medium, others fairly soft. Surfaces pale brown to pale red-brown. Break ABC/D/A **5** pale brown with thick mauve core, ABV/Y/Z **7** brown with red core, others pale brown all through (most) or with red core. Fairly plentiful poorly sorted sand. Fairly plentiful fine and coarse veg to 1.0. More limestone than usual in a Nile fabric, to 0.1 and ABC/D/A **5** one piece 0.2. In ABV/Y/Z **7** (0.7) and UP 159 **4** (0.5), each one piece of grey material, probably refired pottery ('grog'). Uncoated. Not polished or burnished.

Phase	Context & No.	Grid ref	Dia rim (top)	Fig
ii/ii	ABN/ABR (UP 11) **5**	Area 13	?	
iv (Pt II?)	ABS (UP 20) **19**	Area 13	*c.*12	
iv (Pt II?)	ARU=ARZ (UP 204) **13**	Area 13	?	
iv (Pt II?) x3	ABV/ABY/ABZ **7**	Area 13	*c.*13	
iv (Pt II?)?	BWZ? (UP 1041) **6**	Area 12	?	
vi	ABG (UP 235) **52**	Area 13	?	
Mamluk/Mamluk/vii	ABC/ABD/ABA (UP 69) **4★**	Area 13	*c.*12	
Mamluk/Mamluk/vii	ABC/ABD/ABA (UP 69) **5★**	Area 13	?	

Phase	Context & No.	Grid ref	Dia rim (top)	Fig
Mamluk/vii	AKJ/AKI (UP 144) **11†**	Area 14	11	
Mamluk/vii	AKJ/AKI (UP 159) **4****	Area 14	10	
Mamluk/vii	AKJ/AKI (UP 159) **5+6+7****	Area 14	10	2h

* Different vessels

** Almost certainly same vessel

† Different vessel from AKJ/AKI (UP 159) **4–7**

2278 **<u>24</u>** Fig. 2i–k

Crudely shaped, with direct, inward-leaning rim. Considerable variability, but only of detail. Surfaces wiped but uneven. Where no 'As' entry appears in the table, either the closest similarity is to AAA East **18**, or the piece is too fragmentary to classify.

<u>Nile B2 near C.</u> Fired fairly soft. Surfaces pale brown to red-brown. Break pale brown to red-brown, all through or with red or (most) grey core. Fairly plentiful poorly sorted sand. Fairly plentiful fine and coarse veg to 1.0 or in a few cases 1.5. Sparse limestone to 0.1, and some examples a few pieces to 0.3/0.5. Uncoated. Not polished or burnished.

Phase	Context & No.	Grid ref	Dia rim (top)	Fig & notes
o	BEO **81**	14/15-S04/S05	*c*.14	
ii	AIY under Room 1 **162**	09 to 12-03/04	?	
ii	ABR **4**	Area 13	?	
ii	AYG **4**	Area 13	*c*.8	
ii/ivb	AIY/AVB **56**	10 to 14-01/S01/S02	10	
iii	BCB **54**	01 to 04-04/05/06	*c*.11	
iii	BWK (UP 1025) **5**	Area 12	?	
iii/iva	BDR/BCP **7**	10/11-04/05	?	
iii/iva/?	BPD/BHR/BPV **15**	03/04-22/23	?	
iv (Pt II?)	ABY **6**	Area 13	?	
iv (Pt II?)	ADC **182**	Area 13	?	As 2j
iv (Pt II?)	ADF North **81**	Area 13	*c*.15	
iv (Pt II?)	ARU=ARZ (UP 204) **7***	Area 13	10	
iv (Pt II?)	ARU=ARZ (UP 204) **8***	Area 13	*c*.11	2j
iv (Pt II?)	ARU=ARZ (UP 204) **9***	Area 13	*c*.10	
iv (Pt II?)	ARU=ARZ (UP 204) **10***	Area 13	11	2k
iv (Pt II?)	ARU=ARZ (UP 204) **11***	Area 13	10	
iv (Pt II?)	BWY **4**	Area 12	*c*.10	
iv (Pt II?)	BWX **5**	Area 12	*c*.10	
iv (Pt II?)?	BWZ? (UP 1041) **26**	Area 12	?	
iva	AIW **7**	17/18/19-S01	10	
iva	AJH under AVH **18**	05–04/05/06	*c*.12	
iva	BAX **30**	06/07/08-03/04	*c*.12	

Phase	Context & No.	Grid ref	Dia rim (top)	Fig & notes
iva	BDU **28**	16/17/18-06/07/08	?	
iva/ivb	BHR/BTG **17**	01-20/21	12	
ivb	AFL **12**	04/05/06-01/02	9	As 2k
ivb	BDB **17**	01/02/03-04	12	
ivb	BEJ **4**	13/14-S02/S03	?	
ivb–c/v/vi	AGL/AAN/AGK **6**	06-02	11	As 2j
ivd	AMU **7**	14 to 20-S03	?	As 2j
v	DAF **19**	Area 2	?	
v	AZG (UP 195) **1**	Area 13	?	
vii	AAA East **18**	Area 1	14	2i
vii	ARD (UP 1031) **18**	Area 12	?	
?	UP 19 **52**	Area 12	9	
?	UP 1044 **14**	Area 12	?	
?	UP 1048 **11**	Area 12	?	As 2k
?	UP 1048 **12**★★	Area 12	*c.*10	
?	UP 1048 **13**★★	Area 12	?	

★ The five examples from ARU=ARZ (UP 204) all appear to be from different vessels

★★ Probably from the same vessel, but not the same vessel as UP 1048 **11**

639C <u>25</u> Fig. 3a

Slightly thickened rim.

<u>Nile C</u>. Fired fairly soft. Surfaces pale brown. Break red-brown all through. Fairly plentiful poorly sorted sand. Plentiful fine and coarse veg to 0.8. Sparse limestone to 0.05. One piece grog(?) 0.6 × 0.3. Uncoated. Not polished or burnished.

Phase	Context & No.	Grid ref	Dia rim (top)	Fig
iii–iva	ACE **97**	01 to 05-08 to 12	*c.*10	3a

898 <u>26</u> Fig. 3b–d

Simple direct rim. The variable stances, from slightly incurved to slightly outcurved, reflect the lack of standardisation of these handmade vessels.

<u>Nile C</u>. Fired fairly soft to medium. Exterior brown, interior brown or grey. Break red-brown to brown, most with grey core which in several examples extends to the interior surface, from stacking or inverting in the kiln. Fairly plentiful poorly sorted sand. Fairly plentiful to plentiful fine and coarse veg to 0.5–0.8. More limestone than usual, some with pieces to 0.3/0.4. AQE **32** one piece bone 0.2. Uncoated, but probably wet-smoothed. Not polished or burnished.

Phase	Context & No.	Grid ref	Dia rim (top)	Fig
o	BEO **79**	14/15-S04/S05	11	3b
ii	AQE **32**	19/20-01/02	*c.*10	3c

Phase	Context & No.	Grid ref	Dia rim (top)	Fig
ii	BET **114**	14/15-02/03	*c.*15	
iii–iva	ACE **24**	05-06/07/08	?	
iii–iva	ACE **209**	01 to 05-08 to 12	*c.*13	3d
iva	BAX **4**	06/07/08-03/04	*c.*14	
ivc	BHN **33**	03-22	*c.*10	
ivd	ATY **247**	18/19-06/07/08	?(*c.*20?)	

2276 <u>27</u> Fig. 3e–f

The rolling of the rim is clearly intentional but crudely done; on ARU=ARZ **6** and AJY **18** part of its length is not rolled and it is similar to <u>24</u>. Surfaces wiped but uneven. AJY **18** retains part of a thin, pale red-brown clay lining.

<u>Nile C</u>. Fired fairly soft. ARU=ARZ **6** surfaces red-brown, others pale brown. Break AJY **18** pale brown with faint, diffuse pink core, ARU=ARZ **6** red-brown with pink core, ANG **3** exterior half brown, interior half grey, except brown close to rim. Fairly plentiful poorly sorted sand. Fairly plentiful veg, AJY **18** fine to 0.2, others fine and coarse to 0.5. Sparse limestone to 0.2. Uncoated. AJY **18** has areas of whitewash on the exterior. Not polished or burnished.

Phase	Context & No.	Grid ref	Dia rim (top)	Fig
ii	AJY **18**	17 to 20-S04/S05	?	3e
iv (Pt II?)	ARU=ARZ (UP 204) **6**	Area 13	13	As 3f
?	ANG (UP 336) **3**	Area 14	*c.*11	3f

639B <u>28</u> Fig. 3g–h

Red slipped.

<u>Nile C</u>. Fired fairly soft. ACE **68** surfaces pale yellow-brown, DBW/DBU **33** pale brown. Break ACE **68** yellow-brown with pink core, DBW/DBU **33** red-brown with pinkish mauve core. Fairly plentiful poorly sorted sand. Plentiful fine and coarse veg to 1.0/1.6. ACE **68** no visible limestone, DBW/DBU **33** sparse to 0.1 and one piece 0.7 × 0.1. Areas of red slip on exterior only. Perhaps polished where slip survives.

Phase	Context & No.	Grid ref	Dia rim (top)	Fig
iii–iva	ACE **68**	08-09	*c.*10	3g
ivc–d(?)/ivd(?)	DBW/DBU **33**	Area 1 28-S31	*c.*11	3h

2274 <u>29</u> Fig. 3i–k

Crudely rolled rim with groove below. Some variability of form. Surfaces wiped but uneven.

<u>Nile C</u>. Fired fairly soft. AJH under AVH **16** and AKU **9** surfaces brown, AAA Lower **15** orange-brown, others red-brown. Break AJH under AVH **16** and AKU **9** brown with red core, AAA Lower **15** orange with red zones and grey core, others red-brown with grey core. Fairly plentiful poorly sorted sand. Plentiful fine and coarse veg to 0.5/1.0. AJH under AVH **16** more limestone than usual, with pieces 0.7 × 0.3 and 0.4 × 0.1; others sparse, AYY **2** and AKU **9** to 0.05, AJH under AVH **17** and AAA Lower **15** to 0.2, AAA Lower **15** also one void 0.3. Uncoated. Not polished or burnished.

Phase	Context & No.	Grid ref	Dia rim (top)	Fig & notes
iv (Pt II?)	AYY **2**	Area 13	?	As 3j
iva	AJH under AVH **16***	05-04/05/06	*c.*10	3i
iva	AJH under AVH **17***	05-04/05/06	*c.*9.5	3j
v–vi	AKU (UP 186) **9**	Area 14	*c.*10–13	**
vii	AAA Lower **15**	Area 2	*c.*9	3k

* Different vessels

** Shoulder as AAA Lower **15**, rim as AJH **17**

639A **30** Fig. 3l

Obviously folded rim.

Nile B2. Fired fairly soft. Surfaces pale brown, exterior where slip lost. Break red-brown all through. Fairly plentiful poorly sorted sand. Fairly plentiful fine and coarse veg to 0.4. Only one piece limestone, 0.2 × 0.1, visible. Traces of red slip on exterior of body only. No visible polish or burnish.

Phase	Context & No.	Grid ref	Dia rim (top)	Fig
vii	AAA (UP 23) **200**	06-05	*c.*10	3l

2272A **31** Fig. 4a

Short, upright direct rim. Surfaces wiped but uneven.

Nile B2 near C. Fired fairly soft to medium. BKC **17** exterior pale brown, interior somewhat misfired grey, others surfaces pale brown. Break pale brown to red-brown, with red core, red zones and grey core, or grey core. Fairly plentiful poorly sorted sand. Fairly plentiful fine and coarse veg to 1.2. More limestone than usual in a Nile fabric, to 0.3. Uncoated. Not polished or burnished.

Phase	Context & No.	Grid ref	Dia rim (top)	Fig & notes
ii	BDX **66**	02/03-04	*c.*11	As 4a
iv (Pt II?)	ARU=ARZ (UP 204) **12**	Area 13	*c.*10	As 4a
ivb	AVB **96**	10/11-S01/S02	?	As 4a
ivc	BKC **17**	06/07-26	9	4a
ivd	ACB **4**	04-07/08	*c.*11	As 4a
v	AZG (UP 331) **3**	Area 13	?	*

* Shoulder as 4a but rim closer to 4b of **32**

2272B **32** Fig. 4b

Similar to **30** but with rolled, not direct, rim. Surfaces wiped but uneven.

Nile B2 near C. Fired medium, somewhat misfired. Surfaces grey. Break grey with thick red core. Fairly plentiful poorly sorted sand. Fairly plentiful fine and coarse veg to 0.7. Sparse limestone to 0.1. Uncoated. Not polished or burnished.

Phase	Context & No.	Grid ref	Dia rim (top)	Fig
o	ADU (UP 330) **4**	Area 13	10	4b

810 **33** Fig. 4d–g

Bases from thick-walled jars of 'beer jar' type. ARU=ARZ **5**, only, has spiral ridges on interior which imply wheel assistance. Otherwise handmade, with finger impressions on interior, and exterior uneven but not excessively so, with no visible scraping marks.

Nile D near C. Fired fairly soft. Surfaces red-brown. Break red-brown with grey core, especially where thickest; ARU=ARZ **5** also thin red zones. Fairly plentiful poorly sorted sand. Moderate qty to fairly plentiful fine and coarse veg to 1.0. More limestone than usual in a Nile fabric, with pieces to 0.3. Uncoated. Not polished or burnished.

Phase	Context & No.	Grid ref	Fig & notes
o	BDY **62**	01 to 03-07/08	As 4e
iii	BCB **111**	01 to 04-04/05/06	As 4d
iv (Pt II?)	ABW **1**	Area 13	As 4g but less massive
iv (Pt II?)	ARU=ARZ (UP 204) **3**	Area 13	4d
iv (Pt II?)	ARU=ARZ (UP 204) **4**	Area 13	4e
iv (Pt II?)	ARU=ARZ (UP 204) **5**	Area 13	4f
?	UP 1033 **1**	Area 12	4g
?	UP 1048 **1**	Area 12	As 4e

4 **34** Not illustrated

Body sherds, probably from 'beer jars' rather than bread moulds. Although they cannot contribute much, they broaden the context base for the coarsest vessels. The exteriors of ARU **1, 2** and ANG (UP 1009) **3** have vertical channels made with the fingers. The white plaster(?) inside two examples (see table), which is quite thick, occurs also in several in Rzeuska's corpus (2006, 446–48) and in some examples of **598** and **659**.

Nile C. Ware as rims and bases of 'beer jars'. Fired fairly soft (most) to medium. Surfaces pale brown (most) to red-brown. Break pale brown all through or with grey core (most), or red-brown with grey core. Fairly plentiful poorly sorted sand. Fairly plentiful fine and coarse veg to 0.6/0.7. Sparse limestone to 0.1, a few examples with pieces to 0.2 and BDR **72** one piece 0.6 × 0.3. Uncoated. Not polished or burnished.

Phase	Context & No.	Grid ref	Notes
o	ADU (UP 330) **1**	Area 13	Whitewash on exterior
ii/ii	ADG/ADH **9**	Area 13	
ii/ii/ivc	AJX/AJY/BRS **1**	21/22-S01/S02/S03	
iii	BDR **72, 76**	11/12/13-03/04/05	
iii	BDR **82**	11/12/13-03/04/05	
iv (Pt II?)	ARU=ARZ (UP 343) **1, 2, 3**	Area 13	
iv (Pt II?)	ARU=ARZ (UP 343) **4**	Area 13	White plaster inside
iv (Pt II?)	BWQ **3, 4, 5, 6, 7**	Area 12	

Phase	Context & No.	Grid ref	Notes
iv (Pt II?) ×2	ARP=ARS/AYY **3**	Area 13	
iv (Pt II?)?	BWZ? (UP 1041) **1–5, 7–10, 14, 24, 25**	Area 12	
iv (Pt II?)?	BWZ?(UP 1041) **11–13**	Area 12	Whitewash on exterior
iv (Pt V)	BWR **1**	Area 12	
iva	AFZ **3**	17 to 20-S01	
iva	BHR **179**	02/03-21/22/23	
iva/ivb	BHR/BTG **90**	02-20/21	
ivc	BQG **20**	Area 2	
ivc(?)	DBN **5**	Area 1 29-S31	
v/v	BNN/BNR (I) **3**	W06/W07-S01/S02/S03	
v–vi	CBU **61**	06/07/08-33/34/35	
vii	AAA (UP 23) **208**	01 to 10-01 to 10	
vii	ARD (UP 1031) **6–14, 16**	Area 12	
?	BEP **101**	16 to 20-01/S01	Whitewash on exterior
?	ANG (UP 1000) **42**	Area 14	Whitewash on exterior
?	ANG (UP 1000) **74**	Area 14	Whitewash on exterior, white plaster inside
?	ANG (UP 1009) **1, 3**	Area 14	
?	ARY **1**	Area 13	Whitewash on exterior
?	ARY **2, 3**	Area 13	
?	UP 1034 **4**	Area 12	
?	UP 1035 **4, 7, 8, 12, 13, 15, 17**	Area 12	
?	UP 1039 **1**	Area 12	Whitewash on exterior
?	UP1044 **3+4, 5–10, 12, 13, 16–22, 25**	Area 12	
?	UP 1045 **2**	Area 12	
?	UP 1046 **2**	Area 12	
?	UP 1048 **2–7, 9, 10, 16–18**	Area 12	
?	UP 1048 **8*, 14***	Area 12	Red slip on exterior

* Almost certainly same vessel

35 Small beer jar with straight rim and cylindrical body (Rzeuska 2006, Form 6, Pl. 20)

Although the rim diameter is smaller than Rzeuska's examples', and the finish is a whitewash instead of a red slip, this appears to be a small beer jar, the rim form being close to that of Rzeuska's [45]. This parallel is preferred to a similar high stand (Form 219, Pl. 155) because the stands are wheel assisted and in no case white washed.

2788 **35** Fig. 4c

Handmade. The groove below the rim and the impress below it were almost certainly for or from string-tying.

Nile B2. Fired fairly soft. Exterior concealed by wash; interior pale brown. Break pale brown with red core. Fairly plentiful poorly sorted sand. Fairly plentiful fine and coarse veg to 1.0. Sparse limestone to 0.1. Whitewash on exterior and top of rim, and irregularly down *c*.1.0 on interior. Not polished or burnished.

Phase	Context & No.	Grid ref	Dia rim (top)	Fig
ivc	ACP **75**	01 to 05-10	7	4c

36 Flat base of wide-mouthed jar (Rzeuska 2006, Form 15, Pl. 37)

Little survives, but **36** resembles only this one form in Rzeuska's material. The four bases recorded there ([117–120]) are in Nile B1, Nile B2 and P.60 (two) fabrics; the Nile B1 example is eroded but the others are all wheel assisted with scraped base like **36**, and the Nile B2 example is red slipped.

713 **36** Fig. 4h

The small base area may indicate a small vessel. Ridges on the interior prove wheel assistance, but the exterior has scraping marks in groups at various angles, to shape the base (some of them contain slip, so were made prior to slipping, as expected).

Nile B2. Fired medium. Exterior red-brown where slip lost; interior surface pink. Break red-brown with pink 'core' near interior surface, or one pink zone and grey 'core' where thickest. Fairly plentiful fine and medium sand with a few larger grains. Medium qty fine veg to 0.3. Sparse limestone to 0.1. Red slip on exterior and underside; interior uncoated. Traces of polish where slip survives.

Phase	Context & No.	Grid ref	Dia base	Fig
ivc/vii	BKP/AAA **17**	07/08-23	2.2	4h

37–38 Medium-sized jars with direct rim and slim body (not present in Rzeuska 2006)

Rather too slim to fit into Rzeuska's Forms 21–24 (Pls 43–47). There is a better match (dia 7) from late OK Abusir (Kaiser 1969, I, Typ 6), red slipped and, if one of the majority, polished. This is preferred to the basic Fourth Dynasty form (Wodzińska 2007, Fig. 11.7 [AB1]), which, although similar, has a more upright neck and only a white or pinkish wash.

319 **37** Fig. 4i

All four examples are from different vessels. ACE **204** is distorted and the dia uncertain.

Nile B2. Fired medium. Surfaces pale brown to red-brown, exterior where uncoated or slip lost. Break, ABC/D/A **6** red-brown with dark brown zones and red-brown core, UP 588 **561** pale brown all through, others red-brown with red zones and grey core. Fairly plentiful fine and medium sand with a few larger grains. Fairly plentiful fine and coarse veg to 0.7, and ABC/D/A **6** one piece 1.0. Sparse limestone to 0.05/0.1, ABC/D/A **6** also one piece 0.3 and UP 588 **562** one 0.4 × 0.2. Red slip on exterior of UP 588 **561** (to top of rim) and **562** (carried over the rim and down 2.0 on interior); others weathered but slip possible on exterior. Probable traces of polish where slip survives.

Phase	Context & No.	Grid ref	Dia rim (top)	Fig
iii–iva	ACE **204**	01 to 05-08 to 12	*c*.16 (?)	Similar to 4i
Mamluk/ Mamluk/vii	ABC/ABD/ABA (UP 69) **6**	Area 13	11	Similar to 4i

Phase	Context & No.	Grid ref	Dia rim (top)	Fig
vii	AAA (UP 588) **561**	01/02-31/32/33	9	Similar to 4i
vii	AAA (UP 588) **562**	01/02-31/32/33	9	4i

2268 38 Fig. 4j

Nile B2. Fired medium. Surfaces pale red-brown where uncoated or slip lost. Break red-brown with grey core towards interior surface where thickest,. Fairly plentiful poorly sorted sand. Fairly plentiful fine and some coarse veg to 0.3. Sparse limestone to 0.1. Small areas of red slip on exterior, carried over the rim and running down interior. No visible polish or burnish.

Phase	Context & No.	Grid ref	Dia rim (top)	Fig
vii	AAA (UP 157) **68**	06 to 10-11/12	6	4j

39–40 Medium-sized jars with modelled rim and ovoid body (Rzeuska 2006, Form 21, Pl. 43)

Part of Rzeuska's series of tall (as distinct from globular or squat) jars of various sizes. The white slip is not attested for this series but many are red slipped. The closest match for **39** is probably her [147]; for **40** it is [151] in P.60. For a white slip, see a good match for **39** (dia top 9) from Herakleopolis dated to the late OK/early FIP (Bader 2009a, Fig. 11f).

2284 39 Fig. 5a

Nile B2. Fired fairly hard. Surfaces red-brown, exterior where slip lost. Break red-brown with thick grey core. Moderate qty fine and medium well-sorted sand. Fairly plentiful fine and medium veg to 0.6. Sparse limestone to 0.05. Fairly thick but unevenly applied white slip on exterior, carried over the rim and irregularly down to max 1.4 on interior. The slip does not disguise the veg voids. Not polished or burnished.

Phase	Context & No.	Grid ref	Dia rim (top)	Fig
vii	AAA (UP 38) **67**	12 to 15-11	7	5a

2286 40 Fig. 5b

The rim, at least, is wheel assisted.

Nile B2. Fired medium. Surfaces red where uncoated or slip lost. Break red with pink core tending to mauve. Moderate qty fine and medium sand with a few larger grains. Moderate qty fine and coarse veg, mostly to 0.4 but a few pieces to 0.9. More limestone than usual, to 0.05 and one piece 0.2 × 0.1. Small surviving areas of slip on exterior, and on interior down to 1.0, fired variably white and pink. No visible polish or burnish.

Phase	Context & No.	Grid ref	Dia rim (top)	Fig
vii	AAA (UP 108) **25**	29 to 34-S06	6	5b

41 Gracile medium-sized jar with modelled rim (not present in Rzeuska 2006)

Although the rim form is similar to that of **40**, the neck appears to be longer; it probably finds a counterpart at Abusir (Kaiser 1969, II, Typ 28), also slipped and highly polished. A rather larger (dia top 18) and more angular example from Giza is red slipped and recorded as burnished (Hawass and Senussi, 47 [35]).

2218 **41** Fig. 5c

Nile B2. Fired fairly soft. Surfaces pale brown where slip lost. Break dark brown with pale brown core. Fairly plentiful poorly sorted sand. No visible veg. Sparse limestone to 0.05. A few tiny dark rock particles. Areas of thick orange slip survive on both surfaces. Both surfaces highly polished.

Phase	Context & No.	Grid ref	Dia rim (top)	Fig
ivc	AAD **45**	09-06	9	5c

42 Medium-sized jar with squared rim (nearest, Rzeuska 2006, Form 26, Pl. 49)

In Rzeuska's series, the squared upper part of the rim is best matched by [181] of her Form 26, in uncoated Nile B2, but more closely by an example in wet-smoothed Marl A4 from First Dynasty Elephantine (Raue 1999, Abb. 36 [5]). Between these in date we find one of the Fourth Dynasty in slipped and burnished Marl A1 from Giza (Nazlet el-Samman) (Hawass and Senussi 2008, 180 [H27]). The form appears to be long-lived so it is not possible to date **42** closely. See also Archaic **10** and **11**.

635A **42** Fig. 5d

Nile B2. Fired fairly hard. Surfaces pale red-brown. Break pale brown with red zones and grey core. Fairly plentiful poorly sorted sand. Fairly plentiful fine veg to 0.2. Sparse limestone to 0.1. Uncoated. Not polished or burnished.

Phase	Context & No.	Grid ref	Dia rim (top)	Fig
vi	ABG (UP 235) **4**	Area 13	10	5d

43–57 Medium-sized to large globular jars (Rzeuska 2006, Forms 26–29, Pls 49–51)

The Anubieion examples are never preserved very far down the body, though the angle of the neck and shoulder is usually sufficient to betray their globular shape, rather than the slimmer profile of the 'tall' jars of Rzeuska's Forms 21–25. However, the rim and upper shoulder are often very similar in the two forms so the identification is not always certain. The best matches to most of the Anubieion examples are [175–182] of Rzeuska's Form 26, but none approaches the rim diameter of **53**. To **56** the best matches are probably [185] and [191] of Rzeuska's Forms 27 and 29, and to **48** [189] of her Form 28.

In Rzeuska's material, Forms 26–29 may be uncoated or red slipped on the exterior, with more of the latter. In contrast to the Anubieion series, only [184] is recorded as polished, but this may be due to the conditions of preservation.

These jars are heirs to a tradition stretching back into the Predynastic Period, and there is great variability of form. The fragmentary condition of the Anubieion examples, and sometimes the small scale or simplified outlines of published material, limit the confidence with which comparisons can be made. Even when resemblances are close and the fabrics similar, ambiguities remain: **44** and **46** are very like the rim of a wet-smoothed strainer-neck jar of the late First Dynasty from Elephantine (Raue 1999, Abb. 36 [8]), but also close to various of Rzeuska's Form 26, some of which are slipped and others not. Again, uncertainties in the dating of some published series may leave open the date of Anubieion examples, however similar the vessels may be: thus **52** may well be from a pre-Teti jar (cf Chłodnicki *et al.*, Fig. 8 [24]). However, it is noted that Raue's jars of similar form, most of which pre-date the reign of Teti, are never slipped, increasing the chances of the slipped Anubieion examples' being later.

892 **43** Fig. 5e

Nile B2. Fired fairly hard; slightly misfired. Exterior concealed by slip, interior surface dark brown where uncoated. Break brown with thick grey core. Fairly plentiful poorly sorted sand. Fairly plentiful mostly fine veg to 0.3. Sparse limestone to 0.1. Thick reddish brown slip on exterior, carried over the rim and down about 2.5 inside, firing dark brown inside below the minimum diameter. Polished where slipped.

Phase	Context & No.	Grid ref	Dia rim (top)	Fig
iii–iva	ACE **17**	05-06/07/08	10	5e

647 __**44**__ Fig. 5f–g

ADU NW **5** is wheel assisted but hand finished. DAG **31** shows no evidence.

<u>Nile B2.</u> Fired fairly hard. ADU NW **5** surfaces purple-brown, DAG **31** red-brown where slip lost. Break, ADU NW **5** pale brown with red zones and grey core, DAG **31** orange with thin dark brown zones, and pink core close to interior surface. ADU NW **5** plentiful, DAG **31** fairly plentiful, fine and medium well-sorted sand. Fairly plentiful fine veg to 0.3. ADU NW **5** carefully smoothed, perhaps self-slipped, but no coloured slip, DAG **31** thick white slip on all surfaces. Not polished or burnished.

Phase	Context & No.	Grid ref	Dia rim (top)	Fig
o	ADU (UP 122) NW **5**	Area 13	10	5f
iv	DAG **31**	Area 2 W09-S52/S53/S54	9.5	5g

665A __**45**__ Fig. 5h

The smaller diameter AMB/AAA/AMA **22** is also slighter.

<u>Nile B1.</u> AMB/AAA/AMA **22** fired fairly soft, AON **31** medium. Surfaces red-brown where slip lost. Break red-brown, AMB/AAA/AMA **22** with diffuse red core, AON **31** with thick pink core. Fairly plentiful fine and medium well-sorted sand, AMB/AAA/AMA **22** with a few larger grains. Small qty fine veg to 0.2. Sparse limestone to 0.05, AON **31** also one piece 0.2. Thick red-brown slip on all surfaces. All surfaces highly polished.

Phase	Context & No.	Grid ref	Max dia rim	Fig
o/vii/?	AMB/AAA/AMA **22**	04/05-14/15	8	Similar to 5h
ii	AON **31**	05/06-S01/S02	11.5	5h

2298 __**46**__ Fig. 5i

The rim is wheel assisted.

<u>Nile B2.</u> Fired fairly hard. Surfaces red-brown where slip lost. Break red-brown with thick pale grey core. Fairly plentiful fine and medium well-sorted sand. Fairly plentiful fine and coarse veg to 0.3. Sparse limestone to 0.05. Surviving area of red-brown slip, in part discoloured grey from fire, on both surfaces. Highly polished where slip survives.

Phase	Context & No.	Grid ref	Dia rim (top)	Fig
iv (Pt II?)	ADC **103**	Area 13	12	5i

890 __**47**__ Fig. 5j

The rim appears to be wheel assisted.

<u>Nile B2.</u> Fired medium. Exterior concealed by slip, interior dark brown. Break brown with one dark brown

zone near exterior, and deep red core. Plentiful poorly sorted sand. Fairly plentiful mostly fine veg to 0.5. Rather more limestone than usual, to 0.1, also one piece 0.2 and one 0.3. Thick brown slip on exterior, carried over the rim to a straight edge at the minimum diameter, the final 1.0 inside black, from lack of oxygen in the kiln. Polished where slipped.

Phase	Context & No.	Grid ref	Dia rim (top)	Fig
vi/vi/vi	AEP/AEQ/AER **29**	01 to 04-07/08	10	5j

2923 **48** Fig. 5k

Rather poorly made.

Nile B2. Fired fairly soft. Surface red-brown where slip lost. Break red-brown with dark brown core. Fairly plentiful poorly sorted sand. Fairly plentiful fine veg to 0.2. Sparse limestone to 0.1. Traces of red slip on exterior, and on interior to 2.0 from rim, but too little survives on interior to show any further slip. Traces of polish where slipped.

Phase	Context & No.	Grid ref	Dia rim (top)	Fig
?	BEP **65**	14 to17-01/S01	*c.*13	5k

934 **49** Fig. 5l

Nile B2. Fired medium. Surfaces red-brown where slip lost. Break red-brown with red zones and purple-grey core towards the interior surface. Fairly plentiful poorly sorted sand. Fairly plentiful fine veg to 0.2. Sparse limestone to 0.1. Small areas of red slip survive on exterior of body and rim, and a larger area on interior down to minimum diameter. Polished where slip survives.

Phase	Context & No.	Grid ref	Dia rim (top)	Fig
(vi–)vii	AAB **14**	22/23-09/10	7	5l

894 **50** Fig. 5m

Nile B2. Fired fairly soft. Surface pale brown where slip lost. Break pale brown with red zones and mauve core. Fairly plentiful fine and medium sand with a few larger grains. Fairly plentiful fine veg to 0.3. Sparse limestone to 0.1. Small areas of red slip survive on both surfaces as far down as preserved. Both surfaces polished where slip survives.

Phase	Context & No.	Grid ref	Dia rim (top)	Fig
ii	BGL**78**	15/16/17-04/05	9	5m

2062 **51** Fig. 6a

Perhaps handmade.

Nile B2. Fired fairly soft. Surfaces brown, exterior where slip lost. Break brown with diffuse red core. Fairly plentiful poorly sorted sand. Fairly plentiful fine and coarse veg to 0.6. Sparse limestone to 0.05. Thin red slip on exterior, carried over the rim and down interior to point of minimum diameter. Not polished or burnished.

Phase	Context & No.	Grid ref	Dia rim (top)	Fig
ivc	BTX **108+109**	02/03-19/20	11	6a

2064 **52** Fig. 6b

Nile B2. Fired fairly soft. Surfaces red-brown. Break pale brown with thin red zones and diffuse pinkish mauve core. Fairly plentiful poorly sorted sand. Fairly plentiful fine and coarse veg to 0.5. Sparse limestone to 0.05. Exterior probably only wet-smoothed, with no visible slip; interior uncoated. Not polished or burnished.

Phase	Context & No.	Grid ref	Dia rim (top)	Fig
iii	AIK **6**	01/02-02/03	10	6b

653 **53** Fig. 6c

Low bulge in short neck. The rolled rim, at least, appears to be wheel assisted.

Nile B2. Fired medium. Exterior surface pale red-brown where slip lost; interior weathered. Break red-brown with pink core. Fairly plentiful fine and medium sand with a few larger grains. Moderate qty fine veg to 0.3. Sparse limestone to 0.1 and one piece 0.5. Red slip on exterior, carried over the rim and down at least 2 cm on interior, then weathered. Probable traces of polish on exterior and rim where slip survives.

Phase	Context & No.	Grid ref	Dia rim (top)	Fig
iii or before	CFT **1**	08/09-22	16	6c

888 **54** Fig. 6d

The rim, at least, appears to be wheel assisted.

Nile B2. Fired medium. Exterior concealed by slip; interior dark brown. Break red-brown with grey core extending to interior surface. Fairly plentiful poorly sorted sand. Fairly plentiful fine and coarse veg to 0.8. Sparse limestone to 0.05 and one piece 0.5 × 0.3. Red slip on exterior, carried over the rim to a straight edge about 2.0 down; the slip is fired black in interior, from lack of oxygen in the kiln. Lightly polished where slipped.

Phase	Context & No.	Grid ref	Dia rim (top)	Fig
ivb	AVO **2**	12-S01/S02	10	6d

635B **55** Fig. 6e

Wheel assisted but hand finished.

Nile B2. Fired fairly hard. Surfaces pale brown. Break purple-brown with grey core. Fairly plentiful poorly sorted sand. Fairly plentiful mostly fine and some coarse veg to 0.5. More limestone than usual in a Nile fabric, to 0.2. Uncoated. Not polished or burnished.

Phase	Context & No.	Grid ref	Dia rim (top)	Fig
v	DAC **10**	Area 2 W06/W07/W08-S52/S53/S54	10	6e

447 **56** Fig. 6f

Nile B2 Sandy. Fired fairly hard. Exterior concealed by slip, interior surface brown. Break pale brown with thin red zones and grey core. Fairly plentiful fine and medium sand with a few larger grains. Moderate qty fine veg to 0.3. Sparse limestone to 0.05. Thick orange-red slip on exterior, carried over the rim and down to a straight edge just below the minimum diameter on the interior. Polished where slipped.

Phase	Context & No.	Grid ref	Dia rim (top)	Fig
iv (Pt II?)	ADF North **62**	Area 13	9	6f

1430 **57** Fig. 6g

The rim, at least, is wheel assisted,

Nile B1. Fired hard, rather misfired. Exterior concealed by slip, interior brown. Break dark brown, with red-brown zone next to interior surface and deep pink core. Fairly plentiful fine and medium well-sorted sand. Small qty fine veg to 0.2. Only one piece limestone 0.1 visible. Brown slip on exterior, carried over rim and down about 1.5 on interior to a less careful edge than usual, then running down. Polished where slipped, except where running down.

Phase	Context & No.	Grid ref	Dia rim (top)	Fig
iii–iva	ACE **90**	01 to 05-08 to 12	10	6g

58 Small globular jar (Rzeuska 2006, Form 31, Pl. 52)

Although Rzeuska's Form 31 (which is also uncoated) is not a perfect match, it is similar in both form and size. On the other hand, another such small jar type, from Fourth Dynasty Giza (Wodzińska 2007, Fig. 11.13 [ABM2]), may be a closer match, having a diameter range 4–6 and all examples being red slipped.

663 **58** Fig. 6h

Nile B2. Fired medium. Surfaces red-brown. Break red-brown with red zones and pale purple core. Fairly plentiful fine and medium sand with a few larger grains. Small qty fine veg. Sparse limestone to 0.1. Slip on exterior and top of rim only, fired pink. Polish on exterior only.

Phase	Context & No.	Grid ref	Max dia rim	Fig
v	DAC **13**	Area 2.W06W07/W08-S52/S53/S54	5	6h

59 Large cylindrical handmade base (not present in Rzeuska 2006)

Bases of closed forms are seldom published, and no entirely convincing match has come to light. It could be from a tall Predynastic jar such as one from Hierakonpolis (Adams and Friedman 1992, Fig. 7 [2a, left]), but this suggestion is offered with reservations, and the Archaic type of 'jar with a flat, flaring base', at Helwan (Köhler and Smythe 2004, 133 and Pl. 5 [19]), although not dissimilar, is not close enough to be totally convincing. More probable is a footed bowl like one from Akhmim (Hope and McFarlane, 2006, Fig. 3 [DIIIa.1]). Rzeuska's Form 221, Pl. 157, offers somewhat similar bases of high stands in Nile B2 and Nile C fabrics but only one of the six is handmade.

735 **59** Fig. 6i

Somewhat damaged but retaining part of the interior surface. Underside rough where it stood before firing; no evidence of string cutting, but in any case unlikely. Handmade.

Nile C. Misfired. Exterior surface partly grey, partly red-brown; underside and interior grey. Break grey all through. Fairly plentiful poorly sorted sand. Fairly plentiful fine and coarse veg to 0.7. Sparse limestone to 0.1 and two pieces each 0.2. Uncoated. Not polished or burnished.

Phase	Context & No.	Grid ref	Dia base	Fig
ii	BGG **142**	11/12-S04/S05	6	6i

60 Scraped base of handmade(?) jar (not present in Rzeuska 2006?)

Tapering base from a jar, with a rounded end. Apparently handmade, but so carefully that the interior is smooth. Exterior also carefully smoothed, but some vertical scraping marks are just visible. Best match is probably Rzeuska's Form 17 (Rzeuska 2006, Pl. 39) but the three examples there are all in mixed clay. Although the careful finish limits the number of potential parallels, it is not sufficient to establish the vessel type.

822 **60** Fig. 6j

Nile B2. Fired fairly soft. Surfaces pale brown, lowest part of interior tending towards grey. Break pale brown with red zones and grey core. Fairly plentiful poorly sorted sand. Fairly plentiful fine veg to 0.4. Sparse limestone to 0.1. Both surfaces smoothed, the exterior vertically but very carefully, leaving no facets. No visible slip or polish or burnish, and unlikely to have had any.

Phase	Context & No.	Grid ref	Fig
vi/vi/vi	AEP/AEQ/AER **32**	02-04 to 07	6j

61–63 Scraped bases of wheel-assisted jars

These three bases each combine wheel-ridged interior and scraped exterior. In addition, **62** appears to preserve wheel ridges on the exterior at the upper break, from the wheel-assisted upper body. The vessels would have been made on a slow wheel in the first instance, but instead of being returned to it inverted for the finishing of the base, as was the practice in later periods, they were scraped down to a rounded shape by hand. This technique continues as late as the beginning of the Eighteenth Dynasty and cannot be used to date the vessels closely. The many 'beer jars' in Rzeuska's series (2006, Pls 9–34) are all entirely handmade, so the present examples should be from large jars of other types.

61 Scraped base of wheel-assisted jar (Rzeuska 2006, nearest, Form 13, Pl. 35)

The narrowing shape and thick base probably derive from a pointed-based jar of Rzeuska's Form 13, although these are usually uncoated. It relates reasonably well to one of the outline forms in the lengthy Sedment series (Petrie and Brunton 1924a, Pl. XXXII [62f]). An example in marl clay from Qau is dated to the FIP (Bourriau 1981, 53 [89]).

247 **61** Fig. 7a

Wheel assisted, with wheel ridges on interior, but hand finished, with vertical scraping marks on central area of exterior and traces on lower body. Identification numbers partly lost from sherd before cataloguing.

Nile B2. Fired fairly soft. Surfaces pale brown where slip lost. Break outer half pale brown with red core, inner half grey. Fairly plentiful poorly sorted sand. Fairly plentiful fine and coarse veg to 0.8. Sparse limestone to 0.1. Traces of red slip on exterior, on mid and lower body; interior uncoated. No visible polish or burnish, but weathered.

Phase	Context & No.	Grid ref	Max dia body	Fig
ivd	(ATY? **154**?)	2(8?)-(02?) to S05	8	7a

62–63 Scraped bases of wheel-assisted jars (Rzeuska 2006, Forms 24, 26–30, Pls 47–51)

The more rounded **62** and **63** accord more closely with Rzeuska's Form 24, or in the case of **63** perhaps the more globular Forms 26–30.

249B **62** Fig. 7b

Wheel assisted, with ridges on the interior. Exterior vertically scraped.

Nile B2. Fired fairly soft. Surfaces pale brown (exterior where slip lost). Break pale brown with red core. Fairly plentiful poorly sorted sand. Fairly plentiful fine and coarse veg to 0.5. Sparse limestone to 0.05. Red slip on exterior. Probable traces of polish where slipped.

Phase	Context & No.	Grid ref	Fig
vii	AAA (UP 23) **564**	01/02-31/32/33	7b

2706 **63** Fig. 7c

Sherd from near the base of a round-based jar. Wheel assisted, with ridges on the interior. Exterior vertically scraped, with one set of scraping overriding and partly obliterating another at a slightly different angle.

Nile B2. Fired fairly soft. Exterior concealed by slip; interior surface pale brown. Break pale brown with faint red core. Fairly plentiful poorly sorted sand. Moderate qty fine veg to 0.2. Sparse limestone to 0.1 and one piece 1.0 × 0.5. Red slip on exterior only. No visible polish or burnish.

Phase	Context & No.	Grid ref	Fig
?	ARY **4**	Area 13	7c

64 Squat jar with short neck (Rzeuska 2006, Form 34, Pl. 53)

Although the diameter is nearly twice as great as that of [202] of Rzeuska's Form 34, the shape is similar and each has the same unusual white slip. For a similar rim, with max dia rim 11.5, see the Abusir series (Kaiser 1969, II, Typ 26), said to be highly polished, implying a slip. Other such rim shapes are found in the MK (Aston D.A. 2004b, Pls 225–27 [872/76/77]) but when they are slipped, the slip is red.

2288 **64** Fig. 7d

Nile B2. Misfired, brittle. Surfaces grey-brown where slip lost. Break grey-brown with thick red core. Fairly plentiful poorly sorted sand. Fairly plentiful fine and coarse veg to 0.6. Rather more limestone than usual, but to 0.1 only. Thick white slip on both surfaces. Not polished or burnished but misfiring would destroy it.

Phase	Context & No.	Grid ref	Max dia rim	Fig
ivc	CGQ **42**	02 to 05-33 to 37	9	7d

65 Squat jar with modelled rim and long neck (Rzeuska 2006, Form 35, Pl. 54)

Although the wide-shouldered body and flat base do not survive, this is such a perfect match for Rzeuska's [209] (in Nile A) for form, size and finish there is little doubt of the vessel type.

331 <u>65</u> Fig. 7e

<u>Nile B1.</u> Fired fairly hard. Surfaces concealed by slip. Break red-brown with pink zones and grey core. Fairly plentiful poorly sorted sand. Sparse fine veg to 0.2, and a few pieces coarse to 0.5. Sparse limestone to 0.1. Thick red-brown slip on all surfaces, patchy on interior. All surfaces polished.

Phase	Context & No.	Grid ref	Max dia rim	Fig
vii	AAA **24**	Area 1	8.5	7e

<u>66–67</u> *Nmst* jars (Rzeuska 2006, Form 37, Pl. 55)

Among the flat-based closed vessels in Rzeuska's material, her Forms 35 and 37 are the only ones with slip on the exterior only. The base diameter range from 6.5 to 11 accords with that of the Anubieion examples, and although <u>66</u> is too poorly preserved to confirm the form, <u>67</u> is a reasonably close match for some of the variants.

707A <u>66</u> Not illustrated

Not recorded whether handmade or wheel assisted.

<u>Nile B2.</u> Fired medium to hard. Interior red, exterior concealed by slip. Break red with grey core. Fairly plentiful fine and medium well-sorted sand. Small to moderate qty fine veg. Sparse limestone to 0.05 or 0.1. Red slip on exterior (including underside), interior uncoated. Polished where slipped.

Phase	Context & No.	Grid ref	Dia base	Notes
o/ii	AQG/AJY **9**	21/22-S04/S05/S06	*c.*9	Not illustrated*

* Insufficiently preserved to show form

709A <u>67</u> Fig. 7f

Probably wheel assisted. Underside smoothed.

<u>Nile B2.</u> Fired fairly soft. Exterior concealed by slip, interior pale brown. Break pale brown with red zones, and grey core where thickest. Fairly plentiful fine and medium well-sorted sand. Moderate qty fine veg to 0.2. Sparse limestone to 0.05. Pink slip on exterior (including underside), interior uncoated. Highly polished where slipped.

Phase	Context & No.	Grid ref	Dia base	Fig
vii	AAA (UP 445) **37**	Area 2	*c.* 6.5	7f

<u>68–69</u> Cosmetic jars(?) (not present in Rzeuska 2006)

Although not represented in Rzeuska's material, these find parallels in the Qau-Matmar cemeteries, conveniently analysed by Stephan Seidlmayer (Seidlmayer 1990). <u>68</u> corresponds to Seidlmayer's K-B72.02 (Abb. 75, upper left) and K-B72.04 (Abb. 75, upper right), with max diameters 9 and 8 respectively. They are described (*ibid.*, 175) as crucibles ('Tiegel') but this is unlikely in the case of <u>68</u>, or indeed the Qau-Matmar examples, given their cemetery contexts. <u>69</u> corresponds to Seidlmayer's K-B73.01 (Abb. 75, upper left and upper right), each with max diameter 7, described as ointment vessels ('Salbgefässe') and specified (*ibid.*, 175) as in most cases red polished. Seidlmayer observes that they imitate stone vessel forms (*ibid.*, 174) and quotes Brunton (1937, 106) as saying that they chiefly occurred in the graves of women; one suspects that <u>68</u> fulfilled a similar function. The paucity and ambiguity of external dating evidence obliged Seidlmayer to state only that the Qau-Matmar series begins in the late OK. However, the form of <u>68</u> can be traced back at least to Naqada IIdI (Payne 1993, Fig. 52 [1004]), and a range of small jars similar to <u>69</u> is included in the Fourth Dynasty corpus of Reisner (1965, Fig. 87).

715 **68** Fig. 7g

Handmade. Scrape marks at various angles around exterior of base, and ridges on underside. Not string-cut.

Nile B2. Fired medium. Exterior pale brown where slip lost; interior dark brown. Break pale red-brown with dark purple-brown core extending to interior surface. Fairly plentiful fine and medium sand with a few larger grains. Small qty fine veg to 0.3. Sparse limestone to 0.1. Thin red slip on exterior, including underside; interior uncoated. Traces of polish on exterior, including underside.

Phase	Context & No.	Grid ref	Dia base	Fig
ii	ABR North (UP 51) **14**	Area 13	3	7g

719 **69** Fig. 7h

Handmade. Thick white deposit on interior: contents or lining.

Nile B2. Fired fairly hard. Exterior concealed by slip; interior surface red where surface deposit lost. Break red-brown near exterior, with pink zones and grey core. Fairly plentiful fine and medium sand with a few larger grains. Sparse fine veg to 0.2. No visible limestone. Thick red-brown slip on exterior, including underside; interior uncoated. Polished where slipped.

Phase	Context & No.	Grid ref	Max dia body	Fig
vii	AAA (UP 445) **80**	Area 2	5.5	7h

70 Long-necked bottles (not present in Rzeuska 2006)

Long-necked bottles with smooth transition from rim to shoulder. Although not present in Rzeuska's material, elongated round-based bottles are common in the FIP (e.g Petrie and Brunton 1924a, Pl. XXXV [89b–y]); Arnold, Do 1993, Fig. 20 (left)). There are many and varied examples from Lisht in Nile B2 at the end of the FIP (Arnold Do. 1988, Fig. 52 [9–14], Fig. 53 [9–13], Fig. 54 [9–12]). Although not illustrated, at Lisht one (*ibid.*, 107 MMA [32.1.60]) is described as having a neck 'straight and set off from the shoulder by a groove' and another (*ibid.*, 109 MMA [32.1.9]) with 'straight neck…set off by a groove'; these vessels must surely have been similar to ADU **9**.

725 **70** Fig. 7i

The groove around the upper body of ADU **9** should be for string-tying. The rims appear to be wheel assisted.

Nile B2. ACE=AJH **98** fired medium, remainder fairly soft. Exterior surface pale brown where slip lost, interior grey except pale brown close to rim. Break ACE **98**, BGE **33** and CBS **26** pale brown with grey core, remainder with red core. Fairly plentiful poorly sorted sand. Fairly plentiful fine and coarse veg to 0.4/0.8. ACE=AJH **98** more limestone than usual, others sparse, to 0.05/0.1. Thin red slip on exterior, except ADU **9** and ACE=AJH **98** discoloured grey in part, former from proximity to another in the kiln. Except ADU **9**, possible traces of polish on exterior.

Rims

Phase	Context & No.	Grid ref	Dia rim (top)	Fig
o	ADU (UP 122) **39**	Area 13	*c.*3.5	As 7i
o	ADU (UP 330) **9**	Area 13	3.9	7i
iii–iva=iva	ACE=AJH **98**	05 to 09-06 to 09	*c.*3.8	As 7i

Neck fragments

Phase	Context & No.	Grid ref
o	ADU (UP 122) NE **1**	Area 13
iva	BGE **33**	12-02/03
ivb	CBS **26**	04/05-30/31/32

71 Spouted bowl (not present in Rzeuska 2006)

Sharply rounded sherd with about 50 per cent of the base of a spout, the hole pushed through from the exterior. Apparently handmade: the interior surface is slightly irregular and without wheel-ridges. Appears to be from the shoulder of a large spouted bowl, the spout being set just above or just below the shoulder. Bowls of this type include some of the Sixth Dynasty from Abusir (Kaiser 1969, XLVI and XLVII) and some of the Twelfth Dynasty from Tell el-Dab'a (Czerny 1999, [Nf 226/27/40/41]). Both series include red slipped and polished examples, and insufficient of **71** survives to allocate it to either.

727 **71** Fig. 7j

Nile B2. Fired fairly soft. Surfaces pale brown, exterior where slip lost. Break pale brown all through. Plentiful poorly sorted sand. Sparse fine veg to 0.2. Sparse limestone to 0.1 and one piece 0.2. Red-brown slip on exterior; interior uncoated. Exterior polished.

Phase	Context & No.	Grid ref	Max dia body	Fig
v	DAF **42**	Area 2 W10-S50	?	7j

72–74 Detached spouts (Rzeuska 2006, Form 38, Pl. 57)

No vessel with a preserved spout was recorded by Rzeuska, but three detached examples of widely differing shape were grouped as Form 38. Of these, only [225] resembles the Anubieion examples at all closely.

The Anubieion spouts divide into two types according to method of manufacture: the two examples grouped as **72** appear to have been formed integrally with the vessel, whereas **73** and **74** were clearly made separately and luted on over a hole previously pierced in the vessel wall. Rzeuska's [225] is more probably of the integral type.

There is no dearth of comparative material from other sites, but usually drawn too schematically or reproduced at too small a scale to show details of manufacture. The integral type is recorded at Giza on large, deep, red slipped and polished basins in the Fourth Dynasty (Wodzińska 2007, Figs 11.25/26 [CD 22]) and again on large, deep, red slipped bowls, some polished, at Tell el-Dab'a in the Twelfth (Czerny 1999, [Nf 218/26/27/29, 240/41/45]). Spouts are plentiful at Abusir on large bowls in the Fifth Dynasty (Kaiser 1969, XLV–XLVII); the first two of these groups are specified as red slipped and polished, and unless the drawings are simplified, the spouts are of the integral type. In Middle Kingdom contexts at Memphis (Kom Rabia) among a number of detached spouts, there were at least two of the integral type, one each in Nile B1 and Nile B2, both red slipped on the exterior but not polished or burnished (Bader 2009, 260 and Abb. 166 [4064]; 338 and Abb. 199 [5091]).

At Tell el-Dab'a, the luted-on type is clearly shown on most of the slightly later bag-shaped jars (Aston D.A. 2004b, Pls 16–19 [81–87]), though these are usually uncoated and (in keeping with the usual practice at this time) apparently never polished. The probability must be that the Anubieion examples, all of them polished, are of the OK or FIP, or the Twelfth Dynasty at the latest.

723A **72** Fig. 8a

Fragments of wall with part of integral spout. The polished slip on the interior of BCW/BDE **24** indicates an unrestricted form; BDR **44** preserves no part of the vessel wall, but the form of the spout is similar.

Nile B2. Fired fairly hard. Surfaces pale brown, exteriors where slip lost. Break pale brown with grey core. Fairly plentiful poorly sorted sand. BDR **44** moderate qty mostly fine veg to 0.3, BCW/BDE **24** small qty fine to 0.2. Sparse limestone to 0.05. BDR **44** small area of red slip survives on exterior, BCW/BDE **24** red-brown slip on both surfaces, not extending into interior of spout. Polished where slipped.

Phase	Context & No.	Grid ref	Dia spout (tip)	Fig
iii	BDR **44**	12/13/14-04/05/06	3.7	As 8a
ivb–c/ivb	BCW/BDE **24**	17/18-08	*c*.2.8(?)	8a

723B

73 Fig. 8b

Fragment of wall of large diameter vessel, with part of spout attached. Hole pushed through from the interior; spout made separately and fitted over the hole. The polished slip on the interior implies an unrestricted form and the diameter at the point of attachment of the spout would have been about 40.

Nile B2. Fired fairly hard. Surfaces concealed by slip, except interior of spout brown. Break brown with grey core. Fairly plentiful fine and medium sand with a few larger grains. Small qty fine veg to 0.2. Sparse limestone to 0.05. Red-brown slip on all surfaces, except interior of spout; slip applied after spout was attached because it spills on to its interior at one point. Polished where slipped.

Phase	Context & No.	Grid ref	Dia spout (tip)	Fig
ivd/ivd	ASZ/ATB **34**	05/06-S05	3.6	8b

2483

74 Fig. 8c

Fragment of wall of a vessel with rather less than 50 per cent of a spout attached. Hole pushed through from the interior; spout made separately and fitted over the hole. The polished slip on the interior implies an unrestricted form, but the spout is much smaller and slighter than 73. The surface slip is crazed, as often in the OK.

Nile B2. Fired medium. Surfaces concealed by slip, except part of 'stump' in interior red-brown. Break red-brown with mauve core. Fairly plentiful poorly sorted sand. Small qty fine veg to 0.3. Sparse limestone to 0.05. Thick red slip on all surfaces, except 'stump' in interior; slip applied after spout was attached. Polished where slipped.

Phase	Context & No.	Grid ref	Dia spout (tip)	Fig
?	CIC **11**	02 to 05-33	2.0	8c

75–76 Platters with groove close to rim (not present in Rzeuska 2006)

Although scarcely to be separated from the following series, these may be of a slightly earlier date. There is a similarity to Fourth Dynasty examples from both Giza (Wodzińska 2007, Fig. 11.15 [CD1]) and Dahshur (Faltings 1989, Abb. 9e [A36, A52]; Abb. 10b [A47, A49]). Platters of these types are all red slipped on all surfaces (as **76** but not **75**), at Giza polished on the interior, at Dahshur on all surfaces.

874A

75 Fig. 8d

Nile B2. Fired fairly soft. Surfaces pale brown. Break brown all through. Plentiful fine and medium sand with a few larger grains. Moderate qty fine veg to 0.3. Sparse limestone to 0.1. One red mineral inclusion 0.1. Smoothed but uncoated. Not polished or burnished.

Phase	Context & No.	Grid ref	Max dia rim	Fig
All iv (Pt II?)	ABK/S/U/V/Y/Z **2**	Area 13	?(30+?)	8d

874B **76** Fig. 8e

Nile B2. Fired fairly soft. Surfaces pale brown where slip lost. Break brown with red zones, and grey core where thickest. Plentiful fine and medium sand with a few larger grains. Moderate qty fine veg to 0.3. Sparse limestone to 0.05. Thick pinkish-red slip on all surfaces (exterior mostly weathered off). Polished where slip survives.

Phase	Context & No.	Grid ref	Max dia rim	Fig
iv (Pt II?)	ADF **17**	Area 13	? (30–40?)	8e

77–89 Platters (Rzeuska 2006, Forms 39–52 and 59–76, Pls 58–64 and 66–70)

Rzeuska's series illustrates a great range of handmade and wheel-assisted platters, with diameters (where measurable) in the wide range 14.5–38.5 cm. Because of the coarse fabric, and often hand manufacture, a perfect match with the fragmentary Anubieion examples is not to be expected, but a general resemblance is evident; the Nile B2 and Nile C fabrics also accord with all but a few of the smallest of Rzeuska's. Her platters are either uncoated or red slipped on the interior (though often on the exterior of the rim also), except that a few have a whitewash instead, and this can be on either surface (Rzeuska 2006, 398). The Anubieion examples are within the same diameter range or in a few cases above its upper limit. The polished surfaces are not paralleled, but predecessors of the Fourth Dynasty, very similar to some of Rzeuska's forms, are normally polished (see Wodzińska and Faltings, entry under **75–76**).

The 'best matches' are probably:
77 Rzeuska's [229], Form 39, Pl. 58; [251], Form 46, Pl. 62
78 Rzeuska's [238/40], Form 43, Pl. 60; [251], Form 46, Pl. 62
79 Rzeuska's [243], Form 44, Pl. 60
80 Rzeuska's [252], Form 46, Pl. 62; [257], Form 50, Pl. 63
81 Rzeuska's [255], Form 49, Pl. 63
82 Rzeuska's [257/58], Form 50, Pl. 63
83 and **84** Rzeuska's [262], Form 53, Pl. 64
85 Rzeuska's [277/78], Form 60, Pl. 66; [297], Form 70, Pl. 69
86 Rzeuska's [281], Form 62, Pl. 67; [295], Form 69, Pl. 69*
87 Rzeuska's [232/33], Form 41, Pl. 59
88 Rzeuska's [304], Form 75, Pl. 70
89 Rzeuska's [305], Form 76, Pl. 70

* **86** is also very similar to an unnumbered MK platter from the South Building at Dahshur (Arnold Do, unpublished), dated to the reign of Amenemhat III. Nor can a NK date be entirely ruled out (Bourriau 2010, Fig. 52 [17.1.7])!

866 **77** Fig. 8f

String-impression at an angle on exterior, from tying before firing. Handmade.

Nile C. Fired fairly soft. Surfaces pale yellow-brown. Break yellow-brown with pink core. Fairly plentiful poorly sorted sand. Plentiful fine and coarse veg to 1.0. One piece limestone 0.1. Thin pale red-brown slip on exterior; interior uncoated but slip perhaps weathered off. No visible polish or burnish.

Phase	Context & No.	Grid ref	Max dia rim	Fig
iva/ivb	BDG/BRT **4**	12/13/14-03/04/05	*c*.38	8f

854 **78** Fig. 8g

Surfaces uneven, lower part scraped. Wide, shallow groove just below rim was probably for string-tying.

Nile C. Fired medium. Surfaces brown where uncoated or slip lost. Break brown with thin red zones and thick grey core. Plentiful poorly sorted sand. Fairly plentiful fine and coarse veg to 1.3. Sparse limestone to 0.1. Red slip survives on interior of rim, and on exterior in the wide groove, but surfaces otherwise weathered or affected by salt. Traces of polish on interior of rim only.

Phase	Context & No.	Grid ref	Max dia rim	Fig
All iva	AQV/AQW/AQX/AQY/AQZ **6**	11-13/14/15	*c.*10–15	8g

886 **79** Fig. 8h

The thickening of the wall towards the lower break implies a shallow vessel.

Nile B2. Fired fairly soft. Surfaces pale brown where slip lost. Break pale brown with grey core. Fairly plentiful poorly sorted sand. Fairly plentiful fine and coarse veg to 0.7. Sparse limestone to 0.1. Thick red slip on both surfaces. Both surfaces polished.

Phase	Context & No.	Grid ref	Dia rim (top)	Fig
o	ADU (UP 122) SW **32**	Area 13	*c.*35–40	8h

896 **80** Fig. 9a

Crude, handmade. Surfaces uneven, but interior smoothed; exterior left rough.

Nile C. Fired medium. Exterior red-brown, interior surface pale purple (from stacking in the kiln). Break red-brown, with grey core extending to exterior surface. Fairly plentiful poorly sorted sand. Fairly plentiful fine and coarse veg to 1.0. Sparse limestone to 0.1, and voids probably from limestone to 0.3. Uncoated. Not polished or burnished.

Phase	Context & No.	Grid ref	Dia rim (top)	Fig
ii	BDX **4**	05-07/08	*c.*20–25	9a

858 **81** Fig. 9b

Two very clear rows of impressions from string-tying. Perhaps handmade.

Nile B2. Fired medium. Surfaces brown where slip lost. Break brown with thick red core. Plentiful fine well-sorted sand. No visible veg. Sparse limestone to 0.2. Thick red slip on interior, and surviving traces on exterior. All surfaces polished where slip survives.

Phase	Context & No.	Grid ref	Max dia rim	Fig
vi	ABI (UP 7) **94**	Area 13	*c.*40(?)	9b

1492 **82** Fig. 9c

Surface uneven: probably handmade.

Nile B2 Sandy. Fired soft. Surfaces brown. Break brown all through. Plentiful poorly sorted sand. Small qty fine veg to 0.3. Sparse limestone to 0.05. One piece pale grey stone 0.2 × 0.1; one piece deep red stone 0.1; two pieces probably 'grog' 0.1. Interior, and exterior down to 1.0, smoothed not slipped; surface of exterior below 1.0 lost. No visible polish or burnish.

Phase	Context & No.	Grid ref	Max dia rim	Fig
iva/ivb	BHR/BTG **150**	02-21	*c.*20(?)	9c

2925 **83** Fig. 9d

The groove on the exterior, below the lightly rolled rim, may have been for string-tying.

Nile B2. Fired fairly soft. Surfaces pale brown where slip lost. Break pale brown with thick grey core. Fairly plentiful fine sand with a few larger grains. Fairly plentiful fine veg to 0.2. Sparse limestone to 0.1. Small areas of red slip survive weathering on top of rim and in the fold under the rim on the exterior. Polished where slip survives.

Phase	Context & No.	Grid ref	Max dia rim	Fig
iva	AFZ **13**	18 to 20-01	*c.*23	9d

2828 **84** Fig. 9e

Almost certainly handmade, with veg inclusions at various angles.

Nile B2. Fired medium. Surfaces orange, with one large mauve patch on exterior where against another in the kiln. Break orange with thick pink core extending to exterior where surface is mauve. Fairly plentiful poorly sorted sand. Fairly plentiful fine and coarse veg to 0.4. Rather more limestone than usual, to 0.15. No surviving slip on surfaces, but some veg voids on both surfaces contain red, probably slip. Not polished or burnished as preserved.

Phase	Context & No.	Grid ref	Dia rim (top)	Fig
ivb	AFV East **7**	11-04/05	*c.*20–28	9e

826 **85** Fig. 9f

Rim of large diameter flat-rimmed bowl with thick wall. The interior surface is weathered but a tiny surviving area shows that not much thickness is lost. Handmade.

Nile B2. Fired medium. Exterior surface brown, interior lost. Break brown with thin red zones and thick grey core. Fairly plentiful poorly sorted sand. Fairly plentiful fine and coarse veg to 1.0. Sparse limestone to 0.2. Surfaces too weathered to retain slip, or polish or burnish.

Phase	Context & No.	Grid ref	Max dia rim	Fig
iv (Pt II?)?	BWL? (UP 1040) **5**	Area 12	? (30+?)	9f

932 **86** Fig. 9g

The lower part of the interior may have turned inwards rather than as drawn, but the coarse fabric precludes certainty.

Nile C. Fired fairly soft. (Presumed) exterior surface brown, interior concealed by slip or wash. Break brown near exterior surface, with one red zone, and grey core extending to interior. Plentiful poorly sorted sand.

Plentiful fine and coarse veg to 1.0. Sparse limestone to 0.3. Thin whitewash on top of rim and on (presumed) interior to depth 1.5, then fired grey. Not polished or burnished.

Phase	Context & No.	Grid ref	Dia rim (top)	Fig
iva	BHR **71**	02-22	*c* 35–40?	9g

2296 **87** Fig. 10a

Two similar rims, differing only in a slightly deeper overhang to BDR **92**.

Nile C. Fired fairly hard. Surfaces yellow-brown where uncoated or slip lost. Break brown, BDR **92** with thin pink zones and thick grey core, AMJ **3** red zones and mauve core. Fairly plentiful fine and medium sand with a few larger grains. Plentiful fine and coarse veg, BDR **92** to 0.5, AMJ **3** to 0.9. No visible limestone. Areas of red slip survive on flat underside of AMJ **3**, but all other surfaces weathered. AMJ **3** highly polished where slip survives, BDR **92** too weathered for polish or burnish to survive.

Phase	Context & No.	Grid ref	Max dia rim	Fig
iii	BDR **92**	11/12/13-03/04/05	*c*.40(?)	Similar to 10a
vi	AMJ **3**	18/19/20-10	*c*.30–35	10a

868 **88** Fig. 10b

The wide, shallow exterior groove has a faint impress from string-tying, which has compressed it into its present form. The underside is rough from standing on the ground before firing. Handmade.

Nile C. Fired medium. Interior concealed by slip, exterior and underside red-brown. Break red-brown with thin red zones and thick grey core. Fairly plentiful poorly sorted sand. Plentiful fine and coarse veg to 1.0. Sparse limestone to 0.1. Thin red slip on interior, probably not carried over the rim; exterior and underside uncoated. Not polished or burnished.

Phase	Context & No.	Grid ref	Max dia rim	Fig
?	UP 1044 **2**	Area 12	? (30+?)	10b

870 **89** Fig. 10c

The underside is rough and uneven. Handmade.

Nile C. Fired fairly soft. Surfaces pale brown where uncoated or slip lost. Break pale brown with red core. Plentiful poorly sorted sand. Fairly plentiful fine and some coarse veg to 1.0. Sparse limestone to 0.1. Pink slip (colour from soft firing) on interior and just over rim on to exterior, perhaps continuing down white for a further 1.0. Below this uncoated. Not polished or burnished.

Phase	Context & No.	Grid ref	Max dia rim	Fig
iv (Pt II?)	ARU=ARZ (UP 204) **14**	Area 13	? (30+)	10c

90–96 Large platters with grooved interior wall (Rzeuska 2006, Forms 77–84, Pls 71–74)

Rzeuska illustrates three series of open forms with parallel grooves in the upper body, or in a few cases the rim. The most numerous are the platters, with thick walls and flat (or almost flat) bases. There are also a few examples of bell-shaped bowls (her Forms 143–144) and bent-sided bowls (her Forms 176–178). It has to be said that the smallest and thinnest of the platters (on Pl. 76) are scarcely to be distinguished from the other two types, which are themselves sometimes very similar; this is a problem of classification all ceramicists have to grapple with, and one to which there is no ultimate solution.

The Anubieion series appears to correspond only to the platters. Rzeuska (2006, 398) states that they functioned as portable ovens, with the grooves ensuring essential airflow. They are divided into large (max dia 30 and above) and medium large (19.5–29), with one small example (16.5) and one 'diverse' (26); several are of uncertain diameter. The diameters are all approximate, owing to the small size of the sherds, but the Anubieion series corresponds only to the 'large' group. Where vessels with such thick walls are concerned, there is certain to be a wide range of forms, and exact duplication is not to be expected.

Each of Rzeuska's series contains some Nile B2 and some Nile C examples. The interiors of the 'large' group are red slipped and the exteriors uncoated, except that [311] is apparently slipped overall. This accords exactly with the Anubieion, where with the exception of **92** it is the interiors only which are fully red slipped. The methods of manufacture again agree exactly, Rzeuska describing pounded bases and coiled walls finished off on the wheel.

Kaiser publishes grooved-rim vessels of similar types in red slipped Nile fabric (Kaiser 1969, XLII, Type 213–16). These are sufficiently preserved to show that at least some examples were supported on three low 'feet', a feature which also survives on a few of Rzeuska's sherds.

The unexpected unfired example (**93**) among the Anubieion material was presumably placed in a tomb, possibly as a lid. A coloured slip should have been visible, even in an unfired state, but a self-slip may not have been.

910 **90** Fig. 10d

Rim and upper half of body smoothed and apparently wheel assisted; lower half and underside handmade, left rough, with veg impressions and scratches from sand-grains. The smoothing clearly over-runs the roughness. No visible string-impressions.

Nile C. Fired soft. Interior concealed by slip, exterior pale brown where uncoated. Break brown with faint red zones and grey core. Fairly plentiful poorly sorted sand. Fairly plentiful fine and coarse veg to 0.6 and a few pieces to 1.0. Sparse limestone to 0.1. Thick red slip on interior, carried over rim and down 1.0 on exterior to a straight edge. Interior and top of rim polished, exterior probably polished where slipped, but not otherwise.

Phase	Context & No.	Grid ref	Max dia rim	Fig
o	ADU (UP 330) **20**	Area 13	*c.*50–55	10d

864A **91** Fig. 10e

Handmade.

Nile C. Fired medium. Upper surface concealed by slip, lower brown. Break brown with thin grey zones near surface, then red zones and grey core. Fairly plentiful poorly sorted sand. Fairly plentiful fine and coarse veg to 0.9. Sparse limestone to 0.1. Thin red slip on upper (grooved) surface, underside uncoated. Possible traces of polish where slip survives.

Phase	Context & No.	Grid ref	Max dia rim	Fig
o/o	AQG/BEO **7**	21-S06	30–40(?)	10e

840 **92** Fig. 10f–g

Wheel assisted as far as preserved. BJF **17** has shallow external grooves, probably for string-tying, while AAD **47** has deeper external grooves and clear string-impressions.

Nile B2. Fired fairly hard. Surfaces concealed by slip. Break, BJF **17** red with thin dark brown zones near surfaces and thick grey core, AAD **47** orange-red all through. BJF **17** fairly plentiful, AAD **47** plentiful, poorly sorted sand. BJF **17** fairly plentiful fine and coarse veg to 0.5, AAD **47** plentiful to 1.3. BJF **17** sparse limestone to 0.1, AAD **47** more than usual, to 0.2. Thick red slip on both surfaces, except underside of BJF **17**, where slip is thinner and fired white in places. BJF **17** only interior polished, AAD **47** both surfaces.

Phase	Context & No.	Grid ref	Max dia rim	Fig
iva	BJF **17**	17/18-06	*c*.40(?)	10f
ivc	AAD **47**	09-06	*c*.35(?)	10g

844 **93** Fig. 11a

Grooves unusually wide and widely spaced. The top 8 cm of the exterior are smoothed, slightly undulating and scored, probably from the assistance of a wheel, while the 2.5 cm remaining to the break are rough and probably handmade. Clearly marked, long string-impressions on exterior, about one to 1.5 cm below rim; cf AAD **47** of **92** but longer and located further down (though the flat edge of the rim may betray a second string which has left no marks).

Nile B2 unfired. Grey on surfaces and throughout break. Fairly plentiful poorly sorted sand. Fairly plentiful fine and some coarse veg to 0.8. Sparse limestone to 0.8. No visible slip, or polish or burnish.

Phase	Context & No.	Grid ref	Max dia rim	Fig
vii	CAA **44**	Area 26	*c*.45	11a

842 **94** Fig. 11b

No visible string-impressions. Interior partly blackened from smoke or ash.

Nile C. Fired fairly soft. Surfaces pale brown, interior where slip lost. Break brown with red zones and thin grey core. Fairly plentiful poorly sorted sand. Plentiful coarse veg to 0.8. Sparse limestone to 0.1 and one piece 0.4 × 0.3. Thick red slip on interior, carried over rim to just below mid-point; exterior uncoated. Polished where slipped.

Phase	Context & No.	Grid ref	Max dia rim	Fig
iii–iva	ACE **187**	01 to 05-08 to 12	30–40(?)	11b

838 **95** Fig. 11c

Rim formed on a slow wheel. The underside lacks wheel-grooves or scratches but has regular undulations. Faint string-impressions at an angle around part of edge of rim, from string-tying.

Nile B2. Fired fairly soft. Surfaces pale brown where uncoated or slip lost. Break pale brown with red zones and grey core. Fairly plentiful poorly sorted sand. Fairly plentiful fine and coarse veg to 0.6. Sparse limestone to 0.05, one piece 0.2 and one fossil shell fragment 0.8 × 0.3. Thick red slip on interior, carried over rim and down 3.0 on exterior to a straight edge; exterior otherwise uncoated. Polished where slipped, interior only on the ridges between the grooves.

Phase	Context & No.	Grid ref	Max dia rim	Fig
vii	AAA East **25**	Area 1	*c*.42	11c

853 **<u>96</u>** Fig. 11d

Upper body and rim of large diameter flat form. Lightly ribbed on interior. Thin grooves on exterior near lower break, perhaps indicating a second throwing to shape the base. No visible string-impressions.

<u>Nile C.</u> Fired fairly soft. Interior concealed by slip, exterior red-brown. Break pale red-brown with thick red core. Plentiful poorly sorted sand. Fairly plentiful fine and coarse veg to 0.5 and a few pieces to 1.0. Rather more limestone than usual in a Nile fabric, to 0.1. Red slip on interior; exterior uncoated. Not polished or burnished. The edge of the rim appears to have been painted dark red, this spilling slightly over on to the interior at one point.

Phase	Context & No.	Grid ref	Max dia rim	Fig
ivc	CGV **30**	02 to 05-33 to 36	*c.*39	11d

<u>97</u> Small to medium-sized bowl with interior groove (not present in Rzeuska 2006)

A simple bowl form, but with a conspicuous groove just inside the rim. An exact match is published by Bader (2009a, Fig. 8l). The fabric is Nile B1 near B2, slipped dark red and polished, with top diameter 16.4, and it is dated as late OK/early FIP. According to Bader (*ibid.*, 30) 'other plates/dishes with thicker walls exhibit horizontal grooves of varying depth and width close to the rim, mostly on the inside of the vessels (Fig. 8.l-m)' so the groove is not coincidental.

431 **<u>97</u>** Fig. 11e

Wheel assisted as far as preserved.

<u>Nile B1.</u> Fired fairly soft. Surfaces pale brown where slip lost. Break pale brown all through. Fairly plentiful fine and medium well-sorted sand. Small qty mostly fine veg to 0.3. Sparse limestone to 0.05. Thin red-brown slip on both surfaces. Both surfaces polished.

Phase	Context & No.	Grid ref	Dia rim (top)	Fig
iv (Pt II?)/?	AYP/AYJ **22**	Area 13	*c.*15	11e

<u>98–101</u> Shallow bowls with direct rim (not present in Rzeuska 2006)

Although by the time the Teti pyramid was constructed, more complicated vessel forms were in vogue in the Memphite area, simple deep and shallow bowls with direct rim had been common in earlier times; at Saqqara they go back to the First Dynasty (Emery 1938, Pls 9/24/27). The shallower forms, at least, are still current at Giza in the Fourth Dynasty (Kromer 1978, Taf. 27 [1/2]); Wodzińska 2007, Figs. 11.15–18 [CD1–CD4]). The shallow **<u>98</u>** and **<u>99</u>** with lightly rounded base resemble Wodzińska's Type CD2, which is handmade and red slipped, the interior (only) being polished. The deeper **<u>100</u>**, with flaring rim, is probably part of the CD3 series, while the incurved **<u>101</u>** resembles CD4. It is not specified whether CD3/4 were handmade or wheel assisted, but most were red, brown or black slipped, and polished on both surfaces or on the interior only. The diameter ranges of all four series CD1–4 were 15–40 cm; many were recorded as burnt on both surfaces or on the interior only, as **<u>100</u>** and BPV **54** of **<u>101</u>**. At Abu Rawash, similar forms are recorded in contexts of the Fourth to early Fifth Dynasty (Marchand and Baud 1996, Fig. 7 [6–7]).

Although it is possible that these rims were brought to the site in mud bricks, they (like other vessels with Fourth Dynasty counterparts) are more likely to indicate pre-Teti activity in the area.

A similar form to **<u>98</u>** is recorded at Akhmim as late as the end of the OK to the early MK (Hope and McFarlane, 2006, Fig. 1 [BIIa.1]), with red slip and polish(?) ('compacted clay') on both surfaces; it may imply a longer life-span for this form further south.

906 **98** Fig. 11f

Small diameter, thick-walled carinated bowl. Surface irregularities indicate handmade.

Nile B2. Badly fired and beginning to sinter. Surfaces grey, except exterior tinged red near break. Break dark brown all through. Plentiful poorly sorted sand. Small qty fine veg to 0.3. Sparse limestone to 0.1. Firing and weathering make it impossible to tell if slipped, polished or burnished.

Phase	Context & No.	Grid ref	Max dia rim	Fig
iva	AJH under AVH **41**	05-04/05/06	*c*.15	11f

1500 **99** Fig. 11g

Perhaps wheel assisted.

Nile B2 with extra limestone. Fired fairly soft. Surfaces concealed by slip. Break brown all through. Fairly plentiful to plentiful poorly sorted sand. Moderate qty fine veg to 0.3. More limestone than usual in a Nile fabric, to 0.1. Thick red-brown slip on all surfaces. All surfaces polished.

Phase	Context & No.	Grid ref	Max dia rim	Fig
iv (Pt II?)	BWX **6**	Area 12	*c*.20(?)	11g

2040 **100** Fig. 11h

Cannot tell whether handmade or wheel assisted.

Nile B2. Fired fairly soft. Surfaces concealed by slip. Break pale brown all through. Fairly plentiful fine and medium sand with a few larger grains. Moderate qty fine and coarse veg to 0.5. No visible limestone. Two orange mineral particles, each 0.1. Thick slip on both surfaces, pink on exterior but black on interior, probably from smoke or ash rather than so fired. Both surfaces polished.

Phase	Context & No.	Grid ref	Max dia rim	Fig
ivc	BQU **19**	Area 2	*c*.16–20	11h

2010 **101** Fig. 12a

On BPV **54** evidence of burning or contact with ash. Deep criss-crossing scratches on exterior of AJI **14** indicate handmade; rims too damaged to show whether or not wheel assisted.

Nile B2. Fired fairly soft. Surfaces brown, AJI **14** where slip lost. Break brown, AJI **14** with red core, or red zones and dark brown core where thickest; BPV **54** all through, probably from burning. Moderate qty fine and medium sand with a few larger grains. AJI **14** plentiful fine and coarse veg to 0.8, BPV **54** fairly plentiful to 0.5. Sparse limestone to 0.05, BPV **54** also one piece 0.2 × 0.1 and one 0.1. BPV **54** two orange mineral or grog fragments 0.05 (cf **6**). AJI **14** interior, and exterior top 2 cm only, smoothed; BPV **54** interior smoothed, exterior weathered. AJI **14** red slip on all surfaces (much damaged), BPV **54** too burnt and weathered to tell. AJI **14** traces of high polish on both surfaces, BPV **54** probable traces on exterior.

Phase	Context & No.	Grid ref	Max dia rim	Fig
ivd	AJI **14**	22/23-01	?(*c*.20–25?)	12a

Phase	Context & No.	Grid ref	Max dia rim	Fig
?	BPV **54**	03/04-21	?	Similar to 12a

102 Thick-walled plate with long-ledged rim (Rzeuska 2006, Form 94, Pl. 79)

Although with its thick wall it is not a perfect match, **102** is close in form, size and surface treatment to this unique example within Rzeuska's series of bent-sided plates.

1486 **102** Fig. 12b

Nile B2. Fired fairly soft. AQG/AJY **31** interior orange, exterior red-brown, ACP **72** surfaces pale brown where uncoated or slip lost. Break, AQG/AJY **31** orange with thin red zones and thick purple core, ACP **72** pale brown with red zones and grey core. Fairly plentiful poorly sorted sand. Fairly plentiful to plentiful fine and coarse veg to 0.8. Sparse limestone to 0.1. AQG/AJY **31** small area of red slip survives on top of rim only; top 2.5 of exterior and whole interior smoothed, but lower exterior rough. ACP **72** thin pink slip on interior, exterior uncoated but smoothed as far as preserved. Polished where slip survives.

Phase	Context & No.	Grid ref	Max dia rim	Fig
o/ii	AQG/AJY **31**	19/20-04/05	(20–30?)	Similar to 12b
ivc	ACP **72**	02 to 05-09	?	12b

103–13 Bent-sided plates (Rzeuska 2006, Forms 92–98, Pls 78–81)

The bent-sided plates are a shallower version of Rzeuska's much longer series of bent-sided bowls (Forms 161–69 but also spout-rims Forms 170/71/73–75 and grooved Forms 176/77). The Anubieion series is so shallow as to come unambiguously under the heading of plates, but the diameter range extends beyond the largest of Rzeuska's.

Each series consists of a mixture of Nile B1 and Nile B2 fabrics in about the same proportion of 3:1 (Rzeuska also has one in Nile A). As with the bent-sided bowls, many are not polished while all at the Anubieion are, though this may be due to the conditions of preservation. **107** is fired black, not burnt.

1668K **103** Fig. 12c

Nile B1. Fired fairly hard. Surfaces concealed by slip. Break red-brown with grey core. Fairly plentiful fine and medium well-sorted sand. Small qty fine veg to 0.2. Sparse limestone to 0.05. Pale red-brown slip on both surfaces. Both surfaces polished.

Phase	Context & No.	Grid ref	Dia rim (top)	Fig
?	ANS (UP 1000) **25**	Area 14	*c.*45	12c

2050 **104** Fig. 12d

Large diameter, thickened rim and sharp change of angle on the interior. Exterior wall almost flat. Form well standardised.

Nile B1. AIW **8** fired medium, others fairly soft. Surfaces pale brown or red-brown where slip lost. Break, AIW **8** pale brown with red zones and grey core, others brown or red-brown all through, or with grey core, or red zones and grey core. Moderate qty to fairly plentiful sand, BHW **171** poorly sorted, others fine, or fine and medium, BGO East/BGQ **19** and BQQ **12** with a few larger grains. Sparse fine veg to 0.2 or none visible. Sparse limestone to 0.05 or none visible. CBY **9** surfaces lost, otherwise slip on both surfaces: BDQ **13** and BGQ/BGO East **19** pink, ADC **101**, AIW **8** and ACP **82** orange-brown, remainder red-brown. Both surfaces polished where slip survives.

Nile B2. Fired fairly soft to medium. Surfaces pale brown or red-brown where slip lost. Break red-brown with red core or red zones and grey core. Fairly plentiful sand, BSE (**26?**) poorly sorted, others fine and medium, AJH under AVH **51** and BML **31** with a few larger grains. Moderate qty to fairly plentiful fine veg to 0.2/0.3. Sparse limestone to 0.05/0.1. Slip on both surfaces, BSE (**26?**) traces of pale pink, others pale red-brown to red-brown, AJH under AVH **51** mostly burnt black. Polished where slip survives.

Phase	Context & No.	Grid ref	Dia rim (top)	Fabric	Fig
ii	BET **30**	12-01/02	*c.*40–45	B1	
iii	BDP (UP 647) **268**	01 to 05-07	*c.*45	B2	12d
iii	BDQ **13**	01 to 05-07/08	*c.*40	B1	
iii	BHW **171**	02-21/22	30+	B1	
iii/iva	BGQ/BGO East **19**	07-01	?	B1	
iv (Pt II?)	ADC **101**	Area 13	*c.*30–35(?)	B1	
iva	AIW **8**	17/18/19-01	30+	B1	
iva	AJH under AVH **51**	05-04/05/06	*c.*40	B2	
iva	BHR **No. lost**	02/03-21 to 24	*c.*30–35(?)	B2	
iva	BML **31**	06-13/14	*c.*40(?)	B2	
ivc	ACP **82**	01 to 05-10	*c.*35(?)	B1	
ivc	BQQ **12**	Area 2	?	B1	
ivd	CBY **9**	04/05-34	?	B1	
vi	AEP **42**	03-03/04	*c.*30(?)	B1	
?	BSE (**26?**)	Area 2	35–40(?)	B2	

2052 **105** Fig. 12e–f

Similar to **104** but with concave exterior wall and most examples thinner. Again, little variability.

Nile B1. BHR **51** and BRP **16** fired fairly soft, remainder medium to fairly hard. ADU **7** and AAB **39** surfaces concealed by slip, others red-brown to brown where slip lost. Break BHR **51** and BRP **16** brown with grey core, others red-brown or brown with mauve or grey core, except AAB **39** red core. Moderate qty to fairly plentiful fine, or fine and medium, sand, BHR **51** and AKN **31** with a few larger grains. Small qty fine veg to 0.2. Sparse limestone to 0.05/0.1. BTX **162** surfaces weathered off, others both surfaces slipped, though some in small areas only: BRP **16** burnt black, ADU **7** and AKN **31** orange, remainder red-brown. Polished where slip survives.

Phase	Context & No.	Grid ref	Dia rim (top)	Fig
o	ADU (UP 335) **7**	Area 13	*c.*28	12e
iva	BHR **51**	02-22	30+(?)	As 12f
ivb	BRP **16**	06-32/33	20+(?)	As 12e
ivc	BTX **162**	02/03-19/20	20+(?)	As 12e
ivd	ATY **37**	22/23-02/03	30–40(?)	As 12e
ivd	BHE **24**	04/05-22	?	As 12e
vi	AKN (UP 233) **31**	Area 13	*c.*30–35	As 12e
vi–vii	AAB **39**	01/02-33/34	*c.*40	12f

1668J **106** Fig. 12g–h

Nile B1. Fired fairly hard. Surfaces concealed by slip. Break red-brown with grey core. Fairly plentiful fine well-sorted sand. Small qty fine veg to 0.2. Sparse limestone to 0.05. Red-brown slip on both surfaces. Both surfaces polished.

Nile B2. Fired fairly soft. Surface pale brown where slip lost. Break pale brown with red zones and grey core. Fairly plentiful fine and medium sand with a few larger grains. Moderate qty to fairly plentiful fine veg to 0.3. Sparse limestone to 0.1. Red-brown slip on both surfaces. Both surfaces lightly polished.

Phase	Context & No.	Grid ref	Dia rim (top)	Fabric	Fig
iii	BDR **127**	11/12/13-03/04/05	25	B1	12g
?	ANS (UP 1000) **46**	Area 14	31	B2	12h

2922 **107** Fig. 13a

Nile B2. Fired fairly hard. Surfaces brown where slip lost. Break brown with darker brown areas. Fairly plentiful fine well-sorted sand. Moderate qty fine veg to 0.2. Sparse limestone to 0.1. Black slip on both surfaces. Both surfaces polished.

Phase	Context & No.	Grid ref	Dia rim (top)	Fig
v	BXJ **1**	Area 13	? (25+, perhaps 35+)	13a

1488 **108** Fig. 13b

Nile B2. Fired medium. Interior concealed by slip, exterior red-brown where uncoated. Break red-brown with thick grey core. Fairly plentiful poorly sorted sand. Fairly plentiful fine and coarse veg to 0.8. Sparse limestone to 0.05. Red slip overall on interior, carried over rim and down 0.5 on exterior; remainder of exterior uncoated. Polished where slipped.

Phase	Context & No.	Grid ref	Dia rim (top)	Fig
vii	CAA **43**	Area 26	*c.*26	13b

1600 **109** Fig. 13c

The well-marked groove below the carination and fainter ones above and in the break are probably from string-tying.

Nile B1. Fired medium. Surfaces concealed by slip. Break brown with red zones and brown core, and areas of dark brown and reddish brown, either oil-staining or from firing method. Fairly plentiful fine and medium sand with a few larger grains. Sparse fine veg to 0.2. Only one piece limestone 0.2 visible. Probable thin slip on both surfaces, fired pinkish grey except red-brown on exterior above carination. Both surfaces polished.

Phase	Context & No.	Grid ref	Dia rim (top)	Fig
ivc	ACP **85**	01 to 05-10	24	13c

1602 **110** Fig. 13d

Surfaces blotchily stained black, perhaps from oil.

Nile B1. Fired medium. Surfaces concealed by slip. Break red-brown all through except for a thin black streak close to each surface, probably from the staining. Fairly plentiful fine well sorted sand. No visible veg. Sparse limestone to 0.1. Thin red slip on both surfaces, with blackened areas. Both surfaces polished.

Phase	Context & No.	Grid ref	Dia rim (top)	Fig
iii	BKR **18**	02-21/22	*c*.20–24	13d

323 **111** Fig. 13e

Nile B2. Fired fairly soft. Surfaces pale brown where uncoated or slip lost. Break brown, ARU=ARZ **35** with grey core, BWQ **1** with red core. Fairly plentiful poorly sorted sand. BWQ **1** fairly plentiful fine and coarse veg, others small to medium qty fine, all to 0.3. Sparse limestone to 0.05. Thin brownish red slip: ARU=ARZ **35**, preserved to the greatest depth, is slipped overall on the interior but only down to 3.0 on the exterior; the others are slipped on both surfaces as far as preserved. ARU=ARZ **35** also shows horizontal and vertical wipe marks on the slipped interior near the rim. Lightly polished where slipped, and ARU=ARZ **35** also polished by compaction on the uncoated exterior near lower break, perhaps evidence of a secondary shaping of the base on a slow wheel.

Phase	Context & No.	Grid ref	Dia rim (top)	Fig
iv (Pt II?)	ABW **24**	Area 13	*c*.30	Similar to 13e
iv (Pt II?)	ADC **105**	Area 13	*c*.26	Similar to 13e
iv (Pt II?)	ARU=ARZ (UP 204) **35**	Area 13	24	13e
iv (Pt II?)	BWQ **1**	Area 13	26	Similar to 13e

1534 **112** Fig. 13f–h

At the lower end of the diameter range for the series.

Nile B1. Fired variably, from fairly soft to fairly hard. Surfaces concealed by slip, or as break where slip is lost. Break, softer fired are brown or red-brown all through, or with red or grey core, harder are red-brown with thin pink zones and grey core. Fairly plentiful fine, or fine and medium, well-sorted sand, some with a few larger grains. Small qty fine veg to 0.2/0.3. Sparse limestone to 0.05/0.1. Slip on both surfaces, AHR/AEF **28** orange-red, others red-brown to brown, on many surviving in small areas only. Both surfaces polished where slip survives.

Phase	Context & No.	Grid ref	Dia rim (top)	Fig
ii	AQE **51**	19/20-01/02	*c*.19–24	As 13g
ii	AQE **72**	19/20-02/03	21	13f
ii	BDS **20**	03-07	?	As 13g
iii–iva	ACE **61**	05-06/07/08	?	As 13f
iii–iva	ACE **215**	01 to 05-08 to 12	*c*.20	As 13g
iv (Pt II?)/?	AYQ/AYR **6**	Area 13	21	13g
iva	BHR **61**	02-20/21	17	Between 13g & 13h
ivb/vi	AHR/AEF **28**	10 to 14-04/05	*c*.17–22	13h
ivc	BQV **72**	Area 2	22	As 13g
ivd	ATY **36**	23/24/25-04/05/06	21	As 13g
vii	CAA North **8**	Area 26	22	As 13g
?	UP 1039 **6**	Area 12	22	As 13g

Phase	Context & No.	Grid ref	Dia rim (top)	Fig
?	UP 1046 **7**	Area 12	21	As 13g

1538 <u>**113**</u> Fig. 14a

The carination is not perfectly parallel to the rim. Scraping marks on the exterior near the break: some horizontal, some at an angle.

<u>Nile B2.</u> Fired medium. Surfaces pale brown where slip lost. Break pale brown with thin pink zones and thick grey core. Fairly plentiful fine and medium sand with a few larger grains. Moderate qty fine veg to 0.5. Sparse limestone to 0.1 and one piece 0.5 × 0.2. Red-brown slip on both surfaces, fired almost red on lower interior, probably from stacking in the kiln. Both surfaces polished.

Phase	Context & No.	Grid ref	Dia rim (top)	Fig
vi	AER **51**	02-08	26	14a

<u>114</u> Straight-walled plate with inner groove (nearest, Rzeuska 2006, Form 106=108, Pl. 86)

No perfect match has been found, but the closest is probably [403] of Form 106=108, most examples of which are red slipped on both surfaces. The general form continues into the early MK (Czerny 1999, 141 [Nf 74/75]), where similar examples (dias 21–30) are slipped and sometimes polished.

876 <u>**114**</u> Fig. 14b

Probably handmade, but uncertain because weathered.

<u>Nile B2.</u> Fired medium. Surfaces brown. Break brown with thick red-brown core. Fairly plentiful fine and medium well-sorted sand. Fairly plentiful fine veg to 0.5. Sparse limestone to 0.1. Surfaces too weathered for slip, or polish or burnish, to survive.

Phase	Context & No.	Grid ref	Max dia rim	Fig
iv (Pt II?)/?	AYP/AYJ **19**	Area 13	*c.*25–30(?)	14b

<u>115–17</u> Straight-walled plates with inner groove (Rzeuska 2006, Forms 106=108–117, Pls 86–90)

A small number of Anubieion plates were classified individually because of their unusual form. All fit well into the medium-size series of straight-walled plates, though some should be classified as large. Although all Rzeuska's examples are red slipped, wholly or in part, none is recorded as polished.

<u>**115**</u> is a close match for Rzeuska's [393] (and [392]) of Form 106=108 (Pl. 85). It is also similar to the slightly smaller [436] of Form 121 (Pl. 91)
<u>**116**</u> is very similar to Rzeuska's [398] of Form 106=108 (Pl. 86), slightly distorted by string-tying
<u>**117**</u> is a close match for Rzeuska's [419] of Form 113 (Pl. 89)

2034 <u>**115**</u> Fig. 14c

<u>Nile B2.</u> Fired fairly soft. Surfaces brown where slip too thin to cover. Break brown with red core. Fairly plentiful fine and medium sand with a few larger grains. Fairly plentiful fine veg to 0.2. Sparse limestone to 0.05. Thin red slip on both surfaces. Both surfaces polished.

Phase	Context & No.	Grid ref	Max dia rim	Fig
ivc	BSG **19**	Area 2	25	14c

1490 **116** Fig. 14d

Top of rim squared. The deep groove on the exterior has the impression of a thin string from string-tying. Smoothing marks at various angles visible on exterior beneath the slip.

Nile B2. Fired fairly soft. Surfaces concealed by slip. Break, brown with red core. Fairly plentiful poorly sorted sand. Fairly plentiful fine and some coarse veg to 0.5. Sparse limestone to 0.05. Red-brown slip on all surfaces. All surfaces polished.

Phase	Context & No.	Grid ref	Max dia rim	Fig
v	BQJ **22**	Area 2	*c.*30	14d

2328 **117** Fig. 14e

Exterior surface abraded.

Nile B2. Fired fairly soft. Surfaces pale brown where slip lost. Break pale brown with red core, or red zones and grey core where thickest. Fairly plentiful fine and medium sand with a few larger grains. Fairly plentiful fine veg to 0.4. Sparse limestone to 0.05. Areas of red-brown slip survive on both surfaces. Highly polished where slip survives.

Phase	Context & No.	Grid ref	Dia rim (top)	Fig
ii	BGG **137**	04/05/06-S01/S02/S03	*c.*20–25	14e

118–25 Straight-walled plates, and deep bowls with modelled rim (Rzeuska 2006, Forms 99–121, Pls 82–91 and Forms 149–54, Pls 104–05 respectively)

Most of the Anubieion series was not recorded in such a way as to make a clear distinction between these two groups. This is partly due to a difference of emphasis (the Anubieion series attempts to distinguish wider and narrower rim-roll where no other difference presents itself) and partly to the generally worse state of preservation of the Anubieion sherds, which are not in their contexts of primary deposition and were doubtless broken up when redeposited. The drawn examples are usually the best preserved, and the 'typing' of others to them relates to the form of rim and upper body rather than to stance. Even in Rzeuska's series the difference of stance can be quite slight (as between Forms 111–12 and 150, for example).

The use of both Nile B1 and Nile B2 is common to the Anubieion and Rzeuska's series (for a marl example, see **344**). They are wheel assisted, but at the Anubieion insufficiently preserved to show how the base was formed. Most are less highly polished than the majority of fine wares of the period.

1668C **118** Fig. 14f

Nile B2. Fired fairly soft. Surfaces concealed by slip. Break pale brown all through. Fairly plentiful fine and medium sand with a few larger grains. Moderate qty fine veg to 0.3. No visible limestone. Thin red-brown slip on both surfaces. Both surfaces polished.

Phase	Context & No.	Grid ref	Max dia rim	Fig
v–vi	BKX **14***	07-25/26	?	As 14f
v–vi	BKX **17***	07-25/26	21	14f

* Rim sherds from the same vessel but do not join

1668B **119** Fig. 15a–c

Major series with narrow roll.

Nile B1. AWZ **7** fired fairly hard, others fairly soft. UP 197 **8** pale brown where slip lost, others, surfaces concealed by slip. AWZ **7** pale brown with pink zones and grey core, others pale brown all through. AWZ **7** moderate qty fine only, others moderate qty fine and medium, well-sorted sand. Small qty fine veg to 0.2. Sparse limestone to 0.05. Red-brown slip on both surfaces. Both surfaces polished.

Nile B2. Fired fairly soft to medium, none harder. Surfaces pale brown to red-brown where slip lost, otherwise concealed by slip. Break pale brown to red-brown all through, or with red core, or with red zones and grey core. Fairly plentiful fine and medium sand, a small number with a few larger grains. Moderate qty to fairly plentiful fine or mostly fine veg to 0.2/0.5. Sparse limestone to 0.05/0.1. Red-brown slip on both surfaces. Both surfaces polished.

Phase	Context & No.	Grid ref	Max dia rim	Fabric	Fig & notes
o	AQG **74**	12/13/14-S04/S05	25	B2	15a
o	BEO **82**	14/15-S04/S05	*c*.20	B2	As 15a
o	ADU (UP 122) NW **27**	Area 13	*c*.20–25	B2	As 15a
ii	AIY **125**	05 to 08-04/05/06	24	B2	As 15c
ii	BDS **8**	04-09	*c*.32	B2	As 15b
ii	BGG **97**	08/09/10-S02/S03	*c*.20	B2	As 15b
ii	BGG **98**	08/09/10-S02/S03	*c*.17(?)	B2	As 15a
ii	BGG **120****	04/05/06-S01/S02/S03	25	B1	15b
iii	BDR **152****	12/13-04/05	25	B1	15b
iii	CHB **9**	08/09-25/26	?	B2	As 15c
†	UP 197 **8**	Area 13	20	B1	As 15b
iii–iva/iva	ACE=AJH **45**	05 to 09-06 to 09	*c*.35–40	B2	As 15c
iv (Pt II?)	ADC **100**	Area 13	*c*.20–25	B2	As 15a
iv (Pt II?)	ADC **113**	Area 13	*c*.38	B2	As 15c
iv (Pt II?)	ADF North **24**	Area 13	? (30+)	B2	As 15c
iv (Pt II?)/?	AYP/AYJ **20**	Area 13	22	B2	As 15c
iv (Pt II?)/?	AYP/AYJ **23**	Area 13	*c*.23	B2	As 15b
iv (Pt II?)/?	AYQ/AYR **5**	Area 13	*c*.20	B2	As 15b
iv (Pt II?)?	BWZ? (UP 1041) **23**	Area 12	?	B2	*
iva	AEF **58**	08 to 14-03/04	?	B2	As 15c
iva	AEF **75**	08 to 14-03/04	*c*.30–40	B2	As 15c
iva	AWZ **7**	08-04/05/06	*c*.20(?)	B1	As 15c
iva	BQW **14**	Area 2	?	B2	*
iva/ivd	AIF/AAT **44**	05/06-04/05	?	B2	*
ivb	AIH **53**	10 to 14-01	?	B2	*
ivb	BCT **69**	18/19-08/09	*c*.25(?)	B2	As 15c
v	BAC **438**	02/03-S01	25	B2	As 15b

Phase	Context & No.	Grid ref	Max dia rim	Fabric	Fig & notes
Mamluk/ Mamluk	ARC/AZR **23**	Area 12	?	B2	*
vii	AAA (UP 588) **567**	01/W01-31/32/33	?	B2	As 15a
vii	AAA (UP 445) **87**	Area 2	?	B2	15c
?	APG (UP 322) **16**	Area 14	22	B2	As 15a

* Insufficiently preserved to be compared with the drawn examples

** Join

† 'Phase iv construction'. No context designation was assigned

1666 **120** Fig. 15d

Narrow but thick inwardly-rolled rim, and a horizontal incised line (rather than a groove) on exterior.

Nile B2. BKN **76** fired fairly hard, others fairly soft to medium. Surfaces concealed by slip, except BJJ **37** and AEF **44** brown where slip lost. Break, BNU **10** and BHL/BHN **13** brown all through, BKN **76** red-brown with grey core, others brown with grey core. Fairly plentiful fine and medium well-sorted sand, BJJ **37** with a few larger grains. BKN **76** medium qty, others small qty, fine veg to 0.2/3. AJX/AJY/BRS **17** one piece limestone 0.1, BJJ **37** and BKN **76** sparse to 0.05, others none visible. All surfaces slipped: BNU **10** pink, BKN **76** red-orange, others red-brown. All surfaces polished.

Phase	Context & No.	Grid ref	Max dia rim	Fig
ii/ii/ivc	AJX/AJY/BRS **17**	21/22/23-S02/S03	*c.*24	As 15d
iii	BJJ **37**	18-06	?	As 15d
iii	BNU **10**	08-S02	?	As 15d
iva	AEF **44**	08 to 14-03/04	*c.*30–35(?)	As 15d
ivb	BKN **76**	02-21	*c.*27	As 15d
ivc/ivc	BHL/BHN **13**	05/06-22/23	*c.*30(?)	15d

1496/1668E **121** Fig. 15e–g

Wide roll, all of similar form.

Nile B1. Fired fairly hard. Surfaces red-brown where slip lost. Break red-brown with grey core. Fairly plentiful fine well-sorted sand. Small qty fine veg to 0.2. No visible limestone. Small areas of red slip survive on both surfaces. Polished where slipped.

Nile B2. ADV **1** fired fairly hard, others fairly soft. Surfaces where slip lost, ADV **1** pale orange-brown, others pale red-brown. Break, AQG **300** pale red-brown with red zones and mauve core, ADV **1** orange-brown with pink zones and grey core, AAD **14** pale brown all through, AAA East 4 pale red-brown with red core, BFB **59** red-brown with grey core. AAD **14** plentiful poorly sorted sand, others fairly plentiful fine and medium with a few larger grains. BFB **59** small qty fine veg to 0.2, others moderate qty to fairly plentiful, mostly fine, to 0.3/0.4. Sparse limestone to 0.05. Slip on both surfaces, ADV **1** pink, AAD **14** red, others red-brown. All surfaces polished.

Phase	Context & No.	Grid ref	Max dia rim	Fabric	Fig
o	AQG **300**	18/19/20-S04/S05	*c.*25(?)	B2	As 15e
iv (Pt II?)	ADV **1***	Area 13	23	B2	15e

Phase	Context & No.	Grid ref	Max dia rim	Fabric	Fig
ivc	AAD **14**	05/06/07-06	*c*.30(?)	B2	15f
Mamluk/ Mamluk/vii	ABC/ABD/ABA (UP 69) **7**	Area 13	*c*.45	B1	As 15e
vii	AAA East **4**	Area 1	26	B2	As 15e
vii?	BFB **59**	Area 1	23	B2	15g

* Embedded in a brick, top course of wall A where it passed under terrace wall

1498/1668D **122** Fig. 16a–d

Major series with wide roll.

Nile B1. Fired fairly soft. Surfaces concealed by slip. Break, ADU **18** red-brown all through, others brown: CIC **32** with grey core, AKJ/AKI **35** with red core, AAA **98** with red zones and grey core. CIC **32** plentiful, others fairly plentiful, fine and medium well-sorted sand, AKJ/AKI **35** also a few larger grains. Small qty fine veg to 0.2. Sparse limestone to 0.05/0.1, except ADU **18** none visible. Red-brown slip on both surfaces. Both surfaces polished.

Nile B2. Fired fairly soft. Surfaces pale brown where slip lost. Break pale brown all through. Fairly plentiful sand, BJJ **18** fine and medium well sorted, others poorly sorted. Moderate qty fine or mostly fine veg to 0.3. Red-brown slip on both surfaces. Both surfaces polished.

Phase	Context & No.	Grid ref	Max dia rim	Fabric	Fig
o	ADU (UP 330) **18**	Area 13	?	B1	As 16d
iii	BJJ **18**	17/18-05/06	*c*.25–30	B2	16a
ivc	AAV **5**	04 to 08-03/04. Level 62.28-38	?	B2	As 16c
ivd(?)	CIC **32**	02-32/33	*c*.40	B1	16b
Mamluk/vii	AKJ/AKI (UP 141) **35**	Area 13	*c*.46	B1	16c
vii	AAA (UP 23) **603**	09-05	18	B2	As 16a
vii	AAA (UP 445) **98**	Area 2	41	B1	16d

1668F **123** Fig. 16e

Small group with little variability of form. Wide but thin internal roll with almost flat top. Exterior of body wall almost flat.

Nile B1. Fired medium. Surfaces concealed by slip. Break, pale brown with pink zones and grey core. Fairly plentiful fine and medium sand with a few larger grains. Small qty fine veg to 0.2. Sparse limestone to 0.05. Red-brown slip on both surfaces. Both surfaces polished.

Nile B2. Fired fairly soft to medium. ARU=ARZ **41** surfaces concealed by slip, BMB **17** red-brown and others pale brown, all where slip lost. Break, ARU=ARZ **41** red-brown with red zones and mauve core, BNN/BNR (I) **10** pale brown with grey core, BMB **17** red-brown with mauve core, ANS **47** dark brown with red core. Fairly plentiful sand, BMB **17** fine and medium well sorted, others poorly sorted. Moderate qty fine or mostly fine veg to 0.3/0.5. ANS **47** no visible limestone, others sparse to 0.05 and ARU=ARZ **41** one piece 0.1. Slip on both surfaces, ARU=ARZ **41** red, BNN/BNR (I) **10** orange-pink, others red-brown. Both surfaces polished.

Phase	Context & No.	Grid ref	Max dia rim	Fabric	Fig
iv (Pt II?)	ARU=ARZ (UP 204) **41**	Area 13	*c*.25	B2	As 16e
v/v	BNN/BNR(I) **10**	W06/W07-S01/S02/S03	*c*.40(?)	B2	As 16e
v–vi	BMB **17**	18-S01/S02	*c*.24(?)	B2	As 16e
vii?	BFB **12**	Area 1	*c*.25–30	B1	As 16e
?	ANS (UP 1000) **47**	Area 14	*c*.40	B2	16e

1668G **124** Fig. 16f

Unique example, with thick rim-roll undercut on the interior with a tool.

Nile B1. Fired fairly soft. Surfaces concealed by slip. Break pale red-brown with faint greenish grey core. Fairly plentiful fine well-sorted sand. Small qty fine veg to 0.2. Sparse limestone to 0.05. Thick red-brown slip on all surfaces. All surfaces polished.

Phase	Context & No.	Grid ref	Max dia rim	Fig
vii	ANJ (UP 132) **1**	Area 14	*c*.30	16f

2921 **125** Fig. 16g

Lightly rolled, rounded rim.

Nile B2. Fired fairly soft. Surfaces concealed by slip. Break brown all through. Fairly plentiful fine and medium well-sorted sand. Fairly plentiful fine veg to 0.2. Sparse limestone to 0.05. Pale pink slip on both surfaces, presumably an underfired red slip. Both surfaces polished.

Phase	Context & No.	Grid ref	Dia rim (top)	Fig
iii	CDU **14**	08/09-22/23	*c*.24–28	16g

126 Small thick-walled plates with round to flat base (Rzeuska 2006, Forms 118/20, Pl. 91)

1484 **126** Fig. 17a

One profile (ABG **1**) showing full technology, and two rim sherds, from similar but not quite identical thick-walled plates. ABG **1** exterior, except near rim, left rough with criss-crossing scratches and, towards the centre, scuffing and impressions of straw or matting acquired before firing; interior, and exterior near rim, smoothed but uneven. ABG **49** is sufficiently preserved to show the same roughness on the lower exterior. Wheel assisted, but bottom scraped.

Nile B2. Fired soft. Surfaces pale brown where uncoated or slip lost. Break ABG **1** pale brown with red zones, and grey core where thickest; remainder pale brown all through. Fairly plentiful poorly sorted sand. Fairly plentiful fine and coarse veg: ABG **49** to 0.3, others mostly to 0.8 but ABG **1** a few pieces to 1.5. Sparse limestone to 0.1. Thin brownish red slip on interior, ABG **49** down 1.5 cm on exterior, others just over rim, each to a straight edge. Possible traces of polish where slipped.

Phase	Context & No.	Grid ref	Max dia rim	Fig
iv (Pt II?)	ADC **170**	Area 13	*c*.20	Similar to 17a

Phase	Context & No.	Grid ref	Max dia rim	Fig
vi	ABG (UP 235) **1**	Area 13	16	17a
vi	ABG (UP 235) **49**	Area 13	*c.*19	Similar to 17a

127–28 Plates with rounded rim (and ring-base) (Rzeuska 2006, Form 119, Pl. 91)

Although the walls are a little thinner, so the rounded rims are less apparent, these have the same exterior swelling as Rzeuska's Form 119, the diameters are almost identical and so is the slip (though, as often, only the Anubieion examples are recorded as polished). Unfortunately the separately attached base-ring of Form 119 is not preserved on the Anubieion examples.

A similar rim is noted at Akhmim from the late OK to the early MK, with red slip on both surfaces and the interior 'compacted' (= polished?) (Hope and McFarlane, 2006, Fig. 1 [AIVb.5]).

1696 **127** Fig. 17b

The exterior swelling has been developed into a wide, shallow cordon, perhaps decorative. Appears to be at least wheel assisted, as far as preserved.

Nile B1 near B2. Fired medium. Surfaces concealed by slip. Break pale brown with red-brown zones and grey core. Fairly plentiful fine and medium well-sorted sand. Sparse fine veg to 0.2. Sparse limestone to 0.05. Thick red-brown slip on all surfaces. Both surfaces polished.

Phase	Context & No.	Grid ref	Max dia rim	Fig
vii	AAA (UP 157) **133**	18/19/20-14	21	17b

2318 **128** Fig. 17c

The exterior swelling is slightly less pronounced. Cannot tell whether handmade or wheel assisted.

Nile B1. Fired fairly hard. Surfaces concealed by slip. Break pale red-brown with pink zone, and grey core extending to interior surface. Fairly plentiful fine and medium sand with a few larger grains. Moderate qty fine veg to 0.3. Sparse limestone to 0.1. Thick slip on both surfaces; brownish red on exterior and down 1.2 on interior to a straight line, then black, due to stacking in the kiln; interior surface, both red and black, is crazed. Both surfaces highly polished.

Phase	Context & No.	Grid ref	Max dia rim	Fig
ivb	AOK **6**	09-01/02/03	20	17c

129–34 Bowls with simple rim, not grooved on the exterior (Rzeuska 2006, Forms 124–25, Pls 92–93)

Bowls of simple form, most of them incurved, with rounded to narrowed rim. The absence of grooves on the exterior differentiates them from Rzeuska's Forms 146–148, though it is probably only a question of whether or not string-tying was needed. Form 124 has a single groove on the interior near the rim, absent from the Anubieion examples, but the top diameters of 13.5 and 16 are nearer to their size than the 19–28 of Form 125.

A virtual duplicate of **129** derives from the nearby excavations of the Australian Centre for Egyptology, though attributed to the NK (Sowada 1999, Pl. 46 [TNE 94:90]). This may be an error, understandable as it was 'unstratified', i.e. in a sand layer, like much in the present volume.

1736A **129** Fig. 17d

A slight depression near the rim is insufficient to qualify as an exterior groove. Appears to be handmade.

Nile B2. Fired fairly soft. Surfaces concealed by slip. Break brown with red core. Moderate qty fine and medium sand with a few larger grains. Moderate qty fine veg to 0.2. Sparse limestone to 0.05. Thick red-brown slip on all surfaces, except that interior and top of rim are dark brown, perhaps from stacking in the kiln, and there is a paler brown band 0.5 deep on interior just below rim (cf **134**). All surfaces polished.

Phase	Context & No.	Grid ref	Dia rim (top)	Fig
v–vi	AFF **14**	19/20-S02/S03/S04	10	17d

1736B **130** Fig. 17e

Handmade; uneven surfaces.

Nile B2. Fired fairly soft. Surfaces concealed by slip. Break brown with red core. Moderate qty fine and medium sand. Fairly plentiful fine veg to 0.3. Sparse limestone to 0.1. Thick red-brown slip on all surfaces. All surfaces polished.

Phase	Context & No.	Grid ref	Dia rim (top)	Fig
iva	AJH **100**	04/05/06-05 to 08	*c.*16	17e

1734 **131** Fig. 17f

Handmade: body profile variable around.

Nile B2. Fired medium. Surfaces concealed by slip. Break red-brown with thick pale grey core extending to exterior surface. Fairly plentiful fine and medium sand with a few larger grains. Moderate qty fine veg to 0.2. Sparse limestone to 0.1. Thick slip on both surfaces, interior red-brown, also exterior to a diagonal 0.5–1.0 down, then a grey band 0.5 wide, then pink below, where stacked untidily in the kiln. Both surfaces highly polished.

Phase	Context & No.	Grid ref	Dia rim (top)	Fig
vii	AAA (UP 445) **130**	Area 2	10	17f

2024 **132** Fig. 17g

The examples preserved to the lowest point are visibly handmade, with uneven surfaces.

Nile B2. AJY **159** fired fairly soft, others medium to fairly hard. Surfaces mostly concealed by slip. Break, see table. Moderate qty to fairly plentiful fine and medium sand, some with a few larger grains. Small to moderate qty veg, AJY **159** and DAC **35** fine and coarse to 0.5, others fine to 0.2/0.3. Sparse limestone to 0.05. For surviving slips, see table (where grey, probably refired or burnt in use). Polished where slipped.

Phase	Context & No.	Grid ref	Dia rim (top)	Slip	Break	Fig
ii	AJY **159**	21/22/23-S01/S02/ S03	?	Both, red-brown	6	
ii	BET **65**	12/13-02/03	(*c.*20–25?)	Int & rim, grey	4	
ii/ivb	AJY/AVB **69**	10 to 14-01/S01/S02	*c.*22	Int only, grey	5	

Phase	Context & No.	Grid ref	Dia rim (top)	Slip	Break	Fig
iii	BCB **6**	01-05	?	Surface lost	1	
iii/iva/ ivb	BPU/BHR/ BKN **7**	02/03-21/22	*c.*17	Ext red, int grey	3	
iv (Pt II?)	ADC **96**	Area 13	18	Rim only, pink	7	
iva	AJH (Lower) **7**	05 to 08-04/05/06	16	Rim only, orange	8	
ivc	CGD **27**	04/05-35	*c.*17–20	Both, grey	2	
v	DAC **35**	Area 2 W06/ W07-S55/S56	15	Int only, orange	1	17g

Break colours: 1 orange with grey core, 2 red-brown with grey core, 3 dark brown with red zones and grey core, 4 dark brown with red core, 5 dark brown all through, 6 pale brown all through, 7 pale brown with red zones and mauve core, 8 red-brown all through

2018 **133** Fig. 17h

Nile B2. Fired medium. Surfaces orange-brown where slip lost. Break orange-brown with pink zones and thin grey core. Fairly plentiful fine and medium sand with a few larger grains. Small to moderate qty fine veg to 0.3. Sparse limestone to 0.1. Surfaces weathered, but traces of thick red-brown slip on both. Highly polished where slip survives.

Phase	Context & No.	Grid ref	Dia rim (top)	Fig
ivb/ivc	AUW **6**	15-S01/01	*c.*18	17h

2000 **134** Fig. 17i

Nile B2. Fired fairly soft. Surfaces concealed by slip. Break pale brown with red core. Fairly plentiful fine and medium sand with some larger grains. Small qty fine veg to 0.2. No visible limestone. Thick red-brown slip on both surfaces, except for a band 0.5 deep around interior of rim, where it is thinly applied (cf **129**). Both surfaces highly polished where slip is thick.

Phase	Context & No.	Grid ref	Dia rim (top)	Fig
Mamluk/Mamluk/vii	ABC/ABD/ABA (UP 155) **25**	Area 13	(*c.*15–20?)	17i

135–36 Shallow bowls with slightly thickened rim. (Rzeuska 2006, nearest, Forms 126–27, Pl. 93)

2004 **135** Fig. 17j

Nile B2. Fired fairly hard. Surfaces orange. Break orange with pink core. Fairly plentiful fine and medium sand with a few larger grains. Fairly plentiful fine veg to 0.2. Sparse limestone to 0.1. Surfaces weathered, but several tiny areas of probable red slip survive on exterior only. No polish or burnish as preserved.

Phase	Context & No.	Grid ref	Dia rim (top)	Fig
?	ANS (UP 1000) (**24?**)	Area 14	(18–28?)	17j

2002 **136** Fig. 17k

Little preserved, but stance apparently as illustrated. Probably handmade.

Nile B2. Fired fairly hard. Surfaces orange-brown where slip lost. Break brown with thin purple zones and thick purple-brown core. Fairly plentiful fine sand with a few larger grains. Fairly plentiful mostly fine veg to 0.3. Rather more limestone than usual, to 0.1. Thick red slip on interior and traces, fired or refired purple-brown, on exterior. Highly polished where slip survives.

Phase	Context & No.	Grid ref	Dia rim (top)	Fig
ivb	AFV East **12**	11-04/05	25 35(?)	17k

137–38 Hemispherical bowls with inner modelled rim (Rzeuska 2006, Forms 126/28, Pl. 93)

337C **137** Fig. 18a

Nile B1. Fired medium. Surfaces concealed by slip. Break reddish brown with thick paler brown core. Moderate qty fine and medium sand. Sparse fine veg to 0.2. Sparse limestone to 0.1. Red-brown slip on both surfaces. Both surfaces polished.

Phase	Context & No.	Grid ref	Dia rim (top)	Fig
o	ADU (UP 122) NW **13**	Area 13	16	18a

2226 **138** Fig. 18b

Nile B2. Fired fairly soft. Surfaces concealed by slip. Break dark brown with paler brown core. Fairly plentiful fine and medium sand with a few larger grains. Moderate qty fine veg to 0.3. Sparse limestone to 0.1. Thick slip on both surfaces, fired grey. Both surfaces polished.

Phase	Context & No.	Grid ref	Dia rim (top)	Fig
iva	AEF **71**	08 to14-03/04	*c.*16–22(?)	18b

139 Fairly small diameter flat-based bowl with sharply incurved rim (no close parallel in Rzeuska 2006 but the incurved rim relates to Form 126, Pl. 93)

Perhaps an exaggerated version of a bowl from Abusir (Kaiser 1969, XXVI, Typ 156), which preserved enough of the base to suggest it was rounded; this was diameter 24, brown slipped and polished. For a similar rim on a shallower bowl of coarser fabric, again diameter 24, see Mendes Phase III (Fourth to Sixth Dynasties) (Adams 2009, Fig. 49 [7]). At Tell el-Dab'a in the MK and SIP, a series of similar bowls includes both imports and local copies (Aston D.A. 2004b, Pls 80–84 [232–52]; Pls 261–64 [942–60]), the base either flat or a very low ring, in approximately equal numbers. Again, most are around 50 per cent larger than **139** and of coarser fabrics, but some preserve a flat base, many are red slipped and some are polished. There is a similar bowl rim in Nile B2 from Dahshur, Valley Temple V, with the top diameter only 10.5, assigned to the Thirteenth Dynasty (Arnold Do. unpublished, III 103).

429 **139** Fig. 18c

Unique bowl with unusually sharply incurved thin rim, and preserving part of an apparently flat base.

Nile B1. Fired fairly soft. Surfaces concealed by slip. Break red-brown all through. Fairly plentiful fine and medium well-sorted sand. Small qty fine veg to 0.2. Sparse limestone to 0.1. Thick red slip on all surfaces. All surfaces highly polished.

Phase	Context & No.	Grid ref	Dia rim (top)	Fig
vii	AAA UP (108) **43**	21 to 35-S01 to S07	14	18c

140–41 Bowls with inner modelled rim (Rzeuska 2006, Form 129, Pl. 93)

140, although of a much smaller diameter than the max 25 of Rzeuska's example, is similar in having the carinated form, the modelling of the inner surface of the rim and the slip on both surfaces. **141** resembles Rzeuska's Form 129 in all respects.

1724 **140** Fig. 18d

Cannot tell whether handmade or wheel assisted.

Nile B2. Fired fairly soft. Surfaces concealed by slip. Break red-brown with pink core. Fairly plentiful fine and medium sand with some larger grains. Sparse fine veg to 0.2. Sparse limestone to 0.1. Thick orange slip on both surfaces. Both surfaces polished.

Phase	Context & No.	Grid ref	Max dia rim	Fig
v/v	BNN/BNR (I) **12**	W06/W07-S01/S02/S03	13	18d

433 **141** Fig. 18e

Nile B2. Fired fairly soft. Interior concealed by slip, exterior pale brown where slip lost. Break pale brown with diffuse red core. Fairly plentiful poorly sorted sand. Small to moderate qty fine veg to 0.3. Sparse limestone to 0.1. Thick red-brown slip on both surfaces, partly lost on exterior. Both surfaces polished.

Phase	Context & No.	Grid ref	Max dia rim	Fig
iv (Pt II?)	ADF North **18**	Area 13	*c.*20–26	18e

142 Medium-diameter deep bowl with slight internal thickening of rim (Rzeuska 2006, nearest, Form 130, Pl. 93)

Although there is no close parallel in Rzeuska's series, the slipped and polished surfaces probably indicate the OK, and **141** appears to be a less sharply modelled version of her Form 130. For a very similar form, slipped (dark red) on both surfaces but much larger (dia 38), see an example from Herakleopolis (Bader 2009a, Fig. 10j) dated to the late OK/early FIP.

2036 **142** Fig. 18f

Probably wheel assisted.

Nile B2. Fired medium. Surfaces red-brown where slip lost. Break orange-brown with thick pink core. Fairly plentiful fine and medium sand with a few larger grains. Fairly plentiful fine and coarse veg to 0.4. Sparse limestone to 0.05. Fairly thick orange-red slip on both surfaces. Both surfaces polished.

Phase	Context & No.	Grid ref	Dia rim (top)	Fig
vii	AAA (UP 23) **544**	09-09	17	18f

143–53 Medium-sized and large bowls with grooved rim (Rzeuska 2006, Forms 131–33/35, Pls 94–96 and 153–54, Pl. 105) (See also Forms 183 and 189, Pls 129 and 134)

This series is so close to some of the 'Meidum' bowls that classification is very difficult. The Anubieion sherds were originally distinguished on the grounds of what were perceived as rounded rims, as opposed to the thinner rims of the 'Meidum' bowls, but the illustrations confirm that the distinction is slight. It is clear that Rzeuska had the same difficulty: among the medium-size bowls some of her Forms 131 and 183, for example [456–458] and [651], appear at least as similar as pairs within the same form; among the larger bowls the same is true of Form 153 and Form 189. Since a decision must be made, the original distinction, based on observation in the field, will be adhered to. Objection could also be raised that the difference between groups within the Anubieion series is slight and that some may overlap; again the only answer is that the grouping suggested seemed the most logical, given that hardly any two examples are really identical. Some justification may be found in the way the division between Nile B1 and Nile B2, carried out much later, mostly followed the same lines. Neither the forms nor the fabrics are co-variable with the diameters. The groove may have been for string-tying.

333A **143** Fig. 18g–h

Groove narrow and shallow. Form not very variable.

Nile B1. Fired fairly hard. Surfaces concealed by slip. Break red with grey core, except ABF/AZH **12** pale brown with red zones and thin grey core. Fairly plentiful fine and medium well-sorted sand, some with a few larger grains. Small qty fine veg to 0.2/0.3. Sparse limestone to 0.05/0.1. Brown slip on both surfaces. Both surfaces polished.

Nile B2. Fired fairly soft. Surfaces concealed by slip. Break brown with thin red zones and purple core. Fairly plentiful fine and medium sand with a few larger grains. Moderate qty fine veg to 0.2. More limestone than usual, to 0.1. Red-brown slip on both surfaces. Both surfaces polished.

Phase	Context & No.	Grid ref	Dia rim (top)	Fabric	Fig
o	AQG **195**	09/10-S03/S04	17	B1	18g
o	AQG **237**	19/20-S06/S07	21	B1	18h
ii	BDX **61**	03/04-07	*c.*22	B2	Between 18g and 18h
iv (Pt II?)	ADF **62**	Area 13	*c.*19	B1	As 18h
v–vi/?	BEQ/BEP **26**	16/17-S01/S02	?	B1	As 18h
vi/vi	ABF/AZH **12**	Area 13	*c.*19	B1	As 18h

337A **144** Fig. 18i–k

Some variability of form, but rounded shoulder and groove below rim. All in **144** approach **143**.

Nile B1. AZO **8** fired fairly hard, others fairly soft. Surfaces concealed by slip. Break, AZO **8** red-brown with thin red zones and grey core, BDG/BRT **38** brown with red core, UP 1034 **5** pale brown all through. Fairly plentiful fine and medium sand with a few larger grains. Small to moderate qty fine veg: AZO **8** to 0.3, remainder to 0.2. Sparse limestone to 0.05. Red-brown slip on both surfaces. Both surfaces polished.

Nile B2. Fired fairly soft. BCU etc **39** surfaces concealed by slip, others brown where slip lost. Break, BGL **122** and UP 23 **413** brown with red zones and mauve core, remainder brown with red core. Fairly plentiful fine and medium sand, CBS/AAA **28** with some larger grains. Moderate qty fine veg to 0.2. Sparse limestone, BGL **122** to 0.1, remainder to 0.05. Slip on both surfaces, BCU etc **39** orange-red, remainder red-brown. Both surfaces polished.

Phase	Context & No.	Grid ref	Dia rim (top)	Fabric	Fig
ii	BGL **122**	14/15-01/S01/S02	20	B2	As 18i
iv (PtV)	AZO (UP 300) **8**	Area 13	22	B1	18i
iva/b/b/ b/b/c	BCU/BCI/BCL/BCN/ BCQ/BCC **39**	05-06/07/08	*c.*21	B2	As 18j
iva/ivb	BDG/BRT **38**	10 to 14-03/04/05	21	B1	18j
v–vi/vii	CBS/AAA **28**	01/W01-28/29/30	20	B2	18k
vii	AAA (UP 23) **413**	08–09	16	B2	As 18i
?	UP 1034 **5**	Area 12	*c.*20	B1	As 18i

1654 **145** Fig. 18l

Nile B2. Fired fairly soft. Surfaces concealed by slip. Break pale brown with red core. Fairly plentiful fine and medium sand with a few larger grains. Fairly plentiful fine veg to 0.3. Sparse limestone to 0.05. Brownish red slip on both surfaces. Both surfaces polished.

Phase	Context & No.	Grid ref	Dia rim (top)	Fig
ivc	BQS **24**	Area 2	*c.*16	18l

2224 **146** Fig. 18m

Nile B2. Fired fairly soft. Surfaces concealed by slip. Break brown, ARP=ARS/AYY **No. lost** with faint red core, CBS/AAA **13** with red zones and thin purple core. Fairly plentiful poorly sorted sand. Moderate qty fine veg to 0.2. Sparse limestone to 0.05. Thick brownish red slip on both surfaces. Both surfaces polished.

Phase	Context & No.	Grid ref	Dia rim (top)	Fig & notes
iv (Pt II?)/iv (Pt II?)	ARP=ARS/AYY **No. lost**	Area 13	20	Similar to 18m*
vi/vii	CBS/AAA **13**	01/W01-29/30	17	18m

* Slightly thicker wall and wider, shallower groove

441 **147** Fig. 19a–b

Slightly thinner wall than **148**.

Nile B2. DAW **11** fired fairly hard, others fairly soft to medium. AAA **49** surfaces concealed by slip, others pale brown where slip lost. Break, CDB **23** burnt; DAW **11** pale red-brown with pink zones and thick grey core; others pale brown, AEW **50** with red zones and thin mauve core, AAA **48** with dark brown zones and thick pink core, AAA **49** with faint red core. AEW **50** and AAA **49** fairly plentiful poorly sorted sand, others moderate qty to fairly plentiful fine and medium well-sorted. Small to moderate qty fine veg to 0.3. Sparse limestone to 0.05. Slip on both surfaces: DAW **11** and AAA **48** orange-brown, AEW **50** and AAA **49** red-brown, CDB **23** pink where not burnt. Both surfaces polished.

Phase	Context & No.	Grid ref	Dia rim (top)	Fig
ivb	CDB **23**	08/09-23	*c.*30(?)	As 19a
iv+	DAW **11**	Area 2 W11-S60	*c.*20	As 19b
v	AEW **50**	04-02 to 07	*c.*17	As 19a
vii	AAA **48**	Area 1	*c.*20	19a

Phase	Context & No.	Grid ref	Dia rim (top)	Fig
vii	AAA **49**	Area 1	*c*.23	19b

439 **148** Fig. 19c–e

No two rims identical but narrow range of forms.

Nile B1. AJH **106** and UP 157 **167** fired medium, others fairly soft. Surfaces concealed by slip. Break, AJH **106** pale red-brown with red core, UP 157 **167** pale red-brown with pink core; others red-brown, DAW **10** all through, AAA East **15** with red core, others with grey core. Fairly plentiful fine and medium sand, some with a few larger grains. Small to moderate qty fine veg to 0.3. Sparse limestone to 0.05/0.1. Slip on both surfaces, UP 157 **167** orange-brown, remainder red-brown except interior surface of ADU NW **11** black from stacking in the kiln. Both surfaces lightly polished.

Phase	Context & No.	Grid ref	Dia rim (top)	Fig
o	ADU (UP 122) NW **10+14***	Area 13	29	As 19c
o	ADU (UP 122) NW **11***	Area 13	*c*.29	As 19c
o	ADU (UP 122) NW **12* ****	Area 13	32	19c
o	ADU (UP 330) **15* ****	Area 13	32	19c
iva	AJH **106**	04/05/06-05 to 08	*c*.27	As 19d
iv+	DAW **10**	Area 1 W11-S60	28	19d
vii	AAA (UP 157) **167**	06 to10-11/12	31	19e
vii	AAA East **15**	Area 1	*c*.35–40(?)	As 19c

* The ADU examples appear to derive from three different vessels

** Join

437 **149** Fig. 19f

Narrow range of forms.

Nile B1. UP 588 **335**, ACS/AUP **44** and ADU SW **6** fired medium to fairly hard, others fairly soft. Surfaces concealed by slip, or pale brown where slip lost. Break UP 588 **335** and ACS/AUP **44** pale brown with red zones and grey core, ADU SW **6** red-brown with thick grey core; others pale brown, AAA East **16** all through, UP 157 **168** and AEF **73** with grey core, others with red core. Fairly plentiful fine and medium sand, UP 588 **335** and ABF/ABG **11** with a few larger grains. Small to medium qty fine veg to 0.3. Sparse limestone to 0.05/0.1. Slip on both surfaces, some only traces or small areas, UP 588 **335** orange, remainder shades of red-brown. Both surfaces lightly polished where slip survives.

Nile B2. BDP **25** fired fairly soft, AAC **148** medium. Surfaces concealed by slip. Break, BDP **25** pale red-brown with red zones and mauve core, AAC **148** red-brown with thin pink zones and thick grey core. Fairly plentiful fine and medium sand, BDP **25** with a few larger grains. Fairly plentiful fine veg to 0.5. BDP **25** sparse limestone to 0.1, AAC **148** none visible. Red-brown slip on both surfaces. Both surfaces lightly polished.

Phase	Context & No.	Grid ref	Dia rim (top)	Fabric	Fig
o	ADU (UP 122) SW **6**	Area 13	*c*.31	B1	
ii/ivb	AIY/AVB **39**	13/14-01/S01	*c*.35	B1	
iii	BDP (UP 534) **25**	01/02-08/09	26	B2	19f
**	UP 197 **7**	Area 13	34	B1	

Phase	Context & No.	Grid ref	Dia rim (top)	Fabric	Fig
iva	AEF **73**	08 to 14-03/04	*c.*30	B1	
ivc/ivc	ACS/AUP **44**	08-S01 to S04	*c.*36	B1	
vi/vi	ABF/ABG (UP 158) **11**	Area 13	*c.*40	B1	
vi–vii	AAC **148**	28 to 34-05 to S05	*c.*36	B2	
vii	AAA (UP 157) **168**	11 to16-11/12	29	B1	
vii	AAA (UP 588) **335**	05/06-25/26/27	?	B1	
vii	AAA East **10***	Area 1	27	B1	
vii	AAA East **16***	Area 1	*c.*32	B1	

* From two different vessels

** 'Phase iv construction'. No context designation was assigned

2134 __**150**__ Fig. 19g

Unique rim form. The rough surface of the groove may be from a thick string tied around before firing.

<u>Nile B1 near B2.</u> Fired fairly soft. Surfaces concealed by slip. Break red-brown all through. Fairly plentiful fine and medium sand with a few larger grains. Moderate qty fine veg to 0.3. Sparse limestone to 0.1. Thick brownish red slip on both surfaces. Both surfaces polished.

Phase	Context & No.	Grid ref	Dia rim (top)	Fig
vii	AAA (UP 157) **170**	18 to 20-10 to 12	27	19g

1656 __**151**__ Fig. 20a

<u>Nile B2.</u> Fired medium to fairly hard. Surfaces pale brown where slip lost. Break pale red-brown with thin red zones and grey core. Fairly plentiful well-sorted sand: AQG **239** fine and medium, BET **134** fine. AQG **239** fairly plentiful fine veg to 0.4, BET **134** small qty to 0.2. Sparse limestone to 0.1 and BET **134** one piece 0.2. Slip on both surfaces, AQG **239** red-brown, surviving in some areas only and interior black near lower break from stacking in the kiln, BET **134** red. Both surfaces lightly polished.

Phase	Context & No.	Grid ref	Dia rim (top)	Fig
o	AQG **239**	19/20-06/07	27	20a
ii	BET **134**	14/15-02/03	*c.*30	As 20a

2118 __**152**__ Fig. 20b

Narrow groove, almost certainly from string-tying.

<u>Nile B2.</u> AMJ **21** fired fairly soft, ARC/AZR **24** medium. Surfaces concealed by slip. Break, AMJ **21** brown with thin grey core, ARC/AZR **24** red with pink core, or pink zones and grey core where thickest. Fairly plentiful poorly sorted sand. Moderate qty to fairly plentiful fine veg to 0.3. Sparse limestone, AMJ **21** to 0.05, ARC/AZR **24** to 0.1. Slip on both surfaces: AMJ **21** thin red-brown, ARC/AZR **24** thick orange-brown. Both surfaces polished, AMJ **21** lightly, ARC/AZR **24** highly.

Phase	Context & No.	Grid ref	Dia rim (top)	Fig
vi	AMJ **21**	18/19/20-10	*c.*26	20b
Mamluk/Mamluk	ARC/AZR **24**	Area 12	*c.*20(?)	As 20b

333B **153** Fig. 20c

Nile B1. Fired fairly hard. Surfaces concealed by slip. Break orange with thick grey core. Fairly plentiful fine and medium well-sorted sand. Small qty fine veg to 0.3. Sparse limestone to 0.1. Reddish orange slip on both surfaces. Both surfaces highly polished.

Phase	Context & No.	Grid ref	Dia rim (top)	Fig
ivd	AFT **6**	08/09-04/05	19	20c

154–55 Deep, thick-walled bowls with grooved rim (Rzeuska 2006, Form 133, Pl. 96)

Although little is preserved below the rim, the thick walls of these bowls appear to equate to Rzeuska's Form 133. **154**, in particular, is thicker than most Anubieion bowls. For a vessel with a similarly thick wall but a rounder body, see a slipped and polished bowl (dia 21.5) from Herakleopolis (Bader 2009a, Fig. 2j) dated as FIP/early MK. Conversely, for a more upright thick-walled form, again slipped and polished (several examples) (dias 20–26 and one 32) see Tell el-Dab'a (Czerny 1999, 149 [Nf 188]), dated to the early MK. The grooves are likely to have been for string-tying.

1698 **154** Fig. 20d

Nile B2. Fired medium. Surfaces concealed by slip. Break brown with thick grey core. Fairly plentiful fine and medium sand with a few larger grains. Moderate qty fine and coarse veg to 0.3. Sparse limestone to 0.1. Pink or pale brown slip on both surfaces but extensively blackened, probably post-firing. Both surfaces polished.

Phase	Context & No.	Grid ref	Max dia rim	Fig
iv (Pt II?)	ADC **137**	Area 13	20	20d

2078 **155** Fig. 20e

Nile B2. ADF North **64** fired medium, AJH under AVH **58** fairly soft. Surfaces concealed by slip. Break brown, ADF North **64** with red zones and purple-grey core, AJH under AVH **58** with faint, diffuse red core. Fairly plentiful fine and medium sand with a few larger grains. Mostly fine veg, ADF North **64** fairly plentiful to 0.3, AJH under AVH **58** moderate qty to 0.3 but one piece 0.7. Sparse limestone to 0.1. Slip on both surfaces: ADF North **64** thin, probably discoloured by burning, perhaps originally red brown; AJH under AVH **58** thick, brownish red. Both surfaces polished.

Phase	Context & No.	Grid ref	Max dia rim	Fig
iv (Pt II?)	ADF North **64**	Area 13	*c.*30–40	20e
iva	AJH under AVH **58**	05-04/05/06	*c.*30–40(?)	As 20e

156–61 Bowls/jars with outside-modelled rim and rounded body (Rzeuska 2006, Form 135, Pl. 96)

Several Anubieion examples are similar to the 'Meidum' bowls with maximum diameter at the body (Rzeuska's Forms 179–182, Pls 126–128), but have thicker rims. In spite of the differences between them, these all bear a closer resemblance to Rzeuska's [473] of Form 135, and except for the smaller Anubieion **156** all are similar in diameter to its 20 cm. The fine line between the 'Meidum' bowls and some other types is nowhere better demonstrated.

It is also the case that some forms (especially **156–58**) continue at least into the early MK: one with a spout from Tell el-Dab'a (dia range 20–25) is slipped and three of the four examples are polished (Czerny 1999, 154 [Nf 241]). There is even some resemblance to an Eighteenth Dynasty form (Bourriau 2010, Figs 25 and 81 [7.4.1]), though this has a thinner 'neck'.

1636 **156** Fig. 20f

Varying thickness of rim indicates hand manufacture, though probably wheel assisted.

Nile B1. Fired medium. Surfaces concealed by slip. Break red-brown with thin red zones and pinkish mauve core. Fairly plentiful fine and medium well-sorted sand. Moderate qty fine veg to 0.3 with a few pieces coarse to 0.8, probably accidental. Sparse limestone to 0.1. Red slip on both surfaces. Both surfaces lightly polished.

Phase	Context & No.	Grid ref	Dia rim (top)	Fig
vii	CAA **No. lost**	Area 26	13	20f

2776 **157** Fig. 20g

Nile B2. Fired fairly soft. Surfaces brown where slip lost. Break brown all through. Fairly plentiful poorly sorted sand. Fairly plentiful fine veg to 0.2. Sparse limestone to 0.1. Red slip on both surfaces. Probable trace of polish on top of rim and possible traces on both surfaces.

Phase	Context & No.	Grid ref	Dia rim (top)	Fig
ii/iva	AJY/AQH **12**	11/12-S01/S02/S03	*c.*17	20g

1634 **158** Fig. 20h

Nile B1 near B2. Fired medium. Surfaces pale red-brown where slip lost. Break pale red-brown with red core. Fairly plentiful fine and some medium well sorted sand. Small qty fine veg to 0.3. Sparse limestone to 0.05 and one piece 0.3 × 0.1. Thick pale red-brown slip on both surfaces. Both surfaces polished.

Phase	Context & No.	Grid ref	Dia rim (top)	Fig
iva	BDU **31**	16/17/18-06/07/08	18	20h

2056 **159** Fig. 20i

Some blackening of interior, almost certainly from use as a cooking pot.

Nile B1. Fired fairly hard. Surfaces concealed by slip. Break red-brown with grey core. Fairly plentiful fine well-sorted sand. Sparse veg to 0.2. Sparse limestone to 0.1. Brownish orange slip on both surfaces. Both surfaces highly polished.

Phase	Context & No.	Grid ref	Dia rim (top)	Fig
iii–iva	ACE **230**	01 to 06-08/09/10	19	20i

2128 **160** Fig. 21a

Nile B1. Fired fairly soft. Surfaces concealed by slip. Break pale brown all through. Fairly plentiful fine well-sorted sand. Small qty fine veg to 0.2. Sparse limestone to 0.05. Pink slip on both surfaces. Both surfaces polished.

Nile B2. Fired medium. Surfaces concealed by slip. Break thin brown zones, then pink zones and faint, diffuse grey core. Fairly plentiful fine and medium sand with a few larger grains. Moderate qty fine veg to 0.3. Sparse limestone to 0.1. Thick red-brown slip on both surfaces. Both surfaces highly polished.

Phase	Context & No.	Grid ref	Dia rim (top)	Fabric	Fig
iv (Pt II?)?	BWL? (UP 1040) **9**	Area 12	?	B1	As 21a
ivc	AAF **21**	05-06/07	23	B2	21a

2060 **161** Fig. 21b

Nile B2. Fired fairly soft. ADC **141** surfaces pale red-brown; BDP **295** weathered. Break BDP **295** pale brown with thick red zones and thin diffuse grey core, ADC **141** pale red-brown all through. Fairly plentiful poorly sorted sand. Fairly plentiful fine and coarse veg to 0.7/0.8. In ADC **141**, one unincorporated red clay nodule 0.2 × 0.1 visible. Sparse limestone to 0.05, and ADC **141** one piece 0.2 × 0.1. BDP **295** too weathered to retain slip, or polish or burnish; ADC **141** has carefully smoothed surfaces, and polished slip appears to survive in the void of a lost inclusion 0.3 in top of rim.

Phase	Context & No.	Grid ref	Dia rim (top)	Fig
iii	BDP (UP 647) **295**	01 to 05-07	? (20–30?)	As 21b
iv (Pt II?)	ADC **141**	Area 13	*c.*23	21b

162–64 Bowls with outside-modelled rim and rounded body (Rzeuska 2006, Form 136, Pl. 96)

2058 **162** Fig. 21c

Nile B2. Fired medium. Surfaces red-brown. Break red-brown with two thin grey-brown zones instead of the more usual grey core. Fairly plentiful poorly sorted sand. Fairly plentiful fine and coarse veg to 0.4. Sparse limestone to 0.1. One piece probable bone, 0.2 × 0.1. Several nodules unincorporated clay to 0.1. Surfaces weathered but well smoothed; no visible slip or polish but perhaps lost.

Phase	Context & No.	Grid ref	Dia rim (top)	Fig
ivb	BKN **220**	02-20/21/22	22	21c

1684 **163** Fig. 21d

The rim of AHV ii/AAT **3** is wheel assisted, and the rims of the other two may be.

Nile B2. Fired medium. Surfaces concealed by slip. Break, ADF North **60** brown with thin red zones and purple core, BNJ **10** orange-red with grey core, AHV ii/AAT **3** orange-red all through. Fairly plentiful to plentiful poorly sorted sand. Moderate qty fine veg to 0.2. All a little more limestone than usual, to 0.1, and AHV ii/AAT **3** one piece 0.5 × 0.2. Slip on both surfaces: ADF North **60** brownish red, others orange-red. Both surfaces polished.

Phase	Context & No.	Grid ref	Dia rim (top)	Fig & notes
iv (Pt II?)	ADF North **60**	Area 13	22	21d
ivb	BNJ **10**	06/07-13	?	*
ivc/ivd	AHV ii/AAT **3**	05/06-05/06	*c.*30	As 21d

* Top flatter than 21d and with faint exterior groove 1.5 down, but too little preserved to illustrate

1686 **164** Fig. 21e

Nile A. BJS i **22** fired fairly soft, others fairly hard. Surfaces concealed by slip. Break BJS i **22** red with diffuse brown core, others red with grey core. Fairly plentiful fine sand with only a few larger grains. Small qty fine veg to 0.2. Sparse limestone to 0.1, UP 627 **38** also one void 0.7 × 0.2 from a burnt-out piece. Red-brown slip on both surfaces. Both surfaces polished. Black deposit on BJS i **22**, inside and outside, probably embalming material.

Phase	Context & No.	Grid ref	Dia rim (top)	Fig
ivc	BJS i **22**	06/07-13/14	? (30–35?)	As 21e
vii	AAA (UP 627) **38**	W01/W02-13 to 20	29	21e
vii?	BFB **56**	Area 1	21	As 21e

165 Small bowl with outside-modelled rim and rounded body (nearest, Rzeuska 2006, Form 136, Pl. 96)

A small version of Form 136. Rzeuska publishes a small (dia 12) red slipped version of the similar Form 137 (2006, Pl. 97 [476]), and small (again dia 12) uncoated versions occur at Abu Rawash in the Fourth or early Fifth Dynasty (Marchand and Baud 1996, Fig. 7 [9–10]). There is a medium-sized (dia 16.5) slipped and polished version from FIP/early MK levels at Herakleopolis (Bader 2009a, Fig. 2h).

1650 **165** Fig. 21f

Two indentations from handling before firing.

Nile B1. Fired medium. Surfaces concealed by slip. Break red with grey core. Fairly plentiful fine and medium well-sorted sand. No visible veg. Sparse limestone to 0.05. Red-brown slip on both surfaces. Both surfaces polished.

Phase	Context & No.	Grid ref	Dia rim (top)	Fig
o	ADU (UP 122) NW **7**	Area 13	8	21f

166–67 Bowls with outside-modelled rim and hemispherical body (Rzeuska 2006, Forms 137/39, Pl. 97)

Although consisting of only five examples, Rzeuska's Form 137 varies widely. The more globular [476/77] are similar to **166**, while the shallower [478–80] resemble **167**; [482] of Form 139 is also fairly similar to the latter.

1632 **166** Fig. 21g

Both surfaces blackened, either from use as a cooking pot, or after breaking.

Nile B1 near B2. Fired fairly hard. Surfaces orange where slip lost. Break orange with thin dark brown zones, and a faint greenish tinge at the core. Fairly plentiful fine and medium sand with a few larger grains. Small qty fine veg to 0.3, and one piece 0.7 on the surface probably accidental. A little more limestone than usual to 0.1, and two pieces each 0.2. Slip on both surfaces: greyish red on top of rim but otherwise blackened. Both surfaces polished.

Phase	Context & No.	Grid ref	Dia rim (top)	Fig
vii	AAA (UP 445) **61**	Area 2	14	21g

2906 **167** Fig. 21h

Short post-firing scratches along the top are probably from tool-sharpening (cf **686**, with references).

Nile B2. Fired fairly soft. Surfaces concealed by slip. Break brown all through. Fairly plentiful poorly sorted sand. Unusually, no visible veg. No visible limestone. Slip on both surfaces, (re?)fired brown. Interior polished and probably exterior also.

Phase	Context & No.	Grid ref	Dia rim (top)	Fig
ivc/vii	BHM/AAA **49**	01/02-21/22	? (20+)	21h

168 Fairly small, shallow, carinated bowl with a single groove. (Rzeuska 2006, Form 140, Pl. 97)

2020B **168** Fig. 21i

The groove was almost certainly for string-tying.

Nile B2. Fired fairly hard. Surfaces concealed by slip. Break red with grey core, which extends to the interior surface below 0.2, almost certainly from being fired with another vessel inside. Fairly plentiful fine and medium sand with only a few larger grains. Small to moderate qty fine veg to 0.5. Sparse limestone to 0.1. Thick slip on both surfaces: exterior red, interior grey with crazed surface from 'nesting' in the kiln. Both surfaces polished.

Phase	Context & No.	Grid ref	Dia rim (top)	Fig
vii	AAA (UP 38) **151**	14-03	? (15+?)	21i

169–76 Bell-shaped bowls with outside-modelled rim (Rzeuska 2006, Forms 141/42, Pls 98/99)

The existence of apparently unstable bowls with a small flat base is attested by the complete profile of several of Rzeuska's examples. The rims are confusingly similar to those of several high stand forms, and although the latter usually have more steeply sloping sides, this is not always the case, especially where stand Form 217 (Pl. 153) is concerned. Furthermore, Nile B1 is commonly used for both series. The most reliable distinction is the fact that, while (like the bowls) the stands are often red slipped and sometimes polished, the slip is only on the exterior. The diameter range of the Anubieion bowl series is greater than Rzeuska's, 15–34 as against 20–24.5, but this has not been felt to outweigh the internal surface treatment.

The 'square' ends to the rims of **169** are not closely matched in Rzeuska's series and these two bowls were at first thought to be of New Kingdom date, but their form has not been found among published material. There is some resemblance to a burnished 'flat-bottomed bowl with outward flaring rim', so clearly of similar type, from Fourth or Fifth Dynasty Giza (Hawass and Senussi 2008, 114 [55]), but this lacks the smooth curve of **169** and may be a predecessor. 'Square'-ended examples, but with deeper overhang, occur at Abusir in the late Old Kingdom (Kaiser 1969, XLI, Type 210–12).

832 **169** Fig. 22a–b

Nile B2. Fired fairly hard. AIY/AVB **43** surfaces pale red-brown where slip lost, ACE **257** surfaces concealed by slip. Break red-brown with thick grey core. Fairly plentiful fine and medium sand with a few larger grains. Fairly plentiful fine and coarse veg to 0.3. Sparse limestone to 0.1. Thick red slip on all surfaces. All surfaces polished.

Phase	Context & No.	Grid ref	Max dia rim	Fig
ii/ivb	AIY/AVB **43**	13/14-01/S01	29	22a
iii–iva	ACE **257**	01 to04-08	*c*.34	22b

2666 **170** Fig. 22c

The complete loss of slip from the rim is not easily explained, but it is not a normal wear pattern, even of a stand. It may indicate use as a scoop or tool when already a sherd.

Nile B2. Fired fairly soft to medium. Surfaces pale brown where slip lost. Break brown with red zones and grey core. Fairly plentiful poorly sorted sand. Fairly plentiful fine and coarse veg to 0.4. Sparse limestone to 0.1. Brownish red slip on exterior and interior, but entire rim area uncoated, slip having apparently worn off. Polished where slipped.

Phase	Context & No.	Grid ref	Max dia rim	Fig
iii–iva	AFS **82**	01/02/03-07	*c*.24	22c

529A **171** Fig. 22d

Some evidence of string impressions on exterior of rim, on its inner edge and in the groove of the overhang; these may have caused the loss of the slip, which has occurred in this area only.

Nile B1. Fired fairly soft. Surfaces brown where slip lost. Break brown with red core. Fairly plentiful fine and medium sand with a few larger grains. Moderate qty fine veg to 0.2. Sparse limestone to 0.1. Red slip on both surfaces, weathered off rim. Both surfaces polished.

Phase	Context & No.	Grid ref	Max dia rim	Fig
iv (Pt II?)/iv (Pt II?)	ARP=ARS/AYY **10**	Area 13	28	22d

529B **172** Fig. 22e

Nile B1. Fired fairly soft. Surfaces concealed by slip. Break pale brown with purple-brown core. Fairly plentiful fine and medium sand with a few larger grains. Fairly plentiful fine veg to 0.2. Sparse limestone to 0.1. Thick red-brown slip on all surfaces. All surfaces highly polished.

Phase	Context & No.	Grid ref	Max dia rim	Fig
iv (Pt II?)	ADC **63+106**	Area 13	28	22e

529C **173** Fig. 22f

Each has a probable thin string impression in the fold of the overhang.

Nile B1. Fired fairly soft to medium. CIE **30** surfaces pale brown, UP 23 **312** orange, both where slip lost. Break CIE **30** pale brown with red zones and mauve core, UP 23 **312** orange with dark pink core. Fairly plentiful sand, CIE **30** fine and medium with a few larger grains, UP 23 **312** fine well sorted. CIE **30** moderate qty fine and coarse veg to 0.7, UP 23 **312** none visible. Sparse limestone to 0.05. CIE **30** pinkish brown slip on all surfaces, UP 23 **312** small areas of pink slip on top of rim and in groove of overhang. Polished where slip survives.

Phase	Context & No.	Grid ref	Max dia rim	Fig
ivb	CIE **30**	02 to 05-33 to 37	*c*.20	22f
vii	AAA (UP 23) **312**	06-08	?	Similar to 22f

529D **174** Fig. 22g

Thin string impression in the fold of the overhang.

Nile B1. Fired fairly soft. Surfaces concealed by slip. Break red-brown with faint red core. Fairly plentiful mostly fine well-sorted sand. Small qty fine veg to 0.2. Sparse limestone to 0.1. Red-brown slip on all surfaces. All surfaces highly polished.

Phase	Context & No.	Grid ref	Max dia rim	Fig
?	AAA (UP 23) **396**	10-08	16(–18?)	22g

529E **175** Fig. 22h

String impression in the fold of the overhang.

Nile B1. Fired medium. Surfaces red-brown where slip lost. Break red-brown with pink zones and grey core. Fairly plentiful fine and medium well-sorted sand. Moderate qty fine and coarse veg to 0.4. Sparse limestone to 0.1. Red-brown slip on all surfaces. All surfaces highly polished.

Phase	Context & No.	Grid ref	Max dia rim	Fig
o/vii/?	AMB/AAA/AMA **23**	04/05-04/05	15	22h

529F **176** Fig. 22i

Slip worn off inner edge of rim roll.

Nile B1. Fired fairly soft. Surfaces pale brown where slip lost. Break pale brown all through. Fairly plentiful fine and medium well-sorted sand. Fairly plentiful fine veg to 0.2. Sparse limestone to 0.05. Red-brown slip on all surfaces. All surfaces highly polished.

Phase	Context & No.	Grid ref	Max dia rim	Fig
v	BXN **1**	Area 13	15	22i

177 Bell-shaped bowl with sharp-edged rim (Rzeuska 2006, Form 145, Pls 100/01)

1682 **177** Fig. 22j

Nile B1. Fired medium. Surfaces concealed by slip. Break red-brown with grey core. Fairly plentiful fine and medium sand, with a few larger grains. Small qty fine veg to 0.2. Sparse limestone to 0.1. Thick orange slip on all surfaces including top of rim. All surfaces highly polished.

Phase	Context & No.	Grid ref	Max dia rim	Fig
vii	AAA (UP 23) **407**	09-06	25	22j

178–91 Bell-shaped bowls with sharp-edged rim, and bent-sided bowls with rounded or modelled rim (and bent-point in middle of body) (Rzeuska 2006, Forms 145, Pls 100/01 and 164–66, Pls 111–15 respectively)

Some of the rim forms divided by Rzeuska into these two series are very similar. She was able to distinguish them by the straight walls of Form 145 (Rzeuska 2006, 407) and the bent point of Forms 164–66, though the latter comprise only a small part of a long series. At the Anubieion the preserved sherds are too small for this distinction to be made. The rims indicate wheel assistance, but no attached bases survive to show the finishing method. The groove or grooves around beneath the rim would surely have been for string-tying, desirable with such large diameters.

As to the fabric, Rzeuska's examples are almost all in Nile B1, whereas those at the Anubieion are almost evenly divided between Nile B1 and Nile B2. No great significance should be attached. As so often, the Anubieion examples are all slipped and polished while most of Rzeuska's are recorded as slipped only; this may be due to the conditions of preservation.

1708 **<u>178</u>** Fig. 22k

<u>Nile B2.</u> Fired fairly soft. Surfaces concealed by slip. Break brown with red core. Moderate qty fine well-sorted sand. Fairly plentiful fine and coarse veg to 0.5. Sparse limestone to 0.05. Thick red-brown slip on both surfaces. Both surfaces polished.

Phase	Context & No.	Grid ref	Dia rim (top)	Fig
ivc	BCC **3**	05-06/07/08	*c.*30(?)	22k

1710B **<u>179</u>** Fig. 23a

<u>Nile B2.</u> Fired fairly soft. Surfaces concealed by slip. Break red with a black zone below each surface, probably from firing fluctuation rather than oil staining Fairly plentiful poorly sorted sand. Fairly plentiful fine and coarse veg to 0.5. Sparse limestone, mostly to 0.1 but a few pieces to 0.3. Red-brown slip on both surfaces. Both surfaces polished.

Phase	Context & No.	Grid ref	Dia rim (top)	Fig
vi/vi	ABF/AZH **14**	Area 13	28	23a

1688 **<u>180</u>** Fig. 23b–d

<u>Nile B1.</u> BGG **138** fired medium, others fairly soft. Surfaces pale brown where slip lost. Break BGG **138** red with pink zones and grey core, others brown with red zones and grey core. Fairly plentiful fine and medium sand, most with a few larger grains. Small qty fine veg to 0.2. Sparse limestone, except BGG **138** more than usual, to 0.05/0.1. Red-brown (BGG **138** pale red-brown) slip on both surfaces. Both surfaces polished.

Phase	Context & No.	Grid ref	Dia rim (top)	Fig & notes
ii	BGG **138**	04/05/06-S01/S02/S03	*c.*30–32	23b
iii–iva	ACE **179**	01 to 05-08 to 12	36	Sim to 23d*
ivb	BTG **23**	02-21	25	23c
vii	AAA **63**	Area 1	26	As 23b
?	APG (UP 322) **12**	Area 14	28	23d

* Differs from APG **12** in having one wide external groove instead of two narrow ones

1706 **<u>181</u>** Fig. 23e

<u>Nile B2.</u> Fired fairly soft. Surfaces concealed by slip. Break brown with thick grey core. Fairly plentiful poorly sorted sand. Moderate qty fine and coarse veg to 0.2. Sparse limestone to 0.1. Thick red-brown slip on both surfaces. Both surfaces polished.

Phase	Context & No.	Grid ref	Dia rim (top)	Fig
iv (Pt II?)	ADF North **52**	Area 13	*c.*24	23e

2222 **<u>182</u>** Fig. 23f

Exceptionally large diameter.

<u>Nile B1.</u> Fired fairly soft. Surfaces concealed by slip. Break brown with red zones and purple-grey core. Fairly plentiful fine and medium well-sorted sand. Fairly plentiful fine veg to 0.2. Sparse limestone to 0.05. Thick

brownish red slip on both surfaces. Both surfaces polished.

Phase	Context & No.	Grid ref	Dia rim (top)	Fig
iii–iva	ACE **91**	01 to 05-08 to 12	*c*.45	23f

2220 **183** Fig. 23g

Nile B1 near B2. Fired fairly soft. Surfaces concealed by slip. Break pale brown with very faint red core. Fairly plentiful fine and medium sand with a few larger grains. Fairly plentiful fine veg to 0.2. Sparse limestone to 0.05. Thick brownish red slip on both surfaces. Both surfaces polished.

Phase	Context & No.	Grid ref	Dia rim (top)	Fig
iv (Pt II?)/iv (Pt II?)	ADS/ARP=ARS **6**	Area 13	? (20–25?)	23g

1680 **184** Fig. 23h

Nile B1. Fired fairly soft. Surfaces concealed by slip. Break pale brown with red zones and mauve core. Fairly plentiful fine and medium sand with a few larger grains. Fairly plentiful fine veg to 0.3. More limestone than usual in a Nile fabric, to 0.1. Fairly thin pale red-brown slip on both surfaces. Both surfaces polished.

Phase	Context & No.	Grid ref	Dia rim (top)	Fig
ivc	AAD (UP 409) **33**	05/06/07-06	*c*.33	23h

1710D **185** Fig. 24a

Nile B2. Fired fairly soft. Surfaces concealed by slip. Break red all through. Fairly plentiful fine and medium sand with a few larger grains. Fairly plentiful fine and coarse veg to 0.5, and one piece 0.8. Sparse limestone, mostly to 0.1 but one piece 0.7 × 0.5! Red-brown slip on both surfaces. Both surfaces polished.

Phase	Context & No.	Grid ref	Dia rim (top)	Fig
vii	ANJ (UP 203) **2**	Area 14	*c*.24–28	24a

1710C **186** Fig. 24b

Nile B1. Fired fairly hard. Surfaces concealed by slip. Break red with thick grey core. Fairly plentiful fine and medium well sorted sand. Fairly plentiful fine veg to 0.2. Sparse limestone to 0.1 and one piece 0.5 × 0.2. Red-brown slip on both surfaces. Both surfaces polished.

Phase	Context & No.	Grid ref	Dia rim (top)	Fig
vii	AAA (UP 445) **138**	Area 2	28	24b

1704 **187** Fig. 24c

Flat top to rim.

Nile B2. Fired fairly hard. Surfaces concealed by slip. Break red with thick grey core. Fairly plentiful fine and medium sand with a few larger grains. Moderate qty fine veg to 0.3. Sparse limestone to 0.1. Thick red slip on both surfaces. Both surfaces polished.

Phase	Context & No.	Grid ref	Dia rim (top)	Fig
o	ADU (UP 330) **2**	Area 13	*c*.30(?)	24c

1690 **188** Fig. 24d

The rim was undercut with a tool.

Nile B2. Fired fairly soft. Surfaces concealed by slip. Break dark brown with lighter brown core. Fairly plentiful poorly sorted sand. Fairly plentiful fine veg to 0.3. Sparse limestone to 0.05. Slip on both surfaces, fired black, almost certainly from original firing not subsequent burning. Both surfaces polished.

Phase	Context & No.	Grid ref	Dia rim (top)	Fig
v	DAC **18**	Area 2 W06/W07/W08-S52/S53/S54	*c*.30–35	24d

1694 **189** Fig. 24e

Nile B1 with extra limestone. Fired fairly hard. Surfaces concealed by slip. Break red-brown with grey core, clearly defined and lacking the usual 'shading off'. Plentiful fine and medium sand with a few larger grains. No visible veg. More limestone than usual in a Nile fabric, to 0.1. Red-brown slip on both surfaces. Both surfaces lightly polished.

Phase	Context & No.	Grid ref	Dia rim (top)	Fig
ii/ivb	AIY/AIH **14**	13/14-02/03	*c*.38	24e

1710A **190** Fig. 24f

Nile B2. Fired fairly soft. Surfaces concealed by slip. Break red with faint, diffuse purple core. Fairly plentiful poorly sorted sand. Fairly plentiful fine and coarse veg to 0.5. Sparse limestone to 0.1. Red-brown slip on both surfaces. Both surfaces polished.

Phase	Context & No.	Grid ref	Dia rim (top)	Fig
iii	BCB **101**	01 to 04-04/05/06	? (20+)	24f

1668H **191** Fig. 24g

Nile B1. Fired medium. Surfaces concealed by slip. Break brown with thin red zones and grey core. Fairly plentiful fine and medium well sorted sand. Small qty fine veg to 0.2. Sparse limestone to 0.05. Red-brown slip on both surfaces. Both surfaces polished.

Phase	Context & No.	Grid ref	Max dia rim	Fig
?	ANS (UP 298) **3**	Area 14	40–50	24g

192–93 Flat bases of bell-shaped bowls (Rzeuska 2006, Forms 141–45, Pls 98–102)

Almost all examples of these forms are slipped on all surfaces, and several are recorded as polished. Most have concave lower walls as **192**, but [515/16] of Rzeuska's Form 145 are convex and similar to **193**.

707B **192** Fig. 25a–b

Not recorded whether handmade or wheel assisted.

Nile B2. AJY **147** and UP 1047 **1** fired medium to hard, others soft. Surfaces concealed by slip. Break AJY **147** and UP 1047 **1** red with grey core, others brown with grey core. UP 1047 **1** fairly plentiful fine and medium well-sorted sand; remainder poorly sorted, AJY **141** small qty, others fairly plentiful. Small to moderate qty fine veg. Sparse limestone to 0.05/0.1. Red slip on all surfaces. All surfaces polished.

Phase	Context & No.	Grid ref	Dia base	Fig
ii	AJY **141***	17 to 20-S04/S05	*c.*12	25b
ii	AJY **147***	17 to 20-S04/S05	?	As 25a
?	UP 19 **35**	Area 12	9	As 25a
?	UP 1047 **1**	Area 12	?	25a

* From two different vessels

709B **193** Fig. 25c–d

Both probably wheel assisted. The flat undersides are smoothed and show no string-cutting, but ABG **35** has marks from a scraped finish.

Nile B2. ABG **35** fired medium to fairly hard, AKJ/AKI **3** fairly soft. Surfaces concealed by slip. Break ABG **35** pale brown with thin red zones and thick grey core, AKJ/AKI **3** brown with faint red zones and grey core. Fairly plentiful sand, ABG **35** poorly sorted, AKJ/AKI **3** fine and medium well sorted. Moderate qty fine and coarse veg to 0.3. Sparse limestone to 0.05. Red-brown slip on all surfaces. All surfaces highly polished.

Phase	Context & No.	Grid ref	Dia base	Fig
vi	ABG (UP 235) **35**	Area 13	*c.*6.5	25d
Mamluk/vii	AKJ/AKI **3**	Area 14	*c.*6	25c

194–202 Medium-sized and large bowls with externally grooved rim (Rzeuska 2006, Forms 147/48, Pl. 103)

Both the Anubieion examples and Rzeuska's counterparts vary considerably in stance and degree of curvature. Most of the Anubieion examples are smaller. The grooves which define the Types may be no more than the impressions left by string tied around, as visible on **196**. An example from Abu Rawash with both form and dimensions similar to **197** (Marchand and Baud 1996, Fig. 10 [5]) is again dated to the Sixth Dynasty.

1702 **194** Fig. 25e–g

The black colour of BHN **46** appears to be intentional rather than a firing error or smoke-blackening in use; the dark brown of UP 1048 **22** is probably a firing error and the sherd is distorted.

Nile B1. More variable than in most types but basically the same ware. AQC **196** and AQI **28** fired fairly soft; BHN **46** and UP 1048 **22** medium; AEN/AEO **41** fairly hard. Surfaces concealed by slip. Break AQC **196** and AQI **28** brown with pink core, also faint diffuse grey core streak in AQI **28**; BHN **46** black with brown core; AEN/AEO **41** red with grey core; UP 1048 **22** brown with grey core. Fairly plentiful (BHN **46** and AEN/AEO **41** plentiful) fine and medium sand with a few larger grains, AEN/AEO **41** almost all fine. BHN **46** no visible veg; others small to moderate qty fine to 0.3. Sparse limestone to 0.1. Slip on both surfaces: AQC **196** and AEN/AEO **41** brownish red, AQI **28** pink, BHN **46** black, UP 1048 **22** dark brown. Both surfaces polished.

Nile B2. Fired fairly soft. Surfaces concealed by slip. Break brown all through. Fairly plentiful fine and medium sand with a few larger grains. Moderate qty fine veg to 0.3. One piece limestone 0.1 × 0.05 visible. Red-brown slip on both surfaces. Both surfaces polished.

Phase	Context & No.	Grid ref	Dia rim (top)	Fabric	Fig & notes
iii	BPW **7**	07-27	*c.*16	B2	25e
iva	AQC **196**	02/03-10	15	B1	25f
ivb–ivc	AQI **28**	16/17/18-04/05/06	19	B1	25g
ivc	BHN **46**	03-22	*c.*17	B1	As 25e*
v/v	AEN/AEO **41**	17-S02	*c.*18	B1	As 25e
?	UP 1048 **22**	Area 12	14	B1	As 25e

* BHN **46** has a faint third groove between the other two

337B **195** Fig. 25h

Nile B1. CAA **31** fired fairly hard, others fairly soft. Surfaces concealed by slip. Break, ADU NW **16** grey all through, CAA **31** red-brown with grey core, BFB **28** pale brown with red zones and mauve core, BEP **47** pale brown with two thin dark brown zones. Fairly plentiful fine and medium sand with a few larger grains. Small to moderate qty fine veg to 0.1/0.2. Sparse limestone to 0.05. Slip on both surfaces, ADU NW **16** black, others red-brown. Both surfaces polished.

Nile B2. AYG **2** fired fairly hard, others fairly soft. Surfaces concealed by slip. Break brown, AYG **2** with red zones and grey core, AYQ/AYR **7** all through, BKX **9** with red core. Fairly plentiful sand, AYG **2** poorly sorted, others fine and medium with a few larger grains. Small to moderate qty fine veg to 0.2/0.3. Sparse limestone to 0.05, AYQ/AYR **7** also one piece 0.1. Slip on both surfaces, AYG **2** discoloured grey by burning, remainder red-brown. Both surfaces polished.

Phase	Context & No.	Grid ref	Dia rim (top)	Fabric	Fig
o	ADU (UP 122) NW **16**	Area 13	13	B1	As 25h
ii	AYG **2**	Area 13	20	B2	As 25h
iv (Pt II?)/?	AYQ/AYR **7**	Area 13	?	B2	As 25h
v–vi	BKX **9**	07-25/26	?	B2	As 25h
vii	CAA **31**	Area 26	22	B1	25h
vii?	BFB **28**	Area 1	?	B1	As 25h
?	BEP **47**	14 to 17-01/S01	18	B1	As 25h

1652 **196** Fig. 26a

The groove shows clear marks of a thin string tied around before firing.

Nile B2. Fired fairly soft. Surfaces concealed by slip. Break pale brown with red core. Fairly plentiful fine and medium sand with a few larger grains. Moderate qty fine veg to 0.2. Sparse limestone to 0.05. Red slip on both surfaces. Both surfaces polished.

Phase	Context & No.	Grid ref	Dia rim (top)	Fig
v–vi	ALE **17**	Area 14	14	26a

1700A **197** Fig. 26b

Nile A. Fired medium. Surfaces concealed by slip. Break brown with red zones and grey core. Fairly plentiful fine well-sorted sand. No visible veg. No visible limestone. Red-brown slip on both surfaces. Both surfaces polished.

Phase	Context & No.	Grid ref	Dia rim (top)	Fig
v/?	ANN/ANO (UP 189) **1**	Area 14	*c.*20	26b

1730 **198** Fig. 26c

Handmade. The grooves around, variable in width and depth, are probably from unusually elaborate string-tying. Rim blackened, and some blackening of exterior, probably from use as a cooking pot.

Originally published in Vol. II (Pl. 63 [26]); the diameter and description are now slightly amended.

Nile B2. Fired fairly soft. Surfaces concealed by slip. Break pale brown with red zones and purple core. Fairly plentiful poorly sorted sand. Fairly plentiful fine and coarse veg to 0.7. Rather more limestone than usual, to 0.1. Thin red slip on both surfaces. Polished on top of rim and possible trace on exterior;

Phase	Context & No.	Grid ref	Dia rim (top)	Fig
ii	AJY **148**	18/19/20-S04/S05	29	26c

2026 **199** Fig. 26d

Nile B2. AXX/AXY **19** fired fairly soft, AYP/AYJ **21** medium. Surfaces concealed by slip. Break AXX/AXY **19** brown with red core; AYP/AYJ **21** orange-brown with pink core. Fairly plentiful fine and medium sand with a few larger grains. AXX/AXY **19** moderate qty, AYP/AYJ **21** fairly plentiful, fine veg to 0.2, AYP/AYJ **21** also a few pieces to 0.5. Sparse limestone to 0.05. Thick red-brown slip on both surfaces. Both surfaces polished.

Phase	Context & No.	Grid ref	Dia rim (top)	Fig & notes
iv (Pt II?)/iv (Pt II?)	AXX/AXY **19**	Area 13	*c.*15(?)	Similar to 26d*
iv (Pt II?)/?	AYP/AYJ **21**	Area 13	*c.*14	26d

* The upper groove is faint

1700B **200** Fig. 26e

Nile B1. Fired medium. Surfaces concealed by slip. Break pale brown with grey core. Fairly plentiful fine and medium well sorted sand. Small qty fine veg to 0.2. Sparse limestone to 0.05. Red-brown slip on both surfaces. Both surfaces polished.

Nile B2. AIY/BDR/AWZ **14** fired medium, AOK **32** fired fairly soft. Surfaces concealed by slip. Break, AOK **32** brown with red core, AIY/BDR/AWZ **14** pale brown with thin pink zones and grey core. Fairly plentiful fine and medium sand with a few larger grains. Fairly plentiful fine veg to 0.2. Sparse limestone to 0.1. Slip on both surfaces, AIY/BDR/AWZ **14** pale brown, AOK **32** orange. Both surfaces polished.

Phase	Context & No.	Grid ref	Dia rim (top)	Fabric	Fig & notes
o	AQG **76**	12/13/14-S04/S05	*c.*18	B1	As 26e
ii/iii/iva	AIY/BDR/AWZ **14**	07/08-06/07	*c.*20	B2	26e
ivb	AOK **32**	08/09-03/04	?	B2	As 26e*

* AOK 32 has three grooves instead of two

335 **201** Fig. 26f–g

Each example has two grooves around, just below rim.

Nile B1. BJJ **36** fired fairly soft, ADF North **15** medium, remainder fairly hard. Surfaces concealed by slip. Break, BJJ **36** red-brown with pink core, ADF North **15** brown with red zones and grey core, others red-brown with grey core. Fairly plentiful fine and medium well sorted sand. Small to moderate qty fine veg to 0.2. Sparse limestone to 0.05. Slip on both surfaces, ADF North **15** pink, CBU **42** misfired grey-brown and surface crazed, others red-brown. All surfaces polished.

Nile B2. Fired fairly soft. Surfaces concealed by slip. Break red-brown with thin deep brown zones and pink core. Fairly plentiful fine and medium sand with a few larger granules. Moderate qty fine and coarse veg to 0.3. Sparse limestone to 0.05. Slip on both surfaces, AQG **124** red-brown, BDG/BRT **8** orange and crazed. All surfaces polished.

Phase	**Context & No.**	**Grid ref**	**Dia rim (top)**	**Fabric**	**Fig**
o	AQG **124**	13/14-S01/S02	*c.*40	B2	26f
iii	BJJ **36**	18-06	*c.*30	B1	As 26g
iv (Pt II?)	ADF North **15**	Area 13	*c.*28	B1	As 26g
iva/ivb	BDG/BRT **8**	12/13/14-03/04/05	?	B2	As 26g
v–vi	CBU **42**	08-34	25	B1	As 26g
vii	AAA (UP 157) **128**	06 to 10-11/12	*c.*40–45	B1	26g
vii	AAA **47**	Area 1	34	B1	As 26g

2122 **202** Fig. 26h

Nile B1 near B2. Fired fairly soft. Surfaces concealed by slip. Break brown with diffuse red core. Fairly plentiful fine and medium well-sorted sand. AMJ **13** moderate qty, ABH Top **54** small qty, fine veg to 0.3. Sparse limestone to 0.05. Brownish red slip on both surfaces. Both surfaces polished.

Phase	**Context & No.**	**Grid ref**	**Dia rim (top)**	**Fig & notes**
vi	AMJ **13**	20-10	*c.*20	26h
vi	ABH Top **54**	Area 13	15–20	Similar to 26h*

* Lower groove wider than on AMJ **13**, and closer to groove above

203 Deep bowl with modelled rim (Rzeuska 2006, Form 151, Pl. 104)

The slightly incurved rim, with its elongated shape and narrow tip, is closely paralleled in Rzeuska's Form 151 [529]. The latter lacks the external groove but this, though deep, is not typologically significant, as it almost certainly results from string-tying, perhaps necessary only if a batch of vessels had been made with softer clay than usual. [529] is wheel assisted and in Nile B1, red slipped and polished on both surfaces; the diameter is larger at 36 cm.

2824 **203** Fig. 27a

Rim probably wheel assisted. Both surfaces partly smoke blackened, probably from use as a cooking pot.

Nile B2. Fired fairly soft. Surfaces brown where uncoated or slip lost. Break brown with faint, diffuse red core. Fairly plentiful poorly sorted sand. Moderate qty fine veg to 0.2. Sparse limestone to 0.05. Thin red slip (mostly blackened) on interior, and exterior down to just below groove. Polished where slipped.

Phase	**Context & No.**	**Grid ref**	**Dia rim (top)**	**Fig**
vi to Mamluk	ABA to ABG (UP 3) **20**	Area 13	*c.*20–24	27a

204 Deep bowl with 'straight' rim (Rzeuska 2006, Form 155, Pl. 106)

A large thick-walled bowl with inward-sloping direct rim. The resemblance to Rzeuska's Form 155 is close, though its similarity to other Anubieion bowls with apparently more rounded body (e.g. **205/06**) does counsel caution.

1506 **204** Fig. 27b

Nile B2. Fired medium. Surfaces brown where slip lost. Break brown with thick red core. Fairly plentiful poorly sorted sand. Fairly plentiful fine and coarse veg to 0.3. Sparse limestone to 0.1. Surfaces weathered but traces of red slip on interior near lower break, so probably originally on both surfaces. Polished where slip survives.

Phase	Context & No.	Grid ref	Dia rim (top)	Fig
vii	AAA (UP 588) **320**	05/06-25/26/27	*c.*30(?)	27b

205–16 Sundry medium-sized to large bowls with maximum diameter at the body and simple, unthickened or slightly thickened rim (Rzeuska 2006, nearest, Form 155, Pl. 106, and Form 190, Pl. 135)

Most of the bodies, as preserved, are too rounded to be identified with the 'deep bowls with straight rim' of Rzeuska's Form 155 (which itself fits uneasily into her series), yet do not really accord with the high-shouldered 'Meidum' bowl Form 190. The rims are mostly of the simplest, and of the same thickness throughout.

Among the examples from the SCA excavations and the trenches of the Greater Cairo Waste Water Project at Giza (Hawass and Senussi 2008), several bear a close resemblance to the Anubieion series. Thus **205** is matched by 43 [9], **212** by 43 [10] and 44 [13], **211** by marl clay 53 [78], **207** by 54 [90] and 65 [150], **207** again and **208** by 154 [A20], and AAA Upper **28** of **213** by 167 [A83]. The marl clay [78] is classified as Type D1c and dated to the Fourth Dynasty, the remainder as Type D1b and dated to the Fourth and Fifth (*ibid.*, 200–01).

212 and **213** also find close parallels at Abu Rawash, dated (after Kaiser) to Khafra to Neferirkare but probably not later than Radjedef (Marchand and Baud 1996, 276, Fig. 7 [3–4]). However, the forms are so varied, and most Anubieion examples and potential comparatives so fragmentary, that any attempt to match them is fraught with difficulties. Thus **212/13** are similar to a form in Kaiser's typology (1969, 81 [33.1.59 = Reisner G 2200 C]) which would locate them as 'Chefren to Neferirkare', but similar also to one in the corpus from Herakleopolis (Bader 2009a, Fig. 9k) which would have them in the late OK/early FIP. **207** and **208** bear some resemblance to one at Herakleopolis (*ibid.*, Fig. 2h) dated FIP/early MK and, together with **209** and **210**, to one from Tell el-Dab'a (Czerny 1999, 153 [Nf 234]) from levels of the Twelfth Dynasty. Finally, the upright **205** may owe its flowing lines to freedom from the string-tying that distorted two examples of the FIP/early MK at Herakleopolis (Bader 2009a, Fig. 3h/j); or is it so slim that it should be something else entirely?

On balance, it seems best to attribute all to the later Old Kingdom and FIP, rather than some to the MK.

1518 **205** Fig. 27c

Two similar but not quite identical examples.

Nile B1. Fired medium. Surfaces concealed by slip. Break red-brown with red core. Fairly plentiful fine well-sorted sand. Small qty fine veg to 0.2. Sparse limestone to 0.05. Red-brown slip on both surfaces. Both surfaces polished.

Nile B2. Fired medium. Surfaces pale brown where slip lost. Break pale brown with red zones and grey core. Fairly plentiful fine and medium sand with a few larger grains. Small to medium qty fine veg to 0.3. Sparse limestone to 0.05. Mid brown slip on both surfaces, perhaps discoloured by secondary burning. Both surfaces polished.

Phase	Context & No.	Grid ref	Fabric	Dia rim (top)	Fig
ivc	BQI **97**	Area 2	B2	*c.*20–25	As 27c
vii	AAA (UP 445) **126**	Area 2	B1	*c.*20	27c

1512 **206** Fig. 27d

Nile B2. Fired medium. Surfaces pale brown where slip lost. Break, BQA to BQJ **18** brown with pink zones and mauve core, UP 445 **43** orange-brown with pink zones and grey core. Fairly plentiful fine to medium sand with only a few larger grains. Fairly plentiful fine veg to 0.4. Sparse limestone to 0.1, BQA to BQJ **18** also one piece 0.2. Slip on both surfaces: BQA to BQJ **18** thick pink, UP 445 **43** orange red with the thick slip of the exterior carried over the rim and down 0.5 on interior to a straight edge, below which the slip is thinner, thickening again lower down; apparently slipped in two stages, probably the interior first. Both surfaces polished.

Phase	Context & No.	Grid ref	Dia rim (top)	Fig
Various ivc/ivd/v	BQA to BQJ **18**	Area 2	*c*.40	As 27d
vii	AAA (UP 445) **43**	Area 2	*c*.30–35	27d

1510A **207** Fig. 27e

Nile B2. Fired fairly soft to medium. Surfaces pale brown to brown where slip lost. Break AHC/AIU **24** pale brown with thin dark brown zones and mid brown core; UP 117 **13** brown with red zones and grey core; others brown with red core. Fairly plentiful fine and medium sand with some larger grains. Fairly plentiful veg to 0.5, AGH/AGI **19** and AAC **11** fine, remainder fine and coarse. Sparse limestone, UP 117 **13** to 0.1, others to 0.05. Slip on both surfaces: UP 117 **13** red-brown, others pale brown.

Phase	Context & No.	Grid ref	Dia rim (top)	Fig
ivd/ivd	AGH/AGI **19**	06/07/08-04/05	*c*.30	As 27e
vi/vi	AHC/AIU **24**	15/16-07/08	*c*.26	As 27e
(vi–)vii	AAC **11**	06-04	?	As 27e
vii	AAA (UP 117) **13**	01 to04-01/S01/S02	*c*.30	27e

1510B **208** Fig. 27f

Nile B2. Fired medium. Surfaces brown where slip lost. Break brown with red core. Fairly plentiful fine and medium sand with some larger grains. Fairly plentiful fine and coarse veg to 0.5. Sparse limestone to 0.05. Pale brown slip on both surfaces.

Phase	Context & No.	Grid ref	Dia rim (top)	Fig
vi/vi	AJJ/AMJ **45**	12/13-05/06	*c*.26	27f

1522 **209** Fig. 28a

Nile B1. ARP=ARS/AYY **9** fired fairly soft, BFB **95** medium. Surfaces concealed by slip. Break ARP=ARS/AYY **9** brown with red core, BFB **95** pale orange-brown with grey core. Fairly plentiful fine and medium well-sorted sand. Moderate qty fine veg to 0.3. Sparse limestone to 0.05. Slip on both surfaces, ARP=ARS/AYY **9** brown, BFB **95** orange. Both surfaces polished.

Nile B2. Fired fairly soft. Surfaces pale brown where slip lost. Break pale brown, BJM **16** all through, with darker areas possibly staining from contents, BFB **30** with one red zone and mauve core close to interior surface. Fairly plentiful poorly sorted sand. Moderate qty fine and some coarse veg to 0.3. Sparse limestone to 0.1. Slip on both surfaces: BJM **16** brownish red, BFB **30** red but interior below 0.5 grey where 'nested' in kiln. Both surfaces polished.

Phase	Context & No.	Grid ref	Dia rim (top)	Fabric	Fig
iv (Pt II?)/iv (Pt II?)	ARP=ARS/AYY **9**	Area 13	*c.*21	B1	As 28a
ivc	BJM **16**	03/04/05-S04/S05/S06	24	B2	As 28a
vii?	BFB **30**	Area 1	*c.*20	B2	28a
vii?	BFB **95**	Area 1	16	B1	As 28a

1520 **210** Fig. 28b

Nile B2. AFV North **No. lost** and AJS **6** fired fairly soft, others fairly hard. Surfaces pale brown to brown where slip lost. Break, BKR/BPU **30** red-brown, AFV North (**No. lost**) pale brown with thick pink core, AJS **6** brown all through, UP 445 **38** pale brown; each with thin dark brown zones and thick pink core. Fairly plentiful sand, UP 445 **38** fine well sorted, others fine and medium with a few larger grains. Small to medium qty fine (BKR/BPU **30** also coarse) veg to 0.3/0.4. Sparse limestone to 0.05/0.1. Slip on both surfaces, BKR/BPU **30** red-brown, others pale red-brown. All surfaces polished.

Phase	Context & No.	Grid ref	Dia rim (top)	Fig
iii/iii	BKR/BPU **30**	02/03-21/22/23	24	As 28b
ivb	AFV North **(No. lost)**	08 to 12-04/05	? (22–30?)	As 28b
ivb	AJS **6**	04/05-13/14/15	23	As 28b
vii	AAA (UP 445) **38**	Area 2	*c.*26	28b

1504 **211** Fig. 28c

Nile B1. Fired fairly hard. Surfaces brown where slip lost. Break brownish red with thick grey core. Fairly plentiful fine and medium well-sorted sand. Fairly plentiful mostly fine veg to 0.4. Sparse limestone to 0.1. Brownish red slip on both surfaces. Both surfaces polished.

Phase	Context & No.	Grid ref	Dia rim (top)	Fig
v–vi/vii	CBS/AAA **3**	01/W01-31/32	*c.*30(?)	28c

1658 **212** Fig. 28d

Nile B1. Fired fairly soft. Surfaces brown where slip lost. Break, AIY **55** brown all through, UP23 **400** brown with red zones and purple core, others brown with red core. Fairly plentiful fine and medium sand, AIY **55** and CAA North **9** with a few larger grains. Small qty fine veg to 0.3. Sparse limestone, CAA North **9** to 0.1, others to 0.05. Slip on all surfaces, AIY **55** dark brown with some burnt areas; CAA North **9** orange, lower exterior pale grey where 'nested' in kiln; others pale red-brown. All surfaces polished.

Phase	Context & No.	Grid ref	Dia rim (top)	Fig
ii	AIY **55**	13/14-01/S01	?	As 28d
ivd	AJK **3**	17/18-08/09	*c.*22	28d
vii	AAA (UP 23) **400**	10-07	*c.*25(?)	As 28d
vii	CAA North **9**	Area 26	*c.*22	As 28d

1524C/1526 **213** Fig. 28e–f

The surfaces of BGY **8** and AAA Upper **28** are burnt.

Nile B1. Fired fairly soft to medium. Surfaces pale brown or brown where slip lost. Break various, about 30 per cent with grey core. Fairly plentiful fine and medium sand, about 50 per cent with a few larger grains. Small to medium qty fine veg, most to 0.3/0.4. Sparse limestone to 0.05/0.1. Slip on all surfaces, ARP=ARS **8** pink, ANJ **15** red, others various shades of red-brown. Both surfaces polished.

Nile B2. Fired fairly soft. Surfaces pale brown where slip lost. Break pale brown all through. Fairly plentiful fine and medium well-sorted sand. Fairly plentiful fine veg to 0.3. Fairly plentiful tiny limestone flecks, but no larger limestone. Thick brownish red slip on both surfaces. Both surfaces polished.

Phase	Context & No.	Grid ref	Dia rim (top)	Fabric	Fig
ii	AIY **122**	05 to 08-04/05/06	*c.*17–20	B1	As 28f
ii	ABR North (UP 51) **3**	Area 13	?	B1	As 28e
iii	BCB **166**	01 to 05-04/05/06	*c.*23–26	B1	As 28f
iii	BDP (UP 647) **265**	01 to 05-07	?	B1	As 28e
iv (Pt II?)	ADF North **89**	Area 13	*c.*24	B2	As 28f
iv (Pt II?)	ARP=ARS (UP 154) **8**	Area 13	*c.*26	B1	As 28f
iva	AFR **19**	03-08/09	?	B1	28e
iva	BHR **46**	02-22/23/24	21	B1	As 28e
ivb–c	BGY **8**	14-14/05	*c.*28	B1	As 28f
ivd	BKQ **21**	02-21	?	B1	As 28f
v–vi	AUA **19**	09/10-S01/S02/S03	?	B1	As 28f
vii	AAA (UP 23) **677**	09-09	*c.*20	B1	As 28e
vii	AAA (UP 157) **166**	01/02/03-13/14/15	?	B1	As 28f
vii	AAA **68**	Area 1	?	B1	As 28f
vii	AAA (UP 445) **63**	Area 2	?	B1	As 28f
vii	AAA Upper **28**	Area 2	19	B1	28f
vii	ANJ (UP 168) **15**	Area 14	*c.*20	B1	As 28f
?	UP 1048 **21**	Area 12	*c.*20	B1	As 28e

1508 **214** Fig. 28g

Rims wheel assisted. The two examples not illustrated survive only to the bottom of the shoulder, near the maximum diameter; AAQ **80** is handmade from that point down, with a slightly irregular surface.

Nile B2. ADC **82** fired medium, others fairly hard. Where uncoated or slip lost, ADC **82** surfaces red-brown, others orange. Break orange with thick pink core. Fairly plentiful fine and medium sand with a few larger grains. Moderate qty fine and some coarse veg to 0.4/0.5. Sparse limestone to 0.1. AAQ **80** contains nodules of unincorporated clay to 0.1. AAQ **80** weathered, no (surviving) slip; remainder red slip on both surfaces, but ADF North/AYQ/AYR **2** traces only. Polished where slipped.

Phase	Context & No.	Grid ref	Dia rim (top)	Fig
iv (Pt II?)	ADC **82**	Area 13	*c.*25	As 28g
iv (Pt II?)/iv (Pt II?)/?	ADF North/AYQ/AYR **2**	Area 13	*c.*30	As 28g
ivd	AAQ **80**	06-05	*c.*21	28g

1468 **<u>215</u>** Fig. 29a

Thick-walled version of the 'Meidum'-bowl-related bowl. The two examples differ slightly: ATT **80** survives only down to the top of the shoulder but is more sinuous (cf **<u>204</u>**, but ware differs).

<u>Nile B2.</u> Fired medium. Surfaces concealed by slip. Break red, ATT **80** all through, ANJ **2** with purple core. Plentiful fine and medium sand with a few larger grains. Moderate qty fine and coarse veg, ATT **80** to 0.4, ANJ **2** to 0.2. Sparse limestone to 0.05. Red slip on all surfaces. All surfaces polished.

Phase	Context & No.	Grid ref	Dia rim (top)	Fig
ivb	ATT **80**	09/10-05/06	*c*.40	Similar to 29a
vii	ANJ (UP 132) **2**	Area 14	30+(?)	29a

2642 **<u>216</u>** Fig. 29b

Wheel assisted as far as preserved. Joining sherds from widely spaced locations, with old break and AVB **92** much more weathered. Two wide, shallow grooves on interior; three more on exterior, unequally spaced, very probably for string-tying.

<u>Nile B1.</u> Fired fairly hard. Surfaces red-brown where slip lost. Break thin red-brown zones, thin pink zones and grey core. Fairly plentiful fine sand with a few larger grains. Moderate qty fine veg to 0.6. Sparse limestone to 0.05. Thick red-brown slip on all surfaces. All surfaces polished, including interior.

Phase	Context & No.	Grid ref	Dia rim (top)	Fig
ivb	AVB **92**★	10/11-S01/S02	*c*.24	29b
ivb/ivc	BCT **37**★	18/19-08/09	*c*.24	29b

★ Join

<u>217–18</u> Fairly small bowls with maximum diameter at the mouth or (just) at the body, and slightly thickened rim (not present in Rzeuska 2006)

A smaller diameter version of the preceding series (but note that BFB **95** of **<u>209</u>** has diameter 16 only), with body and mouth of almost equal diameter and a groove, probably for string-tying. There is no counterpart in Rzeuska's material: nearest is Form 190 (Pl. 135) but it is not close and the diameters are much greater. On the other hand, there are very similar bowls (dias 17 and 16 respectively) at Herakleopolis (Bader 2009a, Fig. 3b/c) with polished red slip on both surfaces, dated to the FIP/early MK.

1528 **<u>217</u>** Fig. 29c

Wheel assisted as far as preserved.

<u>Nile B1.</u> Fired medium. Surfaces concealed by slip. Break red-brown with grey core. Fairly plentiful fine and medium well-sorted sand. Fairly plentiful mostly fine veg to 0.4. Sparse limestone to 0.1 and one piece 0.3. Red slip on both surfaces. Both surfaces polished.

Phase	Context & No.	Grid ref	Dia rim (top)	Fig
vi	ABI (UP 7) **114**	Area 13	14	29c

1516 **<u>218</u>** Fig. 29d

<u>Nile B1.</u> Fired fairly soft. Surfaces concealed by slip. Break brown with red zones and thin mauve core. Fairly

plentiful fine and medium well-sorted sand. Moderate qty fine veg to 0.2. Sparse limestone to 0.05. Thick red slip on all surfaces. All surfaces polished.

Phase	Context & No.	Grid ref	Dia rim (top)	Fig
iii	BXO **1**	Area 13	16	29d

219–20 Deep bowls with straight rim (Rzeuska 2006, Form 156, Pl. 106)

Deep bowls, corresponding reasonably well with Rzeuska's Form 156. **219** comprises vessels of smaller diameter than Rzeuska's, perhaps a development towards two even smaller bowls of the same form (dias 12 and 13), slipped but unpolished, from the early MK (Czerny 1999, 145 [Nf 145]). A close parallel (dia 20.2) is recorded at Akhmim from the late OK to early MK, with red slip on both surfaces but unpolished (Hope and McFarlane, 2006, Fig. 2 [BVd.1]).

2032 **219** Fig. 29e

The interior has smoothing marks parallel to the rim, which may indicate wheel assistance, but the exterior has parallel marks only close to the rim, with others at various angles lower down.

Nile B1. Fired fairly soft. Surfaces pale brown where slip lost. Break pale brown with red zones and mauve core. Fairly plentiful poorly sorted sand. Small qty fine veg to 0.3. Sparse limestone to 0.05. Red-brown slip on both surfaces. Both surfaces lightly polished.

Phase	Context & No.	Grid ref	Max dia rim	Fig
v–vi	BKX **16**	07-25/26	*c.*27	29e

2020A **220** Fig. 29f

BWQ **1** has smoke-blackened exterior, probably from use as a cooking pot.

Nile B2. BWQ **1** and UP 1045 **5** fired fairly soft, remainder fairly hard. Surfaces concealed by slip. Break BWQ **1** brown with red zones and grey core, UP 1045 **5** brown with red core; others red with pink zones and grey core. Fairly plentiful fine and medium sand with a few larger grains. Small to moderate qty fine veg to 0.2. Sparse limestone to 0.1. Thick slip, ATY **236** red-brown, others brown, on both surfaces. Both surfaces polished.

Phase	Context & No.	Grid ref	Dia rim (top)	Fig
iii–iva/iva	ACE=AJH **40**	05 to 09-06 to 09	16	As 29f
iv (Pt II?)	BWQ **1**	Area 12	*c.*21	As 29f
ivd	ATY **236**	25-04	17	29f
?	UP 1045 **5**	Area 12	*c.*19	As 29f

221 Thin-walled bowl with out-turned rim (not present in Rzeuska 2006)

The basic form is that of a red slipped, thin-walled lightly carinated bowl which occurs in small numbers, most 'well polished', at Abusir (Kaiser 1969, XXIII, Type 141/42); the drawn examples have appropriate dias 24 and 23 respectively.

2202 **221** Fig. 29g

Rim sherd from a bowl, apparently with a flange but this is broken at both ends and the shape of the breaks indicates it was short and perhaps a ledge handle. There is a very low ridge along the highest point, probably where the clay was pushed up as the handle(?) was made. It is not possible to be sure of the form of the rim otherwise, but indications are that it was gently outcurved and simple, most probably from a carinated bowl.

Nile B1 near B2. Fired medium. Surfaces concealed by slip. Break pale red-brown with faint purple core. Fairly plentiful fine and medium well-sorted sand. Moderate qty fine veg to 0.2. Sparse limestone to 0.1. Thick red-brown slip on all surfaces. All surfaces fairly highly polished.

Phase	Context & No.	Grid ref	Dia rim (top)	Fig
iva	BDU **30**	16/17/18-06/07/08	*c*.20–25(?)	29g

222–25 Deep bowls with ledged rim (Rzeuska 2006, nearest, Form 158, Pl. 107)

Although there is little doubt that the Anubieion examples relate to vessel Form 158, none of the rims is a perfect match for Rzeuska's, which are short, thick and 'square'. **222–24** are a closer match to some from Abusir (dias 33–38), all slipped and smoothed, some polished, (Kaiser 1969, XLIV, Type 220–23). In some respects an even better parallel (dia 30) is provided by Herakleopolis (Bader 2009a, Fig. 10h), dated to the late OK/FIP. The wider rim of **225** is more like MK examples (dia 46) (Arnold, Do. 1982, 39–40, Abb. 11 [1]) and (dia 31) (Aston 2004b, Pl. 51 [171]), but these are in marl clay so **225** is more probably of the FIP.

2790 **222** Fig. 29h

Interior surface almost flat, and featureless. Rim undercut by string-tying, which has distorted its form.

Nile B2. Fired medium. Surfaces brown where slip lost. Break brown with red zones and grey core. Fairly plentiful fine and medium sand with a few larger grains. Fairly plentiful fine and coarse veg to 0.8. Sparse limestone to 0.1. Thin slip on all surfaces, fired pale brown on exterior and top of rim, red on interior. Faint traces of probable polish on interior and exterior.

Phase	Context & No.	Grid ref	Dia rim (top)	Fig
ivd	ATZ **22**	22/23-01/02	*c*.25	29h

613 **223** Fig. 29i

Two similar, but not quite identical examples, the rim of ADF **51** protruding less. Unusually thick wall, especially of AHC/AIU **19**.

Nile B2. ADF **51** fired medium, AHC/AIU **19** fairly hard. Surfaces red-brown where slip lost. Break red-brown with thick grey core, ADF **51** also red zones. Fairly plentiful fine and medium sand with a few larger grains. Moderate qty to fairly plentiful fine veg to 0.2. Sparse limestone to 0.1. ADF **51** areas of pink slip on all surfaces; AHC/AIU **19** red-brown slip on exterior, carried over the rim on to the interior, but below 0.5 black from stacking in the kiln. Both surfaces polished, ADF **51** where slip survives.

Phase	Context & No.	Grid ref	Dia rim (top)	Fig
iv (Pt II?)	ADF **51**	Area 13	?	Similar to 29i
vi/vi	AHC/AIU **19**	15/16-06/07	*c*.32	29i

2924 **224** Fig. 30a

Nile B2. Fired fairly hard. Surfaces red-brown where slip lost. Break red-brown with thick pink core. Fairly plentiful fine well-sorted sand. Moderate qty fine veg to 0.4. Sparse limestone to 0.05. Small areas of red slip survive weathering on top of rim and just under rim on exterior. Polished where slip survives.

Phase	Context & No.	Grid ref	Max dia rim	Fig
Mamluk/Mamluk/vii	ABC/ABD/ABA **24**	Area 13	*c.*30(?)	30a

327 **225** Fig. 30b

Nile B2. Fired medium. Surfaces concealed by slip. Break red-brown with thin red zones and grey core. Fairly plentiful, poorly sorted sand. Fairly plentiful fine veg to 0.2. Sparse limestone to 0.1. Thick red-brown slip on all surfaces. All surfaces polished.

Phase	Context & No.	Grid ref	Max dia rim	Fig
o	ADU (UP 122) NW **21**	Area 13	39	30b

226 Flat bases of deep bowls with ledged rim (Rzeuska 2006, Form 158, Pl. 107)

These thick, flat bases should derive from large, heavy vessels such as Rzeuska's Form 158. All three of her examples are red slipped and her [547], with base preserved, is also polished.

707C **226** Fig. 30c

Probably handmade.

Nile B1. Fired medium to hard. Surfaces concealed by slip. Break red with grey core. Fairly plentiful fine and medium well-sorted sand. No visible veg. Sparse limestone to 0.05 or 0.1. Red slip on all surfaces. All surfaces polished.

Nile B2. BCB **51** fired soft, others medium to hard. BEO **88** surfaces concealed by slip; where uncoated or slip lost, BCB **51** surfaces pale yellow-brown, AQG/BGU **20** red. Break BCB **51** pale yellow-brown with grey core where thickest, others red with grey core. Fairly plentiful poorly sorted sand. Small to moderate qty fine veg. Sparse limestone to 0.05 or 0.1. BEO **88** red slip on both surfaces, AQG/BGU **20** (surviving?) on interior only, BCB **51** (surviving?) on exterior only. BEO **88** no (surviving?) polish, others polished where slip survives.

Phase	Context & No.	Grid ref	Dia base	Fabric	Fig
o	BEO **88**	14/15-01	*c.*16	B2	30c
o/ii	AQG/BGU **20**	19/20-S04/S05	11	B2	As 30c
iii	BCB **51**	01 to 04-04/05/06	*c.*15	B2	As 30c
Mamluk	ARN (UP 9) **26**	Area 12	*c.*16–20	B1	As 30c

227–36 Bent-sided bowls

A fairly lengthy series in Rzeuska's corpus, incorporating most of the 'spout rim' examples. Distinguished from the bent-sided plates by greater depth, though as usual some examples of the two series are close in form.

Rzeuska's series and the series from the Anubieion each include examples in Nile B1 and Nile B2 fabrics with B1 predominating, though less so at the Anubieion; Rzeuska has also one Nile A and one Nile E. A difference is the much higher incidence of polishing at the Anubieion, as seen also in the bent-sided plates and elsewhere, but this may be due to the conditions of preservation.

227–28 Bent-sided bowls with simple rim and high-located bent-point (Rzeuska 2006, Form 161, Pls 108/09)

1536 **227** Fig. 30d

The form approaches that of some 'Meidum' bowls, but the absence of slip on the lower exterior confirms its place in the 'bent sided' series. The smoothing is so regular it was probably done with the vessel inverted on a slow wheel.

Nile B2. Fired fairly soft. Interior concealed by slip, exterior pale brown where uncoated. Break pale brown with red core. Fairly plentiful poorly sorted sand. Fairly plentiful fine and some coarse veg to 0.5. Sparse limestone to 0.1. Red slip on interior, and on exterior down to bent-point only, and running down below. Below bent-point, smoothed parallel to rim but not slipped. Both surfaces polished where slipped; uncoated area appears polished, but only from compaction during smoothing.

Phase	Context & No.	Grid ref	Max dia rim	Fig
ivb	CIE **38**	02 to 05-33 to 37	20–25(?)	30d

2054 **228** Fig. 30e

Nile B2. Fired fairly soft. Surfaces brown where slip lost. Break, brown with faint grey core. Fairly plentiful poorly sorted sand. Moderate qty fine veg to 0.3. Sparse limestone to 0.05. Small areas of brownish red slip survive on both surfaces. Both surfaces polished where slip survives.

Phase	Context & No.	Grid ref	Dia rim (top)	Fig
ivc/ivd	AHU/AAT **9**	05/06-05/06	*c.*26–30	30e

229 Bent-sided bowl with simple rim and high- to low-located bent-point (Rzeuska 2006, Forms 161/62, Pls 109/10)

1716A **229** Fig. 30f

The bowl from which this sherd derives seems to have been too deep for a spout-rim type.

Nile B1. Fired fairly soft. Surfaces concealed by slip. Break red-brown with grey core. Fairly plentiful fine and medium well-sorted sand. Sparse fine veg to 0.2. Sparse limestone to 0.05. Red-brown slip on both surfaces. Both surfaces polished.

Phase	Context & No.	Grid ref	Dia rim (top)	Fig
iva/ivd	AIF/AAT **29**	05/06-04/05	24	30f

230 Bent-sided bowl with low-located bent-point (Rzeuska 2006, Form 162, Pl. 110)

Closest to the shape of Rzeuska's [561] of Form 162, with a rounded bulge at the lower break. The diameter of [561] is appropriate at 21 cm; only the interior and the rim of the exterior are red slipped, but the not dissimilar [563] is red slipped on both surfaces.

1514 **230** Fig. 31a

Nile B2. Fired fairly soft. Surfaces concealed by slip. Break brown with red core. Fairly plentiful fine and medium sand with some larger grains. Fairly plentiful fine veg to 0.3. Sparse limestone to 0.05. Thick red slip on all surfaces. All surfaces polished.

Phase	Context & No.	Grid ref	Max dia rim	Fig
iv (Pt II?) ×3	ABV/ABY/ABZ **10**	Area 13	*c*.20–30	31a

231 Bent-sided bowls with simple rim (Rzeuska 2006, Forms 161/62 Pls 108–10)

1716C **231** Not illustrated

Simple-rim sherds apparently from bent-sided bowls but ADU NW **24** preserved only down to top of bend and remainder rims only. Although insufficiently preserved to show the detail of the form, they are included to widen the context base.

Nile B1. Fired fairly soft. Surfaces concealed by slip. Break BDP **293** red-brown, others brown, each with grey core. Fairly plentiful fine and medium sand with a few larger grains. Small qty fine veg to 0.2. Sparse limestone to 0.05. Red-brown slip on both surfaces. Both surfaces polished.

Phase	Context & No.	Grid ref	Dia rim (top)	Notes
o	ADU (UP 122) NW **24*, 28***	Area 13	?	Not illustrated
iii	BDP (UP 647) **293**	01 to 05-07	?	Not illustrated

* Almost certainly same vessel

232–34 Bent-sided bowls with modelled rim (Rzeuska 2006, Form 166, Pls 112–15)

Because so little depth survives, these cannot be related to any specific examples in Rzeuska's lengthy series. However, [577–80] of Rzeuska's sub-form 166A are similar to **233**, the diameters in range 27–31 are appropriate, two of the four are in Nile B2 and all are red slipped (though none is recorded as polished). For the less protruding, rounded rim of **234**, the closest match is [581], with diameter 31, in Nile B1, red slipped and polished. The slight thickening of the wall of **234** may represent the top of the bent-point, which would be located high rather than low as Form 166. Since the three examples of **232** differ slightly, it is not feasible to seek a specific parallel. All differ from **223/24**, above, in the rounded inner edge of the rim, but are otherwise very similar.

1672 **232** Fig. 31b

Nile B1. AWD **21** fired medium, UP 1039 **9** fairly soft,. Surfaces concealed by slip. Break, AWD **21** brown with grey core, UP 1039 **9** pale brown all through. Fairly plentiful fine and medium well-sorted sand. Small to moderate qty fine veg to 0.2. UP 1039 **9** sparse limestone to 0.05, AWD **21** none visible. Thick red-brown slip on all surfaces. All surfaces polished.

Nile B2. Fired medium. Surfaces concealed by slip. In the break, pale brown all through. Fairly plentiful fine and medium sand with a few larger grains. Fairly plentiful fine veg to 0.2. Sparse limestone to 0.05. Thick red-brown slip on all surfaces. All surfaces polished.

Phase	Context & No.	Grid ref	Max dia rim	Fabric	Fig & notes
o	ADU (UP 122) NW **25**	Area 13	*c*.24	B2	31b
ivb	AWD **21**	20-02	?	B1	Sim to 31b*
?	UP 1039 **9**	Area 12	?	B1	Sim to 31b*

* Top of rim more rounded than 31b

2038 **233** Fig. 31c

Surface of rim irregular, so perhaps handmade.

Nile B2. Fired fairly hard. Surfaces red-brown where slip lost. Break orange-red with thin dark brown zones and very thick grey core. Fairly plentiful fine and medium sand with a few larger grains. Fairly plentiful fine veg to 0.4. Sparse limestone to 0.05. Thick orange-red slip on exterior and trace on interior. Highly polished where slip survives.

Phase	Context & No.	Grid ref	Dia rim (top)	Fig
v/v	AEW/AEY **4**	05-02/03	*c.*30–35	31c

2236 **234** Fig. 31d

The thickening of the wall at the lower break may indicate a bend; no other explanation suggests itself.

Nile B1. Fired fairly soft. Surfaces pale brown where slip lost. Break pale brown with red core. Fairly plentiful fine and medium sand with a few larger grains. Fairly plentiful mostly fine veg to 0.3. Slightly more limestone than usual, to 0.1. Brownish red slip on all surfaces. Traces of polish on all surfaces, where slip survives.

Phase	Context & No.	Grid ref	Dia rim (top)	Fig
?	BEP **145**	17/18-01/S01	? (35–40?)	31d

235–36 Bent-sided bowls with simple rim and mid-located bent-point (Rzeuska 2006, Form 167, Pl. 116)

The **235** examples, without string-grooves, resemble Rzeuska's [593]. That the upper body need not be concave but may be slightly rounded as AQE **66**, is shown by [581] of her Form 166B, with modelled rim. **236**, with evidence of string-tying, is similar to Rzeuska's [594]. At Tell el-Dab'a the form of **235** continues into the MK (Czerny 1999, 142 [Nf 90–95]); most of the 79 recorded examples are slipped and polished on both surfaces, but almost all are in the diameter range 16–20, none exceeding 23. **236** is matched at Mendes by an example (dia top 26) slipped and polished on both surfaces (Adams 2009, Fig. 50 [10]), dated to the Fourth to Sixth Dynasties.

1718 **235** Fig. 31e–f

Nile B1. Fired fairly soft to medium. AQE **66** pale brown where slip lost, AAB **10** surfaces concealed by slip. Break AQE **66** pale brown with grey core, AAB **10** red-brown with red zones and purple core. Fairly plentiful fine and medium sand with a few larger grains. AQE **66** moderate qty, AAB **10** small qty fine veg to 0.2. Sparse limestone to 0.05. Slip on both surfaces, AQE **66** red-brown, AAB **10** brown. Both surfaces highly polished.

Phase	Context & No.	Grid ref	Dia rim (top)	Fig
ii	AQE **66**	19/20-02/03	*c.*20	31e
vi–vii	AAB **10**	24/25-07/08	27	31f

1676 **236** Fig. 31g

Nile B1. Fired fairly hard. Surfaces pale brown where slip lost. Break pale brown with one thin dark brown zone, red zones and grey core. Fairly plentiful fine and medium sand with a few larger grains. Moderate qty fine veg to 0.3. Sparse limestone to 0.1. Thick, pale red-brown slip on both surfaces. Both surfaces polished. Some black discolouration of both surfaces, probably from burning in use.

Phase	Context & No.	Grid ref	Max dia rim	Fig
iv (Pt II?)	ADF **56**	Area 13	*c.*28	31g

237–40 Bowls with spout rim (Rzeuska 2006, Forms 170–75, Pls 117–24)

The 'spouts' of this series are not fully enclosed; rather, a pouring lip has been created between two rim sections pushed inwards and (in most cases) upwards. The Anubieion examples are fragmentary. The much better preserved vessels illustrated by Rzeuska are all bowls with the upper body leaning outwards to an unthickened simple rim from a more-or-less carinated point in the middle or the lower half of the wall; the two distorted lengths of rim curve inwards, the most extreme examples almost forming a hook.

All are slipped and polished on both surfaces, but with the guidance of Rzeuska's series, it now seems likely that all sherds of **237** are from the incurved area. **238** preserves the carination and is clearly outcurved, most closely resembling Rzeuska's Form 174 (Pls 122/23). **240** should be from the part of the rim which is not distorted. **239** appears to have a very small diameter, perhaps below 10 cm, but this is so much less than any in Rzeuska's material that it may be unreliable.

An uncoated example from Abu Rawash (Marchand and Baud 1996, Fig. 7 [12]) is dated as Khafra to Neferirkare, and probably no later than Radjedef, and a fragment in a fine Nile fabric from Middle Egypt (Willems, H. *et al.*, 2009, 309–10) is similarly dated to the early Fourth Dynasty; however, spout rims also continue into the early MK.

For a mixed clay example, see **363**.

753 **237** Fig. 32a–e

Rim sherds with 'wavy' form, varying in detail. The diameters are impossible to measure.

Nile B1. BET **96** fired fairly soft, ABI Top **137** fairly hard. Surfaces concealed by slip. Break BET **96** brown all through, ABI Top **137** orange-brown with grey core. Fairly plentiful fine well sorted sand. Fairly plentiful fine veg to 0.4. No visible limestone. ABI Top **137** one fragment of bone 0.1. Slip on all surfaces, BET **96** reddish brown, ABI Top **137** orange. BET **96** lightly polished, preserved on exterior and rim only, ABI Top **137** both surfaces highly polished.

Nile B2. BQE **11** fired fairly soft, ATY **90** medium, ABG **24** fairly hard. Surfaces concealed by slip. Break BQE **11** red-brown with mauve core, ATY **90** pale brown with thin dark zones, red zones and grey core, ABG **24** red-brown with thick grey core. Fairly plentiful sand,

BQE **11** poorly sorted, others fine and medium, ABG **24** with a few larger grains. Fairly plentiful veg, ABG **24** fine to 0.2, others fine and coarse to 1.0. Sparse limestone to 0.05, ATY **90** also two voids each 0.2. Slip on all surfaces, ABG **24** thick red-brown, others thin brown, perhaps self-slip. BQE **11** light polish visible on interior only, ATY **90** possible traces of light polish on interior only, ABG **24** all surfaces highly polished.

Phase	Context & No.	Grid ref	Fabric	Fig
ii	BET **96**	12/13-01/02	B1	32a
ivc(–d)	BQE **11**	Area 2	B2	32c
ivd	ATY **90**	24/25-02/03	B2	32d
vi	ABI Top **137**	Area 13	B1	32b
vi	ABG (UP 235) **24**	Area 13	B2	32e

2908 **238** Fig. 32f

Although so little of this rim survives, the way it varies in thickness and direction points to a 'spout rim' bowl. The bent-point is in the middle of the body and the rim of simple form, both features according with the majority in Rzeuska's corpus. It appears to be from a deeper bowl than any there, but may be incorrectly drawn, the stance being particularly difficult to establish.

Nile B2. Fired fairly soft. Surfaces pale brown where slip flaked. Break pale brown with red zones and mauve core. Fairly plentiful poorly sorted sand. Small qty fine and coarse veg to 0.4. Sparse limestone to 0.1 and one piece 0.2 × 0.1. Slip on both surfaces, fired orange-red on exterior, red-brown, slightly darker, on interior. Both surfaces polished.

Phase	Context & No.	Grid ref	Dia rim (top)	Fig
ivb	BDE **12**	17/18-08	?	32f

2662 **239** Fig. 32g

Small rim sherd, with part of an inward fold. Thin rim, but thick wall compared with what appears to be a diameter of only 6–7 cm where not folded.

Nile B1. Fired fairly soft. Surfaces pale brown where slip lost. Break pale brown all through. Fairly plentiful fine and medium sand with a few larger grains. Fairly plentiful fine veg to 0.2. Sparse limestone to 0.05. Thick red-brown slip on both surfaces. Both surfaces polished.

Phase	Context & No.	Grid ref	Dia rim (top)	Fig
iva	BCP **62**	14 to 17-01/S01	?	32g

2008 **240** Fig. 32h

Nile B2. Fired fairly hard. Surfaces weathered, but brown where slip lost or uncoated. Break brown with thin red zones and grey core. Plentiful poorly sorted sand. Fairly plentiful fine and coarse veg to 0.4. Sparse limestone to 0.05. Small area of thick red-brown slip survives on interior only. Highly polished where slip survives.

Phase	Context & No.	Grid ref	Max dia rim	Fig
?	UP 19 **63**	Area 12	*c.*20(?)	32h

241–60 Carinated, so-called 'Meidum' bowls

Wide-mouthed carinated bowls of so-called 'Meidum' type are very common on OK sites. Rzeuska, discussing the typological development of the series from the reign of Teti onwards, remarks (2006, 408/09) that precise dating 'can pose difficulties' and that these bowls 'cannot be considered as a precise chronological marker for dating particular phases'. She concludes that they may have functioned as luxury ware and been cherished and used for long periods of time before being deposited in tombs. Well-stratified settlement assemblages should permit 'statistical analysis that will facilitate a determination of the changes occurring in the shape'. One may fear that sherds from cherished vessels may be as dispersed in settlement levels as in the necropolis, though careful excavation should certainly reveal the first occurrence of various slightly differing forms. The catch is that settlement sherds are usually small and may not reveal enough of the form for this purpose.

Dietrich Raue carried out just such a study on all the major ceramic types in the Elephantine settlement up to the end of the Fourth Dynasty (Raue 1999, 173–89). The angular shoulders of the early Meidum bowls, present at the Anubieion in a few examples only, are characteristic of this series. In the course of the Fourth Dynasty the angular shoulder develops into a rounder form (*ibid.*, 185) which dominates thereafter. Surveys concentrating on the earlier forms have been published by Lies op de Beeck (2000, 5–14; 2004, 239–80), and a brave attempt at classification of the Fifth and Sixth Dynasty forms was made by Pascale Ballet (1987, 1–16).

By a happy coincidence, the Anubieion series had already been classified according to the same basic classification used by Rzeuska, as also by Ballet and op de Beeck, i.e. according to whether the greater diameter lies at the body or at the mouth, so it was fairly easy to compare the two series. The Anubieion adds a few with body and mouth of equal diameter, and a number insufficiently preserved to measure.

The bowls with the very largest diameter rims, above 27 cm, seldom had equally wide bodies; otherwise expressed, the rim range, which hardly affected the capacity of the bowl, is greater than the shoulder range, which did.

The range of Nile fabrics from Nile A to Nile B2 is similar to Rzeuska's, but there are also examples in marl clay and mixed clay, which are absent from her series. The 'classic' 'Meidum' bowls were in marl fabrics and many, but not all, of those at the Anubieion are demonstrably earlier than the main series on the evidence of their forms.

Because of their striking colour and polish, it is probable that a disproportionately high percentage of the Anubieion pieces were collected, compared with (for example) the OK coarse wares. This should have produced a more statistically reliable sample for analysis of variability and distribution and it may thus be of some significance that they occur unusually frequently in Areas other than Area 5.

<u>241–43</u> 'Meidum' bowls with angular shoulder (not present in Rzeuska 2006)

These bowls are from periods prior to the construction of the Teti pyramid. While Rzeuska's *caveat* that they could have been heirlooms should be borne in mind, it is not a necessary condition for their occurrence since at least one large stone mastaba tomb of an earlier period is present under the south enclosure wall of the temple. Best matches to the types defined by Raue (1999), all in Marl A4 fabric, are:

<u>241</u> Raue Abb. 38.1, dated to the first half of the Third Dynasty
<u>242</u> Raue Abb. 37.1, dated up to about the reign of Zoser
<u>243</u> Raue Abb. 39.1, dated to the later Third Dynasty, up to the early years of the reign of Snefru

At Giza the best matches, all in Nile clay, are to **<u>243</u>** (Hawass and Senussi 2008, 111 [26], 155 [A25], 183 [H45]), perhaps implying continuation of **<u>243</u>** into at least the later Fourth Dynasty. At el-Kab (Op de Beeck 2004, Fig. 3) it is hardly practicable to seek out specific matches among the many examples illustrated, especially since all are in marl clay, but a general conformity to the Third and Fourth Dynasty series is evident.

It is prudent not to date the Anubieion examples closely, since the changes Raue charts are quite subtle, and partly dependent on the complete form rather than the upper part. Also, the Anubieion examples are made of a less malleable clay, and developments at Saqqara and in distant el-Kab and Elephantine may not be contemporary.

See the marl clay and mixed clay series, especially **<u>364</u>**.

1610 **<u>241</u>** Fig. 34a

Handmade, though perhaps some wheel assistance at the rim. Some blackening of exterior below carination, perhaps from use as a cooking pot.

<u>Nile B1.</u> Fired fairly soft. Surfaces concealed by slip. Break red-brown with red zones and grey core. Fairly plentiful fine and medium sand with a few larger grains. Fairly plentiful fine veg to 0.3. Sparse limestone to 0.05 and one piece 0.2. Orange slip on all surfaces. All surfaces polished.

Phase	Context & No.	Grid ref	Dia rim (top)	Fig
vi	ABG (UP 206) **1**	Area 13	19	34a

1612 **<u>242</u>** Fig. 34b

Exterior burnt, except in concavity above carination, perhaps from use as a cooking pot.

<u>Nile A.</u> Fired medium. Surfaces concealed by slip. Break brown with red zones and grey core. Fairly plentiful fine and medium well-sorted sand. Sparse fine veg to 0.2. Only one piece limestone (0.2 × 0.1) visible. Brown slip on all surfaces. All surfaces polished.

Phase	Context & No.	Grid ref	Dia rim (top)	Fig
Mamluk/vii	AKJ/AKI (UP 144) **12**	Area 14	*c.*16	34b

1614 **243** Fig. 34c

Nile B1. Fired fairly soft. Surfaces concealed by slip. Break brown with red zones and grey core. Fairly plentiful fine and medium sand with only a few larger grains. Small qty fine veg to 0.2. Sparse limestone to 0.1. Red slip on all surfaces. All surfaces polished.

Phase	Context & No.	Grid ref	Dia rim (top)	Fig
vi/(vi–)vii	AAH/AAC **1**	09-09	14	34c

244–47 'Meidum' bowls with maximum diameter at the body (Rzeuska 2006, Forms 179–82, 188 and 190/91, Pls 126–28, 133 and 135/36)

Rzeuska's Forms 188, 190 and 191 are thick-walled and of large diameter (almost all 29 and above); only a few of the Anubieion series are as large as this. Rzeuska has divided her Forms 179–82 on the basis of rim shapes, but the distinctions are rather fine. See also **259**.

1624/1628C **244** Fig. 33a–h

Although there is some variability, this series does not divide into deeper and shallower forms as do those with larger rim diameters.

Nile A. Fired fairly hard. Surfaces concealed by slip. Break pale red-brown with grey core. UP 445 **128** fairly plentiful fine well-sorted sand, others fairly plentiful fine and medium with a few larger grains. No visible veg. AAA Lower **47** no visible limestone, others sparse to 0.05. Pale red-brown slip on both surfaces. Both surfaces polished.

Nile B1. Fired fairly soft to fairly hard. A few examples, surfaces pale brown where slip lost. Break, fairly soft are red-brown all through, or with red or grey core; fairly hard are red-brown with thick grey core. Fairly plentiful fine and medium sand, only three examples with a few larger grains. Small to medium qty fine veg to 0.2. Sparse limestone to 0.05, UP 197 **1** also one piece 0.1 and one 0.2. Slip on both surfaces, UP 197 **1**, AJH **183** and ANJ **3** pale red-brown, remainder red-brown. Both surfaces polished.

Nile B1 near B2. Fired fairly soft. Surfaces red-brown where slip lost. Break pale brown with red zones and grey core. Fairly plentiful fine and medium sand with rather more than usual of the larger grains. Moderate qty fine veg to 0.2. Sparse limestone to 0.05. Pink slip on both surfaces, discoloured black except on one area of interior, perhaps after breaking since black extends over breaks. Both surfaces polished.

Nile B2. Fired fairly soft to medium. Surfaces concealed by slip, except ATY **237** red-brown and ABG (UP 206) **2** pale brown where slip lost. Break, DAY **17** pale brown with red zones and mauve core, ABG (UP 206) **2** pale brown with red core, UP 445 **40** red-brown with red core, other two red-brown with pink zones and grey core. Fairly plentiful fine and medium sand, DAY **17** with a few larger grains. Moderate qty fine veg to 0.3/0.5. Sparse limestone to 0.05, except ATY **237** and ABC/D/A **1** 0.1. Red-brown slip on both surfaces. Both surfaces polished.

For similar forms to several here, see **351/68** in the marl clay and mixed clay series respectively

Phase	Context & No.	Grid ref	Dia rim (top)	*	Fabric	Fig & notes
ii	AUQ **105**	08/09-02/03	21	0.6	B1	As 33d††
†	UP 197 **1**	Area 13	19	0.6	B1	As 33e
iv	DAY **16**	Area 2 W10-S63	26	0.4	B1	As 33b
iv	DAY **17**	Area 2 W10-S63	*c.*24	0.4	B2	As 33d††

Phase	Context & No.	Grid ref	Dia rim (top)	*	Fabric	Fig & notes
iva	AJH **183**	05/06-04/05/06	22	1.0	B1	As 33f
ivd	ATY **237**	25-04	*c.*23	0.6	B2	33a
v–vi/?	BEQ/BEP **29**	16/17-S01/S02	22	0.6	B1	As 33d††
vi	AGK **34**	15/16-09/10	*c.*24	0.4	B1	As 33e
vi	ABG (UP 206) **2**	Area 13	23	0.8	B2	33b
vi	ABG (UP 235) **2**	Area 13	*c.*24	0.4	B1	33c
Ma'k/Ma'k/vii	ABC/ABD/ABA (UP 167) **1**	Area 13	*c.*32	0.6	B2	As 33d††
vii	AAA (UP 38) **155**	18-08	22	0.6	B1	33d
vii	AAA (UP 157) **164**	03/04-14/15	20	0.6	B1	As 33f
vii	AAA (UP 445) **10**	Area 2	22	1.0	B1	33e
vii	AAA (UP 445) **40**	Area 2	25	1.0	B2	33f
vii	AAA (UP 445) **51****	Area 2	*c.*18	0.4	B1	As 33e
vii	AAA (UP 445) **128**	Area 2	*c.*24	0.4	A	33g
vii	AAA Lower **47****	Area 2	*c.*21	0.4	A	As 33e
vii	ANJ (UP 127) **3**	Area 14	22	1.0	B1	As 33d††
vii	ARD (UP 1031) **1**	Area 12	27	1.0	B1	As 33f
vii	CAA North **6**	Area 26	20	0.4	B1/B2	33h
vii	CAA North **7**	Area 26	21	0.8	B1	As 33b
?	BSE **20**	Area 2	31	0.4	A	As 33f

* Amount by which body diameter exceeds rim diameter

** Probably same vessel, in spite of diameter difference

† 'Phase iv construction'. No context designation was assigned

†† The concavity in the exterior of the rim is not always as marked as on 33d

1638B **245** Fig. 34d

Nile B2. AEF **52+53** fired medium, others fairly soft. Surfaces pale brown to red-brown where slip lost. Break, AEF **52+53** brown with thin pink zones and grey core, BCU etc **38** brown with red zones and mauve core, BCR **9** pale brown with faint red core. Fairly plentiful sand, AEF **52+53** fine, others fine and medium, with a few larger grains. Moderate qty to fairly plentiful fine veg to 0.3. Sparse limestone to 0.05. Slip on both surfaces: BCR **9** pink interior but white exterior, no doubt a firing effect, others brown. Both surfaces polished.

For a similar form see **367** in the mixed clay series.

Phase	Context & No.	Grid ref	Dia rim (top)	*	Fig
iva	AEF **52+53**	08 to 14-03/04	*c.*30	1.0	34d
iva/b/b/b/ b/c	BCU/BCI/BCL/BCN/ BCQ/BCC **38**	05-06/07/08	*c.*24	0.6+	As 34d
ivd	BCR **9**	18/19/20-10	?	0.2	As 34d

* Amount by which body diameter exceeds rim diameter (BCU etc **38** is broken)

1640 **246** Fig. 34e

Nile B2. Fired medium. Surfaces pale brown where slip lost. Break pale brown with thick pink core. Fairly plentiful fine and medium sand with a few larger grains. Moderate qty fine veg to 0.2. Sparse limestone to 0.1. Pink slip on both surfaces. Both surfaces polished.

Phase	Context & No.	Grid ref	Dia rim (top)	*	Fig
vi/vi	ABF/AZH **13**	Area 13	24	0.4	34e

* Amount by which body diameter exceeds rim diameter

2132 **247** Fig. 34f

Rim wheel assisted.

Nile B2. Fired medium. Surfaces concealed by slip. Break orange-brown with purple core. Fairly plentiful fine well-sorted sand. Small qty fine veg to 0.2. Sparse limestone to 0.1. Thick red-brown slip on both surfaces. Both surfaces polished.

Phase	Context & No.	Grid ref	Dia rim (top)	Fig
vii	AAA (UP 157) **165**	11 to 16-11/12	17	34f

248–49 'Meidum' bowls with mouth and body of equal diameter (not present in Rzeuska 2006)

Although not classified by Rzeuska, these are within her range of forms and the range at the Anubieion.

1642A **248** Fig. 34g–i

Only minor variability of form, and not co-variable with diameter.

Nile B1. Fired fairly soft to medium. ADV **1** surfaces concealed by slip; UP 998 **39** orange and others pale brown where slip lost. Break ADV **1** and UP 998 **39** orange-brown with grey core, UP 157 **171** red-brown with red core, others red-brown with red zones and grey core. Fairly plentiful fine, or fine and medium, sand, UP 157 **171** and UP 998 **39** with a few larger grains. Sparse fine veg to 0.2. AIY **82** no visible limestone, others sparse to 0.05 and CGC **20** one piece 0.1. Slip on both surfaces, ADV **1** and UP 998 **39** pale red-brown, remainder red-brown. Both surfaces polished.

Nile B2. Fired fairly soft to medium. Surfaces where slip lost, BWL? **6** brown, AHC/AIU **25** pale brown, CAA **47** orange-brown; others concealed by slip. Break ACE **150** and AUA **56** red-brown with grey core, remainder red-brown to brown, with red core. Fairly plentiful fine and medium sand, BWL? **6** with a few larger grains. Small to moderate qty fine veg to 0.3/0.4. AUA **56** no visible limestone, others sparse to 0.05 and AHC/AIU **25** also one piece 0.5 × 0.1. Slip on both surfaces, BWL? **6** grey (secondary burning?), AHC/AIU **25** red-brown, others orange-brown to pale red-brown. Both surfaces polished.

For similar forms to ADV **1** see **352/70** in the marl clay and mixed clay series respectively.

Phase	Context & No.	Grid ref	Dia rim (top)	Fabric	Fig
ii	AIY **82**	12/13-02/03	21	B1	As 34g
iii–iva	ACE **150**	01 to 05-08 to 12	?	B2	As 34h
iv (Pt II?)	ADV (UP 339) **1***	Area 13	*c.*25–30	B1	34h
iv (Pt II?)?	BWL? (UP 1040) **6**	Area 12	17	B2	34g
ivc	CGC **20**	02/03-34/35	21	B1	34i
v/vi	AHC/AIU **25**	15/16-07/08	23	B2	As 34g

Phase	Context & No.	Grid ref	Dia rim (top)	Fabric	Fig
v–vi	AUA **56**	17 to 20-S01/S02/S03	20	B2	As 34h
vii	AAA (UP 157) **171**	13 to 16-11/12	?	B1	As 34h
vii	AAA (UP 998) **39**	Area 2	16	B1	As 34h
vii	CAA **47**	Area 26	*c.*23	B2	As 34h

* Sherd 'embedded in brick, from an upper course'

1646 **249** Fig. 34j

Example with thicker wall. Visible beneath the slip, scraping marks both parallel to rim and at 45 degrees; cf **251**, UP 588 **566** *et al.*

Nile B1. Fired fairly hard. Surfaces red-brown where slip lost. Break red-brown with pink core, or pink zones and grey core where thickest. Fairly plentiful fine and some medium well sorted sand. Small qty fine veg to 0.2. No small limestone visible, but one piece 0.5 × 0.4 and void from another 0.6 × 0.3. Red-brown slip on both surfaces. Both surfaces polished.

Phase	Context & No.	Grid ref	Dia rim (top)	Fig
vii?	BFB **38**	Area 1	20	34j

250–58 'Meidum' bowls with maximum diameter at the mouth (Rzeuska 2006, Forms 184/85, 187, 189, 191; Pls 130–32, 134–36)

Rzeuska attempts a distinction between rounded and pointed (= thin) rims, but although some in the Anubieion series are one or the other, there are many intermediate forms. She also distinguishes a shallower version, but the differences are slight and the inferior preservation of the Anubieion examples rules out similar differentiation. Finally, Rzeuska has a separate Form for 'large' examples (dia top 25–35) which actually slightly overlaps the 'small' series and does not seem a very useful distinction.

Specifically, the deeper rim with its slightly hollowed exterior seen in **258** has a counterpart in [687] of her Form 190. The unusual white slip of **256** may be a firing aberration.

1618B **250** Fig. 35a–e

Much duplication of form, even among examples of greatly differing diameter.

Nile B1. Fired fairly soft to fairly hard, in approximately equal numbers. AYQ/AYR **3** and UP 157 **162** surfaces pale brown where slip lost, others concealed by slip. Break, the fairly soft are brown with a red core, a thin grey core, or a thin grey core with red zones; the fairly hard are brown with a thicker grey core, some with thin red zones. Fairly plentiful fine, or fine and medium, sand, a small number with a few larger grains. Sparse fine veg to 0.2/0.3. Sparse limestone to 0.05 (most) or 0.1. Red-brown to pale red-brown slip on both surfaces. Both surfaces polished.

Nile B2. Fired fairly soft to fairly hard, in approximately equal numbers. ABY **57**, UP 23 **676** and UP 157 **163** surfaces pale brown where slip lost, remainder concealed by slip. Break similar to B1 series. Fairly plentiful fine and medium sand, a small number with a few larger grains. Small to moderate qty fine veg to 0.3/0.4. ADU NW **15** and UP 157 **163** more limestone than usual to 0.1, others sparse to 0.05. Red-brown to pale red-brown slip on both surfaces. Both surfaces polished.

For a similar form to UP 445 **69** see **369** in the mixed clay series

Phase	Context & No.	Grid ref	Dia rim (top)	*	Fabric	Fig & notes
o	ADU (UP 122) NW **8**	Area 13	*c.*35	0.8	B1	As 35b
o	ADU (UP 122) NW **15**	Area 13	*c.*26	0.4	B2	As 35b
ii	AQE **112**	14/15/16-01/02	?	0.4	B1	As 35c
ii	ABR North (UP 11) **2**	Area 13	32	0.4	B1	As 35c
iv (Pt II?)	ABY **57**	Area 13	?	0.6	B2	As 35c
iv (Pt II?)	ADC **109**	Area 13	? (20–30)	0.4	B1	As 35a**
iv (Pt II?)	ADF North **88**	Area 13	*c.*27	0.8	B2	As 35c
iv (Pt II?) ×2	ADD/ADE **5**	Area 13	*c.*32	0.8	B1	As 35b
iv (Pt II?) ×2	ARP=ARS/AYY **8**	Area 13	*c.*25	1.2	B2	35a
iv (Pt II?)/?	AYQ/AYR **3**	Area 13	?	0.6	B1	As 35c
iva	AJH **107**	04/05/06-05 to 08	26	0.6	B1	As 35c
iva	AJH **108**	04/05/06-05 to 08	*c.*34	0.8	B1	As 35b
iva	AJH Lower **30**	05 to 08-04/05/06	26	1.0	B1	As 35b
iva	BDU **39**	17/18-07/08	17	1.2	B1	As 35a
iva	BHR **210**	03-23	? (20–30)	0.6	B1	As 35a
ivc	AAV West, top **7**	04 to 08-03/04	22	0.4	B2	As 35b
ivc	CIN **14**	06/07-33	?	0.4	B1	As 35a
ivd	ATA **41**	03/04/05-04/05/06	*c.*35–40	0.6	B1	As 35b
iv+	DAW **9**	Area 2 W11-S60	30	0.8	B1	As 35b
vi	ABI (UP 7) **152**	Area 13	?	0.4	B2	As 35a**
Ma'k/Ma'k	ARC/AZR **2**	Area 12	25	0.6	B2	As 35b
vii	AAA (UP 8) **43**	19/20-06	?	1.0	B1	As 35c
vii	AAA (UP 23) **676**	04-05	? (25+)	0.6	B2	As 35c
vii	AAA (UP 157) **162**	03/04-14/15	*c.*30	0.4	B1	As 35c
vii	AAA (UP 157) **163**	13 to 16-11/12	20	0.4	B2	As 35c
vii	AAA (UP 157) **169**	07 to 10-11	23	0.2	B1	As 35c
vii	AAA (UP 588) **129**	03/04-23/24	?	1.0	B1	As 35c
vii	AAA **69**	Area 1	*c.*22	0.4	B1	As 35c
vii	AAA (UP 445) **41**	Area 2	?	1.0	B1	As 35b
vii	AAA (UP 445) **49**	Area 2	*c.*23	0.4	B2	35b
vii	AAA (UP 445) **69**	Area 2	27	1.0	B2	35c
vii?	BFB **29**	Area 1	22	0.8	B2	35d
vii?	BFB **60**	Area 1	24	0.2	B1	35e
?	BEP **48**	14 to 17-01/S01	*c.*30	0.8	B1	As 35c
?	ANS (UP 1000) **68+79**	Area 14	*c.*29	0.6	B1	As 35c

* Amount by which rim diameter exceeds body diameter

** Wall more upright than wall of ARS/AYY **8**

1626 **251** Fig. 35f–h

Lowest preserved area of UP 588 **566** shows shaping scratches, both parallel to rim and at 45 degrees to it, under the slip.

Nile B1. Fired fairly hard. Surfaces concealed by slip. Break orange-brown with thick grey core, AAB Upper **9** with thin pink zones. Fairly plentiful fine sand with a few larger grains. Small qty fine veg to 0.2/3. Sparse limestone to 0.05. Slip on both surfaces, ATY **57** orange, others pale red-brown. All surfaces polished.

Nile B2. BAC **380** fired fairly hard, others fairly soft. AWJ **28** and UP 588 **566** surfaces pale brown where slip lost, others concealed by slip. Break AWJ **28** pale brown with faint red core; others red-brown, BAC **380** with greenish grey core, UP 588 **566** with red zones and grey core, UP 1043 **2** with red zones and mauve core. Fairly plentiful fine and medium sand, BAC **380** and UP 1043 **2** with a few larger grains. Moderate qty fine veg to 0.2. Sparse limestone to 0.05. Slip on both surfaces, BAC **380** orange-brown, remainder red-brown to brown. All surfaces polished.

Phase	Context & No.	Grid ref	Dia rim (top)	*	Fabric	Fig
ivb	AWJ **28**	19/20-01/02/03	25	1.0	B2	As 35f
ivc	BQQ **40**	Area 2	23	1.4	B1	As 35f
ivd	ATY **57**	23/24/25-04/05/06	*c*.27	0.4	B1	As 35h
v	BAC **380**	02/03-01	*c*.25(?)	1.0	B2	As 35g
vi–vii	AAB Upper **9**	28 to 34-S02/S03/S04	27	0.8	B1	35f
vii	AAA (UP 588) **566**	01/W01-31/32/33	21	0.4	B2	35g
?	UP 1043 **2**	Area 12	24	0.8	B2	35h

* Amount by which rim diameter exceeds body diameter

435 **252** Fig. 36a

Narrow groove at base of neck from string-tying before firing, and possible light string impression below the thickening of the rim.

Nile B2. Fired fairly soft. Surfaces pale brown where slip lost. Break brown with red core. Fairly plentiful fine and medium well-sorted sand. Fairly plentiful fine and coarse veg to 2.3. Sparse limestone to 0.1. Thick red-brown slip on both surfaces. Both surfaces polished.

Phase	Context & No.	Grid ref	Dia rim (top)	*	Fig
ii	BGG **135**	04/05/06-S01/S02/S03	*c*.36	0.5	36a

* Amount by which rim diameter exceeds body diameter

2048 **253** Fig. 36b

Nile B1. Fired medium. Surfaces red-brown where slip lost. Break red-brown with pink zones and grey core. Fairly plentiful fine and medium sand with only a few larger grains. Small qty fine veg to 0.2. Sparse limestone to 0.1. Traces of slip on exterior of body (fired red) and interior of rim (fired orange). Polished where slip survives.

Phase	Context & No.	Grid ref	Dia rim (top)	*	Fig
vii	AAA (UP 445) **90**	Area 2	35	1.0	36b

* Amount by which rim diameter exceeds body diameter

1660 **<u>254</u>** Fig. 36c

<u>Nile B1.</u> Fired fairly soft. Surfaces pale brown where slip lost. Break pale brown with grey core. Fairly plentiful fine and medium sand with a few larger grains. Small qty fine veg to 0.2. Sparse limestone to 0.05 and one piece 0.2 × 0.1. Red-brown slip on both surfaces. Both surfaces polished.

Phase	Context & No.	Grid ref	Dia rim (top)	⋆	Fig
Mamluk	AZR (UP 12) **5**	Area 12	*c*.21	0.4	36c

⋆ Amount by which rim diameter exceeds body diameter

2130 **<u>255</u>** Fig. 36d

<u>Nile B2.</u> Fired fairly soft. Surfaces concealed by slip. Break BTX **181** brown with darker brown core, UP 445 **129** brown with red zones and purple core. Fairly plentiful fine and medium sand, UP 445 **129** with a few larger grains. Small qty fine veg to 0.3. Sparse limestone, BTX **181** to 0.05, UP 445 **129** to 0.1 and one piece 0.2 × 0.1. Embedded in surface of UP 445 **129**, a thin flake of blue faience 0.1 long (not a bead) (cf **<u>405</u>** of the MK and **<u>560/86</u>** of the NK**).** Thick slip on both surfaces, BTX **181** brown, UP 445 **129** pale red-brown. Both surfaces polished.

Phase	Context & No.	Grid ref	Dia rim (top)	⋆	Fig
ivc	BTX **181**	02/03-19/20	?	0.3	As 36d
vii	AAA (UP 445) **129**	Area 2	25–30(?)	0.4	36d

⋆ Amount by which rim diameter exceeds body diameter

451 **<u>256</u>** Fig. 36e

In the groove below the rim, the slip is broken up, probably from string-tying.

<u>Nile B2.</u> Fired fairly soft. Surfaces pale brown. Break pale brown with red core. Fairly plentiful fine and medium sand with a few larger grains. Fairly plentiful fine veg to 0.2. Sparse limestone to 0.05 and one piece 0.4. Thick white slip on both surfaces. Both surfaces polished.

Phase	Context & No.	Grid ref	Dia rim (top)	⋆	Fig
o	ADU (UP 335) **2**	Area 13	*c*.40(?)	1.5	36e

⋆ Amount by which rim diameter exceeds body diameter

1644 **<u>257</u>** Fig. 36f

Two narrow grooves around, probably from string-tying. The thin slip allows smoothing marks parallel to the rim to show through.

<u>Nile B2.</u> Fired fairly soft. Surfaces concealed by slip. Break brown with red core. Fairly plentiful poorly sorted sand. Fairly plentiful fine and coarse veg to 0.5. Sparse limestone to 0.05. Red slip on both surfaces, rather thinner than usual. Both surfaces polished.

Phase	Context & No.	Grid ref	Dia rim (top)	⋆	Fig
ivd	ATY **43**	24/25-05/06	*c*.20	0.4	36f

⋆ Amount by which rim diameter exceeds body diameter

1622 **258** Fig. 36g

A thin groove near the rim on exterior of AJG/AUH **20** is probably from extra string-tying.

Nile B1. Fired medium. Surfaces brown where slip lost. Break AJG/AUH **20** orange-brown with pink core, APE **33** brown with thin red zones and grey core. Fairly plentiful fine and medium well-sorted sand. No visible veg. Sparse limestone to 0.05. Slip on both surfaces, AJG/AUH **20** orange, APE **33** brown. Both surfaces polished.

Nile B2. Fired fairly soft. Surfaces pale brown where slip lost. Break pale brown with thin dark brown zones and red core. Fairly plentiful fine and medium sand. Moderate qty fine veg to 0.3. Sparse limestone to 0.1. Two nodules of unincorporated clay visible, 0.1 and 0.3. Pale pink slip on both surfaces. Both surfaces polished.

Phase	Context & No.	Grid ref	Dia rim (top)	*	Fabric	Fig
ivc/ivd	AJG/AUH **20**	06-01/02/03	?	1.0	B1	Similar to 36g
vii	AAA Upper **16**	Area 2	(22–30)	0.4	B2	36g
?	APE (UP 316) **33**	Area 12	?	0.6	B1	Similar to 36g

* Amount by which rim diameter exceeds body diameter

259 'Meidum' bowl with maximum diameter at the body, approaching jar form (Rzeuska 2006, Form 191; Pl. 136)

This vessel is at the extreme end of the bowl series and would otherwise probably be thought of as a jar. The body diameter would have exceeded that of the mouth by about 3.0.

830 **259** Fig. 37a

At least wheel assisted.

Nile B2. Fired medium. Surfaces concealed by slip. Break pale brown with red zones and grey core. Plentiful fine and medium sand with a few larger grains. Small qty fine veg to 0.2. Sparse limestone to 0.05. Orange-red slip on both surfaces. Both surfaces polished.

Phase	Context & No.	Grid ref	Dia rim (top)	Fig
v–vi	AFD **2**	18-S01/S02/S03	*c.*30	37a

260 'Meidum' bowl rims, insufficiently preserved to show stance (not present in Rzeuska 2006)

1662 **260** Not illustrated

Enough survives to prove these rims derive from 'Meidum' bowls, but not enough to illustrate them.

Nile B1 and B2. Most fired fairly soft, a few medium or fairly hard. Fabric details not recorded. Slip on both surfaces, in the usual range, most brownish red and a few orange. Both surfaces polished.

Phase	Context & No.	Grid ref	Dia rim (top)	Fabric
o	ADU (UP 330) **19**	Area 13	?	B2
iii	BCB **169**	01 to 05-04/05/06	?	B2
iii/iva/?	BPD/BHR/BPV **13**	03/04-22/23	?	B1
iii–iva	ACE **62**	05-06/07/08	22	B1

Phase	Context & No.	Grid ref	Dia rim (top)	Fabric
iii–iva	ACE **64**	05-06/07/08	?	B1
iv (Pt II?)	ADD North **7**	Area 13	*c.*23	B2
iv (Pt II?)	ARP=ARS (UP 152) **5**	Area 13	?	B1
iv (Pt II?)/?	AYQ/AYR **9**	Area 13	*c.*30	B1
iva	AJH **176**	05/06-04/05/06	?	B1
iva	AJH Upper **44**	01 to 04-04/05/06	?	B1
iva/ivb	AQC/AEX **97**	01 to 05-06/07	*c.*30	B1
iva/ivb/ivd	AIF/AIE/AAT **8**	06/07-04/05/06	*c.*30	B1
ivb	AFA **1**	20-S01/S02	*c.*20	B1
ivb	AFV North **14**	08 to10-07/08	?	B2
ivb	BCL **20**	05-06/07/08	?	B1
ivb	BDE **13**	17/18-09	21	B1
ivb	CBH **24**	02-22	?	B2
ivb/ivb–c	BDE/BCW **25**	17/18-08	20	B1
ivb–c	BCT **41**	18/19-08/09	*c.*22	B1
ivb–c	BCW **19**	18/19-07	24	B1
ivb–c	BGW **372**	15 to 18-03/04/05	?	B2
ivb–c	BGY **9**	14-04/05	?	B2
ivb–c	BGZ **11**	14 to17-05	?	B2
ivc	AAF **16**	05-09	?	B1
ivc	BCC **13**	05-07/08	?	B1
ivc	BKC **9**	06/07/08-26/27	?	B1
ivc	BTX **170**	02/03-19/20	26	B1
ivc	CGX **4**	05-33/34/35	? (30+)	B1
ivc	BQG **22**	Area 2	*c.*26	B2
ivc?	DBC **37**	Area 1 29/30-S31	*c.*30	B1
ivc/ivd	AIC/AAT **31**	05/06-04/05	*c.*22	B2
ivd	AJI **12**	22/23-01	24	B1
ivd	AJI **13**	22-01	?	B1
ivd	ASE **7**	18/19-08/09	?	B2
ivd	CEG **22**	02/03/04-33/34	?	B1
v	AEL **30**	15/16/17-S01/02/03	?	B1
v–vi	AUA **12**	09/10-S01/S02/S03	*c.*30	B1
v–vi/?	BEQ/BEP **30**	16/17-S01/S02	?	B2
vi	AEP **70**	08 to14-03/04	?	B1
vi	ABI (UP 7) **160**	Area 13	*c.*20	B1
vi/vi	ABF/ABG (UP 281) **11**	Area 13	21	B1
vii	AAA (UP 23) **678**	01 to 05-06 to 09	22	B1
vii	AAA (UP 23) **679**	08-05	*c.*23	B2

Phase	Context & No.	Grid ref	Dia rim (top)	Fabric
vii	AAA (UP 38) **156**	11 to 20-01 to 10	27	B1
vii	AAA (UP 38) **159**	14-03	?	B1
vii	AAA (UP 68) **85**	06/07/08-S04/S05	?	B2
vii	AAA (UP 108) **80**	29 to 34-S06	?	B2
vii	AAA (UP 445) **52**	Area 2	?	B1
vii?	BFB **35**	Area 1	23	B2
?	UP 1035 **11**	Area 12	?	B1

261 Small bowls (not present in Rzeuska 2006)

The type is attested from Sedment (Petrie and Brunton 1924a, Pl. XXIX [4h]) with rim diameter 10. Seidlmayer (1990, 300, Tab. 78 and Abb. 111 Typ ST301) dates it to the FIP, to a time when OK forms were no longer in use. However, it should develop from a small OK round-based bowl (Marchand and Baud 1996, Fig. 7 [9]; Hawass and Senussi 2008, 119 [79]), which is really only a smaller (dia 10.5) version of a common carinated type.

1648 **261** Fig. 37b

Two similar bowls (or lids, but the interiors are polished). Handmade, rims probably wheel assisted. Scraping facets from the shaping process visible under the slip on the exterior of UP 445 **39**.

Nile B1 near B2. ADU NW **22** fired fairly soft, UP 445 **39** medium. Surfaces concealed by slip. Break, ADU NW **22** brown with red zones and mauve core, UP 445 **39** orange-brown with red zones and grey core. Moderate qty to fairly plentiful fine and medium sand, with only a few larger grains. Small to moderate qty fine veg to 0.2. Sparse limestone to 0.05. Slip on both surfaces: ADU NW **22** reddish brown, UP 445 **39** orange. Both surfaces polished.

Phase	Context & No.	Grid ref	Dia rim (top)	Fig & notes
o	ADU (UP 122) NW **22**	Area 13	10	Similar to 37b*
vii	AAA (UP 445) **39**	Area 2	9	37b

* Carination less sharp and concavity above it less deep

262 Wide-mouthed jar (not present in Rzeuska 2006)

Although there is some similarity to Rzeuska's 'vat' Form 197, this almost straight-sided jar more closely resembles slightly outward sloping Fifth Dynasty examples from Abusir (Kaiser 1969, XLIV, Type 220/22), 'always carefully smoothed and sometimes also polished'. For deep bowls with the same stance, specified as smaller at the mouth than in the body, see Fourth Dynasty examples from Giza (Wodzińska 2007, Fig. 11.28 [CD 24]), most commonly with rim diameter in range 20–25, most often slipped and well polished both inside and out. The rim, however, is more modelled. Comparisons are made more difficult by the fact that **262** is slightly warped, so around the rim some profiles, probably formed to facilitate string-tying, are a little more upright than the one drawn.

Hawass and Senussi include similar forms with a similar stance ([32/33, A19/80, I 123, etc]) in their mainly outward-sloping Type D5 (Hawass and Senussi (2008, 231–32), corresponding to Rzeuska's Forms 145, 164–66 (see **177–93**).

1678 **262** Fig. 37c

The sharp profile looks wheel assisted. The rim was probably shaped for string-tying. Some areas of all surfaces are blackened by fire or ash.

Nile B2. Fired medium. Surfaces red-brown where slip lost. Break red-brown with thin dark brown and pink zones and grey core. Fairly plentiful fine and medium sand with some larger grains. Moderate qty fine veg to 0.3. Sparse limestone to 0.1. Thick red slip on all surfaces, visible in spite of blackening. All surfaces polished.

Phase	Context & No.	Grid ref	Max dia rim	Fig
ivc	ACP **26**	01 to 06-08/09	22	37c

263–94 Vats (Rzeuska 2006, Forms 197–200, Pls 139–41)

Large diameter semi-restricted vessels made of Nile clay, varying in form and size. The term 'vats' is adopted to be consistent with Rzeuska, who divides them into *Medium*, *Large*, and *Large thick-walled*; the same subdivision is followed here, using approximately the same diameter ranges, but the dividing line is arbitrary and the small size of the sherds can rule out an accurate diameter. Furthermore, as often at this period, the variability of form means that a wholly logical arrangement within each subdivision is impossible. The series parallels Rzeuska's closely, though since both vary so greatly in detail, no attempt has been made to match individual examples. The rims of the Anubieion series, like Rzeuska's (2006, 419) appear to be wheel assisted, but the lower parts may not have been.

The more upright form of **279** may be distorted by the two deep string-tying grooves; multiple grooves are not usual but one sherd from Abusir (Kaiser 1969, XLV, Typ 228) has three.

Though spouts are not recorded on these vessels by Rzeuska, **292** clearly had a spout and so probably had **268** and **280**. 'Vats' with spouts are published from, *inter alia*, Giza (Wodzińska 2007, Fig. 11.25 [CD22A]), most slipped and polished, of the Fourth Dynasty; Abusir (Kaiser 1969, XLIV, Typ 223), surface treatment not recorded, of the late OK; Herakleopolis (Bader 2009a, Fig. 3j), slipped and polished on both surfaces, of the FIP/early MK; and Tell el-Dab'a (Czerny 1999, 178 [Ng 129]), uncoated, of the early MK. For spouts broken off vessels, though not necessarily of this type, see Rzeuska's Form 38, Pl. 57, and Anubieion **70–73**.

The principal temper is sand, often with the coarsest fraction removed to produce a hard fabric. Although some surfaces are lost and others have the polish dulled from weathering, it is clear that an overall slip and high polish over both surfaces of the entire upper body were usual.

Since all examples were in secondary contexts, the series cannot be dated except from parallels at other sites. The forms continue throughout the MK, but usually the later examples are not fully slipped and not polished (Aston D.A. 2004b, Pls 178–80). In the Memphite area they may continue to be manufactured until the end of the SIP (Bourriau 2010, 65); occurrences thereafter (*ibid.*, Fig. 15 [950, 1432, 3573]; Fig. 17 [1431, 2376, 3343]; Fig. 18 [2116, 2271, 2604, 3380] are thought to be residual but a series with very similar rim forms (*ibid.*, Fig. 26 [8.7.1/2/3]) replaces them.

263–76 Medium-sized vats

2068 **263** Fig. 37d

Nile B1. Fired medium. Surfaces brown where slip lost. Break brown with red zones and grey core. Fairly plentiful fine and medium well-sorted sand. Small qty fine veg to 0.2. Rather more limestone than usual, but to 0.1 only. Areas of thick brownish red slip survive on interior and in the groove of the exterior. Polished where slip survives.

Phase	Context & No.	Grid ref	Dia rim (top)	Fig
ivc	BHS **35**	05/06-23	25–30(?)	37d

2108 **264** Fig. 37e

Smaller diameter than most, and more upright stance. The rim roll is of irregular width, even along the 3.5 cm of length preserved.

Nile B2. Fired medium, rather misfired. Exterior, and probably interior, concealed by slip. Break thin red-brown zone near exterior, otherwise black and sintering. Fairly plentiful fine and medium sand with a few larger grains. Moderate qty fine and coarse veg, mostly to 0.4 but a few pieces to 1.0. Rather more than usual limestone, with three pieces 0.2. Slip on exterior, affected by firing, with areas of white, brown and red; interior probably also slipped (dark grey, from 'nesting' in the kiln). Possible areas of polish on both surfaces.

Phase	Context & No.	Grid ref	Dia rim (top)	Fig
o	BEO **80**	14/15-S04/S05	17	37e

2780 <u>**265**</u> Fig. 37f

The undercut rolled rim is slightly flattened and the clay pushed inwards, from standing inverted before firing. A thin string was tied around before firing, mainly underneath the rim roll, but showing as an impression where the undercutting is ragged.

<u>Nile B2.</u> Fired medium. Exterior concealed by slip; interior pale red-brown. Break red-brown with pink core with a grey tinge. Fairly plentiful poorly sorted sand. Fairly plentiful fine and coarse veg to 0.5 and one piece 1.0. Sparse limestone to 0.1 and one piece 0.3 × 0.2. Thick red-brown slip on exterior and top of rim; interior uncoated. Traces of polish where slipped.

Phase	Context & No.	Grid ref	Dia rim (top)	Fig
iv (Pt II?)/?	AYQ/AYR **27**	Area 13	17	37f

2619 <u>**266**</u> Fig. 37g

The slightly undercut rim would facilitate string-tying.

<u>Nile B2.</u> Fired medium. Surfaces red-brown where slip lost. Break red-brown with grey core. Fairly plentiful poorly sorted sand. Fairly plentiful fine and coarse veg to 1.0. Sparse limestone to 0.1. Areas of red slip survive on all surfaces. Polished where slip survives.

Phase	Context & No.	Grid ref	Dia rim (top)	Fig
o/ii	AQG/BGU **47**	19/20-S04/S05	? (22–28?)	37g

2126 <u>**267**</u> Fig. 37h

The grooves in and below the rim are probably for or from string-tying.

<u>Nile B1.</u> Fired fairly hard. Surfaces brown where slip lost. Break brown with thin red zones and thick grey core. Fairly plentiful fine and medium well sorted sand. Moderate qty fine veg to 0.2. Sparse limestone to 0.1. Areas of thick pale red-brown slip survive on both surfaces. Polished where slipped.

Phase	Context & No.	Grid ref	Dia rim (top)	Fig
iv (Pt II?)	ADF North **25**	Area 13	*c.*25	37h

2084 <u>**268**</u> Fig. 37i

Smoothing marks almost certainly indicate a lost spout.

<u>Nile B2.</u> Fired medium. Surfaces red-brown where slip lost. Break red-brown all through. Plentiful fine and medium poorly sorted sand. Moderate qty mostly fine veg, with some coarse, to 0.4. Sparse limestone to 0.1.

One piece bone 0.2. Traces of red slip survive on top of rim only, partly burnt (from use as a cooking pot?). Polished where slip survives.

Phase	Context & No.	Grid ref	Dia rim (top)	Fig
ii	BGG **1**	12 to 16-S04/S05	*c.*25–29	37i

611A **269** Fig. 38a

Nile B2. Fired fairly soft. Surfaces brown where slip lost. Break brown with red core. Fairly plentiful fine and medium sand with a few larger grains. Moderate qty fine veg to 0.3. Sparse limestone to 0.1. Areas of red slip survive on both surfaces. Polished where slip survives.

Phase	Context & No.	Grid ref	Dia rim (top)	Fig
ivc	BQQ **13**	Area 2	19	38a

609 **270** Fig. 38b

Nile B2. Fired medium. Surfaces pale brown where slip lost. Break pale brown with thin red zones and thick black core. Fairly plentiful fine and medium sand with a few larger grains. Fairly plentiful to plentiful fine and coarse veg to 0.8. Sparse limestone to 0.1. Red-brown slip on both surfaces. Both surfaces polished.

Phase	Context & No.	Grid ref	Dia rim (top)	Fig
vi/vi	AHC/AIU **22**	15/16-06/07	*c.*26	38b

2088 **271** Fig. 38c

Nile B2. Fired soft. Surfaces pale brown. Break pale brown with diffuse red core. Moderate qty poorly sorted sand. Moderate qty fine veg to 0.3. Sparse limestone to 0.1. Thick brownish pink slip on both surfaces. Both surfaces polished. Brown patches (not visible on surface) may derive from oily contents(?).

Phase	Context & No.	Grid ref	Dia rim (top)	Fig
iv (Pt II?)	ABS **8**	Area 13	*c.*27–30	38c

2106 **272** Fig. 38d

The well-defined groove under the rim has a ragged edge and was probably for string-tying. The shallow groove around the upper body may have served the same purpose.

Nile B2. Fired hard. Interior pale red-brown, exterior red-brown, possibly a (self-?)slip. Break reddish brown with thick grey core. Fairly plentiful fine and medium well-sorted sand. Plentiful fine and coarse veg to 1.0. Sparse limestone to 0.1. Probably uncoated. Not polished or burnished.

Phase	Context & No.	Grid ref	Dia rim (top)	Fig
v	AEK **13**	19/20-S01/S02	*c.*28	38d

611B **273** Fig. 38e

Nile B2. Fired medium. Surfaces brown where slip lost. Break brown with red zones and grey core. Fairly plentiful fine and medium sand with a few larger grains. Fairly plentiful fine veg to 0.2. Sparse limestone to

0.05. Traces of red slip survive in the exterior groove only. No surviving polish.

Phase	Context & No.	Grid ref	Dia rim (top)	Fig
iv (Pt II?)	ADF North **49**	Area 13	*c.*19	38e

621C

274 Fig. 38f

Nile B2. Fired fairly hard. Where slip lost, AFV East **6** orange, AEN/AEO **14** red-brown. Break, AFV East **6** orange with thin dark brown zones and thick grey core, AEN/AEO **14** red-brown with red zones and grey core. Fairly plentiful sand, AFV East **6** poorly sorted, AEN/AEO **14** fine and medium with some larger grains. Moderate qty fine veg to 0.4. Sparse limestone to 0.1. Slip on all surfaces, AFV East **6** red, AEN/AEO **14** brown. Polished where slip survives.

Phase	Context & No.	Grid ref	Dia rim (top)	Fig
ivb	AFV East **6**	11-04/05	?	As 38f
v/v	AEN/AEO **14**	14-S02/S03	*c.*22	38f

2100

275 Fig. 38g

Nile B2. Fired fairly soft. Surfaces pale brown where slip lost. Break pale brown with diffuse red core. Plentiful fine and medium sand with a few larger grains. Fairly plentiful mostly fine and some coarse veg to 0.5. Sparse limestone to 0.1. One piece of bone 0.3 × 0.1. Areas of thick brownish red slip survive on both surfaces; exterior discoloured grey from secondary burning, perhaps from use as a cooking pot. Polished where slip survives.

Phase	Context & No.	Grid ref	Dia rim (top)	Fig
ii	AIY **62**	10-01/02	20–25(?)	38g

2098

276 Fig. 38h

Nile B2. BWL? **7** fired medium, BQU **7** hard. BWL? **7** surfaces weathered, BQU **7** pale brown where slip lost. Break, BWL? **7** pale brown with pink zones and grey core, BQU **7** red-brown with thick grey core. Plentiful fine and medium sand with a few larger grains. Fairly plentiful fine veg, BWL? **7** to 0.3, BQU **7** to 0.5. Sparse limestone to 0.1. BWL? **7** thick bright red slip, surviving only in tiny area on top of rim; BQU **7** thick pinkish red slip on both surfaces Polished where slip survives.

Phase	Context & No.	Grid ref	Dia rim (top)	Fig & notes
iv (Pt II?)?	BWL? (UP 1040) **7**	Area 12	?	As 38h*
ivc	BQU **7**	Area 2	*c.*28	38h

* Groove less marked

277–84 Large vats

2082

277 Fig. 39a

Nile B2. Fired medium. Surfaces yellow-brown where slip lost. Break yellow-brown with thick red zones and grey core. Fairly plentiful poorly sorted sand. Fairly plentiful fine and coarse veg to 0.7, and one piece 2.5, probably a twig. Sparse limestone to 0.1. Thick red slip on both surfaces, but fails to conceal the voids. Traces of polish where slip survives.

Phase	Context & No.	Grid ref	Dia rim (top)	Fig
ii/ivb	AIY/AVB **67**	10 to14-S01/S02	35+	39a

1454 **278** Fig. 39b

Wide, deep groove below rim probably from tying with coarse string or many turns of finer string. It seems to have distorted the wall below it. Cannot tell whether handmade or wheel assisted.

Nile B2. Fired medium. Surfaces red-brown where slip lost. Break red-brown with thick grey core. Fairly plentiful poorly sorted sand. Fairly plentiful fine and coarse veg to 0.9. Sparse limestone to 0.1 and one piece 0.3 × 0.2. Small areas of thin pale red slip on all surfaces. Polished where slip survives.

Phase	Context & No.	Grid ref	Dia rim (top)	Fig
ivc	BQS **12**	Area 2	*c.*33	39b

852 **279** Fig. 39c

Two deep grooves almost certainly for string-tying.

Nile B2 near C. Fired medium. Surfaces concealed by slip. Break pale brown with thick red core. Plentiful fine and medium sand with a few larger grains. Fairly plentiful veg, mostly fine to 0.4, some coarse to 1.0. Sparse limestone to 0.1 and one void 0.5 × 0.3. Thick red slip on both surfaces. Both surfaces polished.

Phase	Context & No.	Grid ref	Max dia rim	Fig
v	DAF **23**	W10-S50/51	*c.*35–40(?)	39c

2102 **280** Fig. 39d

Handmade. Clay adhesions on the exterior probably indicate a lost spout.

Nile C. Fired fairly hard. Surfaces concealed by slip. Break red-brown with pink zones and thick grey core. Fairly plentiful poorly sorted sand. Plentiful fine and coarse veg to 0.5. Sparse limestone to 0.1. Thick red slip on both surfaces, but insufficient to conceal the voids from burnt-out veg. Traces of polish on all surfaces.

Phase	Context & No.	Grid ref	Dia rim (top)	Fig
Mamluk	ANJ (UP 179) **6**	Area 14	(35–40?)	39d

607 **281** Fig. 39e

The groove in the top of the rim of BEQ **21** is probably from string-tying, though unusually located.

Nile B2. Fired medium. Surfaces weathered. Break ARP=ARS **17** red-brown with thin red zones, BEQ **21** brown, each with grey core. ARP=ARS **17** fairly plentiful, BEQ **21** plentiful, fine and medium sand with some larger grains. Moderate qty fine veg to 0.2. Sparse limestone to 0.1. Both weathered: no slip or polish survives.

Phase	Context & No.	Grid ref	Dia rim (top)	Fig
iv (Pt II?)	ARP=ARS (UP 152) **17**	Area 13	*c.*30(?)	As 39e
v–vi	BEQ **21**	16/17-S01/S02	*c.*35	39e

621B **282** Fig. 39f

Nile B2. Fired fairly hard. Surface colours vary: where slip lost, AQG/AWJ **3** red-brown, ADC **155** orange, ABC/D/A **1** yellow-brown, UP 588 **71** pink. Break, AQG/AWJ **3** red-brown, ADC **155** orange with red zones, ABC/D/A **1** yellow-brown with thin red zones, UP 588 **71** pink; each with grey core. Fairly plentiful sand, ADC **155** poorly sorted, others fine and medium with some larger grains. Fairly plentiful fine and some coarse veg, to variable length from 0.4 to 0.9. ABC/D/A **1** no visible limestone, others sparse to 0.1. ADC **155** and ABC/D/A **1** red slip on both surfaces, others weathered. Polished where slip survives.

Phase	Context & No.	Grid ref	Dia rim (top)	Fig
o/ivb	AQG/AWJ **3**	19/20-03/04	?	As 39f
iv (Pt II?)	ADC **155**	Area 13	*c.*40(?)	As 39f
Mamluk/Mamluk/vii	ABC/ABD/ABA(UP 190) **1**	Area 13	32	39f
vii	AAA (UP 588) **71**	01/02-21 to 24	*c.*40(?)	As 39f

2104 **283** Fig. 40a

Nile B2. AQG **152** fired medium, UP 23 **193** hard, somewhat misfired. AQG **152** surfaces red-brown, UP 23 **193** brown, each where slip lost. Break, AQG **152** red-brown with thick pink core, or pink zones and grey core where thickest, UP 23 **193** brown with thick grey core. Fairly plentiful fine and medium well-sorted sand. Small qty fine veg to 0.2. AQG **152** sparse limestone to 0.05, UP 23 **193** slightly more than usual, to 0.1. AQG **152** has brownish red slip surviving in exterior groove but interior weathered; UP 23 **193** areas of thick pale reddish brown slip on both surfaces. Polished where slip survives.

Phase	Context & No.	Grid ref	Dia rim (top)	Fig
o	AQG **152**	13/14-01/02	*c.*40	As 40a
vii	AAA (UP 23) **193**	09-07	*c.*28	40a

623 **284** Fig. 40b

The groove was probably for string-tying.

Nile B2. Fired hard. Surfaces red-brown where slip survives. Break red-brown with thin red zones and thick grey core. Fairly plentiful fine and medium sand with a few larger grains. Small qty fine veg to 0.3. Sparse limestone to 0.1. Areas of red slip survive, thin on interior, thicker in exterior groove and on edge of rim. Polished where slip survives.

Phase	Context & No.	Grid ref	Dia rim (top)	Fig
vi/vi	AAJ/AAK **27**	07-07	*c.*40	40b

285–94 Large thick-walled vats

2124 **285** Fig. 40c

Nile B2. Fired hard. Surfaces pale brown. Break pale brown with thin dark brown zones, thin red zones and thick grey core. Fairly plentiful fine and medium sand with a few larger grains. Moderate qty fine and coarse veg to 0.2. More limestone than usual in a Nile fabric, to 0.1 and 1 piece 0.2 × 0.1. Small areas of brownish red slip survive on both surfaces. Polished where slip survives.

Phase	Context & No.	Grid ref	Dia rim (top)	Fig
ivc	BQV **51**	Area 2	*c*.27	40c

2094 **286** Fig. 40d

Nile B2. Fired fairly hard. Surfaces red-brown where slip lost. Break red-brown with grey core. Fairly plentiful fine and medium sand with some larger grains. Fairly plentiful fine and coarse veg to 0.5. Sparse limestone to 0.1 and BPV **44** two pieces each 0.2. Interior surface of AJH **18** rather rough but surfaces of BPV **44** well smoothed. Red slip where least weathered: AJH **18** on exterior, top and very small area of interior; BPV **44** exterior and top only, in part discoloured from secondary burning. Polished where slip survives.

Phase	Context & No.	Grid ref	Max dia rim	Fig
iva	AJH **18**	04/05/06-05 to 08	40(+?)	40d
?	BPV **44**	03-21	30–35(?)	As 40d

2092 **287** Fig. 40e

String impression in the groove below the rim roll. Top of rim flatter than most, but very uneven and twisted so that at one point the inner edge is higher, at another the outer; the average stance may have been as drawn, or a little less upright. Faint, discontinuous smoothing marks on surface of exterior, which is smooth but uneven, indicating hand manufacture.

Nile B2. Fired fairly soft. Surfaces pale yellow-brown. Break pale yellow-brown with red core. Fairly plentiful fine and medium well-sorted sand. Fairly plentiful fine veg to 0.3. No visible limestone. Surfaces weathered, but probable traces of pink or red slip survive in a thin groove in the top of the rim. No visible polish or burnish.

Phase	Context & No.	Grid ref	Max dia rim	Fig
iva/ivb	BDG/BRT **21**	10 to 14-03/04/05	30+(?)	40e

643 **288** Fig. 40f

Two sharp, narrow grooves below the rim, probably from string-tying.

Nile B2. Fired medium. Surfaces pale brown where slip lost. Break brown with red zones and grey core. Fairly plentiful poorly sorted sand. Fairly plentiful fine and coarse veg to 0.4. Sparse limestone to 0.05. Areas of thick red slip survive on both surfaces. Polished where slip survives.

Phase	Context & No.	Grid ref	Dia rim (top)	Fig
ivb	BAJ **2**	16-02	? (30+)	40f

926A **289** Fig. 41a

Deep groove in body, probably from string-tying, and perhaps a further string groove under the rim.

Nile B2. Fired hard. Surfaces red-brown where uncoated or slip lost. Break red with thick grey core. Fairly plentiful fine and medium sand with a few larger grains. Fairly plentiful fine and coarse veg to 1.0. Sparse limestone to 0.1 and one piece 0.2. Red slip on exterior and just down inside rim, partly blackened, probably from secondary burning; none visible otherwise on interior. Polished where slip survives.

Phase	Context & No.	Grid ref	Internal dia rim	Fig
iii–iva	ACE **245**	01 to 04-08	30–35	41a

926B **290** Fig. 41b

Nile B2 near C. BDP **296** fired soft, UP 1038 **2** hard. BDP **296** surfaces brown where uncoated or slip lost, UP 1038 **2** red-brown. Break BDP **296** pale brown all through, UP 1038 **2** red with thick grey core. Fairly plentiful fine and medium sand with a few larger grains. BDP **296** moderate qty fine veg to 0.2, UP 1038 **2** fairly plentiful mostly fine but some coarse to 0.5 Sparse limestone to 0.1. Both weathered, but BDP **296** retains remains of red slip on exterior and top of rim only, and UP 1038 **2** traces of red slip in the groove under the rim roll and on the interior. BDP **296** has a possible trace of polish on top of rim only, but UP 1038 **2** is polished where slip survives.

Phase	Context & No.	Grid ref	Internal dia rim	Fig
iii	BDP (UP 647) **296**	01 to 05-07	?	As 41b
?	UP 1038 **2**	Area 12	*c.*30–35	41b

627 **291** Fig. 41c

Conspicuously folded rim.

Nile B2 near C. Fired fairly hard. Surfaces red-brown where slip lost. Break red-brown with thin red zones and thick grey core. Fairly plentiful poorly sorted sand. Plentiful fine and coarse veg to 2.0. More limestone than usual, to 0.1 and one piece 0.3. Area of red slip survives on exterior, and in a veg cast on interior. Polished where slip survives. Unusual in the coarseness of the veg, and the qty and size of the limestone.

Phase	Context & No.	Grid ref	Dia rim (top)	Fig
ii	AIY **24**	13/14-01/S01	*c.*32	41c

2086 **292** Fig. 41d

Scar from a spout just below the edge of the rim, the smoothing around it partly flattening the rim roll.

Nile B2. Fired medium. Surfaces red-brown. Break red-brown with diffuse pale grey core. Fairly plentiful fine and medium sand with a few larger grains. Moderate qty fine and some coarse veg to 0.4. Sparse limestone to 0.1. Traces of red slip survive on interior only. Polished where slip survives.

Phase	Context & No.	Grid ref	Dia rim (top)	Fig
?	ASL **1**	16/17-06/07/08	20–30	41d

2090 **293** Fig. 41e

Two grooves around ADF **21**, and perhaps one shallow one around AEP/W/Y **4**, probably for string-tying before firing.

Nile B2. Fired fairly hard. Where slip lost, ADF **21** surfaces red-brown, AEW/Y/P **4** orange. Break ADF **21** red-brown with grey core, AEW/Y/P **4** orange with red core. Fairly plentiful fine and medium sand with a few larger grains. Fairly plentiful fine and coarse veg, ADF **21** to 1.1, AEW/Y/P **4** to 0.6. Sparse limestone to 0.1, and AEW/Y/P **4** one piece 0.2. Both weathered, but ADF **21** retains thick red slip in the exterior groove and AEW/Y/P **4** a small area just inside rim. ADF **21** only, polished where slip survives.

Phase	Context & No.	Grid ref	Dia rim (top)	Fig
iv (Pt II?)	ADF **21**	Area 13	40+(?)	41e
v/v/vi	AEW/AEY/AEP **4**	01/02-09	40+(?)	As 41e

621A **294** Fig. 41f–42b

Nile B2. Fired medium to fairly hard. Surfaces red-brown where visible, except BSI/BSJ **3** pale brown and UP 23 **194** exterior pale brown, interior pale orange-brown. Break, BPE **4** orange-red with dark brown and red zones and red-brown core; BSI/BSJ **3** and UP 23 **194** pale brown with thick grey core, former with red zones; AAQ/AAR/AAS **6** red-brown all through; others red-brown with grey core, AZR **6** with pink zones. Fairly plentiful fine and medium sand, most with some larger grains. BPE **4** small qty fine veg to 0.2, others moderate qty to fairly plentiful mostly fine veg, to variable length from 0.3 to 0.7. Sparse limestone to 0.05/0.1. AJU **24** weathered, others red slip on both surfaces (AAQ/AAR/AAS **6** and UP 23 **194** fired or smoke-stained brown), except BSI/BSJ **3** (interior) and CGQ **44** (exterior) one surface weathered. Polished where slip survives.

Phase	Context & No.	Grid ref	Dia rim (top)	Fig
iii	BPE **4**	02-22/23/24	*c.*33(?)	41f
iva/iva	BSI/BSJ **3**	Area 2	34	42a
ivc	CGQ **44**	02 to 05-33 to 37	*c.*36	As 42a
ivd	AJU **24**	05-10	?	As 42b
ivd/ivd/ivd	AAQ/AAR/AAS **6**	06-06	?	As 42b
Mamluk	AZR (UP 12) **6**	Area 12	*c.*35	As 42b
vii	AAA (UP 23) **194**	08-09	32	42b
vii	AAA (UP 23) **228**	03-08	? (30–40)	As 42b

295–99 Bread Moulds

Bread moulds of similar form were made throughout the Archaic period and the OK, but the series from Tell el-Farkha (Mączyńska 2009, Figs 9–16), which runs from the Late Predynastic Period to about the Third–Fourth Dynasty, and the contemporary examples from Helwan (Köhler and Smythe 2004, 133/35, Pl. 5 [6–9] and Pl. 6 [21–22]), are shallower and bear little resemblance to the Anubieion forms. It is possible that the more rounded rims are early in this sequence (Adams 2009, Fig. 10 [1, 3, 8, 10]; Hawass and Senussi 2008, 79 [253]), but the upper part of a bread mould resembling **295** (BDP **1**) was found among material mostly of the Fifth to Sixth Dynasties at Dahshur (Köpp 2004, 64 [Z 330]). The form of **298** (CBS **8**) is also well matched by a bread mould from the 'Late Old Kingdom/early First Intermediate Period' levels at Herakleopolis Magna (Bader 2009a, 34, 37, Fig. 12d). In his brief study of the Tell el-Farkha bread moulds (Chłodnicki 1995), Chłodnicki remarks that most examples from that site are *c.*25–30 in diameter, smaller ones (*c.*15–20) being present but only in small numbers (in contrast to the situation at the Anubieion). Unfortunately he does not offer dating evidence for the different diameters, nor does he specify whether the measurement is internal or external, a matter of some importance with walls of such thickness, though it appears from his illustrations that the external diameter is meant. Rounded rims decrease from *c.*75 per cent in the Late Predynastic Period to *c.*50 per cent in the (early) Old Kingdom but this figure is still so high that it is scarcely possible to draw any conclusions from it. Flat-topped rims are almost entirely of the Old Kingdom, however, which does accord with the Anubieion evidence as far as it goes.

Anna Wodzińska (2007, 308) says, of practice at Giza, '...used primarily in bread production...(but) recycled and also used in other ways. They served as containers for building materials and pigments and as furnaces in a copper workshop'. This may explain their presence in the Saqqara necropolis, since bread for the necropolis workers would surely have been baked a short distance away at the foot of the cliff, where clay for the moulds as well as grain and water would have been closer at hand.

Body sherds from bread moulds are difficult to distinguish from those of beer jars (33) and some listed there may really belong here.

295 Bread moulds with rounded rim (not present in Rzeuska 2006)

749/1420 **295** Fig. 42c–d

Handmade or moulded.

Nile B2 Sandy. Fired medium. BDP **1** surfaces red-brown, BHW **43** and BKP **20** exterior red-brown, interior grey, others grey. Break BQS **17** interior half red-brown, exterior half grey, others red-brown all through except BDP **1**, which has dark brown zones also. Plentiful poorly sorted sand. BKP **20** and BQS **17** plentiful fine and coarse veg, to 0.7 and 1.5 respectively, others fairly plentiful mostly fine to 0.3. Sparse limestone to 0.1, BDP **1** also one piece 0.2 and BHW **43** one piece 0.6 × 0.4. Uncoated. Not polished or burnished.

Phase	Context & No.	Grid ref	Max dia rim	Fig
o	AIL **4**	02-04	*c.*18	As 42d
iii	BDP (UP 534) **1**	01/02-08/09	18	42d
iii	BHW **43**	02-20/21	17	As 42d
ivc	BKP **20**	07/08-22	*c.*24–26	42c
ivc	BQS **17**	Area 2	*c.*18	As 42d

296 Bread mould (or base of stand?) (Not present in Rzeuska 2006)

Rounded rim, more probably from a bread mould than a tubular stand (Rzeuska 2006, Form 220, Pl. 156) for which it is rather simple, large and crude but possible.

816 **296** Fig. 42e

Nile B2. Fired fairly hard. Surfaces red-brown. Break red-brown with thin dark brown zones and pink core. Fairly plentiful poorly sorted sand. Fairly plentiful fine and coarse veg to 1.2. Somewhat more limestone than usual, to 0.1 and three pieces each 0.2. Uncoated, but there may be a faint red-painted band around top of rim, down 0.2 on exterior, 0.6 on interior. No visible polish or burnish.

Phase	Context & No.	Grid ref	Max dia rim	Fig
iii	BDP (UP 647) **103**	01 to 05-07	16	42e

297–98 Bread moulds with squared rim, some grooved (Rzeuska 2006, Forms 202–15, Pls 143–51)

It is not practicable to classify these rims in detail, as Rzeuska was able to do for her more complete forms. At the Anubieion, as in her corpus, the top of the rim is sometimes horizontal and sometimes out turned. This feature, and the shallow groove which is often but not always present, have no obvious practical, stylistic or chronological significance.

1456 **297** Fig. 42f

Nile B2. Fired soft. Surfaces orange, exterior shading to greyish pink where furthest from rim. Break orange with red core. Fairly plentiful poorly sorted sand. Fairly plentiful fine and coarse veg to 0.5. More limestone than usual in a Nile fabric, mostly to 0.1 but several pieces 0.2 and one 0.7 × 0.1. Too weathered for slip, or polish or burnish, to survive.

Phase	Context & No.	Grid ref	Max dia rim	Fig
vi	AER **18**	01-08/09	12–16	42f

747 **298** Fig. 42g–i, 43a–c

AQC **31** retains part of a brown clay lining, and there are probable traces in AQG **79** and ABR North **13**. The lining of AQC **31** is fired soft and contains fairly plentiful poorly sorted sand and plentiful fine and coarse veg to 1.5.

Nile B2 near C Sandy. Fired fairly soft. Surfaces red-brown. Break red or red-brown all through. Fairly plentiful poorly sorted sand, but in some examples mostly fine and medium only. Fairly plentiful fine and coarse veg, in some examples mostly fine, to 0.5/1.0. Sparse limestone to 0.05/1.0. Most surfaces are smoothed, but none slipped. Not polished or burnished. Many show traces of a thin whitewash, seemingly too frequent to be accidental, over areas of the exterior and/or interior (see table). The examples with finer sand and veg are designated Fabric 1 in the table; only one falls between the two: BQF **2** contains the larger qty of large sand grains but not the coarser veg.

Phase	Context & No.	Grid ref	Max dia rim	Fabric	Fig & notes
o	AQG **16**	20/21/22-S03 to S06	*c.*20	2*	As 43a
o	AQG **79**	11/12-S01/S02	*c.*16	1*	As 43a
o	BEN **6**	14/15-01/S01 to S05	?	1*	As 42i or 43c**
ii	BDS **21**	04/05-09	?	1*	As 42h(?)
ii	BGG **4**	12 to 16-S04/S05	*c.*16	2*	As 42i
ii	ABR North (UP 51) **13**	Area 13	*c.*16	1	As 43c
iii	BDR **28**	10/11/12-05	?	2	As 43a
iv (Pt II?)	BWQ **2**	Area 12	*c.*17	2	42g
iv (Pt II?) ×2	AXX/AXY **3**	Area 13	?	2	As 43a
iva	AQC **31**	02/03-10	*c.*31	2*	43a
iva	BHR **74**	02-22	*c.*25	2*	As 43a
iva/ivb	BHR/BTG **130**	02-20/21	*c.*30(?)	2	As 43a
iva–b	DBX **6**	Area 1 30-S32	*c.*24	1*	As 42i or 43c**
ivc	ACP **16**	02 to 05-09	*c.*22	1	As 42i or 43c**
ivc	BQF **2**	Area 2	?	1/2*	As 43a
ivc	BQO **12**	Area 2	22	1*	As 42i or 43c**
ivd	CEW **7**	06-33/34	*c.*26	2	43b
v	AZG (UP 331) **2**	Area 13	17–20	2*	42h
v–vi	BTB **1**	07-33	?	2	As 43a
v–vi	CBS **8**	04/05-25 to 28	*c.*20	1	42i
?	BNE **6**	09-06/07	*c.*17	2*	As 42h(?)
?	UP 1035 **2**	Area 12	?	2	As 43a
?	CAL **9**	Area 26	19	1	43c

* Traces of whitewash

** Insufficiently preserved to distinguish

__299__ Base and body of bread mould (not present in Rzeuska 2006)

Although the form is very similar to a bread mould of the late Second to early Third Dynasty at Elephantine (Raue 1999, Abb. 37 [9]) and examples from Fourth Dynasty Giza (*inter alia* Wodzińska 2007, Figs 11.38/39 [F2B/C]), where such large, roughly made vessels are concerned, dating should be attempted only with caution.

808 **__299__** Fig. 43d

Handmade. Exterior very rough in lower part, less so towards upper break; interior smooth.

__Nile C.__ Fired fairly soft. Surfaces brown. Break thin brown zones and very thick black (rather than grey) core. Fairly plentiful poorly sorted sand. Fairly plentiful fine and coarse veg to 0.6. Sparse limestone to 0.1, and one piece 0.7. Uncoated. Not polished or burnished.

Phase	Context & No.	Grid ref	Dia at bulge	Fig
?	UP 1035 **1**	Area 12	20	43d

__300–17__ High (Offering) Stands

Although the term 'offering stand' is in more general use, in the present chapter 'high stand' is preferred, to conform to the practice in Rzeuska's volume.

__300__ High stand(?) (not present in Rzeuska 2006)

The form could belong to a ringstand from as early as the Archaic Period, such as a very large one, red slipped and well smoothed, from Buto (Faltings 2000, Abb. 8). A high stand, either the base or the top, might better suit the polished slip, but if Petrie (see below) is correct it should have an integral bowl such as a MK series from Tell el-Dab'a (Aston D.A. 2004b, Pls 25/27/28, [105/06/10–13]) when the capacity might be inscribed on the base (though **__300__** is unlikely to be so late).

Kaiser (1969, XI, Typ 75) interprets red-brown polished bases (dia of illustration 15) as derived from such stands, although no bowls survived. He refers to examples from Giza (Reisner 1955, Figs 76 and 128, Type E-XXI), but the bases do not turn upwards in the manner of **__300__**.

The four pre-firing cuts in the rim (base or top?) place it in a group discussed by Kromer (1978, 70 and Abb. 20), publishing an OK jar from Giza with two such cuts. He cites Petrie's hypothesis (1953, 27–28) that it denotes a capacity of a fraction (in the present case one quarter) of a deben, a theory taken up by Lacau and Lauer (1965, 24–27) when discussing ink inscriptions on pots. Rzeuska (2006, Pl. 62 [162]) illustrates a jar with two rim cuts, the form fairly similar to Kromer's and quite unlike **__300__**. The practice continued until at least the reign of Senusret II (Bourriau 1981, 66 [119]) and Gallorini remarks (2009, 116) that in the Middle Kingdom at Kahun there can be up to five in a row on a rim and sometimes other marks elsewhere on the same vessel.

667 **__300__** Fig. 44a

Thin-walled sherd with intentional vertical cuts on the interior, at a right angle to the edge. These must have been made before firing, as some contain slip.

__Nile B2.__ Fired fairly soft. Surfaces concealed by slip. Break dark brown with red-brown core. Fairly plentiful fine and medium sand with a few larger grains. Small qty fine veg to 0.3 and one piece coarse 0.8. Sparse limestone to 0.1. Thick white slip on all surfaces. All surfaces polished.

Phase	Context & No.	Grid ref	Max dia base	Fig
?	UP 19 **55**	Area 12	16	44a

301–07 'X' shaped and 'A' shaped high stands (Rzeuska 2006, Forms 216–18, Pls 152–54)

Rzeuska records several high stands with splayed base, of which the complete profile or a large part of it was preserved. This permitted her to divide them into 'X' and 'A' shapes, with the least diameter at or above the mid-point respectively, though as usual individual stands vary and this division might break down if applied to large numbers of complete examples. Where the complete profile survives, the smaller diameter rim is held, no doubt correctly, to be the top; because smaller it is usually less splayed than the base, and tops of 'A' shaped stands can even approach a cylindrical form. Clues to the identification of rim sherds are thus available, but even so, a firm conclusion cannot always be reached.

Where only a rim sherd survives, it can also be difficult to distinguish a stand from the mouth of a vessel such as a bell-shaped bowl. Such cases have to be assessed on other evidence, including stance, fabric, diameter, wear pattern and which surface is polished, but may remain uncertain.

301–05 'X' shaped high stands (Rzeuska 2006, Form 217, Pl. 153)

In Rzeuska's series, the simple form of **301/02** and the thin overhang to the rim which characterises **303–05** are confined to 'X' shaped stands. In all cases, both at the Anubieion and with the published examples, it is uncertain whether a rim sherd is from a base or a top. It is also difficult to date such fragments closely: they have much in common with a frequently found Fourth Dynasty type (Faltings 1989, Abb. 9d; Wodzińska 2007, Fig. 11.40 [E1]), though in most cases (as with Rzeuska's series) only the exterior is slipped and polished; the diameter range, from 7 to 36, is remarkably wide. On the other hand, rims similar to **303–05** occur in Tell el-Dab'a in the Twelfth Dynasty (Czerny 1999, 199 [F 44–47]), where they are interpreted as from ringstands, Czerny remarking upon the difficulty of distinguishing them from the rims of jars. At Memphis (Kom Rabia) a Nile B2 rim slipped on both surfaces, from the purposive sample in the lowest level reached, of the early Thirteenth Dynasty but with residual material, duplicates the form of **303** (Bourriau and Gallorini in preparation: Corpus 1; also an uncoated example in the mid Thirteenth Dynasty Corpus 5). In addition, from the mid Thirteenth Dynasty come two in Nile B1, one red slipped on the exterior and one uncoated (latter, Bader 2009, 260 and Abb. 166 [5993]; both, Bourriau and Gallorini in preparation, Corpus 4) which are quite similar to **303–05**. All are interpreted as from offering stands.

1712 **301** Fig. 44b

Nile B2. Fired fairly soft. Surfaces concealed by slip. Break brown with red zones and faint, diffuse purple core. Fairly plentiful poorly sorted sand. Small qty fine veg to 0.2. Sparse limestone to 0.1. Thick red slip on both surfaces. Both surfaces polished.

Phase	Context & No.	Grid ref	Max dia base	Fig
ii/ivd	AIY/AIX **18**	12-01/02	16	44b

2320 **302** Fig. 44c

Nile B2. Fired soft. Surfaces yellow-brown. Break yellow-brown all through. Fairly plentiful fine and medium sand with a few larger grains. Fairly plentiful fine and coarse veg to 0.6. No visible limestone. One orange mineral fragment 0.1 × 0.05. On exterior only, traces of thin pink slip; interior apparently only smoothed, uncoated. Lightly polished where slipped.

Phase	Context & No.	Grid ref	Max dia base	Fig
iv (Pt II?)/iv (Pt II?)	ARP=ARS/AYY **11**	Area 13	13	44c

2208 **303** Fig. 44d

Probable thin string impression in fold of rim overhang.

Nile B2. Fired medium. Surfaces orange. Break orange with thick pink core. Fairly plentiful poorly sorted sand. Fairly plentiful fine veg to 0.3. Rather more limestone than usual, to 0.1. Surfaces too weathered to retain slip, or polish or burnish.

Phase	Context & No.	Grid ref	Max dia base	Fig
?	UP 805 **78**	Area 5	18	44d

425 **304** Fig. 44e

The interior is ridged, perhaps from wheel assistance.

Nile B2. Fired medium. Surfaces concealed by slip. Break red-brown with thin red zones and pink core. Fairly plentiful fine well-sorted sand. Small qty fine veg to 0.2. Sparse limestone to 0.05. Red-brown slip on both surfaces, thicker on exterior than interior. Exterior polished, interior not polished or burnished.

Phase	Context & No.	Grid ref	Max dia base	Fig
o	ADU (UP 122) NW **18+20**	Area 13	18	44e

665B **305** Fig. 44f

Probably tied with thin string under overhang of rim.

Nile B2. Fired medium. Surfaces pale red-brown where slip lost. Break pale red-brown with pinkish mauve core, and grey core where thickest. Fairly plentiful fine and medium well-sorted sand. Moderate qty fine veg to 0.3. Sparse limestone to 0.05 and one piece 0.2 × 0.1. Thick orange-red slip on all surfaces. All surfaces highly polished.

Phase	Context & No.	Grid ref	Max dia base	Fig
ivc	AWF **5**	13/14-S04	12	44f

306–07 'A' shaped high stands (Rzeuska 2006, Form 218, Pl. 154)

Thought to derive from 'A' shaped stands because in Rzeuska's series these are a better match than their 'X' shaped counterparts, though the identification is not certain. The rim form is nevertheless quite close to the 'X' shaped Fourth Dynasty stand published by Faltings (1989, Abb. 9d) and referred to under **301–05**. A similar date is implied by a type of 'X' shaped stand from Abu Rawash (Marchand and Baud 1996, Fig. 8 [19]), stated to exist both with and without slip.

1462 **306** Fig. 44g

Nile B2. Fired fairly soft. Surfaces concealed by slip. Break reddish brown with faint red core. Fairly plentiful poorly sorted sand. Moderate qty fine and some coarse veg to 0.5. Sparse limestone to 0.1. Thick red-brown slip on exterior, similar but thinner on interior. Exterior polished, interior probably not polished or burnished.

Phase	Context & No.	Grid ref	Max dia base	Fig
ii/ii	ADG/ADH **5**	Area 13	12	44g

671 **307** Fig. 44h

Nile B2. ACE **93** fired fairly hard, CCK **67** medium. ACE **93** surfaces weathered, CCK **67** concealed by slip. Break brown with thin red zones and grey core. Fairly plentiful poorly sorted sand. Fairly plentiful fine and coarse veg, ACE **93** to 0.5, CCK **67** to 0.3. Sparse limestone to 0.05, ACE **93** also one piece 0.2, CCK **67** one 0.2 and one 0.4 × 0.2. ACE **93** too weathered for slip, or polish or burnish to survive; CCK **67** slip on all surfaces, fired pink, and all surfaces polished.

Phase	Context & No.	Grid ref	Max dia base	Fig
iii–iva	ACE **93**	01 to 05-08 to 12	16	As 44h
ivc	CCK **67**	08 to 11-25/26	19	44h

308 Base from a high stand(?) (Rzeuska 2006, Forms 216–18/22/Diverse, Pls 152–54/58/59)

More probably from a high stand than a jar because highly polished on the interior, but cannot be allocated to a specific type. Stands with a cut-out 'window' (Rzeuska's Form 222) cannot be distinguished on the basis of the rims alone.

2206 **308** Fig. 44i

Nile B1. Fired fairly soft. Surfaces brown where slip lost. Break brown with faint, diffuse red core. Fairly plentiful fine and medium sand with a few larger grains. Small qty fine veg to 0.3. Sparse limestone to 0.1. Thick pinkish red slip on both surfaces. Both surfaces highly polished.

Phase	Context & No.	Grid ref	Max dia base	Fig
ivd	AJI **10**	22-01	11	44i

309 Large-diameter base of high stand (Rzeuska 2006, Form 218, Pl. 154)

Large, rather simple stands are frequent in the OK, and the size and form of **309** would not be out of place in what may be Fourth Dynasty material from the Red Pyramid at Dahshur (Faltings 1989, Abb. 4 [98/129]), though another very similar piece from the Pyramid Temple is assigned to cult and offering practices of the Fifth to Sixth Dynasties (Köpp 2004, 64, 68, Abb. 5 [Z 330]).

Rzeuska's [791] is also similar, and both size and form may continue into the Thirteenth Dynasty on the evidence of a base from Memphis (Bourriau and Gallorini in preparation). However, the polished surface of **309** favours the OK–FIP, as polishing becomes less popular thereafter, and the Serapieion Way context may tip the balance in favour of a pre-Teti date.

814 **309** Fig. 44j

Regular, though very light, ribbing on interior indicates wheel assistance.

Nile B2. Fired fairly hard. Exterior concealed by slip; interior surface red-brown. Break red-brown with thick grey core. Fairly plentiful fine and medium sand with a few larger grains. Fairly plentiful fine and coarse veg to 0.8. Sparse limestone to 0.1. Red slip on exterior; interior uncoated. Extensive surviving areas of polish on exterior only.

Phase	Context & No.	Grid ref	Max dia base	Fig
iii	BWK **1**	Area 12	22	44j

310 Thick-walled tubular high stand (Rzeuska 2006, Form 219, Pl. 155)

An almost perfect match in form and diameter for the base of Rzeuska's Form 219 [795], though this was neither slipped nor polished. Although not recorded on [795], Rzeuska's similar [792–94] are all described as having the lower rim scraped.

751 **310** Fig. 44k

Perhaps handmade, the shallow grooves on the interior from smoothing only. A shallow groove around near the rim, not quite parallel to it, is probably from string-tying. The end shows diagonal scrape marks.

Nile B2. Fired medium. Surfaces red-brown. Break red-brown with thick grey core. Fairly plentiful poorly sorted sand. Fairly plentiful fine and coarse veg to 0.7. Sparse limestone to 0.05. Small areas of thick red slip survive on exterior only. Polished where slip survives.

Phase	Context & No.	Grid ref	Max dia rim	Fig
ii	AQE **5**	21-S03	10	44k

311 Body fragment from a high stand (Rzeuska 2006, Forms 216–18/22/Diverse, Pls 152–54/58/59)

This tapering body fragment cannot be allocated to a specific form of high stand. Although there are no obvious wheel marks, it was probably wheel assisted, as Rzeuska's were. There is a stand fragment of similar diameter from the Greater Cairo Waste Water Project (Hawass and Senussi 2008, 159 [A43]); this has both surfaces red slipped/washed and the exterior is again polished/burnished. Stands with a cut-out 'window' (Rzeuska's Form 222) cannot be distinguished on the basis of the rims alone.

2917 **311** Fig. 44l

Slanting 'pulling up' marks inside part of the length.

Nile B2. Fired fairly hard. Exterior concealed by slip; interior red, shading to purple-brown in the area of the pull marks. Break red-brown with purple core. Fairly plentiful fine sand with a few larger grains. No visible veg. Sparse limestone to 0.05, and two voids each 0.1. Thick red slip on exterior; interior uncoated. Exterior polished.

Phase	Context & No.	Grid ref	Max preserved dia	Fig
o/?	BJA/BMW **18**	14-04	6	44l

312–13 Thick-walled tubular high stands with out-turned rim (Rzeuska 2006, Form 220, Pl. 156)

Rzeuska's series varies considerably but the form typically turns outwards at the ends of a tubular body.

The best match to **312** is her base [801] (Nile B2), and to **313**, bases [798] (Nile B2) and [800] (Nile C). Like **313** but unlike **312**, all are uncoated; however, the somewhat similar stand bases [821/22] of 'diverse' forms (Pl. 159) are slipped externally, and on [822] the slip is carried inside the rim, as on **312**.

There are similar forms to **312/13**, of Fourth Dynasty date, from Dahshur (Faltings 1989, 140 Abb. 5d [158]; 144 Abb. 8b), though these are slightly smaller.

731 **312** Fig. 44m

Perhaps wheel assisted, but the rim is uneven and the interior close to it has gouges from a tool, so hand finished; there are slanting 'pulling up' marks inside the body.

Nile B2. Fired fairly soft. Surfaces pale brown. Break pale brown with thin red zones and grey core. Fairly plentiful fine and medium sand with a few larger grains. Moderate qty fine veg to 0.2. Sparse limestone to 0.1 and one piece 0.2 × 0.1. Thick red slip on exterior and top of rim, carried 2.5 cm into interior to a careful edge. All slipped surfaces polished, including interior.

Phase	Context & No.	Grid ref	Max dia base	Fig
iv (Pt II?)	ADD North **30**	Area 13	7.5	44m

737 **313** Fig. 45a–b

Apparently handmade as far as preserved, the surfaces very uneven and AJJ/AMJ **32** slightly oval in section. There are slanting 'pulling up' marks inside the body of AFT **12**, though widely spaced ridges on both surfaces may be evidence of coiling.

Nile C. Fired fairly soft. Surfaces reddish brown. Break reddish brown, AFT **12** with red zones and grey core, AJJ/AMJ **32** with red core only. Fairly plentiful poorly sorted sand. Fairly plentiful fine and coarse veg, AFT **12** to 0.8, AJJ/AMJ **32** to 1.6. Sparse limestone to 0.05. Uncoated. Not polished or burnished.

Phase	Context & No.	Grid ref	Max dia base	Fig
ivd	AFT **12**	09/10-04/05	7	45a
vi/vi	AJJ/AMJ **32**	12/13-05/06	7–7.5	45b

314–17 Diverse high stands (Rzeuska 2006, 'Diverse high stands', Pls 158/59)

The unusual interior shape of **317** may relate it to Rzeuska's [823]. Otherwise, the wide mouths and direct rims are a good match for her uncoated [819]. In no case is it certain whether the base or top has survived; perhaps they could even be used either way up. The OK/FIP date is also not guaranteed, but later stands are usually more elaborate and better finished; an example from Akhmim dated as late OK to early MK (Hope and McFarlane, 2006, Fig. 15 [A3]) is similar to **315** in form and dimensions.

2326 **314** Fig. 45c

Interior has ribbing from at least wheel assistance.

Nile B2. Fired fairly soft. Surfaces concealed by slip. Break pinkish brown with grey core. Fairly plentiful poorly sorted sand. Fairly plentiful fine and coarse veg to 0.4. Sparse limestone to 0.1. Slip, too thin to disguise the voids, exterior red, interior fired grey-brown indicating the opening was covered in the kiln. Possible but uncertain traces of polish on interior only.

Phase	Context & No.	Grid ref	Dia rim (top)	Fig
ii	AJY **172**	19/20-S04/S05	12	45c

1341 **315** Fig. 45d

Two similar stands, neither of them complete as to height. There is no abrasion pattern on either example to indicate base or rim, and the way they were placed in the kiln is not an indicator. The central area of BET **112** + BGG **122** was pulled up, presumably with a tool inside, it being too narrow for the potter's fingers to produce ribbing. It is to be noted that the joining pieces are from widely separated contexts (see also **544/627/53**).

Nile B2. Both fired medium but rather misfired. BKP/AAA **18** exterior patchy red and grey, interior red, BET **112** + BGG **122** exterior grey, interior dark grey at end with rim, shading to greyish red at break. Break red with grey core, but BET **112** + BGG **122** red all through where thinnest. Fairly plentiful poorly sorted sand. Fairly plentiful fine and coarse veg to 1.2. Sparse limestone to 0.1, BET **112** + BGG **122** also one piece shell 0.5 × 0.2. Misfiring has affected any slip, but traces of red running down inside BET **112** + BGG **122** and the patchy appearance of BKP/AAA **18** may indicate original slips. Not polished or burnished, but misfiring is likely to have destroyed this.

Phase	Context & No.	Grid ref	Max dia base	Fig
ivc/vii	BKP/AAA **18**	07/08-23	11	As 45d
ii	BET **112**★	14-03	9.5	45d
ii	BGG **122**★	04/05/06-S01/S02/S03	9.5	45d

★ Join

2786 **316** Fig. 45e–f

Irregular internal ribbing, implying wheel assistance rather than wheel throwing. Both are fire blackened on the interior, ACE **168** as far as preserved, CFX **5** from the rim to a straight edge 3.7 down.

Nile B2. Fired medium. Surfaces red-brown where not blackened. Break red-brown, ACE **168** with pink core, CFX **5** red zones and grey core. Fairly plentiful poorly sorted sand. Fairly plentiful fine and coarse veg to 1.0. Sparse limestone to 0.05, and ACE **168** one fossil snail cast 0.4. Uncoated, but wet-smoothed using a great deal of water, CFX **5** with a diagonal wipe mark on the exterior. Not polished or burnished.

Phase	Context & No.	Grid ref	Max dia base	Fig
iii–iva	ACE **168**	01 to 05-08 to 12	17	45f
v–vi	CFX **5**	09-23/24	15	45e

2903 **317** Fig. 45g

Nile B2. Fired fairly hard. Surfaces red-brown. Break red-brown with thick purple-grey core towards the interior surface. Fairly plentiful fine and medium well-sorted sand. Fairly plentiful fine and coarse veg to 0.2. No visible limestone. Surfaces too weathered to show evidence of any slip, or polish or burnish.

Phase	Context & No.	Grid ref	Max dia base	Fig
iva	BHR **197**	01/03-21/22/23	*c.*11	45g

318 Upright ringstand(?) with folded rim (not present in Rzeuska 2006)

The combination of upright form and probable hand construction indicate a pre-Teti date, borne out by the absence of parallels from Rzeuska's corpus. A close match is a ringstand from Giza (Kromer 1978, Taf. 21 [2]), which might be assumed to be Fourth Dynasty, though Kromer prefers the late Second or Third. However, a deep bowl (*ibid.*, Taf. 25 [3]) is similar, and Kromer warns that the form is very variable. The same thickening of the wall is seen on two uncoated ringstands from Abu Rawash (Marchand and Baud 1996, Fig. 8 [17–18]), though the rims are not seen to be folded.

619 **318** Fig. 45h

Variable height of rim overhang and uneven interior surface suggest hand manufacture.

Nile B2. Fired medium. Exterior red-brown, interior surface orange (weathered). Break red-brown/orange with thin dark brown zones near surfaces, red-brown core, or red-brown zones and grey core where thickest. Fairly plentiful fine and medium well-sorted sand. Fairly plentiful fine and coarse veg to 0.4. Sparse limestone to 0.1. Surfaces weathered but possible trace of red slip on top of rim. No visible polish or burnish.

Phase	Context & No.	Grid ref	Dia rim (top)	Fig
iv	DAH **6**	Area 2 W10-S55	10	45h

319–21 Ringstands(?) with thickened rim (not present in Rzeuska 2006)

In Rzeuska's corpus there is a dearth of ringstands of the shorter form so common in later periods, but the Fourth Dynasty Giza corpus (Reisner 1955, Fig. 77) proves their existence already in earlier times and provides fairly closely matching forms. The best parallels (*ibid.*, [60/61]) have rim diameter 11–12 and although the bases and tops are very similar, the tops (as illustrated) are the better match. The form occurs again at Giza from more recent excavations in the Western Cemetery (Hawass and Senussi 2008, 120 [85]), specified as in red slipped and burnished Nile B1 fabric and with diameters 11.7 and 13.4; the dating is a little ambiguous but is certainly Fourth to early Sixth Dynasty. A date as early as the Fourth Dynasty should not be assumed for the Anubieion examples, since the absence of the form from Rzeuska's corpus is likely to be a matter of chance.

2282 **319** Fig. 45i

Appears to be at least wheel assisted. There is a very substantial amount of even wear, facilitated by the fairly soft firing, along the inner edge of the rim, consistent with use as a ringstand.

Nile B2. Fired fairly soft. Surfaces pale brown where slip lost. Break pale brown with diffuse pink core. Fairly plentiful fine and medium sand with a few larger grains. Moderate qty fine veg to 0.3. Sparse limestone to 0.05. Areas of brownish red slip survive on exterior; interior uncoated but weathered. Traces of polish where slipped.

Phase	Context & No.	Grid ref	Dia rim (top)	Fig
ivd/ivd	ASD/BAU **14**	17/18-07/08	11	45i

902 **320** Fig. 45j

Probably handmade. Heavily but patchily impregnated with oil or similar substance.

Nile B1. Fired fairly soft to medium. Surfaces pale brown, exterior where slip lost. Break pale brown all through. Fairly plentiful fine well-sorted sand. Moderate qty fine veg to 0.5. Only one piece limestone, 0.2. Areas of very pale pink slip survive on exterior and top of rim; interior uncoated. Polished where slip survives.

Phase	Context & No.	Grid ref	Dia rim (top)	Fig
?	UP 1034 **3**	Area 12	14	45j

2116 **321** Fig. 45k

Under the overhang of the rim, probably tied with thin string before firing.

Nile B2. Fired fairly hard. Surfaces red-brown. Break red-brown with thin dark brown zones and faint brown core. Fairly plentiful fine and medium sand with a few larger grains. Moderate qty fine and coarse veg to 0.3. More limestone than usual in a Nile fabric, to 0.1 and one void 0.4. Weathered and sand-blasted, but interior (at least) may have been red slipped and polished.

Phase	Context & No.	Grid ref	Dia rim (top)	Fig
iii–iva	ACE **99**	01 to 05-08 to 12	*c.*15	45k

322 Ringstand(?) (not present in Rzeuska 2006)

This rim presented various problems as to both form and fabric. No similar form was recorded from MK or NK Memphis (Kom Rabia), where this fabric is in any case uncommon (Bourriau 2010; Bourriau and Gallorini in preparation). Equally implausible as bowl, lid or stand, it was finally matched to an uncoated but wet-smoothed

Nile B2 rim from early Fourth Dynasty Giza interpreted as a 'concave-sided stand', presumably a ringstand rather than an offering (high) stand (Hawass and Senussi 2008, 141 and 167 [A84]).

Although catalogued as Nile D, the fabric has some characteristics of a marl, notably the firing surface and the small amount of plant matter. This ambiguity suits the early OK better than a later date and to some extent reinforces the identification, even though the Giza example is itself in Nile B2.

2458A **322** Fig. 45l

Nile D. Fired medium to fairly hard. Surfaces covered with a thick white layer, probably a firing surface, not a slip. Break red all through except white zone at surfaces. Fairly plentiful poorly sorted sand. Small qty fine veg to 0.2. Plentiful tiny limestone flecks and fairly plentiful to 0.1. Uncoated(?). Exterior polished overall; interior not polished or burnished.

Phase	Context & No.	Grid ref	Dia rim (top)	Fig
vii	AAA (UP 37) **54**	11 to 20-S01/S02/S03	*c.*11	45l

323 Handmade 'cover'(?) (Rzeuska 2006, Form 225, Pl. 160)

The irregular surfaces and lack of wheel ridges appear to indicate a handmade object. Inverted, it could be the knob from a pierced cover such as Rzeuska's uncoated, handmade [829] of Form 225 (dia 13.5). This turns in at the rim, whereas **323** turns out, but Rzeuska mentions (*ibid.*, 424) that every one is different. In the Fourth Dynasty, such objects had a loop handle rather than a 'knob' (Reisner 1955, Fig. 78 from Giza; Faltings 1989, Abb. 5d [145] from Dahshur).

On the other hand, a very similar MK form from Tell el-Dab'a (Aston D.A. 2004b, Pl. 187 [683]) is a lid.

848 **323** Fig. 45m

Nile B2. Fired fairly soft. Surfaces brown. Break brown with red core, or red zones and grey core where thickest. Fairly plentiful poorly sorted sand. Fairly plentiful fine veg to 0.3, and one piece 0.8. Sparse limestone to 0.1. A few fragments of red (grog? mineral?) to 0.2. Possible traces of red slip on exterior only. Not polished or burnished.

Phase	Context & No.	Grid ref	Max dia base	Fig
v	BAC **290**	02/03-S01	11	45m

324–25 Medium-sized shallow lids/bowls with internal ledge (not present in Rzeuska 2006)

Shallow handmade forms, equally suitable for use as lids or bowls. The form can be traced back to the Archaic Period, but the early examples have narrow rims (Stan Hendrickx, pers. comm.). Mark Lehner dates pottery from some recent work at Giza, which includes the type of **324/25**, to the reigns of Khafre and Menkaure of the Fourth Dynasty (Lehner 2007, 279). Reisner's corpus includes the form (Reisner 1955, Fig. 75 XXXIXC [69]), with a diameter of about 24. Also at Giza, Wodzińska's most common sub-group (2007, 304–05, Fig. 11.30, [CD32A]), usually in Nile B2 (*ibid.*, Table 11.3), is normally in diameter range 18–22 and sometimes the interior of the rim is painted red. This corresponds well with the Anubieion examples, though more of the surface of the latter seems to have been slipped (or painted?). Wodzińska publishes hers as bowls, but quotes Raue (1999, 183) for a possible use as lids, for which the wide-rimmed **324** would be especially suitable. There are several further examples from Giza, from the SCA excavations and the trenches of the Greater Cairo Waste Water Project, mostly similar in form to **324** (e.g. Hawass and Senussi 2008, 55 [98], 76 [239], 166 [A81], 180 [I133]). At Abu Rawash, probably in the Fourth Dynasty, they can be red slipped or uncoated (Marchand and Baud 1996, Fig. 8 [20–21]). A pre-Teti date is almost certain.

315A **324** Fig. 46a

Nile B2. Fired fairly soft. Surfaces pale brown. Break pale brown all through. Fairly plentiful poorly sorted sand. Moderate qty to fairly plentiful fine and medium veg to 0.5. No visible limestone. Two pieces of opaque pale grey stone, 0.3 × 0.1 and 0.2 × 0.1. Surfaces weathered, but possible traces of red slip on exterior. Not polished or burnished as preserved.

Phase	Context & No.	Grid ref	Max dia rim	Fig
iv	DAG **12**	Area 2 W09-S52/S53/S54	19	46a

315B **325** Fig. 46b

Nile B2. Fired fairly hard. Surfaces orange-brown. Break red-brown with thick red core. Fairly plentiful fine and medium sand with a few larger grains. Moderate qty fine and some coarse veg to 1.1. Sparse limestone to 0.1. Probable traces of red slip on both surfaces. Not polished or burnished as preserved.

Phase	Context & No.	Grid ref	Max dia rim	Fig
vii	AAA (UP 445) **134**	Area 2	19	46b

326 Small shallow lid with internal ledge (not present in Rzeuska 2006)

Apparently a smaller diameter version of **324/25**. That a similar form can be slipped and polished (both inside and out) is demonstrated by an example from Fourth Dynasty Giza (dia 18) (Kromer 1978, Taf. 23 [1]), though this is restored with a flat base. The type is confirmed as 'of a fine Nile clay' and with 'well polished' surface, with or without red slip (Wodzińska 2007, 304–05 Type CD32C). Larger (dias 21.6 and 28) examples from Giza (Hawass and Senussi 2008, 166 [A81], 180 [H33]), have respectively burnished red slip on both surfaces and a burnished red rim. Red slipped and polished/burnished examples were also seen at Dahshur many years ago by the author and assumed to be Fourth Dynasty, though details of form and diameter were not recorded. The careful external finish indicates a lid in the case of **326**.

Until recently no published example had been located which had a round base and such a small diameter, and a later (NK?) date was thought just possible. A recently published lid (Malykh 2011, 202 and Fig. 10 [98/6/5]) has, if anything, further complicated the matter. It is similar in form and diameter (10.5) to **326** but crucially lacks the base and is uncoated; furthermore, although dated to the late NK–TIP, it comes from debris in a Giza shaft from which there is also OK pottery, and the dating is based on comparison with a late NK–TIP form (Aston D.A. 1996, Fig. 187h) with a flat base, which may not be appropriate. On balance, **326** is still more likely to be OK than later.

455 **326** Fig. 46c

Low wheel-ridges(?) on interior.

Nile B1. Fired fairly soft. Surfaces pale brown, exterior where slip lost. Break pale brown with red zones and thin grey core. Fairly plentiful poorly sorted sand. Fairly plentiful mostly fine veg to 0.5, and one coarse piece 0.9. Sparse limestone to 0.1. Thick red slip on exterior; rim and interior uncoated. Highly polished on exterior only.

Phase	Context & No.	Grid ref	Max dia rim	Fig
iva	AJH **193**	06/07-04/05/06	10	46c

327 Lid(?) (not present in Rzeuska 2006)

It is difficult to see this object as anything but a lid. OK shallow bowls/lids often have an internal ridge (see **324–26**). If drawn a little too shallow, it could be a square-ended variant of an Elephantine form (dia 26) (Raue

1999, Abb. 39 [5]) dated to the Third or early Fourth Dynasty, though this has no slip or wash. It would then equate to a red slipped Mendes example (dia 18) (Adams 2009, Fig. 49 [17]) of about the Fourth Dynasty and a red slipped and polished one from Giza (dia 18) (Kromer 1978, Taf. 23 [1]) of the Fourth.

882 327 Fig. 46d

Form so complex and sharp it appears to be wheel assisted as far as preserved.

Nile B2. Fired fairly soft. Surfaces red-brown. Break brown with faint diffuse red core. Fairly plentiful fine and medium well-sorted sand. Moderate qty mostly fine veg to 0.3. Sparse limestone to 0.1. All surfaces smoothed. Possible thin whitewash on all surfaces except underside. Not polished or burnished.

Phase	Context & No.	Grid ref	Max dia rim	Fig
iva	AEF **105**	15/16-04	? (15–25)	46d

328–35 Miniatures

The closed forms were recorded in Nile fabric only, but the open forms in both Nile and Mixed Clay P.60 fabrics.

Miniature vessels of pottery were produced in very large numbers and are thought to have been predominantly used, perhaps daily, in above-ground offering rituals (Allen, 2006).

328 Miniature offering stands with flat base (not present in Rzeuska 2006)

Miniature offering stands, to be distinguished from the miniature jars **329–33**. The shallow bowl in the top may normally have held a single fruit or seed, though the bowl of UP 627 **13** contains a black pitch-like residue. Unlike most of the miniatures, the type is quite well standardised in form and dimensions. It is wheel assisted, always in Nile clay, and usually shows evidence of string-cutting.

The solidity of these small vessels has ensured that many survived intact or nearly so, and led to an abnormally high recovery rate during the excavation. The distribution pattern resembles that of the miniature jars, and differs greatly from that of the miniature plates. The concentration in surface and near-surface contexts in Area 5 should result from ancient or recent digging for building materials.

Their absence from Rzeuska's corpus is difficult to explain, but they are generally infrequent among published miniatures. The best match found is from Akhmim (Hope and McFarlane, 2006, Fig. 16 [A12]), dated late OK to early MK, though this is handmade. There is some similarity to miniatures from the excavations of the SCA at Giza (Hawass and Senussi 2008, 86 [278–80]) but the interiors are deeper and the resemblance is not close; they are dated to the Fifth–early Sixth Dynasty (*ibid.*, 21). They are not present in the study of Fourth and Fifth Dynasty miniatures from Abu Rawash by Marchand and Baud (1996).

1260 328 Fig. 46e–i

Nile B2 near D. Fired fairly soft to medium. Surfaces pale brown to red-brown. Break pale brown with red core to red-brown all through, and broken examples mauve core where thickest. Fairly plentiful poorly sorted sand. Small to moderate qty fine veg to 0.2/0.4. Sparse limestone to 0.1, some with pieces 0.2, AAB **16** also one piece 0.4 and UP 588 **426** one piece 0.3. Uncoated. Not polished or burnished.

Phase	Context & No.	Grid ref	Max dia rim	Height	Fig
iii/iva/?	BPD/BHR/BPV **20**	03/04-22/23	(Bowl lost)	?	
iv	DAG **42**	Area 2 W09-S52/S53/S54	(Bowl lost)	?	
iv (Pt V)	AZO (UP 318) **20**	Area 13	4.6	4.2	46e
ivb	BCI **22**	05-07/08	3.8	5.4	46f

Phase	Context & No.	Grid ref	Max dia rim	Height	Fig
ivb/ivb	BCI/BCL **6**	05-06/07/08	4.5	5.0	
ivc	BTX **200**	02/03-19/20	(Bowl lost)	*c*.5.0	
ivc	BQH **26**	Area 2	(Bowl lost)	?	
ivc	BQI **122**	Area 2	4.2	5.5	
ivc/ivc/ivd	AHU/AHV/AAT **5**	06/07-04/05	3.9	5.2	
ivc/ivd	AJG/AUH **18**	06-01/02/03	4.5	(Foot lost)	
ivc/vii	AJA/AAA **1**	03/04-10/11/12	4.0	4.5	As 46h
ivd	ATY **223**	25-04	(Bowl lost)	?	
v	BAC **104**	02/03-S01	3.7	5.4	46g
v	BAC **367**	02/03-S01	3.7	5.3	
vi–vii	AAB **16**	22/23-09/10	4.5	5.0	46h
vii	AAA (UP 23) **647**	01 to 04-01/02	4.0–4.1	5.3	46i
vii	AAA (UP 23) **648**	01 to 04-01/02	4.3	5.5	
vii	AAA (UP 23) **649**	01 to 04-01/02	4.2	5.5	
vii	AAA (UP 23) **650**	02/03-04/05	4.1	5.6	
vii	AAA (UP 23) **651**	10/11-01/02/03	4.5	4.9	As 46h
vii	AAA (UP 38) **153**	20-03	3.9	5.5	
vii	AAA (UP 68) **47**	01 to 20-S03 to S08	4.5	5.2	As 46h
vii	AAA (UP 99) **7**	W01 to W05-01 to 10	3.9	5.3	
vii	AAA (UP 118) **44**	05 to 08-01/02/S01	3.9	5.5	
vii	AAA (UP 157) **141**	06 to 10-11/12	3.5	4.6	
vii	AAA (UP 157) **145**	09/10-19/20	4.2	5.5	
vii	AAA (UP 588) **69**	01/02-21 to 24	4.2	(Foot lost)	
vii	AAA (UP 588) **288**	10/11/12-21 to 24	4.1	(Foot lost)	As 46e
vii	AAA (UP 588) **426**	01/W01-40/41/42	4.1	5.5	
vii	AAA (UP 627) **13**	02/03/04-19	4.2	(Foot lost)	
vii	AAA (UP 627) **410**	W01 to W04-18 to 24	3.9	4.5	As 46h

<u>329–32</u> Miniature footed jars with flat base (Rzeuska 2006, Forms 229/30, Pls 162/63)

At the Anubieion, miniature jars are less numerous than miniature offering stands and plates, but very variable in form. As in Rzeuska's corpus, they are always in Nile clay. Wheel assisted, and where preserved the base is string-cut. Most of Rzeuska's examples are slightly smaller.

That there were similar predecessors or contemporaries at Dahshur is shown by an assemblage from the Red Pyramid area (Faltings 1989, Abb. 7 [N-O-E 39/40]). Exact correspondences are not to be expected, but **<u>329–31</u>** are especially close. More significantly, further material, this time from the Pyramid Temple, is dated to the Fifth to Sixth Dynasties and explained as deriving from cult practices and offerings; it includes a good match to **<u>329</u>**, albeit in marl clay (Köpp 2004, 64–65, Abb. 4 [Z 346]).

At Abusir, the only miniature jars recorded by Kaiser (1969, XII, Type 76–81) resemble the present series rather than the offering stands (**<u>328</u>**), which may be a later development. Again, exact correspondences are not to be expected, but a good match is between Kaiser's 77 and **<u>332</u>**, while 76 and 78 are similar to **<u>331</u>** and 79 is not very different from **<u>329/30</u>**.

At Giza, the excavations of the SCA again yielded similar miniature jars (Hawass and Senussi 2008, 71 [200–02], 86 [277, 281], 112 [33]), dated to the Fifth–early Sixth Dynasty (*ibid.*, 21).

At Abu Rawash, the study by Marchand and Baud (1996) illustrates incurving miniatures of the Fourth (to Fifth?) Dynasty of generally similar form (Fig. 6a [5–7]), but none really close.

2694A **329** Fig. 46j

Clear spiral ribbing internally and externally, from wheel-assistance.

Nile B2 near D. Fired medium. Surfaces pale red-brown. In chips, red-brown. Fairly plentiful poorly sorted sand. Moderate qty fine and coarse veg, mostly to 0.2 but pieces to 1.5. Many tiny limestone flecks, also sparse to 0.1 and one piece 0.2. Uncoated. Not polished or burnished.

Phase	Context & No.	Grid ref	Dia rim (top)	Height	Fig
o	ADU (UP 330) **3**	Area 13	3.2–3.4 variable	5.5–5.9 variable	46j

2694B **330** Fig. 46k

Nile B2. Fired fairly soft. Surfaces pale brown. Break pale brown all through. Fairly plentiful poorly sorted sand. Moderate qty fine veg to 0.3 and a few pieces to 0.8. Sparse limestone to 0.1. Uncoated. Not polished or burnished.

Phase	Context & No.	Grid ref	Dia rim (top)	Height	Fig
(vi–)vii	AAB **45**	01-33/34/35	5.4	? (4.0+)	46k

2694C **331** Fig. 46l

Internal scoring from wheel assistance.

Nile B2. Fired fairly soft. Surfaces pale brown. In chips, red-brown. Fairly plentiful fine and medium sand with a few larger grains. Moderate qty fine veg to 0.3. Sparse limestone to 0.05. Uncoated. Not polished or burnished.

Phase	Context & No.	Grid ref	Dia rim (top)	Height	Fig
vii	AAA (UP 157) **142**	14/15/16-10 to 15	2.6	6.2	46l

2694D **332** Fig. 46m

Nile B2. Fired medium. Surfaces weathered off. In chips, red-brown. Fairly plentiful poorly sorted sand. Fairly plentiful fine veg to 0.2. Sparse limestone to 0.1 and one piece 0.2. Surfaces too weathered to preserve slip, or polish or burnish.

Phase	Context & No.	Grid ref	Dia rim (top)	Height	Fig
vii	AAA (UP 38) **162**	16/17-01/02	3.3	5.0–5.2 variable	46m

333 Miniature jar with flat base (not present in Rzeuska 2006)

Similar capacity to **329–32** but lacking the pedestal base. The rim form relates it to these and thus to Rzeuska's miniature jars. Wheel assisted and string-cut.

2816 **333** Fig. 46n

Nile B2. Fired fairly soft. Surfaces pale brown. Break pale brown all through. Fairly plentiful poorly sorted sand. Moderate qty fine veg to 0.3. Sparse limestone to 0.1. Uncoated. Not polished or burnished.

Phase	Context & No.	Grid ref	Dia rim (top)	Height	Fig
iv+	DAW **4**	Area 2 W11-S60	4.0	4.0	46n

<u>334–35</u> Miniature Plates (Rzeuska 2006, Forms 231/32, Pls 164–68)

Miniature plates, like miniature jars and bowls, abound in cemeteries of this period, the smallest perhaps each holding a single fruit or a small number of seeds. The unrestricted forms, in particular, are so variable as to defy all attempts to subdivide them. At the Anubieion they occur in both Nile clay and mixed clay (**<u>371</u>**), though the Nile clay examples are more numerous and include the 'mini miniatures' **<u>335</u>**, found neither in mixed clay nor in Rzeuska's corpus. The range of forms and sizes is otherwise similar in each material. Some are irregular in height or diameter. Although often distorted from careless handling before firing, they are not carelessly made. Most, including some of the smallest, show evidence of string-cutting, so they were thrown from the top of a clay lump on some sort of wheel; the string-cutting, unlike the shaping, is frequently careless, leaving a downward protrusion.

Forms hardly to be distinguished from those of the Sixth Dynasty and later are prolific at Dahshur in or about the reign of Snefru of the Fourth Dynasty (Faltings 1989, Abb. 3a and 7). From Abusir, Kaiser publishes (Kaiser 1969, XLVIII, Type 238–43) a small selection from nearly 500 examples recorded, corresponding to both **<u>334</u>** and **<u>335</u>**. They do not appear to include the very rounded rims most frequent at the Anubieion, which may be due to chance or have a chronological basis. It is not feasible to match individual vessels. There are similar forms at Abu Rawash (Marchand and Baud 1996, Fig. 6a [8–11]; Fig. 9 [15–19]) but these were not analysed or dated.

At the Anubieion, the distribution is unusual, with very few in Area 5 and many in surface and late contexts from the limited excavations in Areas 1 and 2, and (mostly in Nile clay) Areas 12–14. It may indicate a specific use of those areas in the OK or slightly later. See **<u>371</u>** also.

2808B **<u>334</u>** Fig. 47a–l

DAC **36** has at some time been set upright in wet plaster, which has adhered.

<u>Nile B2.</u> BHR **266** fired fairly hard, others fairly soft. Surfaces pale brown to red-brown. Break BHR **266** red-brown with thin pink zones and grey core, others (where visible) pale brown or red-brown all through, or with faint red or grey core. Fairly plentiful poorly sorted sand. Small to moderate qty fine veg to 0.2/0.4. Sparse limestone to 0.05/0.1, also ADU NW **4** and DAW **5** each one piece 0.2 and BWJ **2** one piece 0.5 × 0.3. BDR **66** one piece opaque pale grey stone 0.1. Uncoated. Not polished or burnished.

For similar forms to BDR **66** and UP 8 **12** see **<u>371</u>** in the mixed clay series.

Phase	Context & No.	Grid ref	Dia base	Max dia rim	Height	Fig & notes
o	ADU (UP 122) NW **3**	Area 13	3.4–3.6	4.9	1.4–1.5*	As 47h
o	ADU (UP 122) NW **4**	Area 13	*c*.3.0	*c*.4.5	1.2	***
o/ii	BDY/BDX **22**	01 to 08-07/08	*c*.3.0	*c*.4.5	1.2	**
ii	ABR North (UP 51) **4**	Area 13	*c*.3.0	*c*.5.0	1.7	As 47h
ii	BWJ **2**	Area 12	*c*.3.0	*c*.4.5	1.1	**
iii	BDR **66**	12/13/14-04/05/06	3.8	*c*.6.0	1.8	47a
iv	DAG **50**	Area 2 W09-S52/S53/S54	3.3	*c*.4.5	1.3	As 47e
iv	DAG **53**	Area 2 W09-S52/S53/S54	3.0–3.5*	4.4–4.5*	1.3–1.8*	(Distorted)

Phase	Context & No.	Grid ref	Dia base	Max dia rim	Height	Fig & notes
iv	DAY **14**	Area 2 W10-S63	4.1–4.5*	6.4–6.6*	1.8–2.2*	47b
iv (Pt II?)	ADC **120**	Area 13	2.6	3.7	1.0	47c
iv (Pt II?)	BWX **10**	Area 12	2.8	*c*.5.0	1.7	As 47c
iv (Pt V)	AZO (UP 318) **21**	Area 13	3.1	4.7–4.9*	1.0–1.1*	†
iva	BHR **112**	02-22/23	*c*.2.5	*c*.4.0	1.4	As 47c
iva	BHR **266**	02/03-21/22	4.0	*c*.6.0	1.6	As 47j
iv+	DAW **5**	Area 2 W11-S60	3.0	4.5	1.4	As 47h
iv+	DAW **6**	Area 2 W11-S60	3.2–3.4*	4.5–4.7*	1.4–1.7*	47d
iv+	DAW **7**	Area 2 W11-S60	2.9–3.1*	4.0–4.4*	1.2–1.5*	As 47j
iv+	DAW **8**	Area 2 W11-S60	3.2	4.4	1.3–1.4*	As 47h
v	BAC **323**	02/03-S01	2.8	*c*.5.0	1.6	As 47l
v	BQJ **23**	Area 2	?	*c*.4.5	1.6	As 47l
v	DAC **17**	Area 2 W06/W07/ W08-S52/S53/S54	3.0	4.6	1.7	As 47g
v	DAC **36**	Area 2 W06/W07-S55/ S56	4.0	6.9	2.2–2.3*	As 47b
v	DAF **24**	Area 2 W10-S50/S51	3.9–4.0*	4.8–4.9*	1.2–1.4*	47e
vi/vi	ABF/ABG (UP 236) **1**	Area 13	3.0	4.4	1.0	47f
vii	AAA (UP 118) **43**	22/23-01/S01	3.1–3.3*	4.8–4.9*	1.4	As 47k
vii	AAA (UP 445) **12**	Area 2	2.9	4.8	1.2	**
vii	AAA (UP 445) **71**	Area 2	*c*.3.2	*c*.4.9	1.2	**
vii	AAA (UP 445) **93**	Area 2	2.8–3.0*	4.7–4.8*	1.6–1.9*	47g
vii	AAA (UP 445) **121**	Area 2	3.0	4.4	1.7	As 47g
vii	AAA (UP 998) **28**	Area 2	3.2–3.3*	4.0–4.2*	1.1–1.2*	As 47e
vii	AAA (UP 998) **29**	Area 2	3.2–3.3*	4.4–4.6*	1.5	47h
vii	AAA (UP 998) **30**	Area 2	3.0–3.1*	4.5	1.4–1.5*	As 47h
vii	ANJ (UP 163) **8**	Area 14	*c*.3.3–3.7*	*c*.4.8	2.0	47i
vii	AAA (UP 8) **12**	Area 12¶	3.2–3.5*	5.2	1.5–1.8*	47j
vii	AAA (UP 8) **30**	Area 12¶	2.8–3.2*	4.1–4.4*	1.2–1.3*	47k
vii	AAA (UP 8) **33**	Area 13¶¶	2.5–2.7*	4.1	1.4–1.5*	47l
vii	AAA (UP 8) **48**	Area 12 (not specific)	4.0	6.1	1.3–1.5*	**

* Variable

** Form as mixed clay AAA (UP 445) **11** in **<u>371</u>** (Fig. 49p)

*** Form between UP 998 **29** and UP 8 **33**

† Form between mixed clay BCB **117** and AAA (UP 445) **11** in **<u>371</u>** (Fig. 49m, p)

¶ 'North–South trench, North extension'

¶¶ 'Against East face of terrace wall'

1262 **<u>335</u>** Fig. 47m–q

Exceptionally small vessels. Where there is an overlap of diameter with **<u>334</u>**, the proportions dictate the grouping. As with the larger version, these are too variable in form to subdivide. The forms are also too variable to compare with any specific illustrated example, but those of similar diameter are usually similar in form. The distribution pattern at the Anubieion is much more normal than that of the larger version.

<u>Nile B2.</u> Fired from fairly soft to fairly hard. Where fairly soft, surfaces pale brown, break (where visible) pale brown all through; where fairly hard, surfaces red, break (where visible) red with grey core. Examples with breaks show fairly plentiful poorly sorted sand, small qty fine veg to 0.2 and sparse limestone to 0.05/0.1, and UP 167 **2** and UP 37 **94** each one piece 0.2. UP 167 **2** has one piece of slag(?) 0.4. Uncoated. Not polished or burnished.

Phase	Context & No.	Grid ref	Max dia rim	Fig & notes
ii/iii	AON/AQR **6**	01/02-03/04	3.2	
iii	BCB **118**	01 to 04-04/05/06	2.9	47m
iii	BDO **41**	01/02/03-07	2.8	
iii	BDR **129**	11/12/13-03/04/05	*c.*3.5	
iv	DAG **51**	Area 2 W09-S52/S53/S54	3.6–3.8★	★★ 47n
iv (Pt II?)	ABW **27**	Area 13	*c.*3.3	
iv (Pt II?)	ADD North **5**	Area 13	2.5	
iva	BHR **26**	02-22/23/24	2.6	
iva/ivb	BDG/BRT **16**	12/13/14-03/04/05	2.9	
ivc	AJG **16**	05-S01/S02/S03	2.6	
ivd	ATY **82**	22/23-03/04	3.1–3.3★	★★
v	BAC **263**	02/03-S01	*c.*3.5	
v/v	BAC/BEI **215**	02/03-S01	2.7	
Mamluk/ Mamluk/vii	ABC/ABD/ABA (UP 69) **1**	Area 13	2.8	
Mamluk/ Mamluk/vii	ABC/ABD/ABA (UP 167) **2**	Area 13	4.0	★★
vii	AAA (UP 37) **94**	11 to 20-S01 to S08	2.8	
vii	AAA (UP 37) **95**	02/03-S01	3.0	47o
vii	AAA (UP 117) **34**	07/08/09-S01/S02/S03	2.6–2.7★	
vii	AAA (UP 588) **395**	W01 to W04-20 to 24	2.5	47p
vii	AAA (UP 588) **397**	06/07/08-24 to 30	3.0	
vii	AAA **31**	Area 1	3.0	★★
vii	AAA **61**	Area 1	3.7	★★ 47q
vii	AAA (UP 998) **27**	Area 2	3.1	

★ Variable

★★ Shows string-cutting

MARL CLAY FABRICS, 336–56

Detailed identification of the marl and mixed clay jar forms is hampered by the small size of the sherds. Few are preserved below the base of the neck, or in the case of the bases very far up the body. The matter is further complicated by the continuation of many of the types into the MK; that MK vessels of other types are present at the Anubieion is proved by unequivocally MK forms in Marl C fabric. Some of the jars catalogued here may therefore be as late as the MK, though those in Marl A1 should not be (Nordström and Bourriau, 1993, 176).

336 Medium-sized jars with wide mouth, spindle body and small flat base (Rzeuska 2006, Form 15, Pl. 37)

The rim is not a perfect match for any of Rzeuska's Form 15 but these vary considerably in any case; it is closest to the largest (dia 8), [116], and to [118]. Three of Rzeuska's are in Nile clay and three (including [116/18]) in P.60, so a marl clay example is feasible.

1428 **336** Fig. 47r

Two overlapping grooves below the rim from string-tying. Cannot tell whether handmade or wheel assisted.

Marl A1. Fired fairly soft. White firing surfaces with red-brown tinge. Break red-brown all through. Fairly plentiful fine and medium well-sorted sand. Sparse fine veg to 0.2. Many tiny limestone flecks and sparse to 0.05. Uncoated. Not polished or burnished.

Phase	Context & No.	Grid ref	Dia rim (top)	Fig
iva	BAX **41**	06/07/08-03/04	*c*.9	47r

337 Jar with short neck and modelled rim (Rzeuska 2006, Form 17B, Pl. 39)

Although Rzeuska's [126] has a rim diameter of only 7, the form is similar. There is a marl jar type of the Fourth Dynasty, sometimes red slipped and with diameter usually 10–11 (Wodzińska 2007, Fig. 11.11 [AB7]); the illustrated example has a shorter neck and the rim is not undercut but on the whole this is the closer parallel. At the other end of the date range, there are marl jars of the same type from the FIP/early MK levels at Herakleopolis Magna (Bader 2009a, 24, Fig. 7d,f)

836 **337** Fig. 47s

The rim is folded over into a hook on the interior, then folded back to the exterior and undercut.

Marl C1 (E1a). Fired fairly hard. Surfaces concealed by slip. Break red-brown with thick grey core. Fairly plentiful fine well-sorted sand. Sparse fine veg to 0.2. Plentiful tiny limestone flecks and sparse to 0.1. Red slip on all surfaces. Traces of polish on exterior and top of rim.

Phase	Context & No.	Grid ref	Dia rim (top)	Fig
ii	BDS **4**	04-09	10	47s

338 Narrow rounded base of jar (Rzeuska 2006, Forms 17A/B, Pl. 39)

824 **338** Fig. 47t

Well-marked vertical scraping on exterior. Handmade, with finger impressions on interior, and the wall not the same thickness all round.

Marl A2. Fired fairly soft. Exterior white firing surface, interior red-brown. Break red-brown with grey core where thickest. Plentiful poorly sorted sand. Moderate qty fine and some coarse veg to 0.5. Many tiny limestone flecks and sparse to 0.1. Uncoated. Not polished or burnished.

Phase	Context & No.	Grid ref	Fig
All iva	AQV/AQW/AQX/AQY/AQZ **10**	11-13/14/15	47t

339–40 Jars with modelled rim and narrow mouth (Rzeuska 2006, Form 19, Pl. 41)

Rzeuska's series shows considerable variability. The Anubieion examples are a close match for some individual rim forms (**339** is especially close to Rzeuska's [131]), but bear only a general similarity to others. Rzeuska's fabrics are Marl C1 and P.60; there are no examples in Marl A1, but this fabric is unlikely to be post-OK.

On the other hand, a similar form (in white slipped fine Nile clay) at Abu Rawash (Marchand and Baud 1996, Fig. 7 [5]) is thought to be no later in date than the reign of Neferirkare.

2074 **339** Fig. 47u

The rim may have been wheel assisted.

Marl A1. Fired medium. Exterior pale orange-brown, interior red, probably firing surfaces. Break pale red-brown with very faint, diffuse darker core towards interior surface. Fairly plentiful fine and medium well-sorted sand. No visible veg. Plentiful tiny limestone flecks, none larger. Smoothed, but probably uncoated. All surfaces lightly polished, but may be from sand-blasting.

Phase	Context & No.	Grid ref	Dia rim (top)	Fig
vii	AAA (UP 588) **429**	W01/01-36/37/38	9	47u

2806 **340** Fig. 47v

Wheel assisted.

Marl A1. Fired medium. Surfaces orange-brown where slip lost. Break pale brown all through. Fairly plentiful fine well-sorted sand. Sparse veg to 0.2. Many tiny limestone flecks and sparse to 0.05. Thick orange-brown slip on all surfaces as far as preserved. All surfaces, including interior, polished as far as preserved.

Phase	Context & No.	Grid ref	Dia rim (top)	Fig
iii	BHW **91**	02-20/21	9	47v

341–42 Large globular jars (Rzeuska 2006, Forms 26–28, Pls 48–50)

Similar to several examples among Rzeuska's Forms 26–28, though these are all in Nile clay. **341** is close to [188] of Form 28, **342** fairly close to [178] of Form 26 and [185] of Form 28. The fabric probably precludes a later date.

763 **341** Fig. 47w

The sharp profile of the rim may indicate wheel assistance. The thin groove around below it appears to be from string-tying.

Marl A1. Fired fairly soft. Firing surfaces: exterior white, interior pale red-brown. Break pale red-brown all through. Fairly plentiful fine and medium sand with a few larger grains. Small qty fine veg to 0.2. Moderate qty tiny limestone flecks and pieces to 0.05. Smoothed but uncoated. Not polished or burnished.

Phase	Context & No.	Grid ref	Dia rim (top)	Fig
vi	AAU **5**	17/18-07/08/09	10	47w

924 **342** Fig. 48a

Marl A1. Fired fairly hard. Exterior surface greyish white firing surface, flaking; interior surface greyish white shading to red. Break red-brown all through. Plentiful fine well-sorted sand with a few large grains. No visible veg. Plentiful tiny limestone flecks but none larger. Uncoated. Not polished or burnished.

Phase	Context & No.	Grid ref	Max dia rim	Fig
ivc	BHI **11**	03/04-24	12	48a

343 Platter (or lid?) (Rzeuska 2006, nearest, Forms 39–55, Pls 58–64)

None of Rzeuska's range of forms has the clay strip present on the Anubieion example (which may have been no more than an attempt to improve the stability of a badly made vessel), and all are in Nile clay, so the parallels are by no means certain. On the other hand, Nile clay examples from the Greater Cairo Waste Water Project trenches are very similar (Hawass and Senussi 2008, 162 [A57], 181 [H37], 186 [H72]). The diameters of these are in range 26–37 and A57 is red washed inside. A series of very shallow platters/lids from Fourth Dynasty Dahshur (Faltings 1989, Abb. 10b), described as 'coming in all sizes and many rim forms' could well include **343**, though there is no applied clay strip on the two best matches illustrated (A47 with dia 28 and A49 with dia 33). A Fourth Dynasty date is therefore more likely than a later one. A similar form of similar size occurs as early as the Archaic Period (Köhler and Smythe 2004, Pl. 5 [5]).

846 **343** Fig. 48b

A strip of clay was applied to the (assumed) underside before firing; it stops just short of a break but the surface of the adjacent area has no firing surface and a second, slightly wider, piece may have become detached. The surviving strip is worn, so may be a form of base-ring.

Marl B (or coarse Marl A1?). Fired fairly hard. Cream-coloured firing surfaces where slip lost. Break pinkish brown all through, also where probable second clay piece lost. Plentiful very fine well-sorted sand. No visible veg. Sparse flat red and white (mineral?) fragments to 0.1. Traces of pink slip on top of both interior and exterior firing surfaces, best preserved on rim. Polish survives on top of rim.

Phase	Context & No.	Grid ref	Dia rim (top)	Fig
iv (Pt II?)	ADF North **55**	Area 13	20–30?	48b

344 Bent-sided plate (Rzeuska 2006, Form 96, Pl. 80), or straight-walled plate (Form 100, Pl. 82)

Two groups very numerous both at the Anubieion and in Rzeuska's material but normally in Nile clay, **344–45** being the only examples recorded in other clays at either site. Too little of the body survives to classify **344** more accurately.

1668A **344** Fig. 48c

Both surfaces grey, perhaps from use as a cooking pot.

Marl A1. Fired fairly soft. Surfaces brown where slip lost. Break brown with red zones and faint greenish grey core. Fairly plentiful fine well sorted sand. Sparse fine veg to 0.2. Many tiny limestone flecks but nothing larger. Red slip (mostly discoloured grey) on both surfaces. Both surfaces highly polished.

Phase	Context & No.	Grid ref	Max dia rim	Fig
iv (Pt II?)	ADF North **21**	Area 13	*c.*36	48c

345 Bowl with inner modelled rim (Rzeuska 2006, nearest, Form 127, Pl. 93)

Rzeuska's example is wheel assisted and in Nile B1 fabric, is smaller (dia 20), and has a less flattened interior to the rim; nevertheless, the resemblance is close. The form may be traced back to Naqada III (Köhler 1992, Fig. 4 [6]) via the late Second to early Third Dynasty (Raue 1999, Abb. 37 [4]).

878 **345** Fig. 48d

No wheel-ridges, and inclusions lie at various angles to the rim, so probably handmade.

Marl B(?). Fired fairly soft. Surfaces cream where uncoated or slip lost. Break pale brown with thin dark brown zones close to surfaces. Fairly plentiful fine sand with a few larger grains. Small qty fine veg to 0.2. Many tiny limestone flecks, and sparse to 0.1. Red slip on interior below rim roll, traces on rim roll itself, and small area on exterior close to top of rim; exterior not otherwise slipped but may have weathered off. Traces of polish or burnish on top of rim and on interior below roll.

Phase	Context & No.	Grid ref	Max dia rim	Fig
ivb/ivb–c/ivb–c	AJE/AUX/AVD **5**	12 to 16-S01	?(25–35)	48d

346 Bent-sided bowl (Rzeuska 2006, Form 164, Pl. 111)

Rzeuska's long series of bent-sided bowls is entirely in Nile clay, but includes several examples, like **346**, with very little modelling of the almost square-ended rim. The closest parallel is probably [569] of Form 164.

1692 **346** Fig. 48e

The slight groove just below the rim may have been for string-tying.

Marl A1. Fired fairly hard. Surfaces red-brown where slip lost. Break red-brown with faint, diffuse dark brown core. Fairly plentiful fine and medium sand with a few larger grains. Sparse fine veg to 0.3. Plentiful tiny limestone flecks and sparse to 0.1. Weathered, but traces of thick orange-brown slip on both surfaces. Highly polished where slip survives.

Phase	Context & No.	Grid ref	Dia rim (top)	Fig
vii	AAA (UP 23) **496**	07-07	*c.*26	48e

347 Bent-sided bowl (Rzeuska 2006, Form 166, Pls 112–15)

Although Rzeuska's long series of bent-sided bowls is entirely in Nile clay, several examples are similar in form to **347**. The closest is probably [585] of Form 166C but others are not very different. There are apparent predecessors in the Fourth Dynasty at Dahshur (Faltings 1989, Abb. 3d) in Nile clay, and Giza (Wodzińska 2007, Fig. 11.27 [CD23]) most in Nile clay but also one marl sherd. For the fabric, see also **352**.

1476 **347** Fig. 48f

The crisp outline suggests at least wheel-assistance.

Marl C (E1), early version with fine plant remains. Fired fairly hard. Surfaces concealed by slip except small area of exterior, where white firing surface visible where slip missed. Break red-brown with thick pale grey core. Fairly plentiful fine well-sorted sand. Fairly plentiful fine veg to 0.2. Plentiful tiny limestone flecks and sparse larger pieces to 0.1. Tiny black rock particles visible at ×25 magnification. Red-brown slip on all surfaces. All surfaces polished.

Phase	Context & No.	Grid ref	Max dia rim	Fig
iva	BED **23**	13/14-S02/S03	? (17–23)	48f

348–55 Carinated, so-called 'Meidum' bowls

For a discussion of this common bowl type, see Nile series **241–60**.

348 Thin-rimmed 'Meidum' bowl with angular shoulder (not present in Rzeuska 2006)

Apparently too late in date (or too distant geographically?) for Raue's Elephantine series (Raue 1999, Abb. 38 [1], Abb. 39 [1/2], Abb. 40 [1/2]) but the length of body above the carination exceeds anything in Rzeuska's corpus. A fairly close match, with similarly long, thin rim, is published by Faltings (1989, Abb. 8d), from the reign of Snefru at Dahshur. There are also examples in red slipped and polished Nile clay from Herakleopolis, dated to the late OK/early FIP (Bader 2009a, Fig. 9h–j); the upper bodies are long but more curved than **348**.

For a similar form, see **365** in the mixed clay series.

1448A **348** Fig. 48g

Marl A1. Fired medium. Surfaces concealed by slip. Break red all through. Plentiful very fine sand with a few larger grains. No visible veg. Plentiful tiny limestone flecks and sparse to 0.05. Thick red slip on all surfaces. Both surfaces polished.

Phase	Context & No.	Grid ref	Dia rim (top)	Neck height	Fig
ii	AJY **163**	18 to 20-S04/S05	? (20+)	1.7	48g

349 Thin-rimmed 'Meidum' bowl (not present in Rzeuska 2006)

The thin, upright rim relates better to a form published by Faltings (1989, Abb. 6b [212]), from the reign of Snefru, than to anything in Rzeuska's material.

2120 **349** Fig. 48h

Marl A1(?). Fired fairly hard. Surfaces concealed by slip. Break red-brown with grey core, the core unusual in this fabric. Fairly plentiful fine well-sorted sand. No visible veg. No visible limestone without magnification, but many very tiny flecks at ×20. Some tiny black rock particles. Thick pale red-brown slip on both surfaces. Both surfaces highly polished.

Phase	Context & No.	Grid ref	Dia rim (top)	Fig
o	AQG **301**	18/19/20-S04/S05	*c*.17	48h

350 'Meidum' bowl with maximum diameter at the body and thin rim (Rzeuska 2006, nearest, Form 179, Pl. 126)

The rim is a little thinner than on bowls in Rzeuska's series.

1448B **350** Not illustrated

Marl A1. Fired fairly soft. Surfaces pale pinkish brown where slip lost. Break pale pinkish brown all through. Plentiful very fine sand with a few larger grains. No visible veg. Plentiful tiny limestone flecks and sparse to 0.05. One red mineral(?) inclusion 0.05. Thin pink slip on both surfaces. Both surfaces polished.

Phase	Context & No.	Grid ref	Dia rim (top)	Neck height	Fig
ivd	BCG **11**	17/18-07	25–30	1.1	Similar to 49j*

* See **365** in the mixed clay series

351 'Meidum' bowls with maximum diameter at the body and thicker rim (Rzeuska 2006, nearest, Form 182, Pls 127/28)

The thicker rim is the commoner form at the Anubieion in both the Nile clay and the marl/mixed clay versions, as it is in Rzeuska's series.

1628A **351** Not illustrated

Marl A1. Fired fairly soft. Surfaces concealed by slip. Break pale red-brown with thick red-brown core. Fairly plentiful fine sand with a few larger grains. No visible veg. Many tiny limestone flecks, and sparse to 0.05. Red-brown slip on all surfaces. All surfaces polished.

Phase	Context & No.	Grid ref	Dia rim (top)	*	Fig
ivd	ATY **143**	24/25-05/06	22	0.4	As 33f**

* Amount by which body diameter exceeds rim diameter

** See **244** in the Nile clay series

352 'Meidum' bowl with mouth and body of equal diameter (not present in Rzeuska 2006)

Although not classified by Rzeuska, these are within her range of forms and the range at the Anubieion. For the fabric, see also **347**.

1642C **352** Not illustrated

Marl C (E1), early version with fine plant remains. Fired medium, misfired. Surfaces brown where slip lost. Break dark brown all through. Fairly plentiful fine and medium sand with a few larger grains. Small qty fine veg to 0.3. Many tiny limestone flecks, and sparse to 0.05. Red brown slip on both surfaces, but interior dark brown below upper part of rim, and crazed. Both surfaces polished.

Phase	Context & No.	Grid ref	Dia rim (top)	Fig
vii	AAA (UP 588) **29**	01/02-21 to 24	*c.*30	As 34h*

* See **248** in the Nile clay series

353 'Meidum' bowls with maximum diameter at the mouth (Rzeuska 2006, Forms 184–87, 189, Pls 130–32, 134–35)

2136 **353** Fig. 48i

Extensively stained by oil or a similar substance, probably while the vessel was intact.

Marl A1. Fired medium. Surfaces concealed by slip. Break orange-brown all through. Moderate qty fine well-sorted sand. Many very tiny limestone flecks, and sparse to 0.05. A few dark rock particles visible at x40. Red-brown slip on both surfaces. Both surfaces highly polished.

Phase	Context & No.	Grid ref	Dia rim (top)	*	Fig
vii	AAA (UP 588) **493**	01/02-25/26	*c.*30–35(?)	0.8	48i

* Amount by which rim diameter exceeds body diameter

354–55 Thin-rimmed 'Meidum' bowls, insufficiently preserved to show stance (not present in Rzeuska 2006)

The thin rim is characteristic of an earlier form than most Anubieion 'Meidum' bowls. There are similar examples from Fourth Dynasty Dahshur (dia 18) (Faltings 1989, Abb. 8d) and Giza (dias 28/24) (Wodzińska 2007, Figs. 11.19/20 [CD6A/B]).

1452 **354** Fig. 48j

Marl B(?). Fired fairly soft. Surfaces grey where slip lost. Break grey-brown all through. Fairly plentiful fine sand with a few larger grains. Sparse fine veg to 0.2. Fewer limestone flecks than usual in a marl fabric, and sparse to 0.05. Orange slip on both surfaces. Both surfaces polished.

Phase	Context & No.	Grid ref	Dia rim (top)	Fig
ivc?	BQG **14**	Area 2	15–20(?)	48j

1524A **355** Fig. 48k

Marl A4. Fired fairly soft. Surfaces pale brown where slip lost. Break pale brown all through. Fairly plentiful fine and medium well-sorted sand. Moderate qty fine veg to 0.2. Plentiful tiny limestone flecks and a few pieces to 0.1. Brownish red slip on both surfaces. Both surfaces polished.

Phase	Context & No.	Grid ref	Dia rim (top)	Fig
ivb	CGZ West **7**	02 to 07-33 to 36	?	48k

356 Small bowl (not present in Rzeuska 2006)

A foundation deposit at Tell Ibrahim Awad (van den Brink 1992, Fig. 4) contained 21 small bowls, diameter range (top) about 7–11, many of which are very similar to **356**; the fabric is not described. The date, on the authority of Dorothea Arnold, is 'early FIP with some reminiscences of Late OK' (*ibid.*, 47). Comparative material cited includes vessels from Sedment, where the form closest to **356** appears to be 23g (Petrie and Brunton 1924a, Fig. XXIX).

1426 **356** Fig. 49a

Unlikely to be a lid because interior smoothed.

Marl A1. Fired fairly soft. Firing surfaces, exterior pale pinkish white, interior pinkish brown. Break red-brown all through. Fairly plentiful fine sand with a few larger grains. Small qty fine veg to 0.2. Plentiful tiny limestone flecks and sparse to 0.05. Uncoated. Interior smoothed, and exterior above carination. Apparent polish on both surfaces, though possibly sand-blasting.

Phase	Context & No.	Grid ref	Dia rim (top)	Fig
ii/ii/ivc	AJX/AJY/BRS **64**	21/22/23-S02/S03	13	49a

MIXED CLAY FABRIC, 357–71

357 Narrow base of jar (Rzeuska 2006, Forms 14/15, Pls 36/37)

Rzeuska's Forms 14 and 15 are from jars with wide mouth and spindle body; see Nile clay base **36** and marl rim **336**. The base of Form 14 is lightly carinated, of Form 15 flat; **357** is somewhere between the two. All three examples of Form 14 and three of the six of Form 15 are in P.60.

820 **357** Fig. 49b

Faint vertical scraping facets on the exterior, pushing the clay down into a small roll at the bottom. Spiral ribbing on the interior proves wheel assistance.

Mixed Clay P.60/Nile D. Fired medium. Exterior pale red-brown firing surface with small area greenish white; interior brown. Break outer half red-brown, inner half greenish to brownish white. Fairly plentiful poorly sorted sand. Sparse fine veg to 0.2. Only sparse limestone to 0.05, visible at ×10. Sparse tiny red mineral(?) particles, and one piece 0.2 × 0.3 which is probably grog. Uncoated. Possible traces of polish or burnish on exterior only.

Phase	Context & No.	Grid ref	Dia base	Fig
vii	AAA (UP 38) **146**	11 to 20-01 to 10	2.1–2.2 variable	49b

358–59 Jars with modelled rim and narrow mouth (Rzeuska 2006, nearest, Form 19, Pl. 41)

Rzeuska's series, in Marl C1 and P.60, shows considerable variability of form, and a case could be made for similarity between **358** and [137], but Rzeuska's have less rounded rims. There is a better match for **358** in a Fourth Dynasty jar from Dahshur (Faltings 1989, Abb. 6d [50]) and for **359** in one of about the same time from Giza (Kromer 1978, Taf. 22 [2]), though the 'brown clay' of the latter may indicate a Nile. A similar form to **358** (in white slipped fine Nile clay) at Abu Rawash (Marchand and Baud 1996, Fig. 7 [5]) is thought to be no later in date than the reign of Neferirkare of the Fifth Dynasty. A pre-Teti date seems indicated.

625 **358** Fig. 49c

Angular folded rim.

Mixed Clay P.60/(Nile D?). Fired fairly soft. Surfaces pale brown. Break brown all through. Plentiful poorly sorted sand. Small qty fine veg to 0.2. Many tiny limestone flecks and sparse to 0.1. Possible trace of red slip on exterior, but otherwise too weathered to show slip, or polish or burnish.

Phase	Context & No.	Grid ref	Dia rim (top)	Fig
iv (Pt II?)/ ?	AYQ/AYR **34**	Area 13	10	49c

765 **359** Fig. 49d

Rolled rim. The irregularity of its lower edge could mean hand manufacture, though it may have been caused by a string impression subsequently weathered.

Mixed Clay P.60/Nile D. Fired fairly hard. Surfaces pale brown. Break pale brown with pale grey core. Small qty poorly sorted sand. A few pieces fine veg to 0.2. Sparse limestone to 0.05. A few very small dark and red-brown mineral inclusions. Smoothed, possibly self-slipped on exterior and just over rim, but no coloured slip. Surfaces appear polished, but probably from sand-blasting.

Phase	Context & No.	Grid ref	Dia rim (top)	Fig
vi	AAH **4**	06-08	11	49d

360–61 Jars with protruding rim and very short, sharply curved neck (Rzeuska 2006, nearest, Forms 25–27, Pls 48–50)

Two similar rims in the same fabric, with a short neck in a sweeping curve ending in an exaggeratedly protruding rim. There is some resemblance to examples of Rzeuska's Forms 25–27, but none of those is as idiosyncratic and all are in Nile clay. A better match (max dia 9) is one from the Fifth Dynasty, (Kaiser 1969, IV, Typ 38), red slipped on interior and inner rim and 'very well polished'. See also Hawass and Senussi (2008, 109 [20]) referred to under **362**. As often, the form continues little changed into the early MK (two examples, dias 10 and 8), still slipped and polished on both surfaces, just with a less thickened rim (Czerny 1999, 159 [Nf 329]. Czerny's are in Nile clay and probably Kaiser's also.

659 **360** Fig. 49e

The crisp finish probably implies it was wheel assisted, but there are no clear ridges.

Mixed Clay P.60/(Nile D?). Fired fairly hard. Surfaces pale red-brown where uncoated or slip lost. Break pale red-brown with thick pale grey core off-centre towards interior. Plentiful fine well-sorted sand. Sparse fine veg to 0.2. Plentiful tiny limestone flecks, and sparse to 0.05. Thick red-brown slip on exterior, extending over the rim down to at least the point of minimum diameter, perhaps lower. Polished where slipped.

Phase	Context & No.	Grid ref	Max dia rim	Fig
ivc	BQU **36**	Area 2	11.5	49e

2212 **361** Fig. 49f

The rim, at least, appears to be wheel assisted.

Mixed Clay P.60/Nile D. Fired medium. Surfaces pale brown where uncoated or slip lost. Break pale red-brown with grey core. Fairly plentiful fine well-sorted sand. Small qty fine veg to 0.3. Moderate qty tiny limestone flecks and sparse to 0.1. Thick orange-red slip on exterior, over rim and down interior to a clear but wavy line at the minimum diameter, then some smudging. Highly polished where slipped.

Phase	Context & No.	Grid ref	Max dia rim	Fig
vii	AAA (UP 118) **7**	24-03 to09	11	49f

362 Jar with protruding rim and very short, sharply curved neck (Rzeuska 2006, nearest, Forms 25–27, Pls 48–50)

Similar to **360–61**. A comparable example of the Fifth or early Sixth Dynasty derives from a Giza tomb (Hawass and Senussi 2008, 109 [20]). Though the curvature of the rim interior is less smooth and the ware is red slipped and burnished Nile B2, it may be sufficiently close in form to date the present piece.

342 **362** Fig. 49g

At first mistakenly thought to be of a later period, this sherd was not fully catalogued. There are thus no available details of the ware, except that it clearly did not employ a Nile clay.

Marl clay, mixed clay or import?

Phase	Context & No.	Grid ref	Max dia rim	Fig
vii	CAA North **5**	Area 26	12.5	49g

363 Bowl with spout rim (Rzeuska 2006, Forms 170–75, Pls 117–24)

The 'spouts' of this series are not fully enclosed; rather, a pouring lip has been created between two sections of rim pushed inwards and upwards. Although the unusual shape of this rim sherd places it in the spout-rim series, too little survives for any reconstruction of the form. The fabric is unique for the form, both at the Anubieion and in Rzeuska's material.

For Nile clay examples, see **237–40**.

1478 **363** Fig. 49h

Rim sherd with a twist which was almost certainly intentional. Cannot tell whether or not wheel assisted, though the twist must have been imparted by hand. It is impossible to assess the diameter.

Mixed Clay P.60/(Nile D?). Fired fairly soft to medium. White firing surfaces. Break pinkish brown all through. Plentiful poorly sorted sand. Sparse fine veg to 0.2. The tiny limestone flecks usual in marl clay are not visible, but there is sparse limestone to 0.1 and one piece 0.2. Uncoated. Not polished or burnished.

Phase	Context & No.	Grid ref	Dia rim (top)	Fig
iva	AJL **1**	05 to 08-03/04	Less than 15?	49h

364–70 Carinated, so-called 'Meidum' bowls

For a discussion of this common bowl type, see Nile series **241–60**.

364 'Meidum' bowl with angular shoulder (not present in Rzeuska 2006)

Bowls with angular shoulders were current prior to the construction of the Teti pyramid. The best match in Raue's Elephantine series is to an example in Marl A4 fabric (Raue 1999, Abb. 38 [1]) dated to the first half of the Third Dynasty. In the series from el-Kab (Op de Beeck 2004, Fig. 3), the best match is [24] in Marl A1 fabric from the Third to Fourth Dynasty necropolis, while others, some from specifically Third or Fourth Dynasty mastabas, are also very similar.

For similar bowls in Nile A and B1 fabrics, see **241–43**.

1438 **364** Fig. 49i

Appears to be handmade with wheel-assisted rim. Traces of burning on both surfaces, probably from use as a cooking pot.

Mixed Clay P.60/Nile D. Fired fairly soft. Surfaces pinkish brown where slip lost. Break pinkish brown with diffuse greenish core. Fairly plentiful poorly sorted sand. No visible veg. Plentiful tiny limestone flecks. Sparse black rock particles. Sparse soft red-brown ochre particles. Red slip on both surfaces. Both surfaces polished.

For similar forms, see 1612/10/14 in the Nile clay series.

Phase	Context & No.	Grid ref	Dia rim (top)	Fig
iv (Pt II?)	ARU=ARZ (UP 204) **33**	Area 13	15	49i

<u>365–66</u> Thin-rimmed 'Meidum' bowls with maximum diameter at the body (not present in Rzeuska 2006).

The thin rim is characteristic of an earlier form than most Anubieion 'Meidum' bowls. There are similar examples from Fourth Dynasty Dahshur (dia 18) (Faltings 1989, Abb. 8d) and Giza (dias 28/24) (Wodzińska 2007, Figs 11.19/20 [CD6A/B]).

1450 <u>365</u> Fig. 49j

The short, almost vertical necks are of different heights. BQA to BQJ **27** is rather thicker walled than the other two but of the same form.

<u>Mixed Clay Fine P.60/(Nile D?).</u> AFA **2** fired medium, others fairly soft. AFA **2** surfaces concealed by slip, BQA to BQJ **27** pinkish grey and BEP **95** pink, each where slip lost. Break pale pink to pink all through. Plentiful fine well-sorted sand. No visible veg. Plentiful tiny limestone flecks and sparse to 0.05, and BQA to BQJ **27** one piece 0.1. On both surfaces, BQA to BQJ **27** traces of pink slip, others thick slip, AFA **2** dark brown with pinkish brown areas, BEP **95** pale red-brown. Both surfaces polished (BQA to BQJ **27** traces only).

For a similar form to AFA **2** see **<u>350</u>** in the marl clay series

Phase	Context & No.	Grid ref	Dia rim (top)	Neck height	Fig
ivb	AFA **2**	20-S01/S02	*c.*17–18	1.0	49j
Various ivc/ivd/v	BQA to BQJ **27**	Area 2	*c.*25?	2.0	Similar to 48g*
?	BEP **95**	20-01/S01	?	*c.*2.0	Similar to 48g*

* See **<u>348</u>** in the marl clay series

1524B <u>366</u> Fig. 49k

Rim slightly thicker and more curved.

<u>Mixed Clay P.60/(Nile D?).</u> Fired medium. Surfaces red-brown where slip lost. Break red-brown with faint greenish core. Fairly plentiful fine and medium sand with a few larger grains. Small qty fine veg to 0.2. Plentiful tiny limestone flecks and a few pieces to 0.1. Red-brown slip on all surfaces. Both surfaces polished.

Phase	Context & No.	Grid ref	Dia rim (top)	Fig
iva/ivb	BHR/BTG **101**	02-20/21	*c.*20	49k

<u>367–68</u> 'Meidum' bowls with maximum diameter at the body and thicker rim (Rzeuska 2006, Forms 179–82, 188, 190–91, Pls 126–28, 133, 135–36)

Thicker rim than **<u>365–66</u>**. This is the commoner form in both the marl clay/mixed clay and the Nile clay versions, as well as in Rzeuska's material. Rzeuska's Forms 188, 190 and 191 are larger diameter and thick-walled versions, with diameter 29 and above. Only a few of the Anubieion series are as large as this. Rzeuska's Forms 179–82 attempt to classify rim shapes, but there is much variability and the distinctions are rather fine.

1638A **367** Not illustrated

Mixed Clay P.60/(Nile D?). Fired fairly soft. Surfaces pale brown where slip lost. Break pale brown with faint thick pink core. Fairly plentiful fine well sorted sand. Moderate qty fine veg to 0.2. Many tiny limestone flecks, also sparse to 0.05 and one piece 0.2 × 0.1. Orange-brown slip on both surfaces. Both surfaces polished.

Phase	Context & No.	Grid ref	Dia rim (top)	*	Fig
ivd	ASD **22**	19/20-07/08/09	?	0.4	As 34d**

* Amount by which body diameter exceeds rim diameter

** See **245** in the Nile clay series

1628B **368** Fig. 491

Mixed Clay P.60/(Nile D?). Fired fairly soft to medium. Surfaces concealed by slip. Break, CGQ **58** red-brown with thick pink core, UP 445 **68** and **127** and A-- **154** red-brown with dark brown core, AAN **1** dark brown with grey core, others red-brown with pink zones and grey core. A-- **154** fairly plentiful fine well-sorted sand, others fine and medium, some with a few larger grains. Sparse fine veg to 0.2/0.3. Sparse limestone, CGQ **58** and BFB **31** to 0.05, others to 0.1. Red-brown slip on both surfaces; UP 445 **68** and BFB **31** some blackening, perhaps in use, AAN **1** interior black, from stacking in the kiln. Both surfaces polished.

Phase	Context & No.	Grid ref	Dia rim (top)	*	Fig
ivc	CGQ **58**	02 to 05-33 to 37	*c.*16	0.4	491
v	AAN **1**	08-04	?	0.6	As 33b**
vi	AAH **12**	09-07	22	0.6	As 33d**
vii	AAA (UP 445) **50**	Area 2	22	1.4	As 33d**
vii	AAA (UP 445) **68**	Area 2	*c.*27	1.0	As 33f**
vii	AAA (UP 445) **127**	Area 2	*c.*23	0.4	As 33e**
vii?	BFB **31**	Area 1	*c.*25	0.6	As 33d**
?	A-- **154**†	--01/02†	26–30	0.2	As 33f**

* Amount by which body diameter exceeds rim diameter

** See **244** in the Nile clay series

† Context and grid reference partly lost from sherd

369 'Meidum' bowl with maximum diameter at the mouth (Rzeuska 2006, Form 184, Pls 130/31)

1618A **369** Not illustrated

Mixed Clay P.60/(Nile D?). Fired fairly soft. Surfaces concealed by slip. Break red-brown all through. Fairly plentiful fine and some medium well-sorted sand. Sparse fine veg to 0.2. Many tiny limestone flecks, and sparse to 0.1. Red-brown slip on both surfaces, shading to orange-brown on interior away from rim. Both surfaces polished.

Phase	Context & No.	Grid ref	Max dia rim	*	Fig
vii	AAA (UP 38) **157**	11 to 20-01 to 10	21	0.8	As 35c**

* Amount by which rim diameter exceeds body diameter

** See **250** in the Nile clay series

370 'Meidum' bowls with mouth and body of equal diameter (not present in Rzeuska 2006)

Although not classified by Rzeuska, this is within her range of forms and the range at the Anubieion. The best match is to Rzeuska's [685] of Form 190.

1642B **370** Not illustrated

Mixed Clay P.60/(Nile D?). Fired medium. Surfaces concealed by slip. Break red-brown all through. Fairly plentiful fine and medium sand with a few larger grains. Small qty fine veg to 0.3. Many tiny limestone flecks, and sparse to 0.05. Red-brown slip on both surfaces. Both surfaces polished.

Phase	Context & No.	Grid ref	Dia rim (top)	Fig
vii	AAA Test trench **4**	Area 2	*c*.24	As 34h★

★ See **248** in the Nile clay series

371 Miniature Plates (Rzeuska 2006, Forms 231/32, Pls 164–68)

A mixed clay version of Nile clay **334**, where further details are to be found. Like the Nile clay examples, they show evidence of string-cutting, so were thrown from the top of a clay lump on some sort of wheel; the string-cutting, unlike the shaping, is frequently careless, leaving a downward protrusion. The distribution follows the unusual pattern of the Nile vessels (see **334**), with very few in Area 5 and many in surface and late contexts from the limited excavations in Areas 1, 2 and 12–14. It may indicate a specific use of those areas in the OK/FIP.

2808A **371** Fig. 49m–p

Mixed Clay P.60/(Nile D?). Fired fairly soft to medium. Surfaces cream or off-white, often with pink or brown areas, to red-brown. Break (where visible), AAB Upper **10** red with a pink core (probably indicating a larger than normal Nile component), AAA **51** cream with pink zones and green core, others pale brown or red-brown all through. Moderate qty to fairly plentiful poorly sorted sand, except BCB **117** fine and medium well-sorted. Small to moderate qty fine veg to 0.2/0.4. Some or many tiny limestone flecks, and in some examples also sparse to 0.1. In some examples sparse tiny red (mineral?) inclusions. Uncoated. Not polished or burnished.

For a similar form to AAA (UP 445) **11** see **334** in the Nile clay series

Phase	Context & No.	Grid ref	Dia base	Max dia rim	Height	Fig & notes
iii	BCB **117**	01 to 04-04 to 06	4.5	5.8–5.9★	0.9–1.1★	49m
iii/iva/?	BPD/BHR//BPV **19**	03/04-22/23	3.4–3.5★	4.4–4.7★	1.4–1.5★	49n
iv	DAY **15**	Area 2 W10-S63	*c*.3.0	*c*.5.0	1.5	As 47a★★
iv (Pt II?) ×2	ARP=ARS/AYY **2**	Area 13	3.4–3.7★	4.6–4.9★	1.4–1.7★	As 47j††
iva	BML **30**	06-13/14	*c*.3.0	*c*.5.0	1.5	As 49p
M'lk/ M'lk/vii	ABC/ABD/ABA (UP 129) **2**	Area 13	3.5	6.0	1.7–1.8★	49o
vi–vii	AAB Upper **10**	28 to34-S02/S03/ S04	3.3	*c*.5.5	1.9	†
vii	AAA **51**	Area 1	3.3	*c*.6.0	1.5	As 49p
vii	AAA **62**	Area 1	*c*.4.0	*c*.6.0	1.5	As 49p
vii	AAA (UP 445) **11**	Area 2	2.6–2.7★	4.7	1.1	49p

Phase	Context & No.	Grid ref	Dia base	Max dia rim	Height	Fig & notes
vii	AAA (UP 445) **53**	Area 2	2.5	4.4	0.9	As 49p
vii	AAA (UP 445) **70**	Area 2	2.9	4.8	1.0	As 49p
vii	AAA (UP 445) **72**	Area 2	2.7	5.1	1.3	As 49p
vii	AAA (UP 445) **75**	Area 2	3.8	4.8	1.1–1.5*	As 49p
vii	AAA (UP 445) **94**	Area 2	3.2	4.3	1.0–1.1*	As 49p
vii	AAA Upper **8**	Area 2	2.7–2.8*	4.5	0.9	As 49p

* Variable

** Form as 47a. See **334** in the Nile clay series

† Form between 47a and 47i. See **334** in the Nile clay series

†† Form as 47j. See **334** in the Nile clay series

CHAPTER 9

The Pottery of the Middle Kingdom

As explained elsewhere (Chapter 3, page 13), activity in the area later used for the Anubieion is likely to have continued uninterrupted from the Old Kingdom, through the First Intermediate Period and into the Middle Kingdom. Middle Kingdom burials are known in the area (Giddy 1992, 2 and Pl. 2; Silverman 2009), though in some cases their exact dates are still a matter of debate. Most of the ceramics evolved gradually, and any division between the First Intermediate Period and the Middle Kingdom is bound to be artificial. Those in the present volume confirm that the Anubieion sequence then continues through the Twelfth Dynasty to at least the second half of the Thirteenth, and quite probably to the end and on into the Second Intermediate Period.

Two developments in the wares help to elucidate the sequence. One is an increased popularity of the marl clay fabric E1 (Marl C), the other a great reduction in the number of polished slips so popular in the Old Kingdom. Marl C does occur earlier: Bettina Bader (Bader 2001, 40–41) refers to occurrences in the Fourth Dynasty, and it may have been current at the Anubieion (this volume, **11**) and at Buto (author's personal observation) as early as the Archaic Period, but it is in the Middle Kingdom that it becomes really popular and used above all for medium and large jars, though also for other vessel forms. Bader's valuable volume on its development and chronology is a testament to its importance at this time.

The use or non-use of the wheel is a more complicated question in the Middle Kingdom than previously. Small vessels were frequently thrown using centrifugal force but larger ones continued to be made by hand, though the rims might be wheel assisted. The practice of inverting vessels on the wheel to form the base at a second throwing was not yet in common use and bases were still usually scraped down to the desired shape.

There is an extensive literature on the ceramics of the Middle Kingdom, as well as several as-yet unpublished corpora. It is impracticable and unnecessary to collect all possible parallels, though a selection is included. In particular, reference is made wherever appropriate to the large and well-published corpus from Tell el-Dab'a, and to the series from the Egypt Exploration Society's excavations at Memphis (Kom Rabia) (Bader 2009b; Bourriau and Gallorini in preparation), because of the obvious connection with the Saqqara necropolis. It must be borne in mind that the Memphis excavations did not continue below the Thirteenth Dynasty levels, though residual sherds may be present from earlier periods not excavated. Unpublished corpora from Dahshur and Lisht North are referred to whenever well-published material is sparse, by kind permission of our colleagues Dorothea Arnold and Susan Allen. Older publications are not often mentioned, in spite of the great importance of the sites concerned, because most of the drawings are too simplified to provide reliable parallels.

Although Nile and marl clay fabrics have been kept as separate groups, within each group, and after much deliberation, the arrangement has been made according to the forms, rather than the fabrics. To do otherwise would have involved splitting up (among others) the beer bottles, hemispherical bowls, stands and ringstands which together constitute a large part of the catalogue. The arrangement is thus consistent with that of the Archaic Period and Old Kingdom, itself largely based upon correspondences with Rzeuska's volume (Rzeuska 2006), but different from that of the New Kingdom, which follows the arrangement adopted at Memphis (Bourriau 2010; Bourriau and Gallorini in preparation).

NILE CLAY FABRICS, 372–452

The individual fabrics are not separated. Present (minor variations excluded): D1 (Nile B1) 13 entries; D3 (Nile C) 11 entries; D4 (Nile B2) 53 entries; D7 (Nile D) 4 entries.

372 Large diameter plate

Too little survives for secure identification, but nothing so shallow is found in Rzeuska's corpus (2006), and the polished slip, frequent in the OK but less so later on, suggests a date no later than the early MK. A reasonable match from this period is one (dia 29) of a multitude from Tell el-Dab'a (Czerny 1999, 140 [Nf 58]); they come in a variety of Nile fabrics, mostly red slipped but only a minority polished/burnished. At Memphis (Kom Rabia) the form occurs in the earliest levels excavated, of the mid Thirteenth Dynasty, and continues into at least the later part of that Dynasty (Bourriau and Gallorini in preparation); some have red slip but the only polish/burnish is on one rim.

2919 **372** Fig. 50a

D4 (Nile B2). Fired medium. Surfaces concealed by slip. Break red-brown with greyish purple core. Fairly plentiful fine sand with a few larger grains. Fairly plentiful fine veg to 0.3. Sparse limestone to 0.05. Red-brown slip on both surfaces. Both surfaces polished.

Phase	Context & No.	Grid ref	Max dia rim	Fig
iii	BDP (UP 647) **205**	01 to 05-07	25–35(?)	50a

373–74 Small diameter bowls with thin, straight walls

Although just small enough to be included in the hemispherical bowl series, these bowls are disqualified by their flat, outward-sloping walls. There are many similar forms from the early MK at Tell el-Dab'a, with multiple examples within the round-based series (Czerny 1999, 65–67 and 136–39 [Nf 1–44]). The fabric of the series is Nile B1/B2 (undivided), almost all are red slipped and some are unpolished; a few are uncoated.

The form of the rim does not suit that of the early MK carinated bowl series (*ibid.*, 142–44 [Nf 88–129]), nor is the combination of rim form, stance and small diameter replicated in the later levels at Tell el-Dab'a (Fuscaldo 2000; Aston D.A. 2004b). However, there are good parallels in mid to late Thirteenth Dynasty contexts at Memphis (Kom Rabia) (Bourriau and Gallorini in preparation: [2a1.1/2] in Nile B1 fabric and [22a2.10] in Nile B2), which can be uncoated or red slipped, the only polish/burnish being on one rim of 2a1.1.

1738 **373** Fig. 50b

D4 (Nile B2). Fired medium. Surfaces pale brown. Break pale brown with red zones and grey core. Fairly plentiful fine and medium sand with a few larger grains. Fairly plentiful fine veg to 0.6. Sparse limestone to 0.05. Both surfaces smoothed but not slipped. Not polished or burnished.

Phase	Context & No.	Grid ref	Dia rim (top)	Fig
iv (Pt II?)/iv (Pt II?)	AXX/AXY **22**	Area 13	14	50b

2732 **374** Fig. 50c–d

D4 (Nile B2). ADU **35** fired fairly soft, ADS/ARP **9** medium. Surfaces concealed by slip. Break ADU **35** brown with red core, ADS/ARP **9** orange-brown all through. Fairly plentiful fine and medium sand with some larger grains. ADU **35** moderate qty fine veg to 0.2, ADS/ARP **9** none visible. Sparse limestone to 0.1. Red slip on both surfaces. Not polished or burnished.

Phase	Context & No.	Grid ref	Dia rim (top)	Fig
o	ADU (UP 122) NE **35**	Area 13	*c.*12–15	50c
iv (Pt II?)/iv (Pt II?)	ADS/ARP=ARS **9**	Area 13	14	50d

375 Medium diameter bowl with thin, curved wall

Too large for a hemispherical bowl. There are many similar forms from the early MK at Tell el-Dab'a, with multiple examples within the round-based series (Czerny 1999, 136–39 [Nf 1–44]). Close matches are Nf 6/15–17/22/24, all in diameter range 19–22 cm. The fabric of the series is Nile B1/B2 (undivided), almost all are red slipped and most are polished. The self-slipped and polished version seems to be absent; nevertheless, a similar date for **375** is implied.

2726 **375** Fig. 50e

Some burning on rim, but probably after the vessel was broken.

D1 (Nile B1). Fired fairly soft. Surfaces brown. Break brown with very faint red core. Fairly plentiful fine well-sorted sand, with a few larger grains. Small qty fine veg to 0.2. Sparse limestone to 0.05. Both surfaces perhaps self-slipped, but no coloured slip. High polish on interior; traces of polish on exterior, where probably only ever perfunctory.

Phase	Context & No.	Grid ref	Dia rim (top)	Fig
o/ii	AQG/AJY **16**	21/22-S04/S05/S06	*c.*19	50e

376 Bowl with thin, outcurved wall

The distinctive rim profile, outcurved and with the highest point on the inside edge, can be found on small uncoated flat-based bowls in Nile B2 from Thirteenth Dynasty Memphis (Bader 2009b, Typ 22c, 262 and Abb. 167 [6190]; Typ 25a, 269–70 and Abb. 169 [3644]). The diameters are 10.8 and 13 and the walls rather thicker than the wall of **376**. That this profile can also occur in a larger (dia 22) version, and in combination with a thinner wall, is demonstrated by another bowl from the same excavations (*ibid.*, Typ 23c, 265 and Abb. 167 [4328]).

2702 **376** Fig. 50f

Marks on the exterior are probably from string-trying before firing.

D4 (Nile B2). Fired medium. Surfaces red. Break orange-brown with red core. Plentiful fine and medium sand with a few larger grains. Small qty fine and coarse veg to 0.3. Sparse limestone to 0.1. Probably self-slipped only, all surfaces. Not polished or burnished.

Phase	Context & No.	Grid ref	Max dia rim	Fig
ii	BET **88**	12/13-01/02	*c.*17	50f

377 Bowl with incurved rim

This exact form does not feature in the major Tell el-Dab'a series, though several fairly similar examples appear among the Twelfth Dynasty material (Czerny 1999, 65–67, 136–37). [Nf 6, 7, 8, 11 and 12] in Nile B1/B2 fabric (not divided) are all similar, with a diameter range of 16.5–19 cm, and although almost all are red slipped and most are polished, a few are neither, as also the illustrated [Nf 5] (diameter 16.5), which differs only slightly. Some among a wide range of such bowls at Memphis (Kom Rabia) all in Nile B2, are similar (Bourriau and

Gallorini in preparation: [22b1.7] and [22a2.13]); the former can occur uncoated, though the latter was found only red slipped, and they are dated to the late Thirteenth Dynasty or the early SIP. There are also similar Nile B2 bowls, some uncoated, from the late Hyksos period at Tell el-Dab'a (Fuscaldo 2000, 53–56, [36–47]), so the type is long-lived. Wet-smoothing in this manner is seen also on bowls **379/81**, **401** and offering stand **432**.

2066 **377** Fig. 50g

The uneven surfaces and angled inclusions may mean hand manufacture, the rim perhaps wheel assisted.

D4 (Nile B2). Fired medium. Surfaces brown. Break pale brown with thin red zones and mauve core. Fairly plentiful fine and medium sand with a few larger grains. Fairly plentiful fine and coarse veg to 0.6 and one piece 1.5. Sparse limestone to 0.05 and one piece 0.3. Probably wet-smoothed only, but with application of a copious supply of water! Both surfaces apparently lightly polished, but perhaps sand-blasting.

Phase	Context & No.	Grid ref	Dia rim (top)	Fig
vii	AAA (UP 588) **326**	05/06-25/26/27	16	50g

378 Small bowl with trimmed rim

For this form of rim, it is unnecessary to look beyond the Memphis (Kom Rabia) excavations. It is found on little dishes/plates in Nile B2, some of which have a surviving flat base, and which may be red slipped or uncoated. Bader publishes an uncoated example (dia 11) (Bader 2009b, Typ 22c, 262 and Abb. 167 [5460]) from Level VI of the late Thirteenth Dynasty. Virtually the same form, again both red slipped and uncoated, can be found in a slightly larger (dia 16–20) size (Bourriau and Gallorini in preparation: [20b3.1]), from levels of about the same date.

The trimmed end does not seem to occur among the many small flat-based dishes from the early Twelfth Dynasty at Lisht (Arnold Do. 1988, Figs 52–55a, 63–64) or at all at Tell el-Dab'a at this earlier time (Czerny 1999).

2710 **378** Fig. 50h

Rim cut almost square and left slightly irregular. Smoothing marks on both surfaces.

D4 (Nile B2). Fired fairly soft. Surfaces brown. Break pale brown with red core. Fairly plentiful poorly sorted sand. Fairly plentiful fine and coarse veg to 0.5 and one piece 0.8. Sparse limestone to 0.1 and two pieces each 0.2. Uncoated. Not polished or burnished.

Phase	Context & No.	Grid ref	Dia rim (top)	Fig
iva	AJH under AVH **50**	05-04/05/06	*c.*12	50h

379–80 Wide-mouthed bowls with direct rim

These fit easily into a series of such bowls at Tell el-Dab'a. Both belong with the smaller diameter group (Aston D.A. 2004b, Pls 5–6 [19–24]) although **379** is slightly below their range of 16.5–25.4 cm. The fabric is Nile B2 or 'B2 near C' and most are uncoated. Aston remarks (*ibid.*, 58) that they are 'generally found in the earlier levels' (there is also a long series, most with diameters in the range 16–26, in Czerny's volume (Czerny 1999, 140–42 [Nf 47–87])) and cites many examples in the older publications. There are larger versions, and it is significant that of the next series (Aston D.A. 2004b, Pls 21–22 [91–95]), diameter range 27–35, in Nile B2 and C and again usually uncoated, Aston says (*ibid.*, 71) 'the inner surface, however, is generally wet smoothed whilst the upper part of the outer surface is often similarly smoothed'.

At Memphis (Kom Rabia), where the excavations did not reach the Twelfth Dynasty levels, although there are many similar vessels, none is a very close match. Among other published examples, one from Lisht (Arnold Do. 1988, Fig. 55a [4]), in 'self-slipped' Nile B2, diameter 13.3, is very similar to **379**; so also is one from Dahshur

(Arnold Do. 1982, 30, Abb. 6 [3]), again B2, diameter 15, and significantly described as wet-smoothed. Thus a Twelfth Dynasty date is to be preferred to one in the Thirteenth.

For other wet-smoothed examples, see bowls **377/81**, **401** and offering stand **432**.

2620 **379** Fig. 50i

Interior lightly ridged from wet smoothing. Groove around just below rim for string-tying.

D4 coarse (Nile B2 coarse). Fired medium. Surfaces red-brown. Break brown with red zones and purple core. Fairly plentiful fine and medium sand with a few larger grains. Fairly plentiful to plentiful fine and coarse veg to 0.6. No visible limestone. Both surfaces probably wet-smoothed only, but with application of copious water! Not polished or burnished.

Phase	Context & No.	Grid ref	Max dia rim	Fig
iv (Pt II?)/?	AYP/AYJ **18**	Area 13	15	50i

2708 **380** Fig. 50j

Probably wheel-made.

D4 (Nile B2). Fired fairly soft. Surfaces brown. Break brown with diffuse grey core. Fairly plentiful fine and medium sand with a few larger grains. Small qty fine veg to 0.2. Sparse limestone to 0.1. Uncoated. Not polished or burnished.

Phase	Context & No.	Grid ref	Dia rim (top)	Fig
iva	BKZ **32**	07-26	*c.*20–25 (?)	50j

381 Bowl with flat-topped rim

Similar to **379**, but appears different because of the flat rim, which is probably fortuitous and due to its standing inverted before firing. The wet smoothing is another feature the two forms have in common; it is found again on bowls **377/79** and offering stand **432**.

2668 **381** Fig. 50k

D4 (Nile B2). Fired medium. Surfaces red-brown. Break red-brown with diffuse red core. Plentiful poorly sorted sand. Fairly plentiful fine and coarse veg to 0.5. Sparse limestone to 0.05. Probably wet-smoothed only, but with application of copious water! Not polished or burnished.

Phase	Context & No.	Grid ref	Max dia rim	Fig
vii	AAA (UP 23) **536**	10-07	13	50k

382 Slightly incurved carinated bowl with rounded rim

Absent from the Memphis (Kom Rabia) MK corpus (Bourriau and Gallorini in preparation) and from the later Tell el-Dab'a levels, this slightly incurved version of the carinated bowl belongs to the Twelfth Dynasty and perhaps also the FIP. Examples from this period at Tell el-Dab'a vary a little in stance, but the upper body is in most cases close to vertical (Czerny 1999, 145–49 [Nf 148–72/77–87]). Closest to **382** are [Nf 159] (rim dia 13) and several in the series with diameter 19+, [Nf 177–87]. Most examples of both series are in Nile B1/B2 (undivided), with a polished red slip, and many carry decoration of one or two incised wavy lines.

2782 **382** Fig. 50l

Upper part of carinated bowl, with slightly incurved body above the carination, and rounded rim.

D4 (Nile B2). Fired fairly soft. Exterior concealed by slip, interior brown where uncoated. Break brown with faint intermittent red core. Fairly plentiful poorly sorted sand. Moderate qty fine veg to 0.3. Sparse limestone to 0.1. Fairly thick red slip on exterior, but only down to 0.2 below carination; continues over the rim on to interior, and down 2.5 to a careful straight edge, with splashes below. Polish on top of rim and probable traces on remainder of exterior, especially clear on the small surviving uncoated area below the carination; interior unpolished.

Phase	Context & No.	Grid ref	Dia rim (top)	Fig
ivc	AJG **27**	05/06-S01/S02/S03	13	50l

383 Slightly outcurved carinated bowl with thin rim

Later in date than **382**, this form is common at Memphis in both Nile B1 and Nile B2 fabrics in the second half of the Thirteenth Dynasty (Bader 2009b, Typ 6b2, 253, Abb. 163 [3217]; Typ 28g1, 285–86, Abb. 175 [4063]; Bourriau and Gallorini in preparation) though few examples are preserved down to the carination. The commonest diameters are 12 and 13, and several examples in both fabrics are red slipped on both surfaces like **383**, though only one example, in Nile B2 (Bourriau 2010, Fig. 94 [4063]), from a level which contained both MK and NK sherds, was burnished (not band-burnished as Bader 2009b, 286) both inside and out, indicating a date late in the MK. This dating is fully in accord with the form of **383**.

1365 **383** Fig. 50m

D4 (Nile B2). Fired fairly soft. Surfaces concealed by slip. Break orange-brown with thin dark brown zones and pink core. Moderate qty fine well-sorted sand. Moderate qty fine veg to 0.3. Sparse limestone to 0.1. Thick red slip on both surfaces, including below the carination. Exterior polished, including below the carination; interior possible traces.

Phase	Context & No.	Grid ref	Dia rim (top)	Fig
ivd	ATY **209**	24/25-05/06	13	50m

384 Rim of carinated bowl(?)

The diameter and stance may indicate a carinated bowl with concave wall such as one in Nile B2 (dia 12.3) at Tell el-Dab'a from the Hyksos period (Aston D.A. 2004b, Pl. 208 [813]), and several in the same fabric at Memphis (Kom Rabia) in levels of the late Thirteenth Dynasty or early SIP (Bader 2009b, Typ 28g2, 287 and Abb. 175 [5569]; Bourriau and Gallorini in preparation, [22a4.8]). Uncoated examples are found at both sites. This form variant thus appears to be late in the series.

2617 **384** Fig. 50n

Wheel-made as far as preserved.

D4 (Nile B2). Fired fairly soft. White firing surfaces. Break pale brown all through. Fairly plentiful fine and medium sand with a few larger grains. Fairly plentiful fine veg to 0.3. Sparse limestone to 0.05. Uncoated. No visible polish or burnish.

Phase	Context & No.	Grid ref	Dia rim (top)	Fig
?	UP 805 **70**	Area 5	*c.*12	50n

385–87 Bases and bodies of carinated bowls

385, with implied rim diameter 13–14, is a good match in fabric, size, form and stance to a similarly preserved example from Memphis (Kom Rabia) (Bader 2009b, Typ 28g3, 286 and Abb. 175 [4153]) except that the latter has a flatter base and the version with only partly slipped exterior was not recorded. The carination of **386** implies a rim diameter of about 12–13, well within the Memphis range.

Base **387**, in the finer Nile B1 fabric, is at the lower end of the range, implying a rim diameter 9–10. There are many of similarly small size at Memphis in the second half of the Thirteenth Dynasty (e.g. Bader 2009b, Typ 6b1, 253 and Abb. 163 [3383]; Typ 6b2, 253 and Abb. 163 [5564]); they occur in both Nile B1 and Nile B2.

1366 **385** Fig. 50o

Base, lacking centre, and lower body. Also non-joining fragments assumed to be from the same vessel. The base is too weathered and damaged to show the method of manufacture.

D4 (Nile B2). Fired fairly soft. Surfaces brown, exterior where uncoated. Break brown with red core, or red zones and grey core where thickest. Fairly plentiful fine and medium well-sorted sand. No visible veg. Sparse limestone to 0.1. Several nodules of unincorporated clay to 0.2. Red slip on exterior of upper body only, down to about 1.5–2.0 cm above carination, and running down; interior uncoated. No visible polish/burnish, but surface weathered.

Phase	Context & No.	Grid ref	Max dia base	Fig & notes
ivc	BTX **68+77+87+101**	02/03-19/20	6	50o
ivc	BTX **76**	02/03-19/20	-	Body sherd
ivc	BTX **100**	02/03-19/20	-	Body sherd with carination

2232 **386** Fig. 51a

D4 (Nile B2). Fired fairly soft. Surfaces pale brown where slip lost. Break brown with red zones and grey core. Fairly plentiful poorly sorted sand, with many larger grains. Fairly plentiful fine and some coarse veg to 0.4. Sparse limestone to 0.1. Fairly thick brownish red slip on both surfaces. Both surfaces probably lightly polished.

Phase	Context & No.	Grid ref	Dia at carination	Fig
ii/ivb	AJY/AVB **20**	10/11/12-S01/S02	*c.*10.5	51a

1604 **387** Fig. 51b

The original surface of the base is mostly lost through weathering, but traces survive near the centre, showing the profile. Base probably wheel-made.

D1 (Nile B1). Fired fairly soft. Surfaces concealed by slip. Break pale brown throughout. Fairly plentiful fine well-sorted sand with a very few larger grains. A few pieces fine veg to 0.2. Sparse limestone to 0.05. Slip on both surfaces, including under base, fired brown-red. Areas of light polish survive on exterior and probably on interior.

Phase	Context & No.	Grid ref	Max dia base	Fig
iv (Pt II?)?	BWL? (UP 1040) **1**	Area 12	3.5	51b

388 Base of open form with applied base-ring

Insufficient of the body survives for identification of the vessel type, though the interior slip confirms an open form. For separately applied base-rings, see Arnold (Arnold Do. 1992, 58, Fig. 65A) and Bader (Bader 2009b,

296); they are not confined to the MK but continue to be made throughout the SIP and into the early NK (Janine Bourriau, pers. comm.).

800 388 Fig. 51c

The base-ring is partly lost, clearly revealing that it was separately made, and added before firing.

D1 (Nile B1). Fired medium. Surfaces red-brown where slip lost. Break pale red-brown with red zones and grey core. Moderate qty fine and medium well-sorted sand. Small qty fine veg to 0.3. Sparse limestone to 0.05. Red slip on all surfaces, except perhaps within the base-ring. Surfaces polished, including the whole of the base-ring but not within it.

Phase	Context & No.	Grid ref	Dia base-ring	Fig
vii	AAA (UP 588) **372**	W01/W02/W03-19 to 24	6–7	51c

389 Pedestal bases from carinated (or incurved?) bowls

Pedestal bases, probably all from carinated bowls of the Twelfth Dynasty or a little earlier. They survive well because of their solidity, but readily detach from the rest of the vessel. They vary in absolute diameter and in the relationship of base to minimum diameter of stem ('base index', max ÷ min × 100). At Tell el-Dab'a they occur only in the earlier levels (Czerny 1999, 147 [Nf 161–63]; 161 [Nf 361–78]). Czerny's examples illustrate the form with a low base index, i.e. where the base does not protrude far beyond the stem, the type of vessel cannot always be established.

The high base index provides the more distinctive form. At Memphis (Kom Rabia), bases were not systematically recorded (Janine Bourriau, pers. comm.); unsurprisingly, only one example with a low base index (137) was noted, but six within the range 175–204, three of which are published (Bader 2009b, 256, Typ 8f [5883]; 295, Typ 31e [4271]; 354, Typ 60e [4314]).

A fine complete carinated bowl with a high base index of about 200 was found in a grave at Matmar (Bourriau 1981, 57 [98]), and the vessel forms survive at, among other sites, Deir Rifeh (Petrie 1907, Pl. XIIIA [13/18/19]), where Seidlmayer (1990, 210–16) places the incurved version in his Phase I and the carinated as overlapping Phases I and II. At Memphis, bases in contexts of the Thirteenth Dynasty are thought to be residual and one is even recorded in a context of the late SIP or early NK (Bourriau 2010, 34 and Fig. 10a [2478]). Bader (Bader 2009b, 255) speculates that they may have been reused as stoppers or gaming pieces. Czerny, too, notes the propensity of such bases to become detached (Czerny 1999, 70).

Although apparently most common in Nile B2 fabric, they occur also in Nile B1 and Nile C.

2674 389 Fig. 51d–g

D4 (Nile B2). Firing variable, fairly soft to medium. Where slip lost, surfaces pale brown through red-brown to red. Break from pale brown all through to red all through, three examples with grey core. Fairly plentiful sand, variable from fine and medium well-sorted (AHC/AIU **10**, UP 108 **48** and UP 445 **137**) through fine and medium with some larger grains to poorly sorted (majority). Moderate qty to fairly plentiful fine veg, mostly to 0.3. Sparse or fairly sparse limestone to 0.1, UP 627 **34** one piece 0.3 × 0.1 and one 0.5 × 0.4, AMJ/AAA **2** one 0.3 × 0.2 and AAA East **9** one 0.2 . Red or red-brown slip on all surfaces including underside, many weathered so only small areas survive. Possible but uncertain light polish on exterior and interior of ACE **137**, and exterior of AAA East **1** and AHC/AIU **10**.

Low Base Index

Phase	Context & No.	Grid ref	Base rim dia/min dia	Base Index	Fig
ii	DAM **5**	Area 2	*c.*4.8/3.9	*c.*123	As 51f
iii–iva	ACE **137**	01 to 05-08 to 12	5.4/4.0	135	As 51f
vi/vi	AHC/AIU **10**	15/16-06/07	5.9/4.4	134	As 51f

Phase	Context & No.	Grid ref	Base rim dia/min dia	Base Index	Fig
vi/vii	AMJ/AAA **2**	22-08/09	6.3/5.2	121	51e
vii	AAA (UP 108) **48**	29 to 34-S06	5.2/4.1	127	51f
vii	AAA (UP 627) **34**	W01/W02-13 to 20	6.5/5.6	116	As 51e
vii	AAA East **9**	Area 1	*c*.5.5/ca 4.1	*c*.134	As 51f

High Base Index

Phase	Context & No.	Grid ref	Base rim dia/min dia	Base Index	Fig
ii	AJY **146**	18/19/20-S04/ S05	6.5/3.9	167	51d
ii	BGL **45**	14/15-S04/S05	*c*.6.0/3.8	*c*.158	As 51g
ii/ivb	AIY/AVB **9**	13/14-01/S01	5.8/3.6	161	As 51g
vi	ABG (UP 235) **27**	Area 13	*c*.6.0/3.5	*c*.171	Between 51d & 51g
vii	AAA East **1**	Area 1	5.7/3.7	154	Between 51d & 51g
vii	AAA East **5**	Area 1	*c*.7.2/*c*. 5.0	*c*.144	Between 51d & 51g
vii	AAA (UP 445) **137**	Area 2	5.6/3.0	186	51g

Uncertain Base Index

Phase	Context & No.	Grid ref	Base rim dia/min dia	Base Index	Notes
o	BDY **31**	01/02/03-S07/S08	5.5+/4.6	120+	(Damaged)

390 Small upright bowl with grooved rim

Differs from the MK hemispherical bowls in the constricted upper body and the series of grooves around, just below, the rim. These should be decorative, string-tying usually being unnecessary on so small a vessel; a slightly different bowl-form from Memphis (Kom Rabia) is similarly decorated (Bader 2009b, Typ 6d1, 253 and Abb. 163 [6265]). Here only one of the many hemispherical bowls (Bourriau and Gallorini in preparation, [22a1.14]) comes close to it in form, though lacking the grooves; the diameter is 11, and it can be either uncoated, or red slipped on the exterior as **390**. The contexts are of the SIP.

At Tell el-Dab'a, similar decorative grooves are a feature of small Hyksos Period jars with wide vertical neck and rounded body (Aston D.A. 2004b, Pls 269–70 [982–89]); the form of **390** falls between the last of these and two series of small, slightly incurved bowls (*ibid.*, Pl. 211 [828–33]; Pl. 225 [839–44]). In respect of his [828–33], Aston comments (*ibid.*, 196) that they represent a line of development at Tell el-Dab'a different from anything south of the Delta, including Memphis. **390** thus appears to represent a rare Memphite combination of form and decoration in the SIP.

2728 **390** Fig. 51h

Three well-marked grooves, and one faint one below them, around just below rim. Wheel-made.

D4 (Nile B2). Fired medium. Exterior concealed by slip, interior red-brown. Break red-brown with thick pink core. Fairly plentiful poorly sorted sand. Fairly plentiful fine veg to 0.4. Sparse limestone to 0.1. Thick red slip on exterior to top of rim, and running down inside. Traces of light polish on exterior only.

Phase	Context & No.	Grid ref	Dia rim (top)	Fig
vii	AAA East **20**	Area 1	10	51h

391–96 Hemispherical bowls

These bowls, which originated in the FIP but were especially abundant in the MK, have been much studied (e.g. Arnold Do. 1988, 140–41; Aston D.A. 2004b, 62–63; Bader 2009b, *passim*). They occur in both Nile B1 and Nile B2, of which B1 is thought on the whole to be the later. Arnold established a chronology of the B1 series based on the vessel index, i.e. the relationship of the rim diameter to the vessel height, following which Bader (Bader 2009b, 250), aware that few preserved fragments were large enough for their index to be calculated, noted that this represented a chronological development from a shallower through an upright to a slightly incurved form. None of the B1 Anubieion examples is sufficiently preserved for the index to be calculated, but on this basis the upright to slightly incurved stance should be Thirteenth rather than Twelfth Dynasty. **392** is distinguished from **391** by being uncoated, though with red rim; **393** is fully incurved and thicker-walled. Among the B2 examples, the diameter and slightly curved wall of **394** should indicate hemispherical bowls of the shallower form, rather than bowls or dishes of another type; the stance would be compatible with a date in the FIP or the early Twelfth Dynasty. The more upright stance of **395** should point to a somewhat later date. Although slipped bowls do not normally appear in Nile B2 until the MK is well established, the diagonal scraping of **396** should be an early feature, perhaps as early as the FIP.

Polish is not recorded on examples from settlement sites and may be due to the desert conditions: either the Anubieion examples are sand-blasted, or they retain a polish destroyed by the much wetter and more complex soils of the valley.

By general consent, a rim diameter of more than about 12 indicates a bowl of a different type.

2230A **391** Fig. 51i

Rims, and one lower body of which too little survives to be illustrated.

D1 (Nile B1). Fired fairly soft. Exterior of ABW **23** and AYE/AYF **2** red, both surfaces of AIY **103** pale brown where slip lost, remaining surfaces concealed by slip. Break brown with red core, except AYE/AYF **2** no core. Fairly plentiful fine and some medium sand with a few larger grains. Small qty fine veg to 0.2 or none visible. Very sparse limestone to 0.05. AYE/AYF **2** has interior burnt black (after firing) but appears to have been red slipped over interior, slip extending over rim and down 0.2 on exterior, the interior being lightly polished. ABW **23** has probable red slip and light polish, on interior only; others red slipped, and probably lightly polished, on both surfaces.

Rims

Phase	Context & No.	Grid ref	Dia rim (top)	Fig
ii	BGG **86**	08/09/10-S02/S03	?	As 51i
iv (Pt II?)	ABW **23**	Area 13	*c.*11	As 51i
iv (Pt II?)	AYE/AYF **2**	Area 13	10	51i

Lower body

Phase	Context & No.	Grid ref	Max dia base
ii	AIY **103**	07/08-06	*c.*8(?)

2230B **392** Not illustrated

D1 (Nile B1). Fired fairly soft. ABW **22** surfaces red-brown, others brown. Break brown with red core, except ABK/S/U/V/Y/Z **5** no core. Fairly plentiful fine and medium well-sorted sand. Small qty fine veg to 0.2, and ABW **22** one piece 0.5, probably accidental. Very sparse limestone, to 0.05. All uncoated but with red-painted rims. On ABK/S/U/V/Y/Z **5**, the paint extends down 0.1 outside and 0.3 inside; on ABW **22** 0.8 outside and 0.1 inside; on BET **29** 0.1 only, outside and inside. ABW **22** lightly polished on red-painted area only; remainder not polished or burnished.

Phase	Context & No.	Grid ref	Dia rim (top)	Fig
ii	BET **29**	12-01/02	?	As 51i
All iv (Pt II?)	ABK/S/U/V/Y/Z **5**	Area 13	?	As 51i
iv (Pt II?)	ABW **22**	Area 13	*c*.11	As 51i

1732 **393** Fig. 51j

Thick-walled and incurved.

D1 (Nile B1). Fired medium. Surfaces pale orange-brown. Break pale orange-brown with pink zones and grey core. Fairly plentiful fine and medium well-sorted sand. Small qty fine veg to 0.2. Sparse limestone to 0.05. Both surfaces carefully smoothed, perhaps self-slipped. On interior, red slip or painted band around rim, 1.3–1.8 deep; on exterior, a patch of the same, perhaps accidental. Interior polished, and just over rim on to exterior.

Phase	Context & No.	Grid ref	Dia rim (top)	Fig
vi/vi	ABF/AZH **11**	Area 13	12	51j

1466/2030 **394** Fig. 51k–l

D4 (Nile B2). Fired medium. AQE **139** surfaces red-brown, AEP/Q/R **49** red. Break AQE **139** red-brown with thick pinkish purple core, AEP/Q/R **49** red with faint pink core. Fairly plentiful poorly sorted sand. Fairly plentiful fine veg to 0.2, AQE **139** also a few pieces to 0.4. Sparse limestone to 0.1. No coloured slip; carefully wet-smoothed or perhaps self-slipped on interiors and on exterior of AEP/Q/R **49**, exterior of AQE **139** less carefully smoothed. Not polished or burnished.

Phase	Context & No.	Grid ref	Dia rim (top)	Fig
ii	AQE **139**	16/17/18-02/03	11	51k
vi/vi/vi	AEP/AEQ/AER **49**	01/02-04 to 08	11	51l

2730 **395** Fig. 51m

Deeper, incurved form.

D4 (Nile B2). Fired fairly soft. AJY **154** surfaces pale brown, BGL **27** red, BHR **265** burnt grey-brown to black. Break, AJY **154** brown with thin, diffuse red core, BGL **27** red with orange-brown core, BHR **265** brown, partly burnt post-firing. Fairly plentiful poorly sorted sand, BGL **27** with fewer coarse grains. BGL **27** no visible veg, others moderate qty fine to 0.2. Sparse limestone to 0.1. Uncoated. Not polished or burnished. BGL **27** (only) has a red-painted rim, the paint extending down 0.1 outside, 0.3 inside.

Phase	Context & No.	Grid ref	Dia rim (top)	Fig
ii	AJY **154**	14/15/16-S03/S04/S05	?	As 51m
ii	BGL **27**	15/16/17-04/05	10–15	51m
iva	BHR **265**	02/03-21/22	?	As 51m

2228A/2916A **396** Fig. 51n–o

Most sherds are small rims and the diameters are difficult to ascertain. The forms are similar to the drawn examples. BDY **22** and ADS/ARP=ARS **7** exhibit diagonal scraping of the exterior, from the shaping of the base, BDY **22** starting only 2 cm but ADS/ARP=ARS **7** 4 cm below the rim.

D4 (Nile B2). Fired fairly soft to medium. Surfaces concealed by slip, or brown to red-brown where uncoated or slip lost. Break brown all through or with red core (usually faint and diffuse), brown with red zones and faint grey core, or red with grey core. Fairly plentiful poorly sorted sand. Moderate qty to fairly plentiful fine veg to 0.2 or 0.3. Sparse limestone to 0.05/0.1. BDP (UP 647) **28** red slip on interior only, others red or brownish red slip on both surfaces as far down as preserved. For polish, see table.

Phase	Context & No.	Grid ref	Dia rim (top)	Polish in/out	Fig
o	BDY **22**	01/02/03-07/08	*c.*12	Both(?)	51n
ii	BGL **115**	14/15-01/S01/S02	*c.*13	No	
iii	BDP (UP 647) **28**	01/02-08/09	*c.*11	No	
iii–iva/iva	BNQ/BMY **11**	04/05-12/13	*c.*14	No	
iv (Pt II?)	ARP=ARS (UP 152) **19**	Area 13	*c.*14	Both	
iv (Pt II?) ×2	ADS/ARP=ARS **7**	Area 13	*c.*14	No	51o
iv (Pt II?) ×2	ADS/ARP=ARS **8**	Area 13	*c.*12	No	
iva	BAX **44**	06/07/08-03/04	*c.*12	Both	
?	BEP **58**	14 to 17-01/S01	*c.*14	Both(?)	

397 Hemispherical or small diameter thin-walled bowls in slipped Nile B2 fabric

Extracted from the hemispherical bowl series as probably too large in diameter, or of uncertain diameter because only a small sherd survives.

2228B/2916B **397** Not illustrated

The forms are all similar to BDY **22** and ADS/ARP=ARS **7**.

D4 (Nile B2). Ware as **396**. Red or brownish red slip on both surfaces. BDR/BCP **9** has a thicker slip inside, taken over the rim, on top of the thinner slip, to give the appearance of a red rim on the exterior. For polish, see table.

Phase	Context & No.	Grid ref	Dia rim (top)	Polish in/out
o	AQG **37**	20/21/22-S03 to S06	?	No
ii	AJY **82**	18 to 20-S04/S05	?	Both
ii	AJY **158**	17 to 20-S04/S05	?	No
ii	BET **80**	10/11/12-01/02/03	?	No

Phase	Context & No.	Grid ref	Dia rim (top)	Polish in/out
ii	BGL **79**	15/16/17-04/05	?	No
iii	BJJ **14***	17/18-05/06	?	Both(?)
iii	BJJ **88***	18-06	?	No
iii/iva	BDR/BCP **9**	10/11-04/05	*c.*16	No
iv (Pt II?) ×2	ADS/ARP=ARS **10**	Area 13	*c.*15	Both(?)
ivc	BJS i **9**	06/07-13/14	?	No

* Perhaps same vessel

398 Hemispherical (or deep?) bowl in externally slipped Nile B2 fabric

Probably from a hemispherical bowl such as one from Tell el-Dab'a (Bader 2009b, Typ 28d1, 282 and Abb. 174 [D35]), which is similarly slipped on the exterior, but possibly from a deeper bowl such as occur there 'in hundreds', uncoated or red slipped on the exterior, as a marker for the Hyksos Period (*ibid.*, Typ 37b, 306 and Abb. 185 [D847]; Aston D.A. 2004b, Pls 212–13 [838–44]).

2028 **398** Fig. 51p

Low parallel horizontal ridges on interior indicate wheel manufacture as far as preserved.

D4 (Nile B2). Fired fairly soft. Exterior concealed by slip, interior brown. Break brown with faint red core. Fairly plentiful poorly sorted sand. Fairly plentiful fine veg to 0.2. Sparse limestone to 0.1. Slightly fugitive thick red slip on exterior; interior uncoated but smoothed, though leaving low wheel-ridges. Not polished or burnished.

Phase	Context & No.	Grid ref	Dia rim (top)	Fig
ii	BET **145**	14/15-02/03	*c.*9	51p

399 Base of hemispherical bowl, beaker or bag-shaped jar

Although the exact vessel form from which this base derives cannot be determined, its size and shape should indicate a hemispherical bowl (Bader 2009b, Typ 28d3, 284–85 and Abb. 174 [4009]), a restricted beaker/ deep bowl (*ibid.*, Typ 28d4, 282 and Abb. 175 [5396]) or a tall bag-shaped jar ('Bechervase') (*ibid.*, Typ 38c1–2, 310–11 and Abb. 186 [2307/19/20, 5845]). Furthermore, all occur at Memphis (Kom Rabia) with a red rim but otherwise uncoated, a treatment compatible with the splash of red slip noted on the interior of **399**.

243A **399** Fig. 51q

The interior has ridges from wheel throwing. The exterior is wiped, probably by the potter's hand, not finished on the wheel or cut in facets, and bears fingerprints.

D4 (Nile B2). Fired fairly soft. Surfaces pale brown. Break pale brown with faint red core. Fairly plentiful poorly sorted sand. Fairly plentiful fine veg to 0.3. Sparse limestone to 0.05. Both surfaces smoothed but not slipped. One tiny red splash on the interior probably betrays a red band around the rim. Not polished or burnished.

Phase	Context & No.	Grid ref	Fig
vii	AAA* **19**	Area 2	51q

* Sherd is marked 'Topsoil West Lower', assumed to be UP 585

<u>400</u> Large diameter bowl with rounded body and protruding rim

Although clearly in the OK tradition, this finds parallels in the Twelfth Dynasty at Tell el-Dab'a (Czerny 1999, 171 [Ng 88/89]). The maximum diameters of Czerny's illustrated examples (42 and 34 respectively) are very similar and all three examples are red slipped, though not polished.

1460 **<u>400</u>** Fig. 52a

Large diameter bowl with thick out-turned rim. The rim appears to be at least wheel assisted.

<u>D4 near D3 (Nile B2 near C).</u> Fired medium. Surfaces orange-brown to brown where slip lost. Break orange-brown with thick pink core. Plentiful poorly sorted sand. Plentiful fine and coarse veg to 0.5. Sparse limestone to 0.1. One fragment of bone 0.1. Red slip on both surfaces, but mostly lost from interior. Traces of polish where slip survives.

Phase	Context & No.	Grid ref	Max dia rim	Fig
iv (Pt II?)	ADD North **28**	Area 13	*c*.38	52a

<u>401</u> Bowl with rounded carination

One of the many MK carinated bowls, this version with the out-turned rim and rounded carination fits better into the Twelfth Dynasty at Tell el-Dab'a (Czerny 1999, 142–44 [Nf 88–129]) than the Thirteenth. The series is in fabric B1/B2 (mostly undivided), almost all red slipped and the majority polished. The best match is to the red slipped but unpolished [Nf 116]. Although the wet-smoothed finish is rare among the Tell el-Dab'a carinated bowls, it is not uncommon at the Anubieion on various MK forms (e.g. **<u>377/79/81</u>**, **<u>432</u>**).

2618 **<u>401</u>** Fig. 52b

Wheel-made.

<u>D4 (Nile B2).</u> Fired fairly soft. Surfaces brown. Break brown with faint red core. Fairly plentiful poorly sorted sand. Fairly plentiful fine and coarse veg to 0.5. Sparse limestone to 0.05. Wet-smoothed using a great deal of water. Uncoated. Not polished or burnished.

Phase	Context & No.	Grid ref	Dia rim (top)	Fig
vii	AAA (UP 23) **342**	10-09	16	52b

<u>402–06</u> Bowls with protruding carination

Another in the MK carinated bowl series, at Tell el-Dab'a this version with the protruding carination again fits better into the Twelfth Dynasty than the Thirteenth (Czerny 1999, 142–44 [Nf 88–129]). The series is in fabric Nile B1/B2 (mostly undivided), almost all red slipped and the majority polished. The best match for **<u>402–04</u>** is to Tell el-Dab'a [Nf 111], where the carination is high on the body, but for **<u>405–06</u>** it is to Tell el-Dab'a [Nf 119], where the carination is placed lower down: both are red slipped and polished and exhibit the same sharp, protruding carination. **<u>404</u>** is uncoated, as a few in the Tell el-Dab'a series, though not the two examples of [Nf 111]; it also has a less protruding carination.

The scratches on **<u>404/06</u>** may indicate a date in the FIP but the forms are not closely matched in Rzeuska's volume (2006).

1714 **<u>402</u>** Fig. 52c

<u>D1 (Nile B1).</u> Fired fairly hard. Surfaces concealed by slip. Break orange-brown with thick grey core. Fairly

plentiful fine sand with a few larger grains. Small qty fine veg to 0.2. Sparse limestone to 0.1. Orange-brown slip on both surfaces. Both surfaces polished.

Phase	Context & No.	Grid ref	Dia rim (top)	Fig
ivd	AUH **9**	06/07-23	23	52c

1716B **403** Fig. 52d

D1 (Nile B1). Fired fairly soft. Surfaces concealed by slip. Break brown all through. Fairly plentiful fine and medium sand with a few larger grains. Moderate qty fine veg to 0.2. No visible limestone. Red-brown slip on both surfaces. Both surfaces polished.

Phase	Context & No.	Grid ref	Dia rim (top)	Fig
o	ADU (UP 122) NW **9**	Area 13	22	52d

325 **404** Fig. 52e

Horizontal scratches on exterior below carination perhaps from shaping with a tool.

D4 (Nile B2). Fired fairly soft. Surfaces pale brown. Break brown with red core. Fairly plentiful poorly sorted sand. Moderate qty fine and coarse veg to 0.4. Sparse limestone to 0.1. Two orange mineral particles, 0.05 and 0.1. Small (bird?) bone 0.3 long embedded in surface. Smoothing marks around exterior above bent-point, but both surfaces uncoated. Not polished or burnished.

Phase	Context & No.	Grid ref	Dia rim (top)	Fig
All iv (Pt II?)	ABK/S/U/V/Y/Z **1**	Area 13	26	52e

421 **405** Fig. 52f

The rounded upper body is probably due to over-tightening of string, which would also account for the form of the rim. With its small diameter it might be expected to need no string, but an example of the same size (Rzeuska 2006, Form 168 [595]) also appears to have been tied.

D4 (Nile B2). Fired fairly soft. Surfaces concealed by slip. Break brown with red zones and diffuse purple core. Fairly plentiful sand, mostly fine and medium but with a few larger grains. Moderate qty fine and coarse veg to 0.2. Sparse limestone to 0.1 and one piece 0.2. One flat fragment of bright blue faience, 0.25 × 0.05 thick, perhaps from an inlay (see also **255** of the OK and **560/86** of the NK). Red-brown slip on both surfaces. Both surfaces polished.

Phase	Context & No.	Grid ref	Dia rim (top)	Fig
vi	AMJ **5**	20-10	16	52f

2909 **406** Fig. 52g

Grooves and finger(?) impression below the carination, from scraping of the lower part.

D1 (Nile B1). Fired fairly soft. Surfaces concealed by slip. Break brown with pinkish mauve core. Fairly plentiful fine and medium sand with a few larger grains. Small qty fine veg to 0.3. Sparse limestone to 0.05. Red-brown slip on both surfaces. Both surfaces polished.

Phase	Context & No.	Grid ref	Fig
ii/ii/ivb/ivc	AJX/AJY/AMV/BRS **13**	21/22/23-S04/S05/S06	52g

407–09 Bowls with folded rim

Dating this long-lived rim form is not easy. With a presumed ancestry in the late OK, in either round-topped deep bowls (Rzeuska Pl. 97 [483]) or straight-walled bowls (*ibid.*, Pl. 101 [511]), these forms seem to run right through the MK. The smaller version represented by **407/08** finds a counterpart at Dahshur (Arnold Do. unpublished, III 287) in Nile C fabric with a top diameter of 15, an almost perfect match for **408**. A published example from Lisht (Arnold Do. 1988, Fig. 64 [108]) is again in Nile C (the exterior at least partly red slipped), with a top diameter of 19, and not very different. At Tell el-Dab'a, similar bowls (Aston D.A. 2004b, Pls 27–28 [110–13]) in uncoated Nile C are set upon integral stands as offering stands; the top diameters are between 19 and 29, bridging the gap to the unusually large diameter **409** vessels. These are very similar to published pieces, starting with another from Dahshur (Arnold Do. 1982, Abb. 6 [6]), in wet-smoothed Nile C with a top diameter of 36, and continuing with various round-, ring- and high-based types at Tell el-Dab'a (Aston D.A. 2004b, Pls 24–25 [103–06]), in uncoated (except [106] rim white?) Nile C, with top diameters in the range 31–59!

The Tell el-Dab'a series then continues into the late Hyksos period with a small example in uncoated Nile B2 (Fuscaldo 2000, Fig. 21g), top diameter 20, and three larger ones in Nile C (*ibid.*, Fig. 25c–e), two of them slipped, with top diameters of 30, 33 and 28. At Memphis (Kom Rabia) not dissimilar bowl forms are found well into the Eighteenth Dynasty, though the vessels tend to be shallower (Bourriau 2010, Fig. 39 [4.18.3/5]). Here the question arises as to whether **408**, with no evidence of hand manufacture, might not be the rim of a funnel-necked jar. There are many from Memphis (Kom Rabia) (Bourriau 2010) and the forms are all somewhat similar, but the red slip on the interior of **408** argues against this interpretation.

If **407/09** really are handmade, a date as early as the FIP may be indicated.

2234 **407** Fig. 52h

Irregular depth of rim, two low, wide horizontal ridges on interior 1.2 apart, and smoothing at an angle, all probably indicate handmade. Appears to have been string tied under the overhang of the rim.

D4 (Nile B2). Fired fairly soft. Surfaces pale brown where uncoated or slip lost. Break pale brown all through. Fairly plentiful poorly sorted sand. Moderate qty fine and coarse veg to 0.5. Sparse limestone to 0.05. Red-brown slip on all surfaces, except for an area of exterior probably accidentally missed. Top of rim polished, and interior and exterior possibly.

Phase	Context & No.	Grid ref	Dia rim (top)	Fig
v/v	AEN/AEO **24**	16-S02/S03	*c.*15	52h

2114 **408** Fig. 52i

The lower edge of the rim is uneven, probably from string-tying before firing. Uncertain whether hand- or wheel-made.

D4 (Nile B2). Fired fairly soft. Surfaces concealed by slip. Break brown with faint, diffuse, greenish grey core. Fairly plentiful fine well-sorted sand. Fairly plentiful fine and coarse veg to 0.9. More limestone than usual in a Nile fabric, to 0.1. One nodule of unincorporated clay 0.8 × 0.7. Thick red-brown slip on both surfaces. Traces of polish on exterior and top of rim; interior uncertain.

Phase	Context & No.	Grid ref	Dia rim (top)	Fig
ivd/ivd	ASD/BAU **5**	17/18-07/08	*c.*16	52i

23B **409** Fig. 52j

The grooves immediately below the rim were almost certainly for string-tying. Probably handmade.

D4 (Nile B2). Fired fairly soft. Surfaces pale brown where slip lost. Break pale brown with red core, BPV **45** also one dark brown zone near exterior. Fairly plentiful poorly sorted sand. Fairly plentiful fine and coarse veg to 1.5. Sparse limestone to 0.1, BPV **45** also one piece 0.2 × 0.1. Areas of red slip survive on all surfaces, except BGG **44** + BGL **57** exterior below lower edge of rim. Traces of polish where slip survives.

Phase	Context & No.	Grid ref	Dia rim (top)	Fig
ii	BGG **44***	08/09/10-S02/S03	30–35(?)	52j
ii	BGL **57***	14/15-S04/S05	30–35(?)	52j
iii	BPV **45**	03-21	? (40+?)	As 52j

* Join

410 Deep bowl(?)

Little of this form survives, but it appears to derive from a deep bowl similar to a Nile C example, diameter 30, red slipped on the exterior only, from Memphis (Kom Rabia) (Bourriau and Gallorini in preparation, [12c2.1]). The context is probably of the SIP, which relates **408** to the lengthy Tell el-Dab'a Hyksos series (Fuscaldo 2000, 53–60 [33–70]), though these are somewhat smaller. The slip need not have extended below the area of the rim.

2310A **410** Fig. 52k

D4 (Nile B2). Fired medium. Surfaces pale brown where slip lost. Break pale brown with red zones and pale grey core. Plentiful poorly sorted sand. Moderate qty to fairly plentiful fine veg to 0.3. Sparse limestone to 0.05. Red-brown slip on both surfaces. Both surfaces polished.

Phase	Context & No.	Grid ref	Max dia rim	Fig
iv (Pt II?)	ABY **19**	Area 13	25–35(?)	52k

411 Large diameter bowl with pre-firing hole

These bowls occur on various MK Egyptian sites, usually but not always in Marl C fabric (Bader 2009b, 77 for additional examples). The form is close to that of a bowl from Dahshur (Arnold Do. 1982, 38–39 and Abb 8 [1]). This is even larger (dia 45) and slightly shallower, and the rim, though similar, is not quite identical. It has a similarly located hole but with a short spout. It is dated to the Twelfth Dynasty, between 1820 and 1760 BC. Also very similar is a Marl C bowl (dia 37) from Elephantine (von Pilgrim 1996, 340 and Abb. 151a) with a slightly more sinuous rim but apparently resembling **411** in lacking a spout. It is dated to the reign of Amenemhat III (*ibid.*, 184), so contemporary with the Dahshur example. It seems appropriate to attribute the same date to **411**.

The quantity of sand and the grain size should imply use as a cooking pot (Müller 2008, 204).

655 **411** Fig. 53a

Wheel-made. Intentional hole (diameter 2.2) made, from the exterior, before firing.

D7 (Nile D). Slightly misfired. White firing surfaces, including interior of hole, except fired red over rim and down *c.*1.0 on interior and exterior, probably where shielded by another vessel in the kiln. Break brick red all through except grey core where thickest. Fairly plentiful poorly sorted sand. Fairly plentiful fine veg to 0.4. Plentiful tiny limestone flecks, and pieces to 0.1. Uncoated. Not polished or burnished.

Phase	Context & No.	Grid ref	Dia rim (top)	Fig
vii	CAA North **4**	Area 26	28	53a

412–13 Thin-walled deep bowls

Deep bowls with flat to rounded rim, **413** slightly undercut. The bowls were (from the Tell el-Dab'a parallels) probably flat-based. The examples at Tell el-Dab'a occur in contexts of both the Twelfth Dynasty (Czerny 1999, 159 [Nf 335–46]) and the Thirteenth (Bader 2009b, 321 and Abb. 190, Typ 39n). The diameter range is 13–18 so **412/13** are at the top end. At Tell el-Dab'a the fabrics are Nile B1/B2 (undivided) with one example in Nile C in the Twelfth Dynasty, and one in Nile B2 in the Thirteenth. Almost all those of the Twelfth Dynasty are red slipped and polished on both surfaces, but of the three Thirteenth Dynasty examples, only one is red slipped and that is not recorded as polished. **412** matches [Nf 336/7] very well; no single example is a perfect match for **413**, but [D932] of Typ 39n comes close; in any case, the Tell el-Dab'a examples vary considerably in stance and in rim form. At Saqqara itself, the Waseda University excavations have yielded a similar form with diameter 17 (Yoshimura, Kawai and Kashiwagi, 2005, 380, Fig. 14 [7]) dated as mid Twelfth to early Thirteenth Dynasty.

Two similar rims from Memphis (Kom Rabia) (Bourriau and Gallorini in preparation, [22b4.2] and [25b2.2]) each have a max diameter of 16 but are in Nile B2 and examples may be slipped or uncoated but not polished. Their contexts are of the mid Thirteenth Dynasty to the early SIP, so they may represent a later development.

The fine fabric and polished slip appear to place **412–13** in the Twelfth Dynasty.

1530 **412** Fig. 53b

Small rim sherd with flat rim, stance probably as upright as drawn but might be less so. Cannot tell whether hand- or wheel-made, because of overall slip.

D1 (Nile B1). Fired fairly soft. Surfaces concealed by slip. Break pale brown with red core. Fairly plentiful fine and medium sand with a few larger grains. Moderate qty fine veg to 0.2. Sparse limestone to 0.05. Red-brown slip on all surfaces. All surfaces highly polished.

Phase	Context & No.	Grid ref	Max dia rim	Fig
*	UP 197 **14**	Area 13	*c.*18–20	53b

* 'Phase iv construction'. No context designation was assigned

2887 **413** Fig. 53c

D1 (Nile B1). Fired fairly soft. Exterior pale brown interior concealed by slip. Break pale brown with thick red core. Fairly plentiful fine and medium well-sorted sand. Fairly plentiful fine and coarse veg to 0.6. No visible limestone. Red slip on interior and top of rim, exterior uncoated. Polished where slipped.

Phase	Context & No.	Grid ref	Max dia rim	Fig
ivb–c	BCW **14**	18/19-01	18	53c

414 Medium-sized jar

The form is not a common one and may be wrongly dated, but is perhaps related to a jar rim (dia 11), apparently in Nile B2, of the early Hyksos period at Tell el-Dab'a (Kopetzky 2004, Typ 22, 246 and Abb. 172). This has a white coating on the exterior and a red one on the interior and rim; it is may be that **414** was not misfired, as thought, but was intended to have a similar appearance. It is even possible that both were imitating slightly earlier Marl C jar types known from Dahshur and Tell el-Dab'a (Arnold Do 1982, Abb. 11.6; Bader 2001, 124 and Abb. 28f–h).

2874 **414** Fig. 53d

Surface slightly uneven, but the shaping of the interior suggests at least wheel assistance.

D4 (Nile B2). Fired medium. Interior surface (mis?)fired grey where uncoated, other surfaces concealed by slip. Break pale brown with thin red zones and purple core. Fairly plentiful poorly sorted sand. Moderate qty fine and coarse veg to 0.5. Sparse limestone to 0.1. Slip, mostly grey but a small area of red, on exterior, top of rim and interior of neck only. Traces of polish where slipped.

Phase	Context & No.	Grid ref	Max dia rim	Fig
(vi–)vii	AAC **156**	28-S05 to 02	12	53d

415 Wide-mouth bowl/jar

Although clearly in the OK tradition in most respects, the detailed form best matches the early MK series of (sometimes?) spouted bowls from Tell el-Dab'a (Czerny 1999, 153–54 [Nf 228–41]). These vessels are all large, with rim diameter up to 30, and with few exceptions red slipped and polished on all surfaces. The closest parallels for the form of **415** are probably [Nf 228/33/39/41], with diameters 29, 24, 21 and 21 respectively, but several others are similar. See also a single example from the same site dated to the first years of the NK (Müller 2008, Fig. 176, column 3). David Aston has pointed out (pers. comm.) that **415** differs slightly in the sharper change of angle between rim and shoulder, and that it might be later than the MK, but no published example combining its form and large diameter has been identified in a later period.

1402 **415** Fig. 53e

D4 (Nile B2). Fired medium. Surfaces red-brown where slip lost. Break red-brown with thick grey core. Fairly plentiful poorly sorted sand. Fairly plentiful fine and coarse veg to 0.3. Sparse limestone to 0.05. Traces of red slip on exterior of body and on interior of body and rim. Polished where slip survives.

Phase	Context & No.	Grid ref	Dia rim (top)	Fig
Mamluk/Mamluk/vii	ABC/ABD/ABA (UP 167) **13**	Area 13	? (24+)	53e

416–17 Wide-mouth bowls/jars

Perhaps two of the many variants of the wide-mouth bowl series, many (all?) with a spout, which developed from OK spouted bowls. The best published series of the MK appears to be from Tell el-Dab'a, early in the period (Czerny 1999, 153–54 [Nf 226–46]). None duplicates the well-developed lid ledge of AKJ/AKI **59**, though [Nf 228] and [Nf 231] do show a slight hollowing at this point and Czerny points out the great variability of the type. The diameter range is 18–30 cm (except one of 15), the fabrics are Nile B1 and B2, and Czerny twice mentions the carefully polished red slip on almost all, which emphasises their OK pedigree. An example in Nile B2 from Lisht North (Allen unpublished, PA 1057), diameter about 25, is quite similar to **417**.

From the slightly later Hyksos period, again at Tell el-Dab'a, Müller illustrates a single poorly preserved sherd of a form said to be Syro-Palestinian (Müller 2008, 204 and Fig. 176, column 2) which exhibits a similar hollowing of the rim.

As to the possibility that **416/17** may be NK, convincing parallels are lacking. The best that can be said is that the form of the rim does somewhat resemble that of big red slipped jars from the tomb of Horemheb (Bourriau *et al.* 2005, 32–33, Figs 13–15). Any distant resemblance to the NK 'meat jars' (e.g. Aston D.A., B.G. Aston and Brock 1998, Pl. 32 [272]) should be discounted, and in any case these are normally made of marl clay (Aston D.A. 1998, 478).

721 **416** Fig. 53f

Lid ledge just inside rim. Too weathered to show whether wheel- or handmade.

D4 (Nile B2). Fired fairly hard. Surfaces where slip lost, ABC/ABD/ABA **8** orange, AKJ/AKI **59** red. Break, ABC/ABD/ABA **8** orange with pink zones and grey core, AKJ/AKI **59** red-brown with thick pink zones and grey core. Fairly plentiful fine and medium well-sorted sand. Fairly plentiful fine and coarse veg to 0.5. Sparse limestone to 0.05. Traces of red slip on exterior and rim of both, but not on interior. ABC/ABD/ABA **8** polished where slip survives, AKJ/AKI **59** too weathered to show polish.

Phase	Context & No.	Grid ref	Max dia rim	Fig & notes
Mamluk/Mamluk/vii	ABC/ABD/ABA (UP 161) **8**	Area 13	*c.*18	Similar to 53f*
Mamluk/vii	AKJ/AKI (UP 141) **59**	Area 14	*c.*20	53f

* Ledge less marked

2664 **417** Fig. 53g

The profile of the rolled rim varies from more to less rounded within 4.5 cm, perhaps indicating hand manufacture.

D4 (Nile B2). Fired medium. Surfaces brown where slip lost, and/or uncoated. Break brown with grey core. Fairly plentiful poorly sorted sand. Moderate qty fine veg to 0.3. Rather more limestone than usual, to 0.05. Traces of red slip on exterior in fold of rim; none visible on interior. No visible polish or burnish.

Phase	Context & No.	Grid ref	Max dia rim	Fig
iv (Pt II?)	ADD North **35**	Area 13	*c.*20	53g

418–20 Large storage jars/restricted basins/vats/cooking pots

David Aston (Aston D.A. 2004b, 167–68) and Vera Müller (Müller 2008, 204) both discuss a possible Egyptian or Levantine origin for these numerous, if variously interpreted, vessels. The form is widespread in the Levant, but that they are already prolific in the later OK is certain from the Saqqara corpus (Rzeuska 2006, Forms 197–200, Pls 139–41) and the parallels from the Anubieion (this volume, **263–94**). Müller stresses the value of sand temper in cooking pots as improving the elasticity of the clay at high temperatures (Müller 2008, 204).

The tradition passes down through the MK (Holladay 1997, Pls 7.6/11/12/14/15/18; Czerny 1999, 174 [Ng 109]; Aston D.A. 2004b, Pls 178–80 [650–58]; Müller 2008, 204 and Fig. 175). At Memphis (Kom Rabia) where they are called 'restricted basins', they occur in Nile B2, C, D and E, and matches can be found to all the MK Anubieion examples. Thus there is a fairly close red slipped parallel to **418** AAT/AIC **5** among residual MK pottery in a NK context (Bourriau 2010, Fig. 44 [2663]), the large diameter of **419** is almost equalled, albeit with a slightly different rim form (Bader 2009b, Typ 63b, 359 and Abb. 210 [3661]; Bourriau 2010, Fig. 7 [2376]), and the sharp angle of **420** is found with a slightly different stance (Bader 2009b, Typ 36d1, 306 and Abb. 185 [5314]). The MK levels produced many further examples (Bourriau and Gallorini in preparation). The form continues through the SIP, where another example similar to **418** AAT/AIC **5** is to be found, though larger and uncoated (Aston D.A. 2004b, Pl. 295 [1088]), and similar vessels continue to be made in Nile clay and mixed clay fabrics at least as late as the early TIP (Aston D.A. and Jeffreys 2007, Figs 49/51/52).

The OK examples are without exception red slipped (three are polished) but mostly very large; many of the MK ones (though strangely few of Müller's) are red or white slipped and if most are again large, a few (e.g. Holladay 1997, Pl. 7.6 [7/8], Pl. 7.12 [2 and 10], Pl. 7.14 [6], Pl. 7.15 [1], Pl. 7.18 [12 and 13 (this last from Syria)]) are in line with the **418** examples. In the NK the forms, sizes and surface treatments are very varied, as shown by the Memphis (Kom Rabia) series (e.g. Bourriau 2010, Fig. 26 [8.7.1/2/3]). With its disturbed deposits, the Anubieion cannot contribute to any analysis of the development of this important vessel type and close dating of the present examples is unfeasible.

2510 **418** Fig. 53h–i

D4 (Nile B2). Fired fairly soft. BKB **121** surfaces brown, AIC/AAT **5** red-brown. Break BKB **121** exterior half red-brown, interior half brown, AIC/AAT **5** pale brown with red core. Fairly plentiful poorly sorted sand.

Moderate qty fine and coarse veg to 0.4. Sparse limestone to 0.1. Red slip (flaking) on exterior and over the rim. No visible polish or burnish, but weathered.

Phase	Context & No.	Grid ref	Dia rim (top)	Fig
ivc	BKB **121**	07/08-23	*c*.13	53h
ivc/ivd	AIC/AAT **5**	05/06-04/05	*c*.12	53i

605 **419** Fig. 53j

D7 (Nile D). Fired fairly soft. Surfaces reddish brown where slip lost. Break reddish brown all through. Fairly plentiful fine and medium well-sorted sand. Moderate qty fine and coarse veg to 0.4. Plentifully speckled with tiny limestone flecks, and sparse limestone to 0.1. Thick brownish red slip on both surfaces, weathered off top of rim. Both surfaces polished.

Phase	Context & No.	Grid ref	Dia rim (top)	Fig
ivd	ASD **16**	19/20-07/08/09	32	53j

2096 **420** Fig. 53k

D7 (Nile D). Fired fairly hard, slightly misfired. Exterior and just inside mouth red (probably slip), interior grey. Break grey all through except close to exterior surface. Fairly plentiful poorly sorted sand. Fairly plentiful fine and medium and some coarse veg, to 0.6. More limestone than usual, mostly to 0.2 but one piece 0.5 × 0.4. Probable red slip on exterior; white surface on interior as far as preserved may be a misfired red. Not polished or burnished.

Phase	Context & No.	Grid ref	Max dia rim	Fig
iii	BDR **169**	08/09-06	*c*.20–25	53k

421 Base of jar ('Bechervase')

Because of the near-impossibility of distinguishing small rim sherds from rims of hemispherical bowls, no rims of tall bag-shaped jars (German 'Bechervasen') were recorded at the Anubieion, but in **421** the combination of fine fabric and thick base indicates a vessel of this type. At Memphis (Kom Rabia) where the ceramics (excluding residual pieces) are of the Thirteenth Dynasty onwards, the type is found only in Nile B2 fabric. On the other hand, at Dahshur, where Twelfth Dynasty material is present, it also occurs in Nile B1 (Arnold Do. 1982, Abb. 6 [22]; Abb. 12 [2]), and B1 examples were found in the Senwosret III temple at Abydos (Wegner 2007, 242 Type 36, Fig. 102.36). It is thought the earlier examples were produced mainly, or even exclusively, in Nile B1 (Bourriau and Gallorini in preparation), so **421** is more likely to be of the Twelfth or early Thirteenth Dynasty than later, a finding consistent with the Nile B2 fabric of the numerous Tell el-Dab'a examples of the late MK and the Hyksos Period (Müller 2008, 103).

243B **421** Fig. 53l

The exterior, although flaking, preserves facets from blade shaping, but there are ridges from wheel-throwing on the interior.

D1 (Nile B1). Fired fairly soft. Surfaces red-brown. Break red-brown with faint red core. Moderate qty fine well-sorted sand. Small qty fine veg to 0.2. No visible limestone. Nodules of unincorporated clay to 0.1. Exterior wet-smoothed or self-slipped but no coloured slip. Not polished or burnished.

Phase	Context & No.	Grid ref	Fig
vi	ABG (UP 206) **7**	Area 13	531

<u>422</u> Undulating neck of small bottle

A distinctive neck on an otherwise unremarkable small bottle. An early example from Sedment is dated by Seidlmayer (1990, Abb. 137) to the early part of his sequence, though another (*ibid.*, Abb. 138) is from near the end. The entire sequence is contained (*ibid.*, Abb. 168) within the Eleventh Dynasty and the very early Twelfth. At Tell el-Dab'a, four Nile B2 MK examples (Aston D.A. 2004b, Pls 197–98 [746–49]) are described as 'presumably votive'. One at Tell el-Dab'a appears in a group of votive vessels dated to the SIP (Fuscaldo 2000, 102, Fig. 58) and they are known from SIP tombs in Upper and Middle Egypt (Bourriau 1997, Fig. 6.17 [6,7]). Anne Seiler (pers. comm.) dates Dra Abu el-Naga examples to the early Eighteenth Dynasty and there is one from Amarna later in the Dynasty (Rose 2007, 258 [477]). The form of the neck, which was clearly either significant or merely popular, recurs in late Ramesside Memphis (Kom Rabia) (Aston D.A. 2007, Fig. 47 [547]) and in the TIP (e.g. Spencer and Bailey 1986, 75 [93] = Aston D.A. 1996, 208, Fig. 106 [93]).

261 <u>**422**</u> Fig. 54a

The interior surface does not follow the line of the exterior, so the wall is especially thick at one point. The interior has almost vertical striations where it was pulled upwards, rather than wheel ridges.

<u>D4 (Nile B2).</u> Fired fairly hard. Exterior red; interior red, shading to grey lower down. Break, exterior half red, interior half grey, but red all through where thinnest. Fairly plentiful poorly sorted sand. Moderate qty fine veg to 0.3. Sparse limestone to 0.1. Exterior too weathered for slip or polish to survive; interior has neither.

Phase	Context & No.	Grid ref	Dia neck (bulge)	Fig
ii	AON **54**	03/04/05-02 to S02	4.5	54a

<u>423</u> Jar with lid ledge(?)

A similar jar with such a lid ledge(?), albeit the whole rather more carefully modelled, is dated to the Thirteenth Dynasty at Dahshur (Arnold Do. 1982, Abb. 19.9). It is in Nile B2 fabric, wet-smoothed but uncoated, and has a top diameter of 8. At Memphis (Kom Rabia) a similar form from the late Thirteenth Dynasty can occur in uncoated Nile B2 (Bourriau and Gallorini in preparation, [29.2.1]) as well as red slipped (Bader 2009b, Typ 39d, 313–14 [5269]); the Memphis examples lack the lid ledge, which may be an uncommon feature.

However, a slightly earlier date may be indicated by a similar, though red slipped, jar from Abydos (Knoblauch and Bestock 2009, 228 and Fig. 7) dated, from comparison with examples from Qau studied by Seidlmayer (1990, 395), to between the end of the OK and the early Twelfth Dynasty.

2306 <u>**423**</u> Fig. 54b

The surfaces and rim profile are uneven, but there are apparent wheel grooves on the interior.

<u>D4 (Nile B2).</u> Fired medium, slightly misfired. Surfaces red-brown, exterior turning grey at lower break. Break red-brown with pink core tending to purple. Fairly plentiful poorly sorted sand. Moderate qty mostly fine veg to 0.3. Sparse limestone to 0.1 and one piece 0.2. Weathered, but probably uncoated. No visible polish or burnish.

Phase	Context & No.	Grid ref	Dia rim (top)	Fig
ivb–ivc	BCT **55**	18/19-08/09	7.5	54b

424 Funnel-necked jar(?)

Although **424** somewhat resembles a ringstand, in fact its proportions are unlike those of the usual MK–SIP ringstands: the waist is too wide in relation to the height and the rim roll unusually thin. It actually matches better a funnel-necked jar (rim dia 8) of the early MK (Czerny 1999, 154 [Nf 252]); this is red slipped on both surfaces and although it is not itself polished, one of the two examples of the adjacent and similar form (*ibid.*, 154 (Nf 251) is polished on both surfaces. Kopetzky has a later but not dissimilar form (dia 11) (Kopetzky 2004, 245 and 274, Abb. 172, Typ 17) from the Hyksos Period, part of a series some of which are again red slipped on both surfaces, though there is no mention of polish.

669 **424** Fig. 54c

Seems to be at least wheel assisted, as preserved.

D4 (Nile B2). Fired fairly hard. Surfaces red-brown where slip lost. Break red with grey core. Fairly plentiful fine sand with a few larger grains. Fairly plentiful fine veg to 0.4. Sparse limestone to 0.1. Thick red slip on all surfaces, beginning to turn grey at furthest point from rim. All surfaces polished.

Phase	Context & No.	Grid ref	Max dia rim	Fig
vii	AAA (UP 157) **91**	05 to 11-11/12	9.5	54c

425–28 'Beer bottles' of the Twelfth Dynasty

Part of a series, most commonly in Nile C fabric, which extends well into the Thirteenth Dynasty (see **429–30**). The authoritative study of their early development is by Dorothea Arnold, primarily using material from Lisht (Arnold Do. 1988, 141–43, Figs 67–71). At Tell el-Dab'a, David Aston (Aston D.A. 2004b, 82–87 and Pls 40–50), continuing this study and building on previous work at Tell el-Dab'a, has constructed a dated typological series from the early Twelfth Dynasty to some time in the Thirteenth (Aston D.A. 2004b, 84/85, Figs 12a/b). Among the many illustrated by Arnold, often with only minor differences, it is difficult to select an exact match but the closest are among the last on her Fig. 69 and most of those on Fig. 70, of the mid to late Twelfth Dynasty. The slight irregularities in the interior profiles of **427/28** find counterparts in Arnold's [65/66/69/86 etc]. The red slip is usual. At Tell el-Dab'a, the counterparts are among Aston's Type 5 (2004b, Pl. 40 [145–46]); see also an example from another part of Saqqara (Yoshimura, Kawai and Kashiwagi, 2005, Fig. 26 [31]).

At Memphis (Kom Rabia) the incidence of 'beer bottles' is high in the lowest excavated levels, where it is largely accounted for by the dumping of Twelfth Dynasty material in order to build up the ground level (Bourriau and Gallorini in preparation). There are thus many parallels to **425–27** (though fewer to **428**) among the Memphis Nile C fabric types (Bourriau and Gallorini in preparation, [19.2/3/4]; for a published parallel to **427**, see Bader 2009b, Typ 67a, 362–64 and Abb. 213 [3237]). The incidence decreases dramatically thereafter.

631A **425** Fig. 54d

D4 near D3 (Nile B2 near C). Fired fairly soft. Surfaces pale brown, exterior where slip lost. Break pale brown with grey core. Fairly plentiful poorly sorted sand. Moderate qty fine and coarse veg to 0.7. Sparse limestone to 0.1. Red slip on exterior, up to centre of rim, with one dribble and one splash on interior. Traces of polish on top of rim only.

Phase	Context & No.	Grid ref	Max dia rim	Fig
o	AQG **21**	20/21/22-S03 to S06	10	54d

631B **426** Fig. 54e

D4 near D3 (Nile B2 near C). Fired fairly soft. Surfaces pale brown, exterior where slip lost. Break pale brown with thin red zones and thick grey core. Plentiful poorly sorted sand. Moderate qty fine and coarse veg to 0.5. Sparse limestone to 0.05. Thin brownish-red slip on exterior, over rim and down 0.5 on interior. Possible traces of polish on exterior only.

Phase	Context & No.	Grid ref	Max dia rim	Fig
ii	AJY **122**	18/19/20-S04/S05	11.5	54e

701 **427** Fig. 54f

Three similar rims, all with slightly irregular surfaces but probably wheel assisted.

D4 (Nile B2). Fired soft to fairly soft. Exterior concealed by slip; interior ABC/D/A **9** pale brown, others red. Break ABC/D/A **9** pale brown with red core where thickest, others red with grey core. Fairly plentiful poorly sorted sand. Fairly plentiful fine and coarse veg to 0.7. Rather more limestone than usual, with some pieces to 0.2. Red slip on exterior and rim only, on ABG **43** ending in a straight edge along the middle of the rim. All, traces of probable polish on exterior only.

Phase	Context & No.	Grid ref	Max dia rim	Fig
vi	ABG (UP 235) **43***	Area 13	11	54f
vi	ABG (UP 235) **47***	Area 13	12	As 54f
Mamluk/Mamluk/vii	ABC/ABD/ABA (UP 161) **9**	Area 13	?	As 54f

* Perhaps same vessel but do not join

703 **428** Fig. 54g

Interior surface uneven near lower break, indicating handmade, but the rim appears to be wheel assisted.

D4 near D1 (Nile B2 near B1). Fired fairly soft. Surfaces red-brown. Break red-brown all through. Fairly plentiful fine and medium well-sorted sand. Sparse veg to 0.2. Sparse limestone to 0.1 and one piece 0.2. Trace of pink slip on rim. No visible polish or burnish.

Phase	Context & No.	Grid ref	Max dia rim	Fig
iv (Pt II?)	ABY **9**	Area 13	11	54g

429–30 'Beer bottles' of the Thirteenth Dynasty

Within Aston's 'beer bottle' series (see above), the two Anubieion rims comprising **429** are his Type 7b of the early Thirteenth Dynasty, and closely resemble his [150] (Aston 2004b, Pl. 42), its type standard. **430** has no close counterpart but [150] is probably again the best. At Tell el-Dab'a all examples of Type 7 are uncoated, but at Memphis (Kom Rabia) these jars also occur red slipped on the exterior. The distinctive concave rims of **429** are similar to two published red slipped Nile C examples (Bader 2009b, Typ 67a/b, 362–66 and Abb. 213 [6207, 3282]). Although the form of **430** is not exactly matched, lacking as it does the normal inturned rim with hollowed interior, the probable trimming of the underside places it in Type 19.5, identified as a specifically Memphite type (Bader 2009b, Typ 67e, 366 and Abb. 214; Bourriau and Gallorini in preparation) present throughout the Thirteenth Dynasty and perhaps on into the SIP. The closest parallel (*ibid.*, Type 19.5.12 [6000]) is from a context dated to the Thirteenth Dynasty but containing residual material.

834 **429** Fig. 54h–i

At least wheel assisted.

D3 (Nile C). Both examples misfired (or refired), with both surfaces blackened and showing incipient sintering. Surfaces concealed by slip. Break, BMG **25** red near exterior, otherwise brown, ABA to ABG **2** dark brown near exterior, otherwise pale brown. Fairly plentiful sand, BMG **25** poorly sorted, ABA to ABG **2** fine and medium with a few larger grains. Fairly plentiful fine and coarse veg to 0.6. Sparse limestone to 0.1, BMG **25** also a void 0.8 where a piece burned out. Dark brown to black slip on both surfaces as far as preserved. Possible but uncertain traces of polish/burnish on exterior.

Phase	Context & No.	Grid ref	Dia rim (top)	Fig
v–vi	BMG **25**	17-S01/S02	10	54h
vi to Mamluk	ABA to ABG (UP 3) **2**	Area 13	*c.*10	54i

2280 **430** Fig. 54j

Carelessly made, with uneven surfaces and veg at various angles. The underside of the rim was probably trimmed with a tool.

D3 (Nile C). Fired fairly soft. Surfaces pale brown. Break pale brown with faint, diffuse red core. Fairly plentiful poorly sorted sand. Fairly plentiful fine and coarse veg to 0.8 and one piece 1.5. Sparse limestone to 0.05, and several voids to 0.5 × 0.3. Uncoated. Not polished or burnished.

Phase	Context & No.	Grid ref	Dia rim (top)	Fig
iv (Pt II?)/iv (Pt II?)	AXX/AXY **7**	Area 13	*c.*9	54j

431 Jar (or ringstand?)

Almost the same form appears at Tell el-Dab'a in the early MK as a jar neck and as a ringstand. Because there seems no good reason to make a ringstand in this specialised fabric, the former is more likely. The closest jar parallels are smaller at diameter 10.5 and 12 (Czerny 1999, 157 [Nf 298/99]), but so is the very similar ringstand at diameter 12 (*ibid.*, 199 [F43]). In spite of the small rim diameters, the groove in each may be from string-tying.

2514 **431** Fig. 54k

D7 (Nile D). Fired medium, but showing signs of misfiring. Surfaces white, probably firing surfaces rather than slip. Break red-brown with narrow brown zones close to surfaces. Fairly plentiful sand, poorly sorted but with fewer than usual of the coarse grains. Fairly plentiful fine and coarse veg, mostly to 0.3 only but one piece 1.2. More limestone than usual, mostly to 0.05 but one piece 0.2. Probably uncoated. Not polished or burnished.

Phase	Context & No.	Grid ref	Dia rim (top)	Fig
ivc	AAD (UP 409) **30**	05/06/07-06	*c.*15	54k

432–33 Smaller diameter offering-stand bases

It is not possible to be certain whether these offering-stand bases did or did not have an integral bowl. Judging by the Tell el-Dab'a series, the latter is more likely. That series (Aston D.A. 2004b, Pls 27–30 [110–16]), all in Nile C, maximum diameter of bases in range 13.0–16.4, includes several examples similar to **432**, of which [113] is closest. There is less similarity to **433**, none being so conspicuously ribbed, but [110] is quite close. The Tell el-Dab'a offering stands, again in Nile C, have much larger bases so are unlikely parallels, though **432** just might be from the top of one of these (cf *ibid.*, Pl. 204 [715]).

At Memphis (Kom Rabia) offering stands are not frequent, perhaps because less appropriate in a purely domestic setting. They appeared so infrequently in the random sample that the base of one in Nile B2 (max dia 14) was included as a 'purposive' sample in Corpus 1 (Bourriau and Gallorini in preparation, Fig 17[a]); it is similar to

432, though the rim is a little more upturned.

The copious use of water for wet-smoothing, as seen on **432**, has also been observed on bowls **377/79/81**, **401**.

699 **432** Fig. 54l

Well-defined ribbing on interior indicates at least wheel assistance.

D4 (Nile B2). Fired medium. Surfaces red-brown. Break pale red-brown with darker brown core. Fairly plentiful poorly sorted sand. Fairly plentiful fine and coarse veg to 0.6. Sparse limestone to 0.1 and one piece 0.3. Both surfaces wet-smoothed with copious water, but probably not slipped. Possible trace of polish on rim only.

Phase	Context & No.	Grid ref	Max dia base	Fig
vi to Mamluk	ABA to ABG (UP 3) **15**	Area 13	15	54l

651 **433** Fig. 54m

Ribbing on both surfaces indicates wheel-made as preserved.

D3 (Nile C). Fired fairly hard, starting to become brittle. Surfaces red. Break red with pink core. Fairly plentiful poorly sorted sand. Plentiful fine and coarse veg to 1.2. Sparse limestone to 0.2. Probable trace of red slip on exterior near rim. No visible polish or burnish.

Phase	Context & No.	Grid ref	Max dia base	Fig
vii?	BFB **23**	Area 1	14	54m

434–35 Larger diameter offering-stand bases

Two uncoated Nile C offering-stand bases from Memphis (Bader 2009b, 373 and Abb. 218 [5531]; Bourriau and Gallorini, in preparation) are very similar to **434** and have almost the same diameter (23 and 22); their contexts are probably of the Thirteenth Dynasty, though that of [5531] could extend into the SIP. At Saqqara, Waseda University excavated two such *in situ*, the larger of which (Yoshimura, Kawai and Kashiwagi, 2005, 380 and Fig. 14 [13]) has a base again similar in size (dia 25) and form; it is dated mid Twelfth to early Thirteenth Dynasty.

Although **435** should derive from an offering stand, bases are normally steeper, the shallow elements being the tops. However, as a base, its shallow form would aid stability. The exterior slip and polish are not conclusive, as tops are not always slipped on the inside.

2294 **434** Fig. 54n

All surfaces weathered, especially interior, but extra wear on inside edge of rim may indicate at least occasional use with this rim uppermost. Nevertheless, the form and size look more like an offering stand than a ringstand.

D3 (Nile C). Fired medium. Surfaces reddish brown but weathered. Break brown with thin red zones and thick grey core. Fairly plentiful poorly sorted sand. Fairly plentiful fine and coarse veg to 0.4. Sparse limestone to 0.1. Exterior uncoated, or slip lost, interior weathered. Not polished or burnished.

Phase	Context & No.	Grid ref	Max dia base	Fig
ivc	BQQ **32**	Area 2	*c.*25	54n

649 **435** Fig. 55a

The edge of the rim is slightly abraded, probably in use.

D3 (Nile C). Fired fairly hard. Exterior concealed by slip, interior brown. Break red with thick grey core. Fairly plentiful poorly sorted sand. Fairly plentiful fine veg to 1.0. Sparse limestone to 0.1. Thick red slip on exterior only. Polish on exterior only.

Phase	Context & No.	Grid ref	Max dia base	Fig
ii	ADG **7**	Area 13	29	55a

436 Offering-stand base with thickened wall

At Tell el-Dab'a, a Nile C offering-stand base (dia 16) with a slightly more developed out-turn to the foot exhibits a similar thickening of the wall (Bader 2009b, 373 and Abb. 218 [D1883]); the context is of the Thirteenth Dynasty. Memphis (Kom Rabia) provides no close parallel.

1404A **436** Fig. 54o

Probably at least wheel assisted.

D4 (Nile B2). Fired medium. Surfaces orange-brown. Break orange-brown with red zones and grey core. Fairly plentiful poorly sorted sand. Fairly plentiful fine and coarse veg to 1.1. Sparse limestone to 0.05. Too weathered to retain slip. Not polished or burnished as preserved.

Phase	Context & No.	Grid ref	Max dia base	Fig
o	AQG **256**	11/12-01/S01	*c.*16–20	54o

437 Narrow-waisted ringstand

Narrow-waisted ringstands are characteristic of the MK, SIP and early NK. The upper rim is usually undercut and the base may be, but a rounded form, as here, is not uncommon (e.g. Aston D.A. 2004b, Pl. 188 [697], Pl. 698 [700]). The ridged central area of **437**, probably from string-tying, is unusual but the alternative interpretation as a ridge-necked bottle is very unlikely in this fabric and would not explain the thickening of the wall at the break.

221 **437** Fig. 55b

About 50 per cent of the height of a small ringstand, and a detached body-fragment from the same object.

D4 (Nile B2). Fired medium. Exterior concealed by slip, interior brown where uncoated. Break brick red all through except near lowest point, where grey core near interior surface. Fairly plentiful poorly sorted sand. Fairly plentiful fine and coarse veg to 1.0. Rather more limestone than usual, to 0.1 and four pieces each 0.2. Reddish brown slip on exterior, over the rim and running down inside. Not polished or burnished.

Phase	Context & No.	Grid ref	Max dia base	Fig
iv (Pt II?)	ADF **75+76+77**	Area 13	12	55b
iv (Pt II?)	ADF **78**	Area 13	-	As 55b

438 Base of ringstand(?)

The form and thickness of the rim should disqualify this as a jar, and the incipient curvature at the upper break indicates too low an object for an offering stand. As a ringstand it duplicates almost perfectly one from the early MK at Tell el-Dab'a (Czerny 1999, 200 [F50a]) except that the latter lacks the out-turn and appears to derive from a taller stand. The maximum diameter is 11 and, unlike **438**, it is red slipped on both surfaces as far as preserved.

683 **438** Fig. 55c

The rim is folded inwards, the fold being visible in one break only.

D4 Sandy (Nile B2). Fired soft. Surfaces pale brown. Break pale brown with scarcely perceptible red core. Fairly plentiful poorly sorted sand. Moderate qty fine veg to 0.5 but mostly less. Rather more limestone than usual, to 0.1. Perhaps self-slipped, but no coloured slip. Not polished or burnished.

Phase	Context & No.	Grid ref	Max dia base	Fig
iva	AJH under AVH **7**	05-04/05/06	14	55c

439 Low, sharply curved ringstand

Similar ringstands are common at Tell el-Dab'a at all stages of the MK and into the Hyksos Period (Aston D.A. 2004b, Pls 188–89, 298–300). They are most commonly in Nile B2 fabric. Aston says (*ibid.*, 175 and 245) that the bases are trimmed with a tool, which may account for what was interpreted as wear on **439**. The diameter is rather (though not impossibly) large for an upper rim, so it is probably a base in spite of its tight curvature.

2210 **439** Fig. 55d

Rim thickened, not rolled. The flattest area of the interior, close to the edge of the rim, appears to be abraded as well as weathered, as would happen to a ringstand but to either the base or the top.

D4 (Nile B2). Fired fairly hard. Surfaces pale brown as preserved. Break pale brown with thin red zones and thick grey core. Fairly plentiful poorly sorted sand. Moderate qty fine and coarse veg to 0.4. Sparse limestone to 0.05. Smoothed, but the surfaces are too weathered for slip, or polish or burnish to survive.

Phase	Context & No.	Grid ref	Max dia base	Fig
Mamluk/vii	AKJ/AKI (UP 141) **51**	Area 14	12	55d

440 Ringstand(?)

Although NK bowls can take a similar form, the rather coarse fabric and especially the abraded edge tend to indicate a ringstand and the possible hand-manufacture favours the MK. If this is the case, the best match is from the early MK at Tell el-Dab'a (Czerny 1999, 199 [F47]), though all four examples (dias 15/16) are red slipped on both surfaces. A possible alternative is as the base of a tall stand with integral bowl, like two more (dias 14/13), again MK from Tell el-Dab'a (Aston D.A. 2004b, Pl. 27 [110], Pl. 29 [114]), uncoated like **440**.

2712 **440** Fig. 55e

Slight ledge or nick. Interior near top/bottom abraded, probably in use. Slightly uneven: perhaps handmade.

D4 (Nile B2). Fired fairly soft. Surfaces red-brown. Break pale brown all through. Fairly plentiful poorly sorted sand. Fairly plentiful fine veg to 0.4. Rather more limestone than usual, to 0.1 and one piece 0.1 × 0.2. Uncoated. Not polished or burnished.

Phase	Context & No.	Grid ref	Max dia base	Fig
iii	BDR **182**	08/09-06	12	55e

441 Ringstand

Although the estimated diameter of CGC **10** seems excessively large and may have been misjudged, according to their forms these are the upper rims of ringstands such as one (max dia 18) from Tell el-Dab'a (Aston D.A. 2004b, Pl. 192 [711]). This happens to be in a marl fabric but others less similar in form are in Nile fabrics, with maximum diameters up to 25.

2310B **441** Fig. 55f

D4 (Nile B2). BGL **10** fired fairly hard, CGC **10** medium. BGL **10** surfaces concealed by slip, CGC **10** brown where slip lost. Break red-brown, BGL **10** with thick grey core, CGC **10** with dark brown zones and red core. Fairly plentiful poorly sorted sand. Moderate qty to fairly plentiful fine veg to 0.3. Sparse limestone to 0.05. BGL **10** red-brown, CGC **10** brown, slip on both surfaces. Both surfaces polished.

Phase	Context & No.	Grid ref	Max dia rim	Fig
ii	BGL **10**	15/16-S01/S02/S03	*c.*15	55f
ivc	CGC **10**	02/03-34/35	25–35(?)	As 55f

442–43 Thick-walled ringstands

Low, thick-walled, stable ringstands of about this size are characteristic of the MK. Nile C examples were recorded at Memphis (Kom Rabia) (Bader 2009b, Typ 70b, 369–71 and Abb. 217 [6071]; Bourriau and Gallorini in preparation) and at Dahshur (Arnold Do. 1982, Abb. 4 [5] and Abb. 7 [19]). The Memphis examples are from contexts dated to the middle of the Thirteenth Dynasty and the two from Dahshur are attributed to the reign of Amenemhat III. Each site also has smaller examples.

The type is plentiful at Tell el-Dab'a: there are two similar examples in Nile C (Aston D.A. 2004, Pl. 190 [704/05]), also two in Marl C (Bader 2001, Abb. 69d/e [404/05]) which Bader dates to the beginning of the Thirteenth Dynasty and the first third to the middle, respectively.

No MK parallel has been found for the polish on **443**, so it may date to the FIP.

679 **442** Fig. 55g

Cracked along larger rim, from misfiring. Inner edge of both rims worn in use.

D3 (Nile C). Misfired, fairly hard but brittle. Surfaces red but partly grey from misfiring. Break red/grey with pink zones and thick black core. Fairly plentiful poorly sorted sand. Fairly plentiful fine and coarse veg to 1.0. Sparse limestone to 0.1, also three pieces each 0.2 and one 0.3. Defective firing has destroyed any evidence of slip. Not polished or burnished.

Phase	Context & No.	Grid ref	Max dia rims	Fig
v	DAF **12**	Area 2 W10-S50 to S53	18 and 20	55g

775 **443** Fig. 55h

Misfired and distorted. From a squat, thick-walled ringstand similar to **442**.

D4 (Nile B2). Fired fairly hard, but in part misfired, brittle. Exterior surface pale red-brown where slip lost. Break red-brown with thick grey core. Fairly plentiful fine and medium sand with a few larger grains. Small qty fine veg to 0.2. Sparse limestone to 0.05. Thick red-brown slip on all surfaces. All surfaces polished.

Phase	Context & No.	Grid ref	Max dia rim	Fig
v	AEW **19**	03/04-03 to 06	*c*.20–22	55h

444–45 Provision jars ('Vorratsgefässe')(?)

Although rim **444** might derive from a late OK beer jar (cf Rzeuska 2006, Pl. 13 [17] and Pl. 30 [85]), it is more probably from a MK provision jar similar to one from Dahshur, also handmade in Nile C fabric and with the same top diameter (Arnold Do. 1982, Abb. 7 [14]). These jars, which have thick, heavy peg-type bases (as **445**) seemingly out of keeping with their unrestricted form, vary greatly in size and shape: several at Memphis (e.g. Bourriau and Gallorini in preparation, [35.2.1]), again some wheel-made and some handmade, in Nile B2 and Nile C, are within the diameter range 13–18 and another from Dahshur (Arnold Do. 1982, Abb. 10 [13]) has a diameter of 22. From Saqqara itself come examples with diameter range 14–20 (Yoshimura, Kawai and Kashiwagi, 2005, 387, Fig. 19 [12–14]; 397, Fig. 24 [11]) dated as mid Twelfth to early Thirteenth Dynasty. The type occurs in both the Twelfth and the Thirteenth Dynasties.

Some publications refer to these vessels as meat jars or meat containers, from the presence of bones in two such vessels (Arnold Do. 1982, 55–56 and Taf. 9c–d).

733 **444** Fig. 55i

Distinctive almost vertical grooves on exterior. Handmade.

D3 (Nile C). Badly fired, brittle. Exterior grey, interior surface red. Break grey near exterior, otherwise red. Fairly plentiful poorly sorted sand. Fairly plentiful fine and coarse veg to 1.2. More limestone than usual, to 0.1, and five pieces 0.2/0.3. Uncoated. Not polished or burnished.

Phase	Context & No.	Grid ref	Dia rim (top)	Fig
iii	CHB **4**	08/09-25/26	12	55i

249A **445** Fig. 55j

Wheel assisted, with wheel ridges on interior, but also pull marks. Exterior vertically scraped.

D3 (Nile C). Fired medium. Surfaces pale red-brown, exterior where slip lost. Break pale red-brown with thick grey core. Fairly plentiful poorly sorted sand. Fairly plentiful fine and coarse veg to 1.1. Sparse limestone to 0.1. Areas of red slip survive on exterior. Possible traces of polish where slip survives.

Phase	Context & No.	Grid ref	Fig
o/vii/?	AMB/AAA/AMA **4**	04/05-14/15	55j

446–48 Small diameter tubular bread moulds

It is not clear why these are present at all. Even if priests and other necropolis workers were living on the desert edge rather than down in the valley, why was their bread made in a place to which all ingredients, containers and fuel would have to be brought? Or is it possible that offerings of bread, in tombs or cult chapels, were brought in their moulds, as a guarantee of authenticity or for ease of transport? In any case, the practice does not appear to have continued into the NK.

The flat rim with slightly concave top of Fig. 55l is in the tradition of the Old Kingdom, but the small size argues for a later date. The other rim forms are matched in the early Middle Kingdom, though with such crude vessels too much should not be expected. At Tell el-Dab'a in the Twelfth Dynasty, two (Czerny 1999, 198 [F 17/19]) resemble Fig. 55k, and two others (*ibid.*, [F 18/21]) are like Fig. 55m; later rims (Aston D.A. 2004b, Pl. 186 [675–78]) are different. At Dahshur in the late Twelfth to early Thirteenth Dynasty a Nile C example

(Arnold Do. 1982, Abb. 7 [12]) lies between the two. In Thirteenth Dynasty Memphis (Kom Rabia) they are not common but matches to Fig. 55l and 55m do occur (Bourriau and Gallorini in preparation).

As to the bases, it is even less realistic to expect exact correspondence; suffice it to say that at all three of the above sites, bases of generally similar form occur, though pinching off the wheel seems not to be mentioned. In Memphis there are matches to Fig. 56b and 56c (Bourriau and Gallorini in preparation).

For a pioneering study of bread-moulds of all periods, see Jacquet-Gordon (1981).

739 **446** Fig. 55k–m

Crudely handmade, the form of the rim varying greatly. The porous interior was lined with a thin layer of a smooth, less porous clay tempered only with very fine sand, and parts of this layer survive in a few cases. The diameters are approximate because the vessels are so crude.

D3 handmade (Nile C). Fired soft to fairly soft, but usually rather fragile. Surfaces red or grey. Break red or grey all through. Fairly plentiful to plentiful poorly sorted sand. Small qty fine veg to 0.2/0.3, mostly surprisingly fine given the coarse fabric. Sparse limestone to 0.1, a few to 0.2. Uncoated. Not polished or burnished.

Phase	Context & No.	Grid ref	Max dia rim	Approx form rim	Fig & notes
o/ii	AQG/AJY **24**	19/20-04/05	*c*.5–6	Rounded	55k★
o/ii	AQG/BGU **13**	19/20-S04/S05	*c*.8	Rounded	
ii	AIY **115**	05 to 08-04/05/06	*c*.8	Intermediate	
ii	BGG **55**	08/09/10-S02/S03	*c*.7	Flat	
iii–iva/iva	BNQ/BMY **1**	04/05-12/13	?	Flat	
iv	DAG **11**	Area 2 W09-S52/S53/S54	*c*.8	Rounded	
iva	BAX **3**	06/07/08-03/04	*c*.8	Flat	55l ★
iva/ivb	BHR/BTG **9**	01-20/21	*c*.7	Flat	
iv+	DAW **2**	Area 2.W11-S60	*c*.7	Intermediate	55m ★

★ Areas of lining survive

741 **447** Fig. 56a–d

Bases of crude handmade bread moulds, of the **446** rim type. Many, but not all, show evidence of having been finished by pinching off, apparently between finger and thumb (see table). As with the rims, many retain parts of a clay lining, which survives well because protected.

D3 handmade (Nile C). Fired soft to medium, usually fairly fragile. Surfaces red-brown, brown or grey according to firing. Break red, brown or grey all through, or with red or grey core where thickest. Fairly plentiful to plentiful poorly sorted sand. Small to moderate qty fine and some coarse veg mostly to 0.5, a few pieces to 1.5. Some examples sparse limestone to 0.05/0.1, but others more than usual, and pieces to 0.3, 0.4 and 0.7 (exploded) seen. Uncoated. Not polished or burnished.

Phase	Context & No.	Grid ref	Base pinched?	Fig & notes
o	AQG **58**	18/19-S05/S06	Yes	
o	AQG **223**	19/20-S06/S07	No	★
o	AQG **302**	18/19/20-S04/S05	Yes	56a
o	BDY **49**	01/02/03-07/08	Yes	★

Phase	Context & No.	Grid ref	Base pinched?	Fig & notes
o	BEN **57**	14/15-01 to S03	?	★
o/ii	AQG/AJY **33**	19/20-04/05	No	★
ii	AIY **116**	05 to 08-04/05/06	?	
ii	AIY **121**	05 to 08-04/05/06	Yes	★
ii	BET **125**	14/15-02/03	?	
ii	BGN **16**	10 to 13-S03/S04/S05	Yes	
ii/ii/ivc	AJX/AJY/BRS **67**	21/22/23-S02/S03	No	56b ★
iii	BCB **161**	01 to 05-04/05/06	Yes	★
iii	BDQ **9**	01 to 05-07/08	Yes	
iii	BEK **3**	07/08-03/04	Yes	56c
iii–iva	ACE **166**	01 to 05-08 to 12	Yes	★
iv (Pt II?)	ADC **176**	Area 13	No	★
ivd	ATY **217**	25-04	Yes	56d
v–vi	CBS **29**	04/05-30/31/32	?	★

★ Areas of lining survive

743 **448** Not illustrated

Body sherds from bread moulds apparently of the same type as rims and bases **446–47**. Small-diameter cylindrical section, and in some examples retaining parts of the finer clay lining.

D3 handmade (Nile C). The ware is as the rims and bases. Some sherds have a grey core.

Phase	Context & No.	Grid ref	Notes
o	AQG **141**	13/14-01/02	
o	BDY **55**	01/02/03-07/08	
o	BEN **58**	14/15-01/S01/S02/S03	
o	BEO **16**	21/22-S06	★
o	BEO **42**	14/15-01/S01/S02	
o/ii	AQG/AJY **10,11**	21/22-S04/S05/S06	★(**11** only)
o/ii	AQG/BGU **14**	19/20-S04/S05	
o/ii	BDY/BDX **8**	01 to 08-07/08	
ii	AJY **177**	17 to 20-S04/S05	
ii	BDX **5**	05-07/08	
ii	BGH **36**	10 to 15-S04/S05	
ii	BGL **2**	15/16-S01/S02	
ii/ii/ivc	AJX/AJY/BRS **23**	21/22/23-S02/S03	
ii/ivb	AIY/AIH **15**	13/14-02/03	
iii	CHD **5**	08/09-25/26	
iii–iva	AFS **87**	03-07	
iv (Pt II?)?	BWL? (UP 1040) **24**	Area 12	★

Phase	Context & No.	Grid ref	Notes
iva	BHR **133**	02-22/23	
v/v	BJG/BJO (H) **28**	W01/01-S01	

* Areas of lining survive

<u>449</u> Base of cylindrical bread mould(?)

A series from the Twelfth Dynasty levels at Tell el-Dab'a (Czerny 1999, 197–98 [F 8–F 13]), all with base diameter 12–15 and all handmade in Nile C except one 'Nile B2 near C', provides a nearly perfect match to this base, except that none is described as slipped. Czerny (*ibid.*, 101) insists that these really are bread (or cake) moulds, while conceding that they hardly occur on any other site. However, there is one from Dahshur (Arnold Do. 1982, Abb. 10.16), from a context dated 1820–1760 BC and one from Elephantine (von Pilgrim 1996, 344 and Abb. 153f) probably of the late Twelfth Dynasty. Also from Elephantine is an example with a low hump in the centre (*ibid.*, 334 and Abb. 148d) and from Abydos one with a very pronounced hump (Wegner 2007, 242 and Fig. 101.35); of the latter it is suggested that it might have been used to produce ring-shaped loaves. Thus it may be significant that the upper surface of **<u>449</u>** is broken away in the central area, where a hump would have stood. The slip might imply a pre-MK date, harking back to the OK, but the form is not present in Rzeuska's (2006) corpus. The type does not appear in Jacquet-Gordon's study (Jacquet-Gordon 1981).

717 **<u>449</u>** Fig. 56e

Certainly an unrestricted form, because of interior slip. Handmade.

<u>D4 (Nile B2).</u> Fired fairly soft. Surfaces pale brown where slip lost. Break pale brown with grey core. Fairly plentiful poorly sorted sand. Fairly plentiful fine and coarse veg to 0.8. Sparse limestone to 0.1. Thick red-brown slip on underside, and areas and traces survive on exterior of wall and on interior of wall and base, so all surfaces originally slipped. Underside polished, and probable traces of polish elsewhere where slip survives.

Phase	Context & No.	Grid ref	Max dia rim	Fig
ii	BGN **3**	10 to 13-S03/S04/S05	*c.*13	56e

<u>450–52</u> Large diameter lids(?)

Even when complete, lids are difficult to identify with confidence unless there is either a knob or a hole at the top, or (with less certainty) a slip or wash on the exterior only. Bader (2009b, 337) makes this point, and remarks that an inverted bowl could often serve as a lid; indeed, there was one such *in situ* at the Anubieion in the Ptolemaic period (personal observation, to appear in a later volume).

It is even more difficult to classify rim sherds such as **<u>450–52</u>**, emphasised by the fact that **<u>450</u>**, the only one with surviving slip on the interior, so the most likely to be from a bowl, has a rim form that seems to rule out this interpretation. A possible function as the base of a large offering stand cannot be excluded: as a lid, the lip would fit snugly around the top of a vessel; as a base, it would improve stability. It is thus unsurprising that there are few published parallels.

Bader (2009b, 337) mentions that at Tell el-Dab'a, where complete examples with inturned rim were common, it was often difficult to know whether these were bowls or lids. The various series of bowls (Aston D.A. 2004b, Pls 81–86 [237–60]; Pls 87–88 [261–64]; Pls 261–64 [942–60]), copying Levantine imports, have similar though not quite identical incurved rims, some flat-topped. Most are in Nile B2 but a few are in the coarser Nile C, D and E fabrics. Unfortunately the best matches to **<u>450</u>** are in the B2 series, which may be red slipped but never burnished, and only the other fabrics, which are coarser and lack the internal lip, can be both. The large diameter of **<u>450</u>** is just within the Tell el-Dab'a range, though the best matches (*ibid.*, Pl. 82 [243]; Pls 261/63 [944/56]) are a little smaller, between 21.0 and 24.6. The wide date range is from the Twelfth Dynasty into the Hyksos period, and very similar lids can apparently occur in the Old Kingdom (Malykh 2011,196 and Fig. 3 [98/3/13]).

That such objects can have an even larger diameter is shown by one from Dahshur (Arnold Do. 1982, Abb. 7 [8]). This is in Nile C, has a maximum diameter of 42 cm, and is rather better modelled; however, its function is equally uncertain.

From Memphis (Kom Rabia) there are in fact many examples. Bader publishes one in Nile B2 (Bader 2009b, Typ 46b, 337 and Abb. 199 [2395]) with a general similarity to **450–52**; one in Nile C (*ibid.*, Typ 74a, 375 and Abb. 219 [6073]) with a more specific resemblance to **452**; and one in Marl C, rare in this fabric (*ibid.*, Typ 173a, 480 and Abb. 268 [5922]), which is quite close to **450**. One in Nile B2 published elsewhere (Bourriau and Eriksson 1997, Fig. 3 [9]; Bourriau and Gallorini in preparation [31b2.6]) falls somewhere between **451** and **452**. Among additional examples are one (*ibid.*, [31b2.5]) in Nile B2 similar to **450** and with the same dip under the foot, and one (*ibid.*, [502c1.4]) in Nile C, fairly similar to **451** and distinctive in being the only example polished/burnished (on the interior and the rim) like **450** as well as red slipped. The Memphis contexts are of the Thirteenth Dynasty to the SIP, the unique [502c1.4] coming from the end of the sequence, within the SIP.

812 **450** Fig. 56f

D4 (Nile B2). Fired medium. Surfaces concealed by slip. Break red-brown with pink core, or pink zones and grey core where thickest. Fairly plentiful fine sand with a few larger grains. Small qty fine veg to 0.2. Sparse limestone to 0.05. Red-brown slip on all surfaces. All surfaces polished.

Phase	Context & No.	Grid ref	Max dia rim	Fig
vii	AAA (UP 23) **606**	09-08	27	56f

900 **451** Fig. 56g

D4 (Nile B2). Fired medium. Surfaces red-brown. Break red-brown with grey core. Fairly plentiful fine and medium sand with a few larger grains. Moderate qty fine veg to 0.3. Sparse limestone to 0.1 and one piece 0.2. Numerous nodules of unincorporated clay to 0.2. Too weathered for slip, or polish or burnish to survive.

Phase	Context & No.	Grid ref	Max dia rim	Fig
iii	BDR **91**	10-03/04/05	?(25+)	56g

928 **452** Fig. 56h

Too weathered to tell whether hand- or wheel-made.

D4 (Nile B2). Fired medium. Surfaces orange-brown. Break orange-brown with thick pink core. Plentiful poorly sorted sand. Fairly plentiful mostly fine veg to 0.4. Rather more limestone than usual, to 0.1. Surfaces weathered: no visible slip, or polish or burnish.

Phase	Context & No.	Grid ref	Max dia rim	Fig
ivb	BDE **14**	14/15/16-06/07/08	?(30+?)	56h

MARL CLAY FABRICS, 453–82

The individual fabrics are not separated. Present: E1A (Marl C1) 22 entries; E1B (Marl C Compact) 1 entry; E1C (Marl C2) 5 entries; E4 (Marl A3) 2 entries; E7 (Marl A2) 1 entry.

453 Plate (or lid) with potmark

The vessel form is absent from Bader's corpus (Bader 2001). A slightly thinner but otherwise matching example is published from Memphis (Kom Rabia), where it occurs (dia 22, in uncoated Marl C2) in Level V of the late SIP to early Eighteenth Dynasty (Bourriau 2010, Fig. 9 [3559]); there is another example (dia 25, in uncoated Marl C1 like **453**) in a SIP context (Bourriau and Gallorini in preparation). In the Lisht North corpus a Marl C thick-walled plate (Allen unpublished, PA 377) has a diameter of only 11 but both form and stance are close to **453**. Aston's Tell el-Dab'a assemblage yields only one example of comparable form (Aston D.A. 2004b, Pl. 188 [686]): published as a lid, this has a maximum diameter of only 9.2 and is in Marl A3 fabric.

None of these has a potmark. The mark on **453** is incomplete but was most probably a simple square as known (applied pre-firing) in the MK at Kahun (Gallorini 2009, 134 Type 3.11.3 and Fig. 6 [6]) and at the Anubieion on 7 of the Archaic Period. In Barbara Ditze's NK series from Qantir there is a very similar square (Ditze 2011, 378–79 [142]), but this was applied before firing and to the exterior of a jar. On the other hand, it may be part of something more complex, such as Bader's 388 (Bader 2001, 210, Abb. 68b).

For a summary of all the potmarks in the present volume, see Appendix 1.

2883 **453** Fig. 57a

The smooth unmarked surfaces probably indicate hand manufacture. On the interior is a deeply scratched potmark, probably done after firing.

E1A (Marl C1). Fired hard. Firing surfaces: interior brown, exterior grey. Break red-brown all through. Fairly plentiful fine and medium sand with a few larger grains. Small qty fine veg to 0.6. Many tiny limestone flecks and sparse to 0.05. Uncoated. Not polished or burnished (but weathered).

Phase	Context & No.	Grid ref	Max dia rim	Fig
vii	AAA (UP 37) **127**	11 to 20-S01/S02/S03	18	57a

454 Bent-sided bowl with direct rim

Rim of a large bowl of common form, as Bader's Typ 12, probably nearest to one (dia 26.4) from Dahshur (Bader 2001, 56 and Abb. 5k [35]) in Marl C (unspecific). The context is dated to 'the last two-thirds of the Thirteenth Dynasty'.

At Memphis (Kom Rabia) the form often occurs but usually of a smaller size. One example in Marl C2 (Bader 2009b, Typ 157c, 463 and Abb. 260 [5412]) has probable diameter 14; another of the same fabric (Bourriau and Gallorini in preparation, [88a2.2]) also has diameter 14. Two which are larger, but in Marl C1, have diameters *c.* 19 and 24 respectively (*ibid.*, [55b1.2 and 56b3.2]). All are from levels of the late Thirteenth Dynasty to the SIP.

2322 **454** Fig. 57b

Faint grooves on the interior indicate manufacture on the wheel.

E1C (Marl C2). Fired fairly soft to medium. Thin white firing surfaces. Break red-brown all through. Plentiful poorly sorted sand. Moderate qty fine veg to 0.3. Many tiny limestone flecks, and sparse to 0.1. Uncoated. Not polished or burnished.

Phase	Context & No.	Grid ref	Dia rim (top)	Fig
ivb	BKN **230**	02-20/21/22	(20–30?)	57b

455 Rim of small wide-rimmed jar

Although no published parallel for its small closed form has been located, Teodozja Rzeuska, who has studied Marl A3 at Elephantine and elsewhere (Rzeuska 2011, 461–530), and who kindly examined this small rim sherd, confirmed the fabric and attributed it to the Middle Kingdom. It conforms to her M2 variant, green or grey-green and containing sand, and probably of the Thirteenth Dynasty (*ibid.*, 468).

However, the form could admit of a slightly later date. At Amarna, where Marl A3 is not listed, a globular jar in Marl A4(?) has a similar though not identical rim and is slipped and burnished (Rose 2007, 285, Type MG 3.2 [637]); it is possibly a mid Eighteenth Dynasty survival (*ibid.*, 137). At Memphis (Kom Rabia) a jar rim of the same type, in Marl A2 or a similar fabric (Bourriau 2010, Fig. 31 [12.10.2]), self-slipped and burnished, is placed in the early to mid Eighteenth Dynasty.

759 **455** Fig. 57c

E4 (Marl A3). Fired medium. Surfaces covered by (self-?) slip. Recent break green all through, though the ancient break has weathered pink. Fairly plentiful fine well-sorted sand. Small qty fine veg to 0.2. Greenish grey probable self-slip on both surfaces Both surfaces polished.

Phase	Context & No.	Grid ref	Max dia rim	Fig
vii	AAA (UP 23) **408**	08-07	10	57c

456 Restricted beaker

In the Memphite region, where the Upper Egyptian Marl A2 fabric is uncommon (Nordström and Bourriau 1993, 176), beakers occur frequently but normally in Nile clays. **456** is at the lower end of the size range. At Lisht, Nile B2 beakers similar in size and form occur in the early Twelfth Dynasty (Arnold Do. 1988, 129, Fig. 66 [50, 168]). At Dahshur there were two in Nile clay (Arnold, Do. 1982, Abb. 2 [1] and 7 [3]) while a third, more fragmentary, unpublished example from the same site is an even better match to **456**, with the same wide, shallow groove just below the rim and a top diameter of 5.5. All three are dated to the reign of Amenemhat III or shortly thereafter (*ibid.*, 36–38).

Numerous similar but not identical rims are recorded from Memphis (Kom Rabia) again in Nile fabrics. Most are of somewhat larger diameter (Bourriau and Gallorini in preparation, [27b1.1/2/3/6] etc). The contexts are variously dated from the mid Thirteenth Dynasty to the early SIP. At Tell el-Dab'a, similar Nile clay vessels are dated to the Hyksos Period (Aston D.A. 2004b, 224–25, Pls 219–22). Thus it seems impossible to date **456** closely.

2292 **456** Fig. 57d

Wheel-made as preserved.

E7 (Marl A2). Fired fairly soft. Firing surfaces, exterior and top 1.5 of interior white, interior then pale red-brown. Break red-brown all through. Moderate qty fine and medium well-sorted sand. Small qty fine veg to 0.2. Very many tiny limestone flecks, and sparse to 0.05. Uncoated. Not polished or burnished.

Phase	Context & No.	Grid ref	Dia rim (top)	Fig
ivd	AJF **3**	06-02/03	5.5	57d

457–58 Necks of bottles/narrow-necked jars

457–58 should belong to the series of bottles or narrow-necked jars already present in both Marl C1 and Mixed Clay P.60 fabrics in the late OK (Rzeuska 2006 Pl. 41, Form 19). No close parallel to **457** has been found in Bader's series of these vessels in marl fabrics; **458** resembles one of her Typ 42 (Bader 2001, 123, Abb. 28h) but has a deeper rim. However, at Memphis (Kom Rabia) there is an almost exact duplicate of **457** in Marl C2, of the late Thirteenth Dynasty (Bourriau and Gallorini in preparation, [95.2.5]). Closest in form to **458** is an example in Marl C1 (Bourriau 2010, Fig. 8 [2485]) but this is from a late SIP to early Eighteenth Dynasty context where it may be residual.

The Nile clay version was analysed in detail by Dorothea Arnold (1988, 141–43, Figs 67–71) (see **425–28**). **457–58** are similar to her Figs 68/69 [46/48/70/95/177] and the diameter range embraces both the Anubieion examples. [46/48/95] all belong to her Cluster 2, which she dates to the reign of Senwosret II ([70/177] are not among those analysed). David Aston (Aston D.A. 2004b, 82–83) takes the discussion further and his Type 9b of the Thirteenth Dynasty is quite similar in form to **457–58**.

2252 **457** Fig. 57e

Rim slightly irregular in shape and some smudging of the rim roll, so the diameter is uncertain. Regular horizontal smoothing marks should indicate wheel assistance, in spite of the distortion of the form.

E1A (Marl C1). Fired fairly hard. Exterior thick white firing surface, partly concealed by probable self-slip; interior grey. Break red with faint, intermittent grey core. Fairly plentiful fine and medium sand with a few larger grains. Sparse fine veg to 0.2. Numerous tiny limestone flecks, none larger. Exterior probably self-slipped, the slip being of irregular thickness. Not polished or burnished.

Phase	Context & No.	Grid ref	Dia rim (top)	Fig
ii	AIY **133**	09/10-07/08	*c.*8	57e

2622 **458** Fig. 57f

Regularity of form should indicate wheel assistance. The groove below the rim is probably from string-tying.

E1A (Marl C1). Fired medium. White firing surfaces. Break red-brown, shading to a slightly darker brown core. Fairly plentiful poorly sorted sand. Small qty fine veg to 0.2. Many tiny limestone flecks, and moderate qty to 0.1. Uncoated. Exterior appears to be lightly polished, but perhaps only sand-blasted.

Phase	Context & No.	Grid ref	Dia rim (top)	Fig
iv (Pt II?)	ADC **117**	Area 13	10	57f

459 Jar with folded rim

Similar jars have a long history in the MK. There are early Twelfth Dynasty examples in Marl C from Tell el-Dab'a (Czerny 1999, 194 [Mc 158/59/62]), but others from Memphis (Bader 2009b, 441 and Abb. 248 [5662]; 471 and Abb. 263 [6225]), in Marl C1 and Marl C2 respectively, are of the late Thirteenth Dynasty or early SIP.

3945 **459** Fig. 57g

E1C (Marl C2). Fired medium. Surfaces cream. Break pink all through. Plentiful fine and medium well-sorted sand. No visible veg. Matrix limestone and one piece 0.2. Several nodules of unincorporated clay to 0.2. Probably uncoated. Not polished or burnished, but weathered.

Phase	Context & No.	Grid ref	Dia rim (top)	Fig
vi	ABI Top **118**	Area 13	10	57g

460 Decorated lower neck and shoulder of jar

Marl A3 fabric originates in Upper Egypt in the Eleventh or early Twelfth Dynasty (Nordström and Bourriau 1993, 177). Allowing time for diffusion, at Saqqara it is unlikely to be earlier than the Twelfth Dynasty.

A wide-mouthed jar from el-Kab (Bourriau 1981, 68 [123]) has motifs like the combed ones on **460**, and a narrower-necked jar from the same site (Quibell 1897, Pl. XVI [70]), probably the type of which **460** is a fragment, seems to have such decoration in combination with horizontal incised lines, though the drawing does not admit of certainty. The combed decoration reappears on the exterior of two wide-mouthed bowls from Lisht North (Allen unpublished, PA 77/408); the fabrics are marls within the range A3–B.

For a recent in-depth study of the Marl A3 storage-transport jars, with additional parallels, see now Rzeuska (Rzeuska 2011).

757 **460** Fig. 57h

The diameter of the illustration is only approximate. Uncertain whether or not wheel assisted.

E4 (Marl A3). Fired medium. Surfaces greenish cream. Break greenish cream with faint pink streaks. Fairly plentiful fine and some medium well-sorted sand. Sparse fine veg to 0.2. Sparse limestone to 0.05. Probably uncoated. Not polished or burnished. Combed decoration at the junction of neck and shoulder, with remains of a different incised(?) motif below.

Phase	Context & No.	Grid ref	Fig
ii	BDX **3**	05-07/08	57h

461 Rim of jar with vertical cut

Perhaps from a funnel-necked jar such as Bader's 199 of Typ 44 (2001, 123, Abb. 28j) in Marl C1, with a top diameter of 11. If so, early Twelfth Dynasty (*ibid.*, 125). For the cut in the rim, which may be part of an indicator of capacity, see **300** of the OK.

2918 **461** Fig. 57i

Preserved down to the base of the neck, the out-turn for the body just perceptible in the lower break. Cannot tell whether or not wheel assisted, but this would be usual. Small vertical cut in rim, apparently post-firing.

E1A (Marl C1). Fired hard, beginning to be misfired. Surfaces grey, showing white (firing surfaces?) near lower break. Break grey all through. Fairly plentiful poorly sorted sand. No visible veg. Plentiful tiny limestone flecks and sparse to 0.1. Cannot tell whether or not slipped. No visible polish or burnish.

Phase	Context & No.	Grid ref	Dia rim (top)	Fig
o/ii	BDY/BDX **20**	01 to 08-07/08	*c.*12	57i

462 Jar with direct rim and 'cordon'

Often included in the series of 'jars with grooved/corrugated neck' (see **463/64**), vessels like **462** actually have a smooth neck except for a bulge, amounting almost to a cordon, at its base. Parallels are found at Memphis (Kom Rabia) (Bourriau and Gallorini in preparation, [61.15.1] and [96.3.2]) in Marl C1 and Marl C2 fabrics respectively. The former is dated to the mid Thirteenth Dynasty, the latter to the late Thirteenth to the SIP. The long Marl C series from Tell el-Dab'a published by Czerny (1999, 191–92, [Mc 78–117]) includes many forms very similar to **462** and provides a Twelfth Dynasty date.

2246 **462** Fig. 57j

Horizontal smoothing marks and scratches on interior appear to indicate wheel assistance.

E1A (Marl C1). Fired fairly hard. Exterior white firing surface, interior surface red. Break red with thin grey core where thickest. Fairly plentiful poorly sorted sand. No visible veg. Plentiful tiny limestone flecks and sparse to 0.1. Uncoated. Not polished or burnished.

Phase	Context & No.	Grid ref	Dia rim (top)	Fig
ivd	ATY **187**	23/24-06/07	10	57j

463 Jar in Marl C1 fabric with folded rim and corrugated neck

For an example in Marl C Compact and discussion of this jar type, see **464**.

This particular form, with grooves carried up to the rim, has close parallels from Memphis (Kom Rabia) (Bourriau and Gallorini in preparation, [63.2.4] in Marl C1; [96.5.1] in Marl C2). The jar type in general occurs there throughout the Thirteenth Dynasty. Quite close also are two examples of Bader's Typ 46 (Bader 2001, 128, Abb. 29f/j) from Tell el-Dab'a, respectively in Marl C Compact dated to the end of the Twelfth Dynasty or the beginning of the Thirteenth, and in Marl C1 dated to the beginning of the Thirteenth Dynasty.

2244 **463** Fig. 57k

Exterior ribbing and regular light horizontal scratches on interior appear to indicate wheel assistance.

E1A (Marl C1). Fired fairly hard. White firing surfaces. Break red, with thin grey core where thickest. Fairly plentiful poorly sorted sand. No visible veg. Plentiful tiny limestone flecks and sparse to 0.1. Several nodules of unincorporated clay. Uncoated. Not polished or burnished.

Phase	Context & No.	Grid ref	Dia rim (top)	Fig
vii	AAA (UP 118) **103**	26/27/28-08/09/10	12	57k

464 Jar in Marl C Compact fabric with folded rim and corrugated neck

Marl C Compact fabric appears to be used predominantly for large jars, both bag-shaped and symmetrical, though they also occur in Marl C1 (see **462–63**). These jars were used for both storage and transport and were widely distributed. The neck is very varied in thickness and form, depending on the amount of pressure applied by the potter's fingers and whether or not this was maintained right up to the rim.

The closest parallel found is in the very comprehensive Lisht North Marl C corpus (Allen unpublished, PA 529); the form is similar and it has about the same thickness as **464** while most of the other 28 drawn examples are thinner. It is Typ 46 in Bettina Bader's Marl C corpus (Bader 2001, 129–44, Abb. 29–38) but there is no close match. Nor is there one at Memphis (Kom Rabia) though the inward roll is present on a rather larger *zir* rim in Marl C1 (Bourriau and Gallorini in preparation, [67.6.2]).

That they can be found as early as the Twelfth Dynasty is indicated by an occurrence at Tell el-Dab'a at this date (Czerny 1999, 191 [Mc85]); the fabric is Marl C (undivided). At Memphis (Kom Rabia) although Marl C Compact fabric rarely occurred, there is evidence of its continuation into the Thirteenth Dynasty. Bader states (*ibid.*, 129) that a chronological series is impossible at present, especially since such jars may have been in domestic use before being incorporated into burials.

2248 **464** Fig. 57l

The inward roll of the rim appears to be intentional, unlike on **471**. Smoothing marks on the exterior are horizontal on the upper neck, at 45 degrees below; on the interior they are horizontal, light and regular, apparently indicating wheel assistance.

E1B (Marl C Compact). Fired fairly hard. White firing surfaces. Break red with grey core. Moderate qty, fine well-sorted sand. No visible veg. Plentiful tiny limestone flecks and sparse to 0.1. Uncoated. Not polished or burnished.

Phase	Context & No.	Grid ref	Dia rim (top)	Fig
vii	AAA (UP 445) **34**	Area 2	11.5	57l

465 Large storage jar with deep, folded rim

Among Bader's long series of Typ 57 jars from Tell el-Dab'a (2001, 154–95, Abb. 42–64), the rim forms are very variable but still fail to include anything identical to **465**; the best match is probably an unstratified example (*ibid.*, 186, Abb. 60b).

The Memphis (Kom Rabia) series includes a close parallel in Marl C1 (max dia rim 18) (Bourriau and Gallorini in preparation [67.4.3]), dated to the late Thirteenth Dynasty.

The long Marl C series from Lisht North also includes many very similar to **465** (Allen unpublished, PA 78/194/721/22/1125). The maximum rim diameters are respectively 17, 25, 29, 22 and 26. The chief difference of most from **461** is a concave exterior surface to the rim, but within the series itself there are again many variables.

Dorothea Arnold has published several examples from Dahshur, including two in Marl C (max dias 25 and 22), from an undated context, which are again similar (Arnold Do. 1982, Abb. 11 [3–4]); however, an unpublished one, again in Marl C and with maximum diameter 25 (Arnold Do. unpublished, II [110]), provides an even closer parallel and is dated to the Thirteenth Dynasty.

2254 **465** Fig. 57m

Deep, slightly rounded rim and sloping shoulder. Smoothing marks on exterior are horizontal above groove, at 45 degrees below it; on interior, horizontal, light and regular, apparently indicating wheel assistance. Interior partly soot-blackened, probably post-firing.

E1A (Marl C1) near E1C (Marl C2). Fired fairly hard. Exterior white firing surface, interior surface blotchy red and white. Break red with thin grey core in one part only. Plentiful fine and medium sand with a few larger grains. No visible veg. Numerous tiny limestone flecks and sparse to 0.1. Uncoated. Not polished or burnished.

Phase	Context & No.	Grid ref	Dia rim (top)	Fig
iv (Pt II?)	AXA 'sealed under wall ABX' **1**	Area 13	*c.*20	57m

466–67 Large storage jars in Marl C1 fabric with round, folded rim

Bettina Bader publishes a long series of large bag-shaped to globular jars from Tell el-Dab'a as her Typ 57 (Bader 2001, 155–94, Abb. 42–64) 'large provision jars (zeirs)', the *zeir* or *zir* being the modern Egyptian equivalent form, though normally used to hold water. The bases of **466–67** would have been flat and of large diameter, and the vessels bag-shaped. The rounded rims place them early in Bader's series, as 57a (*ibid.*, 159, Abb. 44). Both have visibly folded rims. The rim diameters accord with her stated range 25–31. Bader places her Typ. 57a in the Twelfth Dynasty, and David Aston (Aston D.A. 2004b, 98) concurs; this date is confirmed by the very similar forms in Czerny's corpus (1999, 190 [Mc 74/75/77]).

The rim form is present in Marl C1 in Thirteenth Dynasty Memphis (Kom Rabia) (Bader 2009b, 449, Abb. 252 [4154]; Bourriau and Gallorini in preparation [67.1.1]) but since these jars can continue in use for many years they may have been manufactured much earlier.

1442 **466** Fig. 58a

Top of rim abraded, probably either from damage caused while the jar was sunk in the ground (a common practice) or from reuse of complete detached rim as a ringstand.

E1A (Marl C1). Misfired, rather brittle. Grey firing surfaces, or pink where abraded. Break grey with light brown zones near surfaces. Plentiful poorly sorted sand. A few impressions probably of fine veg, to 0.2. Plentiful very small limestone flecks and sparse to 0.1. Large qty of unmixed clay to 0.5. Uncoated. Apparent traces of burnish on exterior and about 1.0 down on interior, but this would be unusual and may be desert weathering.

Phase	Context & No.	Grid ref	Dia rim (top)	Fig
ii	AJY **13**	18/19/20-S04/S05	*c.*24	58a

2240 **467** Fig. 58b

Sufficiently preserved for interior to show irregular surface characteristic of hand-manufacture. Smoothing marks inside and out, at 45 degrees to rim.

E1A (Marl C1). Fired fairly hard. Exterior a white firing surface, interior red. Break red with grey core. Fairly plentiful fine and medium sand with some larger grains. No visible veg. Plentiful tiny limestone flecks and sparse to 0.1. Uncoated. Not polished or burnished.

Phase	Context & No.	Grid ref	Dia rim (top)	Fig
v	DAF **29**	Area 2.W10-S57	29	58b

468 Large storage jar in Marl C2 fabric with round, folded rim

Similar to **466–67** in E1a (Marl C1); see above. Probably Twelfth Dynasty.

1444 **468** Fig. 58c

The rim is visibly folded and wheel assisted, but the body would have been handmade.

E1C (Marl C2). Fired medium. Surfaces concealed by slip. Break brown with grey core. Fairly plentiful poorly sorted sand. A few pieces fine and coarse veg to 1.0 on surface only Plentiful tiny limestone flecks and sparse to 0.1. Thick white slip on both surfaces. Interior and top of rim horizontally burnished, and traces on exterior, which has thinner slip and is more weathered.

Phase	Context & No.	Grid ref	Dia rim (top)	Fig
iii	BEK **1**	07/08-03/04	28	58c

469–70 Large storage jars

Judging by the rim diameters and the shape of the shoulders, these rims are from very large jars. The rim forms are not identical: **470** is taller, less rounded internally and narrower at the top. Nevertheless, each is probably best understood as belonging to Bader's Typ 57b (2001, 159, Abb. 44d) in Marl C1, though the illustrated example is again slightly different. Bader notes that the lower edge of the rim is trimmed with a tool, but this was not recorded on the Anubieion examples. Her examples, from Tell el-Dab'a, are dated to the late Twelfth to early Thirteenth Dynasty. No closely matching jars were recorded at Memphis (Kom Rabia), though a somewhat similar Marl C1 rim to **469**, thought to derive from a restricted-form basin (Bourriau and Gallorini in preparation, [78d1.1]), was found in a Thirteenth Dynasty context where it may be residual.

2250 **469** Fig. 58d

E1A (Marl C1). Fired fairly hard. Exterior and interior white firing surfaces. Break red-brown all through. Fairly plentiful poorly sorted sand. No visible veg. Plentiful tiny limestone flecks and sparse to 0.1. Horizontal but irregular smoothing marks inside and out, need not indicate wheel assistance. Uncoated. Not polished or burnished.

Phase	Context & No.	Grid ref	Dia rim (top)	Fig
iva	BAX **9**	06/07/08-03/04	*c*.30(?)	58d

2778 **470** Fig. 58e

E1A (Marl C1). Fired fairly hard. Thick white firing surfaces. Break red-brown with thick grey core. Fairly plentiful poorly sorted sand. Small qty fine veg to 0.2. Many tiny limestone flecks, and sparse to 0.1. Uncoated. Not polished or burnished.

Phase	Context & No.	Grid ref	Dia rim (top)	Fig
iva	AWZ **14**	08/09-04/05/06	? (30+)	58e

471 Large storage jar with undercut rim

On some Tell el-Dab'a Marl C examples of similar diameter to **471** published by Czerny the hook-like roll inside the rim is incipient (1999, 189 [Mc 54/56]) and on others in the same series fully developed (*ibid.*, 190 [Mc 65/66/68]). This is Bader's Typ 48, which she specifies (2001, 146) as predominantly from the beginning of the Twelfth Dynasty, and there is a parallel in Marl C1, though with a rounded projection instead of a hook, from contemporary Lisht (Arnold Do. 1988, 134, Fig. 74 [60]).

Although there is no perfect match in the Memphis series, there are closely related forms (Bader 2001, Typ 48, 149 and Abb. 40d [3286]); (Bader 2009b, Typ 142a, 447 and Abb. 251 [5872]). The context is of the Thirteenth Dynasty to the SIP but they may be residual.

2242 **471** Fig. 58f

Smoothing marks on exterior at 45 degrees to rim. Very regular horizontal smoothing marks on interior, down to 7 cm below rim, may indicate wheel assistance. The low roll on the interior of the rim is clay pushed inwards, perhaps when the vessel stood on its rim prior to firing. Interior partly soot-blackened, probably post-firing.

E1A (Marl C1). Fired fairly hard. Both surfaces white but in part refired greyish. Break brown with grey core. Fairly plentiful poorly sorted sand. No visible veg. Plentiful tiny limestone flecks, and moderate qty to 0.1. Some unincorporated clay nodules, causing unevenness of the exterior surface. Uncoated. Not polished or burnished.

Phase	Context & No.	Grid ref	Dia rim (top)	Fig
vii/?	AAA/AMA **1**	08/09-13/14/15	21	58f

472 Low ring-base of restricted-form vessel(?)

Most marl ring-bases of the MK derive from unrestricted forms and all examples from Memphis conform to this pattern, but **472** looks too deep, and the wall too thick at its maximum, for such a vessel. The only ring-bases at all similar in Bader's original Marl C1 series are her [370/71/73] (2001, 202, Abb. 66n/p/q); they are attributed to (unspecific) closed forms but the diameters are in the range 5.4–6.6 only. Dorothea Arnold publishes one from Dahshur of diameter 10 (1982, Abb. 8 [13]) but thinner-walled and in the fine Marl A2. Closer in form, in the Lisht North corpus, are one in Marl C and diameter 10 but again thinner-walled (Allen unpublished, PA 1027), and three others (in Nile C, Marl B and Marl C), a better match but each with again a diameter of only 5. Bader's recent comparison of vessels from Tell el-Dab'a and Memphis (Kom Rabia) includes a more convincing Marl C parallel (Bader 2009b, 484, Typ. 179b [D1912]), but the diameter is only 7 and an unrestricted form of vessel is postulated.

This method of manufacturing a ring-base is well attested in the MK (Arnold Do. 1993, 58, Fig. 65A) and was also noted on a carinated bowl from the Anubieion (**388**). The Marl C2 fabric probably indicates a date in the Thirteenth Dynasty or later.

2256 **472** Fig. 59a

Handmade, the base formed separately and attached. The base-ring must originally have been a little taller, since the core is exposed on the underside. Scuffing in the fold above the base may indicate string-tying before firing.

E1C (Marl C2). Fired medium to fairly hard. Underside red, exterior white firing surface, interior brown. Break red with grey core. White surface layer is thin on underside, so probably fired standing upright. Fairly plentiful poorly sorted sand. No visible veg. Plentiful tiny limestone flecks and sparse to 0.1. Uncoated. Not polished or burnished.

Phase	Context & No.	Grid ref	Dia base-ring	Fig
ii/ii	AIY/BET **10**	10-01/02	10	59a

473–74 Flat bases of large storage jars

Almost certainly from jars of Bader's Typ 57 (2001, 154–95, Abb. 42–64). On the whole it appears to be the earlier versions, dated to the Twelfth Dynasty and the early Thirteenth, that have the large diameter flat bases. The polishing of the interior of **474** is assumed to have been produced by the flattening and smoothing process.

2258 **473** Fig. 59b

Small part of base and lower wall. Handmade by coiling. Smoothing marks at 45 degrees on exterior, horizontal on interior and parallel to edge on underside.

E1A (Marl C1). Fired fairly hard. Exterior and underside white firing surfaces, interior red. Break red with very thick grey core. Moderate qty poorly sorted sand. No visible veg. Plentiful limestone, mostly small but one piece 0.8. Uncoated. Not polished or burnished.

Phase	Context & No.	Grid ref	Dia	Fig
ii	AUQ **128**	07/08-01/02	15–25(?)	59b

695 **474** Fig. 59c

Small white marks on interior of wall, radiating from the junction (not illustrated), were probably caused by the act of flattening a coil-built vessel.

E1A (Marl C1). Fired fairly soft. Firing surfaces: exterior mottled pink and white, interior red-brown. Break brown, with thick grey core where thickest. Fairly plentiful poorly sorted sand. Small qty fine veg to 0.3. Plentiful tiny limestone flecks and several pieces to 0.2. Some nodules of unincorporated clay to 0.1. Uncoated. Interior polished, exterior not polished or burnished.

Phase	Context & No.	Grid ref	Dia base	Fig
vii/?	AAA/AMA **4**	08/09-13/14/15	*c*.24(?)	59c

475 Round base of jar

It is not possible to assign **475** to any particular type of jar.

2260 **475** Fig. 59d

Part of a thick, round base from a jar. Deep fingermarks on interior. Exterior smoothed but slightly irregular, with no visible marks.

E1A (Marl C1). Fired hard. Exterior blotchy brown and white, interior pale red-brown. Break red with diffuse grey core. Fairly plentiful poorly sorted sand. Small qty fine veg to 0.3. Numerous tiny limestone flecks and sparse to 0.3. Probably uncoated. Not polished or burnished.

Phase	Context & No.	Grid ref	Fig
?*	BNE **48**	09/10-04/05	59d

* Sherds in BNE prove a Phase ivd or later date

476 Shoulder of large jar

It is not possible to assign **476** to any particular type of jar.

2262A **476** Fig. 59e

E1A (Marl C1). Details not recorded.

Phase	Context & No.	Grid ref	Fig
ii	BGL **81**	14/15-01/S01/S02	59e

477 Jar body sherd with painted potmark

It is not possible to assign **477** to any particular type of jar. The potmark may be part of a motif/hieroglyph as Bader's 383 (2001, 209 and Abb. 67i [383]), tentatively identified as the hieroglyph *sr* (Gardiner 1964, 496, O 33); in the lists from Kahun and Gurob (Petrie 1891, Pl. XV) it appears in various guises halfway down the first column. A very similar incised potmark occurs already on a bread mould which is no later than the early OK (Mączyńska 2009, 106, Fig. 17 [16]), but a black-painted motif, again very similar, is published from Memphis (Fischer 1959, 32 [109]) where the NK date is assured by red- and blue-painted bands above it, and it appears again at Deir el-Medina in the reign of Ramesses II (Aston D.A. 2009a, 60, Fig. 13 lower [7]). See also ATY **199** of **478**.

For a summary of all the potmarks in the present volume, see Appendix 1.

2262B **477** Fig. 59f

From the upper body of a jar.

E1A (Marl C1). Fired fairly hard. Surfaces concealed by self-slip. Break red with grey core. Inclusions not recorded. Both surfaces apparently self-slipped. Exterior lightly polished or burnished. Potmark painted in black before firing.

Phase	Context & No.	Grid ref	Fig
v	DAF **18**	Area 2.W10-S50/S51	59f

478 Jar shoulder sherds with potmarks

It is not possible to assign either sherd to any particular type of jar. The potmark on ATY **199** resembles one on a Marl C1 jar from Tell el-Dab'a (Bader 2001, 209 and Abb. 67i [383]). Barbara Ditze's NK Qantir corpus includes various similar trellis-like marks (e.g. Ditze 2011, 378–79 [143–44]). See also the painted **477**.

The fragment on AJY/AQH **11** cannot be identified with certainty; part of a hieroglyph is possible, but it may have been no more than a simple small circle such as occur in Ditze's NK Qantir corpus (Ditze 2011, 402–05 [180–86]) and on a small bread mould which is no later than the early Old Kingdom (Mączyńska 2009, 100, 106, Fig. 13 [2].

For a summary of all the potmarks in the present volume, see Appendix 1.

2262C **478** Fig. 59g–h

E1A (Marl C1). Fired fairly hard. White firing surfaces, interiors patchy. Break AJY/AQH **11** red, ATY **199** brown, each with grey core. Fairly plentiful poorly sorted sand. AJY/AQH **11** sparse fine veg to 0.5, ATY **199** none visible. Plentiful tiny limestone flecks, AJY/AQH **11** also sparse to 0.1, ATY **199** also fairly plentiful to 0.2. Uncoated. Not polished or burnished. Potmarks incised before firing.

Phase	Context & No.	Grid ref	Fig
ii/iva	AJY/AQH **11**	11/12-S01/S02/S03	59g
ivd	ATY **199**	21/22/23-02/03/04	59h

479 Scraped lower bodies of jars

It is not possible to assign any of the four sherds to a particular type of jar. The scraping technique (Bourriau 1981, 53 [89]) may indicate a date in the early MK or even the FIP.

2262D **479** Fig. 59i

Sherds from the lower bodies of narrow-based jars. All show irregular vertical facets resulting from scraping to shape the base; BAY/BCC **1** is less clear than the others but probable. ABR North **11** may be drawn too upright.

E1A (Marl C1). No ware details were recorded, except that ABR North **11** was polished on exterior.

Phase	Context & No.	Grid ref	Fig
ii	ABR North (UP 51) **11**	Area 13	59i
ii	AYG **7**	Area 13	Similar to 59i
iv(Pt II?)/?	AYQ/AYR **18**	Area 13	Similar to 59i
ivc	BAY/BCC **1**	05/06-07/08	Similar to 59i

480 Body sherds in Marl C1 fabric

Included to widen the context base, with many sherds from Phases o and (especially) ii, and a number from Areas 2 and 12–14. Most are from restricted forms, but it is not possible to assign any to a particular type of jar. Without potmarks and not from scraped lower bodies. For a discussion of 'gaming pieces' such as AQE **38** see Bader's Typ 72 (2001, 216, Abb. 70f). Bader's list of sites where they occur (*ibid.*, 218–19) is far from complete.

2262E **480** Fig. 60a–b

AJY **65** has been reused as a scraper and AQE **38** as a large 'gaming piece' or a jar closure.

E1A (Marl C1). All sherds are in Marl C, and certainly or probably Marl C1. Ware details were not recorded.

Phase	Context & No.	Grid ref	Fig
o	AQG **63**	12/13/14-S04/S05	
o	AQG **138**	13/14-01/02	
o	AQG **257**	11/12-S03/SO4	
o	BDY **57**	01/02/03-07/08	

Phase	Context & No.	Grid ref	Fig
o	BEO **60**	14/15-S04/S05	
o/ii	AQG/AJY **23**	19/20-04/05	
o/ii	BDY/BDX **6**	01 to 08-07/08	
o/ii	BDY/BDX **19**	01 to 08-07/08	
o/iva	BJA/BMW **9**	14-04	
ii	AIY **65**	10-01/02	
ii	AIY **97**	07/08-06	
ii	AIY under Room 10 **154**	09 to 12-03/04	
ii	AJY **7**	21/22/23-S05/S06	
ii	AJY **45**	22/23-S05/S06	
ii	AJY **65**	21/22-S05/S06	60a
ii	AJY **120**	21/22-S05/S06	
ii	AQE **38**	19/20-01/02	60b
ii	AQE **47**	19/20-01/02	
ii	AUQ **96**	08/09-02/03	
ii	AUQ **177**	08-03	
ii	BDX **77**	02/03-07	
ii	BET **8**	12-01/02	
ii	BET **32**	14-S01/S02	
ii	BET **38, 41**	12/13-02/03	
ii	BGG **6**	12 to 16-S04/S05	
ii	BGG **30**	08/09/10-S02/S03	
ii	BGG **39**	08/09/10-S02/S03	
ii	BGG **105, 114**	04/05/06-S01/S02/S03	
ii	BGG **143, 145, 146**	11/12-S04/S05	
ii	BNK **2**	11 to 14-05	
ii	ABR North (UP 51) **10**	Area 13	
ii/ii/ivb/ivc	AJX/AJY/AMV/BRS **11**	21/22/23-S04/S05/S06	
ii/iva	AJY/AQH **8**	11/12-S01/S02/S03	
ii/ivb	AIY/AVB **47, 53**	10 to 14-S01/S02	
ii/ivb	AJY/AVB **4, 15**	11/12-S01/S02	
iii	BCB **83**	01 to 04-04/05/06	
iii	BDP (UP 647) **221**	01 to 05-07	
iii	BDQ **6**	01 to 05-07/08	
iii	BDR **69, 74, 79**	11/12/13-03/04/05	
iii	BJJ **13, 15**	17/18-05/06	
iii–iva	ACE **113**	01 to 05-08 to 12	
iv (Pt II?)	ABS (UP 20) **33**	Area 13	
iv (Pt II?)	ABY **13, 14**	Area 13	

Phase	Context & No.	Grid ref	Fig
iv (Pt II?)	ARP=ARS (UP 152) **13**	Area 13	
iv (Pt II?)	ARP=ARS (UP 154) **5**	Area 13	
iva	AQH **58**	19/20-S04/S05	
iva	BML **23**	05-13/14	
iva	CJV **2**	09-29/30	
iva/ivb	AEF/AHR **12**	10 to14-04/05	
ivb	ACS **5**	09-S01/S02/S03	
ivb	AVB **15, 86, 118**	10/11-S02/S03	
ivb	AVB **21**	11/12-S02/S03	
ivb	CGZ **3***	05/06-33/34	
ivb/ivb–c/ivb–c/ivb–c/ ivb–c/ivd	AVA/AUW/AUX/AVD/AVE/AJE **8**	13 to 16-01/S01	
ivc	ATE **20**	03/04/05-S04/S05/S06	
ivc	CGF **6**	02 to 05-33 to 36	
ivc	CGQ **78**	02 to 05-34 to 37	
ivc	BQI **24, 29**	Area 2	
ivc–d(?)/ivd(?)	DBW/DBU **29**	Area 1. 28-S31	
v	AOO **8**	05-10/11	
v	DAF **27**	Area 2. W10-S57	
v/v	BJG/BJO(H) **21**	W01/01-S01	
v–vi	BKX **1**	07-25/26	
v–vi	BPZ **3**	07/08-28	
v–vi	CBU **62***	06/07/08-33/34/35	
vi	ABG (UP 235) **16**	Area 13	
Mamluk	ARN (UP 9) **69**	Area 12	
vii	AAA (UP 108) **14**	29 to 34-S06	
vii	AAA (UP 445) **78**	Area 2	
vii	AAA Lower **39**	Area 2	
?	BEP **78**	16 to 20-01/S01	
?	UP 805 **23**	Area 5	
?	UP 1044 **27, 28, 32**	Area 12	

* Join

481 Body sherds in Marl C2 fabric

All probably from restricted forms, but it is not possible to assign any to a particular type of jar. The Marl C2 fabric probably indicates a date in the Thirteenth Dynasty or later.

2266 **481** Not illustrated

The three sherds are all from different vessels. All handmade.

E1C (Marl C2). Fired fairly hard to hard. Exteriors white firing surfaces; BGG **53** interior brown, others red.

Break BDG/BRT **18** red-brown all through, others red-brown with grey core. Fairly plentiful sand, AYN/AZG **20** poorly sorted, others fine and medium well-sorted. No visible veg. Fairly plentiful tiny limestone flecks, and AYN/AZG **20** sparse to 0.1. BDG/BRT **18** has nodules of unincorporated clay to 0.4. Uncoated. Not polished or burnished.

Phase	Context & No.	Grid ref
ii	BGG **53**	08/09/10-S02/S03
iva/ivb	BDG/BRT **18**	10 to14-03/04/05
v/v	AYN/AZG **20**	Area 13

482 Base of offering stand(?)

Unusually large for either the upper body of a bowl or the base of an offering stand, but more probably the latter. Unsurprisingly, nothing comparable has been located among published material. In Nile C fabric, a similar form with maximum diameter only 16, and one with only a small lip but diameter 24, occurred at Dahshur (Arnold Do. unpublished). It cannot be closely dated; the MK is likely but the FIP also possible.

691 482 Fig. 60c

Handmade by coiling. Both surfaces uneven, and a single groove in the interior is discontinuous.

E1A (Marl C1). Fired fairly soft. White firing surfaces, except top of rim red-brown where it stood in the kiln. Break brick-red all through. Fairly plentiful poorly sorted sand. Moderate qty fine veg to 0.5. Plentiful tiny limestone flecks, and sparse to 0.1. Uncoated. Not polished or burnished.

Phase	Context & No.	Grid ref	Max dia base	Fig
vii	AAA (UP 627) **40**	01/W01/W02-17 to 20	*c*.35	60c

CHAPTER 10

The Pottery of the Second Intermediate Period, the New Kingdom and the Third Intermediate Period

The dense cluster of shaft tombs which occupied the area of the Anubieion during, just before and just after the New Kingdom forms a small part of a much larger cemetery extending far to the north (Sowada *et al.* 1999; personal observation of SCA excavations 2006–09), and at least a short distance to the south and west (Vol. II, Pl. 4). The regular arrangement of those within the excavation area (*ibid.*, Pl. 5) indicates an overall plan, and when we allow for the former presence of above-ground tomb chapels and subterranean chambers, both occupying a greater area than the shafts themselves, it is clear that little space could have remained between them. Thus the probability is that all within the Anubieion area were constructed within a short space of time, marching in rows a little way back from the cliff of the desert edge, into which others as yet undiscovered may have been cut. It might therefore be expected that the pottery associated with them, and in the main derived from vessels deposited with the burials, would all be of more-or-less the same date.

It is clear that this was by no means the case, and although offerings subsequently deposited in the chapels could have included some pottery vessels, the explanation must lie chiefly in the reuse of the tombs for later burials, a practice common throughout Egypt. Even the single excavated shaft and associated tomb chambers proved to contain mixed material, including Ptolemaic sherds, inevitable since the shaft would have stood open at various times. Since the majority of the sherds in the chambers were of Ramesside date, this should prove the use of those chambers for the burial of one or more fairly affluent individuals at that time, but not that the burials were the first to occupy them.

The construction of the tombs must probably be dated by the earliest pottery found around them, and even if the disputed early dates for black-rimmed bowls and Cypriot Base Ring Ware are set aside, parallels with Deir el-Ballas, and some vessels from other sites, appear to indicate a date in the early Eighteenth Dynasty or even the Second Intermediate Period. Use of the area would thus have been more-or-less continuous from the Middle Kingdom (and earlier) onwards. This interpretation is somewhat at odds with that proposed by Giddy, who held that the original burials were Ramesside or from the late Eighteenth Dynasty at the earliest (Vol. II, 6–7). Unfortunately the hieroglyphic inscriptions and reliefs found were so fragmentary that the great majority could be dated only in a general way to the New Kingdom, though a very few were considered to be more specifically of the Eighteenth Dynasty (*ibid.*, 20–27), as was one of the few scarabs (*ibid.*, 29), and these need to be taken into consideration.

That there must have been intensive use of the tombs in the Ramesside period is beyond doubt, since pottery of distinctively Ramesside style occurred in quantity in the sand, in accord with the date of most of the shabtis (*ibid.*, 27–29). When this use ceased is much less clear. The present volume documents a (relatively small) number of sherds of the later Ramessides and the Third Intermediate Period, and it may be that many of the tomb chambers and shafts were by then becoming full of mummies and any associated offerings. That burials of the Third Intermediate Period were certainly present in the area is attested by the presence of a number of shabtis (*ibid.*, 7, 30–32) and of two burials with coffins contained in outer sarcophagi, not from shafts or tomb chambers but sealed within the limestone chip layer BGL (*ibid.*, 35). These two burials were then succeeded by a great many of a poorer sort (*ibid.*, *passim*), in almost all cases unaccompanied by pottery. Nevertheless, pottery of Late Dynastic date was present in quantity, and will be considered in a subsequent volume.

NILE CLAY FABRICS, 483–730

G1 (Nile B2)

483 Incurved bowl with black rim

The dating of black rims is the subject of debate, and is linked to the disputed chronology of Cypriot Base Ring Ware (**794–96**). One view is that they developed during the late SIP but Aston (Aston D.A. 2007, 279) believes their development to have occurred no earlier than the reign of Amenhotep I. They were certainly in production during the reign of Tuthmosis III, when they were especially popular. A very close match for both form and size is a shallow bowl with very low base-ring from Memphis (Kom Rabia) (Bourriau 2010, Fig. 12 [4.2.1]).

2632 **483** Fig. 61a

G1 (Nile B2). Fired fairly hard. Surfaces concealed by slip. Break orange-red with pink core. Fairly plentiful poorly sorted sand. Moderate qty fine veg to 0.3. Sparse limestone to 0.1. Red slip on both surfaces. Black band carefully painted around rim. Faint traces of probable polish on interior only.

Phase	Context & No.	Grid ref	Dia rim (top)	Fig
vii	AAA East **27**	Area 1	16–17	61a

484 Small incurved bowl

Incurved bowls are plentiful in the NK, though most are larger. The slight irregularity inside the rim is probably insignificant, and a reasonably close parallel may be found in Memphis (Kom Rabia) in a common, albeit rather larger, type (drawn example dia 16) with almost flat base and upturned rim (Bourriau 2010, Fig. 11 etc [4.2.3]). This occurs with red slipped surfaces from the earliest level (late SIP to early Eighteenth Dynasty), where it is polished/burnished on the interior; polish or burnish occurs on both surfaces of such bowls in the next level (early to mid Eighteenth Dynasty) (*ibid.*, Fig. 23). Red slipped and polished/burnished round-based incurved bowls of smaller size (dias 10.4–11.5), but without the sharply upturned rim, derive (Aston B.G. 2005, Pl. 121 [89–91]) from a Saqqara tomb of rather later date, the end of the Eighteenth Dynasty or the beginning of the Nineteenth.

It should be noted that vessels of very similar size and form were made in the later OK (Rzeuska 2006, Pl. 64, Forms 54 [263] and 55 [265/66]. However, although these have a red slip it is on the interior only, and unpolished, so the NK parallels, such as they are, are preferred.

1726 **484** Fig. 61b

G1 (Nile B2). Fired fairly soft. Surfaces brown where slip lost. Break brown with red core. Fairly plentiful fine and medium sand with a few larger grains. Moderate qty fine and coarse veg to 0.5. Sparse limestone to 0.1, one piece 0.2 and one 0.3. Areas of red slip survive on both surfaces. Polished where slip survives.

Phase	Context & No.	Grid ref	Dia rim (top)	Fig
Mamluk	AZR (UP 12) **49**	Area 12	10	61b

485 Bowl with sharply incurved rim

The rim may have been slightly distorted by handling or standing, but the incurved form and the wide, shallow groove below it (from string-tying?) are closely matched by one (dia 17) of a series of uncoated bowls in a Saqqara tomb (Aston B.G. 2005, Pl. 112 [10]). Many bowls at Memphis (Kom Rabia) are incurved but none drawn is quite so similar. However, several in an Amarna series also come close (Rose 2007, 196 [86–88]).

Probably late Eighteenth to early Nineteenth Dynasty.

2692 **485** Fig. 61c

G1 (Nile B2). Fired medium. Surfaces pale brown. Break, thin red-brown zone near exterior, grey core off-centre, brown zone near interior. Fairly plentiful poorly sorted sand. Fairly plentiful fine veg to 0.3. Sparse limestone to 0.1. Uncoated. Not polished or burnished.

Phase	Context & No.	Grid ref	Dia rim (top)	Fig
v–vi	CBU **68**	06/07/08-33/34/35	*c.*22	61c

486–87 Incurved bowls with red rim

Although red rims already occur in the MK, incurved bowls tend to be less than 12 cm in diameter and many, though not all, are in the finer G2 (Nile B1) fabric. In the earliest NK contexts at Memphis (Kom Rabia) these are classified as 'in Middle Kingdom style' (Bourriau 2010, Figs 4, 5 and 15). Larger diameter vessels usually belong to the NK tradition, the practice continuing into the early TIP (Aston D.A. and Jeffreys 2007, Fig. 43 [493/94]). At Kom Rabia, many forms of incurved bowl can be provided with a red rim; a good match for the stance of **486/87** (Bourriau 2010, Fig. 23 [4.2.4]) has a flat base.

802 **486** Fig. 61d

G1 (Nile B2). Fired fairly soft. Surfaces very pale brown, exterior slightly darker than interior. Break pale brown with thin red-brown zones and thin grey core. Fairly plentiful poorly sorted sand. Fairly plentiful fine veg to 0.2 and one piece coarse 0.5. Sparse limestone to 0.1. Probably smoothed but uncoated. Red-painted band around exterior of rim, 0.4 wide and carefully applied; faint traces of a similar band on interior. Not polished or burnished.

Phase	Context & No.	Grid ref	Dia rim (top)	Fig
ivd	ATY **233**	25-04	*c.*20–25 variable	61d

2894 **487** Fig. 61e

G1 (Nile B2). Fired fairly soft. Surfaces pale brown. Break pale brown all through. Fairly plentiful poorly sorted sand. Small qty fine and coarse veg to 0.2 only. Sparse limestone to 0.05. Uncoated. Red-painted band around rim, 0.3 wide on exterior, 0.1 on interior. Not polished or burnished.

Phase	Context & No.	Grid ref	Dia rim (top)	Fig
iva	BEG **6**	09 to12-04/05	*c.*16	61e

488 Small, shallow, thick-walled bowl with direct rim

A good match for both the form and the small diameter is already present at Memphis (Kom Rabia) in the early to mid Eighteenth Dynasty (Bourriau 2010, Fig. 21 [1.1.2]), and by the late Eighteenth to early Nineteenth this can be red slipped on both surfaces, and polished/burnished on both surfaces or on the interior only (*ibid.*, Fig. 47). At Amarna, among several red slipped and polished the nearest is probably one (dia *c.*12) with a similarly thick wall but a slightly more rounded rim (Rose 2007, 196 [74]).

2846 **488** Fig. 61f

G1 (Nile B2). Fired fairly soft to medium. Surfaces concealed by slip. Break reddish brown with thick grey core. Fairly plentiful poorly sorted sand. Fairly plentiful fine only veg to 0.3. Sparse limestone to 0.05. Red slip on both surfaces. Traces of probable polish on both surfaces.

Phase	Context & No.	Grid ref	Max dia rim	Fig
iii	BDQ **17**	01 to 05-07/08	9.5	61f

<u>489–90</u> Small, shallow incurved bowls with rounded direct rim

There is no perfect match for <u>**489**</u> among the published forms from Memphis (Kom Rabia), but a slightly deeper bowl appears in the early Eighteenth Dynasty or shortly before (Bourriau 2010, Fig. 12 [4.2.1]) and recurs in many later contexts, where it was subject to various surface treatments. The two rim sherds in <u>**490**</u> are too badly preserved for the stance to be established. None can be dated more closely than to the NK.

2316 <u>**489**</u> Fig. 61g

Evidence on underside of a second wheel-throwing to shape the base, which is lost.

<u>G1 (Nile B2).</u> Fired fairly soft. Exterior red-brown where uncoated; interior pale brown where slip lost. Break pale brown with red core. Fairly plentiful fine and medium well-sorted sand. Small qty fine veg to 0.3. Sparse limestone to 0.1, and one void 0.2. Thin red slip on interior and over rim, probably down to about 1.3 below rim. Interior polished, exterior uncertain.

Phase	Context & No.	Grid ref	Dia rim (top)	Fig
iv (Pt II?)	ARP=ARS (UP 152) **14**	Area 13	12	61g

2841A <u>**490**</u> Not illustrated

<u>G1 (Nile B2).</u> Fired fairly soft. Surfaces concealed by slip. Break not recorded. Moderate qty to fairly plentiful poorly sorted sand. Moderate qty fine veg to 0.5. Sparse limestone to 0.1. Red slip on both surfaces. Both surfaces polished.

Phase	Context & No.	Grid ref	Max dia rim	Fig
iva	BCP **12**	08 to 12-03 to 06	?	Similar to 61g
ivb	AFL **8**	04/05/06-01/02	?	Similar to 61g

<u>491</u> Small to medium-sized shallow incurved bowls with thin direct rim

A very similar form, of similar diameter, already appears at Memphis (Kom Rabia) in the early Eighteenth Dynasty or a little before (Bourriau 2010, Fig. 11 [3.1.1]). From the outset it may be red slipped on both surfaces and polished/burnished on the exterior, and although polish/burnish on both surfaces is not recorded until the late Eighteenth or early Nineteenth Dynasty, a similar form (*ibid.*, Fig. 21 [3.2.1]) is so treated by the mid Eighteenth and there is no reason why <u>**491**</u> should not be of this date.

AUQ **159+199** was originally published in Vol. II (Pl. 63 [28]); the description is now slightly amended.

2841B <u>**491**</u> Fig. 61h

<u>G1 (Nile B2).</u> BGN **22** fired medium, others fairly soft. Surfaces concealed by slip. Break BGN **22** red with grey core, AUQ **159+199** red all through, others brown with red core or red all through. Moderate qty to fairly plentiful poorly sorted sand, but the largest grains sometimes lacking. Moderate qty fine veg to 0.5. Sparse limestone to 0.1. Red slip on both surfaces. Both surfaces polished.

Phase	Context & No.	Grid ref	Max dia rim	Fig
o	BEO **15**	20/21-S06	17	As 61h
ii	AUQ **159★**	08-03	17	61h
ii	AUQ **199★**	05/06-05	17	61h
ii	BET **89**	12/13-01/02	?	As 61h
ii	BGN **22**	10 to 13-S03/S04/S05	14	As 61h
iv (Pt II?)	ARU=ARZ (UP 204) **34**	Area 13	14	As 61h
ivb	BCT **8**	19/20-08/09	?	As 61h

★ Join

492–93 Medium-sized incurved shallow bowls with rounded direct rim

The form is very common at Memphis (Kom Rabia), appearing already, uncoated, in the late SIP to the early Eighteenth Dynasty (Bourriau 2010, Fig. 11 [1.1.1]). As so often, the version with red slip and polish/burnish on both surfaces is found later, in this case from the early to mid Nineteenth Dynasty (*ibid.*, Fig. 60).

2858A **492** Not illustrated

G1 (Nile B2). Fired fairly soft. Surfaces brown. Break brown with red core. Fairly plentiful poorly sorted sand. Fairly plentiful fine and coarse veg to 0.6. Sparse limestone to 0.05. Uncoated. Not polished or burnished.

Phase	Context & No.	Grid ref	Dia rim (top)	Fig
iva	BDU **14**	16/17/18-06/07/08	*c.*19	As 61i

2858B **493** Fig. 61i

ADG **15** and **16** are from different vessels.

G1 (Nile B2). Fired fairly soft. Surfaces concealed by slip. Break brown, ADG **16** with red zones and grey core, others with red core. Fairly plentiful poorly sorted sand. Fairly plentiful fine and coarse veg to 0.3/0.6. ADG **16** more limestone than usual, others sparse, to 0.05. Red slip on both surfaces. Both surfaces polished.

Phase	Context & No.	Grid ref	Dia rim (top)	Fig
ii	ADG **15**	Area 13	21	61i
ii	ADG **16**	Area 13	16	As 61i
ii	AYG Under ADY **3**	Area 13	?	As 61i
iv (Pt II?)	ADC **165**	Area 13	?	As 61i

494 Shallow bowl with internally modelled rim

The form of the rim might be considered inconsequential, but is surprisingly uncommon. At Memphis (Kom Rabia) it is probably best thought of as variant of a type which occurs frequently and with various surface treatments from the early Eighteenth Dynasty, or a little earlier, onwards (Bourriau 2010, Fig. 12 [4.4.1]). At Qantir the nearest match, uncoated, (dia top 16) is Ramesside (Aston D.A. 1998, 151 [346]). It is not recorded from the Saqqara tombs, though an intentionally thinner carinated rim, red slipped and polished/burnished (Aston B.G. 2005, Pl. 121 [95]), described as perhaps intrusive and from the later NK, may be a developed form.

2845 **494** Fig. 61j

Rim sherd. The combination of fairly thick wall and small diameter sets it apart from **492/93**.

G1 (Nile B2). Fired fairly soft. Surfaces red-brown. Break red-brown with purple-grey core. Fairly plentiful poorly sorted sand. Fairly plentiful fine and coarse veg to 0.5. One piece limestone 0.1 visible. Perhaps self-slipped, but no coloured slip. Not polished or burnished.

Phase	Context & No.	Grid ref	Dia rim (top)	Fig
iv (Pt II?)/iv(Pt II?)/?	ADF North/AYQ/AYR **12**	Area 13	13	61j

495 Shallow bowl with internally thickened rim

Similar to **494** but with a less modelled rim, and slipped and polished. At Memphis (Kom Rabia) the best match is the same type (Bourriau 2010, Fig. 12 [4.4.1]), with various surface treatments from the early Eighteenth Dynasty, or a little earlier, onwards, including red slip on both surfaces and ring burnish on the interior from the outset and the interior fully polished/burnished from late in the Dynasty, though not recorded with both surfaces so treated. A similar form (dia 22), uncoated, is interpreted as a lid in the Middle Kingdom style (*ibid.*, Fig. 6 [3378]).

2891 **495** Fig. 61k

G1 (Nile B2). Fired fairly soft. Surfaces concealed by slip. Break red-brown with purple core. Fairly plentiful poorly sorted sand. Moderate qty fine and coarse veg to 0.3. Sparse limestone to 0.05. Red slip on both surfaces. Both surfaces polished.

Phase	Context & No.	Grid ref	Dia rim (top)	Fig
ivb	AIH **26**	14 to 20-01	*c.*17	61k

496–97 Incurved bowls with thin rim

These bowls, with their thin rim, are similar to a type common at Memphis (Kom Rabia) from the late SIP to the early Eighteenth Dynasty onwards. This is red slipped on both surfaces with the interior polished/burnished from the outset (Bourriau 2010, Fig. 12 [4.2.3]), and both surfaces so treated from the following phase of the early to mid Eighteenth (*ibid.*, Fig. 23).

2820A **496** Fig. 61l

G1 (Nile B2). Fired fairly hard. Surfaces pale brown where slip lost. Break red-brown with thin pink zones and grey core. Fairly plentiful fine and medium well-sorted sand. Moderate qty fine veg to 0.2. Sparse limestone to 0.05. Red-brown slip on both surfaces. Both surfaces highly polished.

Phase	Context & No.	Grid ref	Dia rim (top)	Fig
iv (Pt II?)	ARU=ARZ (UP 204) **37**	Area 13	*c.*16	61l

2820B **497** Fig. 61m

G1 (Nile B2). Fired medium. Surfaces pale brown where slip lost. Break red-brown with red zones and mauve core. Fairly plentiful fine well-sorted sand. Moderate qty fine veg to 0.2. Sparse limestone to 0.05. Red-brown slip on both surfaces. Both surfaces highly polished.

Phase	Context & No.	Grid ref	Dia rim (top)	Fig
v/v	BJG/BJO(H) **19**	W01/01-S01	18	61m

498 Medium-sized shallow bowl

This simple form is similar to several bowls at Memphis (Kom Rabia) but no exact match is found; in any case, the notch in the rim is probably fortuitous. At Amarna there is likewise a general resemblance to a red slipped and sometimes polished series of about the same diameter (Rose 2010, 196 [80–89]).

2006 **498** Fig. 62a

G1 (Nile B2). Fired fairly hard. Surfaces concealed by slip. Break red-brown with thick grey core extending to interior surface. Fairly plentiful poorly sorted sand. Fairly plentiful fine and coarse veg to 0.4. Sparse limestone to 0.1. Thick slip on both surfaces; exterior and over the rim red, interior fired grey where stacked in the kiln. Both surfaces crazed. Both surfaces highly polished.

Phase	Context & No.	Grid ref	Dia rim (top)	Fig
ivb	AVB **42**	09-S01/S02/S03	*c.*19	62a

499–501 Medium-sized to large incurved bowls with upturned direct rim

Although none of the published examples from Memphis (Kom Rabia) matches perfectly the rim of **500**, with its final turn up to the vertical, there is a group from Amarna which does so (Rose 2007, 200, [128–132, especially 130]) and all five examples are red slipped and polished on both surfaces. At Memphis, Nile versions of some forms more usual in marl have a more elongated upturn (Bourriau 2010, Fig. 12 [4.12.2] and Fig. 64 [4.12.7]). **500** may have been drawn with too deep a stance. The form of **499** is not matched at either site: the thickening of the wall so close to the rim emphasises its shallow stance and should indicate a flat base.

2012 **499** Fig. 62b

Shallow bowl with thin, direct rim. Body thickening rapidly towards break.

G1 (Nile B2). Fired fairly soft. Surfaces pale brown. Break pale brown with red core. Fairly plentiful poorly sorted sand. Fairly plentiful fine and coarse veg to 0.5. Sparse limestone to 0.1. Interior smoothed, exterior less so. Uncoated. Not polished or burnished.

Phase	Context & No.	Grid ref	Max dia rim	Fig
ii	BGG **46**	08/09/10-S02/S03	? (30–35?)	62b

2324 **500** Fig. 62c

G1 (Nile B2). Fired fairly soft. Surfaces brown where slip lost. Break brown with red zones and mauve core. Plentiful poorly sorted sand. Moderate qty fine veg to 0.3. Sparse limestone to 0.05. Thick brownish red slip on both surfaces. Both surfaces polished.

Phase	Context & No.	Grid ref	Dia rim (top)	Fig
ii	AIY **108**	07/08-06	*c.*20–25	62c

2014 **501** Fig. 62d

G1 (Nile B2). Fired medium. Surfaces concealed by slip. Break BDY/BDX **21** red-brown all through, BGN **19** red-brown with thin pink zones and thin grey core. Fairly plentiful fine sand with a few larger grains. Fairly plentiful fine veg to 0.2. Sparse limestone to 0.1. Thick red-brown slip on both surfaces. Both surfaces highly polished.

Phase	Context & No.	Grid ref	Dia rim (top)	Fig
o/ii	BDY/BDX **21**	01 to 08-07/08	*c.*25–30	62d
ii	BGN **19**	10 to 13-S03/S04/S05	?	Similar to 62d

502–04 Carinated bowls with incurved upper body

There is no shortage of carinated bowls at Memphis (Kom Rabia) but none provides a perfect match for the simple form of **502/03**. The nearest is probably one (dia 21) with a vertical upper wall (Bourriau 2010, Fig. 38 [4.11.12]) of the mid to late Eighteenth Dynasty and later. Not very different is the shallow version (dia 24) of the early to mid Nineteenth Dynasty, which is the best match to **504** (*ibid.*, Fig. 63 [4.11.21]). All of these are uncoated. However, closer to **502/03** are one (dia 22.4) from Qantir, red slipped (but not polished/burnished) (Aston D.A. 1998, 251 [792]), and an uncoated, flat-based example (dia 23.8) from a Saqqara tomb (Aston D.A. 1997, Pl. 112 [12]), both Ramesside. The latter is also similar to **504**, but the rim is thinner.

2860A **502** Fig. 62e

G1 (Nile B2). Fired medium. Surfaces red where uncoated. Break red with grey core. Fairly plentiful poorly sorted sand. Fairly plentiful fine and coarse veg to 0.8. Sparse limestone to 0.1. Red slip on interior only. Exterior not polished or burnished; interior band burnished (3 bands survive).

Phase	Context & No.	Grid ref	Dia rim (top)	Fig
v/v–vi/v–vi/v–vi	AEZ/AFB/AFC/AFD **6**	19/20-S02/S03/S04	*c.*26	62e

2860B **503** Not illustrated

Slightly thinner wall than **502** but the form is very similar.

G1 (Nile B2). Fired fairly soft. Surfaces concealed by slip. Break pale brown with red zones and purple core. Fairly plentiful poorly sorted sand. Small qty fine and coarse veg to 0.2 and one piece 1.0. Sparse limestone to 0.1. Red slip on both surfaces. Both surfaces polished.

Phase	Context & No.	Grid ref	Dia rim (top)	Notes
o	BEO **90**	14/15-01	? (22–30)	As 62e

2878 **504** Fig. 62f

G1 near G4 (Nile B2 near C). Fired fairly soft. Surfaces red-brown. Break red-brown with red zones and purple core. Moderate qty poorly sorted sand. Plentiful fine and coarse veg to 1.0. Sparse limestone to 0.05. Both surfaces probably self-slipped, but no coloured slip. Not polished or burnished.

Phase	Context & No.	Grid ref	Max dia rim	Fig
vii	AAA (UP 118) **88**	29 to 32-01/02	17	62f

505 Body sherd with pigment

For sherds reused to hold pigment, see red on BEO **63** of **598**, and yellow on AHW **3** and AAA **13** of **745**, all of the New Kingdom.

2896 **505** Not illustrated

Sherd, apparently from the carination point of a carinated bowl. Interior surface splashed with blue pigment, some of it quite thick. It is unlikely that blue-painted pottery was being manufactured at Saqqara, so the possibilities seem to be decoration of a tomb chapel and post-firing decoration of pottery (see **726/74/75**) and in view of the colour, more probably the latter.

G1 (Nile B2). Fired medium. Exterior concealed by slip, interior by sand and pigment. Break brick-red all through. Fairly plentiful poorly sorted sand. Moderate qty fine veg to 0.3. Sparse limestone to 0.1. Red slip on exterior, interior uncoated. Probable polish on exterior only.

Phase	Context & No.	Grid ref
ii	AIY under Room 10 **152**	09 to 12-03/04

506 Spinning or figurine bowl

This poorly preserved fragment proves the presence of either a spinning bowl, or one with a deity figure (usually a rearing cobra) standing in the interior. Spinning bowls, provided with two loops through which thread was passed, in water, are known from many NK sites including Memphis (Kom Rabia) (Bourriau 2010, Fig. 73 [a]), Qantir (Aston D.A. 1998, 525 [2127]) and Amarna (Rose 2007, 60–61 and 202–3 [SD 6], 118–19 and 263 [MC 4]). However, one from Buto (EES Excavations, unpublished), where no MK or NK pottery is known, should be no earlier than *c*.550 BC. They have been quite extensively studied (e.g. Allen 1997).

Bowls with fragments of cobra figures occur at Amarna (Kemp 1981, 14–16, Fig. 6; Rose 2007, 70 and 210 [SD 13.1]) and other sites. A fragment from Memphis (Kom Rabia) is thought to be from such a figure (Bourriau 2010, 228, Fig. 73 [c]).

The present example cannot be identified or dated from the little that survives. Although spinning bowls are more common, a cobra bowl is more likely in a cemetery, where the deity may be Renenutet, the provider of nourishment, rather than the more familiar Wadjet. That she might be acknowledged at Amarna is interesting, though other deities besides the Aten are certainly attested there.

Three further fragments from the Anubieion each have only a single loop on the interior and appear to be of Coptic date; these may be lids (cf Egloff 1977, Pl. 55 [9]) but in the NK such a lid is unlikely.

1369 **506** Fig. 62g

G1 (Nile B2). Fired fairly soft. No surfaces survive (eroded in use?). Break brown with red core. Fairly plentiful poorly sorted sand. Fairly plentiful fine and coarse veg to 0.5. Sparse limestone to 0.1. Too damaged to retain slip, or polish or burnish.

Phase	Context & No.	Grid ref	Fig
ii	AIY Under Room 10 **160**	09 to 12-03/04	62g

507–08 Small shallow bowls

The most likely parallel from Memphis (Kom Rabia) is a rather larger (dia 18) shallow bowl which appears in the early to mid Eighteenth Dynasty (Bourriau 2010, Fig. 23 [4.5.4]), is found throughout the NK levels, and can from the outset have red slip and polish on both surfaces.

2863 **507** Fig. 62h

G1 (Nile B2). Fired fairly soft. Surfaces concealed by slip. Break pale brown with faint red core. Moderate qty fine and medium well-sorted sand. Small qty fine only veg to 0.2. Sparse limestone to 0.05. Red slip on both surfaces. Both surfaces polished.

Phase	Context & No.	Grid ref	Dia rim (top)	Fig
vi	ABI (UP 7) **140**	Area 13	9	62h

2864 **508** Fig. 62i

G1 (Nile B2). Fired fairly soft. Surfaces concealed by slip. Break brown all through. Fairly plentiful fine and medium well-sorted sand. Moderate qty fine veg to 0.3. Sparse limestone to 0.05 and one piece 0.5 × 0.3. Red slip on both surfaces. Interior polished, exterior uncertain.

Phase	Context & No.	Grid ref	Dia rim (top)	Fig
vi	ABI Top (UP10) **153**	Area 13	*c.*11	62i

509–11 Small incurved bowls with thin direct rim

At Memphis (Kom Rabia), similar bowls of simple form but various shallow to fairly deep stances are illustrated as Shape Class 4.1. For the shallow **509** close matches are already present in the late SIP to the early Eighteenth Dynasty (Bourriau 2010, Fig. 11 [4.1.3–5]), with red slip and overall polish/burnish (on the interior only) present on 4.1.5 from the outset. For **510/11** the best match does not appear until the early to mid Nineteenth Dynasty (*ibid.*, Fig. 62 [4.1.9])

2841C **509** Fig. 62j

G1 (Nile B2). Fired fairly soft. Surfaces concealed by slip. Break not recorded. Moderate qty to fairly plentiful poorly sorted sand. Moderate qty fine veg to 0.5. Sparse limestone to 0.1. Red slip on both surfaces. Both surfaces polished.

Phase	Context & No.	Grid ref	Max dia rim	Fig
vii	AAA (UP 118) **77**	28/29-01/02	13	62j

1681 **510** Fig. 62k

G1 (Nile B2). Fired fairly soft. Surfaces concealed by slip. Break red-brown all through. Fairly plentiful poorly sorted sand. Fairly plentiful fine veg to 0.4. Sparse limestone to 0.1. Red slip on both surfaces. Both surfaces perhaps, but not certainly, lightly polished.

Phase	Context & No.	Grid ref	Dia rim (top)	Fig
ivd	ATY **208**	25-04	12	62k

2856A **511** Fig. 62l

G1 (Nile B2). Fired fairly soft to medium. Surfaces concealed by slip. Break not recorded. Fairly plentiful poorly sorted sand. Veg present, details not recorded. Sparse limestone to 0.1. Red slip on both surfaces. Both surfaces polished.

Phase	Context & No.	Grid ref	Dia rim (top)	Fig
vi	ABG (UP 235) **38**	Area 13	13	62l

512 Small white/pink slipped bowl

It is the slip colour, rather than the form, which distinguishes this rim sherd from numerous others. The form is in fact not closely paralleled at Memphis (Kom Rabia), a better match being among the small round-based vessels at Qantir (Aston D.A. 1998, 151 [340]). These are usually uncoated or red slipped. Aston says (*ibid.*, 78) that undecorated open forms with white/pink slip are rare at Qantir, and that any such slip is usually on the interior only; however, cream slip on both surfaces of open forms was recorded at Memphis (Kom Rabia) (e.g. Bourriau 2010, Fig. 36 [3.5.1]; Fig. 49 [4.5.5]; Fig. 50 [4.11.2]).

2897 **512** Fig. 62m

G1 (Nile B2). Fired medium. Surfaces concealed by slip. Break pale brown with reddish purple core. Fairly plentiful poorly sorted sand. Moderate qty fine and coarse veg to 0.3 and one piece 1.0. Sparse limestone to 0.1. Slip on both surfaces, fired pinkish orange, probably intended as white. Probable traces of polish on exterior only.

Phase	Context & No.	Grid ref	Dia rim (top)	Fig
ivb–c	AVZ **8**	19-01/02	*c.*13	62m

513–14 Cups

Cups do not survive well, because of their thin walls, and it is probably unwise to attempt too detailed a comparison with published examples in the almost complete absence of profiles from the Anubieion. The out-turned rim of AQG/BEO **11** of **513** and the less pronounced out-turn of **514**, essentially a thin-walled version of it, may not be of great typological significance, but it may be noted that a common NK version, with upright to incurved rim, is absent at the Anubieion. The best matches are to these two examples: one from surface debris at a Saqqara tomb (Aston D.A. and B.G. Aston 2001, Pl. 41 [53]) and two red slipped from Qantir (Aston D.A. 1998, 259 [846]; 593 [2439]), respectively Ramesside and specifically Twentieth to Twenty-first Dynasty. BGG **16** of **513** shows some similarity to a Saqqara example (Aston D.A. 1997, Pl. 115 [97]) recorded as having incised lines around, whereas the former appears to have only marks from string-tying, as does a similar rim of the eleventh to tenth century BC at Memphis (Kom Rabia) (Aston D.A. and Jeffreys 2007, Fig. 29 [176]). The more rounded, string-tied AAA **139** of **513** somewhat resembles another example recorded with incised lines (Bourriau 2010, Fig. 81 [5.1.4]).

This form belongs to the Nineteenth rather than the Eighteenth Dynasty, when cups are shallower, and continues into the Late Dynastic Period. The out-turned rim is recorded at Elephantine as late as the mid eighth to seventh century BC (Aston D.A. 1996, Fig. 184 [18235h:02, 17805A:06] =Aston D.A. 1999, Pl. 49 [1556], Pl. 61 [1813]), but rather different from the more upright cups of the first part of this period at Buto (*ibid.*, 128 Fig. 26 [1]), well known to the present author.

The base and body sherds are not illustrated and cannot be related to a specific illustrated form. Except where noted, non-joining sherds appear to derive from different vessels, so many must have been present. Several fragments derive from the excavated tomb, supporting the probable Ramesside date.

BGG **16** was originally published in Vol. II (Pl. 63 [31]); the description is now slightly amended.

For context AWG, see page 17.

2722 **513** Fig. 63a–d

The lower body is deeply grooved where preserved, from the second throwing to shape the base. A slight carination sometimes marks the edge of the secondarily worked area. The interior is smooth, except that several examples have similar deep grooves spaced 0.5–1.0 apart, which are mostly in the lower part but may extend almost to the rim.

G1 (Nile B2). Fired variably, fairly soft to medium with a few fairly hard. Surfaces brown to red. Break brown with red core, with or without grey core streak, to red all through, and harder examples red with grey core. Fairly plentiful fine and medium sand with a few larger grains. Moderate qty to fairly plentiful fine veg, mostly to 0.2. Sparse limestone to 0.1, UP 445 **139** also a few pieces to 0.4 × 0.3. Uncoated. Not polished or burnished.

Rims

Phase	Context & No.	Grid ref	Dia rim (top)	Fig
o	AQG **8**	20/21/22-S04/S05	*c.*12	As 63a
o	AQG **29+35+36**	20/21/22-S05/S06	?	As 63c
o/o	AQG/BEO **11**	21-S06	11	63a
o/ii	AQG/AJY **6**	21/22-S04/S05/S06	?	As 63c
ii	AIY **151**	08/09-06	?	As 63a
ii	AON **9**	02-01/02/03	*c.*12	As 63d
ii	AON **68+70**	03/04/05-02 to S02	?	As 63a
ii	AQE **13**	21-S03	?	As 63c
ii	AUQ **37**	07/08-S04	12	As 63a
ii	AUQ **157**	08-03	11	As 63c
ii	BGG **16**	12 to 16-S04/S05	*c.*13	63b
ivb	AVB **48**	09-S01/S02/S03	*c.*10	As 63c
ivc	AWG **8**	20/21/22-S05/S06	11	63c
v	BJO **5**†	03 to W02-S01/S02/S03	10	As 63d
v	BJO **6***†	03 to W02-S01/S02/S03	11	As 63d
v/v	BJG/BJO **18***†	W01/W02/W03/01-S01/S02/S03	11	As 63d
vii	AAA (UP 445) **139**	Area 2	12	63d

* Join

† See also base and body sherds. Almost certainly all one vessel

Base and body sherds

Phase	Context & No.	Grid ref	Vessel part
o	AQG **235**	19/20-S06/S07	Body
o/o	AQG/BEO **10**	21-S06	Body
ii/ivb	AIY/AVB **34**	13/14-01/S01	Body
ivc	ATE **25**	03/04/05-S04/S05/S06	Base
ivc	AWG **10***	20/21/22-S05/S06	Body
ivc	AWG **14***	20/21/22-S03/S04	Body
v/v	BJG/BJO **2+63****	W01/W02/W03/01-S01/S02/S03	Body
v/v	BJG/BJO **14**†	W01/W02/W03/01-S01/S02/S03	Body
v/v	BJG/BJO(A+C) **17****	W01/W02/W03/01-S01/S02/S03	Body
v/v	BJG/BJO(H) **40**†	W01/W02/W03/01-S01/S02/S03	Body
?	BEZ **10**	04/05/06-S03/S04	Base

* Join

** Join

† See also rims. Almost certainly all one vessel

2724 **514** Fig. 63e

BDR **63** and BMG **23** have very light external ribbing, more closely spaced than on most of **513**. Vertical wipe marks on exterior of BDR **63**.

G1 (Nile B2). Fired fairly hard. Surfaces red. Break red with grey (UP 445 **140** pink) core. Fairly plentiful fine and medium sand with a few larger grains. Moderate qty fine veg, mostly to 0.2. Sparse limestone to 0.1. Surfaces smoothed, especially interiors, but uncoated. Not polished or burnished.

Phase	Context & No.	Grid ref	Dia rim (top)	Fig
iii	BDR **63**	12 to 14-04 to 06	10	63e
v–vi	BMG **23**	17-S01	11	As 63e
vii	AAA (UP 445) **140**	Area 2	?	As 63e

515 Small deep bowl with groove around

Two series of Nile B2 bowls similar in size and form to **515** are published from Tell el Dab'a, the earlier (Aston D.A. 2004b, Pl. 13 [68–70]) attributed to the MK, the later (*ibid.*, Pls 205–07 [790–807]) to the Hyksos Period. What many of these have in common with **515** is one or more grooves around. While multiple grooves set high on the body are likely to be decoration, on some other bowls (e.g *ibid.*, [795]) a single groove lower down may well be, as here, at the point where the reshaping of the base at a second throwing finishes. The big difference from the Tell el-Dab'a bowls is in the surface treatment, all the latter being uncoated. Since for small deep bowls a polished red slip on both surfaces is characteristic of the NK (Bourriau 2010, 479–84) rather than the MK, and the evidence for shaping of the base on the wheel is incontrovertible, a date in the Eighteenth Dynasty (or later) seems implied. However, no confirmation of the form has so far been found.

443 **515** Fig. 63f

Rim sherd from medium-sized cup or bowl. There is a horizontal groove in the exterior, at the point where the potter began the secondary throwing to shape the base.

G1 (Nile B2). Fired fairly soft. Surfaces concealed by slip. Break brown with red core. Fairly plentiful poorly sorted sand. Moderate qty mostly fine veg to 0.3. Sparse limestone to 0.05. Highly polished brownish red slip on both surfaces.

Phase	Context & No.	Grid ref	Dia rim (top)	Fig
ii	ABR* **2**	Area 13	12	63f

*'North of grid, near base of Phase ii wall'

516 Small bowl, blue-painted on white slip

For similar examples with blue bands from Amarna, and with a more complex design from the Embalmer's Cache of Tutankhamun, see the detailed study of Amarna decorated pottery by Colin Hope (Hope 1991, Fig. 1). There are two straighter walled blue-painted examples from Memphis (Kom Rabia) (Hope, in preparation) and an undecorated one from Saqqara (Bourriau and D.A. Aston 1985, Pl. 35 [21]); also from Saqqara is a blue-painted rim interpreted as from a funnel-necked jar, but which looks similar (Aston D.A. and B.G. Aston 2001, Pl. 39 [29]). All are slightly larger than **516**. The type occurs also at Malkata and there are fairly similar examples from Luxor tomb KV63 and from Karnak North (all, Colin Hope, pers. comm.). At Qantir a bowl with similar profile but much larger (19.4) diameter has a blue-painted band on the interior (Aston D.A. 1998, 133 [274]). Polishing/

burnishing of painted pottery is recorded only at Memphis, Saqqara and Qantir (see **615/17/18/44//45/47/49–52/700–02**). Late Eighteenth Dynasty.

2758 **516** Fig. 63g

G1 (Nile B2). Fired medium. Surfaces concealed by slip and paint. Break brown shading to orange-brown core. Fairly plentiful poorly sorted sand, although the wall is so thin. Only one piece fine veg visible, but sherd is small. No visible limestone. Both surfaces covered with white slip, and then with blue paint, as far as preserved, white showing where paint is rubbed. Traces of polish on exterior and top of rim.

Phase	Context & No.	Grid ref	Dia rim (top)	Fig
v	BAC **420**	02/03-S01/S02	*c.*6	63g

517–18 'Flower pots' (deep flat-based bowls with lightly modelled rim)

The so-called 'flower pots' exist with unmodelled or modelled rim (Holthoer 1977, Pl. 18 [FP 1–2]), **517/18** all having the latter. Perhaps because distorted, **517** is at the small end of Holthoer's diameter range, which runs from 15 upwards. At Memphis (Kom Rabia) (Bourriau 2010, Fig. 24 [4.10.6–4.10.9]) they occur uncoated, or red slipped on one or both surfaces. They are most common in the reigns of Hatshepsut and Tuthmosis III (Bourriau 2010, 81, with references) but reappear spasmodically thereafter. The published Memphis examples are not polished/burnished; polish seems more frequent at Saqqara, perhaps due to differences in survival conditions, unless the more elaborate examples were selected for funerary use.

For examples in G4 (Nile C), see **718/19**.

2496 **517** Fig. 63h

Distorted in the firing, and weathered.

G1 (Nile B2). Fired fairly hard. Surfaces pale brown where not weathered, small area of exterior misfired grey. Break pale brown with thin red zones and grey core, migrating to exterior where misfired. Fairly plentiful poorly sorted sand. Fairly plentiful fine and coarse veg to 0.5. Sparse limestone to 0.1 and one massive piece 1.2 × 1.0 × 0.6 in the break. Uncoated where surface survives. Not polished or burnished.

Phase	Context & No.	Grid ref	Dia rim (top)	Fig
iii	BCB **112**	01 to 04-04/05/06	*c.*14	63h

818 **518** Fig. 63i–j

BAC **193** has well-marked internal throwing-ridges overlain at an angle by smoothing marks. AOM **8** is abraded low down on interior, close to break, and may have been reused as a scraper, or even as a stand for a smaller vessel.

G1 (Nile B2). BAC **193** fired medium, AOM **8** fairly hard. BAC **193** exterior slipped, interior surface red, AOM **8** surfaces concealed by slip. Break red, BAC **193** with thick pink core, AOM **8** with grey core. Fairly plentiful fine and medium sand with a few larger grains. Small qty fine veg to 0.2. Sparse limestone to 0.1. Red slip, BAC **193** exterior only, AOM **8** both surfaces. Traces of polish or burnish, BAC **193** perhaps exterior only, AOM **8** both surfaces.

Phase	Context & No.	Grid ref	Max dia rim	Fig
v	BAC **193**	02/03-S01	20–30(?)	63i
?	AOM **8**	05/06-11/12	20–30(?)	63j

519 Large deep bowl with flat rim

Best seen as a version of a Memphis (Kom Rabia) bowl with rounded body but weaker rim (Bourriau 2010, Figs 24, 38 and 49 [4.10.2]). This is recorded throughout the Eighteenth Dynasty and perhaps into the Nineteenth, usually uncoated.

2870 **519** Fig. 64a

G1 (Nile B2). Fired medium, tending towards misfired. Exterior concealed by slip; interior brown. Break brown with very thick grey core. Moderate qty fine and medium well-sorted sand. Fairly plentiful fine and coarse veg to 0.6. Sparse limestone to 0.05. Exterior (self-?) slipped, fired purple-brown; interior uncoated. Exterior unpolished for the top 4 cm, then polished down to break, but this coincides with the part thrown a second time to reshape the base, and may well be due to the clay's being leather-hard at that time.

Phase	Context & No.	Grid ref	Max dia rim	Fig
vii	AAA (UP 38) **43**	19-09	34	64a

520 Globular bowl

Nothing closely similar was recorded at Memphis (Kom Rabia) or in the Saqqara tombs; nor is the form recorded by Holthoer (1977). This is probably due to a relatively late date for the form: the closest parallels located are from Luxor in the Twentieth to Twenty-first Dynasties (Aston D.A. 2008, Pl. 67 [1335]; Pl.101 [2018]); each (dia 24) has only a red rim, the latter on a cream/pink slip. At Qantir the most similar bowls (dias 31 and 27.6) are from the same period and fully red slipped (Aston D.A. 1998, 589 [2422/23]).

2861 **520** Fig. 64b

G1 (Nile B2). Fired medium. Surfaces concealed by slip. Break not recorded. Plentiful poorly sorted sand. Fairly plentiful fine and coarse veg to 0.5. More limestone than usual, to 0.1 and one piece 0.2; also one piece of bone or shell 0.3 × 0.1. Both surfaces slipped, intended to be red but discoloured, probably from being stacked in the kiln: most of interior, and lower part of exterior, grey-brown. Surfaces polished.

Phase	Context & No.	Grid ref	Dia rim (top)	Fig
v	AEW **41**	04-02 to 07	*c.*20(?)	64b

521 Shallow bowl with slightly overhanging squared rim

A very similar but perhaps slightly shallower type (dia 26) is already present at Memphis (Kom Rabia) in the late SIP to the early Eighteenth Dynasty (Bourriau 2010, Fig. 11 [3.8.1]), one version being uncoated. An even better match for stance (dia 30) appears in the early to mid Eighteenth Dynasty (*ibid.*, Fig. 25). In each case there is an uncoated version among those recorded.

2842 **521** Fig. 64c

G1 (Nile B2). Fired medium. Surfaces red-brown. Break red-brown with thick grey core. Fairly plentiful poorly sorted sand. Moderate qty fine veg to 0.3. Sparse limestone to 0.1. Perhaps self-slipped, but no coloured slip. Not polished or burnished.

Phase	Context & No.	Grid ref	Max dia rim	Fig
ivd/ivd	ATY/ATZ **28**	22/23-S02/S03	*c.*25–28	64c

522 Large shallow bowls

A range of forms, differing slightly in the shape of the rim. The more rounded version (Fig. 64c–e) is well matched at Memphis (Kom Rabia) by a form of similar diameter (Bourriau 2010, Fig. 11 [4.1.2]) already present, uncoated, in the late SIP to the early Eighteenth Dynasty. By the early to mid Eighteenth Dynasty it also occurs with a red rim on the uncoated surface and with red slip on the interior or on both surfaces, and by the mid to late Nineteenth with polish/burnish on the two red slipped surfaces. Versions continue into at least the Twentieth Dynasty (Aston D.A. and Jeffreys 2007, Fig.20 [6, 10]), dias 30 and 26 respectively, uncoated, the latter with a red rim. The surface treatments are altogether very varied but there are relatively few uncoated examples; and unpolished red slip was not recorded.

2854B/2859 **522** Fig. 64d–f

G1 (Nile B2). All fired fairly soft. Surfaces pale brown where visible. Break pale brown with red or grey core. Moderate qty to fairly plentiful poorly sorted sand. Small qty to fairly plentiful fine and coarse veg, in most examples to 0.5 or less, AJY **149** also one piece 0.6. Sparse limestone to 0.1. For surface treatment, see below.

Uncoated

Phase	Context & No.	Grid ref	Max dia rim	Fig
o/?	BJA/BMW **27**	14-04	?	
ii	BGG **141**	04/05/06-S01/S02/S03	?	
iii	BDP (UP 647) **150**	01 to 05-07	?	
iva	CJV **3**	09-29/30	?	

Uncoated, with red rim

On the preserved sherds, the red bands are of different widths and extend differently on to interior and exterior.

Phase	Context & No.	Grid ref	Max dia rim	Band on interior	Band on exterior	Fig
iii	CHJ **10**	08/09-24	?	0.9	0.4	
iva	AQH **69**	14/15-S03/S04	?	–	0.8	
ivc	ATE **30**	03/04/05-S04/S05/S06	25	0.7	0.4	

Red slip on both surfaces, red rim on top of slip

For the width of the red band, see table.

Phase	Context & No.	Grid ref	Max dia rim	Band on interior	Band on exterior	Fig
iii	CHZ **20**	09-28	27	1.3	0.5	64d

Red slip and polish on both surfaces

Phase	Context & No.	Grid ref	Max dia rim	Notes
o	BEO **12**	20/21-S06	?	
ii	BDX **10**	05-07/08	?	

Phase	Context & No.	Grid ref	Max dia rim	Notes
ii	BET **35**	14-S01/S02	*c.*28	
ii	BGG **132**	04/05/06-S01/S02/S03	?	
iv (Pt II?)	ADF North **35**	Area 13	17–20	
iva	BKZ **31**	07-26	23–27	As 64e
iva	BKZ **93**	02/03-27/28	?	
?	BEP **118**	16 to 20-01/S01	25	

Red slip on both surfaces, polish attested on one surface only

Phase	Context & No.	Grid ref	Max dia rim	Polish on int?	Polish on ext?	Fig
ii	AJY **149**	14/15/16-S03/S04/S05	? (30+)	Yes	?	64e
ivb	AVB **91+109**	10/11-S01/S02	?	Yes	No	
vii	AAA (UP 108) **60**	29 to 34-S06	*c.*25	No	Yes	

Red slip on both surfaces, polish on rim only

Phase	Context & No.	Grid ref	Max dia rim	Fig
ii	AIY **110**	07/08-06	*c.*25	

Red slip and polish on exterior only

Phase	Context & No.	Grid ref	Max dia rim	Fig
iv (Pt II?)	ADC **108**	Area 13	?	

Red slip and polish on interior and upper exterior

On the preserved sherds, the slip extends to different distances down the exterior.

Phase	Context & No.	Grid ref	Max dia rim	Slip on exterior	Fig
ii	AUQ **1**	09/10/11-S03/S04/S05	27	0.5	
ii	AUQ **138**	07/08-01/02	?	0.9	
ii	BGL **59**	14/15-S04/S05	28	4.5	

Red slip on interior and upper exterior, polish on interior only

On the preserved sherds, the slip extends to different distances down the exterior.

Phase	Context & No.	Grid ref	Max dia rim	Slip on exterior	Fig
o/ii	AQG/BGU **49**	19/20-S04/S05	30	3.0	
iii–iva	ACE=AJH **41**	05 to 09-06 to 0.9	?	0.2	

Red slip on interior and upper exterior; no polish on exterior, interior uncertain

All sherds are from a single vessel, joining. The interior is blackened by fire. The slip extends variably 4.5–5.3 down the exterior.

Phase	Context & No.	Grid ref	Max dia rim	Fig
o	AQG **61**★	12/13/14-S04/S05	29	64f
ii	BGG **95**★	08/09/10-S02/S03	29	64f
ii	BGL **60**★	14/15-S04/S05	29	64f
ii	BGL **61**★	14/15-S04/S05	29	64f
ii/ivb	AIY/AVB **66**★	10 to 14-01/S01/S02	29	64f

★ All join

Red slip and polish on exterior and upper interior

On the preserved sherds, the slip and polish extend to different distances down the interior (see table). In spite of the difference in diameter and slip/polish, all three sherds may be from the same vessel

Phase	Context & No.	Grid ref	Max dia rim	Slip on interior	Fig
iii	BJJ **12**	17/18-05/06	*c.*30	0.4	
iii	BJJ **44**	17/18-05/06	?	0.9	
iii/iva/iva	BJJ/BJF/BJI **4**	17/18-05	25	1.5	

Surfaces weathered

AQC **130** has traces of red slip, probably polished, on top of the rim only.

Phase	Context & No.	Grid ref	Max dia rim	Fig
iii	BJJ **52**	17/18-05/06	?	
iva	AQC **130**	02/03/04-04 to 10	*c.*17	

523 Medium-sized outward-sloping bowl with almost flat-topped rim

Similar bowls, with flat base, are common at Memphis (Kom Rabia) throughout the NK. They already appear in contexts of the early to mid Eighteenth Dynasty, when they can be uncoated or red slipped on both surfaces (Bourriau 2010, Fig. 23 [3.10.4]); by the early to mid Nineteenth both surfaces can be polished/burnished.

2844 523 Fig. 64g

G1 (Nile B2). Fired medium. Surfaces concealed by slip. Break red-brown with thin red zones and purple core. Fairly plentiful poorly sorted sand. Fairly plentiful fine and coarse veg to 0.7. Sparse limestone to 0.05. Red slip on both surfaces. Traces of polish or burnish on both surfaces.

Phase	Context & No.	Grid ref	Max dia rim	Fig
?	BPV **47**	04-21	22–24	64g

524 Medium-sized outward-sloping bowl

The rim form, first thickened and then tapering but not turned over, is well matched at Qantir in the reign of Tuthmosis III (not the SIP as published (David Aston, pers. comm.)). This (Aston D.A. 1998, 99 [70]) is one of a number of flat-based bowls in red slipped Nile B2, and the 17.2 diameter is similar. A second example (*ibid.*, 91 [35]) is not quite so close in form but uncoated and its dia of 18 is again similar. An example (dia 22) from Memphis (Kom Rabia) (Bourriau 2010, Fig. 15 [3570]), described as in the Middle Kingdom tradition, takes a very similar form.

344B **524** Fig. 65a

G1 (Nile B2). Not recorded in detail. Assumed to be uncoated, and not polished or burnished.

Phase	Context & No.	Grid ref	Max dia rim	Fig
iva	AJH under AVH **35**	05-04/05/06	15	65a

525–34 Medium-sized to large outward-sloping bowls

There are several similar forms at Memphis (Kom Rabia), some with many examples and many surface treatments. One (drawn example dia 32) appears uncoated in the late SIP to the early Eighteenth Dynasty (Bourriau 2010, Fig. 11 [3.10.2]) and red slipped in the early to mid Eighteenth (*ibid.*, Fig. 22). Another (drawn example dia 30) appears, uncoated and red slipped, in the early to mid Eighteenth (*ibid.*, Fig. 23 [4.4.2]). Both recur at least as late as the mid Nineteenth Dynasty.

Uncoated

2848B/2852A **525** Fig. 65b–c

G1 (Nile B2). Fired fairly soft. Surfaces pale brown. Break pale brown with red core (majority) or red zones and grey core. Fairly plentiful poorly sorted sand. Small qty to fairly plentiful fine and some coarse veg, mostly to 0.3 but a few to 1.0. Sparse limestone to 0.05/0.1. Uncoated. Not polished or burnished.

Phase	Context & No.	Grid ref	Max dia rim	Fig
o	AQG **73**	12/13/14-S04/S05	?	
o	AQG **238**	19/20-S06/S07	19	
o	BEO **86**	14/15-S04/S05	?	
o/ii	AQG/AJY **41**	19/20-04/05	?	
o/?	BJA/BMW **30**	14-04	?	
ii	BET **77**	10/11/12-01/02/03	17	
ii	BGH **39**	10 to 15-S04/S05	*c.*16	
ii	BGH **40**	10 to 15-S04/S05	16	
ii	BGN **21**	10 to13-S03/S04/S05	22–26	
ii/ivb	AIY/AVB **38**	13/14-01/S01	?	
iii	BJJ **16**	17/18-05/06	?	
iii	BJJ **17**	17/18-05/06	*c.*16	
iii	CHJ **12**	08/09-24	*c.*18	65b
iii	CHJ **15**	08/09-24	?	
iii	CHJ **16**	08/09-24	?	

Phase	Context & No.	Grid ref	Max dia rim	Fig
iii	CHZ **4**	09-30/31/32	?	
iv (Pt II?)	ADF North **20**	Area 13	?	
iva/ivb	BHR/BTG **118**	02-20/21	*c.*14	
iva/ivb	BHR/BTG **145**	02-20	*c.*16	
ivb–ivc	BGZ East **10**	14 to 17-05	?	
ivc	CES **17**	06/07-33/34	17	
ivd	BGE **46**	12-02/03	24–28	
v/v	BAC/BEI **25**	02/03-S01	?	
v/v	BAC/BEI **94**	02/03-S01	13	
v/v	BAC/BEI **115+131***†	02/03-S01	20	
v/v	BAC/BEI **117+210†**	02/03-S01	20	
v/v	BAC/BEI **119**	02/03-S01	*c.*17	
v/v	BAC/BEI **122†**	02/03-S01	?	
v/v	BAC/BEI **130****	02/03-S01	16	
v/v	BJG/BJO **25****	W01/01-S01	16	
v/v	BJG/BJO **26*†**	W01/01-S01	20	
v/v	BJG/BJO **27**	W01/01-S01	?	
v/v	BJG/BJO **28**	W01/01-S01	*c.*17	
v/v	BJG/BJO(B/C/H) **7**	W01/01-S01	?	
vi	ABI (UP 7) **116**	Area 13	?	
vii	AAA (UP 118) **81**	28/29-01/02	*c.*16	65c
?	BEP **138**	17/18-01/S01	?	
?	BEP **141**	17/18-01/S01	?	

* Join
** Join
† Probably all one vessel

Uncoated, with red rim

2852B **526** Not illustrated

G1 (Nile B2). Fired fairly soft. Surfaces pale brown. Break not recorded. Fairly plentiful poorly sorted sand. Small qty to fairly plentiful fine and coarse veg to 0.5. Sparse limestone to 0.1. Uncoated, but with red band on top of rim extending 0.9 down each surface. Not polished or burnished.

Phase	Context & No.	Grid ref	Max dia rim	Notes
iii/iii–iva/iva/iva	BDA/ACE/BCS/BCZ **11**	05-06/07/08	?	Similar to 65f

Red slip on both surfaces, not polished

2852C **527** Not illustrated

G1 (Nile B2). Fired fairly soft. Surfaces concealed by slip. Break not recorded. Fairly plentiful poorly sorted sand. Fine and coarse veg to 0.5, qty not recorded. Sparse limestone to 0.1. Red slip on both surfaces. Not polished/burnished.

Phase	Context & No.	Grid ref	Max dia rim	Notes
iva	AJH Lower **29**	05 to 08-04/05/06	25	Similar to 65f

Red slip and polish on both surfaces

2848C/2852D **528** Fig. 65d

G1 (Nile B2). Fired fairly soft. Surfaces concealed by slip. Break not recorded. Fairly plentiful poorly sorted sand. Moderate qty to fairly plentiful fine veg, mostly to 0.3. Sparse limestone to 0.1. Red slip on both surfaces. Both surfaces polished (AIY/AVB **44** and ABI (UP 315) **9** uncertain traces only).

Phase	Context & No.	Grid ref	Max dia rim	Fig
ii	AIY **106**	07/08-06	?	
ii	AJY **162**	21/22-S05/S06	?	
ii	BDS **24**	04/05-09	?	
ii/ivb	AIY/AVB **44**	13/14-01/S01	17	
iii	BDR **36**	10/11/12-05	?	
iii	CHJ **11**	08/09-24	18	
iva	AEF **56**	08 to 14-03/04	?	
iva	AQH **49**	19/20-S04/S05	?	
vi	ABI (UP 315) **9**	Area 13	19	65d
vii	AAA (UP 108) **81**	29 to 34-S06	?	

Red slip and polish on interior and upper exterior

769/2852E **529** Fig. 65e

CAA **30** is broken as a straight horizontal edge 9 cm long; a flat base is unlikely, but possibly along a carination.

G1 (Nile B2). Fired fairly soft. Exterior pale brown; interior concealed by slip. Break brown with red core (CAA **30**), others not recorded. Fairly plentiful poorly sorted sand. Small qty to fairly plentiful fine and coarse veg to 0.5. CAA **30** rather more limestone than usual, to 0.1 and one piece 0.3; others sparse to 0.1. All fully red slipped on the interior but only the top 1.0 (BDX **62**), 0.5–0.7 (variable) (BKC **209**) and 0.2 to 1.3 (variable) (CAA **30**) of the exterior is slipped. Polished only where slipped.

Phase	Context & No.	Grid ref	Dia rim (top)	Fig
ii	BDX **62**	03/04-07	?	
ivc	BKC **209**	06/07-26	24	
vii	CAA **30**	Area 26	26	65e

Red slip and polish on interior, exterior uncoated

2852F **530** Not illustrated

G1 (Nile B2). Fired fairly soft. Interior concealed by slip, exterior pale brown. Break not recorded. Fairly plentiful poorly sorted sand. Fine and coarse veg to 0.5, qty not recorded. Sparse limestone to 0.1. Red slip on interior, exterior uncoated. Interior polished, exterior not polished or burnished.

Phase	Context & No.	Grid ref	Dia rim (top)	Notes
iii	BDR **121**	11/12/13-03/04/05	?	Similar to 65f

Red slip and polish on interior, exterior weathered

2852G **531** Not illustrated

G1 (Nile B2). Fired fairly soft. Interior concealed by slip, exterior pale brown. Break not recorded. Fairly plentiful poorly sorted sand. Small qty to fairly plentiful fine and coarse veg to 0.5. Sparse limestone to 0.1. Red slip on interior, exterior surface weathered off. Interior polished, exterior cannot tell.

Phase	Context & No.	Grid ref	Max dia rim	Notes
ii	AJY **168**	21/22-S05/S06	*c*.20	Similar to 65f
ii	AQE **137**	16/17/18-02/03	?	Similar to 65f
ii	BGH **31+33**	10 to 15-S04/S05	?	Similar to 65f

Red slip and polish on rim, surfaces weathered

2852H **532** Fig. 65f

G1 (Nile B2). Fired fairly soft. Surfaces pale brown. Break not recorded. Fairly plentiful poorly sorted sand. Small qty to fairly plentiful fine and coarse veg to 0.5. Sparse limestone to 0.1. Traces of red slip on rim, surfaces otherwise weathered. Polished where slip survives.

Phase	Context & No.	Grid ref	Max dia rim	Fig
ivc	BHM **84**	01/02-21/22	*c*.30	65f

Red slip on one surface, the other weathered

2852I **533** Not illustrated

G1 (Nile B2). Fired fairly soft. Surfaces pale brown where uncoated. Break not recorded. Fairly plentiful poorly sorted sand. Fine and coarse veg to 0.5, qty not recorded. Sparse limestone to 0.1. BCP **40** red slip on interior, exterior weathered; BKN **170** red slip on exterior, interior weathered. Not polished or burnished.

Phase	Context & No.	Grid ref	Max dia rim	Notes
iva	BCP **40**	08/09-06	*c*.14	Similar to 65f
ivb	BKN **170**	02-20/21/22	?	Similar to 65f

Both surfaces weathered

2848F **534** Not illustrated

No details of the ware were recorded.

Phase	Context & No.	Grid ref	Max dia rim	Notes
iv (Pt II?)	ARP=ARS (UP 152) **20**	Area 13	?	Similar to 65b
iva	BHR **30**	02-23	*c*.26	Similar to 65b

535 Medium diameter ring-burnished shallow bowl

A slightly smaller example of a form first found at Memphis (Kom Rabia) in the late SIP to the early Eighteenth Dynasty (Bourriau 2010, Fig. 11 [1.8.1]) and with ring burnish from the early to mid Eighteenth. Versions recur until at least the mid Nineteenth Dynasty. The diameter range is 26–32.

930 **535** Fig. 65g

Outer part of shallow bowl with slightly thickened rim. Not a lid because of interior slip and burnish.

G1 (Nile B2). Fired medium. Interior concealed by slip, exterior red-brown where uncoated or slip lost. Break red-brown with thin red zones and thick grey core. Fairly plentiful poorly sorted sand. Fairly plentiful fine veg to 0.3. Sparse limestone to 0.05. Red slip on interior and to the centre of the rim; thin pink slip on exterior except rim, where perhaps worn off. Interior carefully burnished with non-overlapping strokes *c.*0.4 wide, parallel to the rim; although the sherd cannot show it, the burnishing would be a series of concentric rings or a spiral. Exterior lightly polished where slipped.

Phase	Context & No.	Grid ref	Max dia rim	Fig
vii	AAA West **2**	Area 2	*c.*25	65g

536 Medium-sized to large bowls with turned-over rim

This very common NK to TIP form, to be found on practically every site of this date, exists with many variations of shape and surface treatment. Its gradations of form and thickness are very slight and some in the present series could almost equally well have been included in **525–33**. At Memphis (Kom Rabia)it is already present in the early to mid Eighteenth Dynasty (Bourriau 2010, Fig. 21 [1.8.1–1.8.4], Fig. 22 [3.10.2]) and continues, with variations, into the Ramesside and TIP levels (Aston D.A. 2007, Figs 40–41). At Buto it still occurs in great numbers, many with sharply down-turned rim, well into the seventh century BC (personal observation).

2848E/2850B **536** Fig 65h–66d

Uncoated

G1 (Nile B2). Fired fairly soft. Surfaces pale brown. Break from pale brown with red core to brown with red zones and grey core. Fairly plentiful poorly sorted sand. Small qty to fairly plentiful fine and coarse veg; where fairly plentiful, to 1.5 but shorter where small qty only. Sparse limestone to 0.1. Uncoated. CHZ **3** has, unusually, one narrow band of burnish on exterior, others not polished or burnished.

Phase	Context & No.	Grid ref	Max dia rim	Fig & notes
o	AQG **75**	12/13/14-S04/S05	*c.*23	†
o/o	AQG/BEO **19**	21-S06	*c.*29	65h
ii	AIY **14**	12/13-01	19	
ii	AQR/AUQ **6****	03/04-03	23–25 variable	65i
ii	AUQ **110**	08/09-02/03	?	†
ii/iva	AJY/AQH **1***	11/12-S01/S02	17.5	66b
ii/iva	AJY/AQH **4***	11/12-S01/S02/S03	17.5	66b
ii/ivb	AJY/AVB **52***	11/12-S01/S02	17.5	66b
ii–iii	AON **2****	02-01/02	23–25 variable	65i
iii	BNV **9**	08-S03	19	

Phase	Context & No.	Grid ref	Max dia rim	Fig & notes
iii	CHZ **3**	09-30/31/32	?	
iva	BHR **267**	02/03-21/22	?	†
ivb	AVB **99**	10/11-S01/S02	*c*.21	†
v	BJO **7**	W01/01-S01/S02	*c*.16	
v/v	BJG/BJO(H) **22**	W01/01-S01	17	66c
vii	AAA **34**	Area 1	*c*.22	66d†

* Join

** Join

† Thinner wall but the same form

Uncoated, with red rim

G1 (Nile B2). Fired fairly soft. Surfaces pale brown. Break pale brown with red core. Fairly plentiful poorly sorted sand. Moderate qty to fairly plentiful fine veg, mostly to 0.3. Sparse limestone to 0.1. Uncoated, but with red band on top of rim extending 0.5 down exterior, variably 1.0–1.5 down interior. Not polished or burnished.

Phase	Context & No.	Grid ref	Max dia rim	Notes
ii/ii	AIY/BET **12**	10-01/02	24	Similar to 66e*

* Thinner wall but the same form

Red slip on both surfaces, not polished

G1 (Nile B2). Fired fairly soft. Surfaces concealed by slip. Break not recorded. Fairly plentiful poorly sorted sand. Veg not recorded. Sparse limestone to 0.1. Red slip on both surfaces (AIY/AVB **68** traces only). Not polished or burnished.

Phase	Context & No.	Grid ref	Max dia rim	Notes
ii/ivb	AIY/AVB **68**	10 to 14-01/S01/S02	*c*.20	As 65i
Mamluk	ARN (UP 270) **18**	Area 12	20	As 65i

Red slip on exterior only, not polished

G1 (Nile B2). Fired fairly soft. Exterior concealed by slip, interior pale brown. Break not recorded. Fairly plentiful poorly sorted sand. Veg not recorded. Sparse limestone to 0.1. Red slip on exterior, interior uncoated. Not polished or burnished.

Phase	Context & No.	Grid ref	Max dia rim	Notes
vii	AAA Lower **50**	Area 2	26	As 65i

Red slip on interior only, some polished

G1 (Nile B2). Fired fairly soft. Interior concealed by slip, exterior pale brown. Break from pale brown with red core to brown with red zones and grey core. Fairly plentiful poorly sorted sand. Small qty to fairly plentiful fine and coarse veg: where fairly plentiful, to 1.5 but shorter where small qty only. Sparse limestone to 0.1. Red slip on interior (AQG **92** and BGL **120** uncertain, BDX **59** recorded as extending just over rim on to exterior), exterior uncoated. For interior polish see table, exterior not polished or burnished.

Phase	Context & No.	Grid ref	Max dia rim	Interior polished?	Fig
o	AQG **92**	10/11-S04/S05	*c.*25	Yes(?)	
ii	AIY **80**	10/11-01/02	23	No	
ii	BDX **59**	03/04-07	31	No	66a
ii	BGG **42+58+103**	08/09/10-S02/S03	24	No	
ii	BGL **58**	14/15-S04/S05	?	Yes(?)	
ii	BGL **120**	14/15-01/S01/S02	?	? (burnt)	
iii	BJJ **35**	18-06	?	No	
iii	BJJ **49+51**	17/18-05/06	27	No	
iii	BPD **10**	02/03-21	*c.*25	Visible on rim only	
v/v	BAC/BEI **120**	02/03-S01	?	Yes	
v–vi	CBS **41**	04/05-25/26/27	?	Yes	
?	BEP **146**	17/18-01/S01	*c.*20	Yes	

537 Small to medium-sized slipped and polished bowls with turned-over rim

In the Saqqara tombs, polished/burnished red slip is uncommon except in the late Eighteenth Dynasty tombs of Maya (largely unpublished) and Horemheb (Aston D.A. 1997, 89). In the latter there is a reasonable match in a round-based bowl with diameter 19.6 (Bourriau *et al.* 2005; Fig. 16 [86]). At Memphis (Kom Rabia) two round-based examples similar in form (Bourriau 2010, Fig. 36 [3.8.3]; Fig. 47 [3.7.1]) are mid to late Eighteenth and late Eighteenth to Nineteenth Dynasty respectively. At Amarna there are plenty with polish/burnish, including some with flat base (Rose 2007, 205 [189, 193]).

2848D/2850A **537** Fig. 66e–g

G1 (Nile B2). Fired fairly soft. Surfaces concealed by slip. Break not recorded. Fairly plentiful poorly sorted sand. Veg not recorded. Sparse limestone to 0.1. Red slip on both surfaces. Both surfaces polished.

Phase	Context & No.	Grid ref	Max dia rim	Fig
iv (Pt II?)	ADF **36**	Area 13	*c.*16	66e
iv (Pt II?)	ARU=ARZ (UP 204) **36**	Area 13	*c.*19	66f
ivd	AHY **86**	16-05/06	14	66g

538 Small diameter slipped and polished thin-rimmed plate

Probably from a round-based plate of a type common at Memphis (Kom Rabia) from the late Eighteenth Dynasty onwards (Bourriau 2010, Fig. 47 [1.2.4]), some examples of which are polished/burnished on both surfaces (*ibid.*, Fig. 77); one is published from Saqqara (Bourriau *et al.* 2005, Fig. 5 [1]), though this is uncoated. A flat-based version with a less rounded rim appears earlier, at the end of the SIP or early in the Eighteenth Dynasty (Bourriau 2010, Fig. 11 [1.8.2]), with a polished/burnished example in the mid to late Eighteenth (*ibid.*, Fig. 36).

2634 **538** Fig. 66h

G1 (Nile B2). Fired fairly soft. Surfaces brown where slip lost. Break brown with pink zones and purple core. Fairly plentiful poorly sorted sand. Moderate qty mostly fine veg to 0.3. Sparse limestone to 0.05. Thick red slip on both surfaces. Both surfaces polished.

Phase	Context & No.	Grid ref	Dia rim (top)	Fig
Mamluk/Mamluk/vii	ABC/ABD/ABA (UP 69) **8**	Area 13	13	66h

539–41 Shallow bowls with almost flat wall

The almost flat wall relates these bowls to a type common at Memphis (Kom Rabia) from the late SIP to the early Eighteenth Dynasty onwards (Bourriau 2010, Fig. 11 [1.2.1]); the version with red slip and polish/burnish on both surfaces does not appear until the early to mid Nineteenth (*ibid.*, Fig. 60). Similar vessels are not difficult to find at other sites in the Ramesside period (e.g. Aston D.A. 2008, Pl. 116 [2370]). The shallow grooves on the interior of **540/41** are unusual but unlikely to be chronologically significant.

2607 **539** Fig. 66i

G1 (Nile B2). Fired fairly soft. Surfaces pale orange-brown where slip lost. Break orange-brown with pale purple core. Fairly plentiful fine and medium sand with a few larger grains. Fairly plentiful fine veg to 0.3. Sparse limestone to 0.05. Red slip on both surfaces. Upper surface and end of rim polished; one burnish band on underside.

Phase	Context & No.	Grid ref	Max dia rim	Fig
?	UP 19 **50**	Area 12	*c.*20	66i

2862 **540** Fig. 66j

G1 near G2 (Nile B2 near B1). Fired fairly soft. Surfaces concealed by slip. Break pale brown all through. Moderate qty fine and medium well-sorted sand. Small qty fine veg to 0.3. Sparse limestone to 0.05. Red slip on both surfaces. Both surfaces polished.

Phase	Context & No.	Grid ref	Max dia rim	Fig
vi	ABG (UP 266) **11**	Area 13	*c.*18	66j

2865 **541** Fig. 66k

G1 (Nile B2). Fired fairly soft. Surfaces pale brown. Break pale brown with grey core. Fairly plentiful poorly sorted sand. Moderate qty fine veg to 0.2. Sparse limestone to 0.05. Probably self-slipped, but no coloured slip. Interior lightly polished, exterior not polished or burnished.

Phase	Context & No.	Grid ref	Dia rim (top)	Fig
iii	CHJ **17**	08/09-24	? (17–22)	66k

542 Shallow slipped and polished bowl with almost flat wall

The flattened form of the rim is probably fortuitous. Similar shallow vessels already appear at Memphis (Kom Rabia) in the late SIP to the early Eighteenth Dynasty (Bourriau 2010, Fig. 11 [1.8.1]) and fully red slipped and polished/burnished in the early to mid Eighteenth Dynasty (*ibid.*, Fig. 21 [1.8.3]).

2848A **542** Fig. 66l

G1 (Nile B2). Fired fairly soft. Surfaces concealed by slip. Break not recorded. Fairly plentiful poorly sorted sand. Moderate qty to fairly plentiful fine veg, mostly to 0.3. Sparse limestone to 0.1. Red slip on both surfaces. Both surfaces polished.

Phase	Context & No.	Grid ref	Max dia rim	Fig
iv (Pt II?)	ABW **25**	Area 13	*c.*26	66l

543 Flat-rimmed bowl

Although some similar forms are classified as lids (see **703–06**), the red slip on the interior (only) shows this was intended to be a bowl. There is no close match at Memphis (Kom Rabia) (though some of the smaller lids are similar in form), nor in the Saqqara tombs. However, a Ramesside bowl from Qantir, in uncoated Nile B2 and with diameter 16.2 (Aston D.A. 1998, 163 [416]), does provide a good parallel and should date **543** to this period.

1470 **543** Fig. 66m

G1 (Nile B2). Fired medium. Exterior pale orange-brown, interior and rim concealed by slip. Break pale orange-brown with thick grey core. Fairly plentiful poorly sorted sand. Plentiful fine and coarse veg to 0.9. No visible limestone. Thin orange-red (self-?) slip on interior and top of rim, extending just over on to exterior; exterior otherwise uncoated. Polished where slipped.

Phase	Context & No.	Grid ref	Max dia rim	Fig
vii	AAA (UP 445) **88**	Area 2	20–21	66m

544 Shallow bowl(s)

It is possible that all the sherds are from a single bowl, since their similarity was only recognised after it was too late to check. It should also be noted how widely separated the two joining pieces were (see also **315/627/53**). The rims are distorted by string-tying, making comparison with published bowls difficult. However, **544** should otherwise resemble one from Memphis (Kom Rabia) already present in the early to mid Eighteenth Dynasty (Bourriau 2010, Fig. 21 [3.2.5]) and which recurs, both uncoated and red slipped, until the mid to late Nineteenth. The modest diameter might not seem to require tying, but a bowl of similar size and shape from Luxor has a rim groove probably caused in the same way (Aston D.A. 2008, Pl. 24 [499]). Roll-rim plates of the Late Ptolemaic–Early Roman period are sometimes also string-tied and quite similar in appearance, but the context of AQE **120**, if trustworthy, legitimises the earlier date.

AQE **120** was originally published in Vol. II (Pl. 63 [27]) before the join to BAG/BAH **5** was found. The ware description was prepared for Vol. II and not revised, as most were, so the criteria may not be consistent.

2873 **544** Fig. 66n

Unlikely to be lid(s) because interior polished.

G1 (Nile B2). AEZ/AFB/C/D **7.** Fired fairly soft. Surfaces pale reddish brown. Break pale reddish brown with red core. Fairly plentiful poorly sorted sand. Moderate qty fine and coarse veg to 0.6. Sparse limestone to 0.1. Probable self-slip on both surfaces, but no coloured slip. Interior lightly polished, exterior not polished or burnished.

AQE **120**+ BAG/H **5**. Firing not recorded. Surfaces brown. Break brown with pink core. Plentiful fine sand. Small qty fine veg. No visible limestone. Probable self-slip on interior, exterior uncertain. Interior polished, exterior not polished or burnished.

Phase	Context & No.	Grid ref	Max dia rim	Fig
ii	AQE **120***	14/15/16-01/02	17	As 66n
ivb–c/ivb–c	BAG/BAH **5***	16/17-06/07/08	17	As 66n
v/v–vi/v–vi/v–vi	AEZ/AFB/AFC/AFD **7**	19/20-S02/S03/S04	19	66n

* Join

545 Straight-walled deep bowl

Well matched at Memphis (Kom Rabia) by a form of the early to mid Eighteenth Dynasty (Bourriau 2010, Fig. 24 [4.10.5]), its thickening wall seems to imply a flat base. The absence of coloured slip precludes close dating, but it may be fairly early in the NK.

2847 **545** Fig. 67a

G1 (Nile B2). Fired medium. Surfaces red-brown. Break pale brown with very thick grey core. Fairly plentiful poorly sorted sand. Fairly plentiful fine and coarse veg to 0.8. Sparse limestone to 0.1. Surfaces probably self-slipped, but no coloured slip. Not polished or burnished.

Phase	Context & No.	Grid ref	Max dia rim	Fig
iii	AIK **3**	01/02-02/03	*c.*30	67a

546–47 Bowls with folded rim

This type of bowl is very popular throughout the NK, but already found in the SIP. Anne Seiler discusses it briefly (Seiler 2005, 148–49), seeing a more incurved version as predecessor of a NK series but also illustrating SIP examples very similar to those from the Anubieion (*ibid.*, Abb. 66–67). Her diameter range of 20–30 cm for each version is also appropriate. At Memphis (Kom Rabia), the form is present from the early to mid Eighteenth Dynasty onwards (Bourriau 2010, Fig. 22 [3.13.1/2] and Fig. 25 [4.14.5]); among the range of surface treatments are a red slipped interior, a red rim, and a red rim on a red slipped interior. The date range at Tell el-Dab'a (Ezbet Helmi) is similar, from late SIP to the reign of Tuthmosis III (David Aston, pers. comm.).

An example of the incurved version (dia *c.*34) is known in the rare Marl H16 fabric (Bourriau 2010, Fig. 35 [o]).

2452A **546** Fig. 67b

G1 (Nile B2). Fired fairly hard. Surfaces weathered. Break red with grey core. Fairly plentiful poorly sorted sand. Small qty fine veg to 0.2. Sparse limestone to 0.1. Possible trace of (self-?) slip on interior. Not polished/burnished.

Phase	Context & No.	Grid ref	Dia rim (top)	Fig
iii	BDR **20**	10/11/12-03/04	*c.*28–30	67b

2472 **547** Fig. 67c

Small areas of black material, probably from a mummification, adhere to the interior and to the top of the rim.

G1 (Nile B2). Fired fairly soft. Surfaces brown. Break brown with red core. Plentiful fine and medium sand with only a few larger grains. Fairly plentiful fine and coarse veg to 0.5. Sparse limestone to 0.1. Red slip on top of rim and perhaps on interior. Possible but uncertain traces of polish on top of rim.

Phase	Context & No.	Grid ref	Dia rim (top)	Fig
?	BSE **26**	Area 2	*c.*18	67c

548 Deep bowls with flat-topped rim

Large jars of similar form and diameter are common in the New Kingdom, but the red slip on the interior should indicate bowls, which also abound, though the bodies are usually more rounded and the diameters greater (e.g. Bourriau 2010, Fig. 25 [4.14.3/4]; Fig. 50 [4.14.7]). A NK date is probable but cannot be further narrowed. A similar thick-walled form in red slipped G1 occurs in the early to mid TIP (Aston D.A. 1999, Pl. 33 [1039]).

2890 **548** Fig. 67d

Two similar rim sherds, but not the same vessel. Out-turned rim with almost flat top.

G1 (Nile B2). AEF **24** fired fairly soft, BCW **15** soft. Exterior pale brown, AEF **24** where slip lost; interior concealed by slip. Break pale brown, AEF **24** with red zones and thick grey core, BCW **15** with thin red core. Fairly plentiful poorly sorted sand. Fairly plentiful fine and coarse veg to 0.6. AEF **24** sparse limestone to 0.05, BCW **15** none visible. Red slip, AEF **24** all surfaces, BCW **15** interior and top of rim, with splashes on exterior. AEF **24** exterior probably polished, other surfaces uncertain; BCW **15** polished on interior and top of rim only.

Phase	Context & No.	Grid ref	Max dia rim	Fig
iva	AEF **24**	08 to 14-03/04	*c*.18	67d
ivb–c	BCW **15**	18/19-07	*c*.18	Similar to 67d

549–50 Small outward-leaning bowls

The forms indicate a flat base. From Memphis (Kom Rabia) a similar bowl (dia 10) (Bourriau and Gallorini in preparation), with a rim groove even more marked than in BCI **6** of **549**, is attributed to the MK, but this is red slipped on both surfaces. Among the mass-produced uncoated small bowls of the NK it would be unrealistic to seek an exact counterpart, but one similar flat-based form (dia 12) (Bourriau 2010, Fig. 21 [3.2.6]) appears in the early to mid Eighteenth Dynasty (though this also exists in a red slipped version). Both larger and smaller examples of the Ramesside period, and shortly before, are plentiful in the Saqqara tombs.

2876 **549** Fig. 67e–f

G1 (Nile B2). BCI **16** fired medium, BAC/BEI **98** fairly soft. BCI **16** surfaces red, BAC/BEI **98** reddish brown. Break BCI **16** red, BAC/BEI **98** reddish brown, all through. Fairly plentiful poorly sorted sand. BCI **16** small qty fine veg to 0.3, BAC/BEI **98** moderate qty fine and coarse to 0.3. Sparse limestone, BCI **16** to 0.05, BAC/BEI **98** to 0.1. Uncoated. BCI **16** not polished or burnished, BAC/BEI **98** lightly polished on exterior only, perhaps sand-blasting.

Phase	Context & No.	Grid ref	Dia rim (top)	Fig
ivb	BCI **16**	05-06/07/08	9	67e
v/v	BAC/BEI **98**	02/03-S01	9	67f

2889 **550** Fig. 67g

G1 (Nile B2). Fired fairly soft. Surfaces weathered. Break pale brown with thin red core. Fairly plentiful poorly sorted sand. Moderate qty fine and coarse veg to 0.3. Sparse limestone to 0.1. Uncoated. Not polished or burnished.

Phase	Context & No.	Grid ref	Dia rim (top)	Fig
ivb	AWD **12**	19/20-01	8	67g

551 Small deep bowl

Probably a small bowl with round or flat base, rather than a ringstand or offering stand. The exact form has not been found in the relevant publications, but a variant of a flat-based bowl from a Saqqara tomb (Aston D.A. 1997, Pl. 115 [88]) is possible. Perhaps early TIP (Sabine Laemmel, pers. comm.).

2817 **<u>551</u>** Fig. 67h

There is burning on the interior near the centre, possibly from use as a lamp but its position is unusual.

G1 (Nile B2). Fired medium. Surfaces red-brown. Break red-brown with faint, diffuse red core. Fairly plentiful poorly sorted sand. Fairly plentiful fine veg to 0.5, and one piece coarse 0.9 visible. Sparse limestone to 0.1 and one piece 0.3. Uncoated. Not polished or burnished.

Phase	Context & No.	Grid ref	Max dia rim	Fig
Mamluk/Mamluk/vii	ABC/ABD/ABA(UP 69) **9**	Area 13	13	67h

552 Small deep bowl

A very similar form (dia 14), uncoated and with a flat base, appears at Memphis (Kom Rabia) in the mid to late Eighteenth Dynasty (Bourriau 2010, Fig. 38 [4.2.7]). The thickening body of **552** at the lower break indicates a similar flat base (see **572**).

2911 **552** Fig. 67i

Almost certainly used as a lamp: the entire length of the rim is blackened and this extends well down both surfaces, especially the interior.

G1 (Nile B2). Fired fairly soft. Where not burnt, exterior pale brown, interior dark brown. Break pale brown with thick grey core. Plentiful poorly sorted sand. Fairly plentiful fine veg, mostly to 0.3 but pieces 0.6 and 1.0. Sparse limestone to 0.1. Uncoated. Not polished or burnished.

Phase	Context & No.	Grid ref	Max dia rim	Fig
ivb–c	BGW **385**	15 to18-03/04/05	11	67i

553 Small shallow bowls

At Memphis (Kom Rabia) a similar bowl type (dia 14) is already present in the early to mid Eighteenth Dynasty (Bourriau 2010, Fig. 21 [3.2.5]) and recurs, both uncoated and red slipped, until the mid to late Nineteenth. The base is not present, but an uncoated, chronologically overlapping type (again dia 14) of the Nineteenth Dynasty (*ibid.*, Fig. 60 [3.2.7]), preserves a flat base, as is probable on at least CGV **6**. That the flat base is commonplace as early as the late Hyksos period is evident from a long series of only slightly larger such bowls, uncoated or with red slipped interior, at Tell el-Dab'a (Fuscaldo 2000, Figs 13–20).

2854A **553** Fig. 67j–k

The thickening of the lower wall of CGV **6** probably indicates a flat base.

G1 (Nile B2). CGV **6** fired medium, AHV i/AAT **7** fairly soft. CGV **6** surfaces red-brown, AHV i/AAT **7** pale brown as preserved. Break, CGV **6** red-brown with pale grey core, AHV i/AAT **7** pale brown with faint red core. Fairly plentiful poorly sorted sand. Fairly plentiful fine and coarse veg, AHV i/AAT **7** to 0.2, CGV **6** to 0.5. CGV **6** more limestone than usual, to 0.2 and one piece 0.8 × 0.2, AHV i/AAT **7** sparse to 0.1. CGV **6** uncoated, and not polished or burnished; AHV i/AAT **7** surfaces lost.

Phase	Context & No.	Grid ref	Max dia rim	Fig
ivc	CGV **6**	02 to 05-33 to 36	*c.*15	67j
ivc/ivd	AHV i/AAT **7**	05/06-05/06	*c.*12	67k

554 White slipped shallow bowl

This thick-walled shallow vessel is distinctive by reason of its white slip, which probably extended over the whole of the surfaces but might have been confined to the rim area. At Memphis (Kom Rabia), as on most sites, white slips are much less common than red but do occur on various bowls, none of which is really similar in form to **554**. In the Saqqara tombs there are four (dias 14.4–19.6) with white rim (Aston D.A. 1997, Pl. 114 [69–71]; Aston D.A. and B.G. Aston 2001, Pl. 41 [67]), all with flat base, but none with rolled rim. A better parallel to the form of **554** is one with a round base from Malkata (drawn example dia 10) (Hope 1989a, Fig. 1c) which can be 'white-coated'. However, a similar form (dia 16) appears, uncoated, as late as the TIP (Brissaud *et al.* 1987, Fig. 14 [166]). It is also possible that **554** was the integral bowl of an offering stand like a white-coated Ramesside example (dia 14) (Hope 1989b, Fig. 9h); such stands are often white coated.

2913 **554** Fig. 67l

G1 (Nile B2). Fired medium, but misfired, becoming brittle. Surfaces brick-red where slip lost. Break brick-red with thick purple-grey core. Plentiful poorly sorted sand. Small qty fine veg to 0.2. More than usual limestone, to 0.1. Thin white slip on all surfaces. Not polished or burnished.

Phase	Context & No.	Grid ref	Max dia rim	Fig
iva	BAX **18**	06/07/08-03/04	*c.*16	67l

555 Small straight-walled bowl with thickened rim

The slipped and polished interior indicates a bowl rather than a lid or a stand base, and reasonably close parallels, also red slipped on the interior, are provided by two examples from the late Hyksos period at Tell el-Dab'a (Fuscaldo 2000, Fig. 21e, f [87, 88]), though these are a little larger with diameters of 17.5 and 20 respectively. The date may be indicative of activity in the Anubieion cemetery at this time, as the form seems to be absent from the Saqqara tombs of the later New Kingdom and from the Amarna corpus, and the only bowl from Memphis (Kom Rabia) which is at all similar (Bourriau 2010, Fig. 12 [4.14.1]) is of about the same date.

2875 **555** Fig. 67m

Fairly small diameter deep bowl. Unlikely to be a lid or stand because interior polished.

G1 (Nile B2). Fired fairly soft. Surfaces red-brown. Break red-brown with thick, faint red core. Fairly plentiful poorly sorted sand. Small qty fine veg to 0.3. Sparse limestone to 0.05. Thin red slip on interior only. Polished on interior only.

Phase	Context & No.	Grid ref	Max dia rim	Fig
v/v	BAC/BEI **6**	02/03-S01	12	67m

556 Flat-based shallow bowls

Simple uncoated small bowls are not easy to date, but recently published examples from Saqqara (Aston B.G. 2011, 202–03 [1–6]) are very similar, and the soft firing of two examples in **556** would not be characteristic of the Late Dynastic at the Anubieion. There is no shortage of generally similar uncoated bowls of the same size in the NK. At Memphis (Kom Rabia) the best parallel is from the early to mid Nineteenth Dynasty (Bourriau 2010, Fig. 60 [3.2.7]). At Amarna the nearest is probably one of the 'crude' offering dishes (Rose 2007, 200 [123]). Holthoer's corpus (Holthoer 1977) has some fairly similar, but lack of detail in the small scale drawings makes comparisons difficult.

2815 556 Fig. 68a

Only AJY **173** preserves the (probably string-cut) flat base, but the form of AGZ **17** also indicates this.

G1 (Nile B2). BET **141** and AGZ **17** fired medium, others fairly soft. AJY **173** surfaces pale brown, BET **141** red-brown, AGZ **17** red, ATC/ATB **37** brown. Break AJY **173** pale brown with grey core, BET **141** red-brown with grey core, AGZ **17** red-brown with thick purple core, ATC/ATB **37** brown with grey core. Fairly plentiful sand, ATC/ATB **37** fine and medium with a few larger grains, others poorly sorted. Moderate qty veg, BET **141** and ATC/ATB **37** fine to 0.2, others fine and coarse to 0.4/0.5. Sparse limestone, ATC/ATB **37** to 0.05, others to 0.1. Uncoated. Not polished or burnished.

Phase	Context & No.	Grid ref	Max dia rim	Fig
ii	AJY **173**	22/23-S05/S06	15	68a
ii	BET **141**	14/15-01	?	As 68a
ivc	AGZ **17**	11-S02/S03	14	As 68a
ivc/ivd	ATC/ATB **37**	04/05-S04/S05	13	As 68a

557 Deep bowl

Slip on the interior only, indicates a bowl rather than a stand or ringstand, and the curvature of the inner wall implies a fairly deep form. The dating is more difficult, as the form and size are reasonably well matched by bowls of the early MK at Tell el-Dab'a (Czerny 1999, 142 [Nf 80/81]; 166 [Ng 39/41]), but at this time the usual practice is to apply slip to both surfaces. On the whole, and for this reason, and although no close match for the form has been found in the NK (the best at Memphis (Kom Rabia) are probably in the 'flower pot' series) (Bourriau 2010, Fig. 24 [4.10.4/5]), this period is preferred. The Memphis examples, of the early to mid Eighteenth Dynasty, do occur, as do many NK bowls, with only the interior red slipped.

2490 557 Fig. 68b

Grooves below rim from string-tying before firing.

G1 (Nile B2). Fired soft. Surfaces pale brown where uncoated or slip lost. Break pale brown all through. Fairly plentiful fine and medium sand with a few larger grains. Fairly plentiful fine veg to 0.3. Sparse limestone to 0.1 and one piece probable fossil shell 0.3. Red slip on interior and top of rim; on exterior on rim-roll only, and probably never slipped below this. Not polished or burnished.

Phase	Context & No.	Grid ref	Max dia rim	Fig
?	AIV **7**	17-06/07/08	19	68b

558–59 Medium-sized to large bowls with folded rim

Although these two bowls are very similar, 558 resembles in form and diameter (23) a type published from Memphis (Kom Rabia) only from a context of the late SIP to the early Eighteenth Dynasty (Bourriau 2010, Fig. 12 [4.14.1]). This is slipped on the exterior only (correction to page 57) and not polished/burnished. 559 is better matched by a slightly different form, which appears in the early to mid Eighteenth Dynasty and continues, so might develop from the other (*ibid.*, Fig. 25 [4.14.3]). The drawn example has a diameter of only 30 but this is the smallest of twelve recorded, which range up to 52 and include diameters of 37, 44 and 46. From the outset it can have a red slip on the interior and by the early to mid Nineteenth Dynasty is recorded with both surfaces slipped and with polish/burnish on the exterior (*ibid.*, Fig. 64), though the fully polished version is not recorded. Similar bowls from the late Hyksos period at Tell el-Dab'a (dia 23, 20) (Fuscaldo 2000, Figs 21d/g [86/89]) are also red slipped, on the interior and on both surfaces respectively.

2648 **558** Fig. 68c

G1 (Nile B2). Fired fairly soft. Surfaces brown, exterior where slip lost. Break brown with red core. Fairly plentiful fine and medium sand with a few larger grains. Fairly plentiful fine and coarse veg to 1.0. No visible limestone. Exterior weathered; pinkish brown slip on interior and top of rim. Possible but uncertain traces of polish where slipped.

Phase	Context & No.	Grid ref	Dia rim (top)	Fig
?	BHY **90**	02-19/20	*c.*20–25	68c

2843 **559** Fig. 68d

Conspicuous impress of a thick string, tied before firing, underneath the overhang, and a less obvious second set lower down.

G1 (Nile B2). Fired fairly soft. Surfaces concealed by slip. Break red-brown with pale pink to purple core. Fairly plentiful poorly sorted sand. Fairly plentiful fine and coarse veg to 0.9. Sparse limestone to 0.1 and two pieces each 0.2. Thick red slip on both surfaces. Traces of polish on both surfaces.

Phase	Context & No.	Grid ref	Max dia rim	Fig
iva	BHR **268**	02/03-21/22	*c.*40	68d

560–61 Bowls/basins with direct rim

At Memphis (Kom Rabia) there is a wide choice of parallels for these large diameter open forms (Bourriau 2010, [3.10.1/4, 4.4.2, 4.10.2]). All are present already in the early to mid Eighteenth Dynasty (*ibid.*, Figs 22–24) and all except [4.10.2] continue to appear until well into the Nineteenth, a testimony to their usefulness. For dating purposes, the significant feature is the appearance in the mid Eighteenth Dynasty of polish/burnish on the red slip (*ibid.*, 139), which should apply to **560**, though not necessarily to **561**.

329 **560** Fig. 68e–g

Variable in thickness and diameter, but all with flat- or almost flat-topped rims and almost straight walls.

G1 (Nile B2). DBW/DBU **67** fired soft, others medium. Surfaces concealed by slip. Break DBW/DBU **67** brown all through, others brown with grey core, or red with grey core. Plentiful or fairly plentiful fine and medium sand with only a few larger grains, except ABV/Y/Z **8** (with the thickest walls) poorly sorted. Fine veg: DBW/DBU **67** very little, ADU **11**, BHR **8** and ATY **235** small qty to 0.2, AEW **39** moderate qty to 0.2, AIY/AIX **14**, ABV/Y/Z **8**, BEP **57** fairly plentiful, **14** to 0.7, **8** to 0.5, **57** to 0.2. Little or no visible limestone, and only to 0.1 except ATY **235** one piece 0.2. ADU **11** has a piece of embedded blue material 0.2 × 0.1, apparently faience rather than bone (cf **255** of the OK, **405** of the MK and **586** of the NK). Brownish red slip on both surfaces, except BHR **8**, which is weathered. Except BHR **8**, both surfaces polished.

Phase	Context & No.	Grid ref	Max dia rim	Fig & notes
o	ADU (UP 330) **11**	Area 13	*c.*32–38	As 68f*
ii/ivd	AIY/AIX **14**	12-01/02	*c.*24	As 68f
iv (Pt II?) ×3	ABV/ABY/ABZ **8**	Area 13	?	68e
iva	BHR **8**	02-23	40+(?)	As 68f
ivc–d(?)/ivd(?)	DBW/DBU **67**	Area 1. 28-S31	?	As 68g but rim not grooved

Phase	Context & No.	Grid ref	Max dia rim	Fig & notes
ivd	ATY **235**	25-04	32	68f
v	AEW **39**	04-02 to 07	?	68g
?	BEP **57**	14 to17-01/S01	?	As 68f

* ADU 11 has a narrow groove around exterior 1.7 below rim

1418 **561** Fig. 68h

Two deep grooves around exterior, from string-tying.

G1 near G4 (Nile B2 near C). Fired fairly soft. Surfaces brown. Break brown with red zones and thick grey core. Plentiful fine and medium sand with a few larger grains. Fairly plentiful fine veg to 0.4. Sparse limestone to 0.1. Probable traces of red-brown slip on exterior and on top of rim. Not polished or burnished.

Phase	Context & No.	Grid ref	Dia rim (top)	Fig
iva	BDA **4**	05-06/07/08	*c.*30(+?)	68h

562 Large shallow bowl with string-tied rim

Because of its soft firing, this shallow bowl has suffered more than most from weathering, but is almost certainly a form found at Memphis (Kom Rabia) in Nile G4 (Bourriau 2010, Fig. 28 [3.10.7]). Because of their large diameter these were string-tied around the overhanging rim before firing, producing a corrugated effect. Eighteenth Dynasty.

2452B **562** Fig. 68i

Large diameter bowl, originally bifurcated but lower projection now lost, together with exterior surface of vessel.

G1 (Nile B2). Fired fairly soft. Exterior weathered; interior pale brown. Break pale brown with thick grey core. Fairly plentiful poorly sorted sand. Small qty fine veg to 0.2. Sparse limestone to 0.1. Exterior weathered, interior perhaps self-slipped. Not polished or burnished.

Phase	Context & No.	Grid ref	Dia rim (top)	Fig
ii	AIY **36**	13/14-01/S01	30–40(?)	68i

563 Carinated(?) bowl

Although only the rim survives, this may well be from a bowl with a gently rounded carination, a type common at Memphis (Kom Rabia) throughout the Eighteenth and Nineteenth Dynasties, uncoated or with various surface treatments (Bourriau 2010, Fig. 23 etc [4.5.1]).

2914 **563** Fig. 69a

G1 (Nile B2). Fired medium. Surfaces brick-red. Break brick-red all through. Plentiful poorly sorted sand. Fairly plentiful fine and coarse veg to 0.3. More limestone than usual, to 0.1. Uncoated. Not polished or burnished.

Phase	Context & No.	Grid ref	Dia rim (top)	Fig
iva	AQC **212**	02/03-10	15	69a

564 Carinated bowl with out-turned rim

Similar carinated bowls, with a variety of surface treatments, are already present in Memphis (Kom Rabia) from the first half of the Eighteenth Dynasty onwards (Bourriau 2010, Figs 23, 38, 49 etc [4.5.5]) but with slightly out-turned rim. The closest parallel for the rim form is a single example (dia 20) from a context of the late Eighteenth to mid Nineteenth Dynasty (*ibid.*, Fig. 61 [3.11.2]), recorded with a red slipped rim on a red slipped (in this case unpolished) interior, which is one possible interpretation of the Anubieion example. A similar bowl (dia 21.6) from Amarna (Rose 2007, 218 [289]) has a slight thickening of the rim; there are possible traces of slip. Among several at Qantir in the Ramesside period, some red slipped, two uncoated examples (dia 20) are the closest (Aston D.A. 1998, 167 [454]; 169 [461]). In the Saqqara tombs a fine ware example (dia 18) with highly polished red slip has an almost identical form but is drawn with a shallower stance (Aston D.A. 1997, Pl. 112 [1]). Probably Nineteenth Dynasty.

2046 **564** Fig. 69b

The interior above the carination is smoothed, leaving no wheel-ridges.

G1 (Nile B2). Fired fairly soft. Exterior brown where uncoated, interior pale brown where slip lost. Break brown with faint red core. Fairly plentiful poorly sorted sand. Small qty fine veg to 0.4. No visible limestone. Thin brownish red slip on interior, over rim and down exterior to a straight edge 2.0 below rim. Polished where slipped.

Phase	Context & No.	Grid ref	Dia rim (top)	Fig
?	UP 1044 **24**	Area 12	*c.*18	69b

565 White washed thick-walled bowl

In spite of the unusually thick wall, the similarity of form, and especially the thin white wash, indicate a deep bowl similar to one of the early to mid Eighteenth Dynasty from Memphis (Kom Rabia) (Bourriau 2010, Fig. 24 [4.10.8]) in the 'flower pot' series. A date in or about the reign of Tuthmosis III is likely (*ibid.*, 81).

1404B **565** Fig. 69c

G1 (Nile B2). Fired medium. Surfaces pale brown where visible. Break pale brown with thick pink zones and diffuse grey core. Fairly plentiful poorly sorted sand. Moderate qty fine veg to 0.3. More limestone than usual, to 0.1. Thin white wash on all surfaces. Not polished or burnished.

Phase	Context & No.	Grid ref	Max dia rim	Fig
ii/iii/iva	AIY/BDR/AWZ **8**	07/08-06/07	*c.*15	69c

566 Medium-sized deep bowls

No close parallel to this form has been found with so upright a stance and it may have been drawn too upright, in which case it should be similar to CHJ **12** of **525** and the form close to a common one from Memphis (Kom Rabia) (Bourriau 2010, Fig. 23 [4.4.2]) which occurs with various surface treatments. The first occurrence is in the early to mid Eighteenth Dynasty, polish/burnish (of both surfaces) appearing in the late Eighteenth to Nineteenth (*ibid.*, Fig. 49).

2857 **566** Fig. 69d

G1 (Nile B2). Fired fairly soft to medium. Surfaces pale brown to red. Break pale brown with red core where soft, red with grey core where medium fired. Fairly plentiful poorly sorted sand. Moderate qty mostly fine veg to 0.3, except BHR **269** to 0.5 and one piece 1.0. Sparse limestone to 0.1. For red slip and polish, see table.

Phase	Context & No.	Grid ref	Dia rim (top)	Red slip?	Polished?	Fig
ii	BDX **50**	03/04-07	?	Int only	No	As 69d
iva	BHR **269**	02/03-21/22	*c.*20	Both	Int/Ext?	69d
ivc	ATE **19**	03/04/05-S04/S05/S06	*c.*20	Ext only	Ext only	As 69d

567 Medium-sized deep bowls

This series equates to two adjacent groups of bowls in the series from Memphis (Kom Rabia) (Bourriau 2010, Fig. 38 [4.2.9]; Fig. 49 [4.2.10]). Both appear during the Eighteenth Dynasty: the former, with a distinct flat base, occurs with a variety of surface treatments but there are no polished/burnished examples until the Nineteenth; the latter, its base less clearly defined, occurs with red slip but is not recorded with polish or burnish. The diameter range of 4.2.9 is fairly wide at 14–25 (though most are 18–20), that of 4.2.10 less so at 18–21 (Janine Bourriau, pers. comm.). The Anubieion examples are thus probably Ramesside.

2856B **567** Fig. 69e

Uncoated

G1 (Nile B2). Fired fairly soft to medium. Surfaces red-brown. Break not recorded. Fairly plentiful poorly sorted sand. Veg present, details not recorded. Sparse limestone to 0.1. Uncoated. Not polished or burnished.

Phase	Context & No.	Grid ref	Dia rim (top)	Notes
o/ii	AQG/AJY **40**	19/20-04/05	?	As 69e

Red slip and polish on both surfaces

G1 (Nile B2). Fired fairly soft to medium. Surfaces concealed by slip. Break pale brown, with or without red core, to red-brown with grey core, with or without red zones. Fairly plentiful poorly sorted sand. Variable veg, from moderate qty fine only to 0.3, to fairly plentiful fine and coarse to 0.9. Sparse limestone to 0.1. Red slip on both surfaces. Both surfaces polished.

Phase	Context & No.	Grid ref	Dia rim (top)	Fig
ii	AIY **81**	10/11-01/02	18	69e
ii	ABR North (UP 51) **18**	Area 13	21	As 69e
iv (Pt II?)	ADF North **76**	Area 13	20–23	As 69e
vi to Mamluk	ABA–ABG (UP 3) **17**	Area 13	21	As 69e
vii	AAA East **26**	Area 1	18	As 69e

Red slip and polish on interior, exterior uncoated

G1 (Nile B2). Fired fairly soft to medium. Exterior pale brown to red-brown, interior concealed by slip. Break not recorded. Fairly plentiful poorly sorted sand. Veg present, details not recorded. Sparse limestone to 0.1. Red slip on interior, exterior uncoated. Interior polished, exterior not polished or burnished.

Phase	Context & No.	Grid ref	Dia rim (top)	Fig
iii–iva	AFS **49**	03-07	?	As 69e

Both surfaces weathered

G1 (Nile B2). Fired fairly soft to medium. Surfaces pale brown to red-brown. Break not recorded. Fairly plentiful poorly sorted sand. Veg present, details not recorded. Sparse limestone to 0.1. Surfaces too weathered to show slip or polish.

Phase	Context & No.	Grid ref	Dia rim (top)	Fig
iva	AJH **96**	04/05/06-05 to 08	*c.*22	As 69e

568 Slipped and polished bowl with almost flat wall

A very similar form already appears at Memphis (Kom Rabia) in the late SIP to the early Eighteenth Dynasty (Bourriau 2010, Fig. 11 [3.10.3]). It recurs throughout the NK and TIP, with a variety of surface treatments, and there is a version with polished red slip on both surfaces from the early to mid Nineteenth Dynasty (*ibid.*, fig 61). The drawn example has a diameter of 24, but slightly shallower ones from a Saqqara tomb have diameters of only 13.5 and 13.6 (Aston B.G. 2005, Pl. 117 [59/61]) so there is a range of sizes. Most published examples are shallower than **568** as drawn, but at least one (Aston D.A. 1999, Pl. 29 [884]) has a similar stance.

2872 **568** Fig. 69f

G1 (Nile B2). Fired fairly soft. Surfaces concealed by slip. Break pale brown with red core. Fairly plentiful poorly sorted sand. Fairly plentiful fine veg to 0.2. Sparse limestone to 0.05. Red slip on both surfaces, and both polished.

Phase	Context & No.	Grid ref	Dia rim (top)	Fig
vii	AAA (UP 23) **541**	10-08	18	69f

569 Slipped and polished deep bowl with almost flat rim

Although the conspicuous feature is the rim shape, it is likely to have been acquired merely through the bowl's being stood inverted before firing. It is probably a version of a Memphis (Kom Rabia) type (dia 27) with an only slightly more rounded rim (Bourriau 2010, Fig. 24 [4.10.2]); this is recorded only uncoated or with unpolished red slip on the interior, but an almost identical vessel with a more rounded rim (dia 32, another example dia 28) from a Saqqara tomb (Aston B.G. 2005, Pl. 121 [94]) is red slipped and polished/burnished, presumably on both surfaces. Eighteenth or early Nineteenth Dynasty.

2016 **569** Fig. 69g

G1 (Nile B2). Fired medium. Surfaces concealed by slip. Break red-brown with grey core. Moderate qty fine and medium well-sorted sand. Plentiful fine and coarse veg to 1.0. Sparse limestone to 0.05 and one piece 0.2. Fairly thick red slip on both surfaces, but it fails to conceal the veg and limestone voids. Both surfaces polished.

Phase	Context & No.	Grid ref	Max dia rim	Fig
ii	BDX **68**	02/03-07	*c.*23	69g

570 Deep bowl/cup with trimmed rim

Although in most respects similar to a commonly occurring form classified at Memphis (Kom Rabia) as a cup (Bourriau 2010, Fig. 24 [5.2.1]), this is distinguished by the knife-trimmed 'square' rim (Colin Hope, pers. comm.). One example (dia 20), dated to the eighth–seventh century BC, looks as though it may have been similarly knife-trimmed (Aston D.A. and Jeffreys, Fig. 33 [298]) but is not so described. Examples of the technique are recorded on much larger bowls from Luxor (Aston D.A. 2008, Pl. 16 [312]; Pl. 45 [890]; Pl. 82 [1005]). Ramesside or TIP.

2784 **570** Fig. 69h

Small traces of burning on surviving interior surface.

G1 (Nile B2). Fired fairly soft. Surfaces pale brown, exterior where slip lost. Break pale brown with diffuse red core. Fairly plentiful fine and medium sand with a few larger grains. Moderate qty fine and a little coarse veg to 0.3. Sparse limestone to 0.1. Small areas of pink (intended to be white?) slip survive on exterior and on top of rim only. Probable trace of polish on top of rim only.

Phase	Context & No.	Grid ref	Dia rim (top)	Fig
ii	AUQ **97**	08/09-02/03	13	69h

571 Pedestal foot of goblet(?) with painted bands

A small area of the vessel interior survives, to which a black remnant of the contents adheres, perhaps from use as an incense burner. Feet of this form are usually from goblets rather than bowls. Eighteenth Dynasty examples tend to be larger (Peet and Woolley 1923, Pl. LII [XLV 1037]; Rose 2007, 218 [293] with cream slip and white coating). Although those of the Ramesside period are often smaller and undecorated (Aston D.A. 1998, 175 [488/90]), at least one larger example (base diameter 13) with black and red bands is published (Hope 1989b, Fig. 14e). Late Eighteenth Dynasty–Ramesside.

2410 **571** Fig. 69i

G1 (Nile B2). Fired fairly hard. Surfaces concealed by slip. Break orange with pink core. Fairly plentiful fine and medium sand with some larger grains. Small qty fine veg to 0.2. Sparse limestone to 0.1.White slip on all surviving surfaces, including underside of foot and interior of body. Red-painted band 0.8 wide around the bottom, and another around the waist, its ends not meeting cleanly but overlapped. Not polished or burnished.

Phase	Context & No.	Grid ref	Dia base (bottom)	Fig
ivd	ATY **81**	23/24/25-04/05/06	6	69i

572 Flat base of bowl

The slip on the interior indicates an open form, perhaps similar to **552** and to a flat-based bowl from Memphis (Kom Rabia) (Bourriau 2010, Fig. 38 [4.2.7]). The latter appears, uncoated, in the mid to late Eighteenth Dynasty but occurs red slipped on both surfaces in the early to mid Nineteenth.

2476 **572** Fig. 69j

Distinct 'step' in interior where an extra clay plug was inserted, for added strength, before firing. Traces of burning on interior and underside.

G1 (Nile B2). Fired fairly soft. Surfaces pale brown where slip lost. Break pale brown with red core, or red zones and grey core where thickest. Fairly plentiful poorly sorted sand. Moderate qty fine veg to 0.3. Sparse limestone to 0.1.Thick red slip on all surfaces, including underside. Possible traces of polish on underside.

Phase	Context & No.	Grid ref	Max dia base	Fig
o	BDY **52**	01/02/03-07/08	*c.*6	69j

573–76 Miniature deep bowls

Miniature vessels can be amongst the most difficult of all to date, because their forms are so simple. The problem is compounded when, as at the Anubieion, the contexts are of little help. Most of the Anubieion miniatures are ascribed to the OK–FIP, on the basis of better-contexted published examples. There does, however, seem to be sufficient reason to date **573–76** to the NK, in spite of their similarity to one from Dahshur (Faltings 1989, Abb. 7 [N-O-E 58]) said to be of the Fourth Dynasty, not to mention a slightly larger version (dia 8.6) of the sixth century BC from Abusir (Smoláriková 1999, Fig. 18 [33]).

At Amarna there is a good match (dia 8.4) to **574** (Rose 2007, 213 [SE 4.1]), and other vessels have a more general similarity to the series (*ibid.*, 211 [SE 1.1]; 221 [SF 2.1]); here, at least, the material should be of a known date. Further parallels include one (dia 7) from Memphis (Bourriau 2010, Fig. 28 [20.1.1]) from the early to mid Eighteenth Dynasty, and a number from the Saqqara tombs area: from Tia and Tia (Aston D.A. 1997, Pl. 112 [25/30/42]; Pl. 102 [115]); from surface debris (Aston D.A. and B.G. Aston 2001, Pl. 40 [42/43]); from Paser and Ra'ia (Bourriau and D.A. Aston 1985, Pl. 35 [22/23]); and from Horemheb (Bourriau *et al.* 2005, Fig. 6 [24–29]).

2818 **573** Fig. 69k–m

Three examples, all slightly different but having in common the general form and pinched base. AJY **178** has a smudged mat-impression on the bottom of the base, and the rims of BGG **140** and AJY **178** are slightly distorted from careless handling before firing.

G1 (Nile B2). Fired fairly soft. Surfaces pale brown. Break brown with faint red core. Fairly plentiful poorly sorted sand. Moderate qty fine veg to 0.3/0.5. Sparse limestone to 0.05, AAA **15** also one piece 0.5 × 0.4. AJY **178** one piece of hard dark red-brown stone 0.2. Uncoated. Not polished or burnished.

Phase	Context & No.	Grid ref	Dia rim (top)	Height	Fig
ii	AJY **178**	10 to 14-S04/S05	5.2	3.5–4.3 variable	69k
ii	BGG **140**	04/05/06-S01/S02/S03	5.7	3.9	69l
vii	AAA **15**	Area 1	6.0	3.1–3.6 variable	69m

2814 **574** Fig. 69n

Interior, except the bottom 1.0, blackened, more probably from use as a lamp or from burning incense than from mummification material. Underside uneven, and rough where it stood before firing, so no clear indication of string-cutting from the clay lump. Some fingermarks on lower exterior.

G1 (Nile B2). Fired fairly soft. Surfaces pale brown. Intact, no break. Fairly plentiful to plentiful poorly sorted sand. Fairly plentiful fine and coarse veg to 1.3. Sparse limestone to 0.1. Uncoated. Not polished or burnished.

Phase	Context & No.	Grid ref	Max dia rim	Height	Fig
vii	AAA (UP 157) **143**	07/08/09-13/14/15	6.4	4.4	69n

2812A **575** Fig. 69o

G1 (Nile B2). Fired medium. Surfaces red-brown. Break red-brown with thick grey core. Fairly plentiful poorly sorted sand. Fairly plentiful fine and coarse veg to 0.5. More limestone than usual in a Nile fabric, to 0.1 with one piece 0.2, two 0.3 and one 0.9 × 0.3. Uncoated. Not polished or burnished.

Phase	Context & No.	Grid ref	Max dia rim	Height	Fig
vii	AAA (UP 998) **26**	Area 2	5.0	3.4	69o

2812B **576** Fig. 69p

G1 (Nile B2). Fired soft. Surfaces pale brown. Break pale brown all through. Fairly plentiful poorly sorted sand. Moderate qty fine veg to 0.3. Sparse limestone to 0.05. Uncoated. Not polished or burnished.

Phase	Context & No.	Grid ref	Max dia rim	Height	Fig
iv	DAG **52**	Area 2 W09-S52/S53/S54	*c.*5.0	3.9	69p

577–78 Large bowls/basins with modelled rim

Both are slightly distorted by string-tying, an understandable precaution on wide-mouthed bowls of such large diameter. At Qantir, they probably equate to an even larger (dia 30) uncoated bowl with no fewer than four string-grooves down to the break (Aston D.A. 1998, 107 [107]). This is from a small corpus now redated to the reign of Tuthmosis III (David Aston, pers. comm.). At Memphis (Kom Rabia) there are several related large-diameter forms to choose from, but the closest appear to be among the 'bowls with carinated contour' (Bourriau 2010, Fig. 24 [4.11.8] and Fig. 63 [4.11.23]). The former, with complete shallow, flat-based profile, first appears in the early to mid Eighteenth Dynasty, the latter only in the early Nineteenth; each can have red slip on all surfaces from the outset. **577** and **578** are from nearby contexts, and could have come from the same tomb.

2080 **577** Fig. 70a

G1 (Nile B2). Fired medium. Surfaces red where slip lost. Break red with thick grey core. Fairly plentiful poorly sorted sand. Fairly plentiful fine and coarse veg to 1.0. Sparse limestone to 0.05. Red slip on all surfaces, but fails to conceal the veg voids. Possible trace of polish on top of rim only.

Phase	Context & No.	Grid ref	Dia rim (top)	Fig
vi	ABI (UP 7) **69**	Area 13	*c.*25	70a

2630 **578** Fig. 70b

The groove is probably from string-tying.

G1 (Nile B2). Fired fairly hard. Surfaces red-brown. Break red with thick pink core, or pink zones and grey core where thickest. Fairly plentiful fine and medium sand with a few larger grains. Fairly plentiful fine and coarse veg to 0.5. Sparse limestone to 0.1. Weathered, but possible traces of red slip on exterior. Not polished or burnished.

Phase	Context & No.	Grid ref	Dia rim (max)	Fig
vi	ANQ (UP 150) **15**	Area 14	*c.*30–35(?)	70b

579 Restricted bowl

Although at Memphis (Kom Rabia) there are many globular jars with similarly flaring rim, most of which can be red slipped (Bourriau 2010, Fig. 27 [11.8.5–8, 11.10.6], Fig. 66 [11.4.3]), these are all too small at diameter 12 or less to compare with **579**, which gives no sign of being distorted. The situation at Amarna and Qantir is similar. It is likely, therefore, that the vessel was a restricted bowl of the uncommon type from a purposive sample at Memphis (*ibid.*, Fig. 34 [c]), the rim of which differs a little but has a diameter of 19, and which is again red slipped, although not polished or burnished.

2506 **579** Fig. 70c

G1 (Nile B2). Fired fairly hard. Surfaces concealed by slip where preserved, otherwise weathered. Break orange-red with pink core. Fairly plentiful poorly sorted sand. Moderate qty fine veg, mostly to 0.3. Sparse limestone to 0.05. Red slip survives on inner edge of rim and midway down exterior of neck only. Traces of polish or burnish on inner edge of rim.

Phase	Context & No.	Grid ref	Dia rim (top)	Fig
ivd/ivd/v/v/v	AHL/AHP/AGW/AHJ/AHK **14**	14-02	*c.*16	70c

580–82 Restricted bowls with modelled rim

An example similar to **581** from Memphis (Kom Rabia), with a slightly taller neck (Bourriau 2010, Fig. 25 [7.6.3]), in uncoated G1 fabric and diameter 26, is dated to the early to mid Eighteenth Dynasty. This is in keeping with a 'family resemblance' to the very much smaller **662**. **582**, on the other hand, seems absent from both Memphis and the Saqqara tombs, but occurs at Qantir in three examples, one with red slip and two blue-painted on a cream/pink slip (Aston D.A. 1998, 309 [982]; 371 [1303/04]); all four have virtually the same diameter. **580**, from the excavated Anubieion tomb, although smaller and closer to the globular jars, is probably of the same type. The date should be Ramesside.

2774 **580** Fig. 70d

Interior blackened, probably before breaking, perhaps from a fire in the tomb.

G1 (Nile B2). Fired fairly soft. Exterior brown where slip lost, interior burnt black. Break brown with red core. Fairly plentiful poorly sorted sand. Fairly plentiful fine and coarse veg to 1.0. Sparse limestone to 0.1. Red slip on exterior, over rim and down about 0.5 inside, then running down. Possible but uncertain traces of polish where slipped.

Phase	Context & No.	Grid ref	Dia rim (top)	Fig
v/v	BJG/BJO(H) **52**	W01/W02W03/01-S01/S02/S03	*c.*15	70d

445 **581** Fig. 70e

Cannot tell whether hand- or wheel-made.

G1 (Nile B2). Fired medium. Surfaces orange-brown where uncoated or slip lost. Break orange with thin dark brown and pink zones and grey core. Fairly plentiful poorly sorted sand. Moderate qty fine and coarse veg to 0.5. Sparse limestone to 0.05 and one piece 0.2. Small areas of thick red slip survive on exterior and interior of rim only. Polished where slip survives.

Phase	Context & No.	Grid ref	Dia rim (top)	Fig
iv (Pt II?)	ARP=ARS (UP 152) **4**	Area 13	30–35	70e

1406 **582** Fig. 70f

G1 (Nile B2). Fired medium. Exterior concealed by slip, interior pale brown. Break not recorded. Plentiful poorly sorted sand. Small qty fine and coarse veg to 0.3. Sparse limestone to 0.1. Thick red slip on exterior, over the rim and down 0.5 on interior to a careful edge. Exterior polished.

Phase	Context & No.	Grid ref	Dia rim (top)	Fig
ii	BET **66**	12/13-02/03	20	70f

583 Restricted bowl(?)

Probably like Nineteenth Dynasty examples from Memphis (Kom Rabia) interpreted as globular jars (Bourriau 2010, Figs 67 and 84 [11.11.2]), which can be red slipped or uncoated, or perhaps like slightly earlier, similar and much better preserved 'carinated basins' from Amarna (Rose 2007, 224 [329]). The upper body of each type can be red slipped; each has a grooved rim, whereas the Anubieion rim is, as preserved, merely thumb-impressed. However, the Amarna vessels have a partly pinched rim with unexplained vertical holes in its thickness and the treatment of **583** may be part of a similar process.

At Luxor, a Ramesside red slipped carinated bowl of diameter 19 (Aston D.A. 2008, Pl. 134 [2736]), if subjected to 'finger pinching' as seen on a larger red slipped bowl (*ibid.*, Pl. 13 [251]), should have had a profile similar to that of **583**.

A similar rim form is found on bag-shaped jars/beakers of both Nile and marl fabrics at Qantir (Aston D.A. 1998, 120–21 [160–62]; 432–33 [1538]); the rim diameter range of the Nile examples is only 11–14 and of the single marl example it is only 20, but **583** could be from a larger version of this form.

2704 **583** Fig. 70g

Sherd, distorted by large thumbprint on top of rim.

G1 near G4 (Nile B2 near C). Fired fairly hard. Surfaces concealed by slip. Break red with brick-red zones and thick grey core. Fairly plentiful poorly sorted sand. Moderate qty mostly fine veg to 0.4. Sparse limestone to 0.1. Red slip on all surfaces. Not polished or burnished.

Phase	Context & No.	Grid ref	Dia rim (top)	Fig
iv (Pt II?)	ABY **50**	Area 13	25–30(+?)	70g

584 Wine jar/bottle with thin neck

Vessels with this neck and rim combination are well known in NK contexts but usually larger, with wider shoulders and a handle from neck to shoulder, and made of marl clay (sometimes decorated). As such, the form appears (rim dia 8–9) in a Saqqara tomb used at the end of the Eighteenth Dynasty and in the early Nineteenth (Aston B.G. 2005, Pls 126–27 [120–24]). There were several examples, in Marl D, in the tomb of Tutankhamun (Holthoer 1993, 64–67, Fig. M and Pl. 35 [41–48]). At Amarna there are similar vessels, again in marl clay (Rose 2007, 269 [569–74]), but including a version of comparable size ([572], rim dia 4.7) and one larger, lacking the rim but with a similarly narrow shoulder ([571]). The much larger version (rim dia 18) in Nile clay (*ibid.*, 259 [483]) should be considered a different type and would have had two handles (David Aston, pers. comm.) but the rim form is again much the same. At Gurob there was a similar vessel (rim dia 4.5) (Brunton and Engelbach 1927, Pl. 39 [80k]), in a fabric simply noted as 'buff' so probably a marl; the rim is slightly deeper but, perhaps significantly, it has no handle.

Although on the basis of their forms a relationship with these published examples seems certain, the combination in **584** of small size, Nile clay and lack of a handle is unusual; perhaps the smaller examples were not always given handles?

The vessel type should belong to the late Eighteenth or (early?) Nineteenth Dynasty while the tomb context may confirm an (early?) Ramesside date.

317 **584** Fig. 70h

Long neck with rim, and upper body, broken in several pieces; also a rim sherd of the same type.

G1 (Nile B2). Fired fairly soft. Exterior concealed by slip, interior of neck red-brown, shading to purple on interior of body. Break AAA **58** red-brown with diffuse red core, others neck brown with diffuse red core, body red-brown near exterior, thin dark brown zone and grey zone near interior. Fairly plentiful to plentiful poorly sorted sand. Fairly plentiful fine and coarse veg to 0.8/1.0. Sparse limestone to 0.1, AAA **58** also one piece 0.2. Fugitive red slip on exterior and on top of rim, carried down inside AAA **58** 1.5, others 1.0. AAA **58** not polished or burnished as preserved; others have surviving areas of polish on exterior and on top of rim.

Phase	Context & No.	Grid ref	Max dia rim	Fig
v/v	BJG/BJO(H) **11+12+26+47***	W01/01-S01	5.3	70h
v/v/v/v	BJG/BJO/BNN/BNR(I) **20+22***	W01 to W07/01-01 to 04/S01/ S02/S03	-	70h
v/v	BNN/BNR **2***	01/02-S01	5.3	70h
vii	AAA **58**	Area 1	*c.*5	As 70h

* Join

585–86 Small globular jars

Two jars of similar small size but slightly differing form. Light internal ribbing proves that both were wheel-thrown, but a seam on the interior of 586 shows it was thrown in two parts (or three if the neck was also separate), which is not unusual for this vessel type (Anne Seiler, pers. comm.). The careful edge to the interior slip indicates a wide mouth. Among his 'carinated vessels' Holthoer offers a selection of similar forms, including several of the appropriate size (Holthoer 1977, Pls 30–32), but the small scale of his illustrations prohibits any definite identifications. In the Memphis/Saqqara area, examples are unexpectedly elusive, unless one with polished red slip but a diameter of 11.5, from near the surface in the earlier Memphis excavations (Fischer 1959, 24 [36]), was of this type. Further afield, there is a single Amarna (descendant?) from old excavations, lacking the neck, with diameter *c.*8.5 but described only as 'rough red; sometimes a poor slip' (Rose 2007, 261 [500]). Eighteenth Dynasty, until end of reign of Tuthmosis III.

265A **585** Fig. 70i

G1 (Nile B2). Fired fairly soft. Exterior concealed by slip, interior brown. Break brown with red core. Fairly plentiful poorly sorted sand. Moderate qty mostly fine veg to 0.4. No visible limestone. Red slip on exterior, carried down 1.3 inside neck and splashing on to interior of vessel. Polished on exterior only.

Phase	Context & No.	Grid ref	Dia rim (top)	Max dia body	Fig
ii	AJY **161**	17/18-S04/S05	4.5	8.7	70i

2488 **586** Fig. 70k

G1 (Nile B2). Fired fairly soft. Exterior concealed by slip, interior brown where uncoated. Break brown with red core. Fairly plentiful fine and medium sand with some larger grains. Moderate qty fine veg, mostly to 0.2. Sparse limestone to 0.05. Scrap of blue material, probably faience, in upper break, see also **255** of the OK, **405** of the MK and **560** of the NK. Red slip on exterior, and just preserved on interior as a straight edge 0.2 below the upper break. Polished on exterior only.

Phase	Context & No.	Grid ref	Max dia body	Fig
ivb	AUN **8**	08-03	8.3	70k

587 Small globular, shouldered jar with direct rim

Such a simple form is difficult to date, but a very similar small jar is to be found in Holthoer's corpus (Holthoer

1977, Pls 41 and 69 [X0 3]), where it is classified as 'occasional' and described (*ibid.*, 174) as 'very rare in NK context'. This example has only a red rim band and 'irregular red dots' (splashes?) on an uncoated surface, but the red slip on **587** may imply greater pretensions; perhaps it was used for ointment. Predecessors in the MK and SIP (Aston D.A. 2004b, Pl. 51 [167]; Pls 195–96 [732–37]; Pls 307–09 [1155–71]) are all uncoated, as is a similar but rather larger (rim dia 9) example from Memphis (Kom Rabia) of the late Eighteenth to Nineteenth Dynasty (Bourriau 2010, Fig. 52 [11.2.1]). For red slipped parallels it is necessary to cite another larger (rim dia 8) Memphis example, of the mid to late Nineteenth Dynasty (*ibid.*, Fig. 84 [11.2.2]) or a smaller one (rim dia 3.5) (with handles) from Amarna (Rose 2007, 261 [517]), the latter polished as well as slipped. A NK date is likely but further precision is not possible.

Originally published in Vol. II (Pl. 63 [24]); the description is now slightly amended.

235A **587** Fig. 70j

The illustration somewhat exaggerates the irregularity of the rim.

G1 (Nile B2). Fired medium. Exterior concealed by slip, interior brown where uncoated. Break red-brown all through. Fairly plentiful poorly sorted sand. Fairly plentiful fine veg to 0.3. Sparse limestone to 0.1. Red slip on exterior, over the rim and down 2.0 inside; interior otherwise uncoated. Not polished or burnished.

Phase	Context & No.	Grid ref	Dia rim (top)	Fig
ii	AUQ **104***	08/09-02/03	5	70j
ii	AUQ **205***	05/06-05	5	70j

* Join

588 Miniature jar

The thick wall indicates a miniature of a type known from Amarna with diameter range 3.6–4.9 (Rose 2007, 261 [496]) and Qurna with range 4.5 and 6.0–8.5 (Myśliwiec 1987, 48 [258–62/67]). None is published from Memphis (Kom Rabia) and they also seem, more surprisingly, to be absent from the Saqqara tombs.

2446 **588** Fig. 70l

Internal ribbing, although rough, indicates throwing on a wheel. Two thin grooves around the upper body appear to be intentional.

G1 (Nile B2). Fired fairly soft. Exterior pale yellow-brown; interior grey, shading to red near upper break. Break pale brown with red zone, and grey core close to interior surface. Moderate qty mostly fine and medium sand with some larger grains. Fairly plentiful fine and coarse veg to 0.9. Sparse limestone to 0.05. Some unincorporated clay nodules to 0.2. Smoothed but probably uncoated. Not polished or burnished.

Phase	Context & No.	Grid ref	Max dia body	Fig
vii	AAA **23**	Area 1	*c.*5	70l

589–99 'Beer Jars' and related forms

One of the commonest of all the NK vessel types throughout Egypt, the 'beer jar', can have inturned, upright or slightly out-turned rim. Inevitably there is some inconsistency in classification, particularly where only rim sherds survive. Until very recently, the most comprehensive series of complete forms was that of Holthoer, but of his four types (Holthoer 1977, Pl.18 [BB1–BB4]) three have little or no shoulder. The fourth is illustrated only by examples with the rim out-turned to varying degrees and their upper parts are scarcely distinguishable from his 'shortnecked funnel-necked jars' (*ibid.*, Pl. 33 [FU 2]) and some 'ordinary globular jars' (*ibid.* Pl. 34 [GJ]). Generally speaking, Holthoer's series does not continue into a late enough period to parallel the Anubieion examples.

Fortunately, we now have from Barbara Aston a dated typology of 'beer jars' from Saqqara together with some additional illustrations (Aston B.G. 2011, 217–21). Her typology takes account of a number of details and dimensions, and although inevitably there is no exact match to the complete Anubieion profile **589** (Fig. 71a), it fits much better into the Ramesside period, and probably the second half of the Nineteenth Dynasty onwards, than the Eighteenth Dynasty. The upright or outward-sloping rims of Fig. 71b/g/h should be of the late Eighteenth or the first half of the Nineteenth Dynasty, while the inward-sloping rims of Fig. 71c–e accord better with the second half of the Nineteenth or the Twentieth Dynasty.

At Qantir, where the first three of Holthoer's types are also lacking, David Aston groups all forms together (Aston D.A. 1998, 182–187 [520–548]; 272–73 [904–10]; 424–25 [1502–04]). At Memphis (Kom Rabia) the inturned are classified as tall jars and divided between a thinner version (Bourriau 2010, Fig. 27 [10.8.3]; Fig. 51 [10.8.17]; Fig. 65 [10.8.32]) and one with a slight thickening of the rim and more upright stance (*ibid.*, Fig. 27 [10.8.3] and Fig. 40 [10.8.5]), though there were many unpublished (and some published) intermediate and variant forms. CFT **15** (Fig. 71f) and AVB **116** of **591** have a taller, upright neck; CFT **15** is at the bottom of the diameter range but appears to be of this type; there are others as small in the main series. The out-turned examples were classified as globular jars (Bourriau 2010, Fig. 27 [11.8.5–11.8.8]). Several varieties of 'beer jar' appear in previous publications of the Saqqara tombs; a good match for **593** (Fig. 71h), without the distortion to the rim, may be noted (Bourriau and D.A. Aston 1985, Pl. 36 [53]). The inward-sloping and upright rims from the Anubieion are listed together, with representative illustrations, and the few outward-sloping are separate. The inward-sloping tend to have a thinner wall than the others. The red slipped version also occurs at Memphis (Kom Rabia), and at Qantir, where it is 'much rarer' than the uncoated (Aston D.A. 1998, 272). The white slip or wash of **592**, though not uncommon on various jars, seems not to be recorded on a 'beer jar' at either Saqqara or Qantir.

The flat, thick, heavy base is usually deeply fingermarked all around the exterior, though whether this was intentional or not is unknown; if accidental, it is strange that it should occur so consistently. Some are pierced with a central hole before firing, as demonstrated by Anubieion examples; this, at least, is clearly no accident but the reason is again not known with certainty. The only other form frequently found with a pre-firing hole is the so-called 'flower pot' **719** (Holthoer 1977, Pl. 18 [FP]); a few (marked ★) of the Anubieion bases may be from this open form, which in any case occurs much less frequently, but some of the unpierced might be from flat-based 'beakers', which are to all intents and purposes 'beer jars' cut off just above mid height (Bourriau and D.A. Aston 1985, Fig. 1 [2]; Aston D.A. 1997, Pl. 115 [94]; Bourriau *et al.* 2005, Fig. 8 [6]).

The date range is from the early NK until the end of the Ramesside, and into the TIP. The inward-sloping version with shoulder (Fig. 71c–e) is absent from the Amarna corpus (Rose 2007, 235–58), but occurs at Memphis in contexts of the early to mid Eighteenth Dynasty. Many Anubieion examples derive from the excavated tomb and its shaft, so probably from the original or subsequent burials in that tomb.

For sherds reused to hold pigment, as on the interior of BEO **63** of **598**, see blue on **505** and yellow on AHW **3** and AAA **13** of **745**, all of the New Kingdom. Note also the evidence of reuse of bases

The sole completely preserved profile is listed first. It was originally published in Vol. II (Pl. 61 [1]); the description is now slightly amended.

Profile

2714A **589** Fig. 71a

Reconstructed from sherds, all from the lowest levels of the excavated tomb shaft. A few small pieces were not recovered. Extra clay was added by the potter to fill a large hole or depression in the underside, pushed into place with the fingers, leaving an irregular fingermarked surface; clay surrounding this area was folded with the fingers around the exterior, partly obscuring the deep finger impressions in the vessel wall.

G1 (Nile B2). Fired fairly soft. Surfaces pale brown. Break pale brown with faint, diffuse red core, or red zones and grey core where thickest. Fairly plentiful poorly sorted sand. Moderate qty fine veg to 0.3. Sparse limestone to 0.1. Uncoated. Not polished or burnished.

Phase	Context & No.	Grid ref	Dia rim (top)	Dia base	Fig
v	BEI **1+3+4+5**★	02/03-S01	8	8.5	71a
v/v	BAC/BEI **11** +unnumbered sherds★	02/03-S01	8	8.5	71a

★ Join

Rims

2650A/2654 **590** Fig. 71b–e

Rim incurved or upright.

G1 (Nile B2). Fired variably, from fairly soft to fairly hard. Surfaces brown to red respectively. Break brown with or without grey core, to red with grey core, respectively. Fairly plentiful poorly sorted sand. Most, moderate qty fine veg but a few examples fairly plentiful with some coarser, all to about 0.3. Sparse limestone to 0.1, AQE **40** also one piece 0.3.

Most are uncoated; exceptions are AQE **40**, red slipped externally and down inside to 1.0 below the rim; BDY/BDX **18** and perhaps BJG(A) **21**, red slipped externally and down inside to break; and BKQ **9**, misfired so that the body is greyish and slightly sintered and the slip, applied externally and down inside to 0.7 below the rim, and presumably intended to be red, is white. None polished or burnished.

Phase	Context & No.	Grid ref	Dia rim (top)	Fig
o	BEO **102**	14/15-01	*c*.11	
o	ADU (UP 122) NE **2**	Area 13	9	71b
o/ii	BDY/BDX **18**	01 to 08-07/08	?	
ii	AQE **40**	19/20-01/02	*c*.7	
ii	ABR North (UP 51) **5**	Area 13	9	71c
iii	BHW **89**	02-20/21	10	
iv (Pt II?)	ABY **10**	Area 13	10	
iv (Pt II?)	ABY **60**	Area 13	?	
iva	BAX **28**	06/07/08-03/04	? (12+)	
iva	BHR **264**	02/03-21/22	?	
ivb	AFV East **23**	11-04/05	*c*.10	
ivb	AVB **116**	10/11-S01/S02	*c*.9	
ivb	BPJ **2**	07-26	?	
ivb–ivc	BCT **38**	18/19-08/09	?	
ivc	AUY **18**	09-S02/03	12	
ivd	ATY **28**	23/24/25-04/05/06	9	71d
ivd	ATZ **12**	22/23-01/02	?	
ivd	BKQ **9**	02-21	7	
ivd(?)	CIC **10**	02 to 05-33	?	
ivd(?)	CIC **16**	02 to 05-33	*c*.10	
v	BJG(A) **21**	W01W02/W03/01-S01/S02/S03	*c*.11	
v	BJG(A) **24**★	W01W02/W03/01-S01/S02/S03	9	
v	BJG(A+C) **5**★	W01W02/W03/01-S01/S02/S03	-	

Phase	Context & No.	Grid ref	Dia rim (top)	Fig
v	BJG(A+C) **17**	W01W02/W03/01-S01/S02/S03	*c.*14	
v	BJG(A+C) **19**	W01W02/W03/01-S01/S02/S03	?	
v	BJG(B+C+H) **4**	W01W02/W03/01-S01/S02/S03	?	
v	BJG(H) **37**	W01W02/W03/01-S01/S02/S03	?	
v/v	BAC/BEI **176**	02/03-S01	?	
v/v	BAC/BEI **211**	02/03-S01	*c.*13	
v/v	BNN/BNR(I) **11**	W06/W07-S01/S02/S03	*c.*15 (?)	
v/v/v/v	BJG/BJO/BNN/ BNR(H) **1**	W01 to W07/01-01 to 04/S01/ S02/S03	*c.*12	
v/v/v/v	BJG/BJO/BNN/ BNR(I) **10**	W01 to W07/01-01 to 04/S01/ S02/S03	?	
vi	AIU **11**	16-07/08	11	
vi–vii	AAB **8**	24/25-06/07	8	
vii	AAA (UP 445) **111**	Area 2	?	
?	BEP **143**	17/18-01/S01	*c.*13	
?	BEP **144**	17/18-01/S01	?	
?	UP 805 **22**	Area 5	10	71e

* Join (BJG(A+C) **5** is a body sherd)

2650B **591** Fig. 71f

Tall rim. CFT **15** has an unusually but not uniquely small diameter.

G1 (Nile B2). Fired fairly soft. Surfaces brown. Break brown with red core. Fairly plentiful poorly sorted sand. Moderate qty mostly fine veg to 0.3. Sparse limestone to 0.1. Uncoated. Not polished or burnished.

Phase	Context & No.	Grid ref	Dia rim (top)	Fig
iii or before	CFT **15**	08/09-23/24	7	71f
ivb	AVB **116**	10/11-S01/S02	*c.*9	As 71f

2656 **592** Fig. 71g

G1 (Nile B2). Fired fairly soft. Surfaces concealed by slip or wash. Break brown with red zones and grey core. Plentiful poorly sorted sand. Moderate qty fine veg, mostly to 0.2. Sparse limestone to 0.1. White slip or wash on both surfaces. Not polished or burnished.

Phase	Context & No.	Grid ref	Dia rim (top)	Fig
ii	BGG **127**	04/05/06-S01/S02/S03	11	71g

2502 **593** Fig. 71h

G1 (Nile B2). Fired medium to fairly hard. Exterior concealed by slip, interior red-brown where uncoated. Break red with pale purple core. Fairly plentiful poorly sorted sand. Fairly plentiful fine and coarse veg to 0.1. Sparse limestone to 0.1. Fairly thick red slip on exterior and down 2 cm inside to a clear edge, then uncoated. Not polished or burnished.

Phase	Context & No.	Grid ref	Dia rim (top)	Fig
iii–iva	ACE **202**	01 to 05-08 to 12	12	71h

2658 **594** Fig. 71i

G1 (Nile B2). Fairly hard, but misfired. Surfaces grey shading to red. Break grey with brick-red core. Plentiful poorly sorted sand. Moderate qty fine veg to 0.3. More limestone than usual, mostly to 0.1 but one piece 0.2 and one 0.3. Possible red slip on exterior but misfired. Not polished or burnished.

Phase	Context & No.	Grid ref	Dia rim (top)	Fig
ii	BGL **121**	14/15-01/S01/S02	11	71i

Bases

2428 **595** Fig. 71j

Small-diameter base, but probably of a larger-diameter vessel. Intentional pre-firing central hole, diameter 2.0. Two adjacent light finger impressions on exterior close to lowest point. Apparently string-cut.

G1 (Nile B2). Fired fairly hard, verging on misfired. Surfaces red with brownish tinge. Break red with brownish tinge, and grey core where thickest. Fairly plentiful poorly sorted sand. Moderate qty fine veg to 0.3. Rather more limestone than usual, to 0.1 and one piece 0.8 × 1.0! Perhaps self-slipped but no coloured slip. Not polished or burnished.

Phase	Context & No.	Grid ref	Dia base	Fig
?	BNE **36**	12/13-07	*c.*4	71j

1378 **596** Fig. 71k

Small-diameter base from a larger-diameter form. String-cut.

G1 (Nile B2). Fired fairly soft. Surfaces red-brown. Break red-brown with faint grey core. Fairly plentiful poorly sorted sand. Moderate qty fine and coarse veg mostly to 0.5, a few pieces to 1.5. Sparse limestone to 0.1. Wet-smoothed or self-slipped, but no coloured slip. Not polished or burnished.

Phase	Context & No.	Grid ref	Dia base	Fig
ii	BKS **10**	02/03-21	5–5.5 variable	71k

2700 **597** Fig. 71l

Thick bases with intentional pre-firing hole, central in AQG **69**, well off-centre in ADS/ARP **3**. Hole in AQG **69** very probably made from exterior; ADS/ARP **3**, cannot tell. Deep finger-prints in ADS/ARP **3**, none in AQG **69**, but weathered. Both string-cut. Holes incompletely preserved but diameter perhaps as large as 2.0.

G1 (Nile B2). Fired fairly soft. Surfaces brownish red. Break brown with red zones and grey core. Fairly plentiful poorly sorted sand. Moderate qty fine veg to 0.3. Sparse limestone to 0.1, ADS/ARP **3** also one piece 0.3. Uncoated. Not polished or burnished.

Phase	Context & No.	Grid ref	Dia base	Fig
o	AQG **69**	12/13/14-S04/S05	*c.*7	As 711
iv (Pt II?)/iv (Pt II?)	ADS/ARP=ARS **3**	Area 13	5	711

2714B **598** Fig. 72a–c

Bases of larger-diameter forms without hole. Where not weathered, usually show string-cutting. Interiors vary from fairly smooth, though with wheel scratches (AFS **80** and the two from Area 13), to quite deeply ribbed.

Evidence of reuse is a thick coating of red pigment on the interior of BEO **63**, and plaster inside BEN **20**, BEO **64**, AON **72** and BET **37**. The plaster in BEO **64** is thick and retains two overlapping rectangular impressions of a thin, flat, probably flexible metal tool 2.0 wide, assumed to be an applicator. Since these four examples all derive from pre-temple levels, their reuse cannot have been in connection with the building of the temple; it is likely to have been in the construction and decoration of tombs in the immediate area, the latest of which is still of the NK. Unless the vessels had been deposited in tomb chapels, or broken while being placed in tombs, it thus appears that the burials were soon disturbed, being either robbed or thrown out/pushed aside to make room for subsequent interments.

For plaster in vessels, see also **34** and **659**.

G1 (Nile B2). Fired variably from fairly soft to hard. Surfaces brown to red respectively. Break brown with red core to red with grey core respectively. Fairly plentiful poorly sorted sand. Small to moderate qty fine and coarse veg, with some pieces to 1.0. Sparse limestone to 0.1; a few also have pieces to 0.3. Uncoated. Not polished/burnished.

Phase	Context & No.	Grid ref	Dia base	Fig
o	AQG **161**	09/10-S03/S04	?	
o	BEN **4**	14/15-01 to S05	?	*
o	BEN **20**	14/15-01 to S03	7	
o	BEO **1****	20/21-S06	8	
o	BEO **63**	14/15-S04/S05	?	
o	BEO **64**	14/15-S04/S05	6.5	72a
o/o	AQG/BEO **12****	21-S06	8	
ii	AON **72**	03/04/05-02 to S02	*c.*7.5	
ii	AON **73**	03/04/05-02 to S02	*c.*7	*
ii	AUQ **197**	05/06-05	7	72b
ii	BET **37**	12/13-02/03	*c.*7.5	
ii/ii	ADG/ADH **13+14**	Area 13	7	72c
iii	BDR **95**	11/12/13-03/04/05	?	
iii	BJJ **27**	18-06	*c.*6.5	
iii–iva	AFS **79**	01/02/03-07	6	
iii–iva	AFS **80**	01/02/03-07	*c.*6.5	
iv (Pt II?)/iv (Pt II?)	ADC/ADE **9**	Area 13	*c.*6	
v	BJG(A) **10**	W01/W02/W03/01-S01/S02/S03	?	
v–vi	CBS **13**	04/05-30/31/32	*c.*8.5	
vii/?	AAA/AMA **6**	08/09-13/14/15	6.6–7 variable	

Phase	Context & No.	Grid ref	Dia base	Fig
?	BEP **23**	14 to 17-01/S01	?	*
?	BEP **82**	20-01/S01	?	

* Perhaps from 'flower pots' (see **517/18**)

** Join

2698 **599** Fig. 72d–e

Bases of smaller-diameter forms without hole (though AQG/AJY **20** not quite sufficiently preserved for certainty). Deep internal wheel-ribbing: exterior fairly smooth, AER **25** has a single deep fingermark. BAC **351** probably string-cut from the wheel, the others certainly.

G1 (Nile B2). AQG/AJY **20** fired fairly soft, BAC **351** medium, AER **25** fairly hard. AQG/AJY **20** surfaces brown, BAC **351** orange-red, AER **25** red. Break, AQG/AJY **20** brown with red core, BAC **351** pinkish-red with orange-red zones, AER **25** red all through. BAC **351** plentiful, others fairly plentiful, poorly sorted sand. AQG/AJY **20** moderate qty fine veg to 0.3, BAC **351** small qty to 0.2, AER **25** fairly plentiful to 0.3. Sparse limestone to 0.1, AQG/AJY **20** also one piece and AER **25** two, each 0.2. Uncoated. Not polished or burnished.

Phase	Context & No.	Grid ref	Dia base	Fig
o/ii	AQG/AJY **20**	19/20-04/05	*c.*4.5	As 72e
v	BAC **351**	02/03-S01	*c.*4.5	72d
vi	AER **25**	01/02-08/09	5	72e

600–01 Wide-mouthed jars

Characteristic of the SIP and the early Eighteenth Dynasty, and apparently a developed form of a MK beaker. Grooves around, near the rim, as **601**, are also characteristic and must have been for (or from) string-tying. At Luxor (Dra'Abu el-Naga) in the Seventeenth Dynasty, the illustrated examples (dias 10–12) have grooves (Seiler 2003, Abb. 26 [ZN 01/418]; Seiler 2005, Abb. 41); they are red slipped but have an additional white band near the rim. At Memphis (Kom Rabia) in the early to mid Eighteenth Dynasty, one resembling **601** (Bourriau 2010, Fig. 26 [10.3.1]) (dia also 10) has well-marked grooves, while a more globular form (*ibid.*, Fig. 35[m]) (dia also 14) is closer to **600** and shows only faint grooving; each has a red slip on the exterior.

2480 **600** Fig. 72f

G1 (Nile B2). Fired medium. Surfaces red, exterior where slip lost. Break red all through. Fairly plentiful poorly sorted sand. Fairly plentiful fine and coarse veg to 0.5. Sparse limestone to 0.1. Red slip on exterior, mostly lost, surviving best where burnished; interior has no (surviving?) slip. Traces of three horizontal burnish bands on exterior.

Phase	Context & No.	Grid ref	Dia rim (top)	Fig
iva/ivb	BHR/BTG **127**	02-20/21	*c.*14	72f

2478 **601** Fig. 72g

G1 (Nile B2). Fired fairly soft. Surfaces brown. Break brown with red core. Fairly plentiful poorly sorted sand. Fairly plentiful mostly fine veg to 0.6. Sparse limestone to 0.1 and one piece 0.3 × 0.1. Surfaces too weathered for slip, or polish or burnish to survive.

Phase	Context & No.	Grid ref	Dia rim (top)	Fig
ii	AIY **63**	10/11-01/02	10	72g

602 Slender jar

One of a long series of tall, slender jars with rounded base, similar to two at Tell el-Dab'a dated to the SIP (Aston D.A. 2004b, Pl. 228 [883]; Kopetzky 2004, Abb. 210, Typ 14, [K3894]). The former and others are in uncoated Nile B2; the latter is red washed. In the Eighteenth Dynasty the rim may still be slightly everted (Aston D.A. 1998, 93 [49]; Budka 2006, Fig. 19 [2]), but is usually direct. The rim form may place **602** in the SIP.

2886 **602** Fig. 72h

String was tightly but carelessly tied before firing, and has left a clear impression. The surfaces, especially the exterior, are 'bumpy'.

G1 (Nile B2). Fired fairly soft. Surfaces red-brown. Break pale red-brown with red zones and purple core. Fairly plentiful poorly sorted sand. Fairly plentiful fine and coarse veg to 0.5 and one piece 1.0. Sparse limestone to 0.05. Exterior probably self-slipped, but no coloured slip. Exterior lightly polished.

Phase	Context & No.	Grid ref	Max dia rim	Fig
ivb–c	AUE **9+10**	14-06	10	72h

603 Globular, necked, shouldered jar

Similar to a type so named at Memphis (Kom Rabia) (Bourriau 2010, Fig. 66 [11.8.17]), which can be red or cream slipped. This is probably the same as one of Holthoer's 'shortnecked, funnel-necked jars' (Holthoer 1977, Pl. 33 [FU 2]). David Aston (pers. comm.) would classify this as a 'beer jar', but in practice it seems not to occur in his Qantir series.

2718 **603** Fig. 72i

G1 (Nile B2). Fired fairly hard. Surfaces concealed by slip. Break red with pink core. Fairly plentiful poorly sorted sand. Fairly plentiful fine veg to 0.2. Sparse limestone to 0.1. Red slip on both surfaces. Not polished or burnished.

Phase	Context & No.	Grid ref	Dia rim (top)	Fig
?	UP 805 **65**	Area 5	10	72i

604–05 Bottles/jars with projection on the neck

604 is the lower neck of an ovoid bottle or jar with a single projection on the neck. (The form is not to be confused with the more common one of the MK and NK with multiple undulations, (e.g. Bourriau 1981, 56 [95]; Aston D.A. and Jeffreys 2007, Fig. 47 [547]).) At Memphis (Kom Rabia) there is a rim in marl fabric H8 of about the same size (Bourriau 2010, Fig. 55 [10.8.16]) and a rather larger one in G1 with painted bands (*ibid.*, Fig. 35 [b]). A complete vessel from Saqqara (Aston D.A. 1991, Pl. 49 [47]) is also slightly larger. The best match of all for the form is among four at Qantir in the red slipped local Nile fabric and all about the same size as the Anubieion example (Aston D.A. 1998, 301 [958–62, especially 960]) and a fragment uncoated but with blue paint (*ibid.*, 361 [1262]). Ramesside.

605 is the body of a similar (but not the same) vessel, the size and bag-shape best matched by examples from Lahun (Petrie, Brunton and Murray 1923, Pl. LX [80M, 80P]) and Matmar (Brunton 1948, Pl. LVII [82Q]). David Aston places the first two, and probably the third also, in the late eighth or seventh century BC (Aston

D.A. 1996, 38/39, 44/45). This seems too late for the thick wall of **605**, but it is clear that the form was long-lived and a date in the TIP is likely.

2484 604 Fig. 72j

G1 (Nile B2). Fired fairly hard. Exterior concealed by slip, interior red. Break red with grey core. Plentiful poorly sorted sand. Moderate qty very fine veg to 0.2. Sparse limestone to 0.1. Red slip on exterior, interior uncoated. Trace of possible polish on swelling only.

Phase	Context & No.	Grid ref	Dia at swelling (ext)	Fig
vii	AAA (UP 445) **142**	Area 2	*c*.7–8	72j

253 605 Fig. 72l

Exterior of base has many fine grooves from secondary throwing.

G1 (Nile B2). Fired fairly soft. Surfaces pale red-brown. Break pale brown with red core. Fairly plentiful poorly sorted sand. Fairly plentiful fine veg to 0.3. Sparse limestone to 0.1 and one piece 0.2. Exterior perhaps self-slipped, but no coloured slip. Not polished or burnished.

Phase	Context & No.	Grid ref	Max dia body	Fig
ii	AON **1**	04-S02	8	72l

606 Tall, slender jar or bottle

Although the surface treatment of the lower body was not fully recorded, it does not appear to be scraped, so a pre-NK date is very unlikely, yet forms of this size and with these proportions, including the gentle reverse curve and relatively thick wall, are surprisingly uncommon in the NK. In the Saqqara tombs, only one jar (dia 15) comes close (Bourriau *et al.* 2005, Fig. 11 [75]). At Memphis (Kom Rabia) few bodies are recorded and in the Eighteenth and Nineteenth Dynasties none is similar; the best matches for the form are two band-painted 'bottles' (dia 12) probably of the eleventh to tenth century BC (Aston D.A. and Jeffreys 2007, [548/49]), both orange slipped on the upper and one red slipped on the lower body. Some confirmation of a late Ramesside or early TIP date comes from a burial at Tanis (Brissaud *et al.* 1987, Fig. 21 [271]). The upper body of **606** is badly weathered and could have been decorated.

245 606 Fig. 72m

Body interior has wheel ridges, with diagonal striations where the neck was pulled upwards.

G1 (Nile B2). Fired fairly hard. Exterior red where slip lost, interior grey-brown shading to red in the neck. Break red with thick grey core. Fairly plentiful poorly sorted sand. Moderate qty fine veg to 0.3. Sparse limestone to 0.1. Thick red slip and polish on exterior only.

Phase	Context & No.	Grid ref	Max dia body	Fig
iii	BDR **21**	10/11/12-03/04	12	72m

607 Rim of small or medium-sized jar(?)

Although this jar rim has a New Kingdom appearance, no close parallel has been found. The dip in the top may simply be accidental or idiosyncratic, in which case it could be from a 'tall jar' like a red slipped example from Memphis (Kom Rabia) (Bourriau 2010, Fig. 108 [10.10.26]) or one of unspecified form with black-painted bands on a cream/pink slip from Ramesside Luxor (Aston D.A. 2008, Pl. 97 [1941]). It may belong in Holthoer's JO 2 Ledged Roundbased Ovoid Jar series (Holthoer 1977, 161 and Pl. 38); it is unfortunate that Holthoer's corpus was not drawn with more detail or reproduced at a larger scale, as this ought to have been the most useful reference source.

1436 **607** Fig. 72k

G1 (Nile B2). Fired fairly soft. Surfaces concealed by slip. Break brown with red core. Plentiful poorly sorted sand. Fairly plentiful fine veg to 0.3. Sparse limestone to 0.1. Thick red slip on all surfaces. Areas of polish survive on all surfaces.

Phase	Context & No.	Grid ref	Dia rim (max)	Fig
iv (Pt II?)?	BWZ? (UP 1041) **22**	Area 12	9	72k

608–18 'Funnel-necked' jars

Many jars in this series would elsewhere be described as 'funnel necked', but the range of forms is so wide that the term is used sparingly in the present catalogue; the same view was taken at Memphis (Kom Rabia) (Bourriau 2010, 12). Barbara Aston has recently made a valiant attempt to distinguish late Eighteenth Dynasty examples from those of the Ramesside period (Aston B.G. 2011, 236–37), but while her study includes some helpful hints (markedly bowed 'convex' necks and short necks are unlikely to be as early as Eighteenth Dynasty), many forms in the two series are more noteworthy for their similarity than for any obvious differences.

For similar necks in G2 (Nile B1) fabric, see **711–12**.

608 Tall, necked, shouldered jars with direct rim: burnished

CGQ **68** etc (Fig. 73a) is preserved down to the maximum diameter, which is twice that of the rim, indicating a somewhat globular form like one from Saqqara (Aston B.G. 2005, Pl. 135 [201]) and placing an otherwise standard 'funnel-necked jar' in a minority among published examples. AEP/AEQ/AER **54** is from a lower neck, lacking rim. Burnishing of unpainted jars of this type seems to be found only in the Memphite region; even at Qantir, where two blue-painted rims were burnished (Aston D.A. 1998, 367 [1294/95]), no unpainted example is recorded. Probably Ramesside, the identification receiving cautious confirmation from Barbara Aston's recent typology (Aston B.G. 2011) (see above).

2684A **608** Fig. 73a–b

Each example has a string-tying groove at the base of the neck and CGQ **68** another a little below.

G1 (Nile B2). Firing, surfaces and break not recorded. Fairly plentiful poorly sorted sand. Fairly plentiful fine and coarse veg, mostly to 0.5. Rather more limestone than usual, to 0.2 except BCQ **5** to 0.3. Red slip on exterior up to top of rim (where preserved), interior uncoated. Horizontally burnished over entire preserved area.

Phase	Context & No.	Grid ref	Max dia rim	Fig
ivb	BCQ **5**	05-06/07/08	11.5	73b
ivc	CGQ **68 to 74***	02 to 05-34 to 37		73a
v–vi	CBQ **52+53+54+55+56***	02 to 06-35/36	13	73a
v–vi	CBU **60***	04-36		73a
vi/vi/vi	AEP/AEQ/AER **54**	01/02-04 to 08	-	

* All join

609 Tall, necked, shouldered jars with direct rim: polished

Necks of two very similar 'funnel-necked jars', unusual in being polished overall. Polishing, like burnishing (see 608), seems to be confined to the Memphite area except for rare blue-painted examples from Qantir. A Ramesside date is again cautiously proposed on the basis of BarbaraAston's series (Aston B.G. 2011) (see above).

2696A 609 Fig. 73c

UP 588 **425+454+455** has two string-tying grooves at the base of the neck.

G1 (Nile B2). Firing, surfaces and break not recorded. Fairly plentiful poorly sorted sand. UP 588 **425+454+455** small qty, DAG **33** moderate qty, mostly fine veg to 0.3. Sparse limestone to 0.1, UP 588 **425+454+455** also one piece 0.3. Red slip on exterior, interior uncoated. Exterior lightly polished.

Phase	Context & No.	Grid ref	Dia rim (top)	Fig
iv	DAG **33**	Area 2 W09-S52/S53/S54	?	As 73c
vii	AAA (UP 588) **425***	01/W01-40/41/42	10	73c
vii	AAA (UP 588) **454+455***	01/W01-41/42	10	73c

* Join

610 Body sherds from 'funnel necked' jars

The sherds are from three different vessels, the form and diameter similar to CGQ **68** etc (Fig. 73a). Each has a string-tying groove around (BCN **7**+BCC **25** has two).

2684B 610 Fig. 73d

G1 (Nile B2). UP 588 **318** misfired, others not recorded. UP 588 **318** exterior red, interior grey, others surfaces brown to red where slip lost. Break UP 588 **318** grey with thin red core, others brown with faint, diffuse red core or red all through. Fairly plentiful poorly sorted sand. Fairly plentiful fine and coarse veg, mostly to 0.5, UP 588 **531+532** also one piece 1.5. Rather more limestone than usual: BCN **7**+BCC **25** to 0.1, UP 588 **531+532** to 0.2, UP 588 **318** to 0.3. Red slip on exterior, interior uncoated. Not polished or burnished.

Phase	Context & No.	Grid ref	Fig
ivb	BCN **7***	05-07/08	73d
ivc	BCC **25***	05-07/08	73d
vii	AAA (UP 588) **318**	05/06-25/26/27	
vii	AAA (UP 588) **531+532**	01/W01-37/38	

* Join

611–12 Tall, necked, shouldered jars with direct rim

The wide range of height, wall thickness and diameter reflect the variability of the 'funnel-necked jars' so common in the NK, especially in the later Eighteenth Dynasty and the Ramesside period. In 611, BKN **35**+BHP **157** (Fig. 74f) has a string-tying groove around the neck, the string nevertheless failing to prevent some distortion. Several others, notably AJY **165** (Fig. 74c), BCC **42,** BHP **127** (Fig. 74i) and especially AJX/AJY/BRS **63** (Fig. 74d), an exceptionally bowed neck almost certain to be Ramesside (Aston B.G. 2011) (see above), have similar distortions, either in spite of string-tying or because of it, though the string was usually finer and left few clear marks; others again have possible string scuffing, and the practice must have been common, especially around the base of the neck, where there is clear evidence on BEO **101** (Fig. 74b), another probably Ramesside jar.

612, a normal jar in other respects, and with a string-groove around the base of the neck, contains excessively large limestone fragments and is misfired into the bargain! The bowed neck again suggests the Ramesside period.

Although rather small, AQG **153** (Fig. 74a) might alternatively be from a mug/carinated bowl (Bourriau 2010, Fig. 80 [4.11.32]); this type is also present at Saqqara (Aston D.A. 1997, Pl. 119 [149]; Bourriau *et al.* 2005, Fig. [107]), where the same problem is acknowledged (Bourriau and D.A. Aston 1985, 42 [25]).

2682A/2696C **611** Fig. 74a–j

G1 (Nile B2). Fired variously, from fairly soft to fairly hard. Most surfaces concealed by slip. Break varies from pale brown with red core to red all through or with grey core. Fairly plentiful poorly sorted sand. Moderate qty to fairly plentiful veg, usually fine to 0.3, a few longer or coarser, seldom more than 0.5 but BKN **35**+BHP **157** to 0.7. Most, sparse limestone to 0.05/0.1; BKN **35**+BHP **157** also several pieces to 0.2; a few, none visible. Most have slip on exterior (see table), interior uncoated. Not polished or burnished, but some are weathered and may have been so originally.

Phase	Context & No.	Grid ref	Dia rim (top)	Slip	Fig
o	AQG **153**	13/14-01/02	9	Red	74a
o	AQG **193**	09/10-S05/S06	*c.*13	None	As 74b
o	AQG **276**	17/18/19-S05/S06	*c.*10	Red	As 74b
o	AQG **299**	18/19/20-04/05	*c.*8	None	As 74b
o	BEO **101**	14/15-01	10.5	Red	74b
o	ADU (UP 122) SW **30**	Area 13	11	Red	As 74g
ii	AJY **165**	22/23-S05/S06	7	None	74c
ii	AJY **166**	18/19/20-S04/S05	10	Red	As 73c
ii/ii/ivc	AJX/AJY/BRS **63**	21/22/23-S02/S03	*c.*15	Red	74d
iii	BCB **87**	01 to 04-04/05/06	12	Red	As 73c
iii	BDR **122+124**	11/12/13-03/04/05	10	Red	As 74g
iii	BJJ **48**	17/18-05/06	16	None	74e
iii	CHJ **13†**	08/09-24	15	Red	Between 73c and 74e
iii	CHJ **14†**	08/09-24	?	Red	Between 73c and 74e
iii/?	BHW/BHY **54**	01-21	14	None	74h
iii–iva=iva	ACE=AJH **43**	05 to 09-06 to 09	8	Red	As 74b
iv (Pt II?)	ABY **11**	Area 13	*c.*10	Red	As 74g
iva	AQH **183+185**	21-S01 to S04	8††	None	74g
ivb	BKN **35****	02-21	11.5–12.5 variable	Red	74f
ivb–c	AQI **12**	17/18-05/06	?	Red	As 73c
ivc	ACP **73**	01 to 05-10	?	No	As 74j
ivc	BCC **42**	05-06/07	*c.*13 (?)	Red	As 74b
v/v	BAC/BEI **62***	02/03-S01	13	Red	As 73c
v/v	BJG/BJO(B/C) **11***	W01/W02/W03/01-S01/S02/S03	13	Red	As 73c

Phase	Context & No.	Grid ref	Dia rim (top)	Slip	Fig
?	BEP **96**	20-01/S01	8	Red	74j
?	BHP **127**	02-22	*c.*14	Red(?)	74i
?	BHP **157★★**	02-22	11.5–12.5 variable	Red	74f

★ Join

★★ Join

† Almost certainly same vessel but do not join

†† Drawn with diameter 7, slightly too small

2686 **612** Fig. 74k

G1 (Nile B2). Misfired. Exterior brown where slip lost, with a large black area starting to collapse inwards, distorting the form; interior patchily red-brown and black. Break red-brown with thick grey core. Fairly plentiful poorly sorted sand. Fairly plentiful fine and some coarse veg, to 0.4. Rather more limestone than usual to 0.1, and some abnormally large pieces: 1.0 × 0.9, 2.0 × 0.8, 0.3. Red slip survives misfiring, over entire exterior and running down interior. Not polished or burnished, but this is unlikely to have survived.

Phase	Context & No.	Grid ref	Dia rim (top)	Fig
ii	BDS **3★**	04-09	9–11 variable	74k
iii–iva	ACE **246★**	01 to 04-08	9–11 variable	74k

★ Join

613 Tall, necked, shouldered jar with direct rim and grooved neck

The combination of the thin wall and the vertical stance of the neck is within the 'funnel-necked jar' range, although uncommon. The potter seems to have lacked confidence in its ability to withstand the hardening and firing processes, as he tied a string twice around the neck.

2682B **613** Fig. 74l

G1 (Nile B2). Fired fairly soft. Exterior concealed by slip, interior brown Break brown with red core. Fairly plentiful poorly sorted sand. Fairly plentiful fine and coarse veg to 0.7. Sparse limestone to 0.1, also one piece 0.3 × 0.1. Red slipped on exterior, interior uncoated. Not polished or burnished.

Phase	Context & No.	Grid ref	Dia rim (top)	Fig
ii	AQE **111★**	14/15/16-01/02	*c.*9	74l
ii/ivb	AIY/AVB **11+36★**	13/14-01/S01	*c.*9	74l

★ Join

614 Tall, necked, shouldered jar(?) with direct rim

Although the combination of upright stance and rounded rim is difficult to parallel, and the original height impossible to establish, this neck is probably from a jar in the 'funnel necked' series. The difficulty in categorising such diagnostic fragments is well illustrated by two essentially identical examples similar to the present piece classified respectively as from 'funnel necked' and 'globular' jars (Aston D.A. 2008, Pl. 60 [1206/07]).

2879 **614** Fig. 74m

G1 (Nile B2). Fired medium. Surfaces pale brown where slip lost. Break pale brown with red core tending towards purple. Fairly plentiful poorly sorted sand. Fairly plentiful fine and coarse veg to 0.5. Rather more limestone than usual, to 0.1. Areas of red slip survive on exterior and rim; interior weathered but probably uncoated. Traces of polish where slip survives.

Phase	Context & No.	Grid ref	Dia rim (top)	Fig
iva	AQC **65**	02/03-10	12	74m

615–16 Tall, necked, shouldered jars with direct rim: blue-painted on cream slip

No example from Memphis (Kom Rabia) so far published, even among the unpainted examples, provides a really close parallel to any of this series. However, the forms of all are quite well matched from Qantir, and UP 588 **471** of **615**, is especially close to one (dia 12) blue-painted on a cream slip (Aston D.A. 1998, 381 [1334]). For **616** the closest form is probably one (dia 14) blue-painted and burnished on a red slip (*ibid.*, 367 [1295]), though some unburnished examples are also similar in form and diameter, on a red (*ibid.*, 363 [1275]), cream (*ibid.*, 381 [1335]) or white (*ibid.*, 409 [1446]) slip. There is a similar but unpainted jar (dia 12) from a Saqqara tomb (Aston B.G. 2005, Pl. 116 [51])

Although the form, at least of **615**, occurs as early as Amenhotep III, in the Eighteenth Dynasty the body may be painted but usually the neck is not, so a Ramesside date is very likely for all. The brownish paint of **616** is consistent with this (Colin Hope, pers. comm.).

Polishing or burnishing of blue-painted pottery is recorded at Memphis only (Bourriau 2010, 253 and 312, Figs 66 [10.10.21] and 82 [10.2.5], Saqqara (Bourriau *et al.* 2005, 53 Fig. 28, 55 [147]) and Qantir (Aston D.A. 1998, 404 [1432]). (See **516/617/18/44//45/47/49–52/700–02**).

See also **617** and **647**.

2764 **615** Fig. 75a–b

G1 (Nile B2). BGL **74** fired fairly soft, UP 588 **471** fairly hard. Exterior concealed by slip, BGL **74** interior brown, UP 588 **471** red. Break BGL **74** brown with red core, UP 588 **471** red with grey core. Fairly plentiful poorly sorted sand, BGL **74** with fewer than usual larger grains. Moderate qty fine veg to 0.3. Sparse limestone to 0.1. Cream slip on exterior. UP 588 **471** two blue-painted bands over the slip, except for a band 1.0 wide bordered by black bands 0.1 wide; BGL **74** weathered but has traces of blue paint over the slip and a probable red-painted band. UP 588 **471** retains traces of polish on blue and unpainted areas, but none (survives?) on BGL **74**.

Phase	Context & No.	Grid ref	Dia rim (top)	Fig
ii	BGL **74**	15/16/17-04/05	*c.*12	75a
vii	AAA (UP 588) **471**	01/W01-32 to 38	13	75b

2766 **616** Fig. 75c

G1 (Nile B2). Fired fairly soft. Surfaces brown, exterior where slip lost. Break brown with diffuse red core. Fairly plentiful sand with fewer than usual of the larger grains. Fairly plentiful fine veg to 0.2. Sparse limestone to 0.1. Thin cream slip overall on exterior and down to *c.*1.5 on interior. Traces of greyish blue paint survive in many places on exterior, the colour poor because the slip is thin. There is an almost horizontal brownish painted band, assumed to lie on top of the blue; this is the manganese-based paint which fires variously from red through brown to black. Not polished or burnished.

Phase	Context & No.	Grid ref	Dia rim (top)	Fig
ii	BGN **20**	10 to 13-S03/S04/S05	13	75c

617 Tall, necked, shouldered jar with direct rim: blue-painted on red slip

As with the blue-painted series on a cream slip, no example from Memphis (Kom Rabia) so far published provides a really close parallel. However, although the form could be as early as Amenhotep III, it is again quite well matched from Qantir. The best is probably one (dia 16) on a cream slip (Aston D.A. 1998, 409 [1440]) but almost as close are two (dia 12) on a red slip (*ibid.*, 363 [1270/75]). The first and last of these three are also very similarly decorated. None is polished. From a Saqqara tomb there is a jar (dia 13) again very similar in form and decoration but again unpolished (Aston D.A. 1997, Pl. 118 [143]).

Polishing/burnishing of blue-painted pottery is recorded only at Memphis, Saqqara and Qantir. See also **516/615/18/44//45/47/49–52/700–02**.

2744A **617** Fig. 75d

Probably the same vessel as AAA **7** of **649**.

G1 (Nile B2). Fired fairly hard. Exterior concealed by slip, interior red. Break red with grey core. Fairly plentiful poorly sorted sand. Moderate qty fine veg to 0.3. Sparse limestone to 0.1. Red slip on exterior, interior uncoated. One blue-painted band flanked by two thin black bands. Exterior polished, apparently before painting. The 'blue' colour is actually a dull grey.

Phase	Context & No.	Grid ref	Dia rim (top)	Fig
vii	AAA **12**	Area 1	15	75d

618 Tall, necked, ovoid jar with lightly modelled rim: blue-painted on cream slip

For a similar form and diameter, drawn a little less upright, see an example from Memphis (Kom Rabia) (Bourriau 2010, Fig. 66 [10.10.21]), also blue-painted and burnished/polished on a cream slip. It occurs only in early to mid Nineteenth Dynasty levels, in accord with the rather thin Ramesside-type rim roll (Colin Hope, pers. comm.) and with a similar but again less upright (unpolished) example from Qantir (diameter 16) (Aston D.A. 1998, 381 [1333]). Polishing/burnishing of blue-painted pottery is recorded only at Memphis, Saqqara and Qantir. See also **516/615/17/44//45/47/49–52/700–02**.

2762 **618** Fig. 75e

G1 (Nile B2). Fired medium. Exterior concealed by slip, interior surface brown. Break brown with orange-brown core. Fairly plentiful poorly sorted sand. Moderate qty fine and very fine veg to 0.2. Sparse limestone to 0.1. Cream slip on exterior only, blue-painted except for an unpainted band 0.6 wide bordered by black bands, immediately below which is a narrow red band; higher up, there are two narrow black bands on top of the blue. Polished on the blue area.

Phase	Context & No.	Grid ref	Dia rim (top)	Fig
vii	AAA (UP 8) **36+44**	Area 12	17	75e

619 Tall, necked, ovoid jars with direct rim

The shorter necks of **619** distance them from most of the 'funnel necked' jars, while their thin, flaring wall still leaves them within the NK. They appear at Memphis (Kom Rabia) in the mid to late Nineteenth Dynasty (Bourriau 2010, Fig. 84 [11.4.6 and 11.10.28]), and are present at Qantir at about the same time (Aston D.A. 1998, 299 [953–57]).

2688/2696D **619** Fig. 75f–h

The narrow groove at base of neck of AQG **249** etc is probably from string-tying.

G1 (Nile B2). AQG **217+**AIY under Room 10 **166** firing, interior surface and break not recorded. Exterior surface concealed by slip. Red slip on exterior.

Others. Fired fairly hard. Surfaces red-brown, AQG **249** shading to brown towards lower break. Break red-brown with thin dark brown zones and grey core. Uncoated.

All. Fairly plentiful poorly sorted sand. Moderate qty fine veg to 0.3. Sparse limestone to 0.1, also BGG **104** and AJY/AVB **43** each one piece 0.2 and AQG **249** one 0.4. Not polished or burnished.

Phase	Context & No.	Grid ref	Dia rim (top)	Fig
o	AQG **217***	09/10-S03/S04	11	75f
o	AQG **249****	11/12-S03/S04	12	75g
ii	AIY under Room 10 **166***	09 to 12-03/04	11	75f
ii	BGG **104**	08/09/10-S02/S03	*c.*12	75h
ii/ivb	AJY/AVB **43****	11/12-S01/S02	12	75g

* Join

** Join

620 Tall, necked, shouldered or ovoid jar with direct rim: white slipped

Dating this piece, and its smaller drawn counterpart AIY under Room 10 **166+**AQG **217** of **619** (Fig. 75f) is not a simple matter. The form could hardly fit the description 'funnel necked' more closely, but it differs from most in the straightness of the wall. A Late Dynastic jar should be ruled out by the height of the neck in relation to its diameter (Aston D.A. and B.G. Aston 2010, Pl.16 [117]; Pl. 17 [129/30]; French and Ghali 1991, 121 [98/99]) though such can be of white slipped Nile clay (*ibid.*, [98 *2nd example*]). On balance, a Ramesside date is most likely: white and cream slips are recorded from Qantir but the best match may be a red slipped rim (dia 10) (Aston D.A. 1998, 293 [935]).

2696B **620** Not illustrated

G1 (Nile B2). Firing, surfaces and break not recorded. Fairly plentiful poorly sorted sand. Moderate qty to fairly plentiful fine veg to 0.3. Sparse limestone to 0.05/0.1. White slip on exterior (not a colour changeling as it was recorded as not misfired), interior uncoated. Not polished or burnished.

Phase	Context & No.	Grid ref	Dia rim (top)	Notes
iva	AEF **40**	08 to 14-03/04	15	As 75f

621 Tall jar with direct rim

Although this form, with its concave neck profile, is close to some varieties of the wide-ranging 'funnel-necked jar' series, it is distinct. It was probably a sinuous, slender jar of a common type (Bourriau 2010, Fig. 39 [9.6.1]), often blue-painted, simply described at Qantir (Aston D.A. 1998, 344, with references to several sites) as an 'ovoid jar'. As such it is a close match to a couple of blue-painted Qantir examples (*ibid.*, 375 [1312/13]) of the Ramesside period.

2696E **621** Fig. 75i

G1 (Nile B2). Firing, surfaces and break not recorded. Fairly plentiful poorly sorted sand. Moderate qty to fairly plentiful fine veg to 0.3/0.5. Sparse limestone to 0.05/0.1 or none visible. Red slip on exterior, interior uncoated. Not polished or burnished.

Phase	Context & No.	Grid ref	Dia rim (top)	Fig
ii	AJY **156**	17/18-S04/S05	*c.*9	75i

622–23 Tall, necked, shouldered jars with modelled rim

Among the published jars from Memphis (Kom Rabia) there is no close match to **622** in a Nile fabric, but two examples in Marl H1 are very similar (Bourriau 2010, Figs 69 and 87 [10.8.27]), the drawn one having rim diameter 10. The dates are respectively early-to-mid and mid-to-late Nineteenth Dynasty. The very extensive Qantir Ramesside corpus yields a close Nineteenth Dynasty match and a similar one in the Twentieth to Twenty-first Dynasty (Aston D.A. 1998, 193 [572]; 579 [2377]) in the local Nile fabric, with rim diameter 14, themselves uncoated though others in the series are red slipped. The presence of BJG(A) **23**+BJG/BJO **18** and BJG/BJO **19** in the chambers of the excavated Anubieion tomb should be evidence for a Ramesside date for either an original or a secondary interment.

623 should be accounted the same type, but the rim form is closer to an example in G1 red 'washed' ware from Saqqara, with the same bowed neck and with rim diameter 13.3 (Bourriau and D.A. Aston 1985, Pl. 36 [65]).

2520/2522 **622** Fig. 75j–k

All non-joining sherds are from different vessels.

G1 (Nile B2). AVB **110** and BJG/BJO **19** fired medium, BJG(A) **23**+BJG/BJO **18** misfired, CBU **65** fired medium to fairly hard and slightly brittle. AVB **110** surfaces pale brown; BJG(A) **23**+BJG/BJO **18** misfired, surfaces pale grey tinged with red; BJG/BJO **19** and CBU **65** exterior concealed by slip, interior pale brown and red-brown respectively. AVB **110** and BJG/BJO **19** break pale brown with red core; BJG(A) **23**+BJG/BJO **18** pale grey with red core; CBU **65** red-brown with red core, or red zones and thin, discontinuous grey core where thickest. Fairly plentiful poorly sorted sand. Moderate qty fine veg to 0.3. AVB **110** and BJG/BJO **19** sparse limestone, others rather more than usual, to 0.1. AVB **110** too weathered to retain slip; BJG(A) **23**+BJG/BJO **18** exterior only, perhaps an intended red slip, fired grey; BJG/BJO **19** and CBU **65** red slip on exterior and over rim, CBU **65** running down inside. BJG/BJO **19** possible trace of polish on top of rim, others not polished or burnished.

Phase	Context & No.	Grid ref	Dia rim (top)	Fig
ivb	AVB **110**	10/11-S01/S02	10	As 75j
v	BJG(A) **23**★	W01/01-S01	10.5	75j
v/v	BJG/BJO **18**★	W01/01-S01	10.5	75j
v/v	BJG/BJO **19**	01/02-S01	*c.*12	75k
v–vi	CBU **65**	06/07/08-33/34/35	13	As 75j

★ Join

2678A **623** Fig. 75l

G1 (Nile B2). Fired fairly hard. Exterior concealed by slip, interior brown. Break brick-red all through. Fairly plentiful poorly sorted sand. Fairly plentiful fine and coarse veg to 0.5. Sparse limestone to 0.1. Weathered, but traces of almost certain red slip. Not polished or burnished.

Phase	Context & No.	Grid ref	Dia rim (top)	Fig
ivd/v/v	ACL/AAN/ACK **5**	07-02	11	75l

624 Tall, globular jars with folded rim

A very close match with the same sweeping curve around the rim is provided by a red slipped 'large ovoid slender jar' from Amarna (Rose 2007, 229 [349]). At Memphis (Kom Rabia) it should fall in category 11.15 or 11.17, 'globular, ovoid/bag-shaped jars with folded rim' (Bourriau 2010, 13) but no published example in these (or any other) categories is so similar. Close parallels are equally elusive elsewhere, perhaps because some drawings are simplified. Late Eighteenth Dynasty.

2312/2526B **624** Fig. 75m–n

G1 (Nile B2). BHR **190** and ABY **59** fired fairly soft, BEP **94** medium, BHR/BTG **109** misfired. BHR **190** and ABY **59** surfaces pale brown, ABY **59** exterior where slip lost; BEP **94** red-brown, exterior where slip lost; BHR/BTG **109** exterior concealed by slip, interior grey. Break BHR **190** and ABY **59** pale brown with red zones, BHR **190** also grey core; BEP **94** red-brown all through; BHR/BTG **109** blackish grey all through. Fairly plentiful poorly sorted sand. BHR **190**, ABY **59** and BEP **94** fairly plentiful fine and some coarse veg to 0.3/0.4 and BEP **94** one piece 1.1; BHR/BTG **109** moderate qty fine to 0.3. BEP **94** rather more limestone than usual to 0.1 and one piece 0.2, remainder sparse to 0.1. BHR **190** uncoated; BEP **94** and ABY **59** red slip and BHR/BTG **109** purple (misfired red?), on exterior and top of rim. BHR **190** and ABY **59** not polished or burnished; BEP **94** has one surviving burnish band on top of rim; BHR/BTG **109** has broad burnish bands, merging into continuous polish, on exterior of body and of rim.

Phase	Context & No.	Grid ref	Dia rim (top)	Fig
iva	BHR **190**	02/03-21/22/23	9	As 75m
iva/ivb	BHR/BTG **109**	02-20/21	10	75m
iv (Pt II?)	ABY **59**	Area 13	*c.*10(?)	75n
?	BEP **94**	20-01/S01	12	As 75m

625 Tall jar with lightly modelled rim

Although a little more elaborate, probably related to the 'tall, necked, ovoid jars with direct rim' beginning at Memphis in the early to mid Eighteenth Dynasty (Bourriau 2010, Fig. 26 [10.4.3]), when a red slip is already attested; the red slip occurs again up to the early to mid Nineteenth Dynasty, but later-contexted sherds could, as always, be residual. Polish/burnish is not recorded.

2456 **625** Fig. 75o

G1 (Nile B2). Fired soft. Exterior concealed by slip, interior pale brown. Break pale brown all through. Fairly plentiful poorly sorted sand. Moderate qty fine veg to 0.2. Sparse limestone to 0.05. Thick red slip on exterior and just over rim; interior uncoated. Traces of polish on exterior and on top of rim.

Phase	Context & No.	Grid ref	Dia rim (top)	Fig
v/v/v–vi	AEN/AEO/AFD **7**	14/15-S01/S02	*c.*14	75o

626 Tall, necked, ovoid jar with modelled rim

This well-made and distinctive concave neck is surprisingly difficult to match, but a shouldered jar is indicated, such as a larger (rim dia 12) red washed example from Amarna (Rose 2007, 253 [456]), rather than a more slender form. A rim from Memphis (Kom Rabia) (dia 8) is similar but the neck appears to have been shorter (Bourriau 2010, Fig. 27 [10.16.1]). There is little doubt of its Eighteenth Dynasty date.

2524 **626** Fig. 75p

G1 (Nile B2). Fired fairly hard. Exterior concealed by slip, interior red. Break red with pink core, or pink zones and thin grey core where thickest. Fairly plentiful poorly sorted sand. Moderate qty fine veg to 0.3. Sparse limestone to 0.1. Red slip on exterior and on top of rim, interior uncoated. Not polished or burnished.

Phase	Context & No.	Grid ref	Dia rim (top)	Fig
vii	AAA (UP 108) **29**	24 to 34-S06	8	75p

627 Tall, necked, ovoid jar with modelled rim

This form first appears at Memphis (Kom Rabia) in the early to mid Eighteenth Dynasty in an uncoated example (Bourriau 2010, Fig 27 [10.10.9]), but the red rim band probably indicates a Ramesside date: one such at Qantir is fully red slipped (Aston D.A. 1998, 299 [952]) (the neck is restored after one from Mayana (Petrie and Brunton 1924b, Pl. LXV [80P])). A similar neck from Saqqara (Bourriau and D.A. Aston 1985, Pl. 35 [41]) has blue- and red-painted bands on an uncoated surface. The wide scattering of the NK sherds is shown by the contexts of the two, which join (see also **315/544/653**).

2678B **627** Fig. 75q

G1 (Nile B2). Fired fairly hard. Surfaces red where uncoated, interior shading to grey near break. Break red all through, Fairly plentiful poorly sorted sand. Fairly plentiful fine and coarse veg to 0.5. Sparse limestone to 0.1. Red slip on rim roll, extending down 0.5 inside and running down outside. Traces of polish on rim but may be sand-blasting.

Phase	Context & No.	Grid ref	Dia rim (top)	Fig
ivd	ATY **7***	25-04	9.5	75q
v–vi/vii	CBS/AAA **10***	W01/01-29/30	9.5	75q

* Join

628–29 Tall, necked, shouldered jars with modelled rim

Although these two jar rims differ slightly, both are probably to be compared with a type which already occurs at Memphis (Kom Rabia) in the early to mid Eighteenth Dynasty (Bourriau 2010, Fig. 27 [10.8.4]) and continues well into the Nineteenth. It is recorded with red slip, both with and without polish/burnish, in the mid to late Eighteenth (*ibid.*, Fig. 40). **629** has also some similarity to another Memphis form which appears at the same time (*ibid.*, Fig. 27 [10.14.5]), and recurs with red slip, again at the same time (*ibid.*, Fig. 40).

904 **628** Fig. 76a

G1 (Nile B2). Fired fairly soft. Exterior concealed by slip; interior pale brown. Break brown with grey core. Fairly plentiful poorly sorted sand. Fairly plentiful fine and coarse veg to 0.9. Sparse limestone to 0.1. Red slip on exterior and top of rim; none visible on interior. Polished where slipped.

Phase	Context & No.	Grid ref	Dia rim (top, centre)	Fig
iv (Pt V)	AZO (UP 318) **9**	Area 13	14	76a

2526A **629** Fig. 76b

G1 (Nile B2). Fired fairly soft. Surfaces pale brown where slip lost. Break pale brown with red core. Fairly plentiful poorly sorted sand. Moderate qty fine veg to 0.3. Sparse limestone to 0.1. Traces of red slip on exterior and on top of rim. Not polished or burnished.

Phase	Context & No.	Grid ref	Dia rim (top)	Fig
ivd(?)	CIC **13**	02 to 05-23	12	76b

630–31 Tall, necked jars with folded(?) rim

The stance and almost triangular rim of **630** are similar to a 'tall necked shouldered jar with folded rim' (dia 10) in uncoated G1 from Memphis (Kom Rabia) (Bourriau 2010, Fig. 51 [10.14.9]), appearing first (unpublished) in the early to mid Eighteenth Dynasty. The pink slip of **631** usually indicates blue-painted decoration or red-painted bands (Aston D.A. 1998, 342); no decoration survives but among the many Qantir Nile fabric 'Funnel Necked Jars', three with closely similar rim form (*ibid.*, 345 [1190]; 385 [1359/60]) have cream/pink slip and two are blue-painted. Evidence from Memphis shows that blue paint on a cream/pink slip was increasingly popular from the mid Eighteenth Dynasty onwards but declined from the mid Nineteenth (Janine Bourriau, pers. comm.). The Anubieion rims were not recorded as folded but the forms suggest they probably were.

2512 **630** Fig. 76c

G1 (Nile B2). Fired fairly hard. Surfaces red-brown. Break red-brown with pinkish purple core. Fairly plentiful poorly sorted sand with many coarse grains. Moderate qty fine veg, mostly to 0.3 but one piece 0.5. Sparse limestone to 0.1. Probably uncoated. Not polished or burnished.

Phase	Context & No.	Grid ref	Dia rim (top)	Fig
ii	BET **110**	13/14/15-02/03	10	76c

2304A **631** Fig. 76d

G1 (Nile B2). Fired medium. Surfaces brown where slip lost. Break pale brown with thick brick-red core. Fairly plentiful fine and medium sand with a few larger grains. Small qty fine veg to 0.2. Sparse limestone to 0.1. Pale pink slip on all surfaces as preserved, except rim roll (weathered). Possible traces of polish where slip survives.

Phase	Context & No.	Grid ref	Max dia rim	Fig
ii	AQE **6**	21-S03	*c.*11	76d

632–33 Tall, necked, ovoid jars with folded rim

Folding is visible on AJY **121** of **633**, assumed on AQG/AJY **7** and **632**. The lower edge of each rim is cut flat, and in spite of minor differences the first two may derive from the same vessel. Cutting of folded rims is not usual, but is noted on a rim of the same form at Memphis (Kom Rabia), a sherd with blue-painted neck band on a cream slip and the much larger diameter of 21 (Bourriau 2010, Fig. 51 [10.16.12]). This was from a context of the late Eighteenth to early Nineteenth Dynasty.

2204 **632** Fig. 76e

G1 (Nile B2). Fired fairly soft. Surfaces pale brown, exterior where slip lost. Break pale brown with red core. Fairly plentiful poorly sorted sand. Moderate qty fine veg to 0.3. Rather more limestone than usual in a silt ware, but to 0.1 only. Thick red slip on exterior, and over rim to an edge just inside. Polished where slipped.

Phase	Context & No.	Grid ref	Dia rim (top)	Fig
ivb	AWD **14**	19-01	*c.*8	76e

2534/2678C **633** Fig. 76f–g

G1 (Nile B2). Fired fairly hard. AQG/AJY **7** surfaces red, exterior where uncoated; AJY **121** exterior pale brown where slip lost, interior red-brown. Break red with grey core, AJY **121** also narrow pink zones. Fairly plentiful poorly sorted sand. Moderate qty to fairly plentiful fine and coarse veg, mostly to 0.5. Sparse limestone to 0.1. Small areas of red slip survive on exterior and on top of rim, AJY **121** also on upper 0.5 of interior. Traces of polish survive on rim only.

Phase	Context & No.	Grid ref	Dia rim (top)	Fig
o/ii	AQG/AJY **7**	21/22-S04/S05/S06	(*c*.9?)	76f
ii	AJY **121**	19/20-S04/S05	10	76g

634 Tall, necked jar with folded or thickened rim

634 closely resembles a folded rim from Memphis (Kom Rabia) (Bourriau 2010, Fig. 27 [10.14.5]). Although little of this survived below the actual rim, the vessel form and early to mid Eighteenth Dynasty date are confirmed by an almost complete jar profile from Amarna (Rose 2007, 258 [481]). At Memphis the type exists with a red slip (also uncoated); at Amarna the illustrated example has a cream slip.

2716 **634** Fig. 76h

G1 (Nile B2). Fired medium. Surfaces red-brown. Break red-brown all through. Fairly plentiful poorly sorted sand. Small qty fine veg to 0.2. Sparse limestone to 0.1. Small surviving area of red slip on top and exterior of rim only. Probable trace of polish on top of rim where slip survives.

Phase	Context & No.	Grid ref	Dia rim (top)	Fig
ii	ABN **12**	Area 13	12	76h

635 Thin-walled long-necked jar

The form may derive from 'beer bottles' of the Thirteenth Dynasty (Seiler 2003, 53, Abb. 16) but is now more gracile, with a less pronounced rim which might still be folded but is perhaps no more than thickened. A jar neck from early to mid Eighteenth Dynasty Memphis (Kom Rabia) (Bourriau 2010, Fig. 27 [10.14.4]) appears to mark a stage in this development, and **635** should not be much, if at all, later.

2492 **635** Fig. 76i

Rim of fairly small jar with slightly tapering neck. Fine wheel-marks on interior.

G1 (Nile B2). Fired medium. Surfaces orange-red. Break orange-red all through. Fairly plentiful fine well-sorted sand, with only a few larger grains. Moderate qty fine veg to 0.2. Sparse limestone to 0.1. Possibly self-slipped but no coloured slip. Not polished or burnished.

Phase	Context & No.	Grid ref	Dia rim (top)	Fig
o/ii	BEO/BGL **18**	14/15-S04/S05	6.5	76i

636 Tall, necked, ovoid jar with folded rim: decorated with painted bands on white slip

Apparently the rim of a tall jar of a type, some in Marl A fabric and some in white slipped Nile B, discussed at length by Colin Hope (Hope 1987, 97–122), both form and decoration closely matching Marl A jars Cairo SC 12071/77. The bodies of these two jars are decorated, respectively, with birds and fish and with horses. The series is dated by Hope to the period from Amenhotep II to Tuthmosis IV and manufacture in Thebes is suggested.

2450 **636** Fig. 76j

G1 (Nile B2). Fired fairly soft. Surfaces concealed by slip. Break red-brown with grey core. Fairly plentiful poorly sorted sand. Moderate qty fine veg to 0.2. Sparse limestone to 0.1. A few lumps of unincorporated clay to 0.2. Thick white slip, showing pinkish from underlying clay colour, on all surfaces as far as preserved. Not polished or burnished. Decorated with two black-painted bands flanking one red.

Phase	Context & No.	Grid ref	Dia rim (top)	Fig
ii	AIY under Room 10 **167**	09 to12-03/04	10	76j

637 Tall, necked, ovoid jar with folded rim: blue-painted on cream slip

Although the rim was not recorded as folded, the form corresponds well to one so described from Memphis (Kom Rabia) (Bourriau 2010, Fig. 51 [10.16.13]). This has a similar diameter (26) and as preserved is also blue-painted on the neck only. Late Eighteenth to Nineteenth Dynasty.

2760 **637** Fig. 76k

G1 (Nile B2). Fired medium. Exterior concealed by slip, interior red. Break red all through. Plentiful poorly sorted sand. Moderate qty fine and fairly fine veg to 0.3. Sparse limestone to 0.05. Cream slip on exterior. Area of blue-painted decoration, on neck only as preserved. Not polished or burnished.

Phase	Context & No.	Grid ref	Dia rim (top)	Fig
ivc	CIN **15**	06/07-33	*c.*20	76k

638 Jar with modelled rim

Jars with a similarly bowed neck occur at Memphis (Kom Rabia) from at least the mid to late Eighteenth Dynasty onwards (Bourriau 2010, Fig. 40 [10.16.8]; Fig. 51 [10.16.11]), and although these are slightly larger with diameters 18 and 17 respectively, there are plenty of smaller examples, albeit with generally slightly different rim forms. Because of damage to the rim, the stance of **638** may not be quite correct: it could have been more upright, like several from Nineteenth Dynasty Luxor (Aston D.A. 2008, Pl. 28 [572]; Pl. 62 [1241], etc). However, it is similar to the stance of jars from the Saqqara tombs of Pay and Raia (Aston B.G. 2005, Pl. 119 [75]), Horemheb (Bourriau *et al.* 2005, Fig. 25 [143]) and Tia and Tia (Aston D.A. 1997, Pl. 113 [50]).

2640 **638** Fig. 76l

G1 (Nile B2). Fired medium. Surfaces brown. Break brown with thin red zones and thick grey core. Fairly plentiful fine and medium sand with some larger grains. Moderate qty fine veg to 0.3. Sparse limestone to 0.1. No visible slip, but weathered. Not polished or burnished.

Phase	Context & No.	Grid ref	Dia rim (top)	Fig
ivd	ATY **182**	21/22-03/04	*c.*13	76l

639 Necked jar with pre-firing pie-crust decoration

A published example from Memphis (Bourriau 2010, Fig. 65 [10.8.28]) is red slipped on both surfaces. Among several unpublished examples from the same site, one (11789 from context RAT 154) is blue-painted on the exterior, as is one from Qantir (Aston D.A. 1998, 419 [1480]), painted above the flange and on the lower neck.

639 is not painted as preserved. Ramesside.

BGL **56** was originally published in Vol. II (Pl. 63 [18]), when thought likely to be Late Dynastic; the description is now slightly amended.

311 **639** Fig. 76m

Non-joining rims almost certainly from one jar, and a (lower neck?) sherd, probably from the same one.

G1 (Nile B2). Fired medium. Exterior concealed by slip, interior red-brown. Break red-brown with thick red core. Fairly plentiful poorly sorted sand. Fairly plentiful fine veg to 0.3. Sparse limestone to 0.05. Thick red slip on exterior, extending to top of rim but not to interior. Polished where slipped.

Phase	Context & No.	Grid ref	Vessel part	Dia rim (top)	Fig
o	BEN **59**	14-S04	Rim	9.5	76m
o	BEO **29**	14/15-S05/S06	Body sherd	-	
ii	BGL **56**	14/15-S04/S05	Rim	9.5	As 76m

640 Small globular jar with direct rim

Small, gracile jar, perhaps to be thought of as a small 'beer jar', though such would not normally have a white slip. The rim form is influenced by string-tying, and cannot be closely matched, though a similar effect is seen from time to time, for example on an otherwise different jar type from Amarna (Rose 2007, 228 [345]). In the NK, a white slip on Nile clay is usually, though not always, blue-painted; on **640** there is no evidence of this.

2652 **640** Fig. 76n

G1 (Nile B2). Fired medium. Surfaces concealed by slip. Break red-brown with grey core. Fairly plentiful fine and medium well-sorted sand. Fairly plentiful fine and coarse veg to 0.5. Sparse limestone to 0.1. White slip on both surfaces as far as preserved. Not polished or burnished.

Phase	Context & No.	Grid ref	Dia rim (top)	Fig
ii/ii/iva	AIY/BDR/AWZ **16**	07/08-06/07	7–10	76n

641 Squat, necked, ovoid jar/'flask'

This rim form has not been identified at Memphis (Kom Rabia), but has counterparts in two types of marl clay vessel from the Saqqara tombs. These are a long-necked 'flask' with vertical loop-handles on the shoulders (Aston B.G. 2005, Pl. 124 [114–16]) and a squat 'amphora' with vertical handles on the body (Aston D.A. 1991, Pl. 50 [56]); a fragment of rim and upper neck from a third tomb (Aston D.A. 1997, Pl. 119 [159]) is described as from a 'flask'.

2696F **641** Fig. 76o

G1 (Nile B2). Fairly plentiful poorly sorted sand. Moderate qty to fairly plentiful veg to 0.3 or 0.5. Sparse limestone to 0.05 or 0.1 or none visible. Uncoated. Not polished or burnished. No other details recorded.

Phase	Context & No.	Grid ref	Dia rim (top)	Fig
iva/iva	BJF/BJI **4**	17/18-05/06	*c.*10	76o

642 Jars/bottles with folded rim

Probably originating with Levantine amphorae, this easily recognisable rim form is not recorded from Memphis (Kom Rabia), where it is probably too late in date for the principal NK levels. At the Anubieion it is related to the slightly inward-sloping **741** in the marl fabric H1; at Tell el-Dab'a a forerunner(?) in Marl A4 is recorded in the early Eighteenth Dynasty (Fuscaldo 2000, Fig. 53g [252]). At Qantir, a similar Levantine form (Aston D.A. 1998, 669 [2760]) is dated Late Bronze I–IIA, while at Luxor there is a red slipped example of the late Nineteenth Dynasty (Aston D.A. 2008, Pl. 60 [1208]) and one with a red rim on a white slip of the Twentieth to Twenty-first (*ibid.*, Pl. 84 [1685]) which has the inward slope of **741**.

2516 **642** Fig. 76p

Two similar sherds from (probably different) short-necked globular jars.

G1 (Nile B2). Fired hard. ADC **119** surfaces brown, ADD/ADE **6** red. Break respectively brown and red, each with grey core. Fairly plentiful fine and medium sand with some larger grains. Moderate qty fine and coarse veg to 0.4. Rather more limestone than usual, to 0.1 and ADC **119** one piece 0.2. Thin white wash (not slip) on exterior, and patchily on interior to 1.5–2.0 down. Possible traces of polish or burnish on both surfaces of each.

Phase	Context & No.	Grid ref	Dia rim (top)	Fig
iv (Pt II?)	ADC **119**	Area 13	*c.*9	76p
iv (Pt II?)/iv (Pt II?)	ADD/ADE **6**	Area 13	*c.*11	As 76p

643 Tall, slender jar with folded rim

Allowing for the small internal roll to be an accidental effect of standing inverted before firing, this large-diameter rim probably derives from a slender jar like an example blue-painted on a pink slip (rim dia 15) from one Saqqara tomb (Aston B.G. 2005, Pl. 122 [105]) and not very different from an unpainted but white washed example (rim dia 24.4) from another (Bourriau *et al.* 2005, Fig. 19 [102]). The type is in Holthoer's corpus (Holthoer 1977, Pl. 17 [ST 3, Variant A, 185/510:5]) but the rim differs. At Memphis (Kom Rabia), the best match is probably one (rim dia 21) blue-painted on a cream slip (Bourriau 2010, Fig. 108 [10.16.34]). Eighteenth to early Nineteenth Dynasty.

2430 **643** Fig. 76q

G1 (Nile B2). Fired fairly soft. Surfaces pale brown. Break yellowish brown with red core. Fairly plentiful poorly sorted sand. Small qty fine veg to 0.2. No visible limestone. Red slip survives in shallow groove in top and on part of exterior; interior uncoated. Traces of polish where slip survives.

Phase	Context & No.	Grid ref	Dia rim (top)	Fig
iv (Pt II?)	ADF North **23**	Area 13	*c.*16	76q

644–45 Body sherds from jars: blue- and red-painted figurative designs on cream slip

Enough survives of **644** to show the motif resembles motifs on two storage jars from the Saqqara tomb of Horemheb (Bourriau *et al.* 2005, Figs 27–28 [146–47]). An inverted bunch of lotus flowers is interspersed with what are probably poppy heads on short stems with buds, drawn in the same manner though the flower heads are smaller. Too little survives of **645** for a parallel to be drawn. Similar black stems on shrubs occur at Amarna. The thinness of the lines is a Memphite characteristic (Colin Hope, pers. comm.).

Polishing/burnishing of blue-painted pottery is recorded only at Memphis (Bourriau 2010, 253 and Fig. 66 [1021]; 312 and Fig. 82 [10.2.5]), Saqqara (Bourriau *et al.* 2005, 53 Fig. 28, 55 [147]) and Qantir (Aston D.A. 1998, 132–33 [271]; 366–67 [1292–96]). See also **516/615/17/18/47/49–52/700–02.**

Probably late Eighteenth or early Nineteenth Dynasty.

2768 **644** Fig. 77a

G1 (Nile B2). Fired medium. Surfaces red. Break brick-red, shading to orange-red at centre. Fairly plentiful poorly sorted sand. Moderate qty fine veg to 0.3. Sparse limestone to 0.1. Cream slip on exterior. On the slip, design of a thick blue stem (blue lotus?), flanked by shorter and much thinner black flower-stems with paired black buds and red flowers. Possible but uncertain traces of polish on the larger red area only.

Phase	Context & No.	Grid ref	Fig
vii	AAA (UP 998) **37**	Area 2	77a

2770A **645** Fig. 77b

G1 (Nile B2). Fired medium. Exterior concealed by slip, interior red-brown. Break red-brown with thick grey core. Fairly plentiful poorly sorted sand. Moderate qty fine veg to 0.3. Sparse limestone to 0.1. Cream slip on exterior. On the slip, parts of red petals from a floral motif and a thin horizontal black line, the defined space being cream slipped; otherwise blue-painted. Traces of polish or burnish on the blue area only.

Phase	Context & No.	Grid ref	Fig
vii	AAA (UP 23) **372**	06 to 10	77b

646 Body sherd from a fluted jar: blue-painted on cream slip

Sherd from the rounded lower body, probably the front, of a medium-sized storage jar (Aston D.A. 1998, 415/16 [1463/64/72/73]). According to Aston (*ibid.*, 414) this decorative style is common at Qantir but very rare elsewhere. He has recently published examples from the tomb of Maya and Merit at Saqqara, among which are two footed globular jars, fluted just below the maximum diameter (Aston D.A. 2011a, 10, 20, 32 [79–80]), probably the type of vessel from which **646** derives. Fluting can occur from Amenhotep III onwards but is never common (Colin Hope, pers. comm.).

2752 **646** Fig. 77c

G1 (Nile B2). Fired fairly hard. Surfaces red. Break red with grey core. Fairly plentiful poorly sorted sand. Moderate qty fine veg to 0.3, and a little coarse to 0.5. Sparse limestone to 0.1, and one piece 0.2. Thick cream slip on exterior only. Blue paint survives in the grooves and extends on to the ungrooved area; across it runs a horizontal black-painted band, but it is uncertain how far below this the blue extended. Not polished or burnished.

Phase	Context & No.	Grid ref	Fig
vii	AAA (UP 588) **551**	W01/01-46+	77c

647 Body sherds from jars: blue-painted lotus petal motifs on cream slip

AQG/BGU **38** (Fig.77d) and ATY/AAA **7** (Fig. 77e) are from the same form as **615**. There were many examples at Karnak North (Hope 1999, 123, Fig. 1b), always with these narrow bands of motifs. Other jars exist with the same narrow bands on the body but a taller neck , which can be decorated.

BAC **267**, ABI **12** and UP 588 **449+528** (Fig. 77 f–h) resemble BGL **118** of **651** though possibly of earlier date. Curvature and decoration point to upper body sherds from small to medium S-shaped jars with wide mouth, direct rim and round base. At Malkata and Amarna the body is fairly wide; in the Ramesside period, perhaps from Horemheb onwards, it is more slender and the height greater. There are several narrow panels with thin outlines to the motifs; the standard arrangement is as UP 588 **449+528**.

AAA **28**, AMJ **16** and AAA Lower **46** (Fig. 77i–k), with thick wall, are possibly larger versions of the preceding, but more probably like a neckless bag-shaped Amarna jar (Rose 2007, 236 [378]), or a painted example of a much slimmer jar (*ibid.*, 228–29 [344–50]) or its taller Malkata counterpart (Hope 1989a, Fig. 10c).

AAA **27** (Fig. 77l) is from the lower body of a fairly large jar. For decoration well below the max dia, and in the lowest panel downward-tapering short petals, see a few at Amarna and Malkata.

AAA **33** and AEK **36** (fig 77m/n), with thick wall, are again possibly from large jars. The illustration of AEK **36** slightly misinterprets the design: the central panel has three narrow black (not black and red) bands only, the central one of varying width and slightly wavy, touching the others in two places.

Polishing/burnishing of blue-painted pottery is recorded only at Memphis, Saqqara and Qantir (see **516/615/17/18/44/45/49–52/700–02**). The petal motif is employed from Amenhotep III to Ramesses II, though blue-painted pottery continues until about Ramesses IV/VI.

2770B **647** Fig. 77d–n

G1 (Nile B2). Fired medium to fairly hard, ABI **12** misfired. Exterior concealed by slip, interior brown or brownish red, except ABI **12** and UP 588 **449+528** grey. Break brown or brownish red with grey core, except ABI **12** red all through. Fairly plentiful poorly sorted sand. Small to moderate qty fine veg, mostly to 0.3. Sparse limestone to 0.1, AMJ **16** also one piece 0.3 × 0.2. Cream slip on exterior, on top of which is painted decoration in blue, outlined with thin black lines. Thick black horizontal lines demarcate the areas of reserved slip, or in a few cases cross areas of blue. AQG/BGU **38**, AEK **36**, and BAC **267** have traces of polish or burnish, confined to the blue areas, and ATY/AAA **7** appears to have been polished or burnished overall.

Phase	Context & No.	Grid ref	Fig
o/ii	AQG/BGU **38**	19/20-S04/S05	77d
ivd/vii	ATY/AAA **7**	20 to 24-02/03	77e
v	AEK **36**	08-S02	77n
v	BAC **267**	02/03-S01	77f
vi	AMJ **16**	18/19/20-10	77j
vi	ABI (UP 315) **12**	Area 13	77g
vii	AAA (UP 108) **33**	22 to 26-S01/S02/S03	77m
vii	AAA (UP 588) **449***	01/W01-41/42	77h
vii	AAA (UP 588) **528***	02-46	77h
vii	AAA Lower **46**	Area 2	77k
vii	AAA (UP 8) **27**	Area 13	77l
vii	AAA (UP 8) **28**	Area 13	77i

* Join

648 Body sherd from a jar: blue-painted panel on cream slip

The sherd is from the upper part of a vessel but is too small for the form to be established. Jars with the blue-painted area restricted to the front occur from Amenhotep III on into the Ramesside period but are not very common (Colin Hope, pers. comm.).

For context AWG, see page 17.

2750 **648** Fig. 78a

Body (probably neck) sherd from a jar, with the blue-painted area as a panel, not a band. A similar combination of red and black horizontal lines and a blue panel (actually a vertical strip 2.5 wide) is published from the tomb of Maya and Merit at Saqqara (Aston D.A. 2011a, 8 and 30 [57]); it is uncertain how many such strips were present but probably only two on the 'front' of the vessel.

G1 (Nile B2). Fired fairly soft. Exterior concealed by slip; interior brown. Break brown with thick red core. Fairly plentiful poorly sorted sand. Moderate qty fine veg to 0.3. Sparse limestone to 0.1. Cream slip on exterior only. Blue-painted panel bordered by vertical black line to left; horizontal black, red, black lines across both cream and blue areas. Not polished or burnished.

Phase	Context & No.	Grid ref	Fig
ivc	AWG **13**	20/21/22-S05/S06	78a

649 Body sherds from jars: blue-painted on red slip

CBS **69** should be from a large jar as smaller ones do not usually have string-impressions. The linear decoration probably indicates the Ramesside period (Colin Hope, pers. comm.). Polishing/burnishing of blue-painted pottery is recorded only at Memphis, Saqqara and Qantir (see **516/615/17/18/44/45/47/50–52/700–02**).

2744B **649** Fig. 78b–c

CBS **69** bears impressions from string-tying. AAA **7** is probably from the same vessel as AAA **12** of 617.

G1 (Nile B2). CBS **69** fired medium, others fairly hard. Exterior concealed by slip, interior red. Break, red with brownish core (CBS **69**), no core (UP 23 **373**, UP 588 **503**) or grey core (others). Fairly plentiful poorly sorted sand. Moderate qty fine veg, mostly to 0.3. Most have sparse limestone to 0.1, but BEN **33** and CBS **69** more than usual, CBS **69** also one piece 0.3 × 0.1 and AAA **7** one piece 0.3 × 0.2. Red slip on exterior: BEN **33,** CBS **69** and AAC **122** a thick, deep red slip, the others a more usual, thinner slip. As preserved, each is decorated with one or more blue bands, with or without black outlines (see table). All except UP 23 **373** and UP 588 **503** polished, before painting. The technique is not very successful, yielding a dull grey colour instead of a bright blue.

Phase	Context & No.	Grid ref	Vessel part and paint details (+ = 'to break')	Fig
o	BEN **33**	14/15-01 to S03	Body sherd. Blue area, width 1.0+	
v–vi	CBS **69**	01/02-24 to 27	Body sherd. As drawn.	78b
vi–vii	AAC **122**	37/38-S01 to S05	Body sherd. Blue area, width 1.8+	
vii	AAA (UP 23) **373**	04-08	Body sherd, probably base of neck*	
vii	AAA (UP 588) **503**	01/W01-25/26/27	Base of neck. As drawn.	78c
vii	AAA **7**	Area 1	Probably neck.**	

* Blue area (width 1.0+), thin black line adjacent, red slip band 0.5 adjacent, black area (width 1.0 +) 0.2 away

** Blue band, width 0.9, flanked by thin black lines 0.15 away

650 Body sherds from jars: blue-painted linear motifs on cream slip

The lines are usually black, sometimes red. This simple design is commoner in the Ramesside period than earlier. Polishing/burnishing of blue-painted pottery is recorded only at Memphis, Saqqara and Qantir (see **516/615/17/18/44/45/47/49/51/52/700–02**).

The drawn sherds illustrate the following features:

- AIY under Room 10 **153** and BJA/BMW **8** (Fig. 78d). Do not join but probably the same vessel, with design overlap. Big area of reserved slip, blue and reserved slip bands, red outlines. Appears to be Ramesside (Colin Hope, pers. comm.)
- BAC/BEI **195** (Fig. 78e). Alternating blue and reserved slip bands, with black bands outlining all. Similar, on wide-mouthed ovoid jars, from Saqqara (Bourriau *et al.* 2005, Fig. 22 [112] and Fig. 23 [125]) and Qantir (Aston D.A. 1998, 375 [1312–20]). See also a 'slender jar' from early to mid Nineteenth Dynasty

Memphis (Kom Rabia) (Bourriau 2010, Fig. 64 [9.6.5]). Although there are two late Eighteenth Dynasty examples from Aniba, a Ramesside date is likely (Colin Hope, pers. comm.). See also 655 with red bands

- BGG **25** (Fig. 78f). Black dots on topmost band; very thin reserve slip band with only one black outline; form of shoulder (other shoulders are UP 588 **482,** BEP **140**, BEQ/BEP **28** and CBU **22**)
- BHR **270** (Fig. 78g). Two red bands on top of cream slip, remaining area blue
- AVB **100** (Fig. 78h). Shoulder with cordon (the only other is BGG **80**). A cordon or scalloped line occurs more often at the base of the 'overlapping petals' motif (Colin Hope, pers. comm.)
- AEW **9** (Fig. 78i). The only example with black lines on top of blue, not merely to outline a blue band. This occurs throughout the period of manufacture of blue-painted pottery, though it is less common than the type with bands (Colin Hope, pers. comm.)
- UP 38 **201** (Fig. 78j). Typical of many: wide reserve slip band with black outlines
- UP 588 **482** (Fig. 78k). Shoulder, with blue band and badly placed black outline
- UP 445 **141** (Fig. 78l). Very thin reserved band swamped by the bad placing of a heavy black outline
- BEP **139** (Fig. 78m). Two black bands on top of cream slip, all otherwise blue

2772 **650** Fig. 78d–m

G1 (Nile B2). Fired variously, from fairly hard to fairly soft. Surfaces as break where uncoated. Break brown with red core, brown with red zones and grey core, or harder fired examples red with grey core. Fairly plentiful poorly sorted sand. Small to moderate qty fine veg, mostly to 0.3. Sparse limestone to 0.1. Cream slip on exterior only, often fired pink, on top of which is painted decoration of horizontal blue bands, usually outlined with black, sometimes red. AJY **155**, ATD **11** and AAB Upper **8** have traces of polish or burnish, confined to the blue areas, while BAC/BEI **195** and probably UP 38 **201** appear to have been polished or burnished overall.

The blue paint on AAA **482** is irregularly applied along the lower edge of the band.

Phase	Context & No.	Grid ref	Fig & notes
o	AQG **150**	13/14-01/02	
o	BEN **52**	14/15-01 to S03	
o	BEO **19**	21/22-S06	
o	BEO **20+21**	21/22-S06	
o/ii	AQG/AJY **29**	19/20-04/05	
o/?	BJA/BMW **2†**	14-04	★
o/?	BJA/BMW **8†**	14-04	78d★
o/?	BJA/BMW **24**	14-04	
ii	AIY under Room 10 **153†**	09 to 12-03/04	78d
ii	AJY **155**	22/23-S05/S06	
ii	BGG **17**	12 to 16-S04/S05	
ii	BGG **25**	12-02/03	78f★
ii	BGG **80¶**	08/09/10-S02/S03	
ii	BGG **161**	11/12-S04/S05	
ii	BGL **75★★**	15/16/17-04/05	
ii	BGL **76★★**	15/16/17-04/05	★
ii	BGN **17**	10 to 13-S03/S04/S05	
ii/ivb	AIY/AVB **42**	13/14-01/02	
ii/?	AHW and just above **5**	14-S01/S02/S03	
iii	BDR **10**	08 to 11-03/04/05	

Phase	Context & No.	Grid ref	Fig & notes
iii	BJJ **50**	17/18-05/06	
iva	BHR **270**	02-22/23	78g
ivb	AVB **100**¶	10/11-S01/S02	78h
ivc	ATD **11**	03/04/05-S04/S05/S06	
ivc	ATE **27**	03/04/05-S04/S05/S06	
v	AEW **9**	04-02 to 07	78i
v/v	BAC/BEI **195**	02/03-S01	78e ⋆
v–vi	CBU **22**	07/08-34/35/36	
v–vi/?	BEQ/BEP **28**	16/17-S01/S02	⋆
(vi–)vii	AAB Upper **8**	28 to 34-S02/S03/S04	
vii	AAA (UP 38) **201**	17 to 20-09/10	78j
vii	AAA (UP 118) **57**	25/26-05/06	
vii	AAA (UP 588) **435**	04/05-26/27/28	
vii	AAA (UP 588) **472**	01/W01-32 to 38	
vii	AAA (UP 588) **482**	01/W01-44/45/46	78k
vii	AAA East **17**	Area 1	
vii	AAA (UP 445) **141**	Area 2	78l ⋆
vii	AAA (UP 8) **24**, **37**	Area 12	
?	BEP **139**	17/18-01/S01	78m ⋆
?	BEP **140**	17/18-01/S01	

⋆ Sherds so large or distinctive that they must be from vessels with only linear, not floral, designs

⋆⋆ Probably same vessel

† Probably all same vessel

¶ Perhaps same vessel

651 Body sherds from jars: blue-painted on cream slip applied between red slipped areas

Body sherds from jars, with red and cream slips applied in zones, and blue paint over the cream (Hope 1991, 21). This technique of blue painting on cream slip with the remainder red slipped is known from various sites including Saqqara (Aston D.A. 2011a, 8, 30, [53]), Malkata (Hope 1989a, 7), Karnak North (Hope 1996, 32), and Amarna (Hope 1991, 21 and Fig. 8e), but the polishing of the blue is very unusual; in any case, polishing/burnishing of blue-painted pottery is recorded only at Memphis, Saqqara and Qantir (see **615/17/18/44/45/47/49/50/52/700–02**). The linear decoration probably indicates the Ramesside period. (All information from Colin Hope, pers. comm.).

2748 **651** Fig. 79a

G1 (Nile B2). UP 588 **406** and AMA **8+9** fired medium, others fairly hard. Exterior concealed by slip, interior UP 588 **406** and AMA **8+9** orange-red, others red. Break, UP 588 **406** orange-red with red core, AMA **8+9** orange-red with red zones and grey core, others red with grey core. Fairly plentiful poorly sorted sand. Moderate qty to fairly plentiful fine veg, mostly to 0.3. Sparse limestone to 0.1, except that BEN **42**, BGL **118** and BCP **31**, all among the harder fired, have more limestone than usual, with one piece 0.3 × 0.2, two 0.3 × 0.1 and 0.5, and one 0.4 × 0.3 respectively.

Thick deep red slip on exterior, not overall, but leaving uncoated zones for a cream slip (or vice versa) in order that the blue paint, on top of the cream, was not dulled. Narrow black bands, generally applied on top of the cream, demarcate the blue from the red, or in the case of AMA **8+9** two blue bands from each other.

The 'cream' slip actually varies from whitish to orange, according to thickness and firing. The red slipped area is always polished. The blue of BGL **118**, UP 588 **406** and AAA **6** is also polished, as is the cream of BEN **42**; the other two are weathered and may have been polished originally.

Designs of undrawn examples:

- BEN **42**: Cream slip close to break. No blue survives but is assumed.
- BCP **31**: Lower neck. Cream band 1.0 wide to break, blue band 0.7 and black band 0.2 alongside, both on the cream.
- UP 588 **406**: Cream band 2.1 wide, with blue band 1.4 wide on top. Black band 0.1 between red slip and one edge of cream, perhaps another along the other edge, perhaps a third outlining the blue.
- AAA **6**: Cream band 2.0 wide to break, with two blue bands 1.3 and 0.5 (to break) wide on top. Space between, 0.2 wide, almost filled by a black band.
- AMA **8+9**: Cream band 4.1 wide, two blue bands 1.5 and 1.6 (to break) wide on top, space between, 0.1 wide, in which is black band 0.05. Another black band 0.1 wide along other edge of 1.5 band.

Phase	Context & No.	Grid ref	Fig
o	BEN **42**	14/15-01/02/03	
ii	BGL **118**	14/15-01/S01/S02	79a
iva	BCP **31**	08 to 12-03 to 06	
vii	AAA (UP 588) **406**	W01 to W04-18 to 24	
vii	AAA **6**	Area 1	
?	AMA **8+9**	07/08/09-12/13	

652 Body sherd from a jar: blue-painted on cream slip applied on top of red slip

The technique of applying a cream slip on top of a polished red slip is very rare, and otherwise known only from Memphis (Kom Rabia), (Colin Hope, pers. comm.). This is the sole example from the Anubieion. Polishing/burnishing of blue-painted pottery is recorded only at Memphis, Saqqara and Qantir (see 615/17/18/44/45/47/49–51/700–02).

2746 **652** Fig. 79b

G1 (Nile B2). Fired medium. Exterior concealed by slip, interior grey. Break brown with grey zone close to interior surface. Fairly plentiful poorly sorted sand. Moderate qty fine veg to 0.3. Sparse limestone to 0.1. Overall red slip on exterior, over part of which is a cream slip, with blue paint and black bands on top. Little paint survives, but the blue was a band at least 0.8 wide on top of a cream slipped area about 2.0 wide. Black outlines to the blue and the cream are *c*.0.2 wide. The exposed red slip has overall polish, and apparent light polish of the cream slip may also be this showing through. Laying the cream slip between the red and the blue appears to be an attempt to brighten the blue.

Phase	Context & No.	Grid ref	Fig
ii	AIY **111**	05 to 08-04/05/06	79b

653 Upper body and lower neck of funnel-necked jar with collar: black-painted bands on red slip

Funnel-necked (and larger) jars are sometimes, as here, reinforced with a collar at the junction of neck and body like an example from Amarna (Hope 1991, Fig. 12a). Just enough of the form survives to indicate a bowed neck as Memphis (Kom Rabia) Type 10.4.5 rather than 10.4.12 (Bourriau 2010, Fig. 51), although it is the latter which has a collar. From surface debris in the New Kingdom Necropolis at Saqqara comes a similar jar (Aston D.A. and B.G. Aston, 2001, Pl. 41 [69]). None of these is painted, but black bands are not uncommon on jars of various types (e.g. Rose 2007, 253 [455]). Some blue-painted examples at Qantir were preserved down to a collar (Aston D.A. 1998, 359 [1258]; 365 [1281]; 379 [1321]). Late Eighteenth Dynasty to Ramesside.

The wide scattering of the New Kingdom sherds is shown by the contexts of the two joining sherds (see also **317/544/627**).

2646 **653** Fig. 79c

G1 (Nile B2). Fired medium. Surfaces red-brown, exterior where slip lost, interior shading to grey towards lower break. Break brick-red with grey core, towards interior surface where thickest, and thin dark brown zones close to surfaces. Fairly plentiful poorly sorted sand. Fairly plentiful fine and coarse veg to 0.4. Sparse limestone to 0.1 and one piece 0.2 × 0.1. Thick red slip on exterior. Not polished or burnished. Decorated with three parallel black-painted bands, the uppermost on and above the cordon.

Phase	Context & No.	Grid ref	Fig
o/ii	AQG/BGU **18**★	19/20-S04/S05	79c
o/?	BJA/BMW **3**★	14-04	79c

★ Join

654 Upper body sherds from jars: black-painted bands on red slip

The jar type is uncertain: it could be funnel-necked as **653** or ovoid as **655**.

2460A **654** Fig. 79d

Two body sherds from different jars.

G1 (Nile B2). Fired medium to fairly hard. Exterior concealed by slip, AQG **258** interior red-brown, UP 8 **11** dark brown. Break orange-brown, UP 8 **11** with red zones and each with grey core towards interior surface. Fairly plentiful poorly sorted sand. Moderate qty to fairly plentiful fine veg to 0.3. Sparse limestone to 0.1, AQG **258** also one piece (shell?) 0.5 × 0.1, UP 8 **11** one piece limestone 0.3. Red slip on exterior. AQG **258** probable traces of polish on exterior; UP 8 **11** none visible. UP 8 **11** decorated with black-painted bands of fairly uniform width, AQG **258** small part of one only, not preserved to full width.

Phase	Context & No.	Grid ref	Fig
o	AQG **258**	11/12-01/S01	
vii	AAA (UP 8) **11**	10-15	79d

655 Upper body of ovoid(?) jar: red-painted bands on white slip

A similar vessel, an ovoid jar decorated with red bands (in company with wider blue ones) on a (probably thick) white 'wash', is published from Saqqara (Bourriau *et al.* 2005, Fig. 22 [112]). Red bands on 'cream/pink slip' also occur at Qantir on a small number of funnel-necked jars (Aston D.A. 1998, 349 [1204–07]). Late Eighteenth Dynasty to Ramesside. See also BAC/BEI **195** of **650**, with black and blue bands.

2460B **655** Fig. 79e

Three joining sherds from the upper body of a jar.

G1 (Nile B2). Fired medium. Exterior concealed by slip; interior dark reddish brown. Break red-brown all through. Fairly plentiful poorly sorted sand. Fairly plentiful fine veg to 0.3. Sparse limestone to 0.1, one piece 0.2 and one 0.9 × 0.7! Pink slip on exterior, perhaps a thin white slip influenced by the clay colour. Not polished or burnished. Decorated with red-painted bands of different widths.

Phase	Context & No.	Grid ref	Fig
iii–iva	ACE **149★**	01 to 05-08 to 12	79e
?	UP 805 **38** + **51★**	Area 5	79e

★ Join

656 Painted handle of jar

Monochrome painted decoration on closed vessels imitates bichrome styles on their imported counterparts (Bourriau 1981, 134 [262]). It is more usual on marl than on Nile fabrics. On handles it commonly takes the form of horizontal stripes, as here (Holthoer 1977, Pl. 14). An almost identical detached handle in Nile B2 from Luxor (Aston, Aston and Ryan 2000, 38 [82]) proved difficult to attribute to a vessel form, the options being a large jug (Hatshepsut/Tuthmosis III) and a flask (Twentieth Dynasty). A Ramesside date is supported by a lone fragment of a jug from Qantir (Aston D.A. 1998, 131 [266]) but for the Anubieion example a vertical loop handle on a squat amphora (Holthoer 1977, Pl. 23 [AH]) and a date in the early to mid Eighteenth Dynasty are preferred, as an H10 marl clay fragment from Memphis, Kom Rabia (Bourriau 2010, Fig. 35e).

2518 **656** Fig. 79f

G1 (Nile B2). Fired fairly hard. Surface red-brown where slip not applied to back of handle. Break red-brown with grey core. Fairly plentiful poorly sorted sand. Small qty fine veg to 0.3. Moderate qty small limestone to 0.05; more than usual in G1 but insufficient for G5. Reddish-brown slip, overall except back of handle, where it was difficult to reach. Black-painted decoration of parallel lines with groups of three and four diagonal cross-bars. Polished where slipped.

Phase	Context & No.	Grid ref	Fig
o	AQG **94**	11/12-S01/S02	79f

657–58 Bichrome (red- and black-) painted body sherds from jars of unknown type

Colin Hope (1987) has discussed a small number of intact and almost intact jars decorated with black and red bands, in one case with black dots as **657**, in conjunction with figured designs. He argues (*ibid.*, 109) that this colour scheme was introduced in the early to mid Eighteenth Dynasty and is typical of the reign of Tuthmosis III. The vessel typology drawn up by Holthoer (1977, Pls 29–40) includes so many jars of various types and sizes with this style of band-painted decoration as to leave no doubt of its popularity in the Eighteenth Dynasty. Examples are published from many sites, including Qurna (Myśliwiec 1987, 33 [22 etc.]). The small size of the Anubieion sherds makes it inadvisable to relate them to any one of Holthoer's jars. For **657**, see also **752** in marl fabric H2.

2474A **657** Fig. 79g

Body sherd with painted decoration which includes black dots.

G1 (Nile B2). Fired fairly soft. Exterior concealed by slip, interior pale brown. Break pale brown with grey core. Fairly plentiful poorly sorted sand. Moderate qty fine veg to 0.3. Sparse limestone to 0.1. White slip on exterior, interior uncoated. Not polished or burnished. Painted decoration of black dots on a black band, flanked by red and black bands..

Phase	Context & No.	Grid ref	Fig
vii	AAA (UP 108) **34**	29 to 34-S06	79g

2474B

658 Fig. 79h–j

Body sherds from jars, with fragmentary painted decoration in red and/or black.

G1 (Nile B2). Fired soft to medium. Exteriors concealed by slip, interiors as break. Break pale brown with red or grey core, to red all through. Fairly plentiful poorly sorted sand (BTX **195** mostly fine and medium). Moderate qty fine veg to 0.3, except BTX **195** to 0.2. Sparse limestone to 0.05/0.1. White slip (UP 588 **569** thick) on exterior; some fired, or influenced by the clay colour, to appear pinkish. UP 445 **145** only, probably polished. All band-painted only: for decoration, see table; bands are horizontal, band dimensions are widths.

Phase	Context & No.	Grid ref	Fig & notes
o/ii	AQG/AJY **43**	19/20-04/05	2 black bands 0.2 & 0.3, white band 0.5 between, & white band 0.6 adjacent
ii	BGG **5**	12 to 16-S04/S05	1 black band 0.4, trace of red band 0.2 away
iva/v–vi	AJW/BRR **2**	21/22/23-S03	2 adjacent red bands & 1 black, each 0.6, 0.3 apart
ivc	BTX **195**	02/03-19/20	79h
vii	AAA (UP 108) **32**	26/27/28-01/S01	79i
vii	AAA (UP 588) **569**	W01/01-41/42	1 red band 0.1
vii	AAA (UP 627) **37**	W01/W02-13 to 20	2 black bands, each 0.3, 0.5 apart
vii	AAA **57**	Area 1	79j
vii	AAA (UP 445) **145**	Area 2	As (UP 108) **32** but bands 0.2 and 0.3 apart

659 Jars (and beakers?) with impressed decoration

These fragments, with their idiosyncratic pie-crust and fingerprint decoration, are numerous but so badly broken up that some of the original forms cannot be reconstructed with certainty. They appear to relate to two distinct types of vessel, a wide-mouthed carinated beaker and a larger bag-shaped jar.

The beaker form is well attested at Saqqara, the closest match being from the tomb of Horemheb (Aston B.G. 2011, 244 and Fig.VI.25 [205]); this example has pie-crust decoration around the rim (dia 13), below which is a horizontal cordon and lower on the body a protruding 'step'. A much larger beaker (rim dia 34) (*ibid.*, 242 and Fig.VI.25 [204]) takes a similar but not identical form and has no pie-crust decoration. Their NK credentials are impeccable as each is blue-painted, the larger one with an elaborate design which includes widely spaced blue and red dots, the smaller with blue bands only. Two contemporary Saqqara tombs have yielded counterparts to the smaller example (Aston D.A 1997, 90 and Pl. 118 [144]; Aston B.G. 2005, 110 and Pl. 118 [68]), the former with blue-painted bands, but in each case the rim is missing.

Better preserved are three beakers from Amarna (Rose 2007, 87–88 and 226 Type SF7 [340–42]). The first two have rim diameters of 28.1 and 29 (the other rim is missing but of similar diameter) so must be considered counterparts of the larger of the Horemheb pair. The surviving rims were not decorated with pie-crust impressions but with roundels inserted from above and the elaborate decoration ([342] only) again included blue paint. Colin Hope, when studying [341–42], reconstructed a similar beaker from Amarna from fragments in the Petrie and Ashmolean Museums (Hope 1991, 29–30 and Fig. 2c–e).

Although none of the Anubieion fragments may have come from such a beaker, a relationship between the decorative elements is clear and must establish a NK date. The Anubieion examples are perhaps best thought of as a 'poor man's' version of the elaborate examples in the élite tombs, with pie-crust replacing the Amarna roundels, and perhaps the finger impressions the painted dots, but retaining the cordons and steps. That one rim and two body sherds (Fig. 80d,e,h) from the Anubieion were from a different form is certain, and although no published counterpart has been located, fortunately an unpublished drawing exists, of a jar (rim dia 18) from the Sacred Animal Necropolis at Saqqara, here reproduced (Fig. 80 insert) by kind permission of the Egypt Exploration Society, which must be of the type concerned. The rim lacks pie-crust decoration but cordons or steps and finger impressions are present. The provenance is recorded as 'below shrine D ramp of temple' so could well relate to a pre-temple level. No NK levels were recognised at the site; on the other hand, there are difficulties in proposing reuse of an older jar: it is recorded as having been full of plaster (as were two other large vessels, at least one of them probably early Ptolemaic), which should imply reuse by plasterers, probably in the animal galleries. However, both the Nile and the marl (**740**) Anubieion examples retain thin plaster traces, some on the exterior, which appear to have been for waterproofing rather than from contents, so probably contemporary with the jars themselves. It seems unlikely that plasterers would have selected exactly the same rare vessels, many centuries old, for reuse at two different Saqqara sites, but a curious coincidence that a jar type waterproofed with plaster in the NK should be selected to hold plaster centuries later. The problem cannot be resolved without further well-stratified examples. In passing, it may be noted that at the Anubieion some of the OK 'beer jars' of **34** had also been used to hold plaster, as had some examples of **598**.

All the parallel examples cited are in Nile (G1) fabric. On the exterior, the Saqqara beakers are variously slipped red, white or pink, while those from Amarna are 'cream coated'. Some from each site also have a red slip on at least the upper part of the interior. That the Anubieion examples are not slipped on the interior increases the probability that all are from the jar form although some are of small diameter.

For a body sherd in marl fabric H1, see **740**. For a parallel in a marl fabric, albeit Marl A4, see a jar body sherd with cordon from Luxor (Aston, D.A., 2008, 284 and Pl. 108 [2188]), dated to the Twentieth to Twenty-first Dynasty.

289/293 **659** Fig. 80

Pie-crust decoration around the rim apparently made with the fingers but some further defined with a tool, probably a sharp stick. In most instances there are finger impressions on the interior also, but the interior of AJH **95** etc (Fig. 80g) has wedge-shaped jab marks from a tool instead. Finger impressions in horizontal rows around at least the upper body. Various grooves, steps and cordons around the body, the grooves almost certainly being for or from string-tying. No handles. The majority of the sherds have areas of thin white plaster on one or both surfaces; none bore any traces of embalming materials.

Found in many contexts, but there were two main areas of deposition: 04 to 09-04/05/06, and 17 to 20-01/02/03. Context AJH was recorded by the excavators as 'redeposited', and this may apply to other contexts also. Many of the non-joining sherds appear to come from only a few vessels.

G1 (Nile B2). Fired fairly soft to medium. Surfaces pale brown to red-brown where unslipped or slip lost. Break red-brown with red zones and grey core (most) or grey core only, or red core only. Fairly plentiful fine and medium sand, some examples with some larger grains. Fairly plentiful mostly fine and some coarse veg, mostly to 0.5/0.7. Sparse limestone to 0.05/0.1, AJH Lower **3** + AJH under AAD **7** also one piece 0.4. Thick red slip on exterior, interior unslipped. Most examples, exterior lightly polished. All, interior not polished or burnished.

Rims

Phase	Context & No.	Grid ref	Dia rim (top)	Fig
ii	AIY **2**★¶	19/20-01/02/03	*c.*20	80d
ii/ivb	AQE/AWJ **27**	19/20-03/04/05	?	Similar to 80g
iii–iva=iva	ACE=AJH **38**	05 to 09-03 to 06	? (15–20)	80b
iii–iva=iva	ACE=AJH **39+40**	05 to 09-06 to 09.	? (20–30)	80a
iva	AIW **4+6**★¶	17/18/19-01	? (17–20)	80d
iva	AJH **24**	05/06-04/05/06	?	
iva	AJH **95**★★	04/05/06-05 to 08	14	80g
iva	AJH **132+151**★★	05/06-04/05/06	14	80g
iva	AJH Lower **26**	05 to 08-04/05/06	?	
iva	AJH under AVH **56**	05-04/05/06	? (15–20)	80c
iva	BJF **4**	17/18-06	?	

Phase	Context & No.	Grid ref	Dia rim (top)	Fig
iva/ivb	AJH/AWX **41★★**	07/08-04/05	14	80g
iva/ivb	AJH/AWX **42**	07/08-04/05	?	
iva/ivb	BDW/ATT **2**	07/08/09-06	*c*.20	80f

★ Join

★★ All join

¶ Probably all same vessel; see bodies also

Bodies

Phase	Context & No.	Grid ref	Fig
ii	AJY **21**	17 to 20-S04/S05	
ii/ivb	AQE/AWJ **4★★¶**	19/20-03/04	80e
ii/ivb	AQE/AWJ **16+19★¶**	19/20-01/02/03	80d
iii–iva=iva	ACE=AJH **17††**	05 to 09-06 to 09	
iii–iva=iva	ACE=AJH **18††††**	05 to 09-06 to 09	
iva	AJH **39††**	04/05/06-05 to 08	
iva	AJH **64★★★★**	04/05/06-05 to 08	
iva	AJH **69**	04/05/06-05 to 08	
iva	AJH **137††††**	05/06-04/05/06	
iva	AJH **138+139+152★★★★**	05/06-04/05/06	
iva	AJH **140+141**	05/06-04/05/06	
iva	AJH **192★★★★**	06/07-04/05	
iva	AJH Lower **3†††**	05 to 08-04/05/06	
iva	AJH Lower **4†**	05 to 08-04/05/06	80h
iva	AJH under AAD **6**	06 to 09-06/07	
iva	AJH under AAD **7†††**	06 to 09-06/07	
iva	BML **17+18**	06-13/14	
iva/ivb	AJH/AWX **40†**	07/08-04/05	80h
iva/ivb/ivd	AIF/AIE/AAT **1**	06/07-04/05/06	
ivb	AWI **1★★★**	19/20-01/02	
ivb	AWI **2**	19/20-01/02	
ivb	AWJ **12★★¶**	19/20-01/02/03	80e
ivb	AWJ **13★¶**	19/20-01/02/03	80d
ivb	AWJ **2,4,6,20,24**	19/20-01/02/03	
ivb/ivb–cx5/ivd	AWD/AVF/G/J/W/Z/AIS **7★★¶**	17-01/02/03	80e
ivb/ivd	AWV/AAT **3**	05/06-04/05	
ivb/?	BCM/ASH **2**	17/18/19-07	
ivb–c	AVZ **4★★★**	19-01/02	
ivc	AOR **3**	05-09/10	80i
ivc	AUY **13**	09-S02/S03	

Phase	Context & No.	Grid ref	Fig
ivd(?)	CIC **5**	02 to 05-33	

* Join
** Join
*** Join
**** Join
† Join
†† Join
††† Join
†††† Join
¶ Probably all same vessel; see rims also

<u>660–62</u> Ovoid jars with modelled rim

Heir to a tradition dating from at least the late OK (Rzeuska 2006, Pl. 43, Form 21 [149/50]; Pl. 48, Form 25 [171]; Pl. 49, Form 26 [178]), the form finds its closest parallels in the taller necks of the SIP and the early Eighteenth Dynasty (Bourriau 1990a, Fig. 4.3 [2]; Fuscaldo 2000, Fig. 30c [119]). From Memphis (Kom Rabia) there is a slightly larger version (Bourriau 2010, Fig. 27 [10.10.5]) from an early to mid Eighteenth Dynasty context. The OK examples are of finer fabrics but the later of G1; some are uncoated, others coated (the Memphis examples with red, cream and white). None is recorded as polished/burnished, but a similar form is (*ibid.*, Fig. 84 [11.16.12]). **<u>661</u>** might be from a ringstand, but the thin wall at the break is inappropriate and a jar of this type more likely.

637 **<u>660</u>** Fig. 81a

<u>G1 (Nile B2).</u> Fired fairly soft. Exterior concealed by slip, interior pale brown. Break red-brown shading, in the body area, to darker brown near the interior. Fairly plentiful poorly sorted sand. Fairly plentiful fine veg to 0.4. Sparse limestone to 0.1. Thick red slip on exterior and rim, running down inside. Exterior and rim polished.

Phase	Context & No.	Grid ref	Dia rim (top)	Fig
ii	AQE **7**	21-S03	10	81a

2498 **<u>661</u>** Fig. 81b

<u>G1 (Nile B2).</u> Fired fairly soft. Surfaces brown. Break brown with red core. Fairly plentiful poorly sorted sand. Fairly plentiful fine veg, mostly to 0.2. Sparse limestone to 0.1. Uncoated. Not polished or burnished.

Phase	Context & No.	Grid ref	Max dia rim	Fig
ivd	ATY **256**	18/19-06/07/08	*c.*11	81b

449 **<u>662</u>** Fig. 81c

Many fine horizontal scratches on interior indicate wheel assistance.

<u>G1 (Nile B2).</u> Fired fairly soft. Surfaces concealed by slip. Break orange-brown with red core. Fairly plentiful fine and medium well-sorted sand. Small qty fine veg to 0.2. No visible limestone. Thick brownish-red slip on both surfaces. Small areas of polish survive on exterior, and on top and interior of rim; interior otherwise not polished or burnished.

Phase	Context & No.	Grid ref	Dia rim (top)	Fig
?	BEP **56**	14 to 17-01/S01	7	81c

663 Ovoid jar with modelled or folded rim

A similar rim and short neck are found on two examples (illustration, dia 12) from Memphis (Kom Rabia), one uncoated, one red slipped (Bourriau 2010, Figs 52 and 108 [11.16.7]), both from the late Eighteenth to Nineteenth Dynasty. This accords with the proposed date of examples (dia 10) from Qantir (Aston D.A. 1998, 305 [964/67]), part of a very variable short red slipped series 'probably...a Ramesside innovation' (*ibid.*, 302). The form is not closely matched in the Saqqara tombs.

2544 663 Fig. 81d

G1 (Nile B2). Fired fairly soft. Exterior concealed by slip; interior brown. Break brown with red core. Fairly plentiful poorly sorted sand. Small qty fine veg to 0.2. No visible limestone. Thick red slip on exterior, over the rim and down 1.0 inside. Traces of polish or burnish on top of rim only.

Phase	Context & No.	Grid ref	Dia rim (top)	Fig
ii	AIY **107**	07/08-06	10	81d

664 Rim of a neckless(?) jar, reused as a ringstand

The chief interest of this fragment resides in its reuse. The upright stance is confirmed by the wear pattern on the top of the rim. Similar forms are not common until the late NK, when they include red slipped neckless jars of the late Nineteenth Dynasty from Luxor (Aston D.A. 2008, Pl. 56 [1109]) and of the TIP from Elephantine (Aston D.A. 1999, Pl. 25 [731]).

2690 664 Fig. 81e

About 15 per cent of the circuit of a jar neck, the lower break carefully ground smooth. In this form the complete circuit would make a practical ringstand, and wear on the top of the rim confirms this use.

G1 (Nile B2). Fired fairly hard. Surfaces red, exterior where slip lost. Break, red shading to purple-brown core. Fairly plentiful poorly sorted sand. Moderate qty fine veg to 0.3. More limestone than usual, to 0.1. Traces of red slip on exterior. Not polished or burnished.

Phase	Context & No.	Grid ref	Dia rim (top)	Fig
ii	BET **31**	12-01/02	11	81e

665–69 Smaller neckless storage jars with rolled/folded rim

Storage jars with a capacious body, and a small opening to minimise contamination, are present at most periods and on many sites. At Memphis (Kom Rabia) an example (dia 13) similar to **668/69**, red slipped and burnished/polished, is dated to the early to mid Eighteenth Dynasty (Bourriau 2010, Fig. 27 [11.15.2]), to be followed in the late Eighteenth to Nineteenth Dynasty by one red slipped but not polished/burnished (*ibid.*, Fig. 52 [11.15.13]) with the more rounded form of **666**, while its folded rim is clearly replicated on a larger (dia 18) and slightly different form in Mixed Clay Fabric 1 (*ibid.*, Fig. 57 [q]). The red slipped series continues through the Nineteenth Dynasty and (dias 10–11.2) into the Twentieth (Aston D.A. and Jeffreys 2007, Fig. 23 [78–80]). A number of red slipped Ramesside examples at Qantir (dias 9–11), some polished/burnished, are also close (Aston D.A. 1998, 311 [1003–06]; 339 [1157–58]). At Luxor there are many similar, mostly red slipped, of both the Nineteenth and the Twentieth to Twenty-first Dynasties (Aston D.A. 2008, *passim*).

The more complex form of **665** occurs much less frequently. At Memphis (Kom Rabia), however, a fragment (illustration, dia 8) which just preserves the important downturn to the narrow body is found from the late Eighteenth to the mid Nineteenth Dynasty (Bourriau 2010, Figs 67 and 84 [11.16.12]) and is recorded with red slip. The date (and diameter) are in accord with the only similar example from the Saqqara tombs (Bourriau *et al.* 2005, Fig. 44 [152]), though its fabric is a slipped and burnished G2.

The more open profile of **667** is similar to another of the early to mid Eighteenth Dynasty from Memphis (Bourriau 2010, Fig. 27 [11.8.5]); none from Qantir is really close but there is a wide range of forms into which it could easily fit.

Three of these jars were originally published in Vol. II. The descriptions are now amended: **665** (Pl. 61 [5]); **668** (AON **74** only, misread as **94,** Pl. 63 [21]) before the joining piece BAC/BEI **56** was found (the illustration is amended); **669** (AQE **21** only, Pl. 63 [23]) before the joining piece AQE **20** was found (the illustration is amended: the rim of **21** is now seen to be distorted and the new drawing is based on AQE **20**).

235B **665** Fig. 81f

AIH **49** does not join but is almost certainly from the same vessel.

Nile G1 (Nile B2). Fired fairly soft. Exterior pale brown where slip lost, interior brown where uncoated. Break pale brown with faint, diffuse red core. Fairly plentiful poorly sorted sand. Fairly plentiful fine and coarse veg mostly to 0.4 but one piece 0.7 and one 1.5 visible. Sparse limestone to 0.1. Fugitive red slip on exterior, over rim and down 1.0 on interior. Not polished or burnished. Pale pink plaster adheres to part of exterior and interior near rim on AQG **122** and AJY/AVB **46**, also small part of exterior of AIH **49**; possibly from attachment of a lid but more probably secondary since there is similar plaster on sherd BCB **109**, thought to be Late Dynastic.

Phase	Context & No.	Grid ref	Max dia rim	Fig
o	AQG **122***	13/14-S01/S02	8	81f
o	AQG **218***	11/12-S01/S02	-	81f
ii/ivb	AJY/AVB **45+46***	11/12-S01/S02	8	81f
ivb	AIH **49**	10 to 14-01	8	

* All join

2528 **666** Fig. 81g

G1 (Nile B2). Fired fairly soft. Surfaces pale brown where uncoated. Break pale brown with diffuse red core. Fairly plentiful poorly sorted sand. Fairly plentiful fine veg to 0.3. No visible limestone. Small traces of red slip survive on inside edge of rim, so exterior probably originally red slipped. Not polished or burnished as preserved.

Phase	Context & No.	Grid ref	Dia rim (top)	Fig
o	AQG **136**	13/14-S01/S02	9	81g

2304B **667** Fig. 81h

G1 (Nile B2). Fired medium. Surfaces brown, exterior where slip lost. Break brown with thick red core. Fairly plentiful fine and medium sand with a few larger grains. Small qty fine veg to 0.2. Sparse limestone to 0.1. Slip on exterior, and probably on to top of rim, fired pale pinkish brown. Possible trace of polish where slip survives.

Phase	Context & No.	Grid ref	Max dia rim	Fig
iii or before	CFT **4**	08/09-22	*c.*11	81h

259 **668** Fig. 81i

G1 (Nile B2). Fired fairly hard. Exterior concealed by slip, interior red, shading to pink at lowest point. Break red with thick grey core. Fairly plentiful poorly sorted sand. Moderate qty fine veg to 0.3. Sparse limestone to 0.1. Thick red slip on exterior and over rim; interior uncoated. Traces of polish on exterior.

Phase	Context & No.	Grid ref	Dia rim (top)	Fig
ii	AON **74**★	03/04/05-02 to S02	10	81i
v/v	BAC/BEI **56**★	02/03-S01	10	81i

★ Join

2745 **669** Fig. 81j

G1 (Nile B2). Fired medium. Surfaces red-brown. Break red-brown with thick grey core. Fairly plentiful fine and medium sand with some larger grains. Fairly plentiful fine and coarse veg to 0.8. Sparse limestone to 0.05. Exterior smoothed or possibly self-slipped. Not polished or burnished.

Phase	Context & No.	Grid ref	Max dia rim	Fig
ii	AQE **20**★	19/20-02/03	12	81j
ii	AQE **21**★	19/20-01/02	10	81j

★ Join

670 Larger neckless storage jar with rolled/folded rim

Although they can resemble the 'restricted basins' which originate in the OK and continue into the NK (Bourriau 2010, Fig. 26 [8.7.1–3]), the large storage jars form a separate category. A close parallel is one of the early to mid Eighteenth Dynasty from Memphis (*ibid.*, Fig. 27 [11.15.2]) with red slip, polished/burnished and of the same size. Further red slipped examples, smaller, are two from the Saqqara tombs (Aston D.A. 1991, Pl. 48 [45]; Aston D.A. 1997, Pl. 116 [112]) but they, and the many similar from Qantir (Aston D.A. 1998, 199 [586–96]; 311 [999–1010]) are better compared for size with the smaller storage jars (**665–69**). Jars of similar form, of similar size (Aston D.A. 2008, Pl. 124 [2542]) or larger (*ibid.*, Pl. 37 [742]), continue into the late Nineteenth Dynasty. Thereafter, they cannot easily be distinguished from the 'meat jar' series.

2508 **670** Fig. 81k

Rim and body sherd forming a substantial part of the rim and upper body.

G1 (Nile B2). Fired fairly soft. Surfaces pale brown, exterior where slip lost. Break pale brown with red zones and grey core. Plentiful poorly sorted sand. Moderate qty fine veg to 0.3. Only one piece limestone 0.2 visible. Exterior red slipped, interior uncoated. Weathered, but probable traces of polish on shoulder.

Phase	Context & No.	Grid ref	Dia rim (top)	Fig
ii	AIY **23**★	13/14-01/S01	*c.*13	81k
ii	AIY **42**★	...14-... (lost)	-	81k

★ Join

671 Hole-mouth (Canopic?) Jar

This unusual form is said to resemble Canopic Jars from Dra'Abu el-Naga (Anne Seiler, pers. comm.) and would fit the plain hole-mouth of the sole NK example illustrated (at very small scale) by Holthoer (Holthoer 1977, Pl. 16 [CA 1]). However, the two grooves, perhaps for string-tying but perhaps decorative or for location of the modelled lid, are not shown by Holthoer, nor are they visible on two Eighteenth Dynasty Canopic Jars (one from Sedment) (Bourriau 1981, 113–14 [227/28]. Another possible parallel is a large red-slipped hole-mouth jar from Amarna (Rose 2007, 235 [376]), but sundry 'beer jar' forms from Luxor (Aston D.A. 2008, 56–58, Pl. 1 [8–10]), some of which bear a degree of resemblance to it, are all uncoated as well as lacking grooves.

761 **671** Fig. 81l

Both surfaces blackened, perhaps from the intentional burning of a newly robbed tomb.

G1 (Nile B2). Fired fairly hard. Surfaces probably concealed by slip, including interior as far as preserved. Break red with thick grey core. Fairly plentiful poorly sorted sand. Fairly plentiful fine and coarse veg to 0.9. Sparse limestone to 0.1. Almost certain slip on both surfaces as far as preserved, black but likely to have been red originally. Traces of polish on exterior.

Phase	Context & No.	Grid ref	Dia rim (top)	Fig
ivc	BQR **29**	Area 2	10.5	81l

672 Storage jar with undercut rim

Although none of the many large 'bottles' recorded from Elephantine in the late NK and TIP (Aston, D.A., 1999, *passim*) has the rim so sharply undercut (the closest is probably Pl. 25 [738]), there is little doubt of the identification of the present vessel with these. Furthermore, Aston records (*ibid.*, 30–32) that they occur in both Nile B2 and Nile D (see **720** in Nile fabric G4) and that most examples were white slipped. He mentions that published examples are hard to find, and his two parallels (*ibid.*, 32, footnotes 55 and 56) have vertical rims and do not resemble **672** and **720**. At Memphis (Kom Rabia) the most similar are from the eleventh to tenth century BC silo deposit (Aston D.A. and Jeffreys 2007, Fig. 48 [561/2]), but the closest match is probably from a TIP burial at Lahun (Petrie, Brunton and Murray 1923, Pl. LIX, [43M]) though unfortunately the drawing is in outline only. The form is therefore of the late Ramesside–TIP, but seems not to occur at Buto in the second half of the eighth century BC (author, personal observation) so by then is probably no longer current.

2613 **672** Fig. 81m

G1 (Nile B2). Fired fairly soft. Surfaces pale red-brown where preserved. Break pale red-brown with pink core. Fairly plentiful poorly sorted sand. Fairly plentiful fine veg to 0.5. Sparse limestone to 0.1. Areas of almost certain white slip on exterior, surviving at one point only, on exterior of rim and in groove below it. Not polished or burnished.

Phase	Context & No.	Grid ref	Dia rim (top)	Fig
iii/iii	BKR/BPU **39**	03/04-21/22	*c.*10–11	81m

673 Amphora(?)

Although amphorae are most commonly made of marl clay, or with a marl component, examples in Nile clay are not unknown and **673**, with its small diameter rim and relatively thick, curved neck, is best matched to an uncoated pair from Qantir (Aston D.A. 1998, 427 [1505/06]) dated to the Ramesside period.

2530 **673** Fig. 81n

G1 (Nile B2). Fired medium. Surfaces orange-brown. Break orange-brown with red core and faint, discontinuous purple core streak. Fairly plentiful poorly sorted sand. Fairly plentiful fine and coarse veg to 0.4. Sparse limestone to 0.1. Uncoated. Not polished or burnished.

Phase	Context & No.	Grid ref	Dia rim (top)	Fig
vi	AEP **14**	02-03/04	10	81n

674 Large red slipped, thin-walled storage jars with modelled rim

Three almost identical large jars with an unusually thin wall, the round base in each case too damaged to show technology, except that vertical smoothing marks are visible on the lowest 10 cm of the exterior of BJJ **4+8+9**. On each, there are string-tying grooves just below the rim and at intervals down the body, but most are unusually thin and shallow. All were surely from the same workshop and, because found so close together, presumably from the same shaft tomb. Apart from AQI **23**, perhaps incorrectly recorded, the context dates imply that this tomb, or possibly only its above-ground chapel, was ransacked when construction of the temple was beginning. The location is within the walls of a large tomb chapel, which should overlie a shaft (Giddy 1992, 3 (1.6) and Pls 3 and 5) and just outside the area of clustered Late Dynastic burials (*ibid.*, Pl. 34).

Rather surprisingly, the jar type is not recognisable at Memphis (Kom Rabia) or among the many large jars from the Saqqara tombs, the constricted form with bowed upper body (see **675**) being generally favoured. Only a single upper body (Aston D.A. and B.G. Aston, 2001, Pl. 41 [63]) is at all similar, and even that retains something of the constriction. However, there is an almost identical jar from Gurob (Brunton and Engelbach 1927, Gurob Pl. XXXVI [40A]), unfortunately dated only 'XVIII–XIX Dynasty'. At Qantir, the one apparently somewhat similar jar (Aston D.A. 1998, 313 [1014]) is largely reconstructed after the Gurob example, so a Ramesside date, though probable, cannot be assumed. It does not feature in Colin Hope's study of Ramesside pottery (Hope 1989b), where the constricted and bowed type still appears.

In addition to those published in this volume, rims from several other large jars were recorded at the Anubieion, including one in Vol. II (Pl. 62 [15]), but all appear to be of Late Dynastic date, to be included in Vol. IV.

1300A **674** Fig. 82

G1 (Nile B2). Fired medium. Surfaces red-brown, exterior where slip lost. Break red-brown with grey core. Fairly plentiful poorly sorted sand. Fairly plentiful fine and coarse veg, mostly to 0.8 but pieces to 2.4. Sparse limestone, but includes pieces to 0.3. Red slip on exterior, interior uncoated. Not polished or burnished.

Phase	Context & No.	Grid ref	Dia rim (top)	Fig
iii	BJJ **2+3**★	17/18-05/06	34	82
iii	BJJ **4+8+9**	17/18-05/06	32	As 82
iii	BJJ **5**★★	17/18-05/06	30	As 82
iii	BJJ **18**★★	18-06	30	As 82
iii	BJJ **19**★	18-06	Body sherd	82
iii/iva/iva	BJJ/BJF/BJI **1+2**★	17/18-05	34	82
ivb–c	AQI **23**★	16/17/18-04/05/06	34	82

★ All join
★★ Join

675–76 Large uncoated storage jars with modelled rim

Further large storage jars similar to **674** but insufficiently preserved to show whether the same type as those or the commoner constricted form with bowed upper body. The latter appears in the Saqqara tombs in both an uncoated version (Aston D.A. 1991, Pl. 49 [46]) and one with the exterior red slipped (Aston D.A. 1997, Pl. 117 [126–27]; Bourriau *et al.* 2005; Fig. 12 [78]). At Gurob the type is represented by two examples (Brunton and Engelbach 1927, Gurob Pl. XXXVII [41A/B]). Late Eighteenth to early Nineteenth Dynasty.

2426 **675** Fig. 83a

Two very similar sherds, though diameter and firing differences rule out a single vessel. Thin, deep rim with shallow depression in exterior and groove beneath, from string-tying before firing. Interior of DAG **1** thickly lime-coated, in places to 0.2.

G1 near G4 (Nile B2 near C). Fired fairly hard. Surfaces red-brown. Break red-brown with pink zones and grey core, except that an area of DAG **1** is misfired grey. Fairly plentiful poorly sorted sand. Fairly plentiful fine and coarse veg to 0.7, and AOZ **10** one piece 1.0. Rather more limestone than usual, to 0.1 and AOZ **10** one piece 0.2 × 0.1. Smoothed or self-slipped, but no coloured slips. Not polished or burnished.

Phase	Context & No.	Grid ref	Dia rim (top)	Fig
iv	DAG **1**	Area 2 W09-S52/S53/S54	*c.*25	83a
ivb	AOZ **10**	02/03/04-10	20	As 83a

2504 **676** Fig. 83b

G1 (Nile B2). Fired fairly hard. Surfaces orange-red. Break brick-red all through. Fairly plentiful sand, poorly sorted but with few of the coarsest grains. Moderate qty fine and coarse veg to 0.5. Rather more limestone than usual, to 0.1. Possible but uncertain traces of red slip on top of rim. Not polished or burnished.

Phase	Context & No.	Grid ref	Dia rim (top)	Fig
ivd	ATY **100**	23/24-04	*c.*25 (+?)	83b

677 Large red slipped and polished storage jar with modelled rim

The upright stance probably indicates a less-constricted jar with tall, upright neck, similar to several at Amarna (Rose 2007, 248–51, [440–50]), most of which are decorated but not polished/burnished. This treatment is actually rare in most of the Saqqara tombs, but one similar jar with the same rim diameter and with red slip and polish/burnish is recorded (Aston B.G. 2005, Pl. 121 [97]). Late Eighteenth to early Nineteenth Dynasty.

2532 **677** Fig. 83c

G1 (Nile B2). Fired medium. Surfaces pale brown, exterior where slip lost. Break orange-brown with red core. Fairly plentiful poorly sorted sand. Moderate qty fine veg to 0.3. Sparse limestone to 0.1. Thick red slip on exterior and on top of rim; interior uncoated. Polished where slipped.

Phase	Context & No.	Grid ref	Dia rim (top)	Fig
iva	BDU **29**	16/17/18-06/07/08	20	83c

678 Body sherd of jar with pre-firing potmark

An unpublished G1 jar base from Memphis (Kom Rabia) has a pre-firing circle incised accurately around the lowest point, with a slash mark within the circle and a fainter circle around it. The diameters of the circles are 2.3–2.6 (variable) and 4.8; the present example appears to be of a similar nature but less accurately aligned and of larger (though uncertain) diameter. For a summary of all the potmarks in the present volume, see Appendix 1.

2836A **678** Fig. 83d

Base of a jar with a deep, well-cut groove in the exterior, not aligned with the throwing-grooves; apparently a segment of a circle.

G1 (Nile B2). Fired medium. Exterior concealed by slip, interior grey. Break grey with thin red zone near the exterior. Fairly plentiful poorly sorted sand. Moderate qty fine veg to 0.2. Sparse limestone to 0.05. Red slip on exterior, interior uncoated. Exterior probably polished.

Phase	Context & No.	Grid ref	Fig
iva	BMA **2**	08/09-03	83d

679 Body sherds of jars with post-firing potmarks.

Both marks are from jars, and apparently from the most usual position close to the base. Although CBU **23** is from a relatively complex design, there is too little preserved for identification; in Barbara Ditze's corpus many bear some resemblance to it but none is identical, the best match perhaps being a post-firing example on an unidentifiable vessel form (Ditze 2011, 388–89 [159]). AUQ **6** may be no more than a simple cross, which is among the most common of all potmarks. Colin Hope's article on those from Malkata (Hope 1999, 143, Fig. 10) shows the former to be similar to post-firing marks Nos. 20, 31, 33 or 37, the latter to 13a–c, 14a–b *et al.* There are many other possibilities.

2836B — 679 Fig. 83e–f

G1 (Nile B2). AUQ **6** fired fairly soft, CBU **23** misfired, brittle. AUQ **6** surfaces red-brown, CBU **23** exterior white (slip?), interior grey. Break AUQ **6** pale brown with red zones and purple core, CBU **23** deep reddish purple all through. Fairly plentiful poorly sorted sand. Fairly plentiful fine and coarse veg, AUQ **6** to 1.3, CBU **23** to 0.5. Sparse limestone to 0.05. AUQ **6** probably uncoated, CBU **23** exterior probably self- or red-slipped, discoloured by firing; interior uncoated. AUQ **6** not polished or burnished, CBU **23** exterior probably polished.

Phase	Context & No.	Grid ref	Vessel part	Fig
ii	AUQ **6**	09/10/11-S03/S04/S05	Lower body(?)	83e
v–vi	CBU **23**	07/08-34/35/36	Lower body(?)	83f

680 Ringstand

Nothing comparable has been located from the Memphis/Saqqara area, but two red slipped examples from the magazines of the mortuary temple of Merneptah at Luxor (each dia 12) (Aston D.A. 2008, Pl. 75 [1496] and especially Pl. 83 [1664]) are very similar. They are dated to the Twentieth to Twenty-first Dynasty, which may indicate at least cult activity in the Anubieion area at this time, and perhaps its continuing use for burials.

661 — 680 Fig. 83g

The clay was flattened on the interior and a small piece forced out on to the surface.

G1 (Nile B2). Fired hard. Exterior concealed by slip(?); interior red. Break red with grey core. Fairly plentiful poorly sorted sand. Small qty fine veg to 0.5. Sparse limestone to 0.1. Almost certainly red slipped on exterior, and up into interior as far as the change of angle. Polished on exterior only.

Phase	Context & No.	Grid ref	Max dia base	Fig
(vi–)vii	AAB **4**	24/25-06/07	9	83g

681 Ringstand

Among a number of similar small ringstands at Memphis (Kom Rabia), the best match is probably a common type (Bourriau 2010, Figs 41, 52, 109 [15.1.14]) with the same thickening of the wall. This occurs with red slip, but was not recorded polished. It appears in the mid to late Eighteenth Dynasty and may continue into the Nineteenth. Another version (*ibid.*, Fig. 27 [15.1.7]) lacks the thickening of the wall but is polished/burnished on an external red slip; it was found only in an early to mid Eighteenth Dynasty context.

745 **681** Fig. 83h

Fairly small diameter but relatively thick-walled. Splayed base.

G1 (Nile B2). Fired medium. Surfaces pale brown, exterior where slip lost. Break pale brown with red zones and mauve core. Fairly plentiful poorly sorted sand. Fairly plentiful fine and coarse veg to 0.5. Sparse limestone to 0.1. Red slip on exterior; interior uncoated. Exterior polished, also interior near the rim, although uncoated.

Phase	Context & No.	Grid ref	Max dia base	Fig
iv (Pt II?)	ADF **63**	Area 13	12	83h

682 Ringstand(?)

The interpretation as a ringstand, in spite of its small diameter, is based upon similar examples (though no better preserved) at Memphis (Kom Rabia). There, the first occurrence is in the early to mid Eighteenth Dynasty (Bourriau 2010, Fig. 27 [15.1.8]), when there is an externally red slipped version, but examples from later contexts even include one with red slip on both surfaces, as here (*ibid.*, Fig. 41), from the mid to late Eighteenth.

Contemporary small bag-shaped and globular jars can yield rather similar rims (Rose 2007, 238 [387/88] and 259 [484–86]) but they are relatively uncommon in such a small size.

265B **682** Fig. 83i

G1 (Nile B2). Fired fairly soft. Surfaces concealed by slip. Break brown with red core. Fairly plentiful poorly sorted sand. Moderate qty mostly fine veg to 0.4. Only one piece limestone 0.05 visible. Red slip on both surfaces. Possible traces of polish on exterior only.

Phase	Context & No.	Grid ref	Dia rim (top)	Fig
iva	BDU **37**	17/18-07/08	7	83i

683 Ringstand

A plausible base or rim form for a ringstand at the lower end of the size range, but nothing published from Memphis (Kom Rabia) is close. Several at Amarna are generally similar, the nearest for form apparently a much larger one (dias 23, 24) (Rose 2007, 188 [27]) with a white or cream coating. However, the flattening of the inner rim is seen to even better advantage on a red slipped example (dia 16.3) from Ramesside Qantir (Aston D.A. 1998, 269 [898]).

1606 **683** Fig. 83j

Clear groove around interior of rim, possibly from string-tying before firing.

G1 (Nile B2). Fired medium. Exterior pale red-brown where slip lost; interior red-brown (slip?). Break red-brown with pink core flanked by two dark brown lines; where thickest, red-brown with pink zones and grey core. Fairly plentiful poorly sorted sand. Fairly plentiful fine veg to 0.3. Sparse limestone to 0.1. Probable thin red slip on exterior, worn or weathered off rim roll; possible but not certain red-brown slip on interior. Not polished or burnished.

Phase	Context & No.	Grid ref	Dia rim (top)	Fig
iii–iva	AFS **81**	01/02/03-07	10	83j

684 Ringstand

Although polished, small and with a slightly unusual profile, this can hardly be other than a ringstand. At Tell el-Dab'a the numerous small ringstands in both the late MK and the SIP/early NK groups include a minority with polish/burnish and the diameters range upwards from 5 cm, though most lie between 7 and 10 cm (Aston D.A. 2004b, Pls 188–89 [690–701]; 298–300 [1095–1107]). At Memphis (Kom Rabia), a few of the illustrated types include polished/burnished examples though none is quite so small or similar in form (Bourriau 2010, *passim*). Because of its small size, probably an upper rim.

2902 **684** Fig. 83k

G1 (Nile B2). Fired soft. Surfaces concealed by slip. Break brown with red core. Moderate qty poorly sorted sand. Fairly plentiful fine veg to 0.4. Sparse limestone to 0.1. Red slip on all surfaces. All surfaces polished.

Phase	Context & No.	Grid ref	Max dia rim	Fig
iva	BHR **111**	02-22/23/24	6	83k

685 Ringstand

A good match for a series of small late Hyksos ringstands (Fuscaldo 2000, Figs 37–38 [145–158], especially Fig. 38c/d [155/56]), most of which are, however, uncoated. At Amarna, none is quite so similar, though several are fairly close. At Memphis, the nearest appears to be a unique cream slipped example (dia 12) from the early to mid Nineteenth Dynasty (Bourriau 2010, Fig. 67 [15.1.17]), but again the resemblance is not close. There is nothing similar from Ramesside Qantir. An SIP or early Eighteenth Dynasty date may be indicated, but is to be applied with caution.

2500 **685** Fig. 83l

G1 (Nile B2). Fired fairly soft. Surfaces brown, exterior where slip lost. Break brown all through. Fairly plentiful poorly sorted sand. Moderate qty fine veg, mostly to 0.2. No visible limestone. Red slip on exterior, and traces on interior of rim. Too weathered to retain polish or burnish.

Phase	Context & No.	Grid ref	Max dia rim	Fig
o/ii	AQG/BGU **45**	19/20-S04/S05	*c.*11	83l

686 Ringstand(?)

Although perhaps from the rim of a jar, part of a ringstand is more probable. Interestingly, a somewhat similar one from Memphis (Kom Rabia) (Bourriau 2010, Fig. 28 [15.1.13]) has three surviving short vertical gouge marks on the interior of the rim, though these are recorded as pre-firing whereas the marks on **686** appear to be post-firing. For a row of at least three such post-firing marks on the rim of a New Kingdom 'meat jar' from Qantir, see now Barbara Ditze's corpus (Ditze 2011, 338–39 [082]).

The two recorded Memphis examples are uncoated, but some of the Amarna series (Rose 2007, 186–89 [8–12]) are slipped on the exterior (none is recorded as polished or burnished, nor has any of them any similar gouge marks).

See also **167** of the OK, though there the post-firing marks are more perfunctory and tool sharpening is a more likely cause.

2888 686 Fig. 83m

Post-firing gouge marks; possibly from tool sharpening?

G1 (Nile B2). Fired fairly soft. Surfaces pale brown where slip lost. Break pale brown with red zones and purple core. Fairly plentiful poorly sorted sand. Moderate qty fine veg to 0.4. Sparse limestone to 0.05. Small areas of red slip survive on exterior and rim, and one spot (accidental?) on interior. Traces of polish on exterior and rim, where slip survives.

Phase	Context & No.	Grid ref	Dia rim (top)	Fig
ivc/ivd	AIC/AAT **3**	05-05	*c.*14	83m

687 Thick-walled ringstand

Although the out-turned rim would allow interpretation as a jar, the wear pattern and the vertical stance near the lower break indicate a ringstand. These are very variable in form, but from Memphis (Kom Rabia) an unpublished example (dia 13) in marl clay fabric H1 (drawing No. 2675) is closely similar; no published example from this site is as close, the best probably being a larger one (dia 22) in white washed G1 of the late SIP to the early Eighteenth Dynasty (Bourriau 2010, Fig. 13 [15.2.1]).

1422 687 Fig. 84a

Considerable wear on interior of rim, extending 3 cm down.

G1 (Nile B2). Fired medium. Surfaces red, except interior grey near break. Break red with grey core. Fairly plentiful poorly sorted sand. Fairly plentiful fine veg to 0.5. Sparse limestone to 0.1 and one piece 0.2. Probably uncoated. Not polished or burnished.

Phase	Context & No.	Grid ref	Max dia rim	Fig
ivd	ACM **19**	03-07	14.5	84a

688 Ringstands

Although there is little doubt that these rims are from ringstands, the forms are so long-lived that their dating poses a problem. Similar ones occur already in the MK or SIP (von Pilgrim 1996, 323, Abb. 142y). However, the polished surfaces of the Anubieion examples are more likely to place them in the NK, when the size and form are well matched by one of a series at Amarna (Rose 2007, 187, SA 2.10 [21].

629 688 Fig. 84b–c

G1 (Nile B2). ADU **43** and ABG **3** misfired, BHR **245** fired fairly soft. ADU **43** exterior concealed by slip, interior grey; BHR **245** surfaces red-brown, exterior where slip lost; ABG **3** exterior concealed by slip, interior red-brown. ADU **43** break red-brown all through; BHR **245** pale brown with red zones and thin grey core; ABG **3** red-brown with diffuse red core.

ADU **43** plentiful, others fairly plentiful, poorly sorted sand. ADU **43** moderate qty fine and coarse veg to 0.5, BHR **245** fairly plentiful fine to 0.3, ABG **3** fairly plentiful fine and coarse to 0.6. Sparse limestone to 0.1, ABG **3** also one piece 0.2. Slip on exterior only: ADU **43** misfired grey with white areas, BHR **245** traces of red, ABG **3** thick red. ADU **43** probably, others certainly, polished where slipped.

Phase	Context & No.	Grid ref	Dia rim (top)	Fig
o	ADU (UP 122) **43**	Area 13	*c.*16	84b

Phase	Context & No.	Grid ref	Dia rim (top)	Fig
iva	BHR **245**	02/03-21/22	?	As 84b
vi	ABG (UP 235) **3**	Area 13	*c.*15	84c

689–90 Ringstands(?)

The exact combination of rim form (see bowl **524**) and small diameter is difficult to match but the most promising parallels are among the Nile B2 ringstands. At Memphis (Kom Rabia), one which occurs uncoated and with red slip on both surfaces or exterior only (Bourriau 2010, Fig. 28 [15.1.14]) is found in contexts of the early-to-mid and mid-to-late Eighteenth Dynasty. Similar examples are found in the Saqqara tombs, one in that of Paser and Raia (Bourriau and D.A. Aston 1985, Pl. 36 [85]) and three in the tomb of Horemheb (Bourriau *et al.* 2005, Fig. 7 [32]); all are uncoated and with diameters 8–10 (though stated to be 17 in the case of Paser and Raia). They accord with a series of eight of the late Hyksos period at Tell el-Dab'a (Fuscaldo 2000, Fig. 37), especially [149] (dia 9.5) and [150] (dia 8.8); these are uncoated but one ([154]) is red slipped. It remains debatable whether the rim form of **689/90** should be regarded as the base or the top, though the published examples favour the top; doubtless a ringstand could be used either way up according to need. Probably Eighteenth Dynasty.

1414 **689** Fig. 84d–e

G1 (Nile B2). AQG/BEO **18** fired medium, ACE=AJH **59** fairly soft. Exterior concealed by slip, interior brown. Break brown, AQG/BEO **18** with pink core, ACE=AJH **59** thin red core. Fairly plentiful fine and medium sand with a few larger grains. Moderate qty fine veg to 0.2. Sparse limestone to 0.1. Red slip on exterior, taken over rim to a careful edge on interior, 0.5 from rim. Not polished or burnished.

Phase	Context & No.	Grid ref	Dia rim (top)	Fig
o/o	AQG/BEO **18**	21-S06	10	84d
iii–iva=iva	ACE=AJH **59**	05 to 09-06 to 09	11	84e

1412 **690** Fig. 84f

Non-joining sherds, almost certainly from the same object.

G1 (Nile B2). Fired medium. Surfaces red. Break red with thick pink core. Fairly plentiful fine and medium sand with a few larger grains. Moderate qty fine veg, mostly to 0.2. Sparse limestone to 0.1. Perhaps self-slipped, but no coloured slip. Not polished or burnished.

Phase	Context & No.	Grid ref	Dia rim (top)	Fig
ii	AUQ **108**	08/09-02/03	11	As 84f
ii	AUQ **109**	08/09-02/03	11	84f

691 Ringstand or offering stand

The large size, form and stance are all compatible with either form; the upright stance might favour a ringstand like some at Amarna, two of which have a white/cream coating on the exterior (Rose 2007, 188 [23–28]). However, an upright one at Malkata is certainly a stand (Hope 1989a, Fig. 5e) and at Tell el-Dab'a one even more upright seems to have been so interpreted (Fuscaldo 2000, Fig. 39d [162]).

2624 **691** Fig. 84g

G1 (Nile B2). Fired medium. Surfaces concealed by slip. Break brown with red zones and purple core. Fairly plentiful poorly sorted sand. Fairly plentiful fine and coarse veg, mostly to 0.5 but pieces to 0.8. Rather more limestone than usual, to 0.1 and three pieces 0.1 × 0.2. White slip on both surfaces. Not polished or burnished.

Phase	Context & No.	Grid ref	Max dia rim	Fig
vii	AAA (UP 588) **236**	W01/W02/01/02-20/21/22	25	84g

692 Ringstand or offering stand

The polished red slip tends to favour the top of a small offering stand, though at Memphis (Kom Rabia) a similarly small and gracile type, often slipped but not polished (Bourriau 2010, Fig. 27 [15.1.9]) was thought to be a ringstand, and this is certainly more likely in a domestic context.

2926 **692** Fig. 84h

G1 (Nile B2). Fired fairly soft. Surfaces pale brown, exterior where slip lost. Break pale brown with red core. Fairly plentiful fine well-sorted sand. Fairly plentiful fine veg to 0.2 and one piece 0.5. Sparse limestone to 0.05. Red slip fired pink on exterior and top of rim, with traces on interior to a depth of 1.0. Exterior and top of rim polished.

Phase	Context & No.	Grid ref	Dia rim (top)	Fig
iii	BPD **8**	02/03-21	*c.*9	84h

693–94 Offering stands

These two white-coated bases appear to be small versions of a NK stand which occurs (base dia 10) at Memphis (Kom Rabia) in a purposive sample of the late Eighteenth to Nineteenth Dynasty (Bourriau 2010, Fig. 57 [i]), and (base dia 11) in a Saqqara tomb of the same period (Bourriau *et al.* 2005, Fig. 18 [100]). The former is uncoated, the latter white washed. The type recurs (base dia 14) at Gurob (Petrie 1891, Pl. XXI [4]) and uncoated at Ramesside Qantir in several versions (base dias 7.5–10) (Aston D.A. 1998, 181 [514–18]). Sometimes the base is closed (as **693** probably was), sometimes open as **694**.

1360A **693** Fig. 84i

Underside rough from standing on the ground before firing.

G1 (Nile B2). Fired fairly soft. Exterior except underside concealed by slip, underside pale red-brown. Break brown with red zones and grey core. Fairly plentiful poorly sorted sand. Fairly plentiful fine and coarse veg to 0.6. Sparse limestone to 0.1. Thin white slip on rim and stem, fired pink from underlying clay colour, surviving best in trough between rim and stem. Not polished or burnished.

Phase	Context & No.	Grid ref	Dia base	Fig
vii	AAA (UP 588) **364**	W01/W02/W03-19 to 24	7	84i

1474 **694** Fig. 84j

G1 (Nile B2). Fired fairly soft. Surfaces reddish brown where uncoated or slip lost. Break reddish brown all through. Plentiful poorly sorted sand. Moderate qty fine and coarse veg to 0.3. More than usual limestone to 0.1. Thin white slip or wash on exterior, and on interior to *c.*1.5 from rim only; the flat underside is partly whitened, probably in transition from exterior to interior. Not polished or burnished.

Phase	Context & No.	Grid ref	Max dia base	Fig
ivb	AVI **41**	04/05-04/05/06	*c*.7	84j

<u>695</u> Large offering stand or ringstand

This massive base is clearly part of a large and heavy structure which could be either a ringstand or an offering stand. No exact parallel has been found, and is not necessarily to be expected, but the details of the ware, and the context, point to the NK and there is no shortage of equally (and more) massive examples, including a number from the mortuary temple of Merenptah at Luxor. Here, large ringstands of a somewhat different form have diameters up to 66 cm (Aston D.A. 2008, Pl. 112 [2285] and Pl. 124 [2553]). These and others (*ibid.*, *passim*) are always uncoated, and in many cases of the coarser Nile C fabric, and this is true of the one most similar to **<u>695</u>** (*ibid.*, Pl. 122 [2497]). The only coated (red slipped) example is interpreted as an offering stand and although of similar diameter (34.4) to **<u>695</u>** it is rather less massive; nevertheless, the surface treatment of **<u>695</u>** favours this interpretation; one with integral bowl is quite possible, although a reasonably similar example (base dia 26) (*ibid.*, Pl. 94 [1862]) is of uncoated Nile C2.

2867 <u>695</u> Fig. 84k

Full thickness not preserved. Slightly inward-leaning wall, and concavity in upper surface, clearly showing an upward continuation.

<u>G1 (Nile B2).</u> Fired fairly soft. Underside pale red-brown where slip worn off, otherwise surfaces concealed by slip. Break pale red-brown with very thick grey core. Fairly plentiful poorly sorted sand. Plentiful fine and coarse veg to 1.2. Sparse limestone to 0.1 and one piece 0.3 × 0.1. Thick 'white' slip, fired pink, on all surfaces. All surfaces polished overall, including underside where slip survives.

Phase	Context & No.	Grid ref	Max dia base	Fig
vii	AAA (UP 998) **13**	Area 2	42	84k

<u>696</u> Offering stand(?)

Originally catalogued as part of the lengthy series of Late Dynastic torches, so there are few details of the ware available. Interpretation as the base of a stand is influenced by the flattened rim and internal grooving, so a bowl is less likely in spite of some resemblance to bowl **<u>524</u>**. No exact parallel in any form has been located; at Luxor none of the many small and medium-sized shallow bowls (Aston D.A. 2008, *passim*) has its curvature. Nearest (*ibid.*, Pl. 8 [118]) is a rim (dia 17) interpreted as a lid, and a lid somewhat in the style of one (dia 13) from Amarna (Rose 2007, 193 [51]) is possible. A ringstand is less likely, because of the very narrow waist.

344A <u>696</u> Fig. 84l

<u>G1 (Nile B2).</u> Assumed to be uncoated and not polished/burnished.

Phase	Context & No.	Grid ref	Max dia base	Fig
vi	AMJ **20**	Not recorded*	15.5	84l

* Probably 18/19/20-10

<u>697–98</u> Firedogs(?)

Firedogs, consisting of a hollow conical body with three solid projections (two long and one short) attached to the top, were apparently used to support vessels over a fire. The fragments described here, if (as seems likely) they derive from such objects, rather than offering stands, would be from the open base. Numerous sites have produced firedogs, little changed in form from the MK to the Ptolemaic Period but mostly dating to the NK and TIP (Aston D.A. 1989, 27–28). Among them are uncoated examples from Amarna (Rose 2010, 194–95 [56–61]) with diameters in the range 13–18.2 and many, dated by the excavators to the TIP and scarcely to be distinguished in form or size from the Eighteenth Dynasty types, from Memphis (Fischer 1959, Fig. 12 [120/34/36] and references; Fischer 1965, Pl. 67 [620/21/24]), all apparently uncoated except the last (with 'buff wash'). Among other sites, they occur in Luxor at about the same time (Myśliwiec 1987, 51 [303/04]).

At the Anubieion, firedogs were perhaps used by cemetery priests or guards rather than buried in tombs; the apparent polish may be due to sand-blasting.

2899 **697** Fig. 84m

G1 (Nile B2). Fired fairly soft. Surfaces pale brown. Break pale brown with red core. Moderate qty poorly sorted sand. Fairly plentiful fine and coarse veg to 0.3. Sparse limestone to 0.05. Self-slipped or wet-smoothed, but no coloured slip. Possible but uncertain traces of polish on both surfaces.

Phase	Context & No.	Grid ref	Max dia base	Fig
ivd	AHY **41**	16-05/06	18	84m

2880 **698** Fig. 84n

Conspicuous vertical wipe marks on exterior.

G1 (Nile B2). Fired fairly hard. Surfaces red-brown. Break red-brown with thin dark brown zones close to the surfaces and thick pink core. Fairly plentiful poorly sorted sand. Fairly plentiful fine and coarse veg with pieces to 1.4. Rather more limestone than usual, to 0.1. Both surfaces probably self-slipped, but no coloured slip. Light polish on interior; exterior unpolished.

Phase	Context & No.	Grid ref	Dia base (bottom)	Fig
iii	BDP (UP 647) **143**	01 to 05-07	*c.*18	84n

699 Conical lid

Though not recorded at Memphis (Kom Rabia), tall conical or domed lids are common in the later Eighteenth Dynasty and the Ramesside period. There are several examples in the Saqqara tombs, some red slipped, others uncoated (Aston D.A. 1991, Pl. 47 [26–27]; Aston D.A. 1997, Pl. 112 [41] and Pl. 115 [101]; Aston D.A. and B.G. Aston 2001, Pl. 41 [56]). All have a maximum diameter in the range 6–8 cm; **699** is 7 cm in diameter at the break so probably little is lost. At Amarna there are counterparts in the same range (Rose 2007, 193 [50]) and larger (*ibid.*, 193 [51]). They can also be elaborately blue-painted (Bourriau 1981, 121–22 [242]).

2486 **699** Fig. 85a

Slight but distinct 'step' in the exterior near the mid-point. Fine wheel-ridging on interior at wider end, then rough interior surface where pulled up.

G1 (Nile B2). Fired fairly soft. Surfaces pale brown. Break brown with red core. Fairly plentiful poorly sorted sand. Moderate qty fine veg, mostly to 0.2. Sparse limestone to 0.1. Exterior too weathered to retain slip or polish; interior has neither.

Phase	Context & No.	Grid ref	Dia at 'step' (exterior)	Fig
ii	BGG **108**	04/05/06-S01/S02/S03	*c.*4	85a

700–01 Small diameter lids: blue-painted on cream slip

Two small lids, the exterior of **700** sufficiently preserved to show the beginning of a central knob. The form matches reasonably well one from Malkata (dia 12) (Hope 1989a, Fig. 12a), not quite so closely an example from Amarna (dia 10) preserving the central knob (Rose 2007, 192 [43]) and one in the Ashmolean Museum (dia 8.9) (Hope 1991, Fig. 15b). All have blue paint on a cream slip on the exterior, and the Amarna and Ashmolean examples a petal design. There are three further blue-painted examples from Malkata, diameters 8, 12 and 12 (Colin Hope, pers. comm.).

The blue-painted lids from Saqqara included in a recent study (Aston D.A. 2011a, 14, 28 [31–41]) do not, as it happens, include any very similar forms, but there are better matches among the unpainted examples (Aston D.A. 1991, 50, Pl. 47 [26], dia 6; Aston D.A. 1997, 86, Pl. 112 [41] dia 7; 88, Pl. 115 [101] dia 7.0–7.7; Aston D.A. and B.G. Aston 2001, 59, Pl. 41 [56] dia 6.7; Aston B.G. 2011, 224–25, Fig. VI.14 [128] dia 10; [129] dia 6.5).

Polishing/burnishing of blue-painted pottery is recorded only at Memphis, Saqqara and Qantir (see **615/17/18/44/45/47/49–51/52/702**).

Probably late Eighteenth Dynasty.

2905 **700** Fig. 85b

G1 (Nile B2). Fired fairly soft. Exterior red-brown where slip lost, interior red-brown. Break brown with red zones and faint, intermittent purple core. Fairly plentiful poorly sorted sand. Moderate qty fine veg to 0.3. Sparse limestone to 0.05. Cream slip on exterior; interior uncoated. Blue-painted area and one narrow black-painted band on top of slip. Probable traces of polish on exterior, on blue and non-blue areas.

Phase	Context & No.	Grid ref	Dia rim (bottom)	Fig
iva	BHR **198**	02/03-21/22/23	*c.*9	85b

2756 **701** Fig. 85c

G1 (Nile B2). Fired medium. Exterior concealed by slip, interior brown. Break brown with red zones and grey core. Fairly plentiful poorly sorted sand. Moderate qty fine veg to 0.3. No visible limestone (but the sherd is small). Cream slip on exterior and rim, extending 0.6 down inside. Blue paint over the slip on both exterior and rim, but not inside except for a small splash. Traces of overall polish where painted.

Phase	Context & No.	Grid ref	Dia rim (bottom)	Fig
v	BAC **362**	02/03-S01	*c.*10	85c

702 Large diameter lids: blue-painted on cream slip

Paralleled by blue-painted examples from Karnak North and by bowls of similar shape, blue-painted on the interior, from Amarna (Colin Hope, pers. comm.). Cream slipped blue-painted lids in the same size range are published from Malkata (Hope 1989a, Fig. 12 [e,f]). At Memphis (Kom Rabia) a similar but even larger (dia 40) form, blue-painted on the exterior, is interpreted as a bowl (Bourriau 2010, Fig. 63 [4.8.9]): early to mid Nineteenth Dynasty. Polishing/burnishing of blue-painted pottery is recorded only at Memphis, Saqqara and Qantir (see **615/17/18/44/45/47/49–51/700–01**).

2754 **702** Fig. 85d

Two rim sherds not joining but perhaps from the same lid.

G1 (Nile B2). Fired medium. Exterior concealed by slip, interior brown. Break brown with red zones and grey core. Plentiful poorly sorted sand, rather more than usual for this fabric. Moderate qty fine and some coarse veg, mostly to 0.3. Sparse limestone to 0.1. Cream slip on exterior, not extending to top of rim or interior.

Blue paint overall on top of slip; single black-painted band on top of blue on UP 627 **70** only, UP 588 **545** not preserved to this depth. Both, traces of overall polish on top of the blue.

Phase	Context & No.	Grid ref	Max dia rim	Fig & notes
vii	AAA (UP 588) **545**	01/02-22/23	25–30(?)	As 85d
vii	AAA (UP 627) **70**	W01-16 to 19	25–30(?)	85d

703–06 Wide-rimmed lids

Among several types of lid recognised at Memphis (Kom Rabia), one (Bourriau 2010, Fig. 67 [16.1.7]) is very similar to the present series, though at diameter 12 the published example is somewhat smaller. It first occurs in the mid to late Eighteenth Dynasty. Another (*ibid.*, Fig. 28 [16.1.2]), is not quite such a close match; the published example has diameter 13 but others range from 10 to 14; it appears in the early to mid Eighteenth Dynasty. Both types are in G1 and uncoated. **703** has a close counterpart (as a bowl) at Amarna (Rose 2010, 204 [169], 206 [198, 206]) and Luxor (Myśliwiec 1987, 38 [52/53]). **704** is closely paralleled (as a bowl) in a Twentieth Dynasty context at Memphis (Aston D.A.and Jeffreys 2007, Fig. 20 [20]) in red slipped (dia 12) and uncoated (dia 14) versions, and is also close to an Amarna bowl (Rose 2007, 206 [199]). Others are generally similar to the Amarna SD series (*ibid.*, 206 [195–211]).

Similar forms in about the same size range occur in many of the Saqqara tombs. One drawn as a bowl has a diameter of 16.4 (Aston D.A. 1991, Pl. 47 [22]); two drawn as lids have diameters of 13.4 and 12.9 (Bourriau and D.A. Aston 1985, Pl. 35 [34/35]). The interpretation as lids is supported by blue paint on a pink slip on the exterior of one example of Memphis [16.1.2] (unpublished because not from a random sample). However, in either a domestic or a necropolis context they could equally well have been used as either lids and bowls.

2738 **703** Fig. 85e

Score marks on exterior near base indicate secondary throwing on the wheel. Remains of plaster on interior (only).

G1 (Nile B2). Fired medium. Surfaces red. Break red with brownish grey core. Fairly plentiful poorly sorted sand. Moderate qty fine veg to 0.2. Sparse limestone to 0.1. Probably self-slipped. Not polished or burnished.

Phase	Context & No.	Grid ref	Max dia rim	Fig
iva	AJH **105**	04/05/06-07/08	14	85e

2819 **704** Fig. 85f

G1 (Nile B2). Fired medium. Surfaces pale red. Break brick-red all through. Fairly plentiful poorly sorted sand. Moderate qty fine veg to 0.2. Sparse limestone to 0.1. Uncoated. Not polished or burnished.

Phase	Context & No.	Grid ref	Max dia rim	Fig
iii/iva	BDR/BCP **10**	10/11-04/05/06	*c.*14–16	85f

2676 **705** Fig. 85g

Exterior very lightly ribbed.

G1 (Nile B2). Fired fairly soft. Surfaces pale red-brown. Break red-brown with thick pink core. Fairly plentiful poorly sorted sand. Moderate qty fine veg to 0.2. Sparse limestone to 0.05 and one piece 0.2 × 0.1. Uncoated. Not polished or burnished.

Phase	Context & No.	Grid ref	Max dia rim	Fig
ivd	BCG **8**	17/18-07	*c.*17	85g

2811/2813 **706** Fig. 85h–i

G1 (Nile B2). Fired soft. Surfaces pale brown. Break pale brown, AQG **194** with red core, AQG/AJY **18** with faint red zones and faint grey core. Fairly plentiful poorly sorted sand. Moderate qty veg, AQG **194** fine and coarse to 0.3, AQG/AJY **18** fine to 0.2. Sparse limestone, AQG **194** to 0.1, AQG/AJY **18** to 0.05. Uncoated. Not polished or burnished.

Phase	Context & No.	Grid ref	Max dia rim	Fig
o	AQG **194**	09/10-S03/S04	16	85h
o/ii	AQG/AJY **18**	21/22-S04/S05/S06	*c.*20	85i

707 Lid with wide, shallow interior groove near rim

The interpretation as a lid, rather than a shallow bowl, is influenced by the exterior slip (and polish?) and by two published examples. One is a very similar, though uncoated, lid (dia 27) from Memphis (Kom Rabia) (Bourriau 2010, Fig. 85 [16.1.13]). The other (dia 20), from Qantir (Aston D.A. 1998, 325 [1078]), is not quite so similar but red slipped on the exterior only. The Memphis example is dated to the mid to late Nineteenth Dynasty and the one from Qantir is also Ramesside.

2893 **707** Fig. 85j

G1 (Nile B2). Fired fairly soft. Exterior concealed by slip, interior pale brown. Break pale brown with thick red core. Fairly plentiful poorly sorted sand. Fairly plentiful fine and coarse veg to 0.3. Sparse limestone to 0.05. Red slip on exterior and over rim, with traces on interior down to 0.5, probably accidental. Probable traces of polish on exterior only.

Phase	Context & No.	Grid ref	Max dia rim	Fig
ivc	BJN **12**	03/04/05-S04/S05/S06	25–28	85j

G2 (Nile B1)

708 Large diameter carinated bowl

The fine ware is unexpected in conjunction with the large diameter of this bowl, which needed string-tying before firing. At Memphis (Kom Rabia) a good parallel (Bourriau 2010, Fig. 24 [4.11.3] is in G1 fabric but even larger, with a diameter of 40. It is described as red slipped and ring burnished on the interior, and dated to the early to mid Eighteenth Dynasty. However, an even more similar form (*ibid.*, Fig. 64 [4.12.7]), again in G1, with diameter 30, white washed in imitation of a marl clay, does not appear until the early to mid Nineteenth, so close dating is not possible.

2869 **708** Fig. 85k

Three faint grooves around just below the rim, apparently for thin string, tied before firing.

G2 (Nile B1). Fired fairly soft. Surfaces greyish brown where slip lost. Break brown all through. Fairly plentiful fine and medium well-sorted sand. Small qty fine veg to 0.3 and one piece 0.5. Sparse limestone to 0.05. Small areas of red slip survive on exterior, interior and rim. Traces of polish on rim only.

Phase	Context & No.	Grid ref	Dia rim (top)	Fig
ivb	ACS **6**	09-S01/S02/S03	*c*.34	85k

<u>709</u> Lentoid ('Pilgrim') flask with painted decoration

David Aston remarks (Aston D.A. 1999, 26) that pilgrim flasks become more popular from the end of the Nineteenth Dynasty and that an increase in those in Nile fabrics is characteristic. He publishes one in uncoated Nile B2 from Elephantine (*ibid*., Pl. 3 [56]) which lacks the rim but is seen from the neck diameter to be even smaller than **<u>709</u>**. There are slightly differing examples from the same site in marl fabric (*ibid*., Pl. 29 [873], Pl. 38 [1180]) which are larger, but marl examples of the smaller size occur in Twentieth to Twenty-first Dynasty Luxor (Aston D.A. 2008, Pl. 65 [1299], Pl. 69 [1394], etc.). There is a red rimmed, white slipped Nile B2 bottle neck (rim dia 8) from the same location and of about the same date (*ibid*., Pl. 101 [2019]) and both this and **<u>709</u>** may be thought of as imitating the colour of the marl examples.

2525 **<u>709</u>** Fig. 85l

Part neck and rim unusual in its painted decoration. There is a clear groove around the centre of the neck. No handle as preserved but surface roughening at the lower break almost certainly from the top edge of one. Remains of thick black coating on interior of neck.

<u>G2 (Nile B1)</u>. Fired fairly soft. Surfaces concealed by slip. Break red-brown all through. Fairly plentiful fine only well-sorted sand. No visible veg. Very sparse limestone to 0.05 or less. All surfaces white slipped, interior slightly brownish. Not polished or burnished. Part of one red-painted band, and above it the end of one, probably the same, the ends not having met.

Phase	Context & No.	Grid ref	Dia rim (top)	Fig
vii	AAA (UP 445) **45**	Area 2	3.6	85l

<u>710</u> Small jar with straight flaring neck

Among the many similar small jars of the MK and NK, it is unusual to find both rounded rim and flat inside surface to the neck. The combination is however found in one example from Luxor dated as Amenhotep III–Akhenaten (Aston D.A. 2008, 64 and Pl. 5 [68]). This is of the coarser Nile B2 fabric, but it too is red slipped (though not polished).

1464 **<u>710</u>** Fig. 85m

Lightly ridged interior of body and rim indicates wheel manufacture.

<u>G2 (Nile B1)</u>. Fired medium. Exterior concealed by slip; interior red-brown where uncoated. Break orange-brown with pink core. Fairly plentiful fine well-sorted sand. Small qty fine veg to 0.2. Sparse limestone to 0.1. Red slip on exterior, carried down inside to base of neck, then running down. Exterior and just inside rim polished, interior otherwise not polished, even where slipped.

Phase	Context & No.	Grid ref	Dia rim (top)	Fig
ivc	AQL (Footings) **12**	05-04/05/06	8	85m

<u>711–12</u> 'Funnel necked' jars

These jars might elsewhere be described as 'funnel necked', but the range of forms is so wide that the term is used sparingly here. For the much more common version in G1(Nile B2) fabric, see **<u>608–18</u>**.

711 Globular jar with internally thickened rim

In the later NK, possibly as early as the Nineteenth Dynasty (Aston B.G. 2011, 209–10 [54]), jar necks tend more towards the vertical, and the inner thickening of the rim seen in **711** develops, a characteristic which persists until about the end of the eighth century BC (author, personal observation). At Qantir, this form appears among pottery of the Twentieth to Twenty-first Dynasties (Aston D.A. 1998, e.g. 547 [2226–33]). It is in evidence on three jars from excavations at Memphis (Fischer 1965, Pl. 58 [411/14/16]), where David Aston, redating Fischer's material (Aston D.A. 1996, 32–34), takes the context of [411] to be Twentieth Dynasty at the latest. It is still common at Buto when the site is reoccupied in the second half of the eighth century BC (*ibid.*, 129, Fig.27 [1]), but disappears shortly thereafter.

343 **711** Fig. 85n

G2 (Nile B1). Fired medium. Surfaces red, exterior perhaps slipped. Break red-brown with thick red to mauve core. Moderate qty fine and medium sand with a few larger grains. Fairly plentiful fine veg to 0.2. Sparse limestone to 0.05. Possible red slip on exterior, but weathered; interior uncoated. Not polished or burnished.

Phase	Context & No.	Grid ref	Dia rim (top)	Fig
?	APE (UP 316) **11**	Area 12	10	85n

712 Tall, necked, shouldered jar with direct rim

Jars of this type are common at Memphis and in the Saqqara necropolis in the second half of the Eighteenth and early Nineteenth Dynasty, but mostly in G1 (Nile B2) fabric (see **611–12**). There are numerous slight variations of rim form and a (fairly narrow) range of diameters. **712** has much the same diameter as a jar from the tomb of Iurudef, which also has internal ribbing and has a similar rim (Aston D.A. 1991, Pl. 48 [44]).

2720 **712** Fig. 85o

G2 (Nile B1). Fired medium. Surfaces brown. Break brown with thin red core. Plentiful fine and medium well-sorted sand. Small qty fine veg to 0.2. Sparse very small limestone to 0.05. Wet-smoothed or self-slipped, resulting in a micaceous surface layer. Not polished or burnished.

Phase	Context & No.	Grid ref	Dia rim (top)	Fig
iva	AQC **199**	02/03-10	*c.*11	85o

713 Conical lid

Central area of a conical lid of Holthoer's type LS1/IP (Holthoer 1977, 72–73, Pl. 15 and Pl. 45 No. 5), called a 'stopper' by Holthoer. This type is recorded as being slipped, generally found together with *hs* jars, and 'very rare' in Nubian contexts (i.e. in the reign of Tuthmosis III).

An apparently rather taller example is published from the Saqqara tomb of Tia and Tia (Aston D.A. 1997, 90 and Pl. 119 [153]), of G1 fabric and blue-painted on a red slip. The context is probably early Ramesside, a date in accord with that of the temple of Seti I at Gurna, from which a further example derives (Myśliwiec 1987, 50–51 [302]), described as painted (slipped?) dark brown.

A more elaborate version of **699** and of a finer fabric.

705 **713** Fig. 85p

The sharpness of the form, especially on and below the flange, indicates wheel manufacture.

G2 (Nile B1). Fired fairly soft. Surfaces red-brown where slip lost. Break red-brown all through. Fairly plentiful fine and medium well-sorted sand. No visible veg. Sparse limestone to 0.05. Thick brownish red slip on all surfaces. All surfaces polished.

Phase	Context & No.	Grid ref	Max dia flange	Fig
ivd	ASD **9**	19/20-07/08/09	12	85p

G4 (Nile C)

714 Large carinated bowl

Large diameter coarse carinated bowls of similar form run right through from the MK (Czerny 1999, [Ng 65–67]; Bourriau 2010, Fig. 6 [3374]) to at least the Eighteenth Dynasty (*ibid.*, Fig. 28 [3.10.7/9]), all the Memphis examples and two of the three from Tell el-Dab'a specified as Nile C. However, the interior profile of **714** is best, and almost perfectly, matched by 'heavy (thick-ware)' examples of the SIP from Tell el-Maskhuta (Holladay 1997, Pl. 7.3 [2], Pl. 7.4 [1, 2]), postulated to derive from Levantine prototypes. The exact profile may or may not be a chronological indicator, but an SIP date seems likely.

23A 714 Fig. 86a

Perhaps handmade. The groove under the flange was almost certainly for string-tying. Exterior below the flange blackened, probably from use as a cooking pot.

G4 (Nile C). Fired fairly soft. Surfaces pale brown where slip lost. Break pale brown with grey core. Plentiful poorly sorted sand. Plentiful fine and coarse veg to 1.1. Sparse limestone to 0.1. Red slip on all surfaces, far too thin to conceal the veg voids. All surfaces polished.

Phase	Context & No.	Grid ref	Dia rim (top)	Fig
o	AQG **46**	18/19-S05/S06	*c*.40–45	86a

715 Large-diameter fairly shallow bowl

The form is common at Memphis in the Nineteenth Dynasty, though always with the upper wall more upright, so **715** may have been drawn a little too shallow. The form exists in both G1 (Bourriau 2010, Fig. 63 [4.11.23]; Fig. 98 [7.6.7]) and G4 (*ibid.*, Fig. 53 [4.11.18]), and even in marl fabric H8 (*ibid.*, Fig. 70 [4.11.24]). The G1 examples have maximum diameters of 37 and 28 respectively and can occur red slipped on both surfaces, while the G4 example (max dia 33) is red slipped on the exterior only.

856 715 Fig. 86b

Thick-walled bowl, preserving the curve to the base. The wide, shallow groove around just below the rim may be for string-tying before firing, and there is a very clear string impression on the curve, certainly from this use.

G4 (Nile C). Fired soft. Surfaces yellow-brown where slip lost. Break yellow-brown with thick red core. Fairly plentiful poorly sorted sand. Plentiful fine and coarse veg to 0.8. Sparse limestone to 0.1. Thick red slip on all surfaces. All surfaces polished.

Phase	Context & No.	Grid ref	Max dia rim	Fig
ivc	BQU **34**	Area 2	*c*.40(?)	86b

716 Large bowl with rounded direct rim

The closest resemblance is to a bowl (top dia 36) from Tell el-Dab'a assigned to the Eighteenth Dynasty (Hein 2004, 185, Abb. 139 [5]), though this is in a marl fabric. At Memphis (Kom Rabia), a bowl of the early to mid Nineteenth Dynasty (max dia 36) in G4 is a little less close in form and uncoated (Bourriau 2010, Fig. 68 [4.1.10]), while an even larger one (max dia 44!) in G1, attributed to the early to mid Eighteenth (*ibid.*, (Fig. 24 [4.11.5]) is slipped and polished/burnished on both surfaces. Among these large string-tied bowls, with their inevitable distortions, exactly corresponding forms are not to be expected.

864B **716** Fig. 86c

Grooves on exterior very probably from string-tying.

G4 (Nile C). Fired fairly soft. Interior concealed by slip, exterior pale brown where uncoated. Break pale brown all through. Plentiful fine and medium well-sorted sand. Fairly plentiful fine and coarse veg to 0.8. Sparse limestone to 0.05. Thin red slip on both surfaces, overall on interior but intermittently on exterior, probably carelessly applied rather than weathered. Traces of polish where slip survives.

Phase	Context & No.	Grid ref	Max dia rim	Fig
iv (Pt II?)	ARU=ARZ (UP 204) **15**	Area 13	?(*c*.35?)	86c

717 Large bowl

This is the large diameter, slightly incurved bowl type from Malkata (Hope 1989a, Fig. 1m) and Amarna (Rose 2007, 198 [114]). The Malkata example is included in the 'Nile B2–D' group, where it can occur with red slip, and the Amarna piece is Nile B2 (there are no Nile C fabrics) with red rim, interior perhaps originally red. Both authors mention string-tying and surface burning (from use as cooking pots?). At Memphis similar vessels occur in G1 (Nile B2), initially in the early to mid Eighteenth Dynasty (Bourriau 2010, Fig. 23 [4.8.4]), some with red slipped surfaces and others a red rim.

872 **717** Fig. 86d

Rim sherd from a large diameter thick-walled deep bowl. Some blackening from fire.

G4 (Nile C). Fired fairly hard. Surfaces red-brown where not burnt. Break red-brown with thin red zones and thick purple core. Fairly plentiful poorly sorted sand. Fairly plentiful fine and coarse veg to 0.5. Sparse limestone to 0.1. On top of rim and rim roll, areas of burning, perhaps a blackened slip. Possible trace of polish on rim where slipped(?).

Phase	Context & No.	Grid ref	Max dia rim	Fig
v	BJG(A) **11**	W01/01-S01	*c*.35–40(?)	86d

718 Rim of 'flower pot'(?)

The thickening of the lower wall probably indicates a so-called 'flower pot'. At Memphis (Kom Rabia) there are several variants in G1 fabric (Bourriau 2010, Fig. 24 [4.10.4–4.10.9]), though none is a perfect match. They were common only in the reigns of Hatshepsut and Tuthmosis III; but at Qantir a Ramesside Nile C bowl with similar rim form and diameter thickens even more rapidly towards the lower break (Aston D.A. 1998, 145 [321]) and may be a later development, so close dating without the base is not feasible. See also **719** and for examples in G1 (Nile B2), see **517/18**.

693 **718** Fig. 86e

The thickening of the wall shows little depth is lost. Wheel made, with wide, shallow, somewhat discontinuous grooves on both surfaces.

G4 (Nile C). Fired fairly soft. Surfaces reddish brown. Break reddish brown with grey core. Fairly plentiful poorly sorted sand. Fairly plentiful fine and coarse veg to 2.0. Sparse limestone to 0.05. Smoothed, possibly self-slipped, but no coloured slip. Not polished or burnished.

Phase	Context & No.	Grid ref	Dia rim (top)	Fig
ivb	CEQ **13**	05-22	*c*.30	86e

719 'Flower pot' base with pre-firing hole

The deep fingermarks and pre-firing hole in a flat base are typical of the so-called 'flower pots' (see **718**) (though some have no holes) (Bourriau 2010, Fig. 45 [b–c]). Holthoer (1977, 83 and Pl. 18) postulated their use in pairs for bread baking, but there are difficulties with this interpretation. Since, with the exception of bread trays, few open forms exist in G4 fabric, **719** is likely to be from a vessel of this same type. Most of the rims from Memphis (Kom Rabia) (Bourriau 2010, Fig. 24 [4.10.4–4.10.9]) are of appropriate diameter (26–35) but all are in G1. 'Flower pots' were common only in the reigns of Hatshepsut and Tuthmosis III, dying out by the reign of Amenhotep III, and the relatively upright form rules out an earlier date (Williams 1992, 34–35).

Smaller-diameter bases with fingermarks, and sometimes a hole, are from the more upright 'beer jars' (see **595/97**).

1381 **719** Fig. 86f

Interior fairly smooth; finger impressions of varying depth around the bottom of the wall. Near the centre of the base, a pre-firing hole made from the exterior, diameter about 1.0 in the exterior, about 2.0 in the interior.

G4 (Nile C). Fired fairly hard. Surfaces red. Break red with thick grey core. Plentiful poorly sorted sand. Fairly plentiful fine and coarse veg to 1.0. Sparse limestone to 0.1. Uncoated. Not polished or burnished.

Phase	Context & No.	Grid ref	Dia base	Fig
vii	AAA West **1**	Area 2	14	86f

720 Storage jars with undercut rim

To be identified with large 'bottles' recorded from Elephantine in the late New Kingdom and TIP (Aston D.A. 1999, *passim*). For further details see **672**, the same form in G1.

773 **720** Fig. 86g–h

G4 (Nile C). Fired fairly hard, tending towards overfired. Surfaces dark brown, except interior of BGW **127** red-brown. Break dark brown with grey core, BGW **127** also with red-brown zone near interior. Fairly plentiful poorly sorted sand. Fairly plentiful fine and coarse veg to 0.7/0.8. BGW **127** sparse, BQQ **31** more than usual, limestone to 0.1. Probably uncoated but cannot be sure. Not polished or burnished.

Phase	Context & No.	Grid ref	Dia rim (top)	Fig
ivb–ivc	BGW **127**	15 to 18-03/04/05	*c*.12	86g
ivc	BQQ **31**	Area 2	14	86h

721 Ringstand(?)

This rather weathered rim appears to be the base of a ringstand or offering stand. Although not ideally suited to either function, it would be more stable as a large diameter squat ringstand such as one in Nile clay from Amarna (Rose 2007, 186 [5]) or one in Marl H8 from Memphis, Kom Rabia (Bourriau 2010, Fig. 31 [15.2.5]). The date would then probably be Eighteenth Dynasty.

2200 **721** Fig. 86i

A much weathered groove around, close to the rim, was probably from string-tying.

G4 (Nile C). Fired medium. Surfaces weathered off. Break red with grey core. Plentiful poorly sorted sand. Fairly plentiful fine and coarse veg to 0.8. Sparse limestone to 0.05. No surviving slip, polish or burnish.

Phase	Context & No.	Grid ref	Max dia base	Fig
ivc	CCK **97**	08 to 11-25/26	*c.*24	86i

G5 (Nile D)

722 Medium-sized jar

Although the form resembles that of some Middle Kingdom 'beer bottles' (e.g. Arnold Do. 1988, Fig. 70 [74]), these vessels are apparently unknown in Nile D fabric. At Memphis, somewhat similar jar rims occur in the early to mid Eighteenth Dynasty, but in marl fabrics (Bourriau 2010, Fig. 30 [10.10.8, 11.8.3], Fig. 31 [11.8.4]). It is more plausibly compared with a Nile D TIP *zir* from Elephantine (Aston D.A. 1999, Pl. 24 [689], though this is much larger at diameter 18 and cream rather than red slipped. As to smaller jars, the same site provides an uncoated example in Nile B2 with diameter 13 (*ibid.*, Pl. 27 [813]), but the rim is less angular.

2638 **722** Fig. 87a

G5 (Nile D). Fired medium. Exterior concealed by slip; interior red-brown. Break red-brown with faint purple core. Fairly plentiful poorly sorted sand. Fairly plentiful fine and coarse veg to 0.5. More limestone than usual, to 0.1 and one piece 0.2. Red slip on exterior, interior uncoated. Not polished or burnished.

Phase	Context & No.	Grid ref	Max dia rim	Fig
iii–iva	ACE **96**	01 to 05-08 to 12	11	87a

723 Storage jar with inturned rim

The rim is smoothed, probably from reuse as a tool, but does retain traces of the white surface; otherwise it might have been the lower body of a carinated bowl, though such a form would be most unusual in G5. Furthermore, a rim of the same form in G1 fabric, diameter 20 at the carination, was found in mid to late Eighteenth Dynasty levels at Memphis (Bourriau 2010, Fig. 45 [m]), where it is thought to have held a lid. A similar rim of pink slipped G1 is recorded from Saqqara (Aston B.G. 2005, Pl. 136 [204]).

2432 **723** Fig. 87b

G5 (Nile D). Fired medium. White firing surfaces(?), brick-red where abraded. Break brick-red with thin, discontinuous pink core. Fairly plentiful fine and medium sand with a few larger grains. Fairly plentiful fine and coarse veg to 1.2. Sparse limestone to 0.1. One piece unincorporated clay 0.5 and voids 0.6 and 1.1. Thick white firing surfaces or slip. Not polished or burnished.

Phase	Context & No.	Grid ref	Dia at carination	Fig
iva	ACE **226**	01 to 06-08/09/10	*c.*17	87b

724 Body and handle of amphora/jar

Although amphorae in Nile fabrics are less common than those in marl clay, they are not uncommon and include Nile D (Hope 1989c, 89); attested surface treatments include a red slip, though the combination of fabric and slip is not specified. Marl clay series ME from Amarna does provide parallels (Rose 2007, 270–73); the closest match (*ibid.*, 271 [584]) is a good deal smaller, but the series includes others less similar (e.g. *ibid.*, 273 [589]) which approach **724** in both diameter and length of handle. **724** is published as drawn, but since it is only a body sherd with attached handle, the stance should perhaps have been more upright. Late Eighteenth Dynasty or perhaps Ramesside.

1446A — 724 Fig. 87c

The handle is distorted and there is a deep thumb impression with marks of textile in it where the handle was manipulated, with a cloth, before firing.

G5 (Nile D). Fired fairly hard. Exterior white firing surface where slip lost, interior pale brown. Break pale brown with grey core. Fairly plentiful poorly sorted sand. Fairly plentiful fine and coarse veg to 0.5. Plentiful limestone to 0.1. Thick red slip on exterior, carelessly applied on and around handle, which was already attached. Not polished or burnished.

Phase	Context & No.	Grid ref	Fig
ii/iii	AON/AQR **3**	01/02-03/04	87c

725 Body sherds in G5

All sherds are apparently from closed forms. Since Nile D, for all its comparative rarity, is found in the MK also, it is not possible to be sure of their date.

1446B/2458B/2626 — 725 Not illustrated

BKR/BPD/BPV **1+2** has a small quantity of black (mummification?) material, adhering to the interior.

G5 (Nile D). Fired medium to fairly hard. Exterior white, probably firing surface, BKR/BPD/BPV **1+2** red where surface lost; interior BHR **154** red, others variously red-brown, brown, dark brown and purple-brown. Break AGZ **5** dark brown with grey core, BHW **139** red-brown with grey core, others red-brown all through. Fairly plentiful poorly sorted sand. Fairly plentiful fine and coarse veg, AJH under AVH **14** to 0.8, BKR/BPD/BPV **1+2** to 1.0, AGZ **5** to 1.5, others to 0.5. Plentiful limestone to 0.1 and most examples also one or more pieces to 0.2 or 0.3. AGZ **5** thick red slip and BKR/BPD/BPV **1+2** probable red slip on exterior, others and interior uncoated. Four examples highly burnished horizontally (see table).

Phase	Context & No.	Grid ref	Burnished?
iii	BDP (UP 647) **89**	01 to 05-07	No
iii	BHW **63***	02-20/21	Yes
iii	BHW **139***	02-20/21	Yes
iii/iii/?	BKR/BPD/BPV **1+2**	02-22	No
iva	AJH under AVH **14**	05-04/05/06	No

Phase	Context & No.	Grid ref	Burnished?
iva	BHR **154**	01-22/23	Yes
ivc	AGZ **5**	11-S02/S03	No
vi to Mamluk	ABA to ABG (UP 3) **11**	Area 13	Yes

* Almost certainly same vessel

G6a

726 Amphora body fragment, blue-painted post firing

It is not possible to identify the specific amphora form from this sherd. Colin Hope (1989c, 90) states that in his experience the majority of ornamented amphorae were decorated after firing, which was not the case at the Anubieion (though see **774/75**). Most have elaborate polychrome decoration but there is no trace of this on the present sherd. Late Eighteenth Dynasty or Ramesside.

For sherds reused to hold pigment, see **505/98/745.**

1310A **726** Fig. 87d

G6a. Fired fairly hard. Exterior concealed by slip; interior dark brown. Break red with grey core. Fairly plentiful poorly sorted sand. No visible veg. Sparse limestone to 0.1. Thick white slip on exterior. Exterior vertically burnished. Blue-painted horizontal band on upper shoulder, paint thickly applied post-firing.

Phase	Context & No.	Grid ref	Fig
vii	AAA (UP 445) **118**	Area 2	87d

727 Amphora base

There is a similar, though not identical, base in G6a fabric from Memphis (Kom Rabia) (Bourriau 2010, Fig. 91[n]). The usual marl slip is absent from **727**, perhaps due to weathering.

2462 **727** Fig. 87e

G6a. Fired fairly hard. Exterior pale red-brown, interior red-brown with grey tinge. Break grey with thin red-brown zones close to surfaces. Fairly plentiful fine well-sorted sand. Moderate qty mostly fine veg to 0.2. Sparse limestone to 0.1. Probably uncoated. Not polished or burnished.

Phase	Context & No.	Grid ref	Fig
vii	AAA **1**	Area 1	87e

728 Amphora handle

2830B **728** Not illustrated

Lower stump of amphora handle attached to thickness of vessel wall.

G6a. Fired very hard. Exterior concealed by slip, interior surface grey. Break red-brown with pink zones and grey core. Fairly plentiful fine and medium well-sorted sand. No visible veg. Sparse limestone to 0.1. Brownish slip on handle (affected by heat?). Probably burnished.

Phase	Context & No.	Grid ref
(vi–)vii/vii	AAB/AAA **2**	28 to 32-04 to S04

729 Body sherds in G6a

2830C **729** Not illustrated

AGD **3** from near the base of an open form, apparently a bowl, with carination. Others from closed forms.

G6a. AGD **3**. Fired very hard. Surfaces concealed by slip. Break red-brown with pink zones and grey core. Fairly plentiful fine and medium well-sorted sand. No visible veg. No visible limestone. Cream to pink slip on both surfaces. Exterior lightly burnished.

Others not recorded in detail. AQH **165** probably uncoated, others cream to pink slip on exterior. Burnish not recorded.

Phase	Context & No.	Grid ref
ii	AYG **6**	Area 13
iva	AQH **165**	21-S01 to S04
ivd	AGD **3**	05/06 01/02/03
ivd/v	AEM/AEO **8**	15/16/17-S01/S02/S03

730 Large lids (or bowls?)

Although the two rims are very similar, small fabric differences and the wide separation of their contexts should rule out a single vessel (however, see **544/627/53**). The form is apparently an addition to the small corpus of known (mostly closed) vessel types in this fabric. It is clearly in the tradition of large bowls with thickened rim that starts in the late Eighteenth Dynasty, occurs in various fabrics, and includes somewhat similar rim-forms (Aston D.A. 1998, 527 [2133]; 621 [2515]; Myśliwiec 1987, 59 [388]; 62 [410]). The series continues until about the beginning of the Saite period (Aston D.A. 1996, 23 and Fig. 26 [4]), but the external thickening and almost flat interior are not usual at any period and may indicate lids rather than bowls.

2424/2830A **730** Fig. 87f–g

G6a. Fired hard. Surfaces concealed by slip. Break CEG **50** red, ADF North **46** red-brown with pink zones, each with thick grey core. Fairly plentiful fine and medium sand, CEG **50** with some larger grains. CEG **50** small qty veg to 0.3, ADF North **46** none visible. Sparse limestone to 0.1. Fairly thick white slip on all surfaces as far as preserved. CEG **50** not polished or burnished, ADF North **46** all surfaces burnished.

Phase	Context & No.	Grid ref	Max dia rim	Fig
ivd	CEG **50**	02/03/04-33/34	*c.*33	87f
iv (Pt II?)	ADF North **46**	Area 13	34	87g

MARL CLAY FABRICS, 731–69

H1 (Marl D)

731 Tall jar (amphora?)

This appears to be an example of the 'tall, necked, shouldered jars with modelled rim' introduced in H1 at Memphis in the mid to late Eighteenth Dynasty (Bourriau 2010, Fig. 42 [10.8.9]) and recurring in H14 in an early to mid Nineteenth Dynasty context (*ibid.*, Fig. 71 [10.8.30]). As preserved, it cannot be distinguished from the main amphora series (see above), though its diameter would put it at the bottom end of the amphora size range.

2400B **731** Fig. 88a

H1 (Marl D). Fired fairly hard. Surfaces concealed by slip. Break pale brownish pink. Moderate qty fine and medium sand with some larger grains. No visible veg. Plentiful limestone to 0.1. White slip on all surfaces, interior shading to pale pink towards lower break. Burnish on top of rim only..

Phase	Context & No.	Grid ref	Dia rim (top)	Fig
ivb	AFL **20**	04/05/06-01/02	10	88a

732 Tall jar(?)

There is not enough surviving neck for certain identification of the vessel form. It may be identified with a 'tall jar' of MK ancestry in Mixed Clay Fabric 1 from Memphis (Bourriau 2010, 85 and Fig. 33 [10.4.4]) (notice a similar discontinuity just surviving at the lower break). Less probably, it might be from a Ramesside globular jar similar to one in Marl D at Qantir (though the drawn diameter of 23 appears to be correct and the stated 13 a misprint) (Aston D.A. 1998, 471 [1748]).

2400C **732** Fig. 88b

H1 (Marl D). Fired fairly hard. Surfaces concealed by slip. Break pale pinkish brown with faint diffuse grey core. Fairly plentiful fine and medium well-sorted sand. No visible veg. Plentiful tiny limestone flecks, also sparse to 0.1 and 1 piece 0.2. Self-slip fired pink, except top of rim white. All surfaces burnished as preserved.

Phase	Context & No.	Grid ref	Dia rim (top)	Fig
(vi–)vii	AAC **141**	28 to 34-05 to S05	*c.*14	88b

733 Small amphora with flat-topped folded rim

This appears to belong to Hope's Type 2b, of the sub-series with vertical loop handles and straight rather than bowed neck (Hope 1969c, 96, 99 and Fig. 6 [5–6]), though it is not of the slipped and burnished mixed clay fabric which he thought standard for the form. Similar vessels occur in the Saqqara tombs of Tia and Tia (Aston D.A. 1997, 91 and Pl. 119 [159]) and Horemheb (Bourriau *et al.* 2005, 60 and Fig. 30 [166–67]) of cream slipped and burnished Marl D (H1), which is a closer fabric match for **733**, especially if a slip on the latter had weathered; the folded rims are not always completely closed at their base. At Qantir, where they are described as flasks, they are found, again cream slipped, of the local 'Marl F' fabric; within the series of rim-forms a close parallel is one with a flat top (Aston D.A. 1998, 515 [2061].

Hope's examples are dated from Amenhotep III to the Nineteenth Dynasty and those from Qantir are Ramesside; Saqqara does not contribute anything further.

2605 **733** Fig. 88c

H1 (Marl D). Fired medium. Firing surfaces: exterior white, top of rim pink (presumably fired inverted), interior pink with whitish sheen. Break orange-brown with thick pink core. Fairly plentiful poorly sorted sand. Small qty fine and coarse veg to 0.4. Plentiful tiny limestone flecks and sparse to 0.1, also one piece 0.2. Uncoated. Not polished or burnished.

Phase	Context & No.	Grid ref	Max dia rim	Fig
vi	AER **21**	01/02-08/09	9	88c

734–36 Long-necked amphorae (tall jars)

Two major long-necked amphora forms occur in the Memphis/Saqqara area in the NK in various fabrics. One has a tapering body and small-diameter pointed base, the other a more ovoid body and much larger, rounded base. Colin Hope (1989c) and David Aston (2004a) have attempted detailed studies but include many variations, especially of body forms, which it is not possible to deduce from the rims alone. Aston, discussing the numerous rim sherds at Qantir (1998, 472), illustrates (*ibid.*, 472, Fig. 5.08) two representative forms from Hope's corpus, one with a tapering, the other with a carinated base. Both are found at Qantir, at Memphis (Kom Rabia) and in the Saqqara tombs of the late Eighteenth to Nineteenth Dynasty.

On the Anubieion site there are rims in marl fabrics H1, H2 and H14 and Mixed Clay Fabric 1. These vary slightly, at the Anubieion as elsewhere, even the unusual CBS **55** (Fig. 88e) finding a reasonably close match at Memphis in H14 (Bourriau 2010, Fig. 74 [f]). The rim forms are not sufficiently distinctive to attribute to one or other amphora type, though it does seem that the long cylindrical or bowed necks did not occur until the mid to late Eighteenth Dynasty, (*ibid.*, 140) rather later than the more waisted form represented (in H14) by **765**. The two carinated bases (**766**) cannot be reliably dated without further evidence, except in a general way to the NK.

BGG **26**+BGH **18** and BGH **1+9+10+13+16** of **735** (Fig. 89a–b) are thought to be from the same vessel, in spite of differences in the temper. The two bodies are from the ovoid amphora type, and the form of the neck, thickened at the curve, is compatible with this (Aston D.A. 1991, Pls 50–51 [56–58]) though the neck fragment should perhaps have been drawn slightly more upright, reducing the diameter of the rim. The other amphora body is from the excavated shaft tomb (see page 25) and likely to be from the original burial equipment.

The handle fragments should be from amphorae but cannot be further identified.

Rims

1344A/2408A **734** Fig. 88d–g

H1 (Marl D). Fired fairly hard. Exterior concealed by slip, interior red-brown to brown. Break red-brown all through (CBS **55** and AAA **56**) or with grey core. Moderate qty fine and medium well-sorted sand. No visible veg. Plentiful limestone to 0.1. Exterior and over rim (self-?)slipped, AAA **56** down to 1.5 on interior. ACE **1** not polished or burnished, others exterior burnished.

Phase	Context & No.	Grid ref	Dia rim (top)	Fig
iii–iva	ACE **1**	05-06/07/08	13	88d
v–vi	CBS **55**	W01/01/02-25/26/27	14	88e
vii	AAA (UP 157) **81**	18/19/20-10/11/12	14	88f
vii	AAA **56**	Area 1	15	88g

Necks and bodies

1344B **735** Fig. 88h–89b

H1 (Marl D). Fired fairly hard. Exterior concealed by slip, interior brown (BGG **26** etc red-brown). Break BJO(A+C) **1** etc brown with thick grey core, others red-brown with grey core. BGG **26** etc moderate qty fine and medium well-sorted sand, others fairly plentiful, poorly sorted. No visible veg. Plentiful tiny limestone and sparse to 0.1 (BGH **1** etc to 0.2). White (self-?) slip on exterior. Exterior burnished.

AQG/BEO **1** was not separately described, except that the exterior had white (self-?) slip and was burnished.

Phase	Context & No.	Grid ref	Vessel part	Fig
o/o	AQG/BEO **1**	21-S06	Neck and shoulder	
ii	BGG **26**★	08/09/10-S02/S03	Neck and shoulder	89a
ii	BGH **1**+**9**+**10**+**13**+**16**	10 to 15-S04/S05	Body	89b
ii	BGH **18**★	10 to 15-S04/S05	Neck and shoulder	89a
v	BJO(A+C) **1**★★	01/02-S01	Body	88h
v/v	BJG/BJO(A+C) **7**+**28**★★	W01/01-S01	Body	88h

★ Join

★★ Join

Handle fragments

1344C/2400A **736** Not illustrated

H1 (Marl D). Not recorded in detail. For burnish, see table.

Phase	Context & No.	Grid ref	Burnished?
ii	AJY **2**	22/23-S05/S06	Yes
ii	BET **2**	17/18-07/08	No
iva	AQH **1**	18-S06	Yes
v	DAF **17**	Area 2 W10-S50/S51	Yes
vii	AAA (UP 23) **99**	09-09	No

737–39 Large globular jars ('Meat Jars')

These large globular or bag-shaped neckless jars occur in Nile, marl and mixed clay fabrics, though not in Niles at the Anubieion. They are not recorded in the funerary assemblages from any of the Saqqara tombs except for one in Mixed Clay Fabric 'H5' (now Mixed Clay Fabric 1) in the tomb chamber of Ramose (Aston D.A. and B.G. Aston 2001, Pl. 38 [5]), but appear in some of the associated embalmers' caches (Aston D.A. 1997, 84 [164] in marl fabric H1; Bourriau *et al.* 2005, Figs 13–15 [79–82] in Nile G1). David and Barbara Aston (2001, 55) drew attention to their rarity in tomb contexts, and in particular their absence from Colin Hope's wide-ranging survey of Ramesside pottery (Hope 1989b) based upon tomb groups. On the other hand, they were plentiful in many fabrics at Memphis (Kom Rabia), where they are called 'globular, ovoid jars with folded rim', from the mid to late Eighteenth Dynasty onwards (Bourriau 2010, 141). They were also very numerous (and very variable in form) at Qantir (Aston D.A. 1998, *passim*). Noting this pattern, Janine Bourriau (pers. comm.) deduces that they were thought less suitable for deposition in tombs than for domestic use. This leaves us asking why they are to be found on the Anubieion site. They may have been left by the embalmers, although there was no trace of embalming material on the sherds; otherwise, possibly they held the food supplies of the necropolis workmen or priests. As to dating, David Aston (Aston D.A. 1998, 478) confirms that the form appeared in the late Eighteenth Dynasty, when Marl D clays became fashionable, and continued to be popular until at least the Twenty-first.

There were several examples at Memphis (Kom Rabia) similar to **737** (Bourriau 2010, note especially Figs 55, 71 and 89 [11.15.15] in H14 and Fig. 88 [11.15.22] in H1). At Saqqara the jar in the tomb of Ramose (Aston D.A. and B.G. Aston, 2001, Pl. 38 [5]) is again similar (in Mixed Clay Fabric 'H5'). At Qantir, where it is difficult to choose among the many on offer, examples in Marl D (Aston D.A. 1998, 481/83 [1805/22]) are perhaps the closest match. As to **738**, it is again at Qantir that the closest parallels are to be found, though examples in Marl A4 (*ibid.*, 443 [1585/87]) are closer than any in Marl D. **739** may owe something of its shape to Levantine jars. It is not found among the many published and unpublished variants at Memphis (Kom Rabia). At Qantir, the rim is not unlike several in the same Marl A4 series (e.g. *ibid.*, 443/45 [1589/93, 1606]) if a little less rounded, and there are quite close matches in Marl A4 at Elephantine in respectively the Nineteenth Dynasty and the 'Libyan Period' (Aston D.A. 1999, Pl. 8 [175]; Pl. 25 [742]). All these are rather larger in diameter (16 to 24) and more upright, and it is possible that the sherd **739** was distorted and seemed smaller and shallower than it really was.

1344D **737** Fig. 90a

As often, the opening was not quite round.

H1 (Marl D). Fired fairly hard. Exterior concealed by slip, interior brown. Break red-brown all through. Moderate qty fine and medium sand. No visible veg. Fairly plentiful tiny limestone flecks and sparse to 0.1. Self-slipped on exterior, over the rim and down a short way inside. Exterior burnished.

Phase	Context & No.	Grid ref	Dia rim (top)	Fig
ivd	AJU **7***	05-10	22	90a
vii	AAA (UP 38) **15***	11 to 20-S01/S02/S03	21	90a

* Join

2643 **738** Fig. 90b

H1 (Marl D). Fired medium. Surfaces cream. Break cream with thick red-brown core. Fairly plentiful fine and medium well-sorted sand. Small qty fine veg to 0.2; several pieces to 1.5 on surface are assumed to be accidental. Matrix limestone but nothing larger. Uncoated. Not polished or burnished.

Phase	Context & No.	Grid ref	Max dia rim	Fig
vii	CAA **35**	Area 26	*c.*20	90b

2418 **739** Fig. 90c

H1 (Marl D). Fired fairly hard. Surfaces red-brown, perhaps modified by weathering. Break thin red-brown zones and thick greenish brown core. Fairly plentiful poorly sorted sand. Fairly plentiful fine veg to 0.5. Fairly plentiful limestone to 0.1. Surfaces too weathered for slip or firing surface, polish or burnish to survive.

Phase	Context & No.	Grid ref	Max dia rim	Fig
?	APE (UP 323) **4**	Area 12	12	90c

740 Body sherds from large jar with cordons and finger impress

Marl version of **659**. See there for discussion. For a parallel in a marl fabric, albeit Marl A4, see a jar body sherd with cordon from Luxor (Aston, D.A., 2008, 284 and Pl. 108 [2188]), dated to the Twentieth to Twenty-first Dynasty.

97 **740** Fig. 90g

Four sherds, of which two join, probably all from a single large jar. Vessel body furnished with cordons and decorated with pre-firing fingerprints. Unillustrated AJH **150** has part of a cordon and one thumbprint, AJD under AAD **13** one thumbprint only. All four have a thin white plaster coating on the interior, probably waterproofing rather than contents.

H1 (Marl D). Fired medium. Exterior probably concealed by slip, interior concealed by plaster. Break green. Fairly plentiful fine well-sorted sand. Small qty fine veg to 0.3. Matrix limestone, and each sherd, except AJH under AAD **12,** also one piece 0.1. More than usual red (mineral?) fragments to 0.1. Probable green (self-?)slip on exterior, interior not visible. Not polished or burnished.

Phase	Context & No.	Grid ref	Max dia body	Fig
iva	AJH **113**★	05/06-04/05/06	*c*.30–35?	90g
iva	AJH **150**	05/06-04/05/06	?	
iva	AJH Under AAD **12**★	06 to 09-06/07	*c*.30–35	90g
iva	AJH Under AAD **13**	06 to 09-06/07	?	

★ Join

741 Globular Jar(?)

The best local match for stance is perhaps a rim of similar size in marl fabric H4 from Memphis (Kom Rabia) (Bourriau 2010, Fig. 88 [11.8.21]), a new type in a context of the mid to late Nineteenth Dynasty, but at Luxor there is a similar stance on a jar with a red rim on a white slip of the Twentieth to Twenty-first Dynasty (Aston D.A. 2008, Pl. 84 [1685]). A similar form but with a slightly more upright stance also occurs at Memphis, the earliest occurrence being in Marl H14 in the early to mid Eighteenth Dynasty (Bourriau 2010, Fig. 32 [10.8.2]). At the Anubieion the more upright stance is found on **790** of unknown Levantine origin, and on **642** in Nile fabric G1, both probably of the late NK or later.

2115 **741** Fig. 90d

H1 (Marl D). Fired medium. Exterior white firing surface, interior brownish pink. Break pale brown. Fairly plentiful fine and medium well-sorted sand.Very small qty fine and coarse veg to 0.3. Matrix limestone, also one piece 0.1 and one 0.3. Uncoated. Light polish on exterior of rim and body, interior not polished or burnished.

Phase	Context & No.	Grid ref	Dia rim (top)	Fig
iv (Pt II?)/?	AYQ/AYR **16**	Area 13	9	90d

742 Body of small squat carinated jar

Similar in size and form to small jars in fine marl clay from the well-known burial of the early NK on or near Mastaba 3507 at Saqqara (Bourriau 1991, Fig. 6 [10, 11]; Aston D.A. 2007, 207–11 and Fig. 2 [17–19, 21]) and probably a smaller version of a decorated Nile clay example from Qau (Brunton 1930, Pl. XXVIII [139]; Bourriau 1981, 134–35 [263]). **742** has no painted decoration but the surface is weathered.There was a slightly larger (dia 18), unpainted example (in Marl A2, assume H10) in a SIP to early NK context at Deir el-Ballas (Bourriau 1990a, Fig 4.3 [14]).

1344E **742** Fig. 90e

H1 (Marl D). Fired fairly hard. Exterior red-brown where slip lost, interior grey-brown. Break red-brown with grey core. Moderate qty fine and medium well-sorted sand. No visible veg. Fairly plentiful limestone to 0.1. Exterior probably self-slipped. Exterior burnished.

Phase	Context & No.	Grid Ref	Max dia body	Fig
ii	AJY **171**	21/22-S05/S06	*c*.12	90e

743 Small Lentoid ('Pilgrim') flask

There are two examples of this form, preserving the shoulder and two complete loop handles, from Malkata (Hope 1989a, Fig 6c, d), where the type is described as becoming more common in the late Eighteenth Dynasty (*ibid.*, 14) than previously. They have the same 'hammerheaded' rim, and the ware is cream slipped and burnished Marl D (*ibid.*, 16). They were probably brought to Thebes (from Memphis?) with precious oils. The Anubieion example is at the lower end of the size range, matching Malkata 6c and a self-slipped and burnished H1 example from the first half of the Eighteenth Dynasty from Memphis (Kom Rabia) (Bourriau 2010, Fig. 29 [11.16.1]) with a slightly different rim. The several Ramesside examples at Qantir (Aston D.A. 1998, 463 [1691–93]; 493 [1944–46]) and one in the tomb of Khay at Saqqara (Aston D.A. and B.G. Aston, 2001, Pl. 39 [30]) have a simplified out-turned rim which appears to represent a later development.

47A — 743 Fig. 90f

Complete neck and scars of two opposed handles.

H1 (Marl D). Fired fairly soft. Exterior concealed by slip, interior white. Break orange-brown shading to deeper brown near interior surface. Small qty poorly sorted sand. Small qty fine veg to 0.2. Plentiful matrix limestone, giving a speckled effect to the break, but all much smaller than 0.05. Weathered, but probable white slip on exterior, fired pale orange where sheltered by a handle; interior uncoated. Not polished or burnished as preserved.

Phase	Context & No.	Grid ref	Max dia rim	Fig
iv (Pt II?)	ADF North **2**	Area 13	3.3	90f

744 Bases of large closed forms

Sherds from the bases of ovoid-body amphorae or 'meat jars'.

1344F — 744 Fig. 90h

H1 (Marl D). AQG **85+155** fired fairly hard. Surfaces grey-brown, exterior where slip lost. Break red-brown with grey core. Moderate qty fine and medium well-sorted sand. No visible veg. Plentiful tiny limestone and sparse to 0.1. White (AQG **85+155** pink) (self-?)slip on exterior. Exterior burnished. Others not described, except that AAA **215** was burnished but AIY/AVB **54** was not.

Phase	Context & No.	Grid ref	Fig
o	AQG **85**★	10/11-S04/S05	90h
o	AQG **155**★	09/10-S03/S04	90h
ii/ivb	AIY/AVB **54**	10 to 14-01/S01/S02	
vii	AAA (UP 23) **215**	08-06	

★ Join

<u>745</u> Body sherds in H1

1344G/2400D

<u>745</u> Fig. 90i–j

Mostly from closed forms. BQS **6** (Fig. 90i), from an open form, has two post-firing holes, probably from a repair but perhaps intentional for cheese-making or a similar function. BJG/BJO(H) **42** (Fig 90j) was reused as a scraper, and two other sherds were also reused, probably during construction and decoration of tomb chapels. The remainder are included to show a concentration in Phase ii contexts and in certain areas of the site.

For sherds reused to hold pigment, as on the interior of AHW **3** and AAA **13**, notice also blue pigment on **<u>505</u>** and red on BEO **63** of **<u>598</u>**, both of the NK.

<u>H1 (Marl D)</u>. Only BQS **6** and BJG/BJO(H) **42** are described in detail. For burnish, see table.

BJG/O(H) **42**. Fired fairly hard. Exterior concealed by slip, interior red-brown. Break brown with grey core. Moderate qty fine and medium well-sorted sand. No visible veg. Plentiful fine limestone and sparse to 0.1. White (self-?) slip on exterior. Exterior burnished.

BQS **6**. Fired fairly hard. Surfaces concealed by slip. Break red-brown all through. Moderate qty fine and some medium well-sorted sand. No visible veg. Plentiful fine limestone and sparse to 0.1. White (self-?) slip on both surfaces. Both surfaces burnished.

Phase	**Context & No.**	**Grid ref**	**Burnished?**	**Fig & notes**
o	AQG **59**	12/13/14-S04/S05	No	
o	AQG **77**	11/12-S01/S02	Yes	
o	AQG **152A****	09/10-S03/S04	Yes	4
o	AQG **184+185,200**	09/10-S03/S04	Yes (both)	
o	AQG **190†**	09/10-S03/S04	Yes	4
o	BEN **9**	14/15-01 to S05	Yes	
o	BEN **55**	14/15-01 to S03	Yes	
o	BEO (**99?**)	14/15-01	Yes	
o/ii	AQG/BGU **2,36**	19/20-S04/S05	Yes (both)	
o/o	AQG /BEO **2,13,14**	21-S06	Yes (all)	3
o–iii	CFT **3**	08/09-22	Yes	
ii	AHW **2,3**	10-S01	Yes	1 (AHW **3** only)
ii	AIY **9**	12/13-01	Yes	
ii	AIY **104**	07/08-06	Yes	
ii	AIY **139**	08/09-06	Yes	
ii	AJX/AJY/BRS **3**	17/18-S04/S05	Yes	
ii	AJY **5**	21-S06	Yes	
ii	AJY **114,123,125**	22/23-S05/S06	Yes (all)	
ii	AJY **124,126**	19/20-S05/S06	Yes (both)	
ii	AON **33**	03/04/05-02 to S02	Yes	
ii	AQE **3,4**	21-S03	Yes (both)	
ii	AQE **61**	19/20-02/03	No	
ii	AQE **76**	14/15/16-01/02	Yes	
ii	AUQ **173**	08-03	Yes	
ii	BDS **2**	04-09	Yes	2

Phase	Context & No.	Grid ref	Burnished?	Fig & notes
ii	BDS **14**★	03 to 06-07	Yes	
ii	BDX **14**★,**16**,**55**	03/04-07	Yes (all)	
ii	BGG **2** ¶	11/12-S04/S05	Yes	4
ii	BGG **6**†	11/12-S04/S05	Yes	4
ii	BGG **27**+**28**†	08/09/10-S02/S03	Yes	4
ii	BGG **29**★★	08/09/10-S02/S03	Yes	
ii	BGG **31**,**72**	08/09/10-S02/S03	Yes (both)	4 (BGG **31** only)
ii	BGG **162**	11/12-S04/S05	Yes	
ii	BGH **2**+**4**+**8**+**12**+**17**¶	10 to 15-S04/S05	Yes	4
ii	BGH **3**+**6**+**7**+**14**†	10 to 15-S04/S05	Yes	4
ii	BGH **5**,**11**,**27**	10 to 15-S04/S05	Yes (all)	4 (BGH **5**,**11** only)
ii	BGL **49**	14/15-S04/S05	No	
ii	BKS **4**	02-20	Yes	
ii/ii/ivc	AJX/AJY/BRS **7**	21/22/23-S02/S03	Yes	
ii/ii/ivc	AJX/AJY/BRS **8**	21/22-S01/S02/S03	Yes	
ii/ivb	AIY/AVB **1**,**2**	13/14-01/S01	Yes	
iii	BCB **63**	01 to 04-04/05/06	No	
iii	BCB **73**	01 to 04-04/05/06	Yes	
iii	BDR **39**	12/13/14-04/05/06	Yes	2
iii	BDR **86**	10-03/04/05	Yes	
iii	BJJ **43**	17/18-05/06	Yes	
iii	CHZ **17**+**18**,**19**	09-28	Yes (both)	
iii/iva/?	BPD/BHR/BPV **6**	03/04 22/23	Yes	
iii/iva/ivb	BPU/BHR/BKN **3**	02/03-21/22	Yes	
iii–iva	ACE **174**	01 to 05-08 to 12	No	
iii–iva	ACE **247**	01 to 04-08	Yes	
iii–iva	AFS **70**★	03-07	Yes	
iv (Pt II?)	ABW **15**	Area 13	Yes	
iv (Pt II?)	ABY **18**	Area 13	No	
iv (Pt II?)/?	AYP/AYJ **2**	Area 13	No	
iv (Pt II?)/iv (Pt II?)	ABK/ABU **2**	Area 13	No	
iva	AQH **2**	19/20-S04/S05	Yes	
iva	AQH **143**††	11/12-S03/S04	Yes	
iva	AQC **170**	02/03-10	Yes	
iva	BHR **256**	02/03-21/22	Yes	
iva/ivb	AQC/AEX **60**	01 to 05-06/07	Yes	
ivb	AEX **6**	04/05-06	No	
ivb	AIH **13**	14 to 20-01	Yes	
ivb	AVB **7**	10/11-S02/S03	Yes	4

Phase	Context & No.	Grid ref	Burnished?	Fig & notes
ivb	AVB **76**††	10/11-S01/S02	Yes	
ivb	AWD **18**	20-02	Yes	
ivb	BTG **4**	02-21	Yes	
ivb	CBH **7**	02-22	No	
ivb	CIE **6**	02 to 05-33 to 37	No	
ivb–c	AUE **3**	14-06	Yes	
ivb–c	BCW **9**	18/19-07	No	
ivc	AQC **170**	02/03-10	Yes	
ivc	BKC **15+16**	06/07-26	Yes	
ivc	CIN **1+2**	06/07-33	Yes	
ivc	BQS **6**	Area 2	Yes (both)	90i
ivc/ivc	ATC/BJL **3**	03/04/05-S04/S05/ S06	Yes	
ivc/ivc	ATD/ATE **7**	05 to 09-S05/S06	Yes	
v	AEK **55**	16 to 18-S01/S02	No	
v/v	BJG/BJO(H) **42**	W01/01-S01	Yes	90j
vii	AAA (UP 23) **43**	10-07	No	
vii	AAA (UP 23) **203**	02-05	No	
vii	AAA (UP 23) **325**	10-08	No	
vii	AAA (UP 23) **326**	10-07	Yes	
vii	AAA (UP 108) **13**	26/27/28-01/S01	Yes	
vii	AAA (UP 108) **55**	28/29-01/02	No	
vii	AAA (UP 588) **416**	01/02-32/33	No	
vii	AAA **13**	Area 1	Yes	1
?	BEP **1**	14 to17-01/S01	Yes	
?	BEP **97**	16 to 20-01/S01	Yes	
?	BPV **37,40**	03/04-21	Yes (both)	
?	CGO **5**	05-25/26	Yes	
?	UP 805 **9**	Area 5	Yes	
?	UP 1034 **1**	Area 12	Yes	

* Join
** Join
† Join
†† Join
¶ Join
1 Yellow pigment on interior and (AHW **3** only) over most breaks
2 Traces of plaster on interior
3 AQG/BEO **13** and **14** probably same vessel
4 Probably all same vessel

H2 (Marl A4)

746 Plate(?)

The vessel form from which this small rim sherd derives is uncertain. It is surely too flat for an offering stand. Some kind of bottle or jar is possible: Holthoer's 'slender bottles' (1977, Pl. 29) are all much too small, but an 'unusual' blue-painted Nile G1 jar with diameter 12, from the Saqqara tomb of Ramose, has a similar rim (Aston D.A. and B.G. Aston, 2001, Pl. 42 [79]). Nevertheless, a plate is the most likely and in G1 can be so small (Aston D.A. 1997, 84 and Pl. 112 [9]); it would be unusual in a marl clay, but plates in red slipped Marl A4 do occur in Ramesside levels at Qantir (Aston D.A. 1998, 447 [1615–18]), albeit with diameter 20–24.

2482 **746** Fig. 91a

H2 (Marl A4). Fired fairly hard. Surfaces white. Break red all through except at surfaces. Plentiful poorly sorted sand. Moderate qty fine veg to 0.2. Plentiful naturally occurring tiny limestone specks. One red (mineral?) fragment 0.1 visible. Uncoated. Not polished or burnished.

Phase	Context & No.	Grid ref	Max dia rim	Fig
iva	BGB **10**	06/07/08-01/02	*c.*13	91a

747 Small incurved bowl

A very common form in the NK but usually of Nile clay (e.g. **483/95**). Memphis (Kom Rabia) examples from early to mid Eighteenth Dynasty levels include some in G1 of about the same size (Bourriau 2010, Fig. 22 [4.1.3/4] and Fig. 23 [4.2.3/5]) though others are larger. Of the same date and in marl clays there are H2 (*ibid.*, Fig. 29 [3.1.4]) and H8 (*ibid.*, Fig. 30 [3.1.3]) examples with diameter 19. However, Colin Hope includes one in 'Uncoated Fine Marl A' (dia 13.5) in his study of Ramesside pottery (Hope 1989b, Fig. 6g) and there are several from Ramesside contexts at Qantir (dias 22–26) in red slipped Marl A4 (Aston D.A. 1998, 447 [1613]; 448 [1621/22]) so an Eighteenth Dynasty date is not assured.

2912 **747** Fig. 91b

H2 (Marl A4). Fired medium to fairly soft. Surfaces pale pinkish brown where surface lost. Break pale pinkish brown all through. Fairly plentiful poorly sorted sand. Fairly plentiful fine and coarse veg to 0.4. Sparse limestone to 0.1. Uncoated, but remains of white firing surface on both faces. Not polished or burnished as preserved.

Phase	Context & No.	Grid ref	Dia rim (top)	Fig
iii	BDR **183**	08/09-06	*c.*15	91b

748 Small straight-sided bowl

Not a common form in marl clay, and even less usual is the string-tying of so small a vessel. It might be from a small carinated dish such as an H2 example (dia 16) at Memphis (Kom Rabia) (Bourriau 2010, Fig. 110 [3.5.3]).

2898 **748** Fig. 91c

Intermittent impressions from string-tying before firing, in spite of small diameter.

H2 (Marl A4)(?). Fired fairly soft. Surfaces pale brown. Break pale brown all through. Small qty poorly sorted sand, including large grains. Small qty fine veg to 0.2. Plentiful tiny limestone flecks and sparse to 0.1. Uncoated. Not polished or burnished.

Phase	Context & No.	Grid ref	Dia rim (top)	Fig
ivb–c	AVZ **2**	20-02	*c.*14	91c

749 Long-necked amphora (tall jar)

See H1 (**734–36**).

2400E **749** Fig. 91d

H2 (Marl A4). Fired fairly hard. Surfaces concealed by slip. Break pale brown all through. Moderate qty fine and medium well-sorted sand. Sparse fine veg to 0.3. Plentiful tiny limestone specks and sparse to 0.05. Slightly misfired greenish slip on both surfaces. Possible traces of burnish on exterior.

Phase	Context & No.	Grid ref	Dia rim (top)	Fig
vii	AAA (UP 588) **502**	W01/01-25/26/27	*c.*11	91d

750 Tall jar ('drop pot')

Rim from a tall jar without handles, probably similar to one from early to mid Eighteenth Dynasty Memphis (Kom Rabia), either slender (Bourriau 2010, Fig. 26 [9.5.1]) or slightly shorter (*ibid.*, Fig. 26 [10.3.1]). Although both are, like the majority, in Nile fabric G1, some unpublished examples in H2 (dia 10), and H2 near H4 (dia 10), were also recorded. Similar examples, respectively in Marl A3 and Marl B, have been published from Deir el-Ballas (Bourriau 1990a, Fig. 4.3 [18 and 21]), where they should be of late SIP to early Eighteenth Dynasty date.

2839 **750** Fig. 91e

H2 (Marl A4). Fired medium. Surfaces creamy buff. Break creamy buff with brown zone near interior surface. Sparse very fine well-sorted sand. No visible veg. Sparse limestone to 0.1. Sparse black, red-brown and clear mineral particles to 0.1. Uncoated. Not polished or burnished.

Phase	Context & No.	Grid ref	Dia rim (top)	Fig
ivc	BHM **130**	01/02-21/22	*c.*12	91e

751 Upper part of jar handle

Although the body diameter could not be measured, the size, shape and angle of attachment of this handle strictly limit the vessel-types to which it could belong. In spite of the firing colour of the interior surface, a long-necked jug (rather than a jar since it has only one handle) is the best candidate: there is a fine Ramesside series in H14/H15 from Saqqara (Aston B.G. 2005, Pls 126–27 [120–24]) but a rim from such a vessel occurs already in a context of the mid to late Eighteenth Dynasty at Memphis (Kom Rabia) (Bourriau 2010, Fig.46 [c]).

2900 **751** Fig. 91f

H2 (Marl A4). Fired fairly soft. Surfaces creamy white. Break pale brown with diffuse greenish core. Fairly plentiful poorly sorted sand. Fairly plentiful fine veg, to 0.3. Plentiful tiny limestone specks and sparse to 0.1. Uncoated. Not polished or burnished.

Phase	Context & No.	Grid ref	Fig
?/?	BHP/BHQ **71**	02-23	91f

752 Bichrome (red- and black-) painted body sherds in H2

Body sherds from jars, with bichrome (red and black) decoration. DAW **12** (Fig. 91j) and DAJ **4** (Fig. 91k) are probably from the same jar, the elongated flat profile of DAJ **4** pointing to a large round-based ovoid type (Holthoer 1977, Pl. 37 [185/599:4]) though the decorative style is found also on various smaller jars (*ibid.*, Pls 37–40). See also **657** in Nile fabric G1. BNE **71** (Fig. 91h) is from the neck of a jar (Holthoer 1977, Pl. 22 [185/520:2]); similar but empty motifs adorn the neck of a bichrome ovoid pedestalled jar in marl fabric H2 from Saqqara (Bourriau and D.A. Aston 1985, Pl. 36 [92]). BAX **47** (Fig. 91g) has decoration similar to that on a small deep bowl in G1 from the surface at Saqqara (Bourriau *et al.* 2005, Fig. 9 [53]); the exact vessel type cannot be established but the pale pink interior may indicate a bowl with another stacked inside it in the kiln. The form of AAB Lower **15** (Fig. 91i) cannot be known with certainty.

Although decoration similar to that on BAX **47** appears on a pedestalled bowl in Fine Marl A fabric apparently as late as the Ramesside period (Hope 1989b, Fig. 13j), the *floruit* of the bichrome style is in the early to mid Eighteenth Dynasty (Hope 1987, 109).

2448 **752** Fig. 91g–k

H2 (Marl A4). All fired fairly soft. Exterior firing surfaces or self-slip: DAJ **4** and DAW **12** interior pink, BAX **47** pale pink, remainder cream. Break, BAX **47** and AAB Lower **15** cream shading to pink towards exterior, remainder pink with faint grey-green core. Moderate qty to fairly plentiful poorly sorted sand. Sparse red mineral fragments to 0.1. Moderate qty fine veg to 0.3, DAJ **4** also one piece coarse 0.9. AAB Lower **15** perhaps firing surface only, remainder self-slipped. Not polished or burnished.

Phase	Context & No.	Grid ref	Fig
iv	DAJ **4***	Area 2 W01/01-S51	91k
iva	BAX **47**	06-04. Level 62.484	91g
iv+	DAW **12***	Area 2	91j
(vi–)vii	AAB Lower **15**	28–34-01/02	91i
?	BNE **71**	09/10-04/05	91h

* Almost certainly same vessel

753 Unpainted body sherds in H2

These body sherds are all from medium-sized jars, except BHW **193** from a small thin-walled jar. They prove the presence of several different H2 jars but are not distinctive enough to illustrate. They cluster at the northern end of the excavation, a sign of New Kingdom tombs in that area, as expected.

2402 **753** Not illustrated

H2 (Marl A4). All fired fairly soft to medium. Exterior concealed by slip, except BHE **19** green; interior BHW **193** cream, BPX **2** brown, CGQ **65** and BHE **19** green, others pink to pale pinkish brown. Break BHW **193** cream, others pink to greenish brown, all through. Moderate qty to fairly plentiful sand, CIE **35** and CGI **44** fine and medium well-sorted, others poorly sorted. CIE **35** moderate qty fine veg to 0.3, others moderate qty to fairly plentiful fine and coarse, mostly to 0.5 but a few longer pieces. BHE **19** has a trace of red slip surviving in a wheel-groove, others self-slipped. For burnish, see table.

Phase	Context & No.	Grid ref	Burnished?
iii	BHW **193**	02-21/22	Yes
iii	BPX **2**	08-26/27	No
iva	BHR **205**	03-23	Yes

Phase	Context & No.	Grid ref	Burnished?
ivb	CIE **35**	02 to 05-33 to 37	Yes
ivb–c/ivb–c/ivd	AUX/AVD/AJE **1**	12 to 16-S01	No
ivc	CGI **44**	03/04-34/35	Yes
ivc	CGQ **65**	02 to 05-34 to 37	No
ivd	BHE **19**	04/05-22	No

H4 (Marl A4)

754 Jar in Middle Kingdom tradition

The form of this jar, with its smooth interior curve, is firmly rooted in the MK, but the thick wall and the quantity of dark grits point to a date in the SIP or early NK. There is a close match from Memphis (Kom Rabia) in self-slipped marl fabric H8 from a context of the first half of the Eighteenth Dynasty (Bourriau 2010, Fig. 31 [10.10.11]) and another from Deir el-Ballas in Nile B2 (G1) of about the same date (Bourriau 1990a, Fig. 4.3 [2]). The traces of colour on the exterior appear to be paint rather the remains of a coloured slip.

2076 **754** Fig. 91l

H4 (Marl A4). Fired medium. Off-white firing surfaces with grey 'blush' areas on exterior. Break off-white with thick pale grey core. Small qty fine and medium well-sorted sand. Small qty fine veg to 0.2. Fairly plentiful tiny dark grits. Sparse limestone to 0.05. Sparse red and orange mineral fragments to 0.05 and one piece 0.1. Traces of orange-red colour on exterior of rim and of darker red on body, probably from painted bands. Traces of polish or burnish where paint/slip survives.

Phase	Context & No.	Grid ref	Dia rim (top)	Fig
iv (Pt II?)	ADC **54**	Area 13	9	91l

755 Jar with black-painted band

The form of the neck indicates a globular rather than a slim jar. The date should be late SIP, or Eighteenth Dynasty down to about the reign of Tuthmosis III. During this period bichrome-painted decoration develops from monochrome brown or black (Hope 1987, 109); although the present piece has only black paint, too little survives to prove there was no red. At Memphis (Kom Rabia) a similar form but undecorated, in the MK fabric Marl C1 (Bourriau 2010, Fig. 20 [c]), is again from a context of the early to mid Eighteenth Dynasty, though the fabric probably indicates earlier manufacture. At Deir el-Ballas the form is recorded in Marl B from the late SIP to the early Eighteenth Dynasty (Bourriau 1990a, Fig 4.4 [10 and 11]). Unsurprisingly, it is absent from the Ramesside tombs at Saqqara.

2734 **755** Fig. 91m

H4 (Marl A4). Fired medium. Surfaces cream. Break pale buff all through, except cream close to surfaces. Moderate qty fine well-sorted sand. Small qty fine veg to 0.3. Sparse limestone to 0.1. Fairly plentiful tiny red mineral fragments. Possibly self-slipped, but no coloured slip. Black-painted band over entire neck surviving, and small black-painted areas just inside the rim may indicate the rim was also painted. Not polished or burnished.

Phase	Context & No.	Grid ref	Dia rim (top)	Fig
iii–iva	ACE **233**	01 to 06-08/09/10	10	91m

756 Decorated shoulder of a squat or globular jar

Small jars, squat and sometimes carinated, have a long prior history in Middle and Upper Egypt but the decorated version, as here, seems to begin in the late SIP and continue into the first half of the NK (Bourriau 1997, Fig. 6.18; Bourriau 2010, 85). For a complete small example in Marl A2 (not A1 as printed) painted in the same way as **756**, see Diospolis Parva (Petrie 1901, Pl. XXXV [89]; Bourriau 1981, 135 [264]). Another is published from Abydos (Peet and Loat, Pl. V [33]). There are similarly decorated shoulder sherds in H10 (Marl A2) from early to mid Eighteenth Dynasty contexts at Memphis (Kom Rabia) (Bourriau 2010, Fig. 35 [d,f,g]). For the rim of a similar jar in H10 fabric, see **763**.

2736 **756** Fig. 91n

H4 (Marl A4). Fired medium. Surfaces greenish cream. Break greenish cream all through. Fairly plentiful fine and medium sand with a few larger grains. No visible veg. Fairly plentiful tiny red mineral fragments, and sparse larger fragments to 0.1. Possibly self-slipped but no coloured slip. Black-painted horizontal band at base of neck and six vertical strokes down from it. Traces of horizontal burnish on exterior.

Phase	Context & No.	Grid ref	Fig
vii	AAA (UP 108) **35**	29 to 34-S06	91n

757 Undecorated shoulder of a fairly large jar

This sherd proves the presence of H4 in this context but is not sufficiently preserved to illustrate.

2915 **757** Not illustrated

H4 (Marl A4). Fired fairly soft. Surfaces off-white, probably firing surfaces. Break pale pinkish brown. Fairly plentiful fine and medium sand with occasional larger grains. Small qty fine veg to 0.3. Sparse limestone to 0.1 and one piece 0.2. Weathered, but no coloured slip, and probably not self-slipped. Not polished or burnished.

Phase	Context & No.	Grid ref	Notes
iv (Pt II?)	ABY **40**	Area 13	Similar to 91n

758 Body sherds in burnished H4

These prove the presence of burnished H4 vessels in these contexts but are not distinctive enough to illustrate.

2404 **758** Not illustrated

Unpainted body sherds with no features, from medium sized to large restricted forms.

H4 (Marl A4). Fired fairly hard. Surfaces greenish cream to green. Break BCB **62** pale greenish brown, remainder green. Fairly plentiful fine well-sorted sand. No visible veg. Limestone not recorded. All, sparse red and dark mineral fragments to 0.1. All self-slipped. All, exterior burnished, BCB **62** only lightly.

Phase	Context & No.	Grid ref
ii	BGL **86**	14/15-01/S01/S02
iii	BCB **62**	01 to 04-04/05/06
(vi–vii)	AAB **18**	27/28-08/09
?	BJP **1**	16/17-05

H8 (Marl B)

759 Bowl (or lid)

Open forms in H8 are not numerous, even where the fabric is more common than in the Saqqara/Memphis area. A similar but not quite identical Marl B example from Deir el-Ballas with diameter 18, dating to the late SIP to the early Eighteenth Dynasty, is interpreted as a bowl rather than a lid (Bourriau 1990a, Fig. 4.3 [23]).

1608 **759** Fig. 92a

Smoothing in two different directions on exterior and very light wheel ridges on interior.

H8 (Marl B). Fired fairly hard. Exterior pale brown, interior white with faint greenish tinge. Break pale pinkish brown. Fairly plentiful poorly sorted sand but with few of the larger grains. No visible veg. Numerous naturally occurring tiny limestone pieces and sparse to 0.1, also one piece 0.2. Possibly self-slipped. Not polished or burnished.

Phase	Context & No.	Grid ref	Max dia rim	Fig
ivc	BHS **250**	05/06-22/23	(*c*.20–30?)	92a

760 Non-rim diagnostic sherds in H8

2414A **760** Not illustrated

Part base of a large drop-pot not reshaped on the wheel, and shoulder and lower neck of a jar.

H8 (Marl B). CCL **3** fired medium, UP 38 **113** fairly hard. CCL **3** exterior cream, interior pink, UP 38 **113** surfaces cream. Break CCL **3** pale pinkish brown, UP 38 **113** pale pink. Fairly plentiful poorly sorted sand. No visible veg. Numerous naturally occurring tiny limestone pieces and sparse to 0.1, UP 38 **113** one piece 0.2. Probably self-slipped but no coloured slips. Not polished or burnished.

Phase	Context & No.	Grid ref	Vessel part
ivc	CCL **3**	09/10-27	Part base
vii	AAA (UP 38) **113**	19-08	Neck and shoulder

761 Body sherds in H8

2414B/2901 **761** Fig. 92b

BDY **3** (Fig. 92b) is from a large open form, the others from amphorae or large jars. AIX/AIY **15** and BDR **40** are from near the base, BDR **40** with wheel ridges on interior of upper part, fingermarks on lower part.

H8 (Marl B). BDR **40** fired medium, others fairly soft. ANS **9** exterior burnt, interior pink; BDY **3** surfaces pink, others surfaces green, exteriors where slip lost. Break ANS **9** pink all through, BDY **3** pink with faint greenish core, others green all through. Fairly plentiful poorly sorted sand but largest grains in ANS **9** only. No visible veg. Numerous tiny limestone flecks, and (except AIY/AIX **15**) sparse to 0.1. White (probable self-) slip on exterior. Not polished or burnished.

Phase	Context & No.	Grid ref	Fig.
o	BDY **3**	01/02/03-A07/S08	92b

Phase	Context & No.	Grid ref	Fig.
ii/ivd	AIY/AIX **15**	12-01/02	
iii	BDR **40**	12/13/14-04/05/06	
?	ANS (UP 1000) **9**	Area 14	

762 Body sherd of storage jar, with post-firing potmark

The well-defined wheel-ridges on the interior would normally indicate a sherd from near the base of the vessel, where potmarks are common. String-tying is more likely on the shoulder (e.g. Aston D.A. 1998, 461 [1683] post-firing and incorporating a cross; Bourriau 2010, Fig. 92 [i] pre-firing, both in H1), but on balance, a base is more probable. The crudely scratched cross is so simple there is little point in seeking parallels, though if the double cross-bar is intentional it is paralleled by two (pre-firing) examples from MK Kahun (Gallorini 2009, 133, Type 3.9.2.) It cuts through the impressions of fine string, one of two lengths tied many times around before firing.

For a summary of all the potmarks in the present volume, see Appendix 1.

2885 **762** Fig. 92c

H8 (Marl B). Fired medium. Exterior cream, interior red-brown. Break brick-red, inner half with green tinge. Plentiful sand, poorly sorted but lacking the largest grains. No visible veg. Only sparse limestone to 0.1 visible, lacking the sprinkling of tiny specks common in marl wares. Exterior probably, interior certainly, uncoated. Probable light polish on exterior.

Phase	Context & No.	Grid ref	Fig
iva/ivb	AQC/AEX **1**	01 to 05-06/07	92c

H10 (Marl A2)

763 Rim of squat ovoid or globular jar

A similar jar form occurs at Memphis (Kom Rabia) in three marl fabrics (Bourriau 2010, Fig. 30 [11.8.2] in H2; Fig. 30 [11.8.3] in H4; Fig. 31 [11.8.4] in H8). At Deir el-Ballas it appears in Nile B2 (Bourriau 1990a, Fig. 4.3 [3]). For a decorated shoulder from a similar vessel in H4, see **756**. For a complete small example in Marl A2 painted in the same way as **756**, see an example from Diospolis Parva (Petrie 1901, Pl. XXXV [89]; Bourriau 1981, 135 [264] (where Marl A1 in error)). Eighteenth Dynasty, until about the reign of Amenhotep III.

2412 **763** Fig. 92d

H10 (Marl A2). Fired medium. Surfaces cream, either firing surfaces or self-slip. Break pink all through except thin zones at surfaces. Fairly plentiful poorly sorted sand. No visible veg. Moderate qty limestone to 0.1. No coloured slip. Probably, but not certainly, polished or burnished (surface is flaking).

Phase	Context & No.	Grid ref	Dia rim (top)	Fig
ii/ivd	AIY/AIX **13**	12-01/02	9	92d

764 Globular Jar

The simple form of the low, rounded rim relates this sherd to a small globular jar. At Memphis (Kom Rabia) it occurs in marl fabric H1 (Bourriau 2010, Fig. 54 [11.15.10]) but also in Nile fabric G1 (*ibid.*, Fig. 52 [11.15.13]). The drawn example has rim diameter 10. The earliest occurrences are in late Eighteenth to Nineteenth Dynasty contexts.

2661 **<u>764</u>** Fig. 92e

<u>H10 (Marl A2)</u>. Fired medium. Exterior concealed by slip, interior brown where uncoated. Break brown. Fairly plentiful fine and medium well-sorted sand. Small to moderate qty fine and coarse veg to 0.4. Matrix limestone and sparse to 0.05. White slip on exterior, over rim and down 1.5 to a straight edge on interior. Not polished or burnished.

Phase	Context & No.	Grid ref	Dia rim (top)	Fig
iii	BDR **176**	08/09-06	12	92e

H14 (Marl D)

<u>765</u> Long-necked amphora (tall jar)

The rather bulbous rim and inward-sloping neck separate this form from the main series of amphorae with cylindrical or bowed neck; it represents an early version of the Egyptian amphora and an early use of the H14 fabric. At Memphis (Kom Rabia), displaying the full 'waisted' neck (dia 14), it appears in marl fabrics H14 and H1 in the early-to-mid and mid-to-late Eighteenth Dynasty respectively (Bourriau 2010, Fig. 32 [10.14.3] and Fig. 42 [10.14.8]), and at the earlier time (dia 10, with slightly differing proportions), in Nile fabric G1 (*ibid.*, Fig. 27 [10.14.4]). There is a larger example (dia 16) in G1 in the late Eighteenth to Nineteenth Dynasty (*ibid.*, Fig. 52 [10.16.10]) and the form reappears in H8 in the mid to late Nineteenth, where it may be residual (*ibid.*, Fig. 89 [10.14.19]). An even better match (dia 16), but with little preserved below the rim, is one in H2 (*ibid.*, Fig. 70 [10.14.17]), again from a mid to late Nineteenth Dynasty context, where it may also be residual.

2406A **<u>765</u>** Fig. 92f

<u>H14 (Marl D)</u>. Fired medium. Surfaces are firing surfaces: exterior white, top of rim pink, shading to interior brown. Break red-brown with thick grey-brown core. Fairly plentiful poorly sorted sand. No visible veg. Plentiful limestone, from tiny flecks to 0.1. Uncoated. Not polished or burnished.

Phase	Context & No.	Grid ref	Dia rim (top)	Fig
iii	BDP (UP 647) **301**	01 to 05-07	*c.*12	92f

<u>766</u> Amphorae (tall jars)

See H1 (**<u>734–36</u>**), and for an earlier form see **<u>765</u>**. The rim of AEP/AEQ/AER **25** (Fig. 92h) is slightly distorted, perhaps from careless handling; there is a similar but less conspicuous example in Mixed Clay Fabric 'H5' (now Mixed Clay Fabric 1) from the Saqqara tomb of Ramose (Aston D.A. and B.G. Aston, 2001, Pl. 37 [6]).

2406B **<u>766</u>** Fig. 92g–h

Two rim sherds from amphorae of slightly differing form.

<u>H14 (Marl D)</u>. Fired fairly soft. Surfaces white, probably firing surfaces. Break pale brown, BHS **235** with red core, AEP/AEQ/AER **25** shading to darker brown towards interior surface. Fairly plentiful poorly sorted sand, AEP/AEQ/AER **25** with few of the larger grains. Small qty fine veg to 0.3. Plentiful tiny limestone and sparse to 0.1. Uncoated. Not polished or burnished.

Phase	Context & No.	Grid ref	Dia rim (top)	Fig
ivc	BHS **235**	05/06-22/23	10	92g

Phase	Context & No.	Grid ref	Dia rim (top)	Fig
vi/vi/vi	AEP/AEQ/AER **25**	03-03 to 08	12	92h

767 Amphora handles

2406C **767** Not illustrated

H14 (Marl D). AIY/BET **1** fired medium, ABG **15** fairly hard. AIY/BET **1** exterior cream, probably firing surface, interior brown; ABG **15** surfaces concealed by slip. Break AIY/BET **1** pale pinkish brown with faint grey core; ABG **15** red-brown with grey core. AIY/BET **1** fairly plentiful poorly sorted sand; ABG **15** moderate qty mostly fine and medium. No visible veg. Fairly plentiful tiny limestone specks and to 0.1. AIY/BET **1** probably uncoated; ABG **15** thick white (probable self-)slip on all surfaces except back of handle at its base. AIY/BET **1** not polished or burnished, ABG **25** burnished where slipped.

Phase	Context & No.	Grid ref	Vessel part	Burnished?	Notes
ii/ii	AIY/BET **1**	10-01/02	Handle stump	No	
vi	ABG (UP 235) **15**	Area 13	Complete handle	Yes	Similar to 89b

768 Globular Jar(?)

No example of this exact combination of rounded rim and short vertical neck has been found, but the latter indicates a globular rather than a tall jar. Memphis (Kom Rabia) provides an approximate parallel in H2 in the mid to late Eighteenth Dynasty (Bourriau 2010, Fig. 43 [11.8.15]). It reappears in the mid to late Nineteenth, but may be residual (*ibid.*, Fig. 88 [11.8.15]), especially since it has not been found in the South Saqqara NK tombs.

2406D **768** Fig. 92i

H14 (Marl D). Fired fairly soft. Surfaces white. Break pale brown all through. Fairly plentiful poorly sorted sand. Small qty fine only veg to 0.3. Plentiful tiny limestone, sparse to 0.1 and one piece 0.3. Uncoated. Not polished or burnished.

Phase	Context & No.	Grid ref	Dia rim (top)	Fig
vii	AAA Lower **41**	Area 2	10	92i

769 Body sherds in H14

2406E **769** Not illustrated

Unlike the H1 series, none shows signs of reuse.

H14 (Marl D). Fired variously, from fairly soft to fairly hard. Exterior white unless concealed by slip, interior red-brown to grey. Break from red-brown, with or without grey core, to grey all through. Fairly plentiful poorly sorted sand. Sparse fine veg to 0.5, or none visible. Plentiful limestone to 0.2. Exterior either firing surface or white self-slip, sometimes firing pink wholly or in part (see table for examples most probably slipped). Some have burnished exterior (see table); others may have lost burnish due to weathering.

Phase	Context & No.	Grid ref	Burnished?	Self-slip?
o	BEN **27**	14/15-01 to S03	Yes	Yes
ii	ABN **2**	Area 13	No	Yes

Phase	Context & No.	Grid ref	Burnished?	Self-slip?
ii	ADG **9**	Area 13	No	
iii	BCB **122**	01 to 05-04/05/06	No	
iii–iva	ACE **178**	01 to 05-08 to 12	Yes	Yes
All iv (Pt II?)	ABK/S/U/V/Y/Z **4**	Area 13	Yes	Yes
iv (Pt II?)	ADF **52**	Area 13	Yes	Yes
iv (Pt II?)/?	AYQ/AYR **24**	Area 13	Yes	Yes
iva	BCP **30**	08 to 12-03 to 06	Yes	
iva/ivb	AEF/AHR **4**	10 to 14-04/05	No	
iva/ivb	BHR/BTG **54**	02-20/21	No	Yes
ivb	BKN **73**	02-21	No	
ivb/ivc	AHZ **2**	17-04	Yes	
ivc	CCK **42**	08 to 11-25/26	No	
ivd	ACM **5**	04-07	No	
ivd	CBY **3**	04/05-34	No	Yes
vi	AAH **6**	06-07	No	
vi/vi/vi	AEP/AEQ/AER **11**	02-04 to 07	No	
vi/vi/vi	AEP/AEQ/AER **18**	01/02-04 to 08	No	Yes
vii	CAA **5**	Area 26	No	
?	BNE **66**	09/10-04/05	No	

MIXED CLAY FABRIC, 770–79

Mixed Clay Fabric 1

This complex fabric was previously classified differently, first as H5 and later as G6b (see page 21).

770 Restricted bowl(?)

Although this rim sherd might derive from an unusually upright 'meat jar', an almost perfect match (albeit with diameter only 30) is provided at Qantir in the shape of a restricted bowl (Aston D.A. 1998, 535 [2189]). Even the ware (Qantir Mixed Clay Fabric III.A with burnished cream slip) is the same (*ibid.*, 68). Ramesside, probably Ramesses I to Merneptah.

1344H **770** Fig. 93a

Mixed Clay Fabric 1. Fired hard. Exterior concealed by slip, interior brown where uncoated. Break red-brown with purple core. Fairly plentiful fine and medium sand. No visible veg. Sparse limestone to 0.05. White marl slip on exterior, over rim and down interior to depth of 3.0, then splashes. Burnished where slipped.

Phase	Context & No.	Grid ref	Dia rim (top)	Fig
vii?	BFB **6**	Area 1	40	93a

771–73 Amphorae (tall jars)

See H1 (734–36). AEP/AEQ/AER **19** (Fig. 93b) is at the upper end of the size range. The bases and body forms occur in the South Saqqara tombs, among others that of Horemheb. Base BHR/AAA **3** (Fig. 93h) and the body fragments derive from the ovoid amphora form (Bourriau *et al.* 2005, Fig. 35 [182] in the same Mixed Clay Fabric 1), base BFB **46+50** (Fig. 93g) from the slender, tapering version (*ibid.*, Figs 31–32 [169/70] in Marl H1). Late Eighteenth Dynasty onwards: BFB **46+50** is of the late Eighteenth Dynasty to the reign of Ramesses II, while the type of BHR/AAA **3** begins in the reign of Ramesses II (Aston D.A. 2004b, 184–200 and pers. comm.).

Rims

2832A **771** Fig. 93b–e

Mixed Clay Fabric 1. Fired fairly hard. Exterior concealed by slip; AEP/AEQ/AER **19** interior also concealed by slip, remainder interior brown. Break red-brown to brown, AEP/AEQ/AER **19** and UP 998 **31** with grey core. Fairly plentiful fine and medium sand, some with a few coarser grains. No visible veg. Sparse limestone to 0.1, and DAF **7** also one piece 0.2. White slip on exterior and over rim, and down a varying distance inside (AEP/AEQ/AER **19** as far as preserved). All burnished, but UP 998 **31** on rim only.

Phase	Context & No	Grid ref	Dia rim (top)	Fig
v	DAF **7**	Area 2.W10-S51/S52/S53	*c.*17	As 93c
vi/vi/vi	AEP/AEQ/AER **19**	02-04 to 07	19	93b
vii	AAA (UP 38) **24**	20-03	13	93c
vii	AAA (UP 38) **135**	11 to 20-01 to 10	11	93d
vii	AAA (UP 998) **31**	Area 2	15	93e

Bodies and handles

2832C **772** Fig. 93f

Mixed Clay Fabric 1. Fired fairly hard. Exterior concealed by slip, interior red-brown to brown. Break red-brown with grey core. Fairly plentiful fine and medium sand, all except UP 998 **4** and **32** also a few larger grains. No visible veg. Sparse limestone to 0.1, DAF **5** also one piece 0.2, DAF **6** also one piece 0.3 × 0.2. White slip on exterior. Burnished, UP 998 **3** with clear vertical strokes.

Phase	Context & No.	Grid ref	Vessel part	Fig
v	DAF **5**	Area 2 W10-S51/S52/S53	Amphora handle	As 93f
v	DAF **6**	Area 2 W10-S51/S52/S53	Amphora handle	As 93f
vii	AAA (UP 998) **3**	Area 2	Amphora handle/body	93f
vii	AAA (UP 998) **4**	Area 2	Amphora handle/body	As 93f
vii	AAA (UP 998) **32**	Area 2	Amphora handle/body	As 93f

Bases

2832Ba **773A** Fig. 93g

Mixed Clay Fabric 1. Fired fairly hard. Exterior concealed by slip, interior red-brown to brown. Break brown with grey core. Fairly plentiful fine and medium sand with a few larger grains. No visible veg. Sparse limestone to 0.1, BFB **46+50** also one piece 0.3 × 0.2. White slip on exterior. Exterior burnished.

Phase	Context & No.	Grid ref	Vessel part	Fig
vii?	BFB **46+50**	Area 1	Amphora base	93g

2832Bb **773B** Fig. 93h

Mixed Clay Fabric 1. Fired fairly hard. Exterior concealed by slip, interior red-brown to brown. Break red-brown with grey core. Fairly plentiful fine and medium sand with a few larger grains. No visible veg. Sparse limestone to 0.1. White slip on exterior. Exterior burnished.

Phase	Context & No.	Grid ref	Vessel part	Fig
iva/vii	BHR/AAA **3**	W01/W02/W03-22/23/24	Amphora base	93h

774 Jar with post-firing painted decoration

The relatively uncommon form of the neck and the chequerboard pattern (which should be on the 'front' of the vessel only, though on the body it certainly reaches around as far as the handle(s)) indicate a Ramesside date; the blue colour is frit (Colin Hope, pers. comm.). For chequerboard on the neck, see the study by Martha Bell (1987, Pl. II [12], Pl. III, Pl. IV [21], Pl.V a [4]); none of these duplicates the body decoration of **774**, or (more surprisingly) the form of the funnel neck.

For post-firing decoration, see also **726/75**. For sherds reused to hold pigment, see **505/98/745.**

1310B/2832F **774** Fig. 94a–c

Various parts, almost certainly of the same large cylinder-neck jar with out-turned rim, but not all join. The decoration is postulated to be added by the necropolis workmen, using the colours and motifs of tomb walls, not by the potters.

Mixed Clay Fabric 1. Fired fairly hard, partly misfired and distorted. Exterior concealed by slip, interior red-brown. Break red-brown with thick grey core. Plentiful poorly sorted sand. Moderate qty fine veg to 0.3. More limestone than usual, mostly to 0.1 but one piece 0.5 × 0.3. Thick white to greenish white slip on exterior. Vertically burnished. Post-firing painted decoration in black, red, white and blue; chequerboard on neck; banded with motifs on body; red bands across handle.

Phase	Context & No.	Grid ref	Vessel part	Max dia rim	Fig
v	DAF **3†**	Area 2 W10-S51 to S53	Upper body	-	94a
v	DAF **8**	Area 2 W10-S51 to S53	Neck	19–21 variable	As 94a
vii	AAA (UP 445) **117★**	Area 2	Body	-	94b
vii	AAA (UP 445) **119★★**	Area 2	Body	-	94c
vii	AAA (UP 734) **2★★**	Area 2	Body	-	94c
vii	AAA (UP 998) **6+7+35+36**	Area 2	Handle & body	-	94a
vii	AAA (UP 998) **9+10+11+34†**	Area 2	Neck & upper body	19	94a
vii	AAA(UP 998) **12★**	Area 2	Body	-	94b

★ Join
★★ Join
† Join

775 Body and handle fragments from jar with post-firing painted decoration

A commoner form than **774** and could be either late Eighteenth Dynasty or Ramesside. Its association with **774** certainly favours the later date. None of the amphorae of similar type illustrated in the studies by Martha Bell (1987) or Colin Hope (1989c) incorporates the handle(s) (all of which are horizontal loops) into the decoration or even decorates the 'sides' of the vessel where the handles are located (assuming two handles only). This is also true of the post-firing-painted amphorae in the tomb of Horemheb (Bourriau *et al.*, 2005, Figs 33–34), although these have vertical handles as **775**.

For post-firing decoration, see also **726/74**. For a technical analysis of the blue pigment, see Appendix 2. For sherds reused to hold pigment, see **505/98/745.**

1310C **775** Fig. 95

Side of a large jar consisting of the lower shoulder and one handle, and a joining body sherd with little surviving paint.

Mixed Clay Fabric 1. Fired fairly hard. Exterior concealed by slip; interior red. Break red with grey core. Fairly plentiful poorly sorted sand. Moderate qty fine veg to 0.3. Sparse limestone to 0.1. Thick white slip on exterior. Burnish visible on handle only. Paint thickly applied post-firing with broad, rough strokes, both blue and red. Burial in the sand has damaged both the blue and the red areas of the design. Horizontal blue band. On the larger piece there is a horizontal blue band above the handle, below it red panels with blue infill to the left of the handle and a sweeping red line with small parts of motifs to the right of it; a crude lotus motif in blue with a red outline is focused on the lower handle join, and there are red lines across the handle.

Phase	Context & No.	Grid ref	Fig
v	DAF **1+2+4***	Area 2 W10-S51/S52/S53	95
vii	AAA (UP 998) **8***	Area 2	95

* Join

776 Large globular jars ('meat jars')

At the Anubieion, these jars also occur in marl fabric H1 (**737–39**), and the two examples of **776** are surprisingly similar to **737–38**, given the wide range of forms exhibited at Memphis (Kom Rabia) and (especially) Qantir. This might indicate contemporary productions, and even the same workshop. At Memphis, a near-perfect match is provided (in H2) in the late Eighteenth to Nineteenth Dynasty (Bourriau 2010, Fig. 54 [11.15.12]); at Ramesside Qantir among a number of very similar examples one in Marl D (Aston D.A. 1998, 483 [1813]) is perhaps the closest.

2832D **776** Fig. 96a–b

Mixed Clay Fabric 1. Fired hard. Surfaces dark grey-brown where slip lost. Break dark grey-brown. Fairly plentiful fine and medium well-sorted sand. No visible veg. Sparse limestone to 0.1. Slipped on both surfaces as far as preserved, BMG **16** fired grey, UP 445 **98** pink. Exterior burnished.

Phase	Context & No.	Grid ref	Dia rim (top)	Fig
v–vi	BMG **16**	19-S01/S02	*c.*26	96a
vii	AAA (UP 445) **144**	Area 2	28	96b

777 Small globular jar

Among the many globular jars of the NK, this simple form is surprisingly uncommon. At Memphis (Kom Rabia) the best matches are in other fabrics: with more elaborate rim, in marl fabric H1 with diameter 10

(Bourriau 2010, Figs 54 and 69 [11.15.10]), reappearing in Nile fabric G1 (*ibid.*, Fig. 84 [11.15.13]); with even less of a rim, again in G1, with diameter only 4 (*ibid.*, Fig. 67 [11.12.1]) or diameter 11 (*ibid.*, Fig. 84 [11.11.4]). At Saqqara, the tomb of Iurudef yielded a small two-handled jar in G1 with suitably small rim (dia 7) (Aston D.A. 1991, Pl. 50 [52]). The date appears to be late Eighteenth to Nineteenth Dynasty.

2832E **777** Fig. 96c

Mixed Clay Fabric 1. Fired medium. Exterior concealed by slip, interior brown. Break red-brown with faint red core. Fairly plentiful fine and medium well-sorted sand. No visible veg. Sparse limestone to 0.1. White slip on exterior, extending just over rim. Burnished where slipped.

Phase	Context & No.	Grid ref	Dia rim (top)	Fig
iva/iva/v–vi	AJW/AQH/BRR **16**	20-S01/S02	6	96c

778 Potmarks

Two pre-firing potmarks on the base area and two post-firing on the shoulder, all probably from amphorae. DAC **20** (Fig. 96f), and probably AAA **49** (Fig. 96g), are of the more ovoid type. The placing of the marks may be only a matter of convenient access: before firing, and probably after firing but before filling, the vessels would be inverted; after filling they would presumably be upright. Thus the marks near the base are more likely to relate to the vessel and the workshop, while those on the shoulder are at least equally likely to describe the contents.

It is unfortunate that none of the four is complete, but some comparisons can be made with the New Kingdom potmarks from Qantir in Barbara Ditze's typology (Ditze, 2007). A remarkably close match for the double potmark AAA **49** (Fig. 96g), was applied pre-firing to the rounded base of a 'meat jar' (Ditze, 469 [274]); both were surely intended to convey the same information, whatever that may have been. The right-hand sign, perhaps an *ankh*, is quite a good match for one similarly made, pre-firing, near the base of a jar (*ibid.*, 437 [223]); the sherd is broken on the left side, so leaving open the possibility that the same combination of signs was present. Better formed examples of an *ankh* are also found apparently standing alone (*ibid.*, 429–31, [211–14]). In Carla Gallorini's study of MK potmarks from Kahun we already find the pre-firing *ankh/nfr* sign twice, once alone and once with a second mark (a vertical stroke) alongside (Gallorini 2009, 141, Types 6.1 and 6.2). The curved sign to the left on AAA **49**, because of its simpler form, resembles more than one from Qantir, (e.g. *ibid.*, 413 [196]), but the most similar is probably one applied in combination with two dots (*ibid.*, 479 [288]); each is pre-firing and from near the base of an amphora.

There appears to be no exact match to the complex BAC **361** symbol (Fig. 96e) in Ditze's corpus, but several in her Category 'B', in all cases post-firing, come close (e.g. *ibid.*, 373 [134], 375 [136], 387 [157]); the first two are from open forms, the last from near the base of a 'meat jar'.

ACE **264** (Fig. 96d) may perhaps read *ms*, though Ditze has a similar form suspended from a loop, pre-firing, from near the base of a jar (*ibid.*, 471 [278]). Gallorini publishes a pre-firing MK *ms*(?) with the central stroke and one other extended (as at the Anubieion) and a cross-stroke to form a triangle (*ibid.*, 142, Type 7.5), and there are at least two post-firing Ramesside examples from the Valley of the Kings (Aston D.A. 2009a, 57, Fig. 7).

Although a few of the many Eighteenth Dynasty potmarks from Malkata (Hope 1999, 140–43, Figs 7–10) bear some resemblance to the Anubieion examples, none is so similar that it may with confidence be regarded as the same mark.

For a summary of all the potmarks in the present volume, see Appendix 1.

2832G **778** Fig. 96d–g

Mixed Clay Fabric 1. Fired fairly hard. Exterior concealed by slip, interior ACE **264** brown, BAC **361** grey-brown, others red-brown. Break ACE **264** brick-red and BAC **361** grey-brown all through, others red-brown with grey core. Fairly plentiful fine and medium well-sorted sand. BAC **361** moderate qty fine veg to 0.3, others none visible. ACE **264** no visible limestone, others sparse to 0.05 (BAC **361** to 0.1). Slip on exterior, ACE **264** fired greenish cream, BAC **361** grey (misfired or burnt?), DAC **20** pink, AAA **49** cream. Burnished.

Phase	Context & No.	Grid ref	Vessel part	Post-/pre-firing	Fig
iii–iva	ACE **264**	01 to 05-08 to 12	Shoulder	Post	96d
v	BAC **361**	02/03-S01	Shoulder	Post	96e
v	DAC **20**	Area 2 W06/W07-S55/S56	Amphora base	Pre	96f
vii	AAA (UP 8) **49**	*	Lower body	Pre	96g

* Not from the excavation, but a surface find a short distance north, near the excavation house

779 Body sherds in Mixed Clay Fabric 1

2408B/2832H

779 Not illustrated

Mixed Clay Fabric 1. Not recorded in detail. Burnish (see table) most frequently as vertical strokes, less often light and overall, but this was not recorded for each individual sherd.

Phase	Context & No.	Grid ref	Burnished?
o	AQG **153A**	09/10-S03/S04	No
o	BDY **42**	01/02/03-07/08	(Not recorded)
ii	AUQ **151**	08-03	Yes
ii	AUQ **194**	05/06-05	Yes
ii	BDX **15**	03/04-07	Yes
ii	BGG **18**	12 to 16-S04/S05	Yes
ii	BGG **34**	08/09/10-S02/S03	No
ii/ii	AIY/BET **7**	10-01/02	Yes
iii	BCB **44**	01 to 04-04/05/06	Yes
iii	BDP (UP 647) **129+132**	01 to 05-07	Yes
iii	BHW **128**	02-21/22	Yes
iii	BPW **3**	07-27	(Not recorded)
iii–iva	ACE **10**	05-06/07/08	Yes
iii–iva	ACE **84**	01 to 05-08 to 12	Yes
iv (Pt II?)	ARE **3**	Area 12	Yes
iv (Pt II?)/iv (Pt II?)	ADC/ADE **3**	Area 13	Yes
iv (Pt II?)/iv (Pt II?)	ADS/ARP=ARS **4**	Area 13	Uncertain
iva	AJH **6**	04/05/06-05 to 08	(Not recorded)
iva	AJH **55**	04/05/06-05 to 08	Yes
iva	AJH under AVH **47**	05-04/05/06	(Not recorded)
iva	CJN **9**	09-31/32	Yes
iva/ivb	BHR/BTG **1**	01-20/21	Yes
ivb	AAG **9**	05 to 08-08/09	Yes
ivb	CGZ East **1**	07/08-33/34/35	Yes
ivc?	DBC **31**	Area 1 29/30-S31	Yes
ivc/ivc	ACS/AUP **3**	08-S01 to S04	No
ivc–d(?)/ivd(?)	DBW/DBU **66**	Area 1 28-S31	(Not recorded)

Phase	Context & No.	Grid ref	Burnished?
ivd	CBY **1**	04/05-34	No
iv+	DAW **1**	Area 2 W11-S60	Yes
v	BJO **1**	W01/01-S01/S02	Yes
v	DAF **14, 39, 40**	Area 2 W10-S50	Yes (all)
vi	ABG (UP 235) **23**	Area 13	No
(vi)–vii	AAB **1**	24/25-06/07	No
(vi)–vii	AAB Lower **31**	28 to 34-01/02/03	Yes
Mamluk/vii	AKJ/AKI (UP 141) **25**	Area 14	Yes
vii	AAA (UP 23) **168**	10-06	No
vii	AAA **18**	Area 1	Yes
vii	AAA **76**	Area 1	Yes*
vii	AAA (UP 998) **33**	Area 2	Yes
vii?	BFB **68**	Area 1	Yes
?	BEP **136**	17/18-01/S01	Yes
?	CAL **13**	Area 26	Yes

* Hole drilled through

OASIS CLAY FABRICS, 780–82

<u>780–82</u> Transport Amphorae

The listing is in numerical order of the fabrics.

Five different fabrics originating in the Egyptian oases were identified in NK Memphis (Kom Rabia) (Bourriau 2010, 292) (not four as *ibid.*, 29–30). Bourriau previously thought one of these (P23) to be of Canaanite origin (Bourriau 1990b, 22*–23*), a view she subsequently revised (Bourriau 2002, 114) but which is still held by most students of this material (David Aston, pers. comm.). In the present volume it remains with the oasis fabrics pending resolution of the matter.

Three of the five fabrics identified at Memphis (P23, P25, P44) are represented on the Anubieion site. At Memphis all were from amphorae or flasks, mostly the former (Bourriau 2010, 29, Figs 44, 71), and present in small numbers only. The amphorae, at least, were present throughout the NK deposits; at Qantir only two fabrics were identified (Aston D.A. 1998, 73), V.01 and V.02 corresponding to P25 and P44(?) respectively, and sherds were rare.

Only <u>782</u> from near the base of the P44 amphora is distinctive enough to illustrate here. The slender body and originally round base are confirmed by a lower body from Saqqara (Aston D.A. 1991, Pl. 51 [62]) and a profile and lower body from Qantir (Aston D.A. 1998, 537 [2202/03]), all in P25 and all early Ramesside in date. The other sherds serve to signal the presence of oasis amphorae on the Anubieion site. All are likely to derive from tombs, where the vessels may have held wine (*ibid.*, 536).

2436 **<u>780</u>** Not illustrated

Amphora body sherd. Well made: finely grooved on exterior and interior from manufacture on a wheel. Small areas of black adhesions on interior, from either waterproofing or residue of contents.

<u>P23.</u> Fired medium. Surfaces reddish brown. Break reddish brown all through. Sparse red mineral inclusions to 0.1. Fairly plentiful poorly sorted sand. No visible veg. Fairly plentiful limestone to 0.15. Red (probably self-) slip. Apparent polish on exterior is probably from sand-blasting.

Phase	Context & No.	Grid ref
iii	BHW **38**	02-20/21

2882 **781** Not illustrated

Amphora body sherd, just preserving the corner of a handle join.

P25. Fired fairly hard. Exterior cream, interior pinkish brown. Break pinkish brown with cream core. No visible sand. Sparse dark mineral inclusions to 0.1. No visible veg. Moderate qty limestone, with pieces to 0.5. Uncoated. Apparent polish on exterior is probably from sand-blasting.

Phase	Context & No.	Grid ref
ii	BET **36**	12/13-02/03

2438/2740 **782** Fig. 96h

Two joining sherds from the lower body of an amphora. Deep, vertical finger impressions on the interior from pressing into a mould, and well-marked scoring around the (otherwise smooth) exterior, probably from finishing on a wheel.

P44. Fired hard. Exterior grey, interior brownish pink. Break one area pink with greenish grey core where thickest, another area brownish pink shading to blue-grey near interior surface. Moderate qty poorly sorted sand. No visible veg. Sparse black, red and pale brown mineral inclusions. Moderate qty limestone to 0.1. Probably uncoated. Not polished or burnished.

Phase	Context & No.	Grid ref	Fig
iii	BDV **1***†	11-05	96h
ivb	AFV East **1***	11-04/05	96h

* Join

† Found inside jar 78/306 inscribed in Greek (Vol I, 82), not seen by the ceramicists

IMPORTED FABRICS—CANAANITE, 783–90

783–90 Transport Amphorae

The listing is in numerical order of the fabrics.

These vessels, also known as Canaanite jars, were imported in large numbers for their contents. At Saqqara they would have been deposited, with their contents, in tombs of the richer sort. It is generally agreed (Hope 1989c, 87; Aston D.A. 1998, 635) that the form inspired that of the Egyptian NK amphorae. In Egypt they are most numerous in the area nearest to their place of origin, i.e. the Eastern Delta. At Qantir they occur in Late Bronze I–IIA (corresponding to the Eighteenth Dynasty from Ahmose to Akhenaten) (Aston D.A. 1998, 627–33 [2541–46/48/51–55/60–63]) but are also prolific, in many fabrics, in Late Bronze IIB (corresponding to the late Eighteenth and Nineteenth Dynasties) (*ibid.*, 635–63/68–77 [2567–2736/51–94]). The same pattern appears in the settlement contexts at Memphis (Kom Rabia), where they were more numerous in the Ramesside period, and especially in the reign of Ramesses II, than in the Eighteenth Dynasty (Janine Bourriau, pers. comm.). These imported fabrics were not catered for by the Vienna System, but many can be equated with the Saqqara/Memphis series (Aston D.A. 1998, 69–71).

The probable places of origin of the five on the Anubieion site have recently been identified (Smith *et al.* 2004, 73, some slightly revised from Bourriau *et al.* 2001, 140–43). P16 is from the Akkar Plain region, P30 from the seaward portion of the Jezreel Valley, west of Affule, P31 from the coastal plain in the Carmel region, P33 from the Lebanese coastal plain and P40 from the region around Ugarit.

783–84 Body sherds in Fabric P16

P16 is Qantir Fabric IV.07.04, not present before LB IIB (Aston D.A. 1998, 69–70, 638). These two fragments signal its presence but are not distinctive enough to illustrate.

2434 **783** Not illustrated

Fairly thin body sherd, finely grooved on exterior and interior from manufacture on a wheel.

P16. Fired medium. Surfaces brownish orange. Break brownish orange all through. Fairly plentiful poorly sorted sand. Sparse larger dark and red mineral inclusions to 0.1, identified (Bourriau *et al.* 2001, 125) as igneous (volcanic) rock. No visible veg. Very sparse limestone to 0.05. Uncoated. Not polished or burnished.

Phase	Context & No.	Grid ref
v/v	BJG/BJO(H) **43**	W01/W02/01/02/03-S01/S02/S03

2884 **784** Not illustrated

Almost flat body sherd with no features. Beginning to laminate, due to weathering.

P16. Fired fairly soft. Exterior white, interior pale pinkish orange. Break, thin zones coloured as surfaces and thick grey core. Fairly plentiful clear, grey, brown and red-brown mineral fragments to 0.1. No visible veg. Limestone pieces 0.1, 0.2 and 1.0 × 1.5(!) visible. Smoothed but uncoated. Not polished or burnished.

Phase	Context & No.	Grid ref
?	UP 19 **56**	Area 12

785–86 Upper part of vessel, base and sherds in Fabric P30

P30 is Qantir Fabric IV.07.05, not present before LB IIB (Aston D.A. 1998, 69–70, 640). The flat shoulder of **785** is also characteristic of LB IIB (and later) periods; shoulder AIY **118** of **786** appears to derive from a similar form. No close parallel to the rim has been found among the published tomb groups from Saqqara, but a similarly flat shoulder and body are illustrated from the Saqqara tomb of Horemheb (Bourriau *et al.* 2005, Fig. 39 [192]) as one of many examples in Fabric P11. At Qantir there are many in P30 with rim forms similar to **785** (Aston D.A. 1998, 643 [2604–28, especially 2618]); in addition, a fabric (IV.07.06) not equated with any at Saqqara/Memphis has several examples, including one close match (*ibid.*, 647 [2637]). The body of **785** may have been drawn too upright. Probably Nineteenth Dynasty.

Base UP 588 **379** of **786** (Fig. 97b) is characteristic of Levantine jars in many fabrics at Qantir (e.g. in P30 *ibid.*, 645 [2629–31]) so is not distinctive enough to provide a close date, though the Nineteenth Dynasty is again likely.

2838 **785** Fig. 97a

Rim, shoulder and body with lower stump of handle, apparently all from a single jar, but do not join.

P30. Fired medium. Exterior mostly red but shading to cream on and around the handle stump, and some other areas mottled; interior pale yellow-brown shading to brownish red near the rim. Break exterior half brownish red, interior half grey. Fairly plentiful clear, grey and white (limestone?) grits to 0.05. No visible veg. Uncoated. Not polished or burnished.

Phase	Context & No.	Grid ref	Vessel part	Dia rim (top)	Fig
iii	CHZ **6**	09-30/31/32	Shoulder	-	97a
iii	CHZ **7+8+9+11+12**	09-30/31/32	Body and stump	-	97a
iii	CIA **5**	01 to 05-3132/33	Rim	10	97a

2440 **786** Fig. 97b

Thick, heavy base UP 588 **379** (Fig. 97b), preserved all round at the bottom, but otherwise only in part. Deep grooves on interior, from manufacture on a wheel. Three body sherds: DAM **1** probably from near base of a thinner-walled vessel; AIY **118** from almost flat shoulder with sharp angle to body wall; AQG **296** probably from similar position. None is from the 785 vessel.

P30. Fired medium, with bicoloured break: interior half and surface grey; exterior half and surface, shades of brown or red-brown. Plentiful poorly sorted sand or similar gritty inclusions. No visible veg. Sparse limestone to 0.1 (base UP 588 **379** to 0.3). Possibly self-slipped, but no coloured slips. Not polished or burnished. AQG **296** interior thickly lime-coated, probably from reuse of sherd.

Phase	Context & No.	Grid ref	Vessel part	Dia base	Fig
o	AQG **296**	18/19/20-S04/S05	Shoulder(?)	-	
ii	AIY **118**	05 to 08-04/05/06	Shoulder	-	
ii	DAM **1**	Area 2 W09-S52	Base fragment	?	
vii	AAA (UP 588) **379**	01/W01 to W04-18 to 23	Base	6	97b

787 Rim and body sherd in Fabric P31

P31 is Qantir Fabric IV.07.10 (Aston D.A. 1998, 69–71, 652), previously thought not to be present before the Ramesside period (LB IIB) but now believed to begin in the Eighteenth Dynasty (Aston 2004a, 176–78). At both Memphis (Kom Rabia) and Saqqara, rims in various fabrics, including P31, bear a general resemblance to BGI **10** (Fig. 97c) but many have a collar around the neck and none is closely similar; the best match for the form is probably in P11, from the tomb of Horemheb (Bourriau *et al.* 2005, Fig. 39 [192], already referred to (above)). At Qantir, on the other hand, there are many to chose from, again in several fabrics, with some fairly close matches to the form (Aston D.A. 1998, 637 [2577] in P39; 639 [2591] in P16; 643 [2618/23] in P30; 653 [2670/73] in P31 itself).

2416 **787** Fig. 97c–d

The two sherds are unlikely to be from the same vessel, the body being altogether thicker and the surface colours lighter. The tall, thin-walled rim is a relatively uncommon form; the body sherd preserves three shallow, horizontal grooves on exterior, similar to the grooves on some Egyptian marl jars of the eighth and seventh centuries BC; it is not possible to know which way up it was and the drawn stance is approximate.

P31. Fired fairly hard. Exterior red-brown, interior grey. Break grey with thin red-brown zone close to exterior. Moderate qty fine colourless grits, perhaps sand. Some voids to 0.2, some apparently from fine veg, others perhaps from inclusions disturbed when the clay was turned on a wheel. Fairly plentiful limestone to 0.1. Exterior appears to be self-slipped. Not polished or burnished.

Phase	Context & No.	Grid ref	Dia rim (top)	Fig
ivc	CGN **2**	06-33 to 37	-	97c
ivd	BGI **10**	12-02/03	10	97d

788 Body sherd in Fabric P33

P33 is Qantir Fabric IV.07.07, in use from LB I to at least Iron 1 (Aston D.A. 1998, 69–70, 630/48/80). As with P16 (above), the sherd signals the presence of this fabric on the Anubieion site but is not distinctive enough to illustrate.

2442 788 Not illustrated

Body sherd, with almost smooth surfaces.

P33. Fired medium to fairly hard. Surfaces cream with a brownish tinge. Break pale brown with grey core. Fairly plentiful clear and dark inclusions, various minerals, sizes as if poorly sorted sand. No visible veg. Moderate qty limestone to 0.1. Perhaps self-slipped, but no coloured slip. Not polished or burnished.

Phase	Context & No.	Grid ref
ivc–d(?)/ivd(?)	DBW/DBU **62**	Area 1 28-S31

789 Body sherds, one with handle, in Fabric P40

P40 is Qantir Fabric IV.07.09, not present before LB IIB but continuing into Iron I (Aston D.A. 1998, 69–70, 650/80). At Memphis (Kom Rabia) the shoulder forms are more rounded than UP 588 **280** (Fig. 97f) until level IIIa of the late Eighteenth to Nineteenth Dynasty, when a carinated shoulder begins to be evident (Bourriau 2010, Fig. 59 [d]). Thereafter, the carination becomes much more marked and the body flatter (*ibid.*, Fig. 76 [e–g]). Too little of UP 588 **280** survives for any but a tentative date, but the late Eighteenth to (early?) Nineteenth Dynasty looks the most likely.

2444 789 Fig. 97f

Two sherds possibly of same vessel but the contexts are widely separated. On the interior, UP 588 **280** is lightly but ADC **53** fairly heavily ribbed.

P40. Fired very hard. ADC **53** exterior brown, interior pale reddish brown, UP 588 **280** exterior pink, interior grey. Break, ADC **53** reddish brown, UP 588 **280** exterior half pink, interior half grey. Fairly plentiful poorly sorted sand. No visible veg. UP 588 **280** moderate qty limestone to 0.2, also appearing on exterior surface, ADC **53** smaller qty and to 0.1 only. ADC **53** has a probable reddish-brown slip on the exterior, UP 588 **280** appears to be uncoated. Not polished or burnished. UP 588 **280** had plaster adhering to the inner surface when found, probably from reuse of the sherd, which could be held conveniently by the handle.

Phase	Context & No.	Grid ref	Vessel part	Fig
iv (Pt II?)	ADC **53**	Area 13	Body sherd	
vii	AAA (UP 588) **280**	03/04-25/26	Vertical handle on body sherd	97f

790 Rim and neck in a Canaanite(?) fabric

The fabric appears to be of foreign origin but cannot be matched to any known. The form is of a Levantine amphora, for example one of LB IIB date at Qantir (Aston D.A. 1998, 669, [2760]). The rim form was much imitated by Egyptian potters (Aston D.A. 2008, Pl. 60 [1208]), though sometimes with a more sloping stance (*ibid.*, Pl. 18 [365]), and is common in the Ramesside period. The earliest occurrence at Memphis (Kom Rabia) is in marl fabric H14 in the early to mid Eighteenth Dynasty (Bourriau 2010, Fig. 32 [10.8.2]). In the Levant the form continues well into the first millennium BC (Sabine Laemmel, pers. comm.), as do the Egyptian copies (David Aston, pers. comm.).

2644 **790** Fig. 97e

Import(?) Fired fairly hard. Surfaces orange-brown. Break orange-brown all through. Fairly plentiful fine well-sorted sand. No visible veg. Fairly plentiful limestone to 0.05. Sparse to fairly plentiful very fine mineral fragments: grey-white, red-brown, dark. Perhaps self-slipped but no coloured slip. Not polished or burnished.

Phase	Context & No.	Grid ref	Dia rim (top)	Fig
vi/vi	ABF/ABG (UP 123) **8**	Area 13	*c.*10	97e

IMPORTED FABRICS—CYPRIOT, 791–96

Small pottery vessels of 'Cypriot' origin were not uncommon in the Saqqara necropolis, to judge by sherds visible on the surface, but unless fairly complete may often have escaped the attention of excavators. Small closed forms containing precious liquids were presumably deposited in tombs for their contents; it is less obvious why open forms should be present, except as exotic objects in their own right.

For the identification of the Cypriot sherds, and for information on origin, dating, etc., the author is indebted to Kathryn Eriksson, who is preparing the Cypriot pottery from Memphis (Kom Rabia) for publication.

Red Lustrous Ware

791–92

Both hand- and wheel-made vessels are found in this ware. **791** appears from the pull-marks in the neck to have been wheel-made, and the body sherds **792** (and **793**) are all thin, of uniform thickness, with parallel, regular, light smoothing marks, so may also have been wheel-made. The neck and handle fragment **791** is from a small restricted form, apparently of pilgrim flask type, though a possible candidate is a spindle bottle from a Saqqara tomb (Aston B.G. 2005, Pl. 126 [127]), and the body sherds **792** (and **793**) are from bowls; all of these are relatively rare in Egypt. The place of origin is not necessarily Cyprus itself, North Syria and Cilicia being other possible candidates (Eriksson 1991, 81–96, with references). In Egypt proper, Red Lustrous Ware does not occur after Amenhotep III, though in Sinai and elsewhere in the Levant it continues into the Ramesside period, presumably reflecting a change in patterns of trade.

2550 **791** Fig. 98a

Upper part of one handle, and segment of neck. Grooves surviving on interior of neck are not horizontal but at about 45 degrees, where the neck was pulled up sharply during manufacture. Heavily weathered from exposure on the surface.

P32. Fired medium. Break and (weathered) surfaces uniform brownish pink. Plentiful light-coloured grits, mostly extremely small; a few larger but still under 0.05. No visible veg. Sparse limestone (?) to 0.05. Small areas of slightly darker brownish colour on the surface may preserve the original shade, but no original surface finish survives.

Phase	Context & No.	Grid ref	Neck dia	Fig
ivd	ATZ **29**	22/23-01/02	ca 3(?)	98a

2910A **792** Not illustrated

Two thin body sherds slightly curved in both dimensions. Form, slip and polish indicate shallow bowls.

P32. Fired medium. UP 23 **383** surfaces salmon pink where slip lost, UP 23 **394** surfaces concealed by slip. Break salmon pink, shading to a brown core. Small qty tiny dark rock particles. Sparse red mineral fragments to 0.05. No visible veg. UP 23 **383** sparse limestone to 0.1, UP 23 **394** none visible. Red slip on both surfaces. Both surfaces polished.

Phase	**Context & No.**	**Grid ref**
vii	AAA (UP 23) **383**	04-09
vii	AAA (UP 23) **394**	09-05

Ware similar to Red Lustrous

793

Body sherd from a bowl, very possibly 'Cypriot' but rather too coarse to be Red Lustrous Ware and perhaps of later date (Kathryn Eriksson, pers. comm.)

2910B **793** Not illustrated

Fairly thin body sherd, slightly curved in both dimensions. Form, slip and polish indicate a shallow bowl.

Cypriot Ware(?). Fired medium. Exterior concealed by slip, interior salmon pink where slip lost. Break salmon pink shading to a brown core. Fairly plentiful tiny dark rock particles. Sparse red mineral fragments to 0.1. No visible veg. Plentiful tiny limestone particles, and sparse to 0.1. Red slip on both surfaces. Both surfaces polished.

Phase	**Context & No.**	**Grid ref**
iva/ivb	BPT/BKN **1**	03-21

Base Ring Ware

794–96

This ware is handmade but with skilful use of turntables (Vaughan 1991, 119–30, with references). **794/95** (Fig. 98b–c) are probably Base Ring I; **796** (Fig. 98d) is Base Ring II. **794** is the neck and rim of a double juglet, on the rim of which is the broken link to its counterpart; many examples have been found in Egypt, including Saqqara. They are less common in Cyprus and may have been made specifically for export, principally to Egypt and Palestine.

When production of this ware started is the subject of lively debate among specialists, with one school favouring an early beginning in the SIP and the other a later one, in or just before the reign of Tuthmosis III. David Aston has recently summarised the competing views (Aston D.A. 2007, with references).

Examples (probably single not double juglets) in surface debris around two Saqqara tombs (Bourriau and D.A. Aston 1985, Pl. 37 [100]; Bourriau *et al.* 2005, Fig. 35 [191]), are from an area where most sherds are rather later in the Eighteenth Dynasty. From the 'Teti Cemetery', at the northern end of the Anubieion enclosure, come a single and a double juglet in Base Ring I ware published as early to mid Eighteenth Dynasty (Sowada 1999, Pls 28 and 53 [TNE94:96/97]) and a single juglet in Base Ring II published as mid Eighteenth (*ibid.*, Pls 28 and 53 [TNE95:148]). **795** preserves half the circumference of a small closed form, probably a juglet but with no surviving handle scar, of the same date as **794**. **796** is from a bowl with a high foot and a 'wish-bone' handle (Eriksson 1993, 123 and Fig. 35 [22]) and dates from the mid Eighteenth to the Nineteenth Dynasty.

1327 **794** Fig. 98b

Horizontal pre-firing slash across half the diameter of the neck, on the side furthest from the join.

P7. Fired fairly hard. Exterior concealed by slip, interior grey. Break grey all through. Sparse sharp-edged grey mineral inclusions. Fairly plentiful limestone to 0.1, and one piece 0.4 × 0.3, with pieces often breaking the surface. No visible veg. Orange-brown (probably self-) slip on exterior, with grey areas. Exterior lightly polished.

Phase	Context & No.	Grid ref	Dia rim (top)	Fig
vii	AAA (UP 157) **147**	08-11/12	2.5	98b

1328A **795** Fig. 98c

On interior, thickening and fingermarks where a separately made neck was attached.

P7. Fired fairly hard. Exterior pale brown where slip lost, interior grey. Break, interior two-thirds grey, exterior third pale brown. Fairly plentiful limestone to 0.1, much of it breaking the surface. Sparse grey and white sharp mineral particles to 0.1. No visible veg. Brown (probably self-) slip on exterior. Exterior polished.

Phase	Context & No.	Grid ref	Fig
vii	AAA (UP 108) **38**	29/30/31-S03/S04/S05	98c

2494 **796** Fig. 98d

Tiny, thin rim sherd. Slight, irregular groove on exterior near rim.

P7. Fired fairly hard. Surfaces concealed by slip(?). Break red with grey zone near exterior. Plentiful tiny dark mineral particles. No visible veg. Fairly plentiful limestone to 0.1. Clay is dense in spite of the numerous inclusions. Probable self-slip, exterior grey, interior grey at rim, shading to brownish red at lower break. Low overall polish on exterior, extending just over the rim.

Phase	Context & No.	Grid ref	Dia rim (top)	Fig
ivd	ASX **16**	04/05-S04/S05/S06	13–17	98d

IMPORTED FABRIC—MYCENAEAN, 797–802

P4

797–802 Stirrup jars and other small closed forms

Fragments of small Mycenaean closed forms are common in the élite Saqqara tombs (Hankey and D.A. Aston 1995) and surprisingly frequent in modest domestic contexts at Memphis (Kom Rabia) (Bourriau 2010, Tables 9–12). The ware, the distinctive nature of which no doubt promotes a high recovery rate, is everywhere referred to as P4, without sub-division. The Saqqara tomb fragments are mostly from stirrup jars and in many cases attributed to Furumark shapes (FS) 178–80/82 of LH III B1/2 (Furumark 1941).

The Anubieion fragments are too small for confident attribution, but some tentative identifications have been made by specialist colleagues, to whom the author extends his thanks. **797** (Fig. 98e) is from a mainland fabric stirrup jar, perhaps FS 178, dated LH IIIA2–B (Vronwy Hankey†), LH IIIB (Professor Basil Hennesey). **798** (Fig. 98f) a stirrup jar shoulder, LH IIIA2, equivalent to the Amarna Period (Kathryn Eriksson). **799** (Fig. 98g–j) stirrup jars, LH IIIA–B or possibly C (Kathryn Eriksson). **800** (Fig. 98k) restricted form, red slip unusual but known, LH III (Kathryn Eriksson). **801** (Fig. 98l) from near the base (or neck?) of a restricted form, LH III (Kathryn Eriksson). **802** (Fig. 98m) LH III (Sabine Laemmel).

The date of the transition from LH IIIA2 to LH IIIB has been variously placed between the reign of Tutankhamun and that of Seti I. However, a recent reassessment (Aston D.A. 2011b) based on the evidence from Gurob and Saqqara, prefers a date in the reign of Ramesses II. The Anubieion fragments cannot contribute to this debate but most can be said to belong to the late Eighteenth or early Nineteenth Dynasty.

1329A **797** Fig. 98e

Thin-walled sherd from the lower body of an angular or squat globular stirrup jar.

P4. Mainland fabric. Fired medium, tending to split parallel to the surfaces (cf CBS **37** of **801**). Exterior pale grey where unpainted, very pale yellow-brown where paint lost. Interior pinkish white. Break pink shading to pale grey near exterior. Moderate qty tiny dark grits and sparse to 0.05. No visible veg. No visible limestone. Self-slip(?) on exterior only. Exterior polished. Painted decoration on exterior, dark brown bands, showing red where paint thinnest, of various widths and variously spaced. Some bands weathered off, leaving only evidence from surface colour difference.

Phase	Context & No.	Grid ref	Max dia body	Fig
vii	AAA (UP 8) **19**	Area 12	*c.*16	98e

2536 **798** Fig. 98f

P4. Fired fairly hard. Surfaces cream. Break pale grey all through. Sparse pale pink mineral fragments to 0.05. No visible veg. No visible limestone. Self-slip(?) on exterior only. Exterior polished. Painted decoration on exterior, of thin pale red-brown bands, partly weathered off.

Phase	Context & No.	Grid ref	Fig
iva	BHR **40**	01-20/21	98f

2540 **799** Fig. 98g–j

Thin-walled body sherds, all very similar but probably (from context location) from two different stirrup jars. ADF **1+2** includes the upturn to a neck (rather than the downturn to a base). The interior of ADF **5** has a thick coating of black pitch-like material, apparently contents; the remainder have a powdery pale brown coating, which, except on BDY **19** where it is thinner, obscures any wheel marks and is probably from contents (oil?) reacting with the clay (Aston B.G. 2005, 117).

P4. Fired fairly soft. Exterior concealed by slip; interior by contents. Break BDY **19** and ADF **5** cream, remainder cream shading to pale pink near interior surface. Moderate qty tiny dark grits. No visible veg. No visible limestone. BDY **19** weathered where not painted, remainder cream to pinkish cream (self-?) slip on exterior. BDY **19** has gloss on paint, otherwise weathered; remainder polished on both painted and unpainted areas. Decorated with painted bands. ADF **1+2** has a single band 1.0 wide, most paint lost but traces perhaps red; ADF **3** small area grey; ADF **4** two bands red-brown of varying shade; ADF **5** two bands well apart, one dark brown 0.5 wide consisting of three close parallel lines of equal width, the other grey 1.2 wide to break (partly lost); BDY **19** grey area 0.8 wide, part of a band. ADF **1+2** bands align with single wheel ridge visible on interior, and with base of neck; ADF **5** bands align with wheel scratches on exterior; ADF **4** small diameter bands do not align with wheel scratches and may not be from the circumference but from a smaller motif.

Phase	Context & No.	Grid ref	Fig
o	BDY **19**	01/02/03-07/08	98g
iv (Pt II?)	ADF **1+2★**	Area 13	98h
iv (Pt II?)	ADF **3★**	Area 13	
iv (Pt II?)	ADF **4★**	Area 13	98i
iv (Pt II?)	ADF **5★**	Area 13	98j

★ Do not join but probably same vessel

2548 **800** Fig. 98k

Fine wheel ridges on interior.

P4. Exterior concealed by slip(?), interior pale, slightly pinkish, brown. Break pale pinkish brown shading to darker brown near exterior surface. Fairly plentiful tiny dark grits. No visible veg. One clear smooth sand-like inclusion 0.1 visible. Thick dark red-brown (self-?) slip on exterior, with small irregularly shaped black areas; interior uncoated. Exterior polished.

Phase	Context & No.	Grid ref	Fig
v	BAC **387**	02/03-S01	98k

2546 **801** Fig. 98l

P4. Fired medium, tending to split parallel to the surfaces (cf **797**). Exterior pale pinkish brown; interior pink. Break exterior half pink, interior half greenish cream, Fairly plentiful tiny dark grits. No visible veg. Sparse limestone to 0.05. Self-slip(?) on exterior only. Exterior polished. Painted decoration on exterior, of narrow criss-crossing dark brown and red-brown lines, approx parallel to the wheel marks. The colour difference is probably due only to paint thickness, and the thinner lines to individual fibres of a brush.

Phase	Context & No.	Grid ref	Fig
v–vi	CBS **37**	04/05-30/31/32	98l

1329B **802** Fig. 98m

Small body sherd similar to **797** but thicker wall and denser clay.

P4(?). Fired medium. Surfaces pale grey. Break dark grey where not weathered, otherwise pale grey. Sparse tiny dark grits. No visible veg. No visible limestone. Self-slip(?) on exterior only. Painted decoration on exterior, of a single dark brown band parallel to the wheel marks, showing red-brown in a narrow strip along each edge, where paint thinner. Exterior polished.

Phase	Context & No.	Grid ref	Fig
iii	BCB **163**	01 to 05-04/05/06	98m

IMPORTED FABRICS OF UNKNOWN ORIGIN, 803–04

803–04 Body sherds of sharply carinated restricted-form vessels

These two body sherds are of a similar fabric but unlikely to be from the same vessel because of the probable slip on **804** (Fig 98o); they were also found some distance apart. They appear to be of Bronze Age rather than Iron Age date and may be from the Mycenaean world but **803** (Fig. 98n), at least, not from Mycenae because painted without a coloured slip. In each case the pale colour of the interior should exclude a pilgrim flask and require a vessel with a larger opening, presumably a jar; **804** is probably too large to be from a lagynos (Kathryn Eriksson and Sabine Laemmel, pers. comm.).

2542 **803** Fig. 98n

Unclassified import. Fired medium. Surfaces pale brown. Break pale brown all through. Plentiful tiny dark grits. Sparse sand-like grains to 0.05. No visible veg. Sparse red mineral fragments to 0.05. Sparse tiny limestone(?) fragments. Possible thin self-slip on exterior but no coloured slip. Painted decoration on exterior, of two horizontal brownish red bands, one darker coloured than the other, parallel to the wheel marks. Traces of polish on painted areas only, but unclear whether originally overall, or paint gloss.

Phase	Context & No.	Grid ref	Fig
ivc	AAD (UP 409) **36**	05/06/07-06	98n

2538 **804** Fig. 98o

Two joining body sherds from the central area of a large, carinated, restricted-form vessel, probably a jar rather than a 'pilgrim flask' because of the pale colour of the interior. Wheel ridges on the interior demonstrate the upper and lower halves were thrown as a unit on the wheel, not thrown separately or moulded. Thin pale brown deposit on interior possibly from contents.

Unclassified import. Fired medium. Surfaces pale brown, exterior where slip or paint lost. Break pale brown. Fairly plentiful fine and medium well-sorted sand, or similar material. No visible veg. Sparse limestone to 0.05. Creamy white surface, probably a slip, survives on one area of exterior where neither painted nor weathered; interior uncoated. Exterior polished where paint or slip survives. Painted decoration on exterior: four bands on one side of carination, trace of one on other side, of various widths and variously spaced. One band is red, remainder brownish red, colour difference probably due to paint thickness only.

Phase	Context & No.	Grid ref	Fig
v–vi	CBQ **14***	02 to 06-34 to 37	98o
v–vi	CBQ **82***	02 to 06-35/36	98o

* Join

APPENDIX 1

The Potmarks

Disregarding cuts in rims, the Anubieion produced only 13 potmarks in the timespan covered in the present volume. One is attributed to the Archaic period, four to the Middle Kingdom and eight to the New Kingdom. Since any such marks noticed would certainly have been recorded, they must have constituted a tiny percentage of all the sherds excavated from these periods (though the policy of not washing the sherds may have led to the loss of some others). David Aston has similarly pointed out the apparent scarcity of these marks in published excavations, that at the best documented New Kingdom settlement sites—Amarna, Malkata and Qantir—(to which one should now add Memphis (Kom Rabia)) they are, relatively speaking, exceedingly rare, and that this is also true of the major New Kingdom cemeteries such as Gurob, Saqqara and Amarna (Aston D.A. 2009a, 52).

The Anubieion potmarks are unusual in that only six were incised before firing; one of the Middle Kingdom being painted on and six incised post-firing. Post-firing marks tend to be much shallower and care has been taken to exclude apparently random scratches both ancient and modern.

In the present volume it was not intended to research all possible parallels or to comment at length on the interpretation of the marks, on which there is an extensive literature. In any case, most of the Anubieion examples are incomplete and can be restored as more than one form.

The complete catalogue is as follows:

Period	Series No.	No.	Type	Fig.
Archaic	7	2895	Pre-firing	11
Middle Kingdom	453	2883	Post-firing	57a
Ditto	477	2262B	Painted	59f
Ditto	478	2262C (AJY/AQH **11**)	Pre-firing	59g
Ditto	478	2262C (ATY **199**)	Pre-firing	59h
New Kingdom	678	2836A	Pre-firing	83d
Ditto	679	2836B (AUQ **6**)	Post-firing	83e
Ditto	679	2836B (CBU **23**)	Post-firing	83f
Ditto	762	2885	Post-firing	92c
Ditto	778	2832G (ACE **234**)	Post-firing	96d
Ditto	778	2832G (BAC **361**)	Post-firing	96e
Ditto	778	2832G (DAC **20**)	Pre-firing	96f
Ditto	778	2832G (AAA **49**)	Pre-firing	96g

APPENDIX 2

Technical Analysis of Blue Pigment

A sample of approximately one gram of blue colour from **775** (DAF 1+2+4) was analysed by William Jay of Monash University as part of an investigation under the supervision of Associate Professor Colin Hope into pigment manufacture and exploitation in the Western Desert of Egypt. The mineralogy was determined by Raman spectroscopy (Department of Chemistry) and the elemental analyses were conducted using an EDS facility fitted to a Focussed Ion Beam microscope (Monash Centre for Electron Microscopy). The sample proved to contain cuproriviate, wollastonite and several copper minerals including pseudomalachite, malachite, chalconatronite and connellite and had been manufactured under reducing conditions at approximately 950 degrees centigrade. These results are consistent with previous analyses of Egyptian blue pigment.

APPENDIX 3

Anubieion Pottery at Giza for Field-School Teaching

The following sherds were transferred to Ancient Egypt Research Associates at Giza for use in field-school teaching. Except where stated, all examples included in the number were transferred.

- *Archaic Period* **1, 4, 6, 8, 9, 12–18, 20**

- *Old Kingdom* **70, 110, 132, 171–176, 198, 204–14/17/18/41–43/63/64/67–77/81–94**, **326/38/43/45/47/49/52/54/55/57–61/63–70/71** (except ARP **2**, AAA (UP 445) **1** and **94**, AAA Upper 8)

- *Middle Kingdom* **382/83/90–92/94/96** (ADS/ARP **7** and **8**, BDY **22** only), **397** (BJJ **88** and **141**, BDR/BCP **9**, AJY **158**, BET **80**, BJS i **9**, ADS/ARP **10** only), **416/30/55/59/62/63/66/67/71/72/82**

- *New Kingdom* **483, 506/10/19/36** (AJY/AQH **1+4** +AJY/AVB **52** and AQR/AUQ **6** +AON **2** only), **571/90** (ADU (NE) **2** and ATY **28** only), **598** (AUQ **197** and BJG(A) **10** only), **609** (UP 588 **454+455** only), **617–19** (AJY/AVB **43**+AQG **249**, BGG **104** only), **626/36/44/45/47–49/51** (except UP 588 **406**), **653/70/71**, **702/15/27/33/52/55/56/59/63/74** (except DAF **8**), **775/81/85–89/91–804**

Bibliography

Adams, B. and R. F. Friedman, 1992. Imports and Influences in the Predynastic and Protodynastic Settlement and Funerary Assemblages at Hierakonpolis, in E.C.M. van den Brink (ed.) *The Nile Delta in Transition: 4th.–3rd. Millennium* B.C. Tel Aviv, 317–38.

Adams, M.J., 2009. The Naqada III–First Intermediate Period Stratification at Mendes 1999–2005, in D. Redford (ed.) *Delta Reports (research in Lower Egypt)*. Vol. I. Oxford and Oakville, 121–206.

Allen, S.J., 1997. Spinning Bowls: Representation and Reality, in J. Phillips *et al.*(eds) *Ancient Egypt, the Aegean and the Near East. Studies in Honour of Martha Rhoads Bell.* Vol. I. Van Siclen, 17–38.

Allen, S.J., 2006. Miniature and model vessels in Ancient Egypt, in M. Bárta (ed.), *The Old Kingdom Art and Archaeology*, Prague 2006, 19–24.

Allen, S.J., unpublished. Corpus of forms from Lisht North.

Arnold, Do., 1982. Keramikbearbeitung in Dahschur, 1976–81, *MDAIK 38*, 25–65.

Arnold, Do., 1988. Pottery, in Di. Arnold, *The South Cemeteries of Lisht I. The Pyramid of Senwosret I.* (MMA Egyptian Expedition XXII). New York, 106–46.

Arnold, Do., 1991. Ägyptische Mergeltone ('Wüstentone') und die Herkunft einer Mergeltonware des Mittleren Reiches aus der Gegend von Memphis, in Do. Arnold (ed.) *Studien zur altagyptischen Keramik.* DAIK. Philipp von Zabern, Mainz am Rhein, 167–91.

Arnold, Do., 1993. Techniques and Traditions of Manufacture in the Pottery of Ancient Egypt, in Do. Arnold and J. Bourriau (eds) *An Introduction to Ancient Egyptian Pottery.* Fascicle I. (DAIK Sonderschrift 17). DAIK. Philipp von Zabern, Mainz am Rhein.

Arnold, Do., unpublished. Corpus of Forms from Dahshur.

Arnold Do. and J. Bourriau (eds), 1993. *An Introduction to Ancient Egyptian Pottery.* (DAIK Sonderschrift 17). DAIK. Philipp von Zabern, Mainz am Rhein.

Aston, B.G., 2005. The Pottery, in M.J. Raven *et al.*, *The Tomb of Pay and Raia at Saqqara.* National Museum of Antiquities Leiden and EES, London and Leiden, 94–128.

Aston, B.G., 2011. The Pottery, in M.J. Raven, V. Verschoor, M. Vugts and R. van Walsem, *The Memphite Tomb of Horemheb* V. Brepols, Turnhout, Belgium, 191–303.

Aston, D.A., 1989. Ancient Egyptian "Fire Dogs"– A New Interpretation, *MDAIK 45*, 27–32.

Aston, D.A., 1991. Pottery, in M.J. Raven, *The Tomb of Iurudef: a Memphite Official in the Reign of Ramesses II.* (EES Excavation Memoir 57). EES and National Museum of Antiquities Leiden, London and Leiden, 47–54.

Aston, D.A., 1996. *Egyptian Pottery of the Late New Kingdom and Third Intermediate Period (Twelfth to Seventh Centuries* B.C.*).* (SAGA Band 13). Heidelberger Orientverlag, Heidelberg.

Aston, D.A., 1997. The pottery, in G.T. Martin, *The Tomb of Tia and Tia.* (EES Excavation Memoir 58). EES, London, 83–102.

Aston, D.A., 1998. *Die Keramik des Grabungsplatzes Q1*, Teil 1, *Corpus of Fabrics, Wares and Shapes.* (Die Grabungen des Pelizaeus-Museums Hildesheim in Qantir–Pi-Ramesse, Band 1). Philipp von Zabern, Mainz am Rhein.

Aston, D.A., 1999. *Elephantine XIX. Pottery from the Late New Kingdom to the Early Ptolemaic Period.* (AV 92). DAIK. Philipp von Zabern, Mainz am Rhein.

Aston, D.A., 2003. New Kingdom pottery phases as revealed through well-dated tomb contexts, in M. Bietak (ed.), *The Synchronisation of Civilisations in the Eastern Mediterranean in the Second Millennium* B.C. Vol. II. (Contributions to the Chronology of the Eastern Mediterranean Vol. IV). ÖAW Vienna, 135–62.

Aston, D.A., 2004a. Amphorae in New Kingdom Egypt. Ä&L XIV, 175–213.

Aston, D.A., 2004b. *Tell el-Dab'a XII: Late Middle Kingdom and Second Intermediate Period Pottery.* (UZK XXIII). ÖAW, Vienna.

Aston, D.A., 2007. Kom Rabia, Ezbet Helmi and Saqqara NK 3507: a study in cross dating, in M. Bietak & E. Czerny (eds), *The Synchronisation of Civilisations in the Eastern Mediterranean in the Second Millennium* B.C. Vol. III. (Contributions to the Chronology of the Eastern Mediterranean Vol. IX). ÖAW, Vienna, 207–48.

Aston, D.A., 2008. *Untersuchungen im Totentempel des Merenptah in Theben.* Band IV: *The Pottery.* (*Beiträge zur*

Ägyptischen Bauforschung und Altertumskunde. Band 17.) Schweizerisches Institut für Ägyptische Bauforschung und Altertumskunde, Kairo. Philipp von Zabern, Mainz am Rhein.

Aston, D.A., 2009a. Theban Potmarks – nothing other than Funny Signs?, in B.J.J. Haring and O.E. Kaper (eds), *Pictograms or Pseudo Script? Non-textual identity marks in practical use in Ancient Egypt and elsewhere.* Nederlands Instituut voor het Nabije Oosten, Leiden. Peeters, Leuven, 49–65.

Aston, D.A., 2009b. *Burial Assemblages of Dynasty 21–25.* (CChEM XXI.) (DÖAW LIV). ÖAW, Vienna.

Aston, D.A., 2011a. Blue-Painted Pottery of the Late Eighteenth Dynasty. The Material from the Tomb of Maya and Merit at Saqqara. *CCÉ* 9, 1–35.

Aston, D.A., 2011b. The LH IIIA2–IIIB Transition: The Gurob and Saqqara Evidence Reassessed, in W. Gauss, M. Lindblom, R. Angus K. Smith and James C. Wright (eds), *Our Cups Are Full: Pottery and Society in the Aegean Bronze Age. Papers presented to Jeremy B. Rutter on the occasion of his 65th birthday.* BAR International Series 2227. Archaeopress, Oxford, 1–12.

Aston, D.A. and B.G. Aston, 2001. The Pottery, in G.T. Martin *et al., The Tombs of Three Memphite Officials: Ramose, K hay and Pabes.* (EES Excavation Memoir 66). EES, London, 50–61.

Aston, D.A. and B.G. Aston, 2010. *Late Period Pottery from the New Kingdom Necropolis at Saqqâra* (EES Excavation Memoir 92). EES and National Museum of Antiquities, Leiden. London and Leiden.

Aston, D.A., B.G. Aston and E.C. Brock, 1998. Pottery from the Valley of the Kings – Tombs of Merenptah, Ramesses III, Ramesses IV, Ramesses VI and Ramesses VII. Ä&L VIII, 137–214.

Aston, D.A., B.G. Aston and D. P. Ryan, 2000. Pottery from Tombs in the Valley of the Kings: KV 21, 27, 28, 45 and 60. *CCÉ* 6, 11–38.

Aston, D.A. and D.J. Jeffreys, 2007. *The Third Intermediate Period Levels.* (The Survey of Memphis III: EES Excavation Memoir 81). EES, London.

Bader, B., 2001. *Tell el-Dab'a XIII: Typologie und Chronologie der Mergel C-Ton Keramik. Materialien zum Binnenhandel des Mittleren Reiches und der Zweiten Zwischenzeit.* (UZK XIX). ÖAW, Vienna.

Bader, B., 2009a. The Late Old Kingdom in Herakleopolis Magna? An interim interpretation, in T. Rzeuska and A. Wodzińska (eds), *Studies on Old Kingdom Pottery.* Warsaw, 13–41.

Bader, B., 2009b. *Tell el-Dab'a XIX: Auaris und Memphis im Mittleren Reich und in der Hyksoszeit.* (UZK XXXI). ÖAW, Vienna.

Ballet, P., 1987. Essai de Classification des Coupes Type *Maidum-Bowl* du Sondage Nord de 'Ayn-Aṣil (Oasis de Dakhla). *CCÉ* 1, 1–16.

Bárta, M., 1996. Several remarks on Beer Jars found at Abusir. *CCÉ* 4, 127–31.

Bell, M., 1987. Regional Variation in Polychrome Pottery. *CCÉ* 1, 49–76.

Bourriau, J.D., 1981. *Umm el-Ga'ab: Pottery from the Nile Valley before the Arab Conquest.* Cambridge University Press, Cambridge.

Bourriau, J., 1990a. The pottery, in P. Lacovara, Deir el Ballas: *Preliminary Report on the Deir el-Ballas Expedition, 1980–1986.* (ARCE Reports 12). ARCE, Winona Lake, 15–22.

Bourriau, J., 1990b. Canaanite Jars from New Kingdom Deposits at Memphis, Kom Rabi'a. *Eretz Israel* 21, Jerusalem, 18*–26*.

Bourriau, J., 1991. Relations between Egypt and Kerma during the Middle and New Kingdoms, in W.V. Davies (ed.), *Egypt and Africa.* London, 129–44.

Bourriau, J.D., 1997. Beyond Avaris: the Second Intermediate period in Egypt outside the Eastern Delta, in E. Oren (ed.), *The Hyksos: New Historical and Archaeological Perspectives.* (University Museum Monograph 96; University Museum Symposium Series 8). University of Pennsylvania, Philadelphia, 159–82.

Bourriau J., 2002. Fabrics of the Oasis Amphorae of the New Kingdom from Memphis, Kom Rabi'a, in R. Friedman (ed.), *Egypt and Nubia: Gifts of the Desert.* British Museum Press, London, 113–31.

Bourriau, J.D., 2010. *Kom Rabia: The New Kingdom Pottery.* (The Survey of Memphis IV: EES Excavation Memoir 93). EES, London.

Bourriau, J.D. and D. Aston, 1985. The pottery, in G.T. Martin, *The Tombs of Paser and Ra'ia at Saqqara.* (EES Excavation Memoir 52). EES, London, 32–55.

Bourriau, J.D. and P.T. Nicholson, 1992. Marl clay pottery fabrics of the New Kingdom from Memphis, Saqqara and Amarna. *JEA* 78, 29–91.

Bourriau, J.D. and K.O. Eriksson, 1997. A Late Minoan Sherd from an Early 18th Dynasty Context at Kom Rabi'a, Memphis, in J. Phillips (ed.), *Ancient Egypt, the Aegean, and the Near East: Studies in Honour of Martha Rhoads Bell.* Vol. I. Van Siclen Books. San Antonio, Texas, 95–120.

Bourriau, J.D., L.M.V. Smith and P.T. Nicholson 2000. *New Kingdom Pottery Fabrics.* (Fourteenth Occasional Publication). EES, London.

Bourriau, J., L. Smith and M. Serpico, 2001. The Provenance of Canaanite Amphorae found at Memphis and Amarna in the New Kingdom, in A.J. Shortland (ed.). *The Social Context of Technological Change. Egypt and the Near East, 1650–1550 B.C.* Oxbow Books, Oxford, 113–46.

Bourriau, J., D. Aston, M.J. Raven and R. van Walsem, with a contribution by C. Hope, 2005. *The Memphite Tomb of Horemheb III. The New Kingdom Pottery.* (EES Excavation Memoir 71). EES, London.

Bourriau, J.D. and C. Gallorini, in preparation. *Kom Rabia: The Middle Kingdom Pottery.* (The Survey of Memphis: EES Excavation Memoir). EES, London.

Brissaud, P., V. Carpano, L. Cotelle, S. Marchand, L. Nouaille, C. Veillard, 1987. Repértoire préliminaire de la poterie trouvée à San el Hagar (2e partie), in P. Brissaud (ed.), *Cahiers de Tanis* I. (Mission Française des Fouilles de Tanis. Éditions Recherche sur les Civilisations 75). Paris, 75–99.

Brunton, G., 1930. *Qau and Badari III.* (BSAE L). BSAE and Bernard Quaritch, London.

Brunton, G.., 1937. *Mostagedda and the Tasian Culture. British Museum Expedition to Middle Egypt, 1927 and 1928.* Bernard Quaritch, London.

Brunton, G., 1948. *Matmar. British Museum Expedition to Middle Egypt 1929–1931.* Bernard Quaritch, London.

Brunton, G. and R.E. Engelbach, 1927. *Gurob.* (BSAE XLI). BSAE and Bernard Quaritch, London.

Budka, J., 2006. The Oriental Institute Ahmose and Tetisheri Project at Abydos 2002–2004: The New Kingdom Pottery. *Ä&L* XVI, 83–120.

Chłodnicki, M., 1995. Some remarks about Late Predynastic, Early Dynastic and Old Kingdom Bread Moulds, *Études et Travaux* XVII, Warsaw, 23–27

Chłodnicki, M., R. Fattovich and S. Salvatori, 1992. The Nile Delta in Transition: a View from Tell el-Farkha, in E.C.M. van den Brink (ed.), *The Nile Delta in Transition: 4th.–3rd. Millennium B.C.* Tel Aviv, 171–190.

Czerny, E., 1999. *Tell el-Dab'a IX: Eine Plansiedlung des frühen Mittleren Reiches* (UZK XV). ÖAW, Vienna.

Ditze B., 2007. Gedrückt – Geritzt – Gekratzt. Die Gefäße mit Topfmarken, in E. B. Pusch (ed.) *Die Keramik des Grabungsplatzes QI – Teil 2,* Hildesheim, 270–502.

Egloff, M., 1977. *Kellia. La Poterie Copte.* (Recherches Suisses d'Archéologie Copte, Vol. III). Geneva.

Emery, W.B., 1938. *The Tomb of Hemaka.* Cairo.

Emery, W.B., 1961. *Archaic Egypt.* Harmondsworth.

Eriksson, K.O., 1991. Red Lustrous Wheelmade ware: a Product of Late Bronze Age Cyprus, in J.A. Barlow *et al.* (eds), *Cypriot Ceramics: Reading the Prehistoric Record.* University Museum Monograph 74; University Museum Symposium Series II). University of Pennsylvania, Philadelphia, 81–96.

Eriksson, K.O., 1993. *Red Lustrous Wheel Made Ware.* (SMA 103). Paul Åströms Förlag, Jonsered.

Eriksson, K.O., 2007. Using Red Lustrous Wheelmade Ware to establish Cultural and Chronological Synchronisms during the Late Bronze Age, in I. Hein (ed.) *The Lustrous Wares of Late Bronze Age Cyprus and the Eastern Mediterranean.* CChEM XIII. (DÖAW XLI). ÖAW, Vienna, 51–69.

Faltings, D., 1989. Die Keramik aus den Grabungen an der nördlichen Pyramide des Snofru in Dahschur. Arbeitsbericht über die Kampagnen 1983–1986, *MDAIK 45,* 133–54.

Faltings, D., 2000. Zweiter Vorbericht über die Arbeiten in Buto von 1996 bis 1999, *MDAIK 56,* 131–53.

Fischer, H.G., 1959. Pottery, in R. Anthes, *Mit Rahineh 1955.* (University Museum Monograph). University of Pennsylvania, Philadelphia, 20–40.

Fischer, H.G., 1965. The Pottery, in R. Anthes, *Mit Rahineh 1956.* (University Museum Monograph). University of Pennsylvania, Philadelphia, 143–61.

Frankfort, H. and J.D.S. Pendlebury, 1933. *The City of Akhenaten.* Part II. (EES Excavation Memoir 40). EES, London.

French, P.G., 1992. The pottery, in L.L. Giddy, *The Anubieion at Saqqara,* II. *The Cemeteries.* (EES Excavation Memoir 56). EES, London.

French, P.G. and H. Ghaly, 1991. Pottery chiefly of the Late Dynastic Period, from Excavations by the Egyptian Antiquities Organisation at Saqqara, 1987. *CCÉ* 2, 93–124.

Friedman, R., 1992. The Early Dynastic and Transitional Pottery of Mendes: the 1990 Season, in E.C.M. van den Brink (ed.), *The Nile Delta in Transition: 4th.–3rd. Millennium B.C.* Tel Aviv, 199–205.

Furumark, A., 1941. *Mycenaean Pottery: Analysis and Classification.* Stockholm.

Fuscaldo, P., 2000. *Tell el-Dab'a X. The Palace District of Avaris: The pottery of the Hyksos Period and the New Kingdom (Areas H/III and H/VI), Part I, Locus 66.* (UZK XVI). ÖAW, Vienna.

Gallorini, C., 2009. Incised marks on pottery and other objects from Kahun, in B.J.J. Haring and O.E. Kaper (eds), *Pictograms or Pseudo Script? Non-textual identity marks in practical use in Ancient Egypt and elsewhere.* Nederlands Instituut voor het Nabije Oosten, Leiden. Peeters, Leuven, 107–42.

Gardiner, Sir A., 1964. *Egyptian Grammar. Third Edition (revised).* OUP, London.

Giddy, L.L., 1992. *The Anubieion at Saqqara,* II. *The Cemeteries.* (EES Excavation Memoir 56). EES, London.

Hankey, V and D.A. Aston, 1995. Mycenaean Pottery at Saqqara: Finds from Excavations by the Egypt Exploration Society of London and the Rijksmuseum van Oudheden, Leiden, 1975–1990, in J.B. Carter and S.B. Morris (eds), *The Ages of Homer. A tribute to Emily Townsend Vermeule.* Austin, 67–91.

Harpur, Y., 2011. Earthenware Vessels in Old Kingdom Two-dimensional Art: Their Manufacture and Direct Use by Minor Human Figures, in D.A. Aston *et al.* (eds), *Under the Potter's Tree: Studies on Ancient Egypt, Presented to Janine Bourriau on the Occasion of her 70th Birthday.* Peeters, Leuven, 441–68.

Harpur, Y. and P. Scremin, 2008. *The Chapel of Ptahhotep. Scene details.* Egypt in Miniature, Vol. II. Oxford Expedition to Egypt. Oxford.

Hartung, U., 2001. *Umm el-Qaab II.* (AV 92). DAIK. Philipp von Zabern, Mainz am Rhein.

Hawass Z. and A. Senussi, 2008. *Old Kingdom Pottery from Giza.* SCA, Cairo.

Hein, I., 2004. Stratum C (18. Dynastie), in I. Hein and P. Jánosi, *Tell el-Dab'a XI: Areal A/V, Siedlungsrelikte der Späten 2. Zwischenzeit.* (UZK XXI). ÖAW, Vienna, 183–86.

Hendrickx, S. *et al.*, 2002. Milk, Beer and Bread Technology during the Early Dynastic Period, *MDAIK 58,* 277–304.

Holladay, J.S. Jr., 1997. The Eastern Nile Delta during the Hyksos and Pre-Hyksos periods: toward a Systemic/Socioeconomic Understanding, in E. Oren (ed.), *The Hyksos: New Historical and Archaeological Perspectives.* (University Museum Monograph 96; University Museum Symposium Series 8). University of Pennsylvania, Philadelphia, 159–82.

Holthoer, R., 1977. *New Kingdom Pharaonic Sites: the Pottery.* (SJE 5:1). Scandinavian University Books, Lund.

Holthoer, R., 1993. The Pottery, in A. el-Khouli *et al. Stone Vessels, Pottery and Sealings from the Tomb of Tut'ankhamun.* Oxford 1993, 37–85.

Hope, C.A., 1987. Innovation in the decoration of ceramics in the mid-18th dynasty. *CCÉ* 1, 96–122.

Hope, C.A., 1989a. The XVIIIth Dynasty pottery from Malkata, in C.A. Hope, *Pottery of the Egyptian New Kingdom: Three Studies.* (Victoria College Archaeology Research Unit, Occasional Papers 2). Victoria College Press, Burwood (Victoria), 3–44.

Hope, C.A., 1989b. Pottery of the Ramesside period, in C.A. Hope, *Pottery of the Egyptian New Kingdom: Three Studies.* (Victoria College Archaeology Research Unit, Occasional Papers 2). Victoria College Press, Burwood (Victoria), 45–84.

Hope, C.A., 1989c. Amphorae of the New Kingdom, in C.A. Hope, *Pottery of the Egyptian New Kingdom: Three Studies.* (Victoria College Archaeology Research Unit, Occasional Papers 2). Victoria College Press, Burwood (Victoria), 87–126.

Hope, C.A., 1991. Blue-Painted and Polychrome Decorated pottery from Amarna: a preliminary corpus. *CCÉ* 2, 17–92.

Hope, C.A., 1996. New Kingdom Painted Pottery from Karnak North. *BCÉ* XIX, 31–33.

Hope, C.A., 1999. Some Remarks on Potmarks of the Late Eighteenth Dynasty, in A. Leahy and J. Tait (eds), *Studies on Ancient Egypt in Honour of H.S. Smith.* (EES Occasional Publications 13). EES, London, 121–46.

Hope, C.A., in preparation. *Kom Rabia: the New Kingdom Blue-Painted Pottery.*

Hope, C.A. and A. McFarlane, 2006. *Akhmim in the Old Kingdom. Part II.* (ACE Studies 7). Aris and Phillips, Warminster.

Hope, C.A. *et al.*, 2002. Oases Amphorae of the New Kingdom, in R. Friedman (ed.), *Egypt and Nubia: Gifts of the Desert.* British Museum Press, London, 95–131.

Jacquet-Gordon, H., 1981. A Tentative Typology of Egyptian Bread Moulds, in Do. Arnold (ed.) *Studien zur altägyptischen Keramik.* DAIK. Philipp von Zabern, Mainz am Rhein, 11–24.

Jay, W.H., unpublished. Pigments from the western desert of Egypt: their characterisation, production and use, Monash University, Melbourne.

Jeffreys, D.G. and H.S. Smith, 1988. *The Anubieion at Saqqara,* I. *The Settlement and the Temple Precinct.* (EES Excavation Memoir 54). EES, London.

Kaiser, W., 1969. Die Tongefässe, in H. Ricke (ed.), *Das Sonnenheiligtum des Königs Userkaf, II: Die Funde.* Beiträge zur Ägyptischen Bauforschung und Altertumskunde, Heft 8. Wiesbaden, 49–82.

Kaplony, P., 1963. *Die Inschriften der Frühzeit*. Vol. III. (ÄA Band 8). Wiesbaden.

Kemp, B.J., 1981. Preliminary Report on the el-'Amarna Expedition, 1980. *JEA* 67, 5–20.

Knoblauch, C.M. and L.D. Bestock, 2009. Four Thousand Years in Abydos: A Preliminary Report on the Architecture and Ceramics of the 2004–05 Excavations in the North Cemetery, West, *MDAIK 65*, 212–252.

Köhler, E.C., 1992. The pre- and Early Dynastic Pottery of Tell el-Farain (Buto), in E.C.M. van den Brink (ed.), *The Nile Delta in Transition: 4th.–3rd. Millennium* B.C. Tel Aviv, 11–22.

Köhler, E.C., 1998. *Tell el-Fara'în · Buto III*. (AV 94). DAIK. Philipp von Zabern, Mainz am Rhein.

Köhler, E.C. and J.C. Smythe, 2004. Early Dynastic Pottery from Helwan. *CCÉ* 7, 123–36.

Kopetzky, K., 2004. Typologische Bemerkungen zur Siedlungskeramik von A/V-p/19, in I. Hein and P. Jánosi, *Tell el-Dab'a XI: Areal A/V, Siedlungsrelikte der Späten 2. Zwischenzeit*. (UZK XXI). ÖAW, Vienna, 237–335.

Köpp, H., 2004. Die Rote Pyramide des Snofru in Dahschur – Bemerkungen zur Keramik, in T. Rzeuska and A. Wodzińska (eds), *Studies on Old Kingdom Pottery*. Warsaw, 61–69.

Kromer, K., 1978. *Siedlungsfunde aus dem frühen Alten Reich in Giseh. Österreichische Ausgrabungen 1971–1975*. Verlag der ÖAW, Vienna.

Lacau, P. and J.-Ph. Lauer, 1965. *La Pyramide à Degrés. Tome V. Inscriptions à l'Encre sur les Vases*. Cairo.

Lehner, M., 2007. Introduction to the Preliminary Ceramic Report, in M. Lehner and W. Wetterstrom (eds), *Giza Reports. The Giza Plateau Mapping Project*. Vol.1. AERA. Hanson, Mass., 279–82.

Mączyńska, A., 2009. Old Kingdom Pottery at Tell el-Farkha. Some Remarks on Bread Moulds, in T. Rzeuska and A. Wodzińska (eds), *Studies on Old Kingdom Pottery*. Warsaw, 95–111.

Malykh, S., 2011. Pottery from the Rock-Cut Tomb of Khafraankh in Giza. *CCÉ* 9, 185–213.

Marchand, S. and M. Baud, 1996. La céramique miniature d'Abou Rawash. *BIFAO* 96, 255–88.

Merrilees, R.S., 1968. *The Cypriote Bronze Age Pottery found in Egypt*. (SMA XVIII). SMA, Lund.

Müller, V., 2008. *Tell el-Dab'a XVII: Opferdeponierungen in der Hyksoshauptstadt Auaris (Tell el-Dab'a) vom Späten Mittleren Reich bis zum Frühen Neuen Reich – Teil 1*. (DÖAW XLV). ÖAW, Vienna.

Myśliwiec, K., 1987. *Keramik und Kleinfunde aus der Grabung im Tempel Sethos' I. in Gurna*. (AV 57). DAIK. Philipp von Zabern, Mainz am Rhein.

Nordström H-Å. and J.D. Bourriau, 1993. Ceramic Technology: Clays and Fabrics, in Do. Arnold and J. Bourriau (eds), *An Introduction to Ancient Egyptian Pottery*. Fascicle 2. (DAIK Sonderschrift 17). DAIK. Philipp von Zabern, Mainz am Rhein, 143–90.

Op de Beeck, L., 2000. Restrictions for the Use of Maidum-Bowls as Chronological Indicators. *CdÉ* LXXV, 5–14.

Op de Beeck, L., 2004. Possibilities and Restrictions for the Use of Maidum-Bowls as Chronological Indicators. *CCÉ* 7, 239–80.

Ownby M., 2009. Petrographic Examination of P.60 Samples, in T.I. Rzeuska and A. Wodzińska (eds), *Studies on Old Kingdom Pottery*. Warsaw, 149–52.

Ownby M., unpublished. Petrographic Analysis of Archaic and Old Kingdom 'P.60' Sherds from the Anubieion at Saqqara.

Payne, J. Crowfoot, 1993. *Catalogue of the Predynastic Egyptian Collection in the Ashmolean Museum*. OUP, Oxford.

Peet, T.E. and W.L.S. Loat, 1913. *The Cemeteries of Abydos*. Part III. *1912–1913*. (EEF Memoir 35). EEF, London.

Peet, T.E. and C.L. Woolley, 1923. *The City of Akhenaten*. Part I. (EES Excavation Memoir 38). EES, London.

Petrie, W.M.F., 1891. *Illahun, Kahun and Gurob*. Reprinted Aris and Phillips, Warminster, 1974.

Petrie, W.M.F., 1901. *Diospolis Parva. The Cemeteries of Abadiyeh and Hu 1898–99*. (EEF Memoir 20). EEF and Bernard Quaritch, London.

Petrie, W.M.F., 1907. *Gizeh and Rifeh*. (BSAE XIII). BSAE and Bernard Quaritch, London.

Petrie, W.M.F., 1953. *Corpus of Proto-Dynastic Pottery*. (BSAE LXVI(B)). BSAE and Bernard Quaritch, London.

Petrie, W.M.F. and G. Brunton, 1924a. *Sedment I*. (BSAE XXXIV). BSAE and Bernard Quaritch, London.

Petrie, W.M.F. and G. Brunton, 1924b. *Sedment II*. (BSAE XXXV). BSAE and Bernard Quaritch, London.

Petrie, W.M.F., G. Brunton and M.A. Murray, 1923. *Lahun II*. (BSAE XXXIII). BSAE and Bernard Quaritch, London.

Petrie, W.M.F., G.A. Wainwright and A.H. Gardiner, 1913. *Tarkhan I and Memphis V*. (BSAE XXIII). BSAE and Bernard Quaritch, London.

Quibell, J.E., 1897. *El Kab*. (BSAE III). Reprinted 1989, London.

Raue, D., 1999. Ägyptische und nubische Keramik der 1.–4. Dynastie, in W. Kaiser *et al.*, Stadt und Tempel von Elephantine, 25./26./27. Grabungsbericht, *MDAIK 55*, 173–89.

Reisner, G.A., 1955. *A History of the Giza Necropolis.* Vol. II. *Completed and revised by William Stevenson Smith.* Cambridge, Mass.

Rose, P.J., 2007. *The Eighteenth Dynasty Pottery Corpus from Amarna.* (EES Excavation Memoir 83). EES, London.

Rzeuska, T., 2006. *Saqqara II. Pottery of the Late Old Kingdom. Funerary Pottery and Burial Customs.* Neriton, Warsaw.

Rzeuska, T., 2009. Pottery of the Old Kingdom – between Chronology and Economy. Remarks on Mixed Clay in the Memphite Region, in T.I. Rzeuska and A. Wodzynzińska (eds), *Studies on Old Kingdom Pottery.* Warsaw, 141–48.

Rzeuska, T., 2011. Grain, Water, and Wine. Remarks on the Marl A3 Transport-Storage Jars from Middle Kingdom Elephantine. *CCÉ* 9, 461–530.

Seidlmayer, S.J., 1990. *Gräberfelder aus dem Übergang vom Alten zum Mittleren Reich. Studien zur Archäologie der Ersten Zwischenzeit.* (SAGA Band 1). Heidelberger Orientverlag, Heidelberg.

Seiler, A., 2003. Bemerkungen zum Ende des Mittleren Reiches in Theben - erste Ergebnisse der Bearbeitung der Keramik aus Areal H, in D. Polz and A. Seiler. *Die Pyramidenanlage des Königs Nub-Cheper-re Intef in Dra' Abu el-Naga.* (DAIK Sonderschrift 24). DAIK. Philipp von Zabern, Mainz am Rhein, 49–72 and Tafel 12.

Seiler, A., 2005. *Tradition und Wandel: die Keramik als Spiegel der Kulturentwicklung Thebens in der zweiten Zwischenzeit.* (DAIK Sonderschrift 32). DAIK. Philipp von Zabern, Mainz am Rhein.

Silverman, D.P., 2000. Middle Kingdom tombs in the Teti pyramid cemetery, in M. Bárta & J. Krejčí (eds), *Abusir and Saqqara in the Year 2000.* (Archiv orientální Supplementa IX). Academy of Sciences, Prague, 259–82.

Silverman, D.P., 2009. Non-Royal Burials in the Teti Pyramid Cemetery and the Early Twelfth Dynasty, in D.P. Silverman, W.K. Simpson & J Wegner (eds), *Archaism and Innovation: Studies in the Culture of Middle Kingdom Egypt.* New Haven and Philadelphia, 47–101.

Smith, L., J. Bourriau, Y. Goren, M. Hughes & M. Serpico, 2004. The provenance of Canaanite Amphorae found at Memphis and Amarna in the New Kingdom: results 2000–2002, in J. Bourriau & J. Phillips (eds), *Invention and Innovation: the Social Context of Technological Change.* Vol. 2: *Egypt, the Aegean and the Near East, 1650–1150 B.C.* Oxbow Books, Oxford, 55–77.

Smoláriková, K., 1999. The Pottery, in L. Bareš, *Abusir IV. The Shaft Tomb of Udjahorresnet at Abusir.* Prague, 87–108.

Sowada, K., T. Callaghan and P. Bentley, 1999. *The Teti Cemetery at Saqqara,* Vol. IV. (ACE Reports 12). Aris & Phillips, Warminster.

Sowada, K., 1999. The Pottery, in K. Sowada, T. Callaghan and P. Bentley, *The Teti Cemetery at Saqqara,* Vol. IV. (ACE Reports 12). Aris & Phillips, Warminster, 73–91.

Spencer, A.J. and D.M. Bailey, 1986. *Ashmunein 1985.* British Museum Occasional Paper 61, London.

van den Brink, E.C.M., 1992. Preliminary Report on the Excavations at Tell Ibrahim Awad, Seasons 1988–1990, in E.C.M. van den Brink (ed.), *The Nile Delta in Transition: 4th.–3rd. Millennium B.C.* Tel Aviv, 43–68.

Vaughan, S.J., 1991. Material and Technical Characterization of Base Ring Ware: A New Fabric Typology, in J.A. Barlow *et al.* (eds), *Cypriot Ceramics: Reading the Prehistoric Record.* (University Museum Monograph 74; University Museum Symposium Series II). University of Pennsylvania, Philadelphia, 119–30.

von Pilgrim, C., 1996. *Elephantine XVIII. Untersuchungen in der Stadt des Mittleren Reiches und der Zweiten Zwischenzeit.* (AV 91). DAIK. Philipp von Zabern, Mainz am Rhein.

Wegner, J., 2007. *The Mortuary Temple of Senwosret III at Abydos.* Pennsylvania-Yale-Institute of Fine Arts Expedition to Egypt 8, New Haven and Philadelphia.

Willems, H., 2008. *Les textes des Sarcophages et la Démocratie.* Éditions Cybele, Paris.

Willems, H. *et al.*, 2009. An Industrial Site at el-Shaykh Sa'id/Wadi Zabayda. Ä&L XIX, 293–331.

Williams, B.B., 1992. *New Kingdom Remains from Cemeteries R, V, S and W at Qustol and Cemetery K at Adindan.* Chicago.

Wodzińska, A., 2007. Preliminary Ceramic Report, in M. Lehner and W. Wetterstrom (eds), *Giza Reports. The Giza Plateau Mapping Project.* Vol.1. AERA. Hanson, Mass., 283–324.

Yoshimura, S., N. Kawai and H. Kashiwagi, 2005. A Sacred Hillside at Northwest Saqqara, *MDAIK 61*, 361–402.

Figures

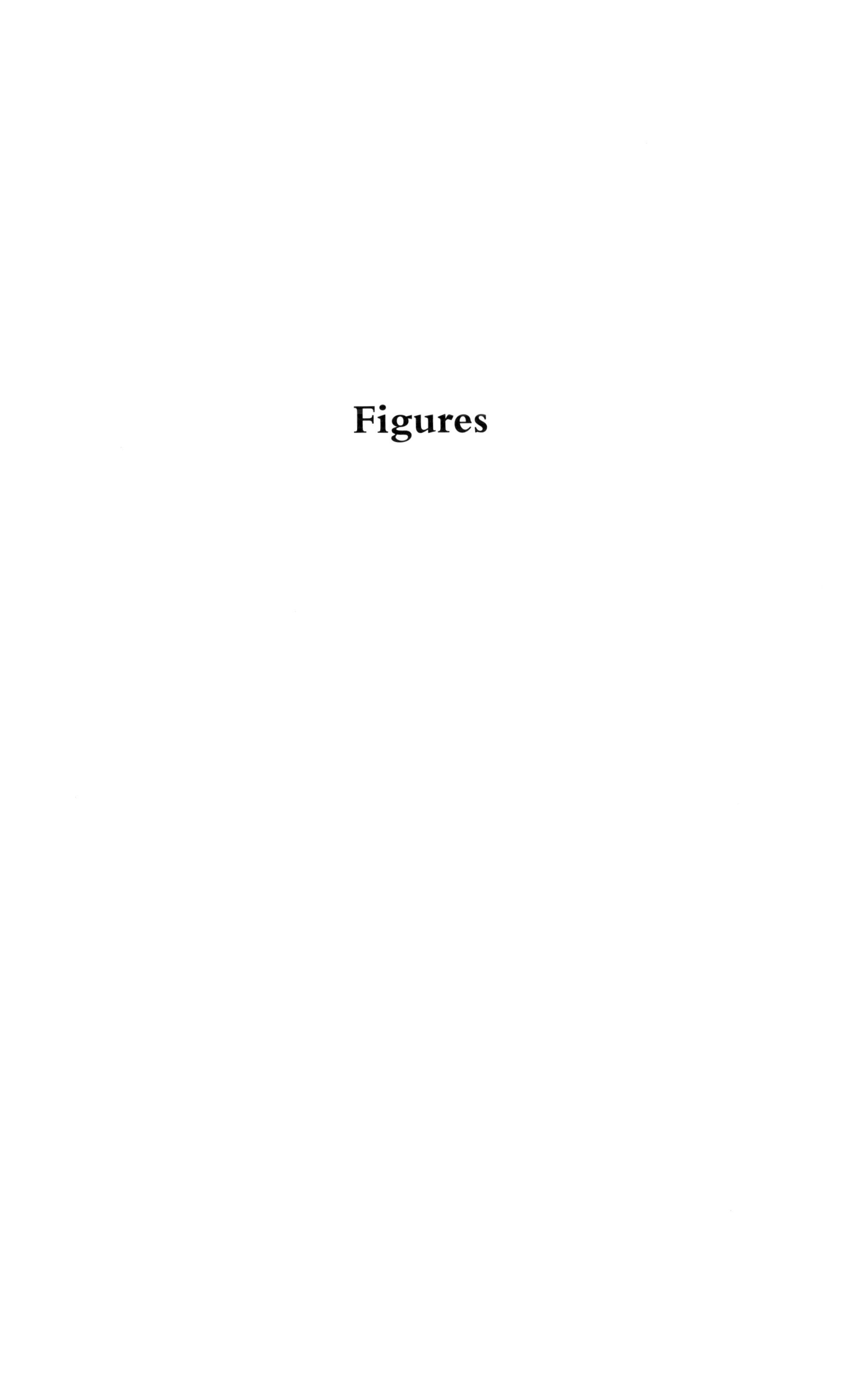

Archaic Period, Various Fabrics

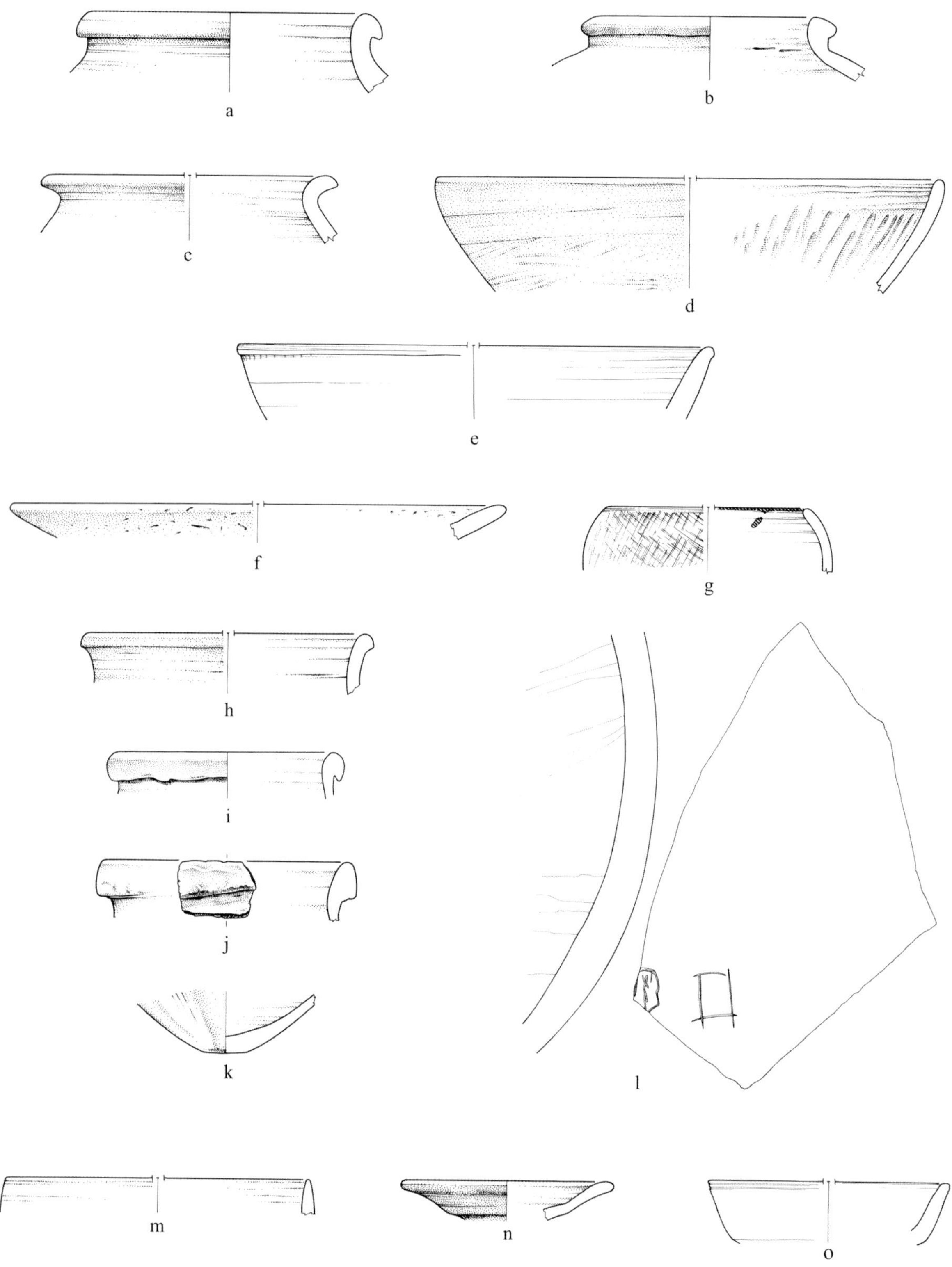

Figure 1. (*a*) 1 (Unclassified Nile); (*b*) 2 (Nile C); (*c*) 3 ARP=ARS/AYY **5** (Nile B1); (*d*) 4 (Nile B2); (*e*) 5 (Nile B2); (*f*) 6 (Nile B2); (*g*) 8 (Unclassified marl); (*h*) 9 (Marl A4); (*i*) 10 (Marl A1); (*j*) 11 (Marl C1); (*k*) 12 (Marl A1); (*l*) 7 (Nile B2); (*m*) 13 (Marl A4); (*n*) 14 (Mixed Clay P.60); (*o*) 15 (Mixed Clay P.60). 1:3

Archaic Period, Various Fabrics, and Old Kingdom and FIP, Nile Fabrics

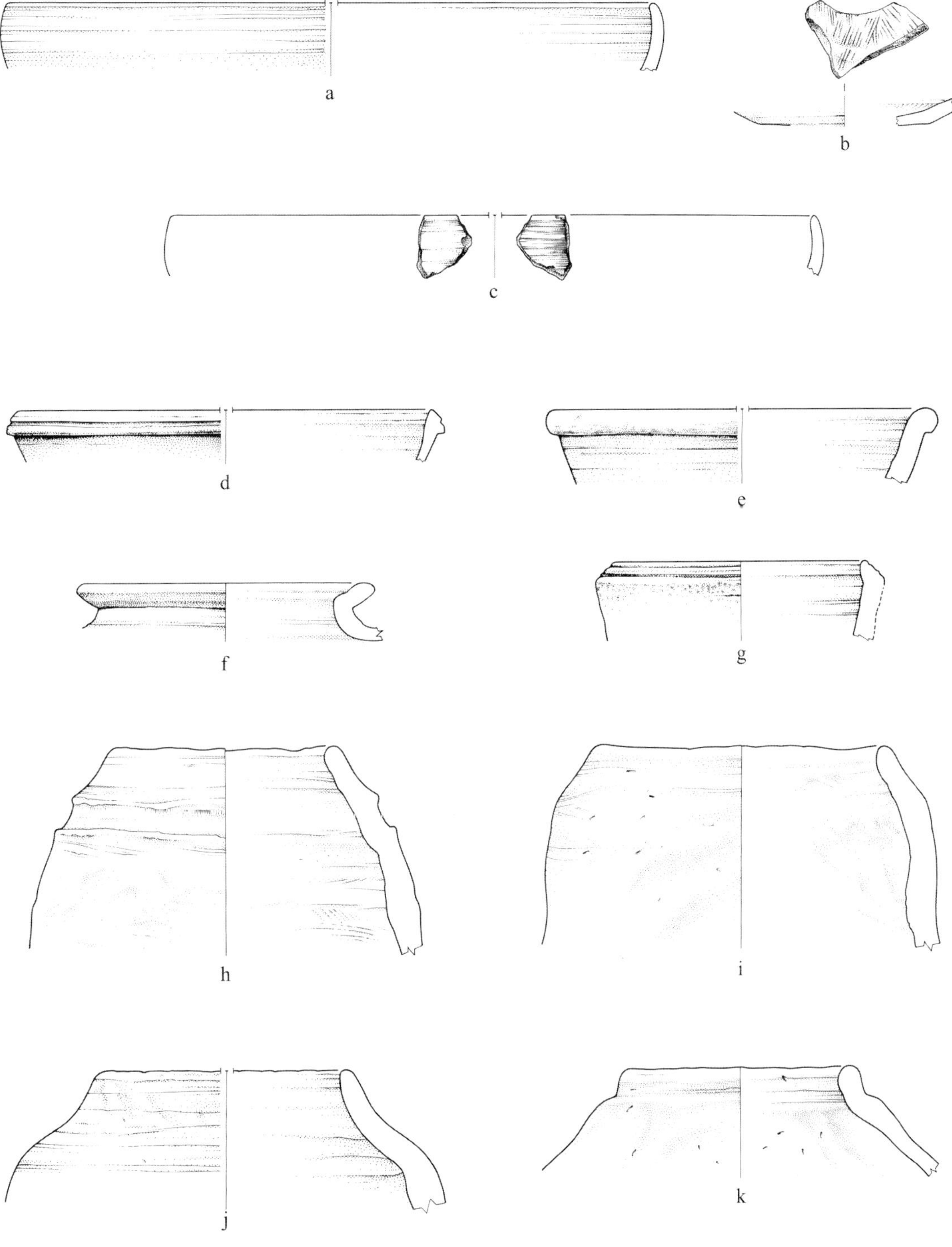

Figure 2. (*a*) **16** (Mixed Clay P.60); (*b*) **17** (Mixed Clay P.60); (*c*) **18** (Mixed Clay P.60); (*d*) **19** (Mixed Clay P.60); (*e*) **20** (Mixed clay P.60); (*f*) **21** (Import); (*g*) **22** (Uncertain fabric); (*h*) **23** AKJ/AKI **5+6+7** (Nile B2 near C); (*i*) **24** AAA East **18** (Nile B2 near C); (*j*) **24** ARU=ARZ **8** (Nile B2 near C); (*k*) **24** ARU=ARZ **10** (Nile B2 near C). 1:3

Old Kingdom and FIP, Nile Fabrics

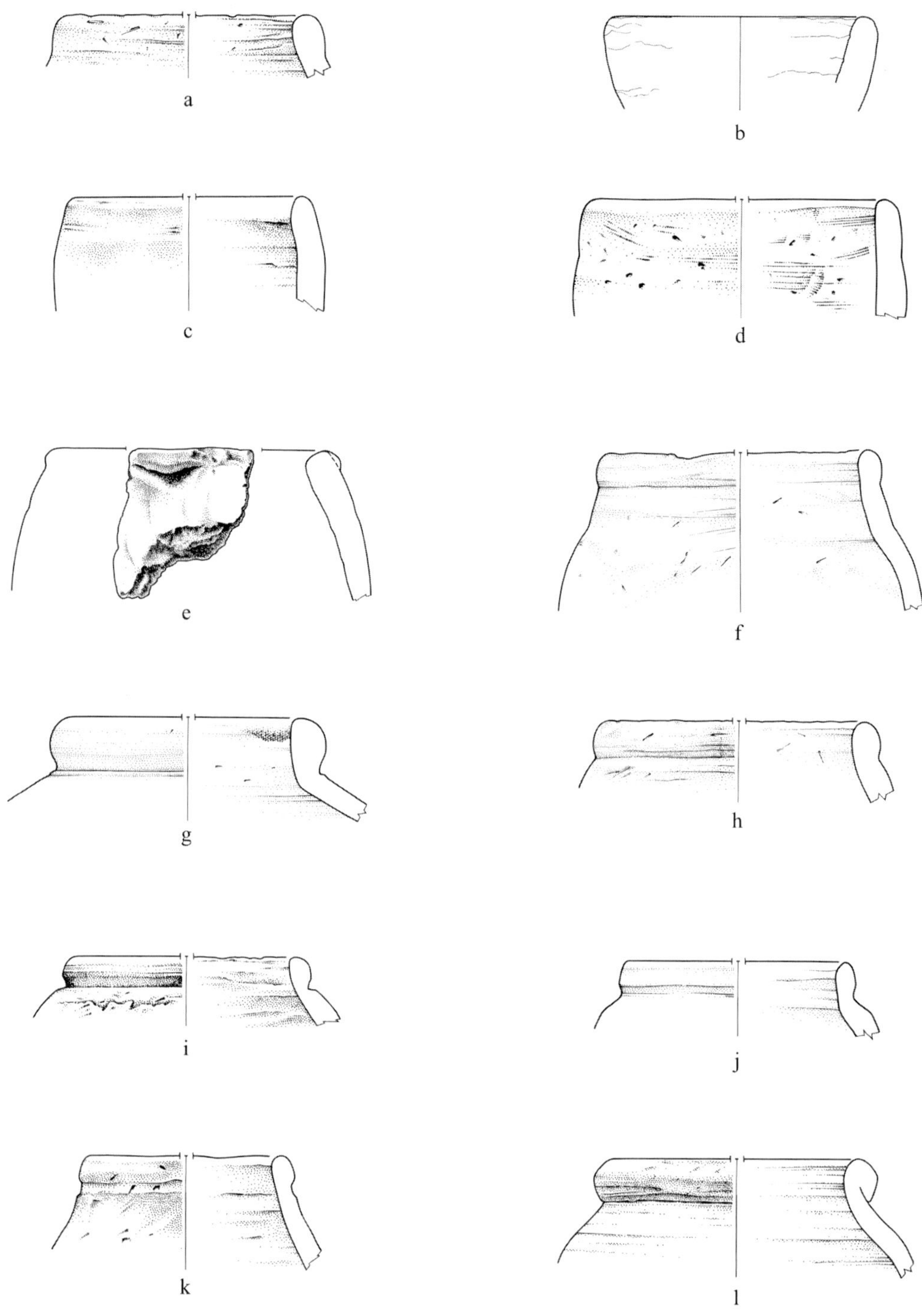

Figure 3. (*a*) **25** (Nile C); (*b*) **26** BEO **79** (Nile C); (*c*) **26** AQE **32** (Nile C); (*d*) **26** ACE **209** (Nile C); (*e*) **27** AJY **18** (Nile C); (*f*) **27** ANG **3** (Nile C); (*g*) **28** ACE **68** (Nile C); (*h*) **28** DBW/DBU **33** (Nile C); (*i*) **29** AJH under AVH **16** (Nile C); (*j*) **29** AJH under AVH **17** (Nile C); (*k*) **29** AAA Lower **15** (Nile C); (*l*) **30** (Nile B2). 1:3

Old Kingdom and FIP, Nile Fabrics

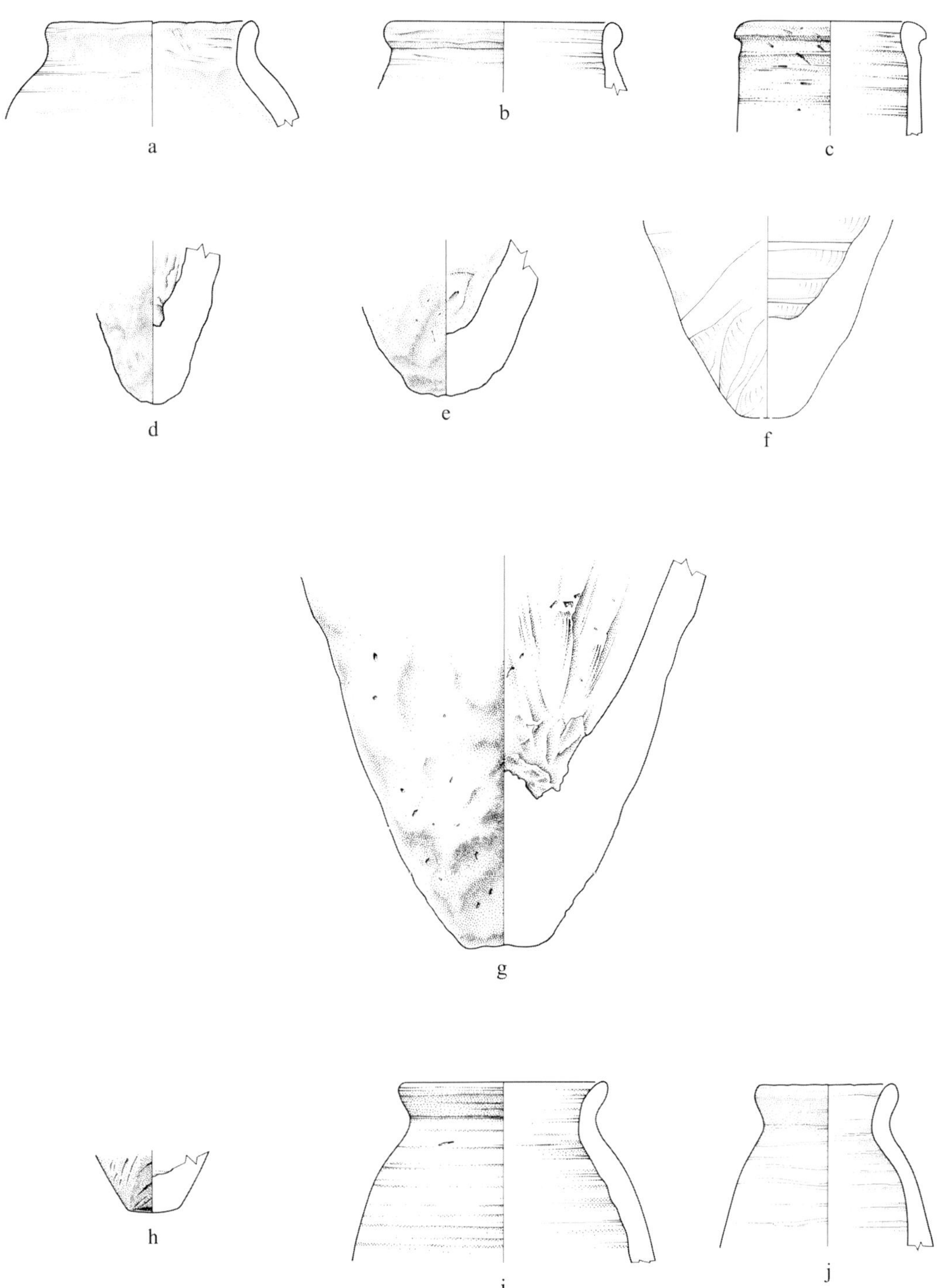

Figure 4. (*a*) **31** BKC **17** (Nile B2 near C); (*b*) **32** (Nile B2 near C); (*c*) **35** (Nile B2); (*d*) **33** ARU=ARZ **3** (Nile D near C); (*e*) **33** ARU=ARZ **4** (Nile D near C); (*f*) **33** ARU=ARZ **5** (Nile D near C); (*g*) **33** UP 1033 **1** (Nile D near C); (*h*) **36** (Nile B2); (*i*) **37** AAA **562** (Nile B2); (*j*) **38** (Nile B2). 1.3

Old Kingdom and FIP, Nile Fabrics

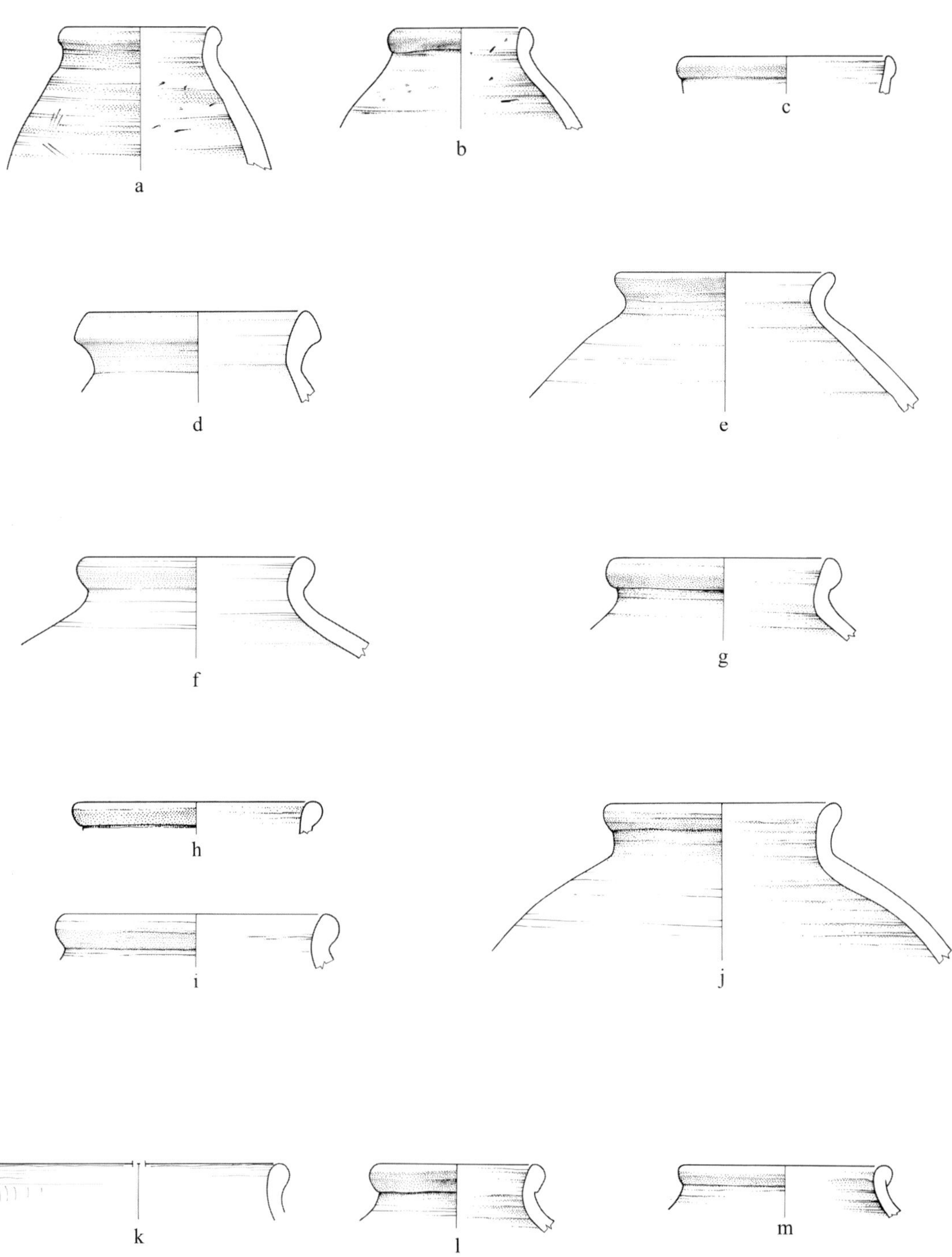

Figure 5. (*a*) **39** (Nile B2); (*b*) **40** (Nile B2); (*c*) **41** (Nile B2); (*d*) **42** (Nile B2); (*e*) **43** (Nile B2); (*f*) **44** ADU **5** (Nile B2); (*g*) **44** DAG **31** (Nile B2); (*h*) **45** AON **31** (Nile B1); (*i*) **46** (Nile B2); (*j*) **47** (Nile B2); (*k*) **48** (Nile B2); (*l*) **49** (Nile B2); (*m*) **50** (Nile B2). 1:3

Old Kingdom and FIP, Nile Fabrics

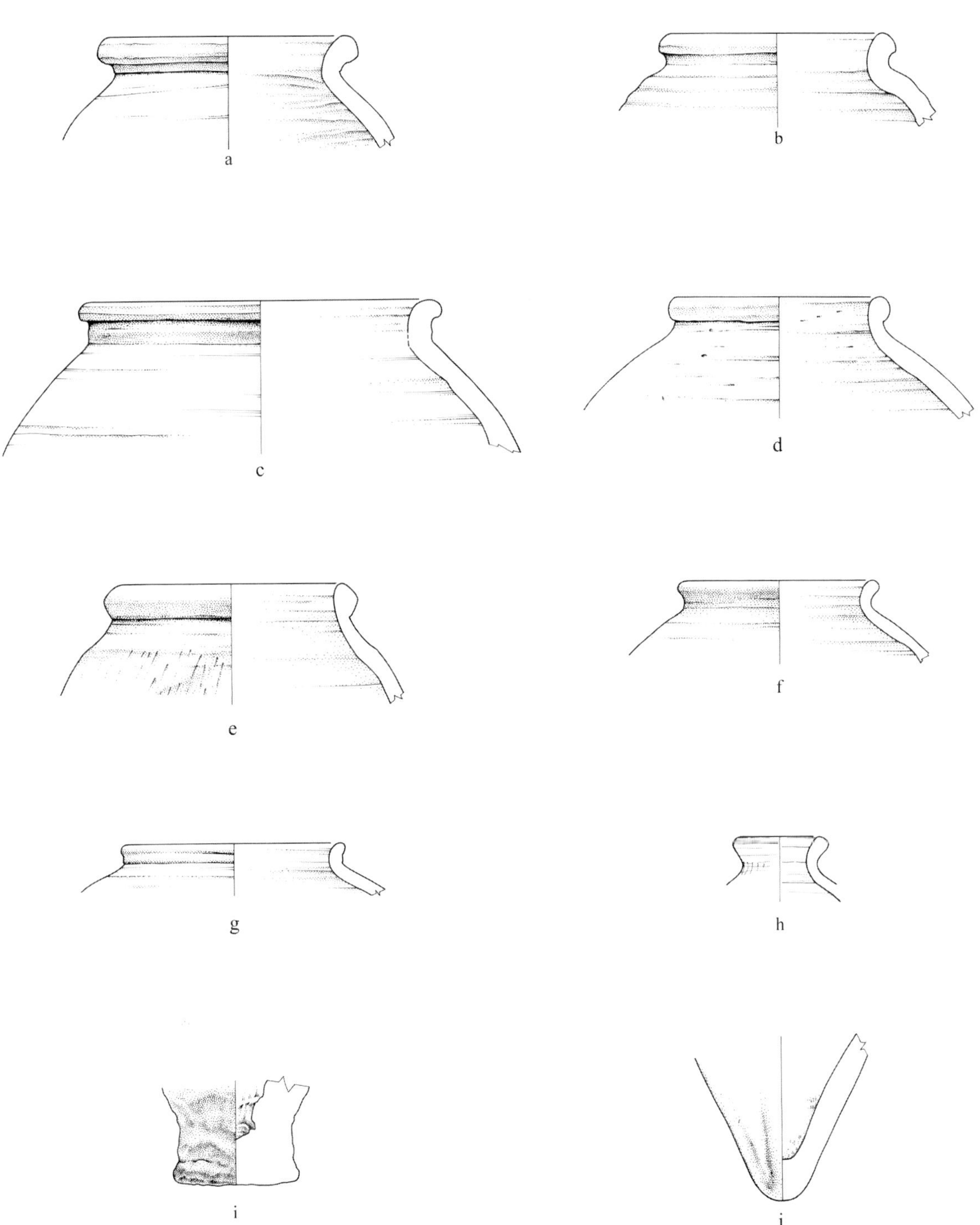

Figure 6. (*a*) **51** (Nile B2); (*b*) **52** (Nile B2); (*c*) **53** (Nile B2); (*d*) **54** (Nile B2); (*e*) **55** (Nile B2); (*f*) **56** (Nile B2 Sandy); (*g*) **57** (Nile B1); (*h*) **58** (Nile B2); (*i*) **59** (Nile C); (*j*) **60** (Nile B2). 1:3

Old Kingdom and FIP, Nile Fabrics

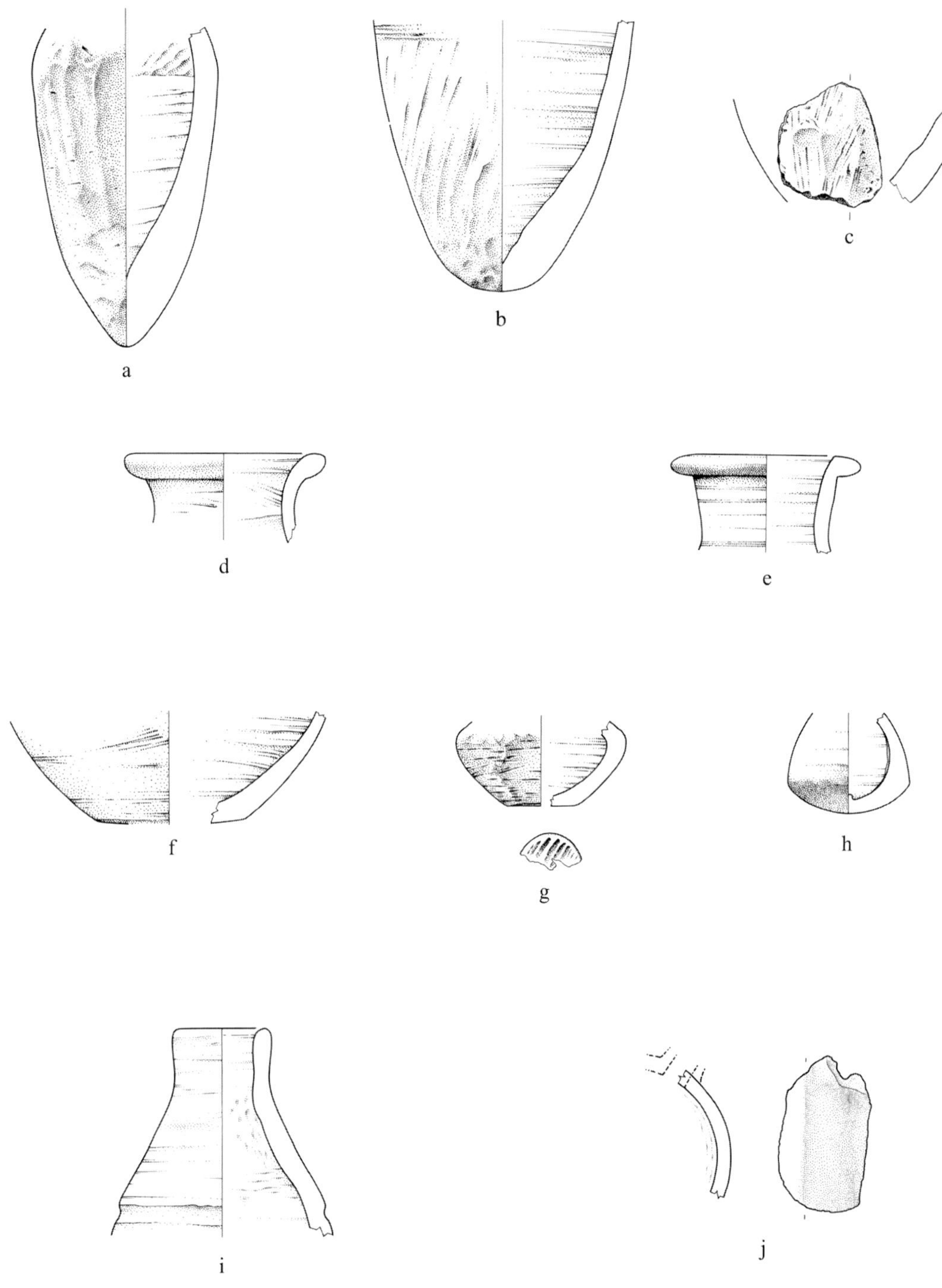

Figure 7. (*a*) **61** (Nile B2); (*b*) **62** Nile (B2); (*c*) **63** (Nile B2); (*d*) **64** (Nile B2); (*e*) **65** (Nile B1); (*f*) **67** (Nile B2); (*g*) **68** (Nile B2); (*h*) **69** (Nile B2); (*i*) **70** ADU **9** (Nile B2); (*j*) **71** (Nile B2). 1:3

Old Kingdom and FIP, Nile Fabrics

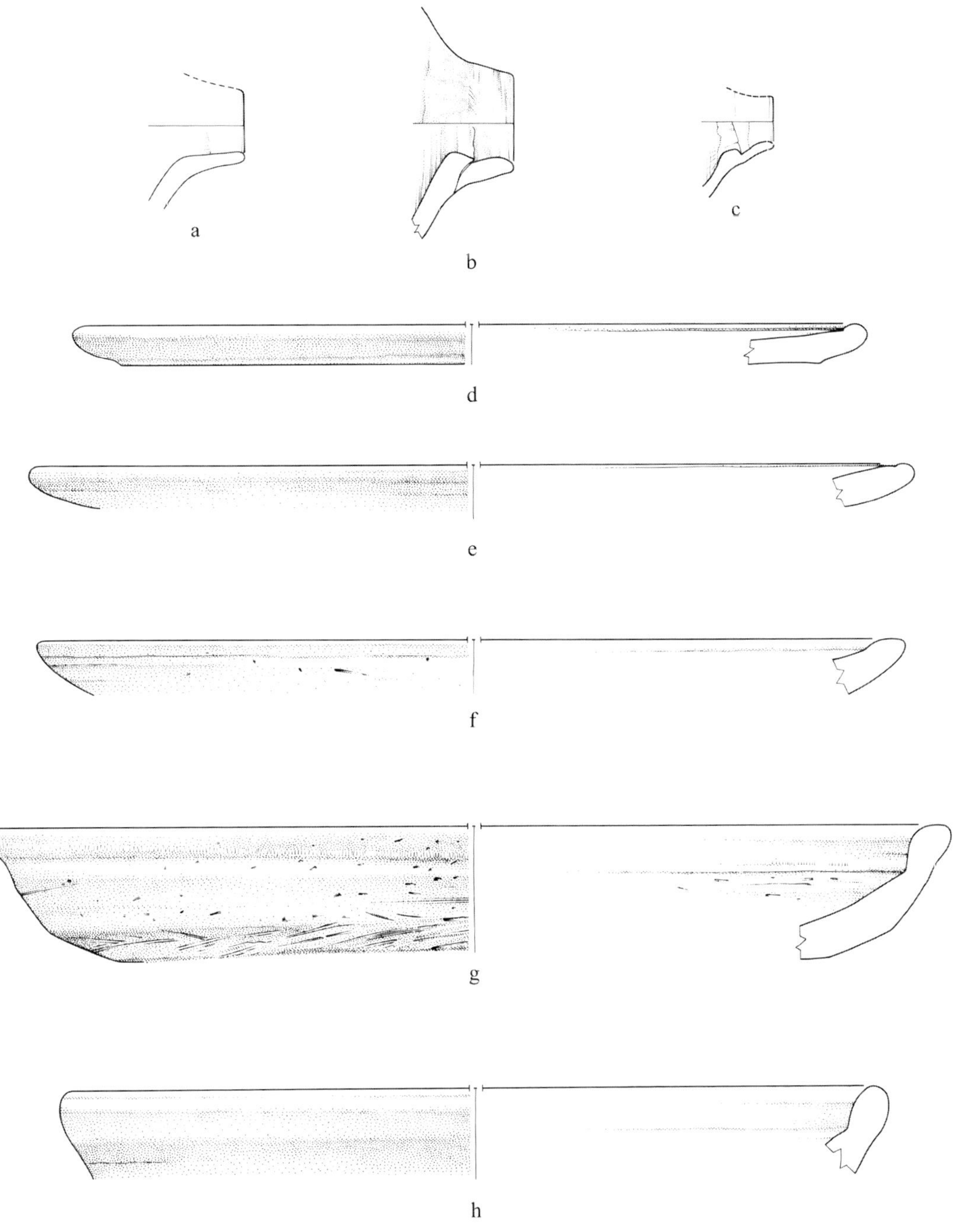

Figure 8. (*a*) **72** BCW/BDE **24** (Nile B2); (*b*) **73** (Nile B2); (*c*) **74** (Nile B2); (*d*) **75** (Nile B2); (*e*) **76** (Nile B2); (*f*) **77** (Nile C); (*g*) **78** (Nile C); (*h*) **79** (Nile B2). 1:3

Old Kingdom and FIP, Nile Fabrics

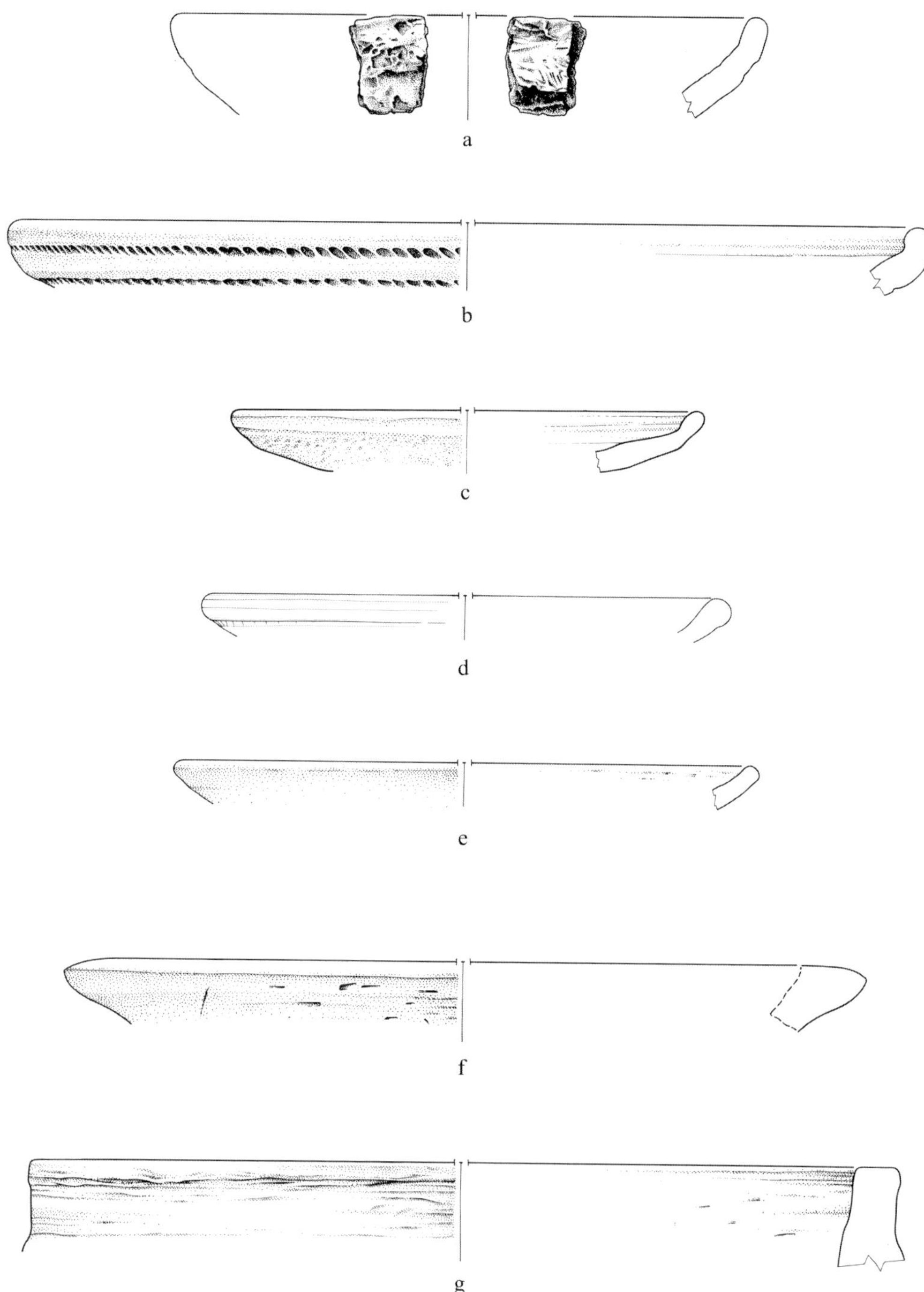

Figure 9. (*a*) **80** (Nile C); (*b*) **81** (Nile B2); (*c*) **82** (Nile B2 Sandy); (*d*) **83** (Nile B2); (*e*) **84** (Nile B2); (*f*) **85** (Nile B2); (*g*) **86** (Nile C).
1:3

Old Kingdom and FIP, Nile Fabrics

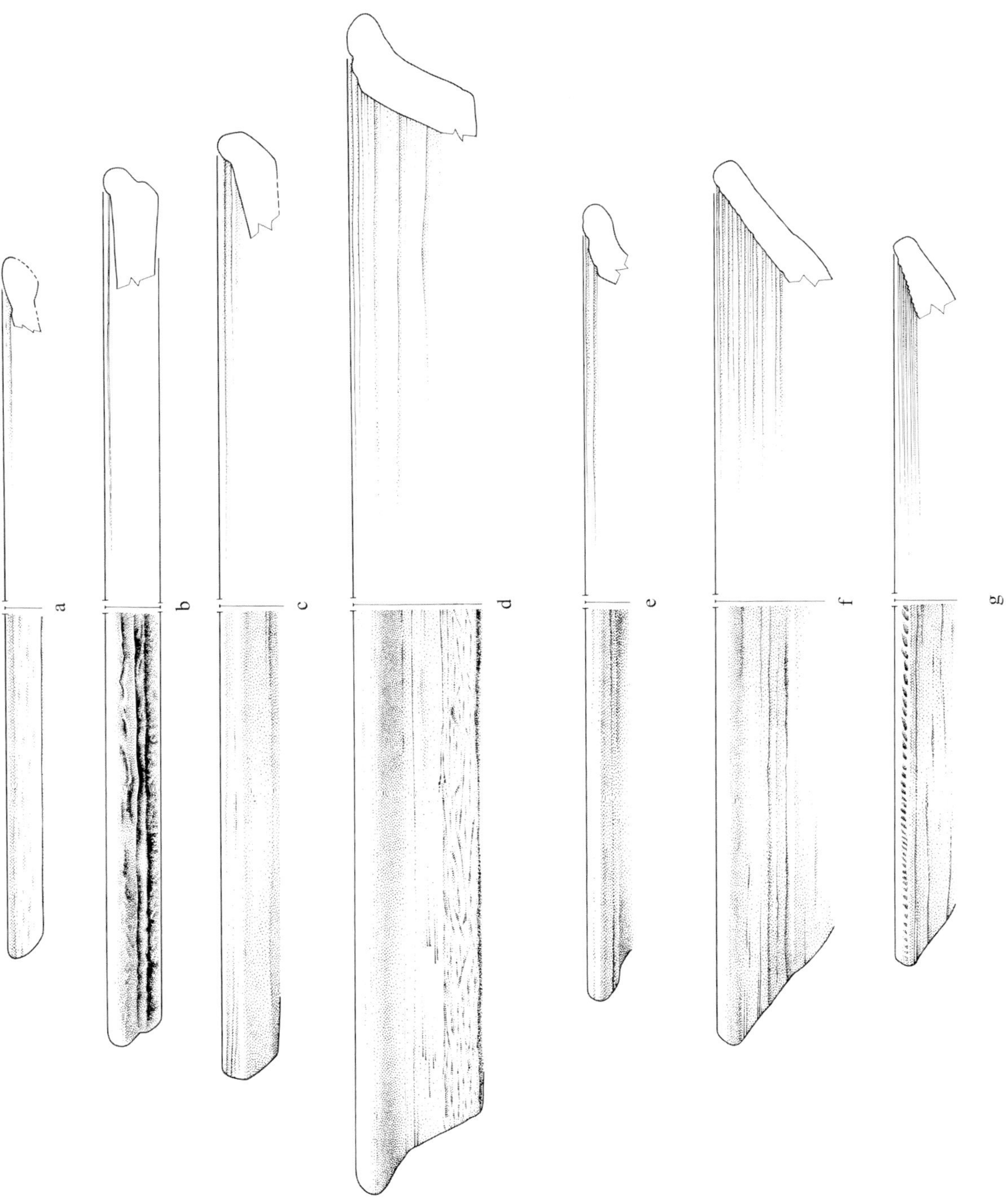

Figure 10. (*a*) **87** AMJ **3** (Nile C); (*b*) **88** (Nile C); (*c*) **89** (Nile C); (*d*) **90** (Nile C); (*e*) **91** (Nile C); (*f*) **92** BJF **17** (Nile B2); (*g*) **92** AAD **47** (Nile B2). 1:3

Old Kingdom and FIP, Nile Fabrics

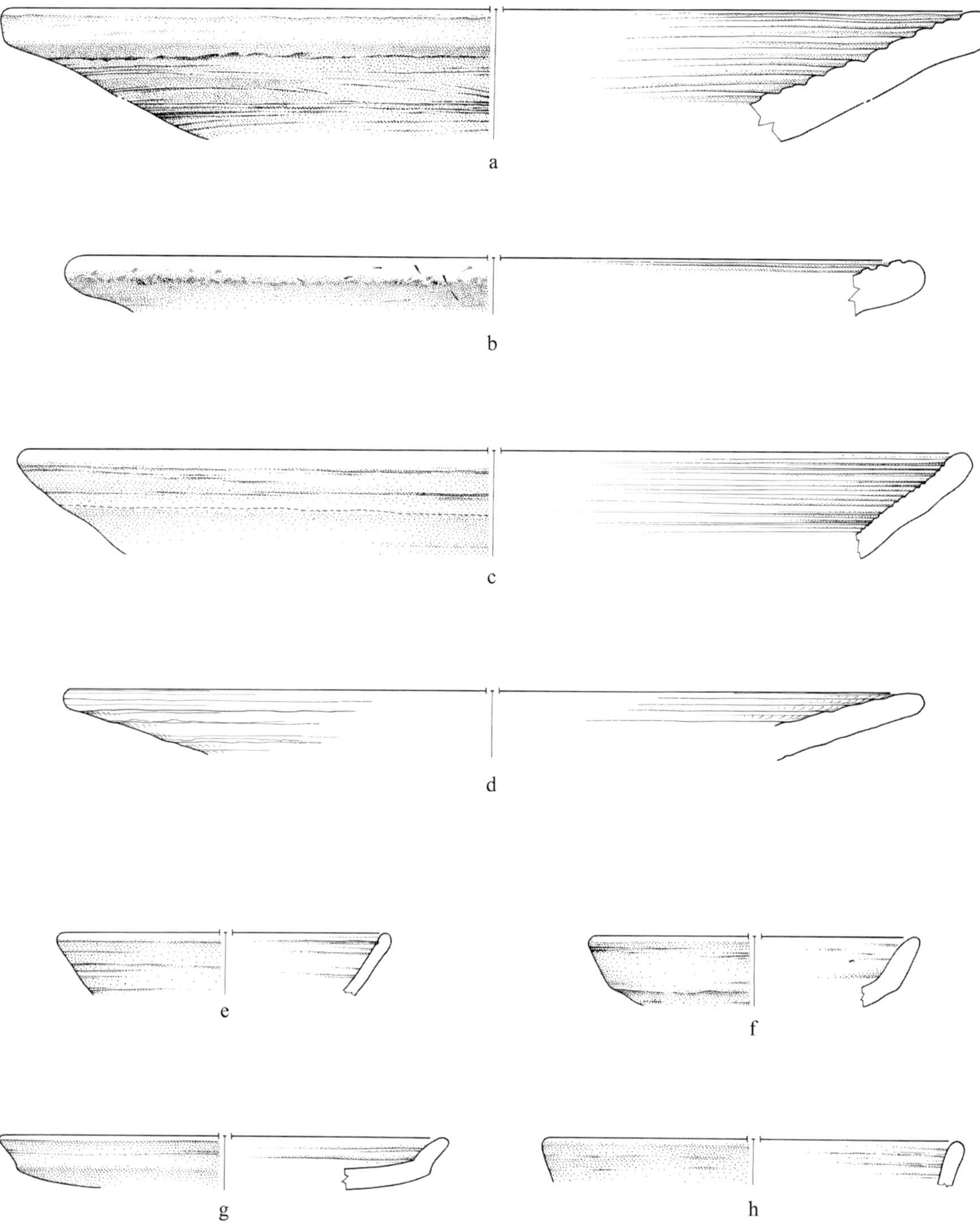

Figure 11. (*a*) **93** (Nile B2 unfired); (*b*) **94** (Nile C); (*c*) **95** (Nile B2); (*d*) **96** (Nile C); (*e*) **97** (Nile B1); (*f*) **98** (Nile B2); (*g*) **99** (Nile B2 with extra limestone); (*h*) **100** (Nile B2). 1:3

Old Kingdom and FIP, Nile Fabrics

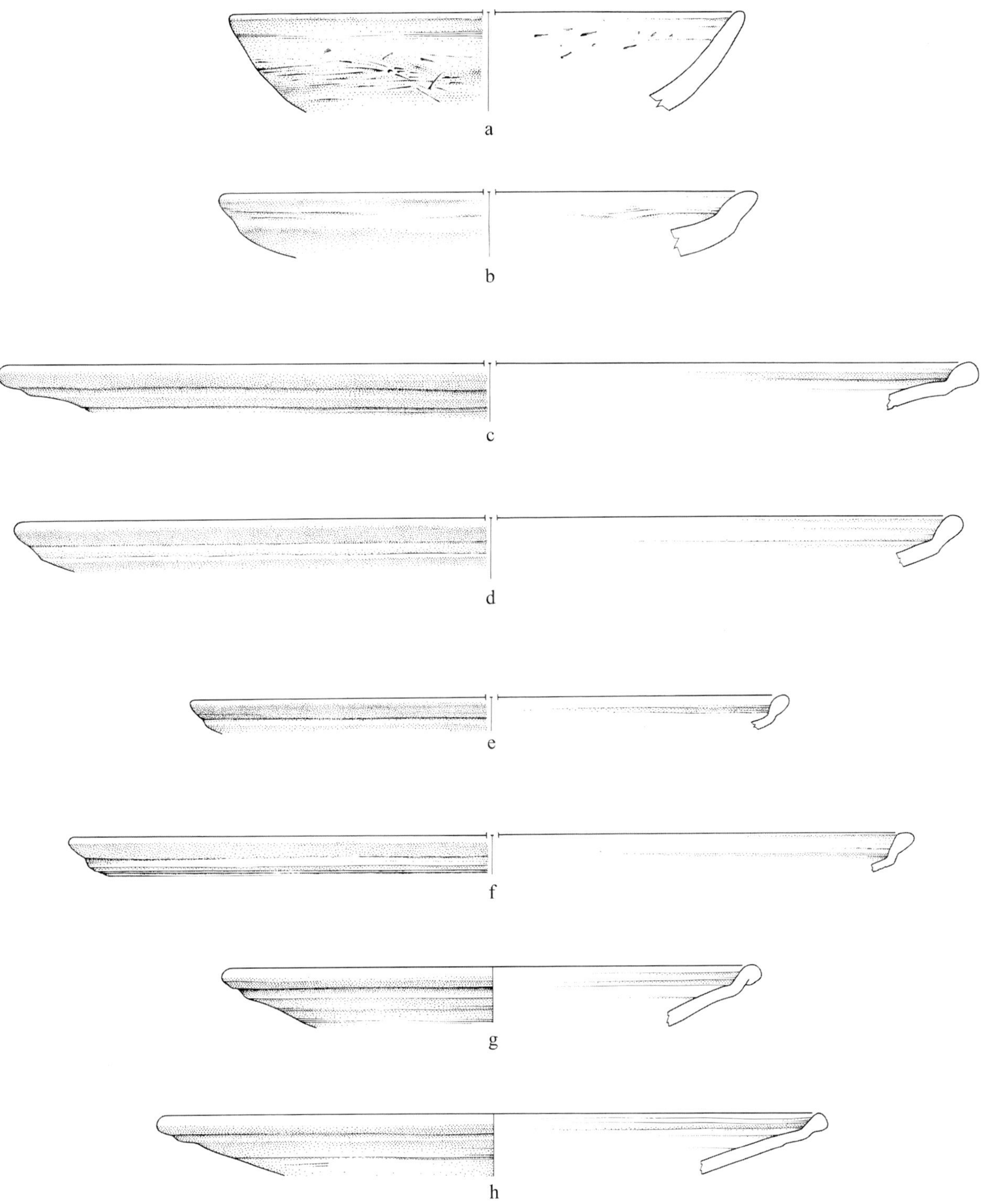

Figure 12. (*a*) **101** AJI **14** (Nile B2); (*b*) **102** ACP **72** (Nile B2); (*c*) **103** (Nile B1); (*d*) **104** BDP **268** (Nile B2); (*e*) **105** ADU **7** (Nile B1); (*f*) **105** AAB **39** (Nile B1); (*g*) **106** BDR **127** (Nile B1); (*h*) **106** ANS **46** (Nile B2). 1:3

Old Kingdom and FIP, Nile Fabrics

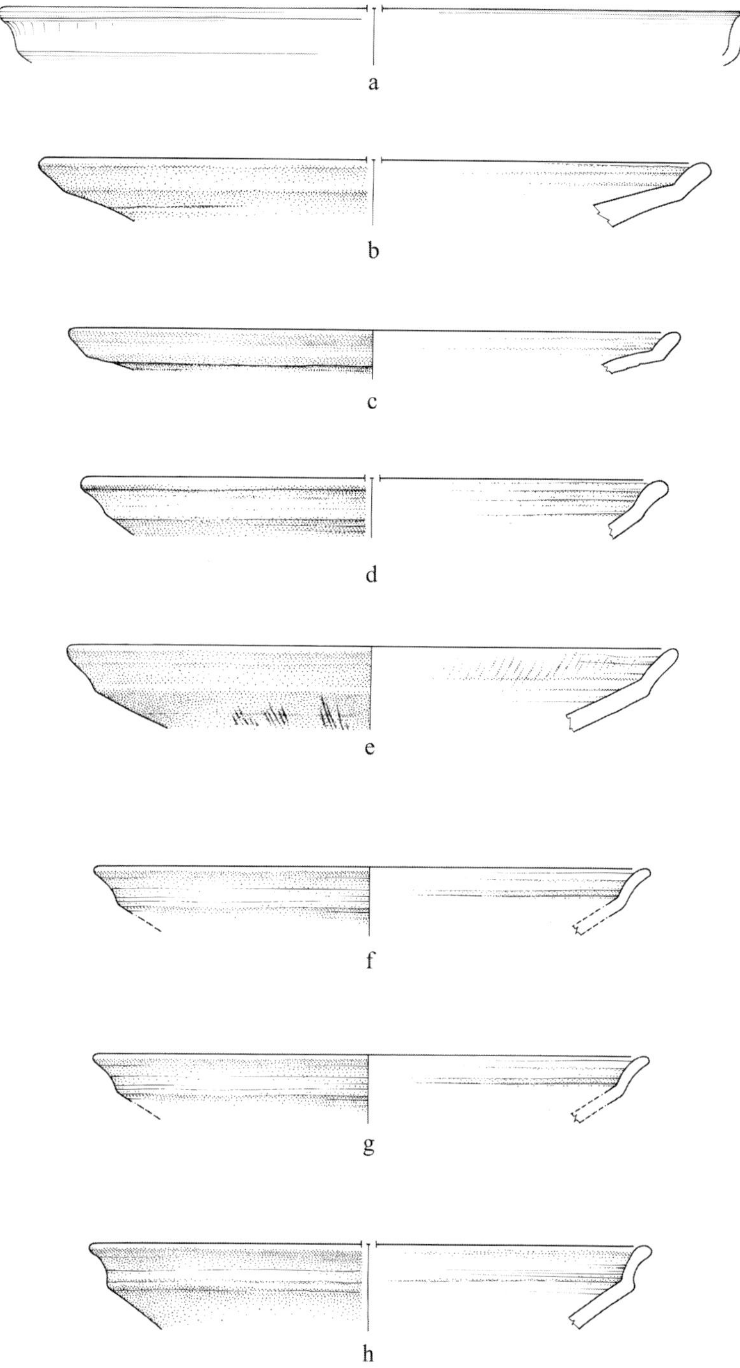

Figure 13. (*a*) **107** (Nile B2); (*b*) **108** (Nile B2); (*c*) **109** (Nile B1); (*d*) **110** (Nile B1); (*e*) **111** ARU=ARZ **35** (Nile B2); (*f*) **112** AQE **72** (Nile B1); (*g*) **112** AYQ/AYR **6** (Nile B1); (*h*) **112** AHR/AEF **28** (Nile B1). 1:3

Old Kingdom and FIP, Nile Fabrics

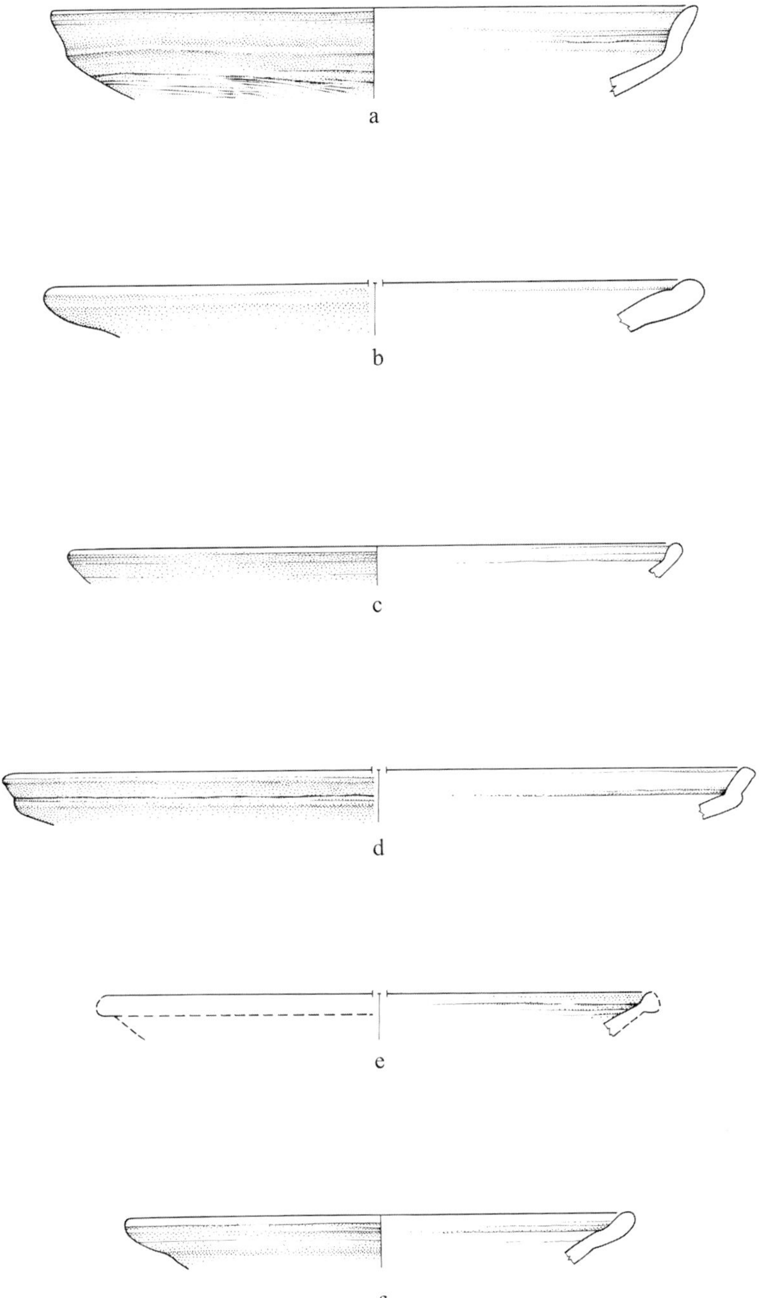

Figure 14. (*a*) **113** (Nile B2); (*b*) **114** (Nile B2); (*c*) **115** (Nile B2); (*d*) **116** (Nile B2); (*e*) **117** (Nile B2); (*f*) **118** BKX **17** (Nile B2). 1:3

Old Kingdom and FIP, Nile Fabrics

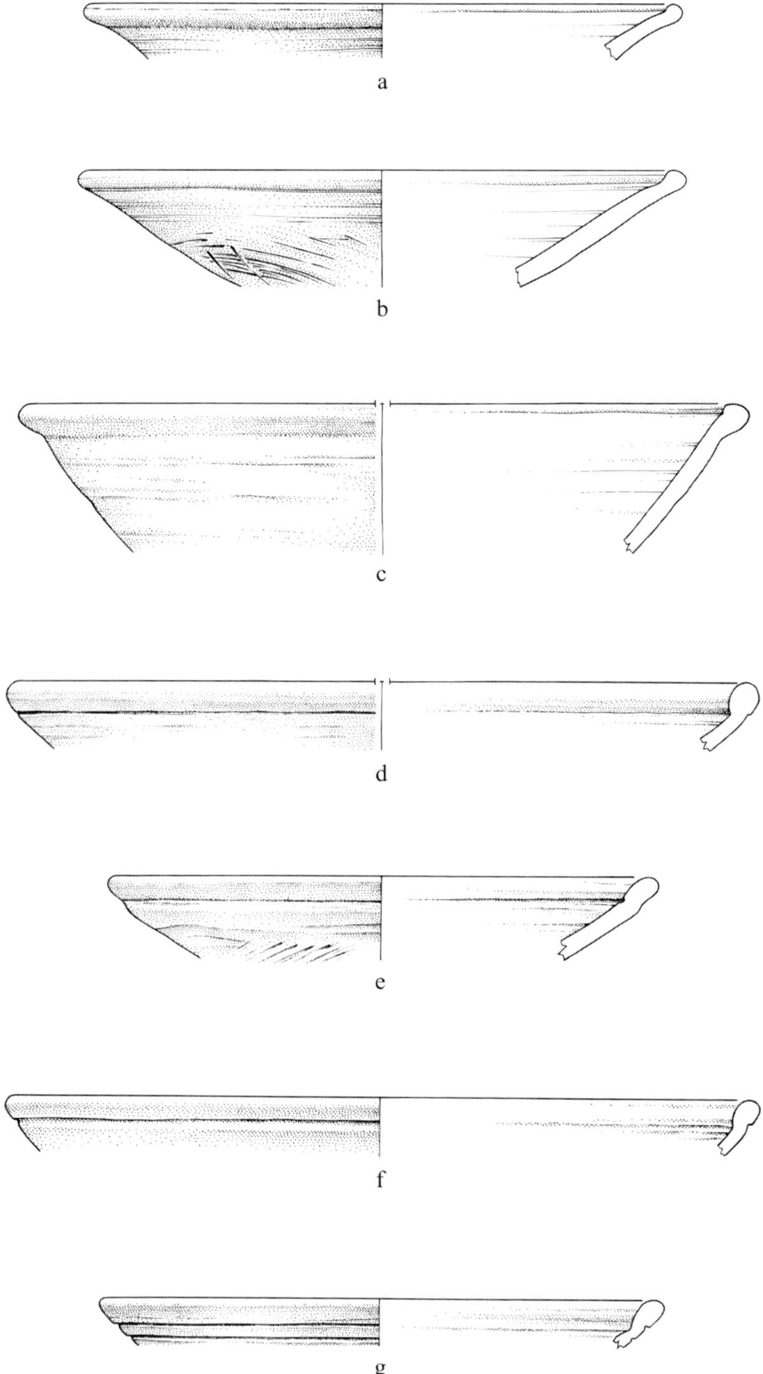

Figure 15. (*a*) **119** AQG **74** (Nile B2); (*b*) **119** BDR **152**+BGG **120** (Nile B1); (*c*) **119** AAA **87** (Nile B2); (*d*) **120** BHL/BHN **13** (Nile B2); (*e*) **121** ADV **1** (Nile B2); (*f*) **121** AAD **14** (Nile B2); (*g*) **121** BFB **59** (Nile B2). 1:3

Old Kingdom and FIP, Nile Fabrics

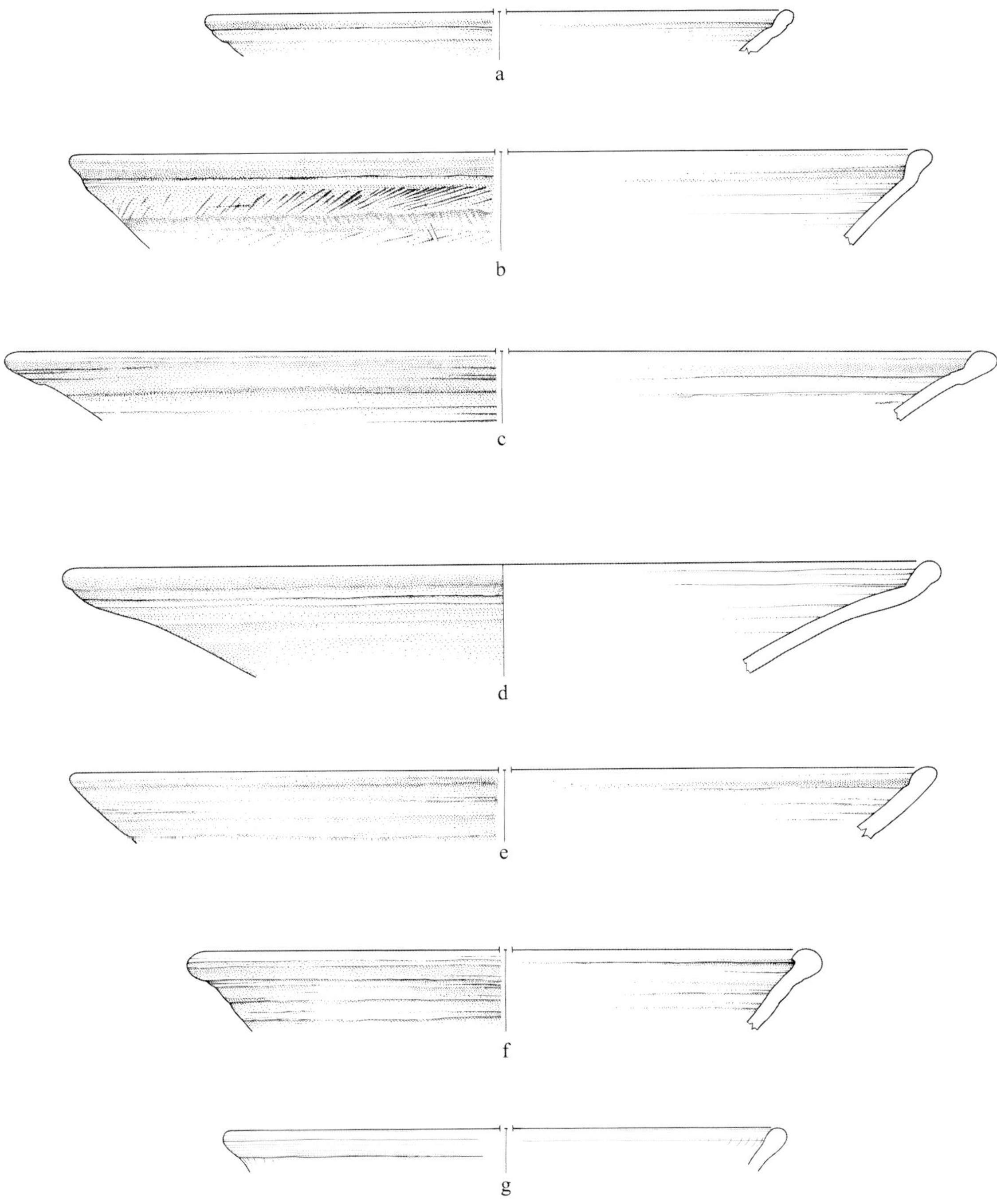

Figure 16. (*a*) **122** BJJ **18** (Nile B2); (*b*) **122** CIC **32** (Nile B1); (*c*) **122** AKJ/AKI **35** (Nile B1); (*d*) **122** AAA **98** (Nile B1); (*e*) **123** ANS **47** (Nile B2); (*f*) **124** (Nile B1); (*g*) **125** (Nile B2). 1:3

Old Kingdom and FIP, Nile Fabrics

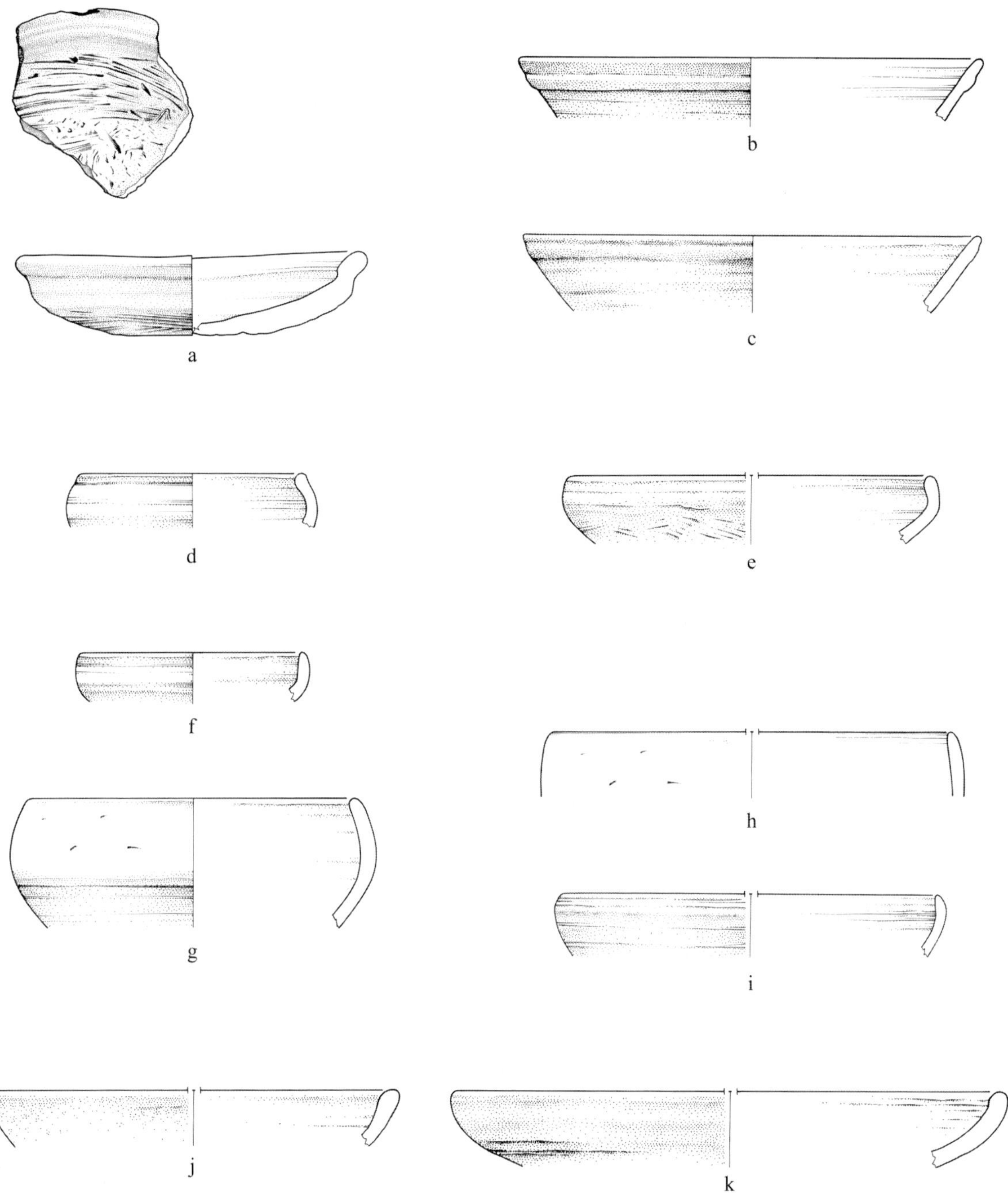

Figure 17. (*a*) **126** ABG **1** (Nile B2); (*b*) **127** (Nile B1 near B2); (*c*) **128** (Nile B1); (*d*) **129** (Nile B2); (*e*) **130** (Nile B2); (*f*) **131** (Nilc B2); (*g*) **132** DAC **35** (Nile B2); (*h*) **133** (Nile B2); (*i*) **134** (Nile B2); (*j*) **135** (Nile B2); (*k*) **136** (Nile B2).
1:3

Old Kingdom and FIP, Nile Fabrics

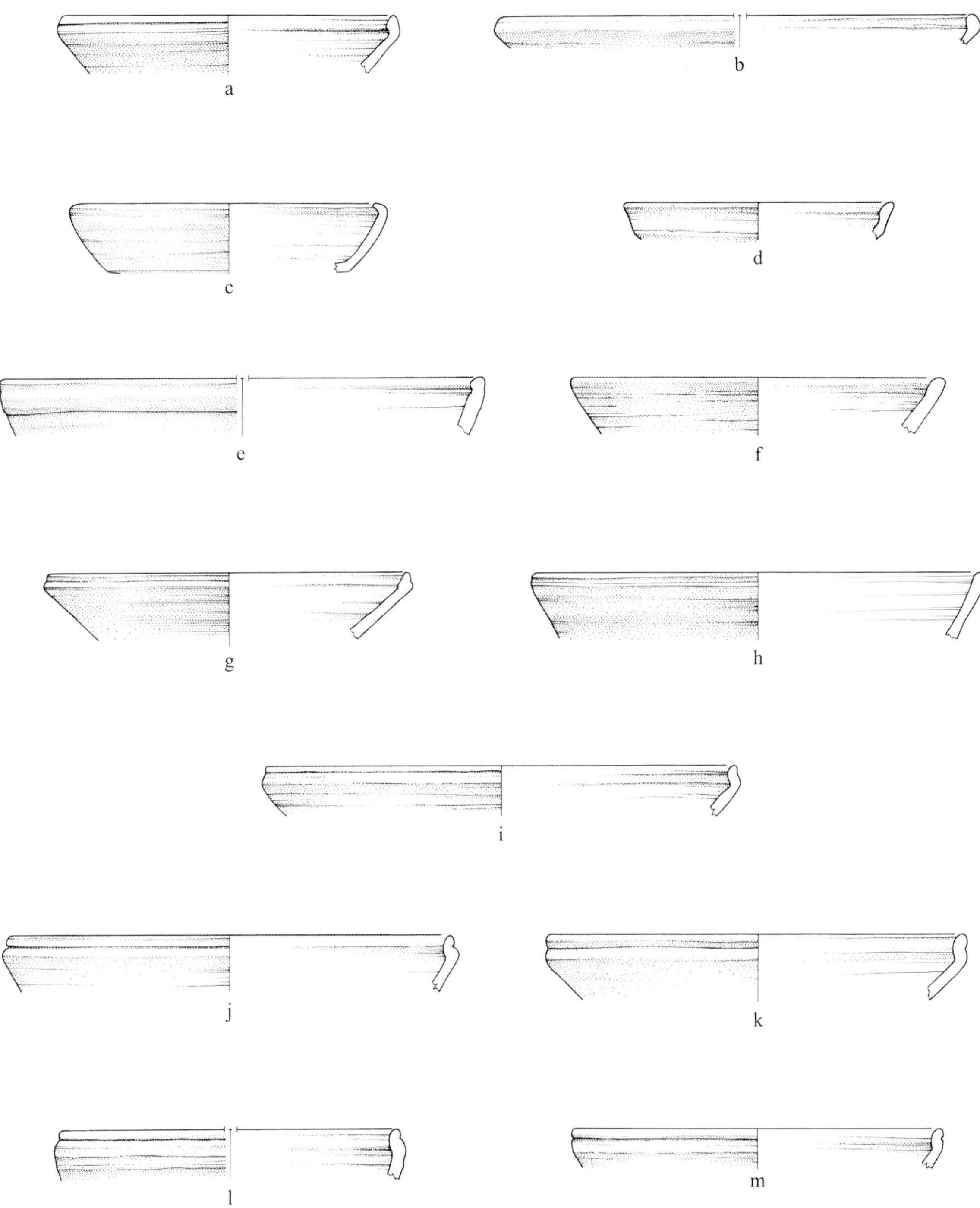

Figure 18. (*a*) **137** (Nile B1); (*b*) **138** (Nile B2); (*c*) **139** (Nile B1); (*d*) **140** (Nile B2); (*e*) **141** (Nile B2); (*f*) **142** (Nile B2); (*g*) **143** AQG **195** (Nile B1); (*h*) **143** AQG **237** (Nile B1); (*i*) **144** AZO **8** (Nile B1); (*j*) **144** BDG/BRT **38** (Nile B1); (*k*) **144** CBS/AAA **28** (Nile B2); (*l*) **145** (Nile B2); (*m*) **146** CBS/AAA **13** (Nile B2). 1:3

Old Kingdom and FIP, Nile Fabrics

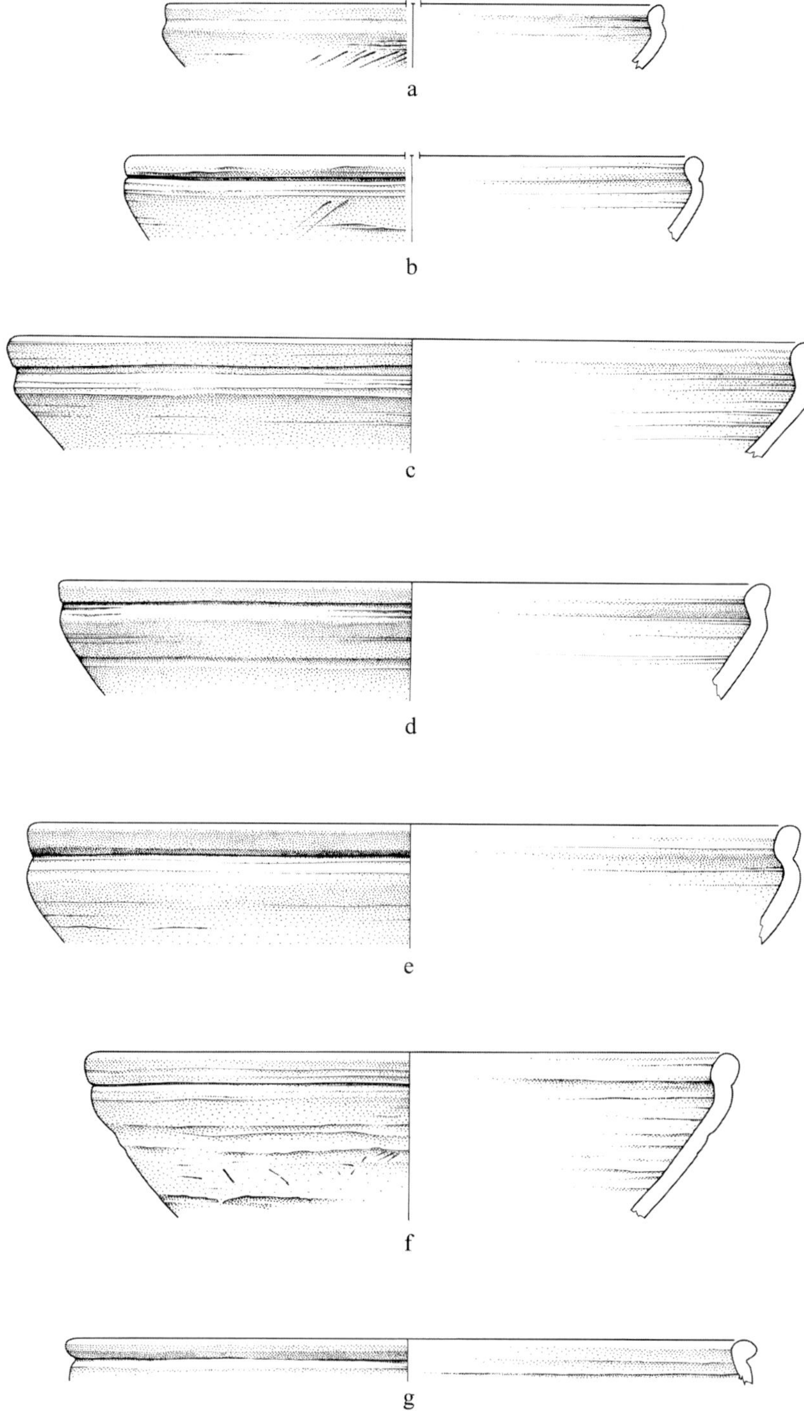

Figure 19. (*a*) <u>**147**</u> AAA **48** (Nile B2); (*b*) <u>**147**</u> AAA **49** (Nile B2); (*c*) <u>**148**</u> ADU **12+15** (Nile B1); (*d*) <u>**148**</u> DAW **10** (Nile B1); (*e*) <u>**148**</u> AAA **167** (Nile B1); (*f*) <u>**149**</u> BDP **25** (Nile B2); (*g*) <u>**150**</u> (Nile B1 near B2). 1:3

Old Kingdom and FIP, Nile Fabrics

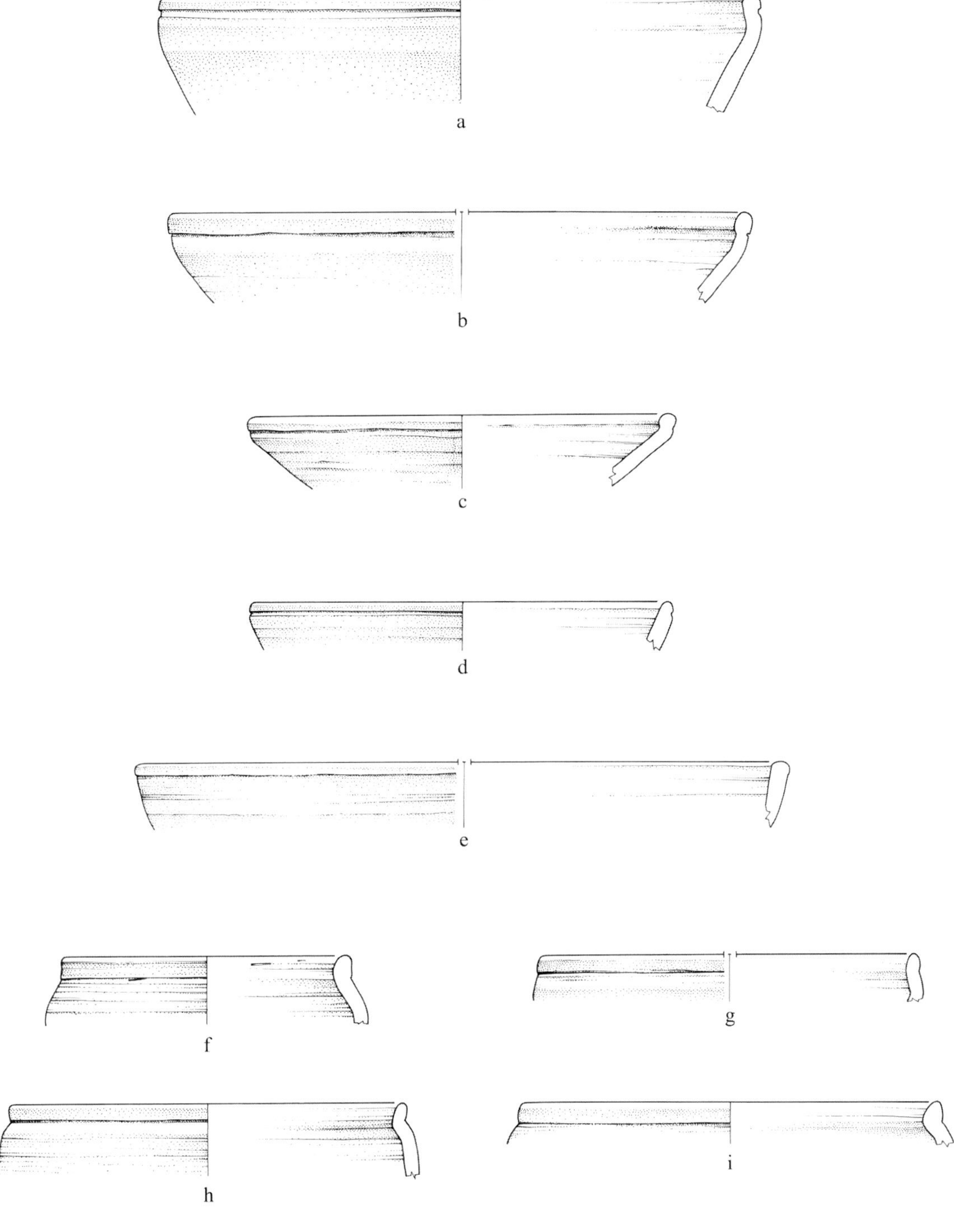

Figure 20. (*a*) **151** AQG **239** (Nile B2); (*b*) **152** AMJ **21** (Nile B2); (*c*) **153** (Nile B1); (*d*) **154** (Nile B2); (*e*) **155** ADF North **64** (Nile B2); (*f*) **156** (Nile B1); (*g*) **157** (Nile B2); (*h*) **158** (Nile B1 near B2); (*i*) **159** (Nile B1). 1:3

Old Kingdom and FIP, Nile Fabrics

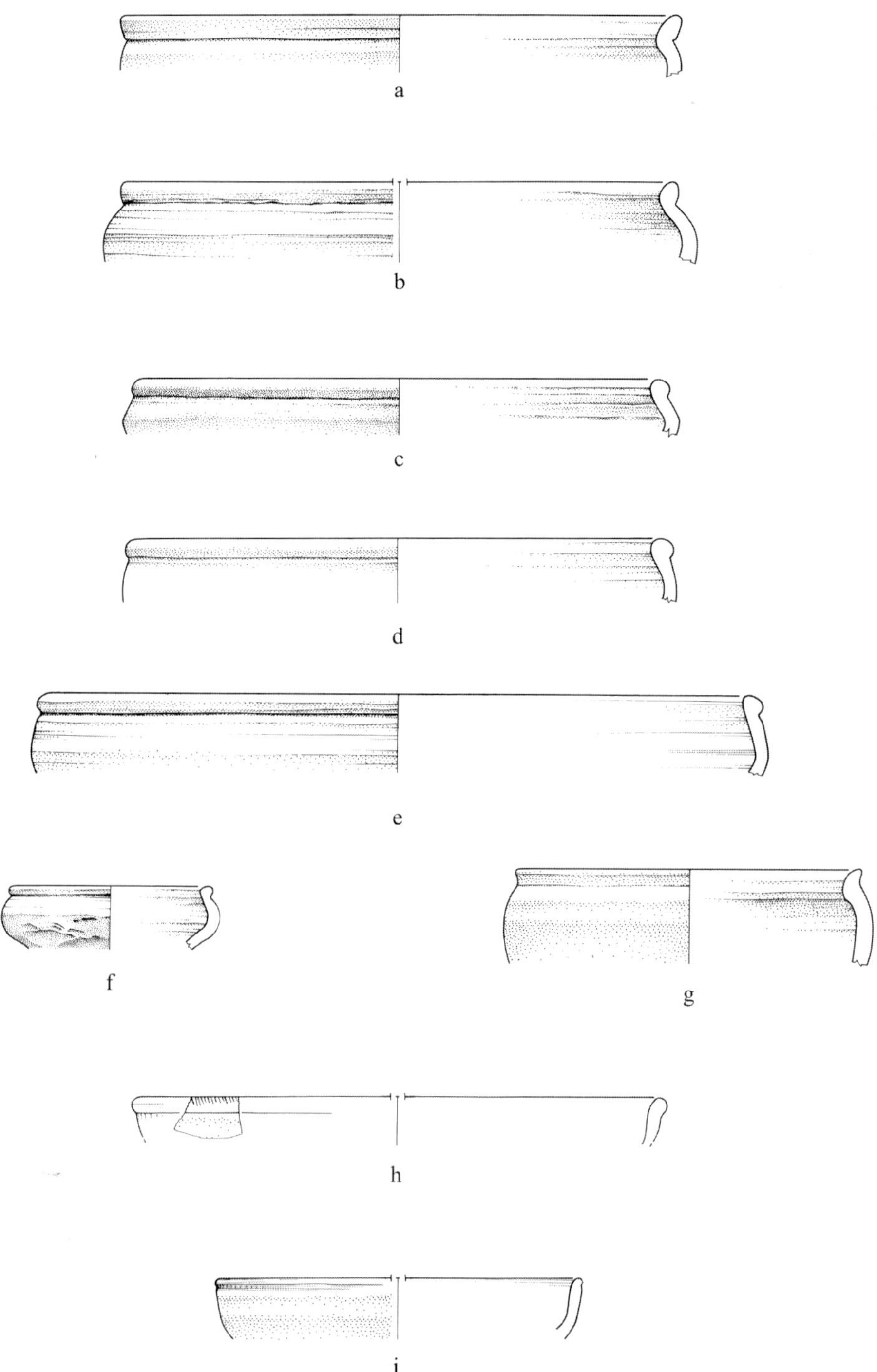

Figure 21. (*a*) **160** AAF **21** (Nile B2); (*b*) **161** ADC **141** (Nile B2); (*c*) **162** (Nile B2); (*d*) **163** ADF North **60** (Nile B2); (*e*) **164** AAA **38** (Nile A); (*f*) **165** (Nile B1); (*g*) **166** (Nile B1 near B2); (*h*) **167** (Nile B2); (*i*) **168** (Nile B2). 1:3

Old Kingdom and FIP, Nile Fabrics

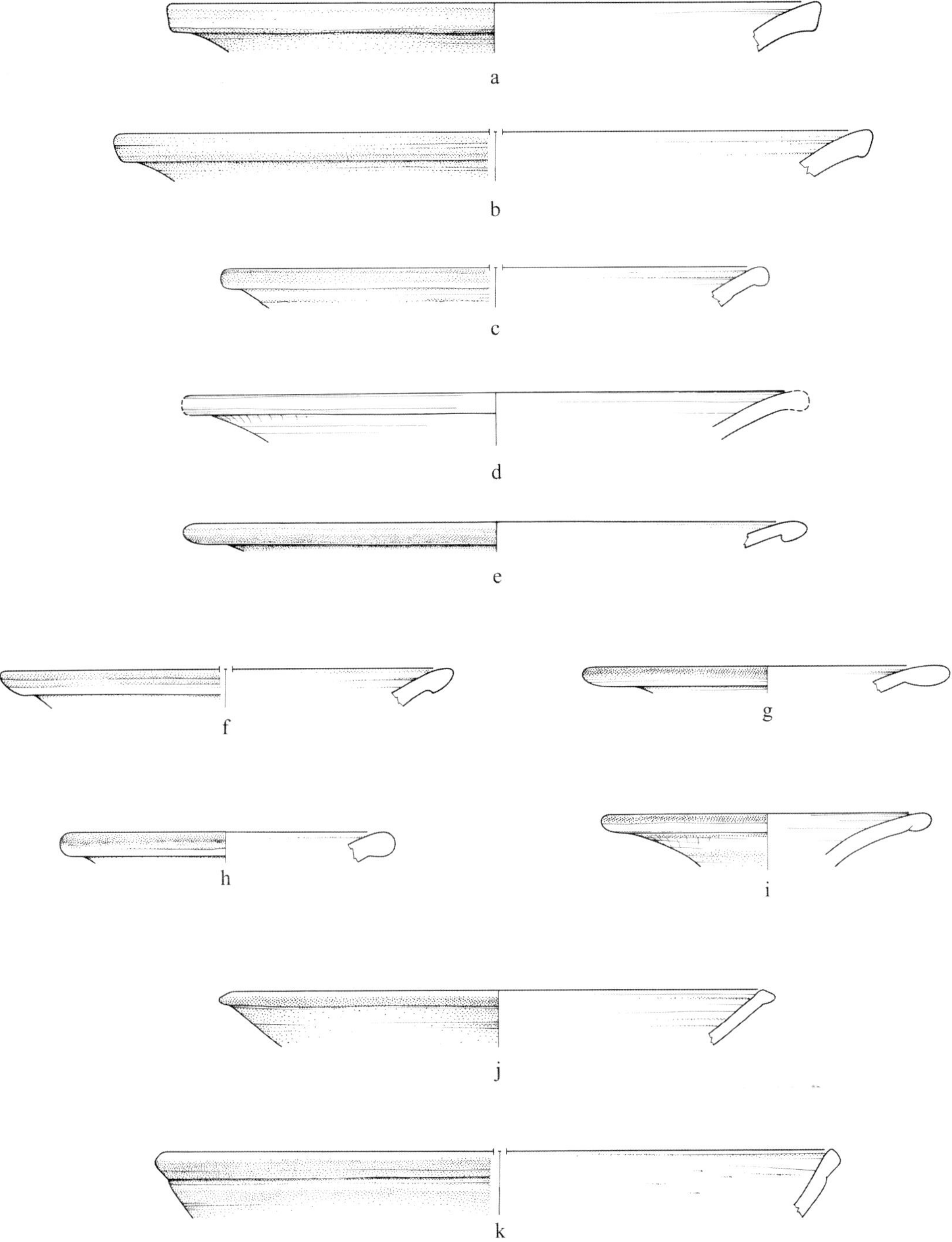

Figure 22. (*a*) **169** AIY/AVB **43** (Nile B2); (*b*) **169** ACE **257** (Nile B2); (*c*) **170** (Nile B2); (*d*) **171** (Nile B1); (*e*) **172** (Nile B1); (*f*) **173** CIE **30** (Nile B1); (*g*) **174** (Nile B1); (*h*) **175** (Nile B1); (*i*) **176** (Nile B1); (*j*) **177** (Nile B1); (*k*) **178** (Nile B2).

1:3

Old Kingdom and FIP, Nile Fabrics

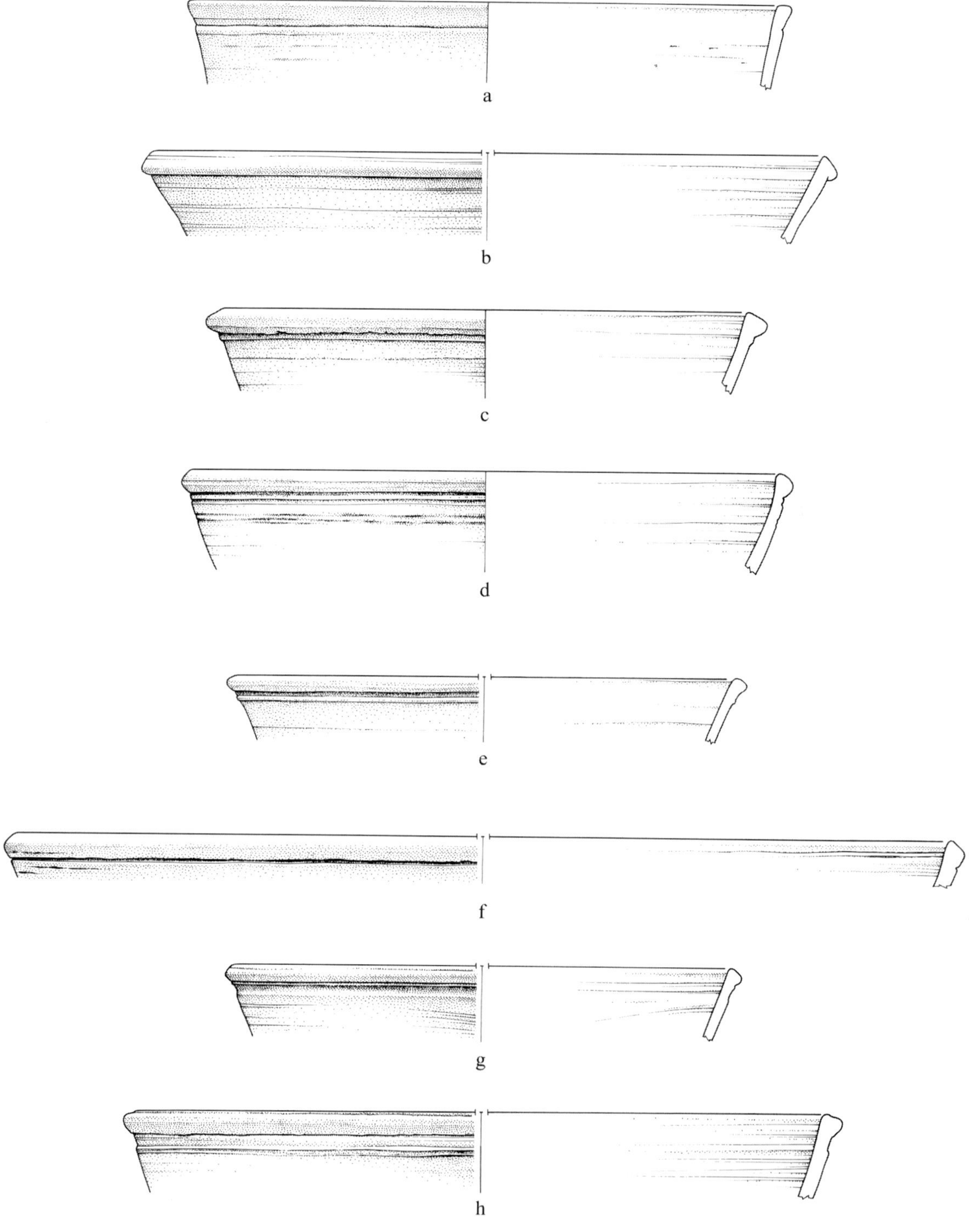

Figure 23. (*a*) 179 (Nile B2); (*b*) 180 BGG **138** (Nile B1); (*c*) 180 BTG **23** (Nile B1); (*d*) 180 APG **12** (Nile B1); (*e*) 181 (Nile B2); (*f*) 182 (Nile B1); (*g*) 183 (Nile B1 near B2); (*h*) 184 (Nile B1). 1:3

Old Kingdom and FIP, Nile Fabrics

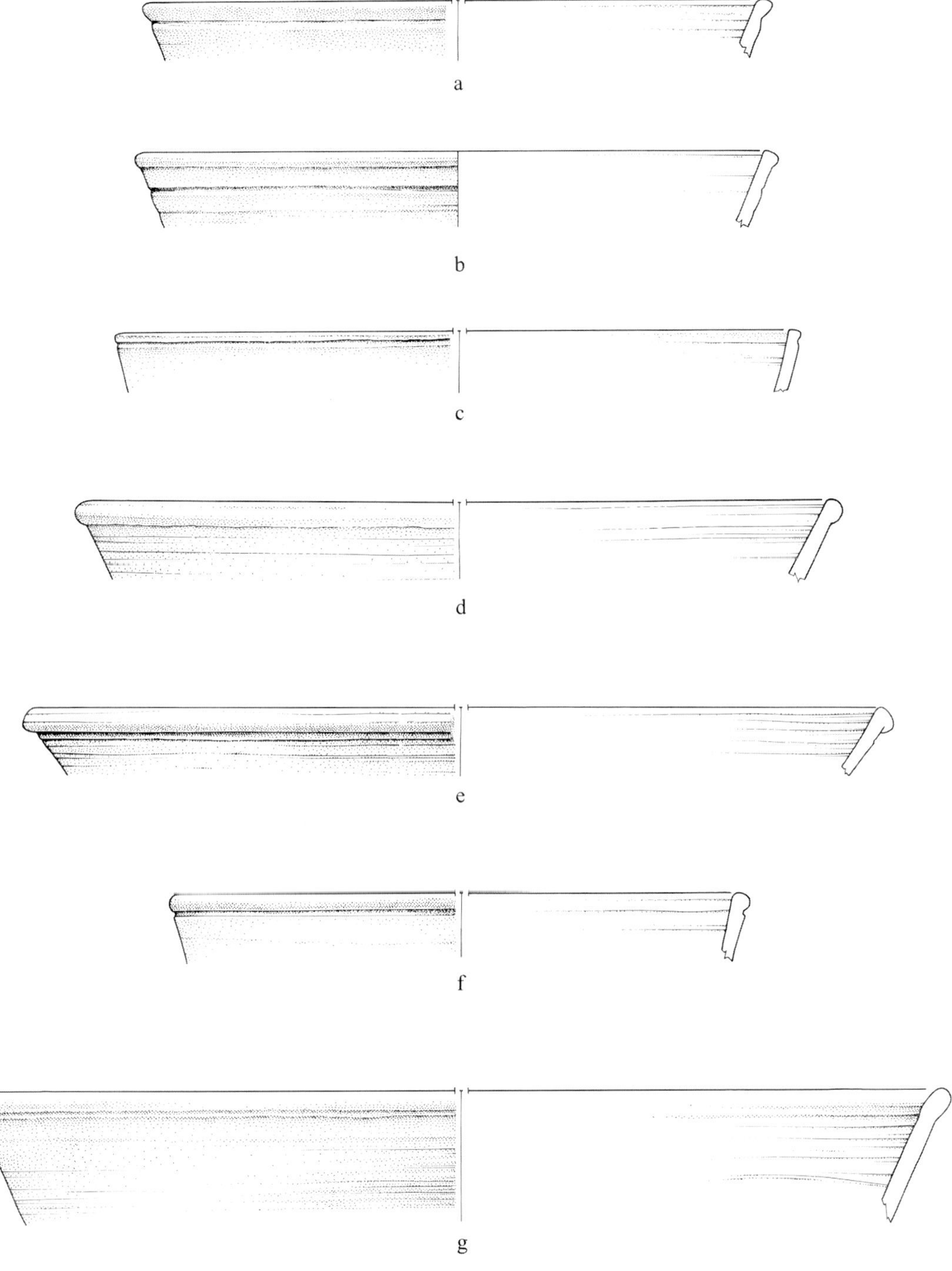

Figure 24. (*a*) **185** (Nile B2); (*b*) **186** (Nile B1); (*c*) **187** (Nile B2); (*d*) **188** (Nile B2); (*e*) **189** (Nile B1 with extra limestone); (*f*) **190** (Nile B2); (*g*) **191** (Nile B1). 1.3

Old Kingdom and FIP, Nile Fabrics

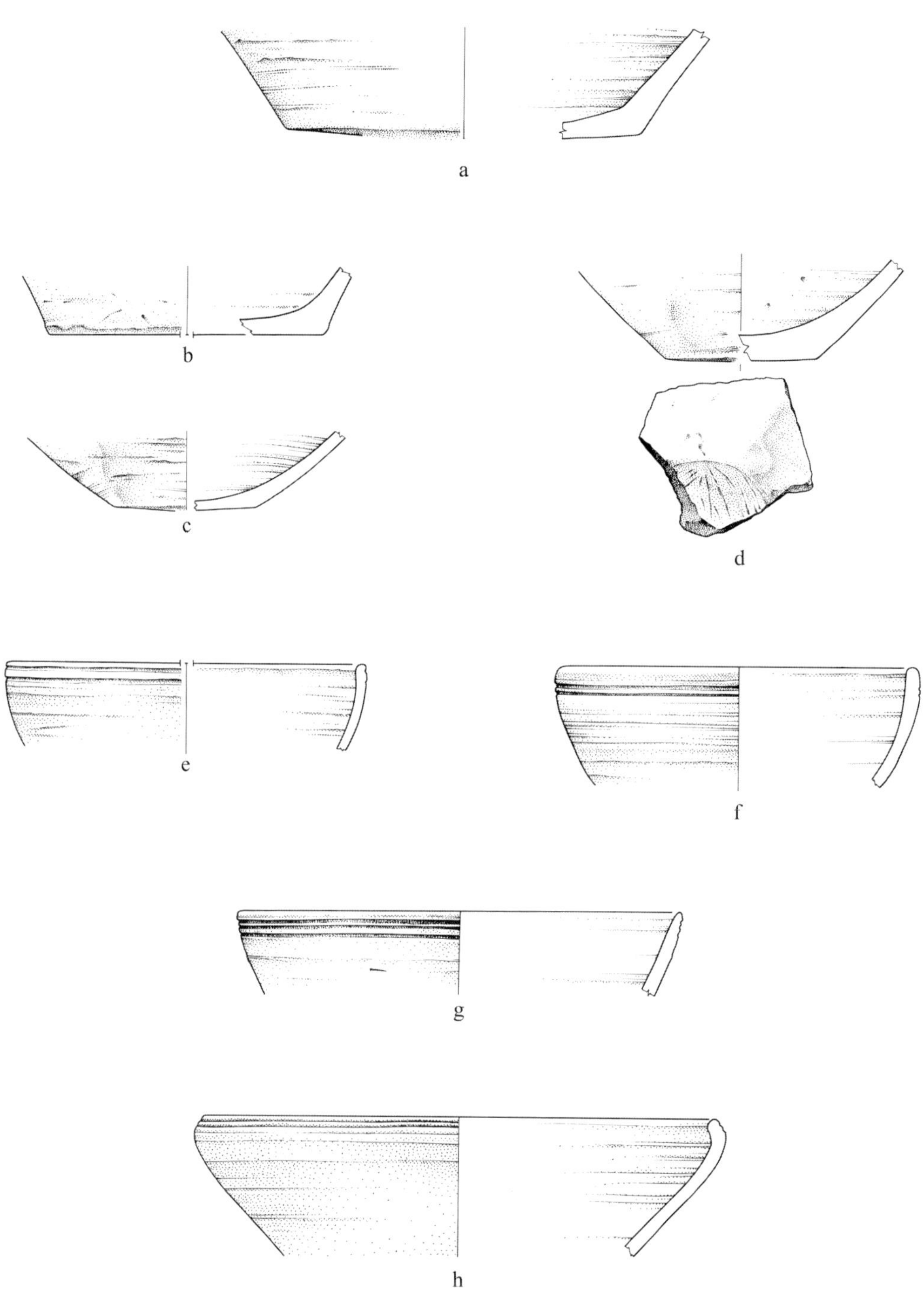

Figure 25. (*a*) **192** UP 1047 **1** (Nile B2); (*b*) **192** AJY **141** (Nile B2); (*c*) **193** AKJ/AKI **3** (Nile B2); (*d*) **193** ABG **35** (Nile B2); (*e*) **194** BPW **7** (Nile B2); (*f*) **194** AQC **196** (Nile B1); (*g*) **194** AQI **28** (Nile B1); (*h*) **195** CAA **31** (Nile B1).
1:3

Old Kingdom and FIP, Nile Fabrics

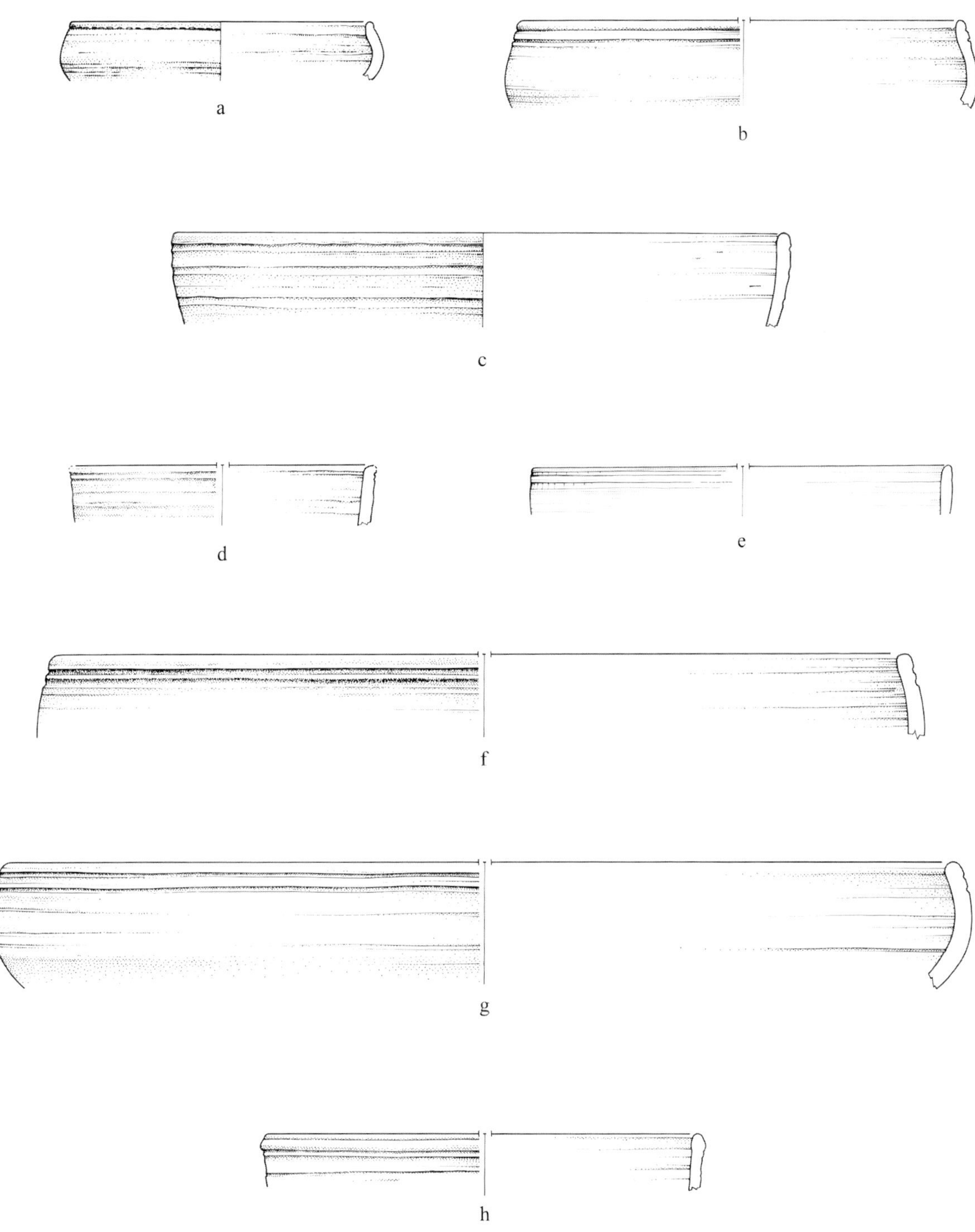

Figure 26. (*a*) **196** (Nile B2); (*b*) **197** (Nile A); (*c*) **198** (Nile B2); (*d*) **199** AYP/AYJ **21** (Nile B2); (*e*) **200** AIY/BDR/AWZ **14** (Nile B2); (*f*) **201** AQG **124** (Nile B2); (*g*) **201** AAA **128** (Nile B1); (*h*) **202** AMJ **13** (Nile B1 near B2). 1:3

Old Kingdom and FIP, Nile Fabrics

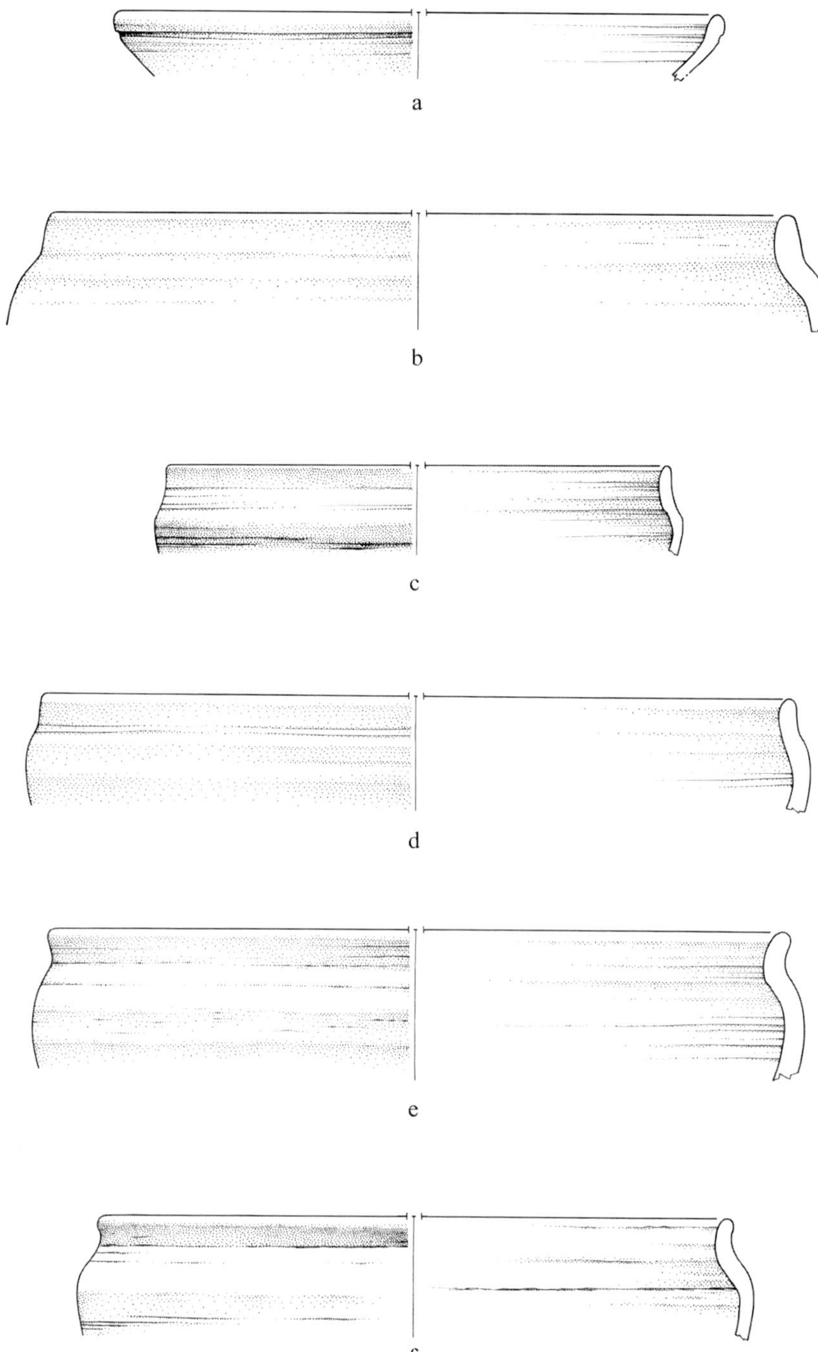

Figure 27. (*a*) **203** (Nile B2); (*b*) **204** (Nile B2); (*c*) **205** AAA **126** (Nile B1); (*d*) **206** AAA **43** (Nile B2); (*e*) **207** AAA **13** (Nile B2); (*f*) **208** (Nile B2). 1:3

Old Kingdom and FIP, Nile Fabrics

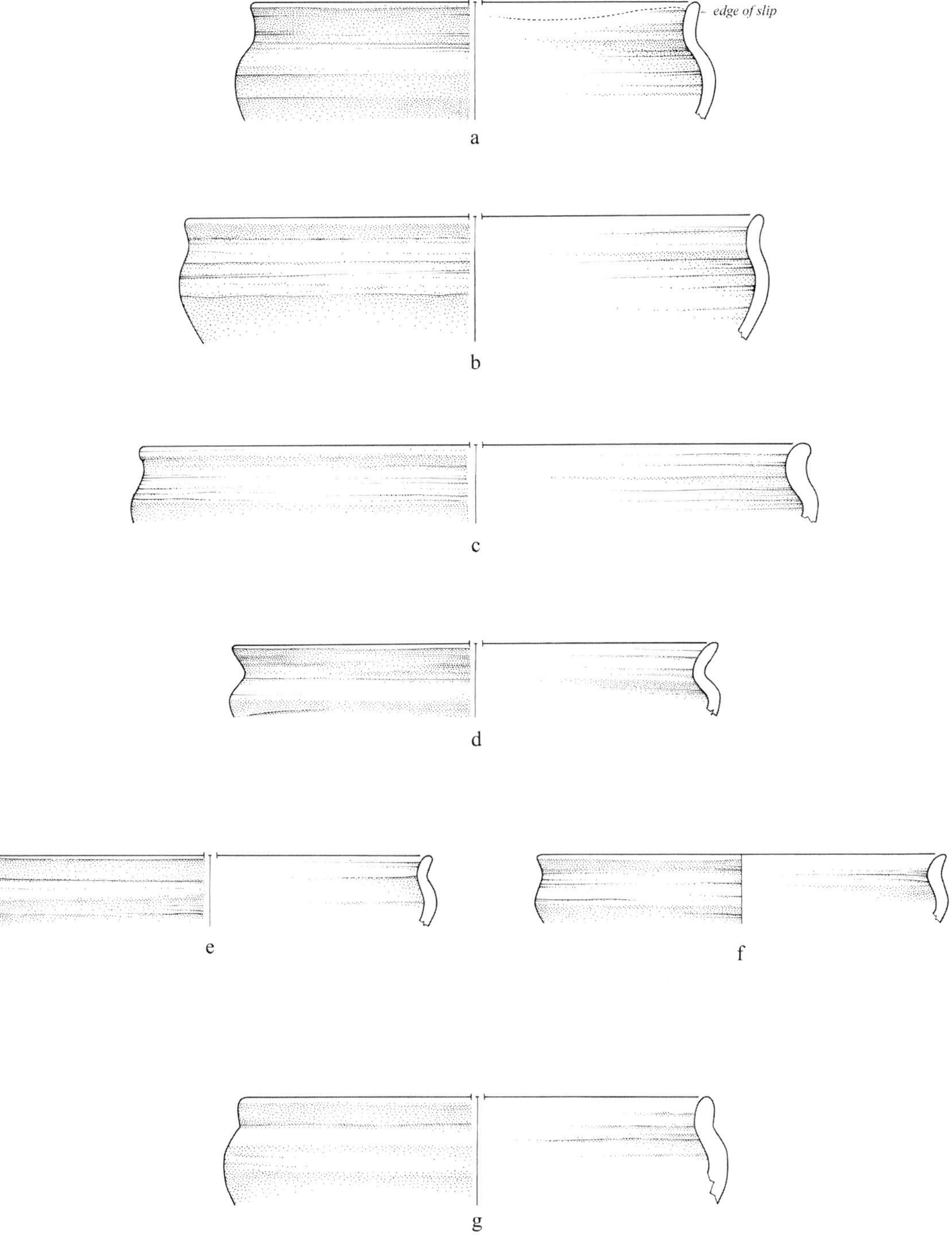

Figure 28. (*a*) **209** BFB **30** (Nile B2); (*b*) **210** AAA **38** (Nile B2); (*c*) **211** (Nile B1); (*d*) **212** AJK **3** (Nile B1); (*e*) **213** AFR **19** (Nile B1); (*f*) **213** AAA Upper **28** (Nile B1); (*g*) **214** AAQ **80** (Nile B2). 1:3

Old Kingdom and FIP, Nile Fabrics

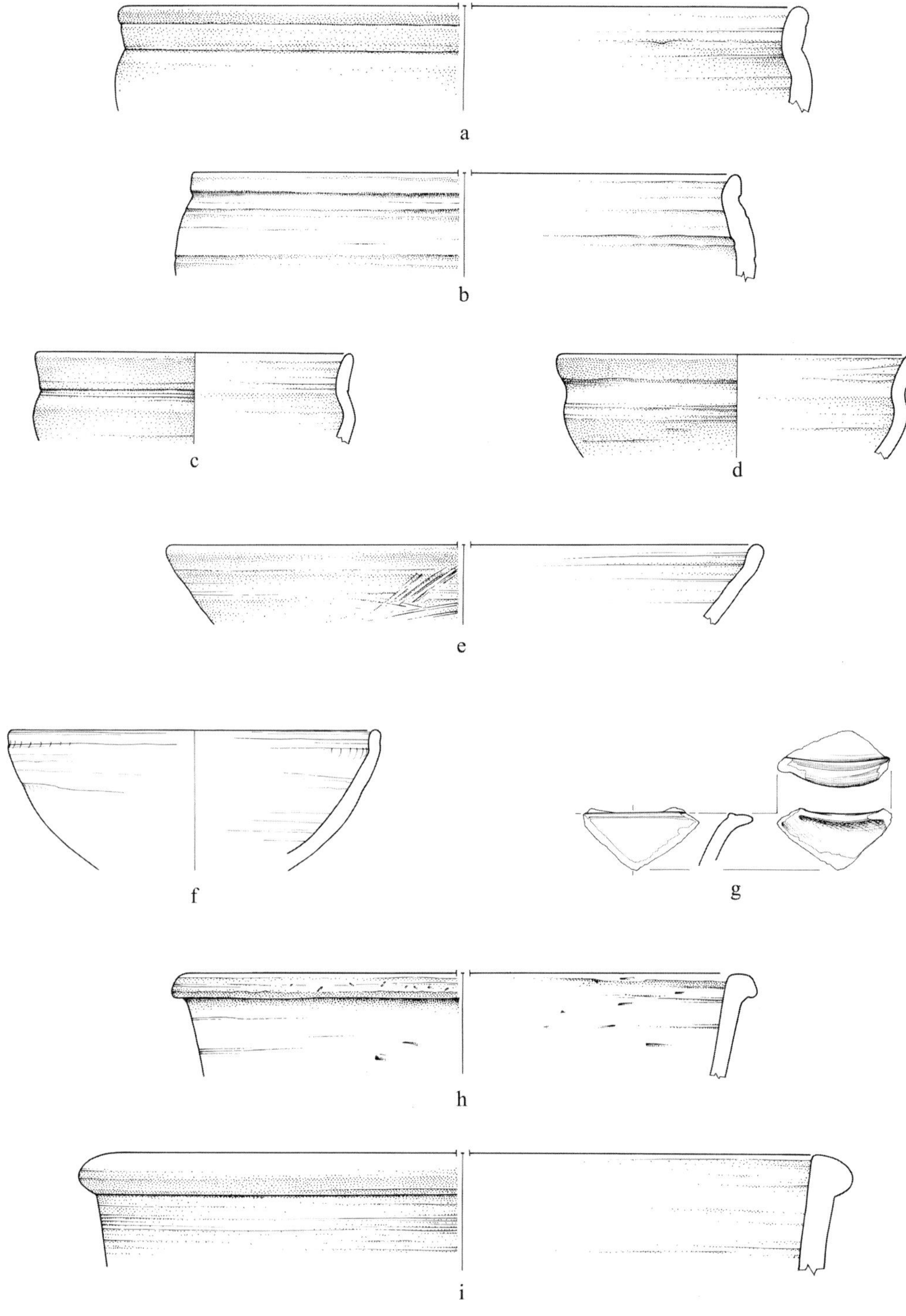

Figure 29. (*a*) **215** ANJ **2** (Nile B2); (*b*) **216** (Nile B1); (*c*) **217** (Nile B1); (*d*) **218** (Nile B1); (*e*) **219** (Nile B1); (*f*) **220** ATY **236** (Nile B2); (*g*) **221** (Nile B1 near B2); (*h*) **222** (Nile B2); (*i*) **223** AHC/AIU **19** (Nile B2).

1:3

Old Kingdom and FIP, Nile Fabrics

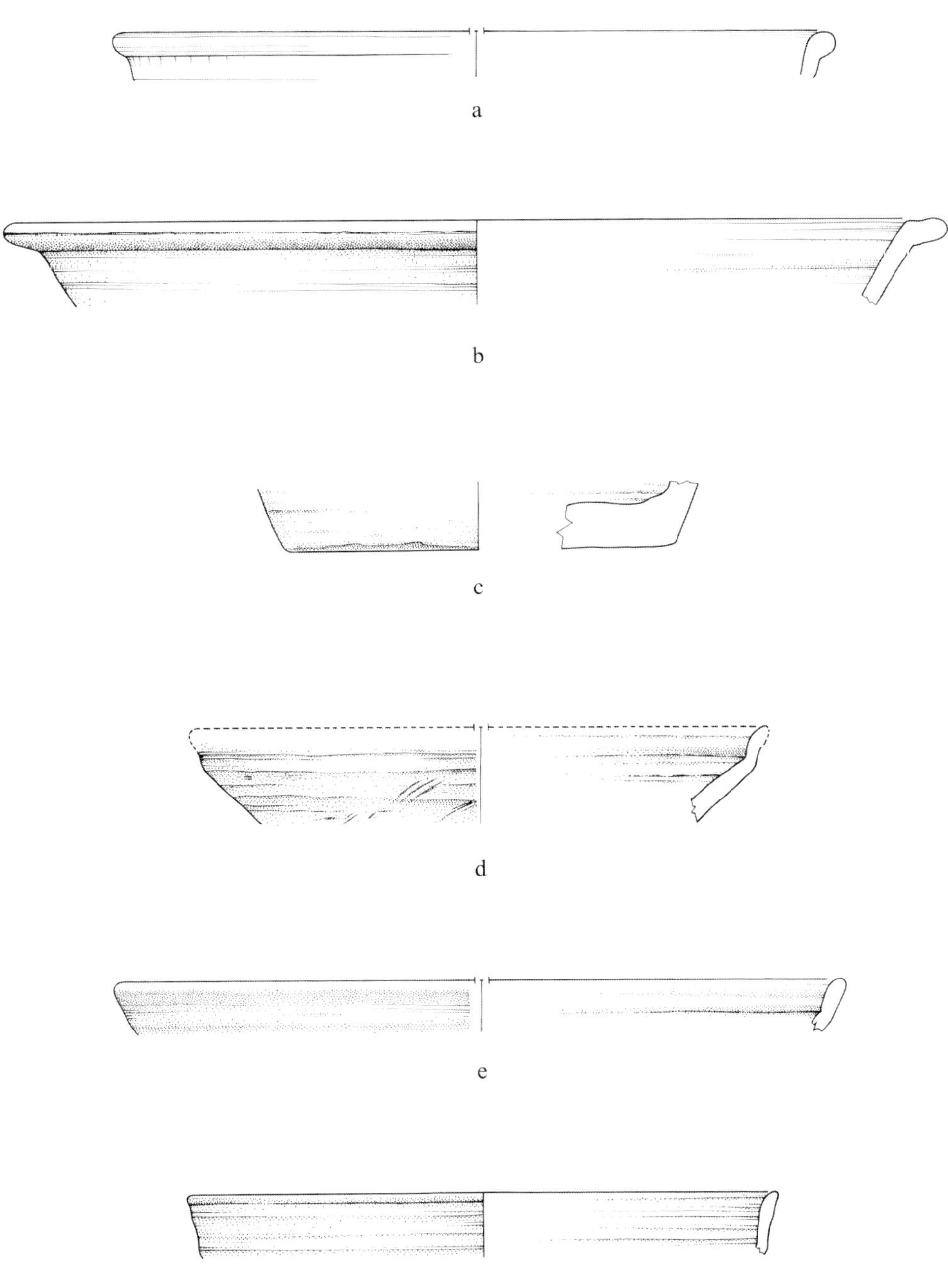

Figure 30. (*a*) **224** (Nile B2); (*b*) **225** (Nile B2); (*c*) **226** BEO **88** (Nile B2); (*d*) **227** (Nile B2); (*e*) **228** (Nile B2); (*f*) **229** (Nile B1). 1:3

Old Kingdom and FIP, Nile Fabrics

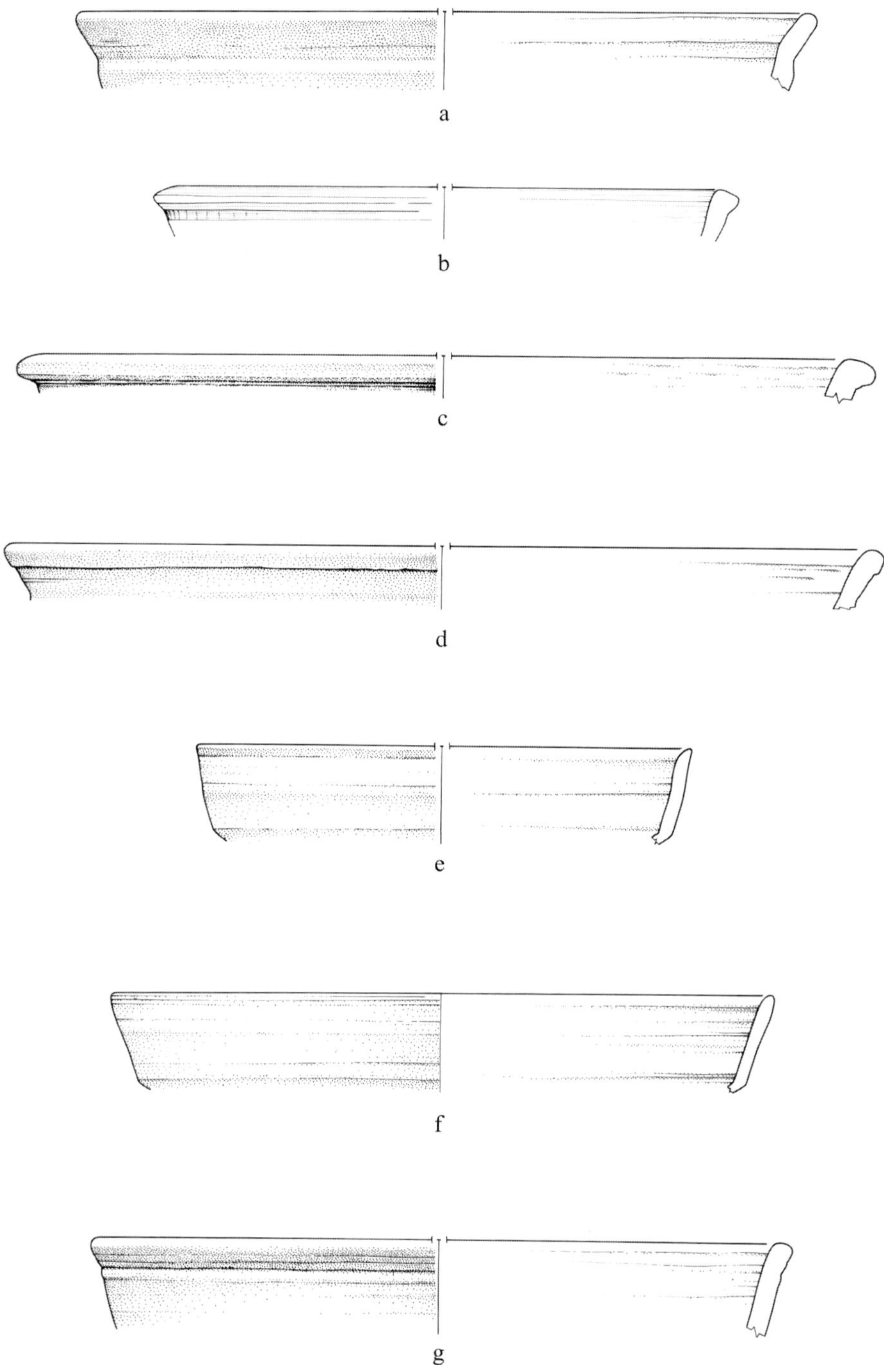

Figure 31. (*a*) **230** (Nile B2); (*b*) **232** ADU **25** (Nile B2); (*c*) **233** (Nile B2); (*d*) **234** (Nile B1); (*e*) **235** AQE **66** (Nile B1); (*f*) **235** AAB **10** (Nile B1); (*g*) **236** (Nile B1). 1:3

Old Kingdom and FIP, Nile Fabrics

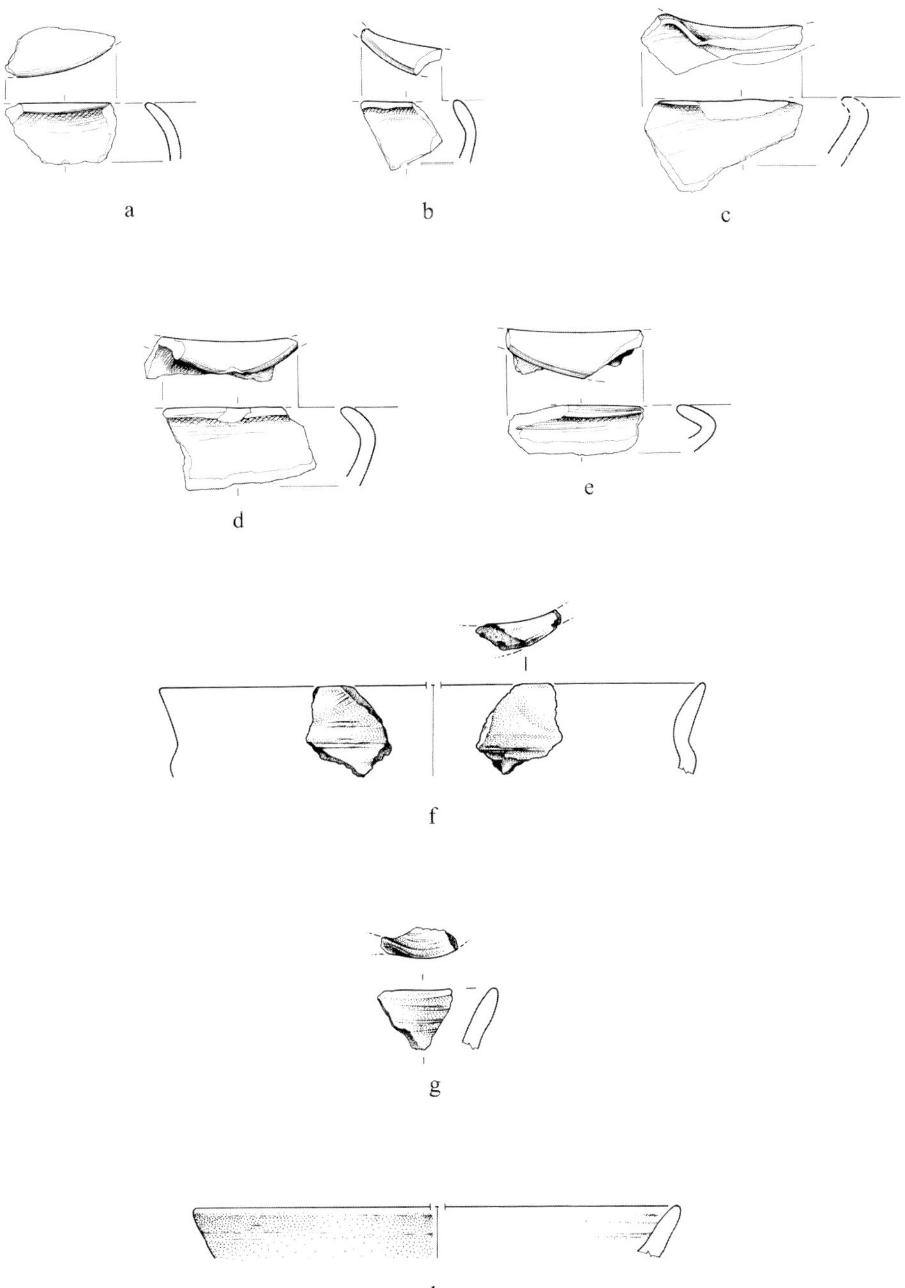

Figure 32. (*a*) **237** BET **96** (Nile B1); (*b*) **237** ABI Top **137** (Nile B1); (*c*) **237** BQE **11** (Nile B2); (*d*) **237** ATY **90** (Nile B2); (*e*) **237** ABG **24** (Nile B2); (*f*) **238** (Nile B2); (*g*) **239** (Nile B1); (*h*) **240** (Nile B2). 1:3

Old Kingdom and FIP, Nile Fabrics

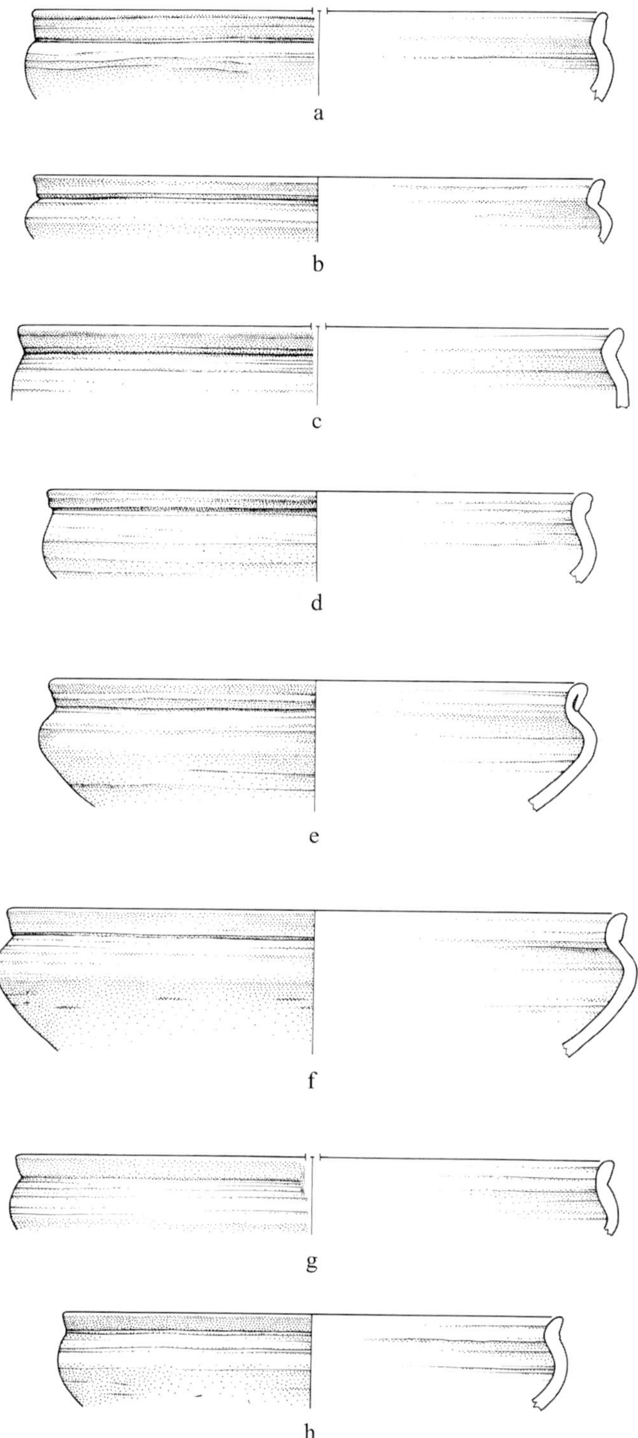

Figure 33. (*a*) **244** ATY **237** (Nile B2); (*b*) **244** ABG **2** (Nile B2); (*c*) **244** ABG **2** (Nile B1); (*d*) **244** AAA **155** (Nile B1); (*e*) **244** AAA **10** (Nile B1); (*f*) **244** AAA **40** (Nile B2); (*g*) **244** AAA **128** (Nile A); (*h*) **244** CAA North **6** (Nile B1/B2).

1:3

Old Kingdom and FIP, Nile Fabrics

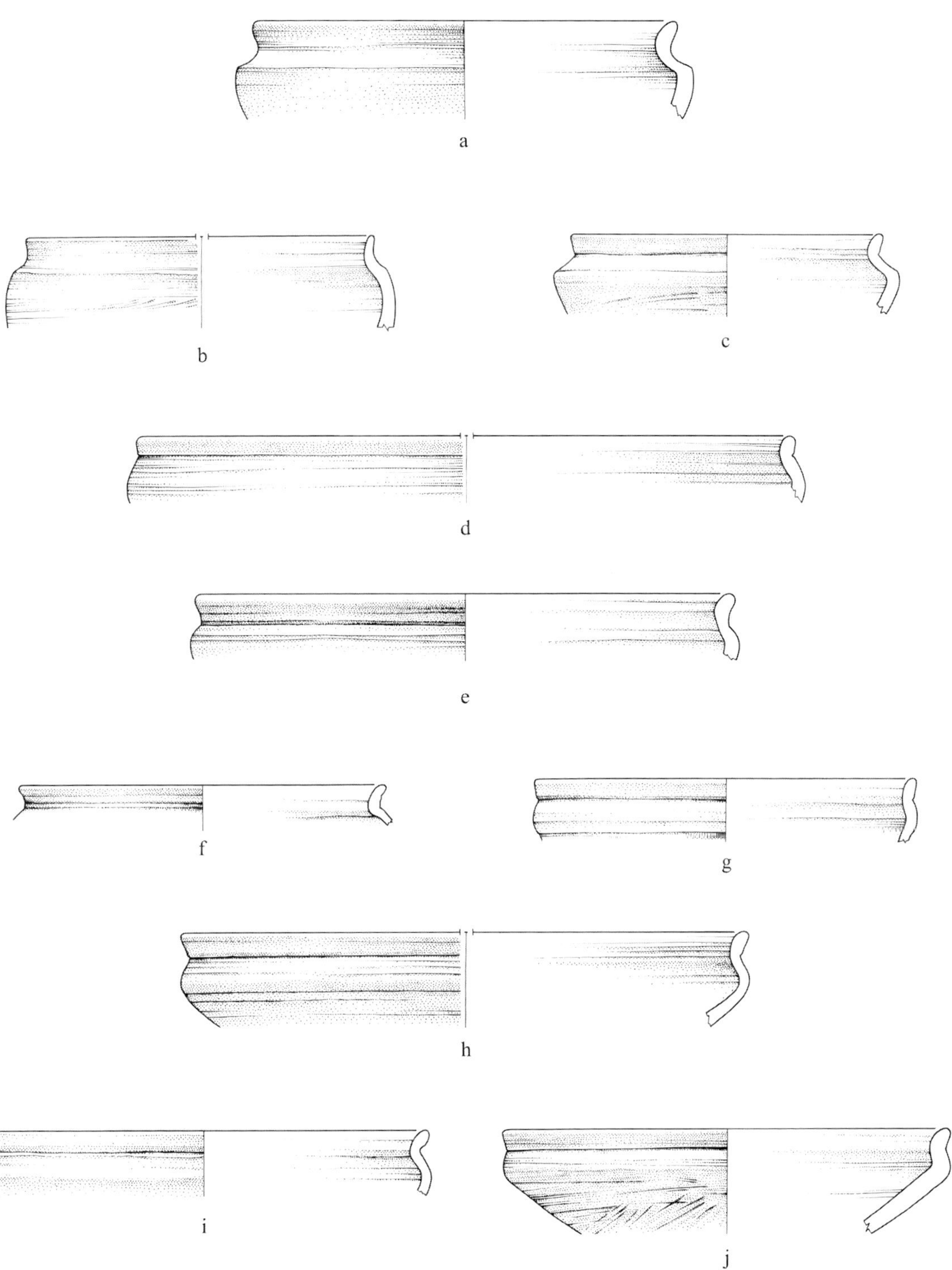

Figure 34. (*a*) 241 (Nile B1); (*b*) 242 (Nile A); (*c*) 243 (Nile B1); (*d*) 245 AEF **52+53** (Nile B2); (*e*) 246 (Nile B2); (*f*) 247 (Nile B2); (*g*) 248 BWL? **6** (Nile B2); (*h*) 248 ADV **1** (Nile B1); (*i*) 248 CGC **20** (Nile B1); (*j*) 249 (Nile B1).
1:3

Old Kingdom and FIP, Nile Fabrics

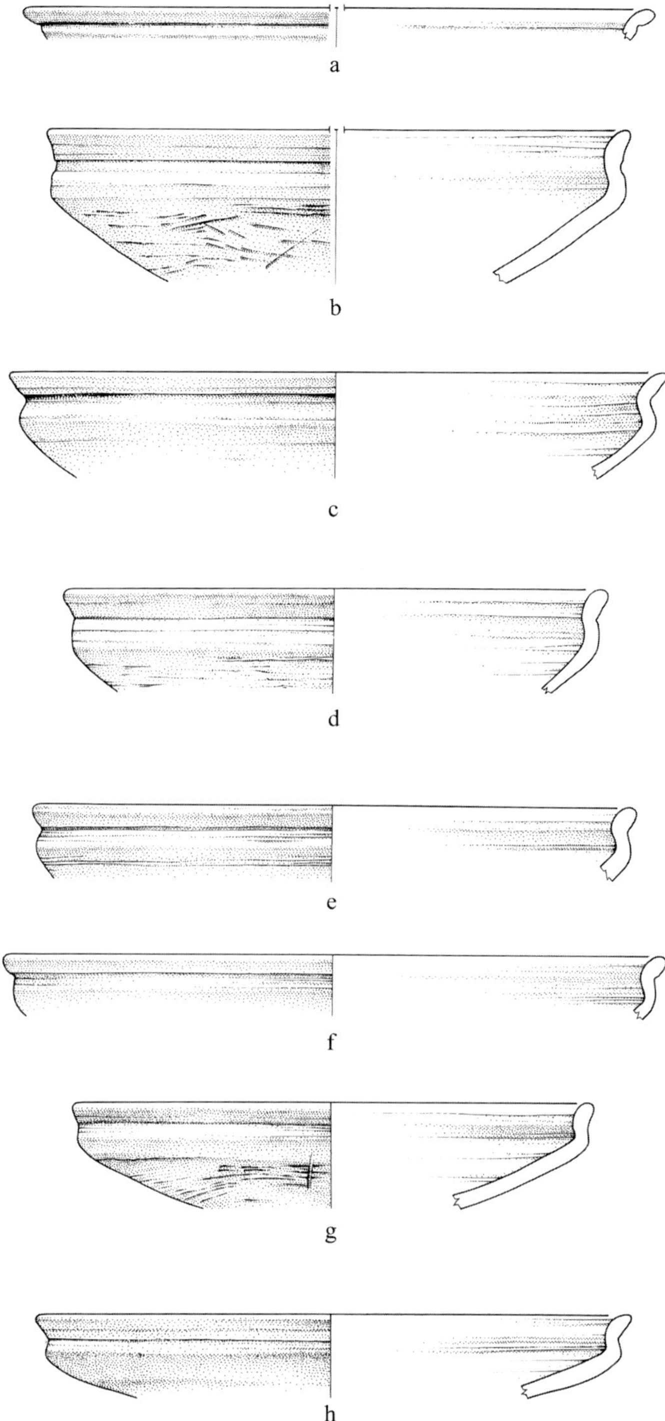

Figure 35. (*a*) **250** ARP=ARS/AYY **8** (Nile B2); (*b*) **250** AAA **49** (Nile B2); (*c*) **250** AAA **69** (Nile B2); (*d*) **250** BFB **29** (Nile B2); (*e*) **250** BFB **60** (Nile B1); (*f*) **251** AAB Upper **9** (Nile B1); (*g*) **251** AAA **566** (Nile B2); (*h*) **251** UP 1043 **2** (Nile B2). 1:3

Old Kingdom and FIP, Nile Fabrics

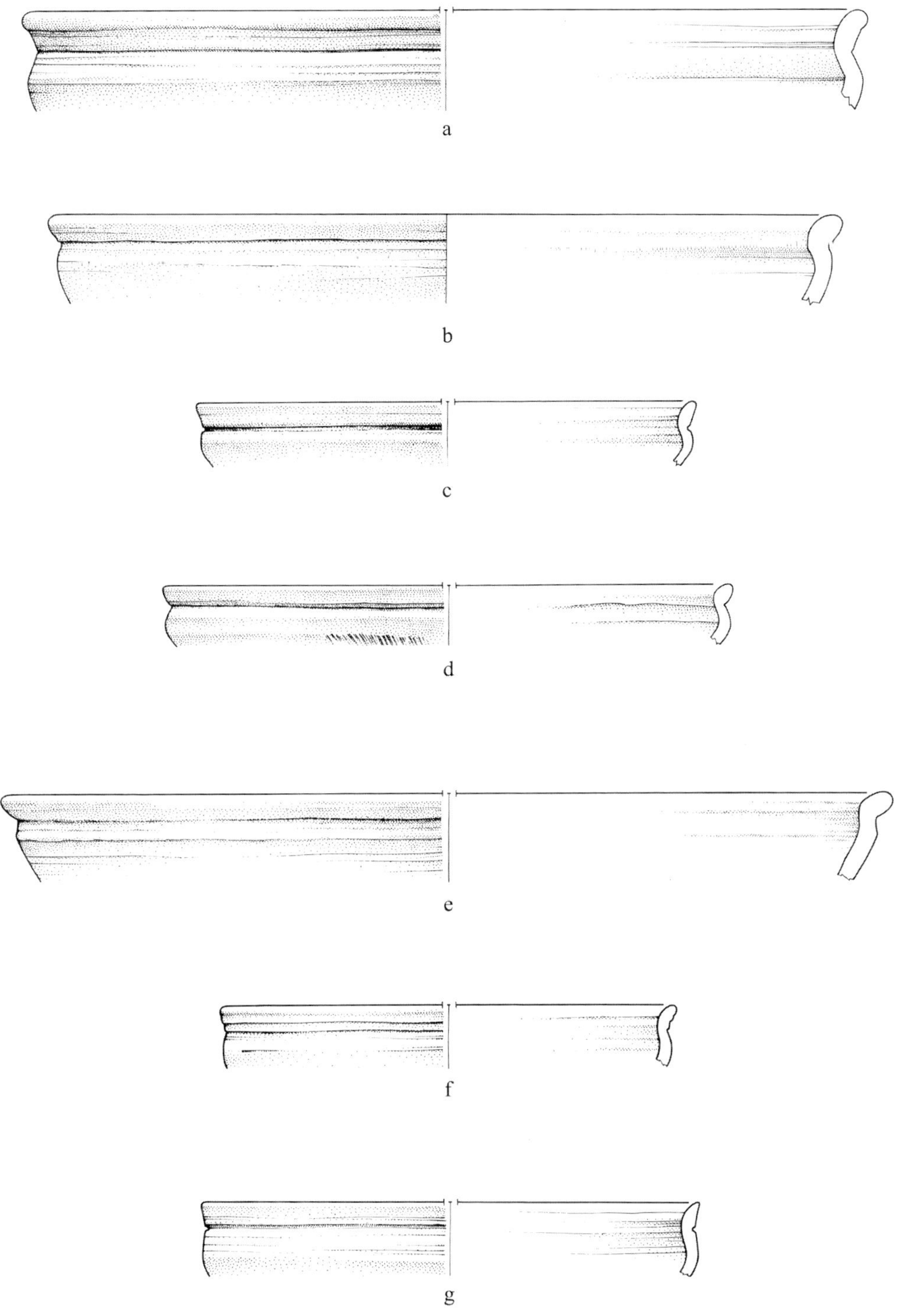

Figure 36. (*a*) **252** (Nile B2); (*b*) **253** (Nile B1); (*c*) **254** (Nile B1); (*d*) **255** AAA **129** (Nile B2); (*e*) **256** (Nile B2); (*f*) **257** (Nile B2); (*g*) **258** AAA Upper **16** (Nile B2). 1:3

Old Kingdom and FIP, Nile Fabrics

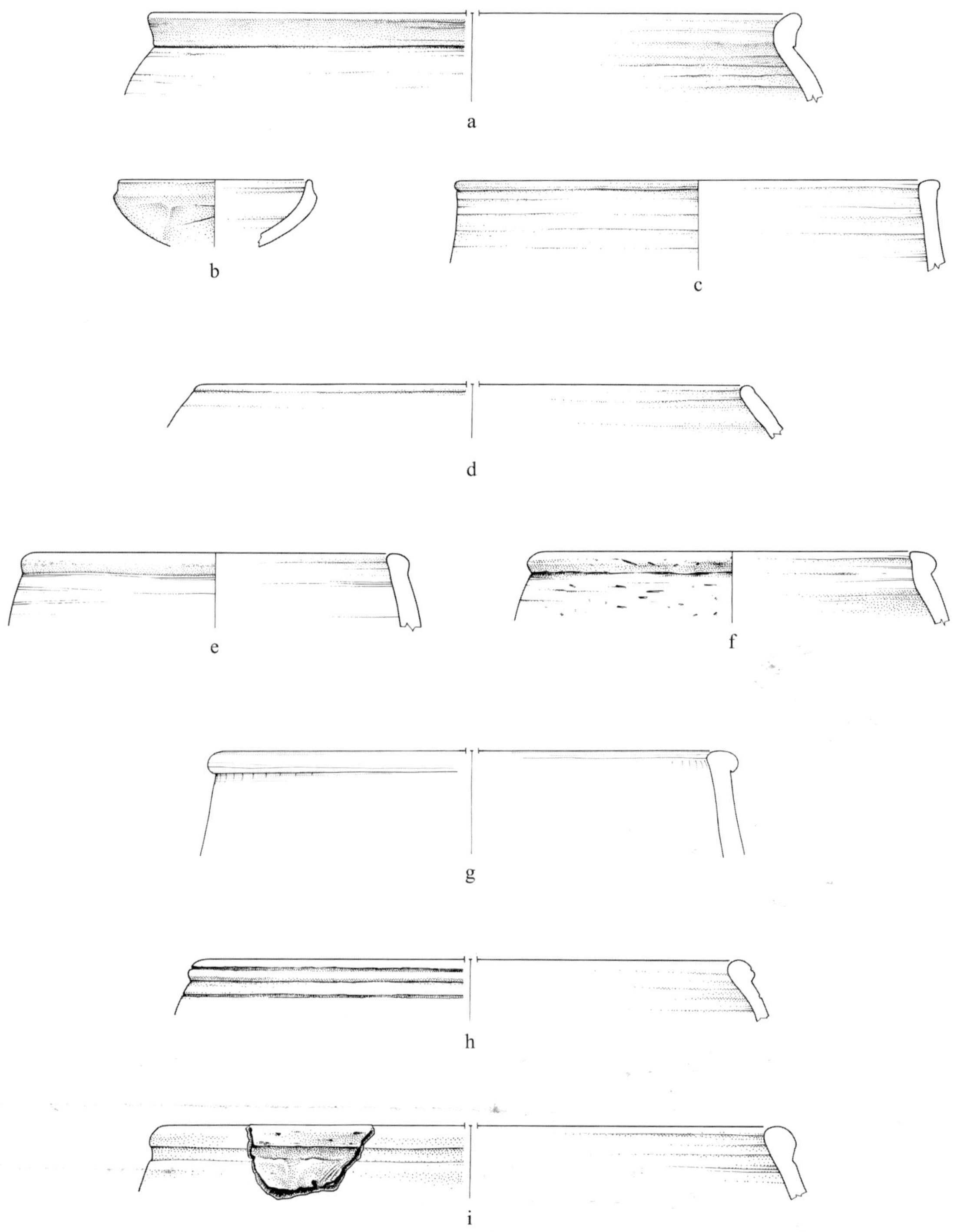

Figure 37. (*a*) **259** (Nile B2); (*b*) **261** AAA **39** (Nile B1 near B2); (*c*) **262** (Nile B2); (*d*) **263** (Nile B1); (*e*) **264** (Nile B2); (*f*) **265** (Nile B2); (*g*) **266** (Nile B2); (*h*) **267** (Nile B1); (*i*) **268** (Nile B2). 1:3

Old Kingdom and FIP, Nile Fabrics

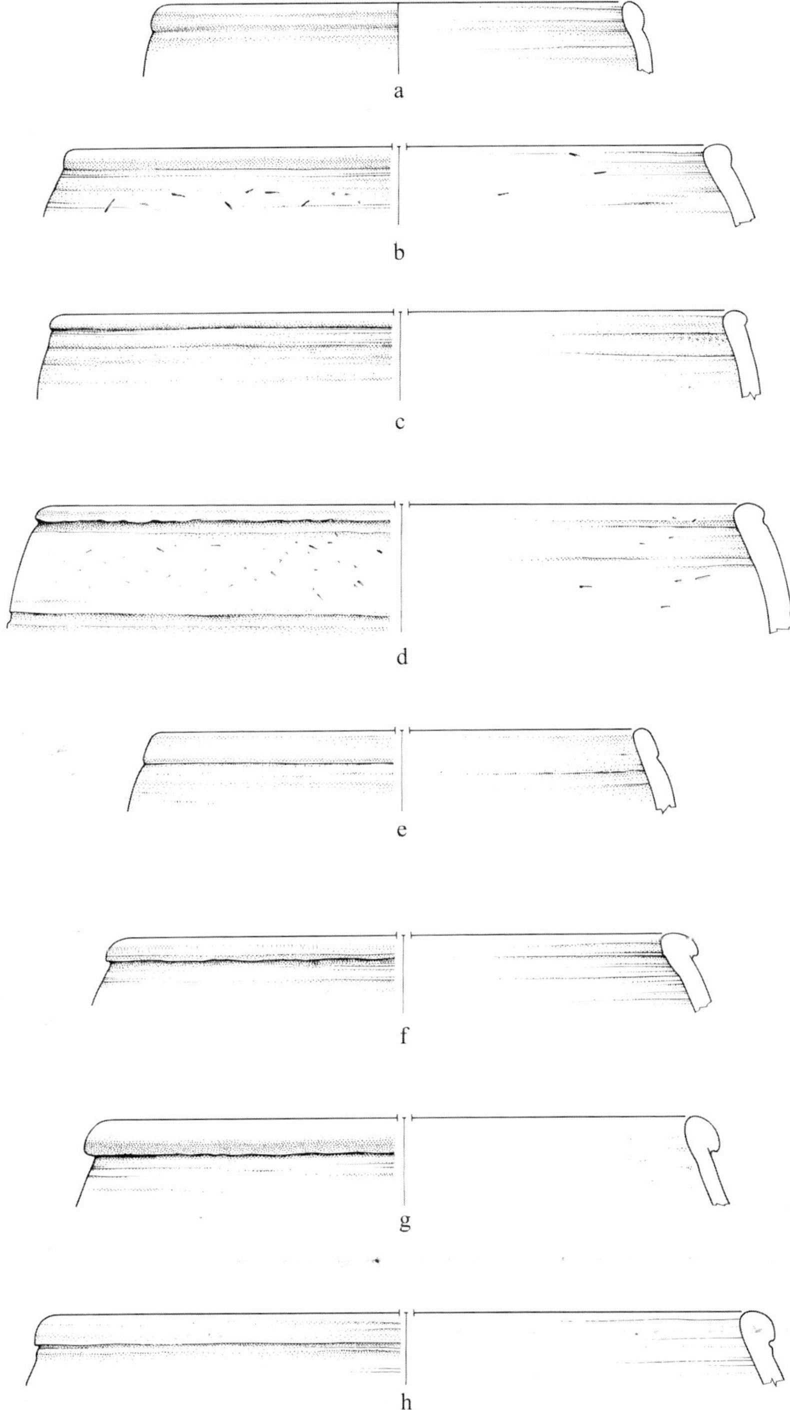

Figure 38. (*a*) **269** (Nile B2); (*b*) **270** (Nile B2); (*c*) **271** (Nile B2); (*d*) **272** (Nile B2); (*e*) **273** (Nile B2); (*f*) **274** AEN/AEO **14** (Nile B2); (*g*) **275** (Nile B2); (*h*) **276** BQU **7** (Nile B2). 1:3

Old Kingdom and FIP, Nile Fabrics

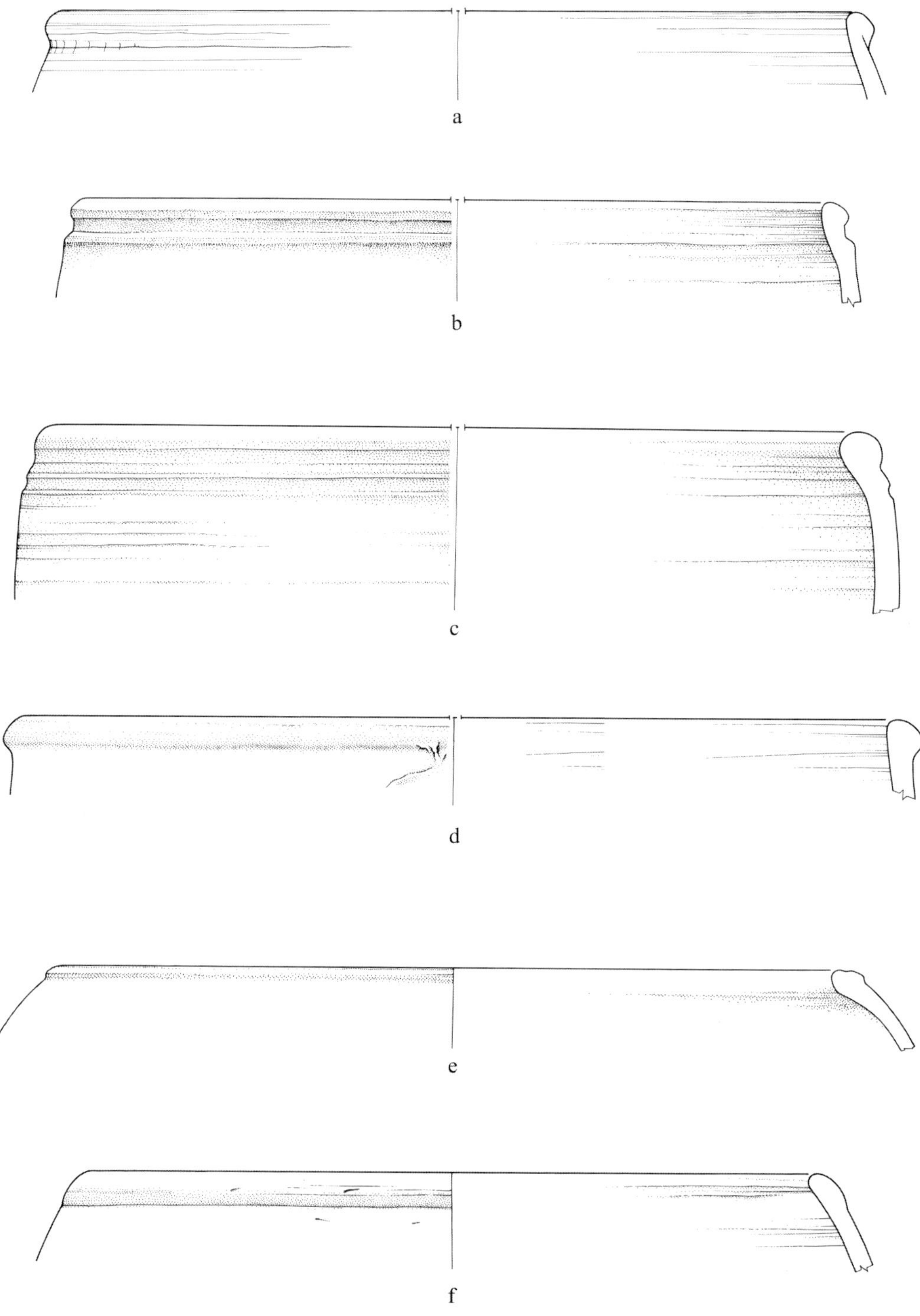

Figure 39. (*a*) **277** (Nile B2); (*b*) **278** (Nile B2); (*c*) **279** (Nile B near C); (*d*) **280** (Nile C); (*e*) **281** BEQ **21** (Nile B2); (*f*) **282** ABC/ABD/ABA **1** (Nile B2). 1:3

Old Kingdom and FIP, Nile Fabrics

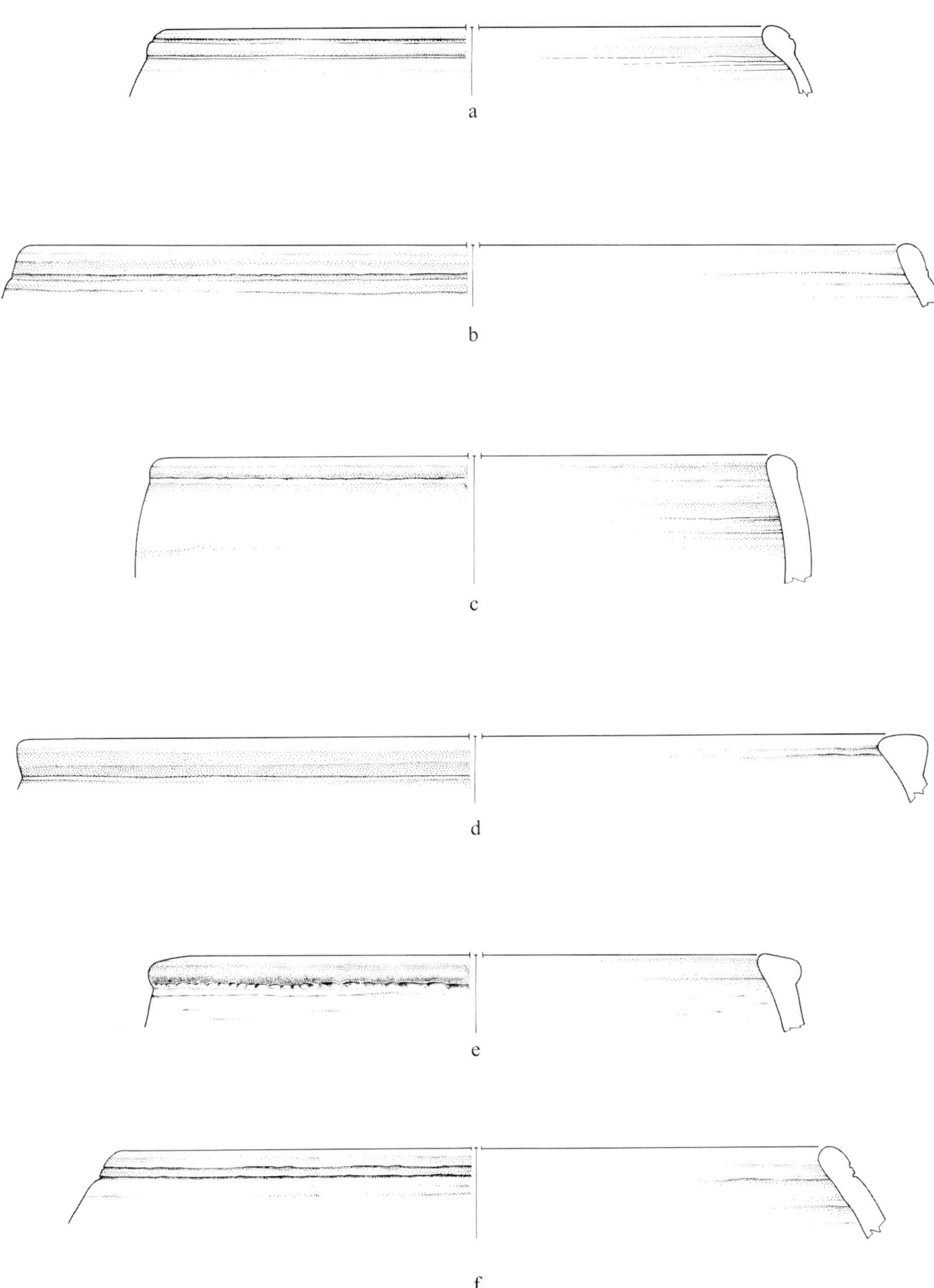

Figure 40. (*a*) **283** AAA **193** (Nile B2); (*b*) **284** (Nile B2); (*c*) **285** (Nile B2); (*d*) **286** AJH **18** (Nile B2); (*e*) **287** (Nile B2); (*f*) **288** (Nile B2). 1:3

Old Kingdom and FIP, Nile Fabrics

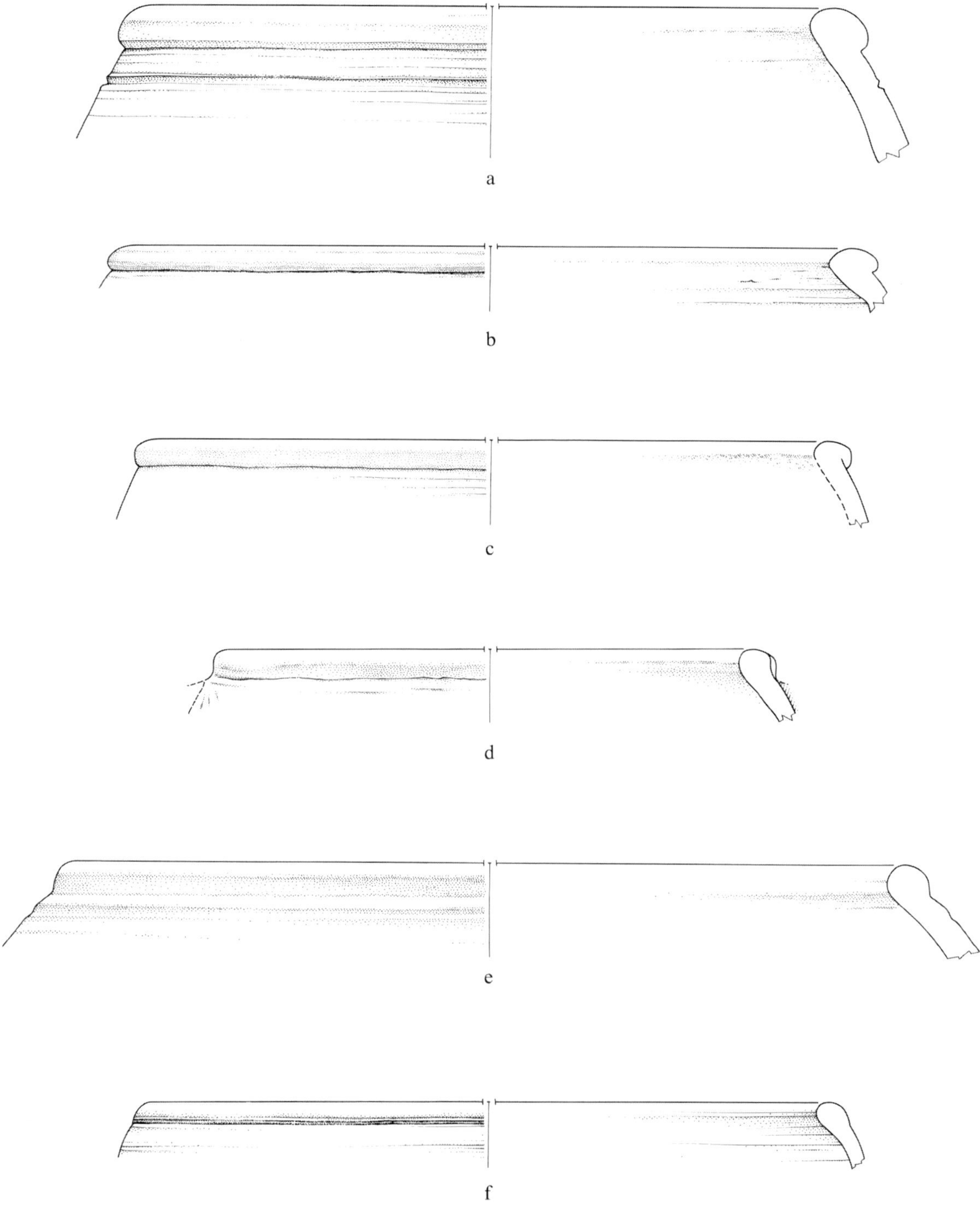

Figure 41. (*a*) **289** (Nile B2); (*b*) **290** UP 1038 **2** (Nile B2 near C); (*c*) **291** (Nile B2 near C); (*d*) **292** (Nile B2); (*e*) **293** ADF **21** (Nile B2); (*f*) **294** BPE **4** (Nile B2). 1:3

Old Kingdom and FIP, Nile Fabrics

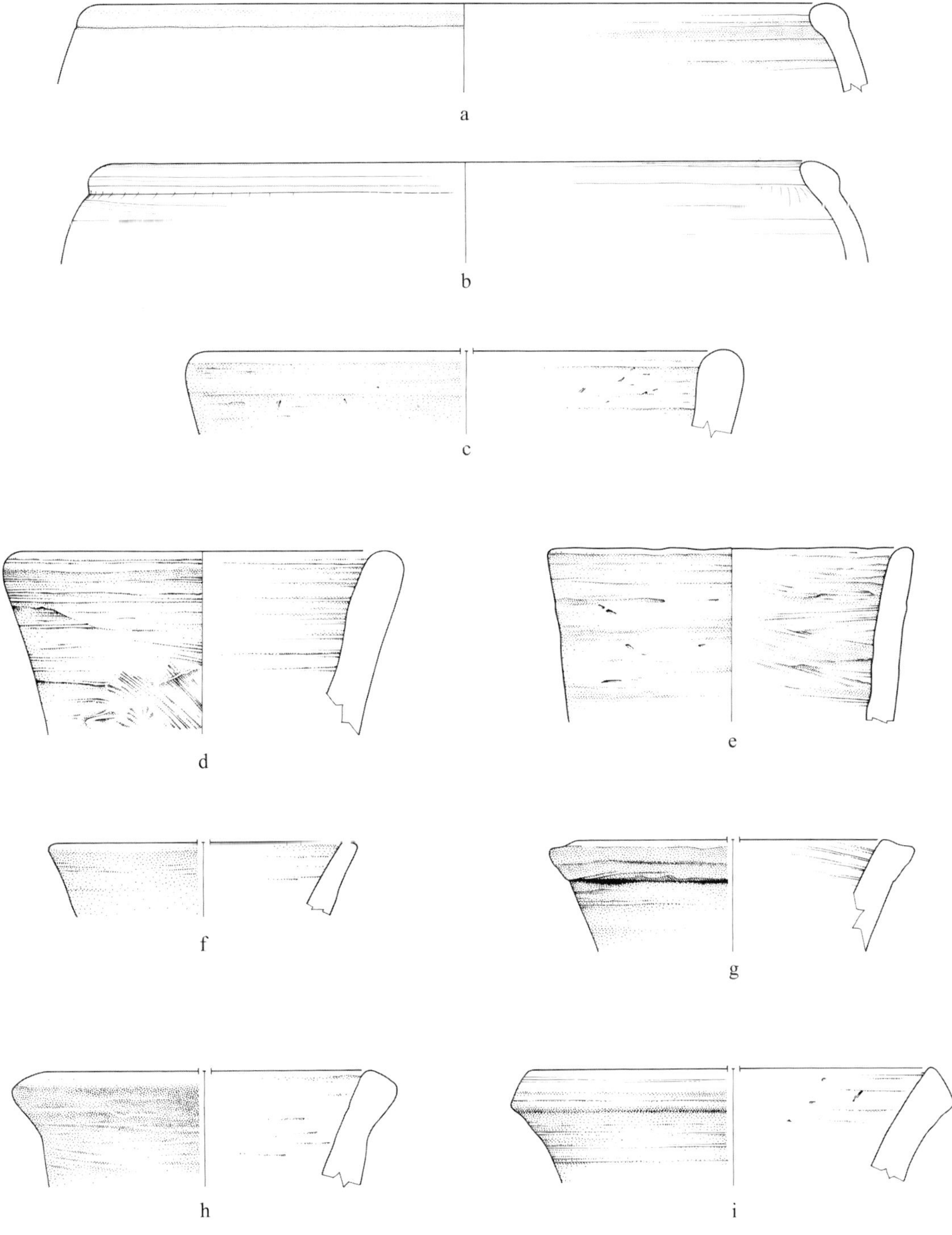

Figure 42. (*a*) **294** BSI/BSJ **3** (Nile B2); (*b*) **294** AAA **194** (Nile B2); (*c*) **295** BKP **20** (Nile B2 Sandy); (*d*) **295** BDP **1** (Nile B2 Sandy); (*e*) **296** (Nile B2); (*f*) **297** (Nile B2); (*g*) **298** BWQ **2** (Nile B2 near C Sandy); (*h*) **298** AZG **2** (Nile B2 near C Sandy); (*i*) **298** CBS **8** (Nile B2 near C Sandy). 1:3

Old Kingdom and FIP, Nile Fabrics

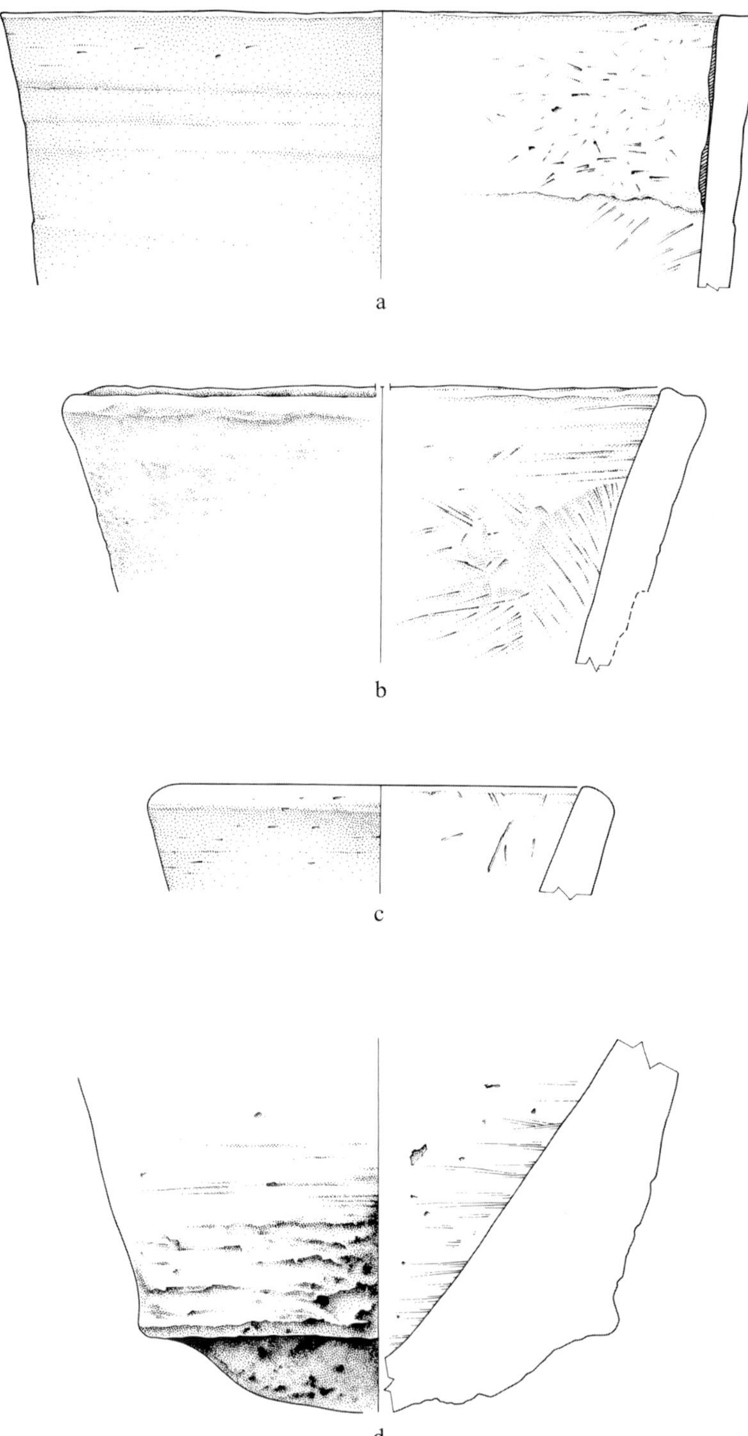

Figure 43. (*a*) **298** AQC **31** (Nile B2 near C Sandy); (*b*) **298** CEW **7** (Nile B2 near C Sandy); (*c*) **298** CAL **9** (Nile B2 near C Sandy); (*d*) **299** (Nile C). 1:3

Old Kingdom and FIP, Nile Fabrics

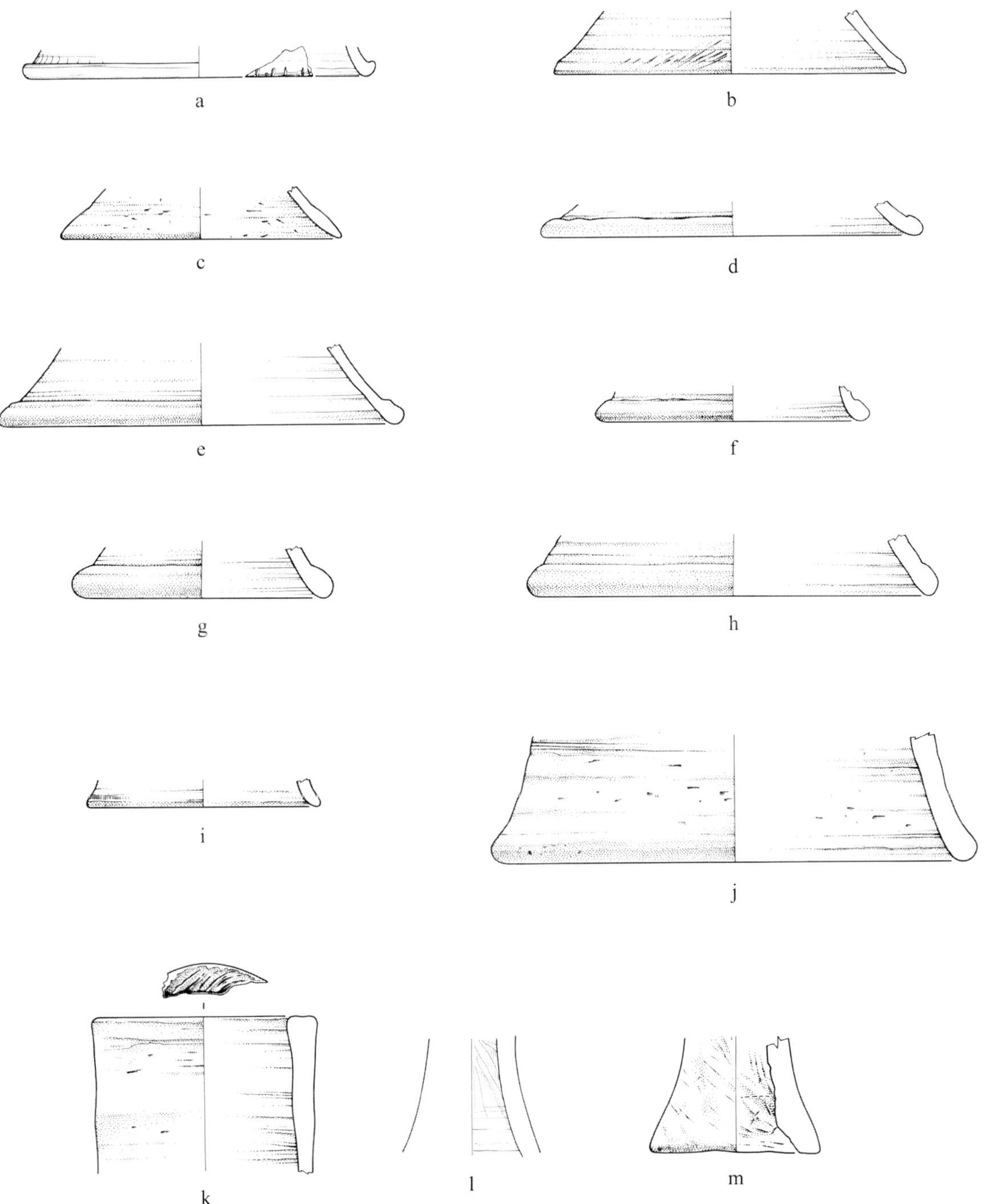

Figure 44. (*a*) **300** (Nile B2); (*b*) **301** (Nile B2); (*c*) **302** (Nile B2); (*d*) **303** (Nile B2); (*e*) **304** (Nile B2); (*f*) **305** (Nile B2); (*g*) **306** (Nile B2); (*h*) **307** CCK **67** (Nile B2); (*i*) **308** (Nile B1); (*j*) **309** (Nile B2); (*k*) **310** (Nile B2); (*l*) **311** (Nile B2); (*m*) **312** (Nile B2). 1:3

Old Kingdom and FIP, Nile Fabrics

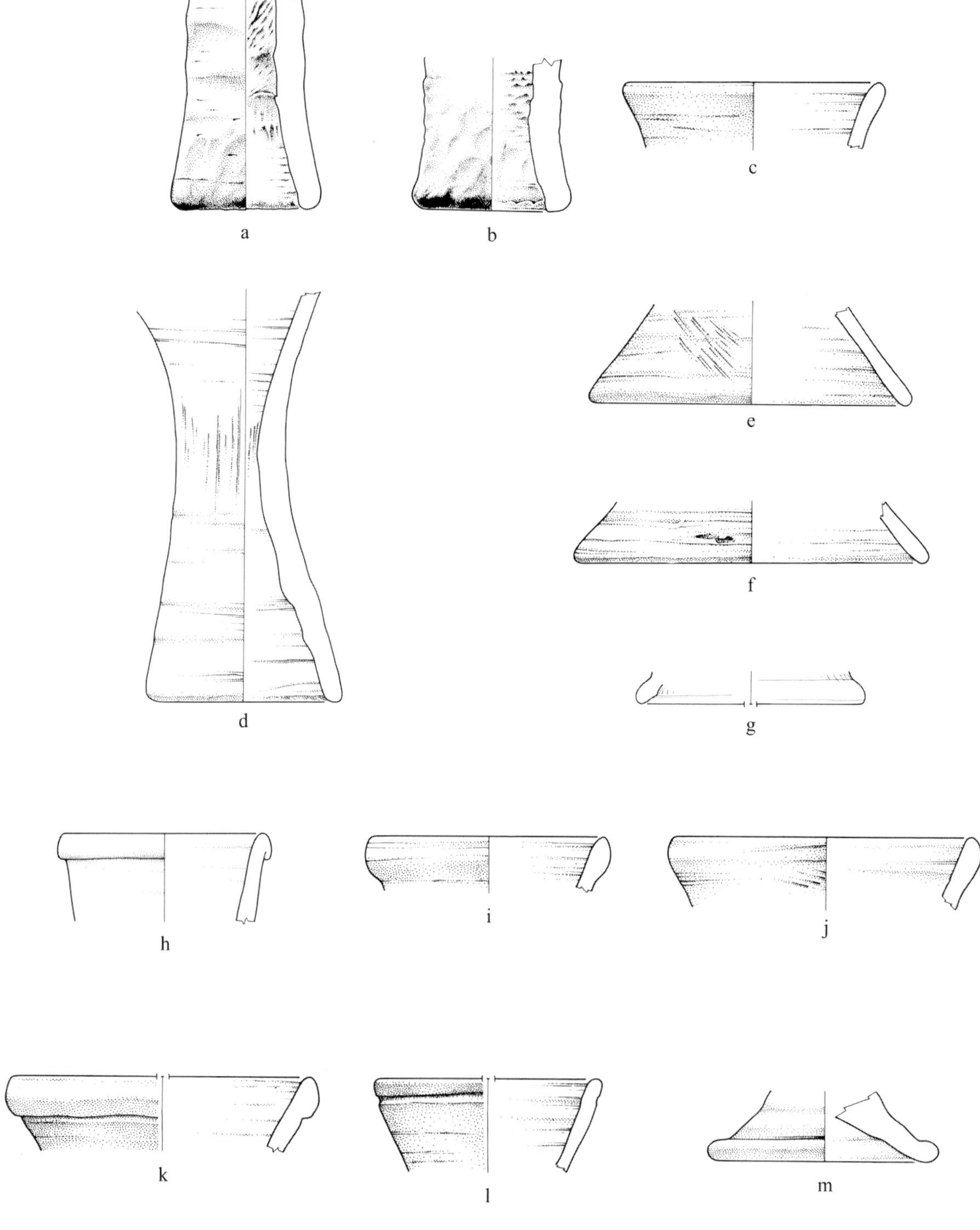

Figure 45. (*a*) **313** AFT **12** (Nile C); (*b*) **313** AJJ/AMJ **32** (Nile C); (*c*) **314** (Nile B2); (*d*) **315** BET **112**+BGG **122** (Nile B2); (*e*) **316** CFX **5** (Nile B2); (*f*) **316** ACE **168** (Nile B2); (*g*) **317** (Nile B2); (*h*) **318** (Nile B2); (*i*) **319** (Nile B2); (*j*) **320** (Nile B1); (*k*) **321** (Nile B2); (*l*) **322** (Nile D); (*m*) **323** (Nile B2). 1:3

Old Kingdom and FIP, Nile Fabrics

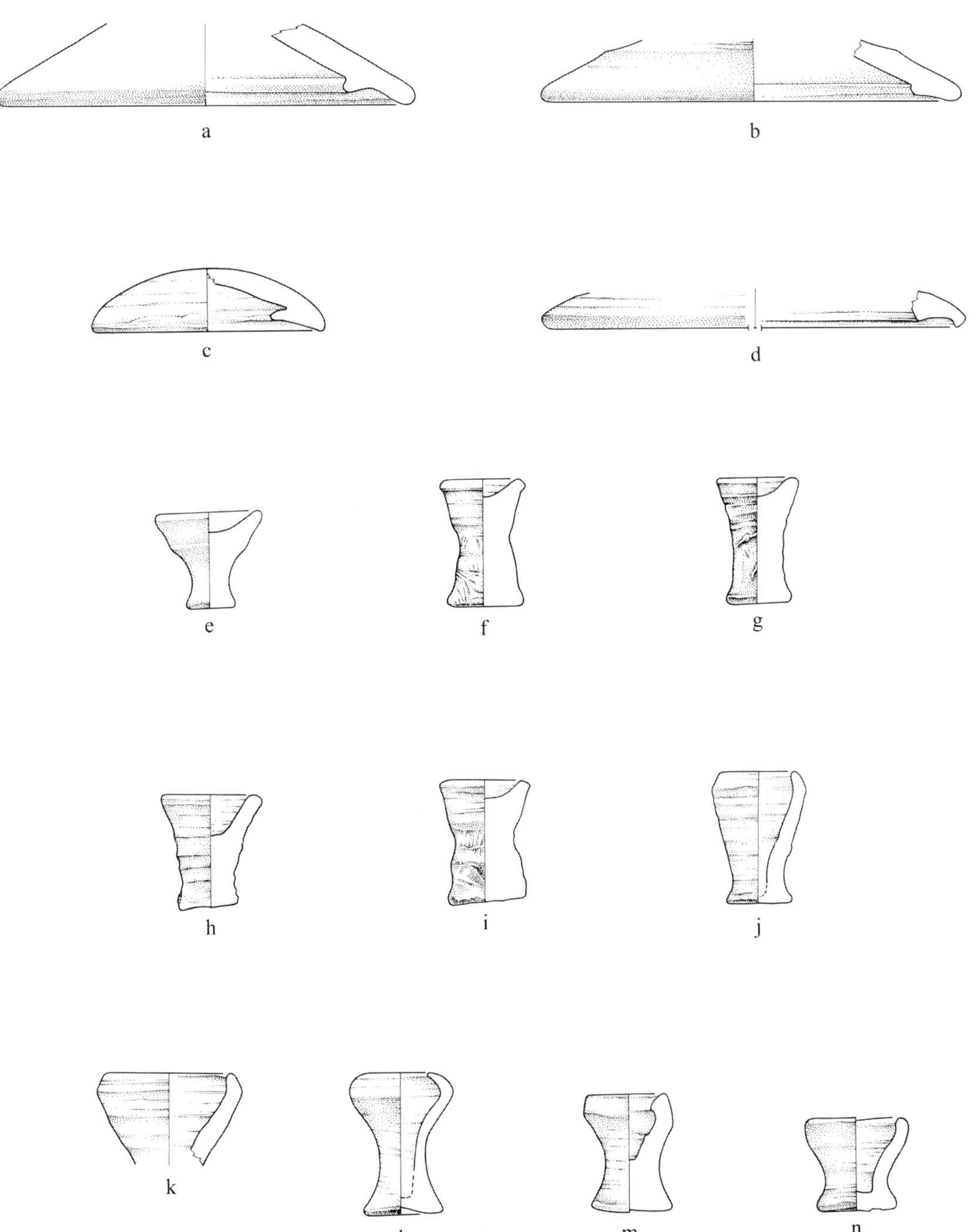

Figure 46. (*a*) **324** (Nile B2); (*b*) **325** (Nile B2); (*c*) **326** (Nile B1); (*d*) **327** (Nile B2); (*e*) **328** AZO **20** (Nile B2 near D); (*f*) **328** BCI **22** (Nile B2 near D); (*g*) **328** BAC **104** (Nile B2 near D); (*h*) **328** AAB **16** (Nile B2 near D); (*i*) **328** AAA **647** (Nile B2 near D); (*j*) **329** (Nile B2 near D); (*k*) **330** (Nile B2); (*l*) **331** (Nile B2); (*m*) **332** (Nile B2); (*n*) **333** (Nile B2). 1:3

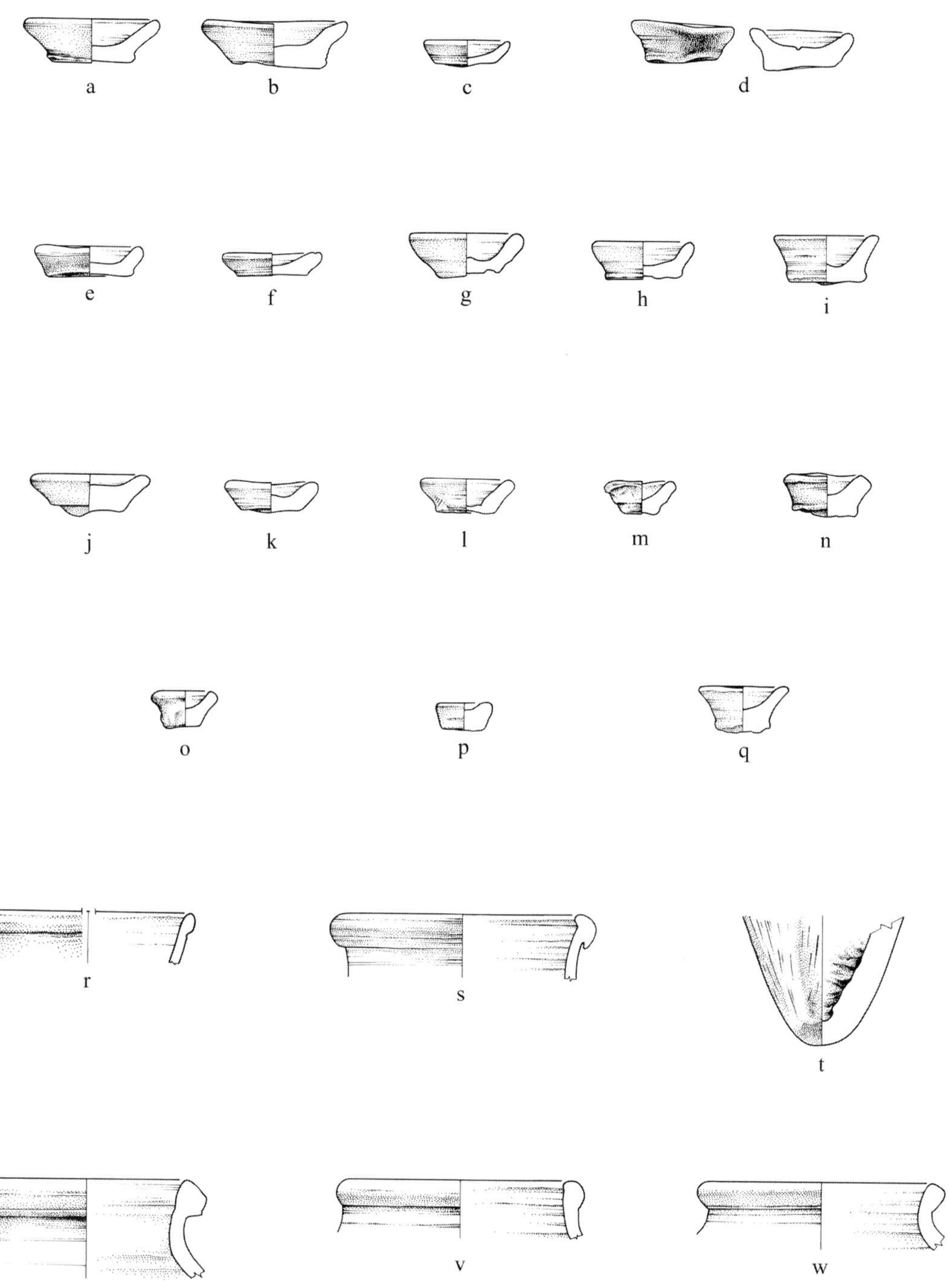

Figure 47. (*a*) **334** BDR **66** (Nile B2); (*b*) **334** DAY **14** (Nile B2); (*c*) **334** ADC **120** (Nile B2); (*d*) **334** DAW **6** (Nile B2); (*e*) **334** DAF **24** (Nile B2); (*f*) **334** ABF/ABG **1** (Nile B2); (*g*) **334** AAA **93** (Nile B2); (*h*) **334** AAA **29** (Nile B2); (*i*) **334** ANJ **8** (Nile B2); (*j*) **334** UP 8 **12** (Nile B2); (*k*) **334** UP 8 **30** (Nile B2); (*l*) **334** UP 8 **33** (Nile B2); (*m*) **335** BCB **118** (Nile B2); (*n*) **335** DAG **51** (Nile B2); (*o*) **335** AAA **95** (Nile B2); (*p*) **335** AAA **395** (Nile B2); (*q*) **335** AAA **61** (Nile B2); (*r*) **336** (Marl A1); (*s*) **337** (Marl C1); (*t*) **338** (Marl A2); (*u*) **339** (Marl A1); (*v*) **340** (Marl A1); (*w*) **341** (Marl A1).
1:3

Old Kingdom and FIP, Marl Fabrics

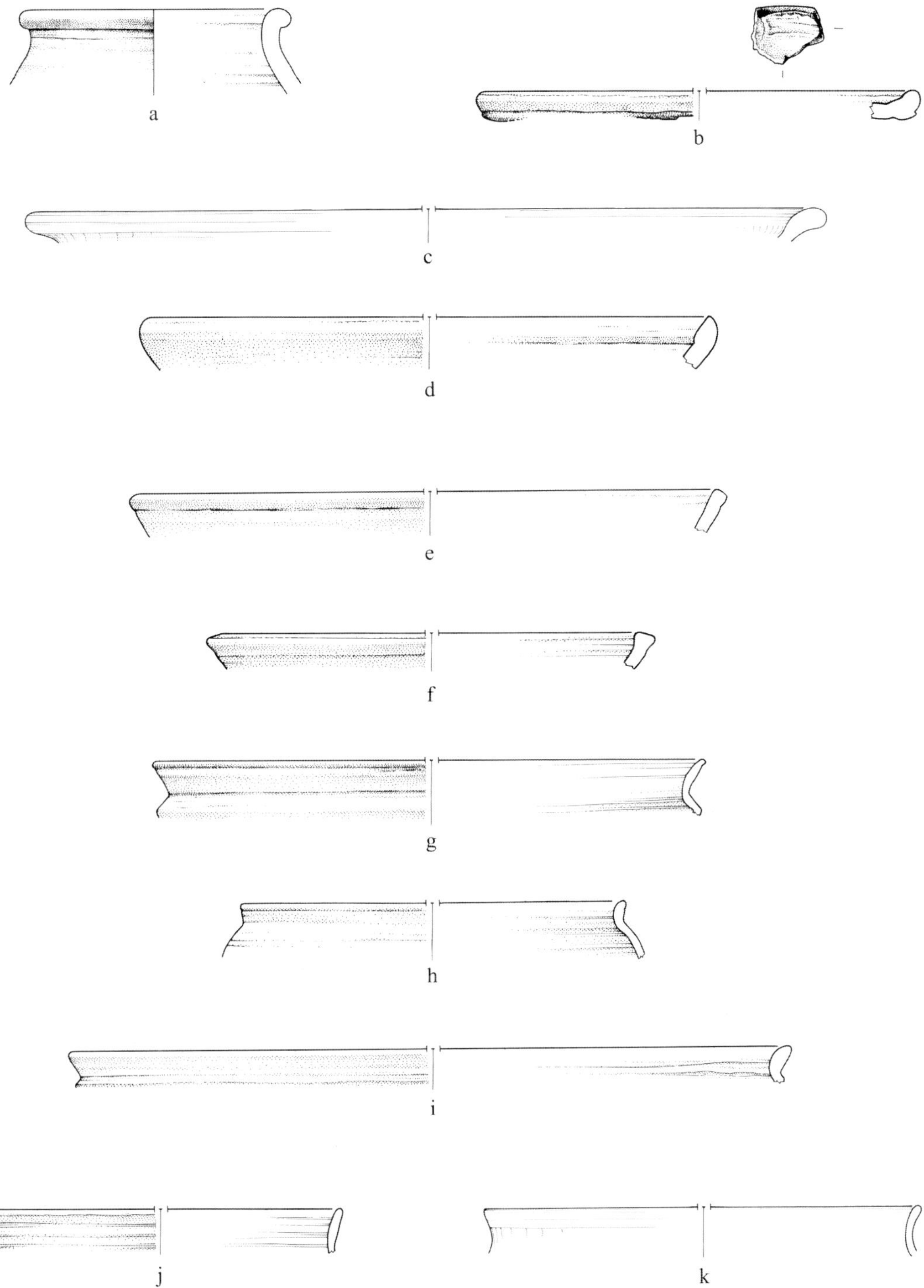

Figure 48. (*a*) **342** (Marl A1); (*b*) **343** (Marl B); (*c*) **344** (Marl A1); (*d*) **345** (Marl B?); (*e*) **346** (Marl A1); (*f*) **347** (Marl C); (*g*) **348** (Marl A1); (*h*) **349** (Marl A1?); (*i*) **353** (Marl A1); (*j*) **354** (Marl B?); (*k*) **355** (Marl A4). 1:3

Old Kingdom and FIP, Marl and Mixed Clay Fabrics

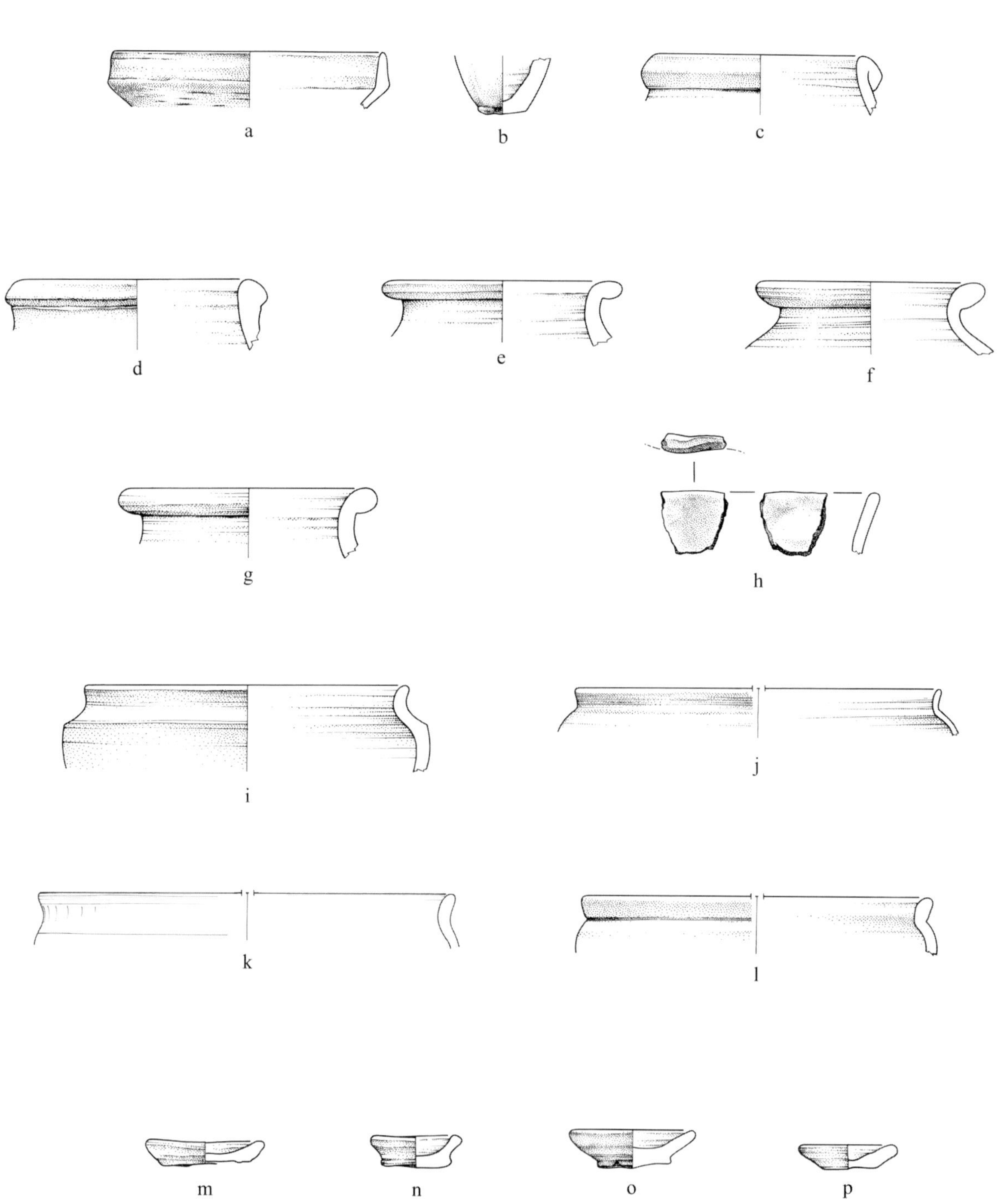

Figure 49. (*a*) **356** (Marl A1); (*b*) **357** (Mixed Clay P.60); (*c*) **358** (Mixed Clay P.60); (*d*) **359** (Mixed Clay P.60); (*e*) **360** (Mixed Clay P.60); (*f*) **361** (Mixed Clay P.60); (*g*) **362** (Fabric uncertain); (*h*) **363** (Mixed Clay P.60); (*i*) **364** (Mixed Clay P.60); (*j*) **365** AFA **2** (Mixed Clay Fine P.60); (*k*) **366** (Mixed Clay P.60); (*l*) **368** CGQ **58** (Mixed Clay P.60); (*m*) **371** BCB **117** (Mixed Clay P.60); (*n*) **371** BPD/BHR/BPV **19** (Mixed Clay P.60); (*o*) **371** ABC/ABD/ABA **2** (Mixed Clay P.60); (*p*) **371** AAA **11** (Mixed Clay P.60). 1:3

Middle Kingdom and SIP, Nile Fabrics

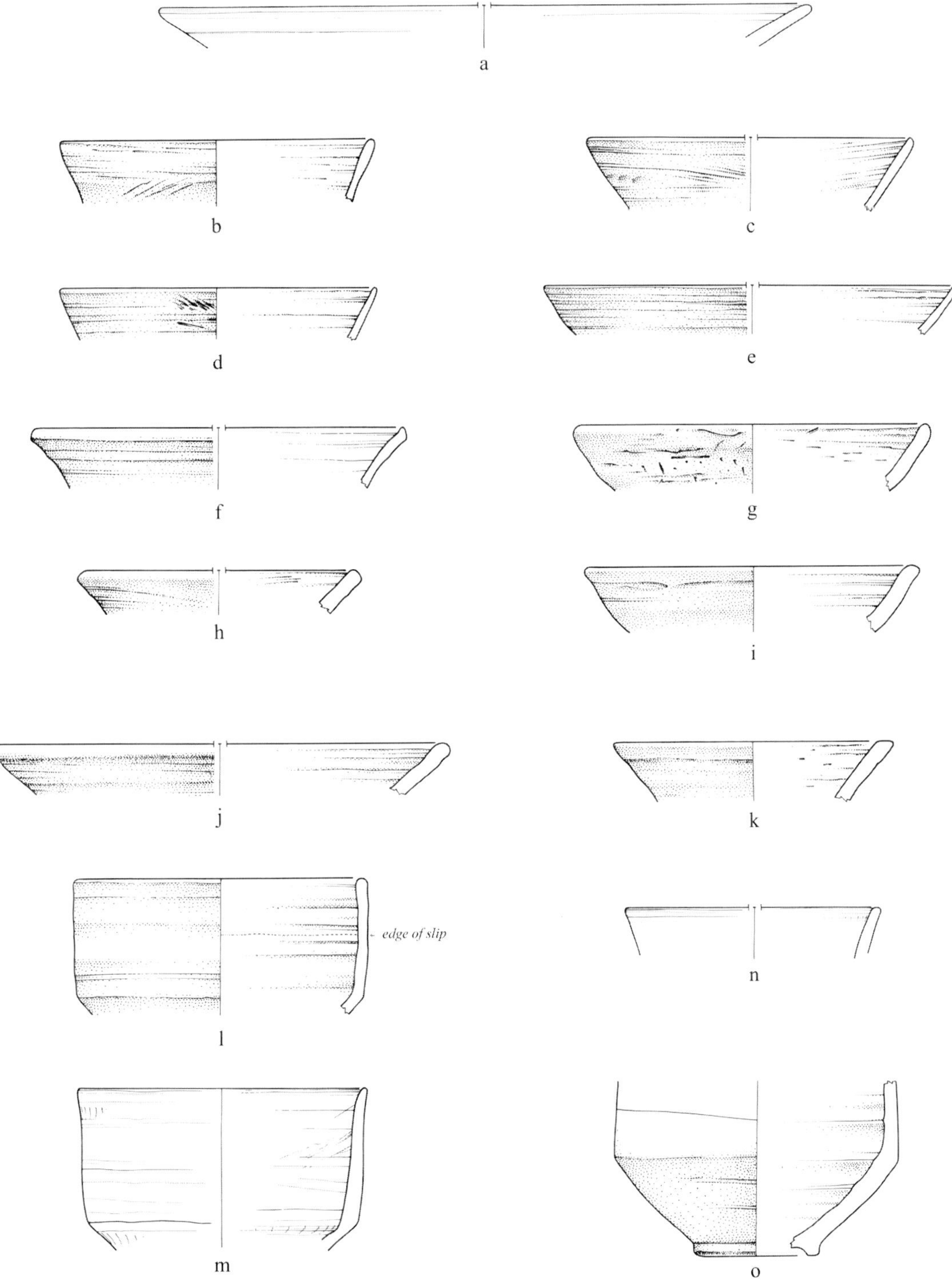

Figure 50. (*a*) **372** (D4-Nile B2); (*b*) **373** (D4-Nile B2); (*c*) **374** ADU **35** (D4-Nile B2); (*d*) **374** ADS/ARP=ARS **9** (D4-Nile B2); (*e*) **375** (D1-Nile B1); (*f*) **376** (D4-Nile B2); (*g*) **377** (D4-Nile B2); (*h*) **378** (D4-Nile B2); (*i*) **379** (D4 coarse-Nile B2 coarse); (*j*) **380** (D4-Nile B2); (*k*) **381** (D4-Nile B2); (*l*) **382** (D4-Nile B2); (*m*) **383** (D4-Nile B2); (*n*) **384** (D4-Nile B2); (*o*) **385** BTX **68 etc** (D4-Nile B2). 1:3

Middle Kingdom and SIP, Nile Fabrics

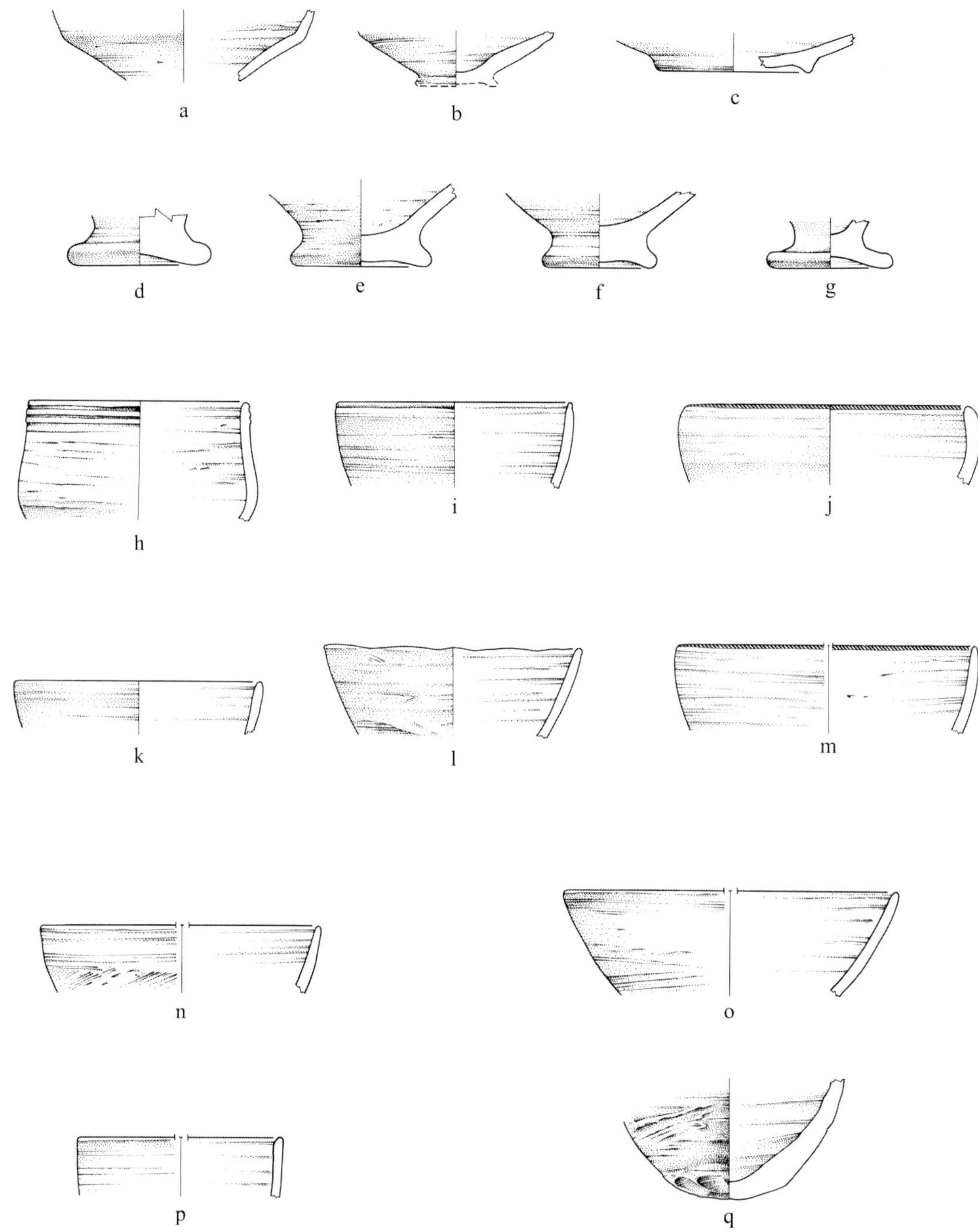

Figure 51. (*a*) <u>**386**</u> (D4-Nile B2); (*b*) <u>**387**</u> (D1-Nile B1); (*c*) <u>**388**</u> (D1-Nile B1); (*d*) <u>**389**</u> AJY **146** (D4-Nile B2); (*e*) <u>**389**</u> AMJ/AAA **2** (D4-Nile B2); (*f*) <u>**389**</u> AAA **48** (D4-Nile B2); (*g*) <u>**389**</u> AAA **137** (D4-Nile B2); (*h*) <u>**390**</u> (D4-Nile B2); (*i*) <u>**391**</u> AYE/AYF **2** (D1-Nile B1); (*j*) <u>**393**</u> (D1-Nile B1); (*k*) <u>**394**</u> AQE **139** (D4-Nile B2); (*l*) <u>**394**</u> AEP/AEQ/AER **49** (D4-Nile B2); (*m*) <u>**395**</u> BGL **27** (D4-Nile B2); (*n*) <u>**396**</u> BDY **22** (D4-Nile B2); (*o*) <u>**396**</u> ADS/ARP=ARS **7** (D4-Nile B2); (*p*) <u>**398**</u> (D4-Nile B2); (*q*) <u>**399**</u> (D4-Nile B2).

1:3

Middle Kingdom and SIP, Nile Fabrics

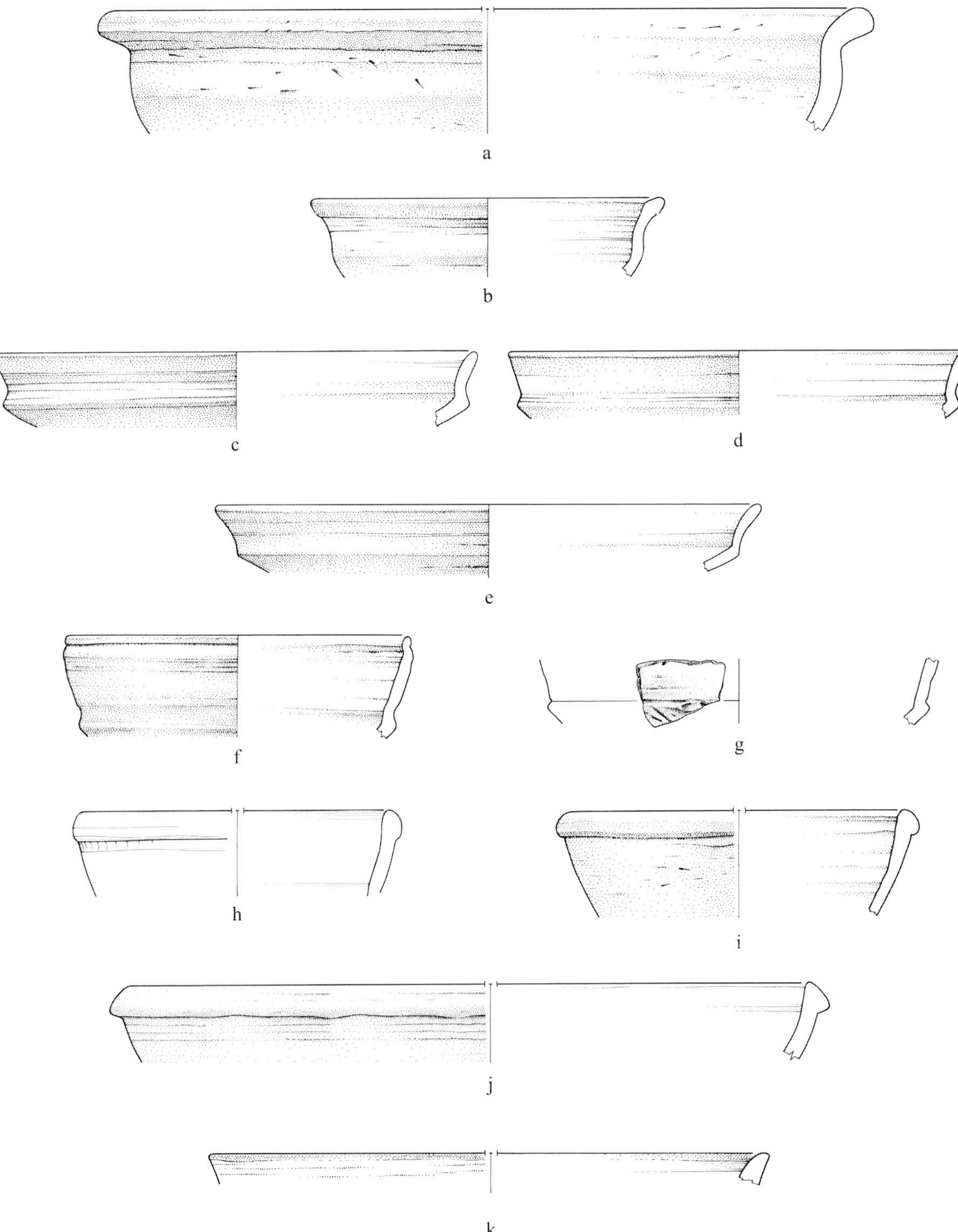

Figure 52. (*a*) **400** (D4 near D3-Nile B2 near C); (*b*) **401** (D4-Nile B2); (*c*) **402** (D1-Nile B1); (*d*) **403** (D1-Nile B1); (*e*) **404** (D4-Nile B2); (*f*) **405** (D4-Nile B2); (*g*) **406** (D1-Nile B1); (*h*) **407** (D4-Nile B2); (*i*) **408** (D4-Nile B2); (*j*) **409** BGG **44**+BGL **57** (D4-Nile B2); (*k*) **410** (D4-Nile B2). 1:3

Middle Kingdom and SIP, Nile Fabrics

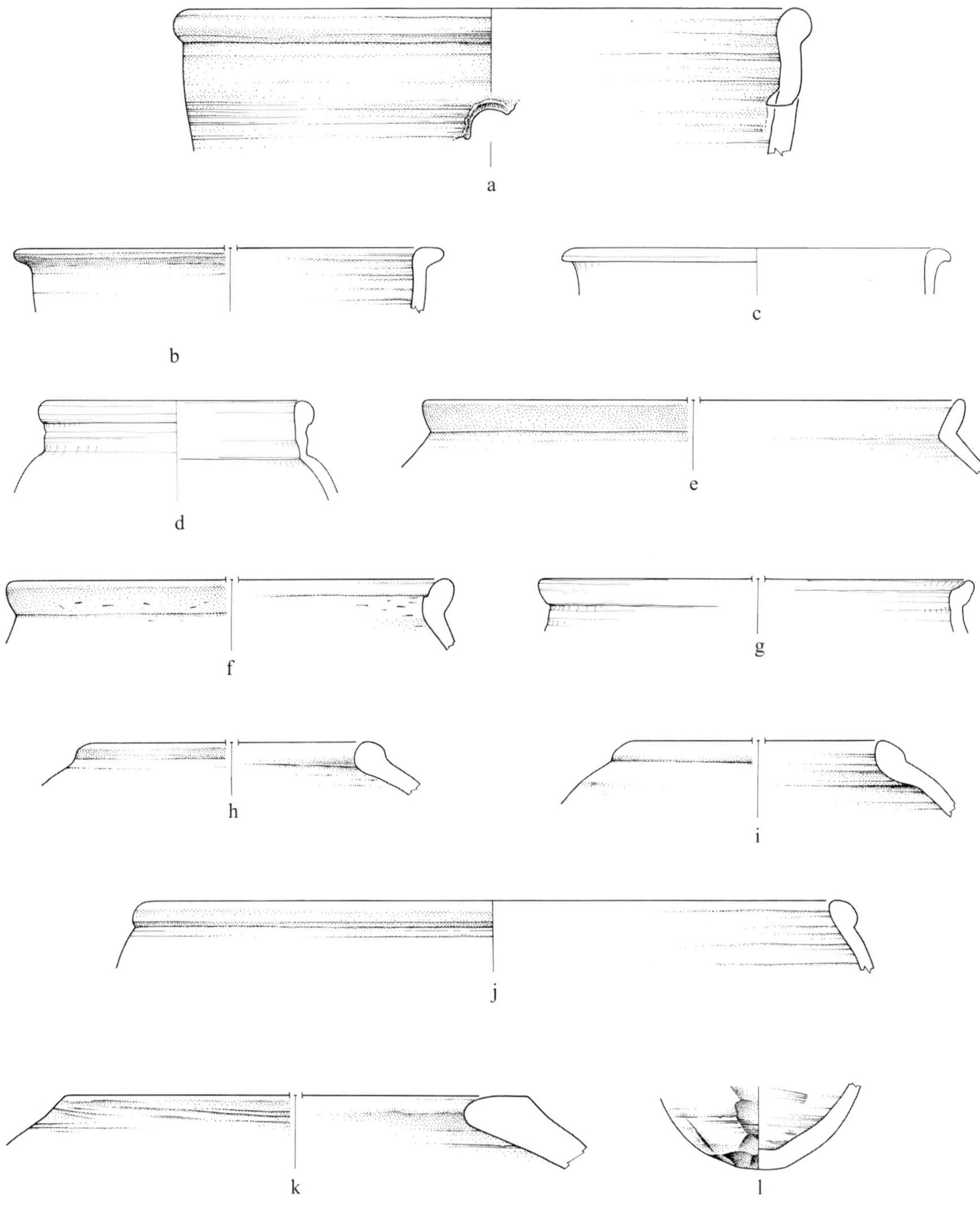

Figure 53. (*a*) **411** (D7-Nile D); (*b*) **412** (D1-Nile B1); (*c*) **413** (D1-Nile B1); (*d*) **414** (D4-Nile B2); (*e*) **415** (D4-Nile B2); (*f*) **416** AKJ/AKI **59** (D4-Nile B2); (*g*) **417** (D4-Nile B2); (*h*) **418** BKB **121** (D4-Nile B2); (*i*) **418** AIC/AAT **5** (D4-Nile B2); (*j*) **419** (D7-Nile D); (*k*) **420** (D7-Nile D); (*l*) **421** (D1-Nile B1). 1:3

Middle Kingdom and SIP, Nile Fabrics

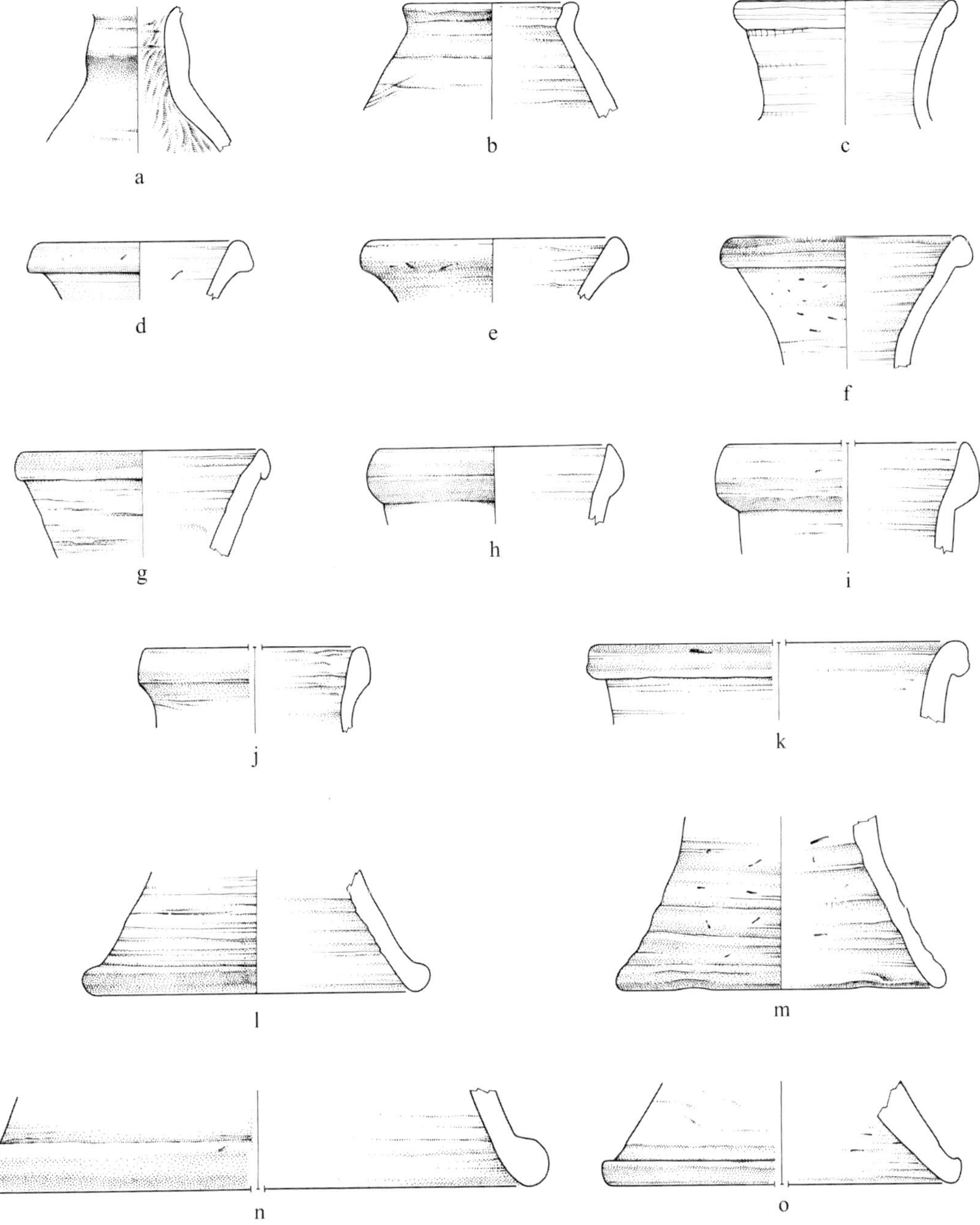

Figure 54. (*a*) **422** (D4-Nile B2); (*b*) **423** (D4-Nile B2); (*c*) **424** (D4-Nile B2); (*d*) **425** (D4 near D3-Nile B2 near C); (*e*) **426** (D4 near D3-Nile B2 near C); (*f*) **427** ABG **43** (D4-Nile B2); (*g*) **428** (D4 near D1-Nile B2 near B1); (*h*) **429** BMG **25** (D3-Nile C); (*i*) **429** ABA to ABG **2** (D3-Nile C); (*j*) **430** (D3-Nile C); (*k*) **431** (D7-Nile D); (*l*) **432** (D4-Nile B2); (*m*) **433** (D3-Nile C); (*n*) **434** (D3-Nile C); (*o*) **436** (D4-Nile B2). 1:3

Middle Kingdom and SIP, Nile Fabrics

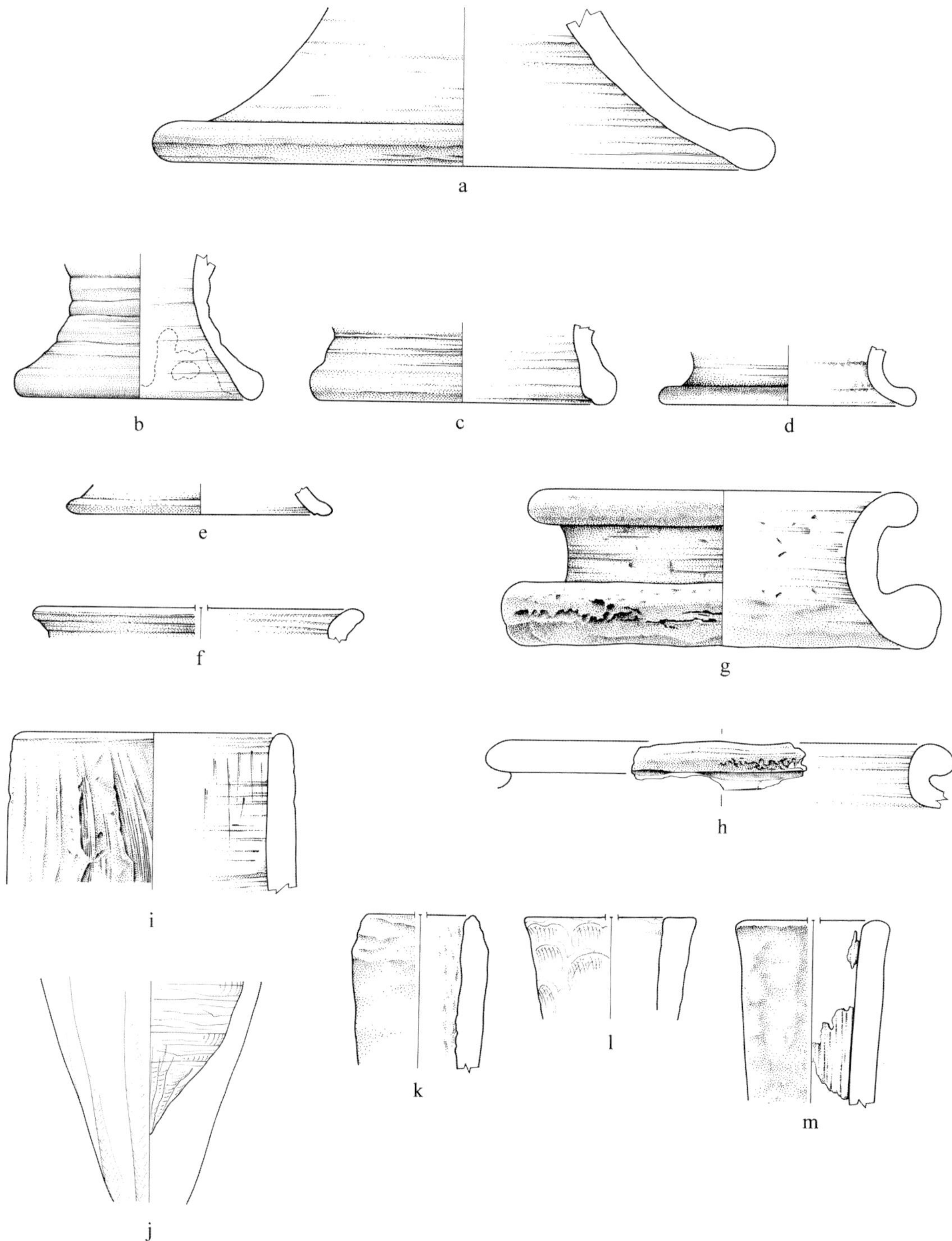

Figure 55. (*a*) **435** (D3-Nile C); (*b*) **437** ADF **75+76+77** (D4-Nile B2); (*c*) **438** (D4 Sandy-Nile B2); (*d*) **439** (D4-Nile B2); (*e*) **440** (D4-Nile B2); (*f*) **441** BGL **10** (D4-Nile B2); (*g*) **442** (D3-Nile C); (*h*) **443** (D4-Nile B2); (*i*) **444** (D3-Nile C); (*j*) **445** (D3-Nile C); (*k*) **446** AQG/AJY **24** (D3-Nile C); (*l*) **446** BAX **3** (D3-Nile C); (*m*) **446** DAW 2 (D3-Nile C).

1:3

Middle Kingdom and SIP, Nile Fabrics

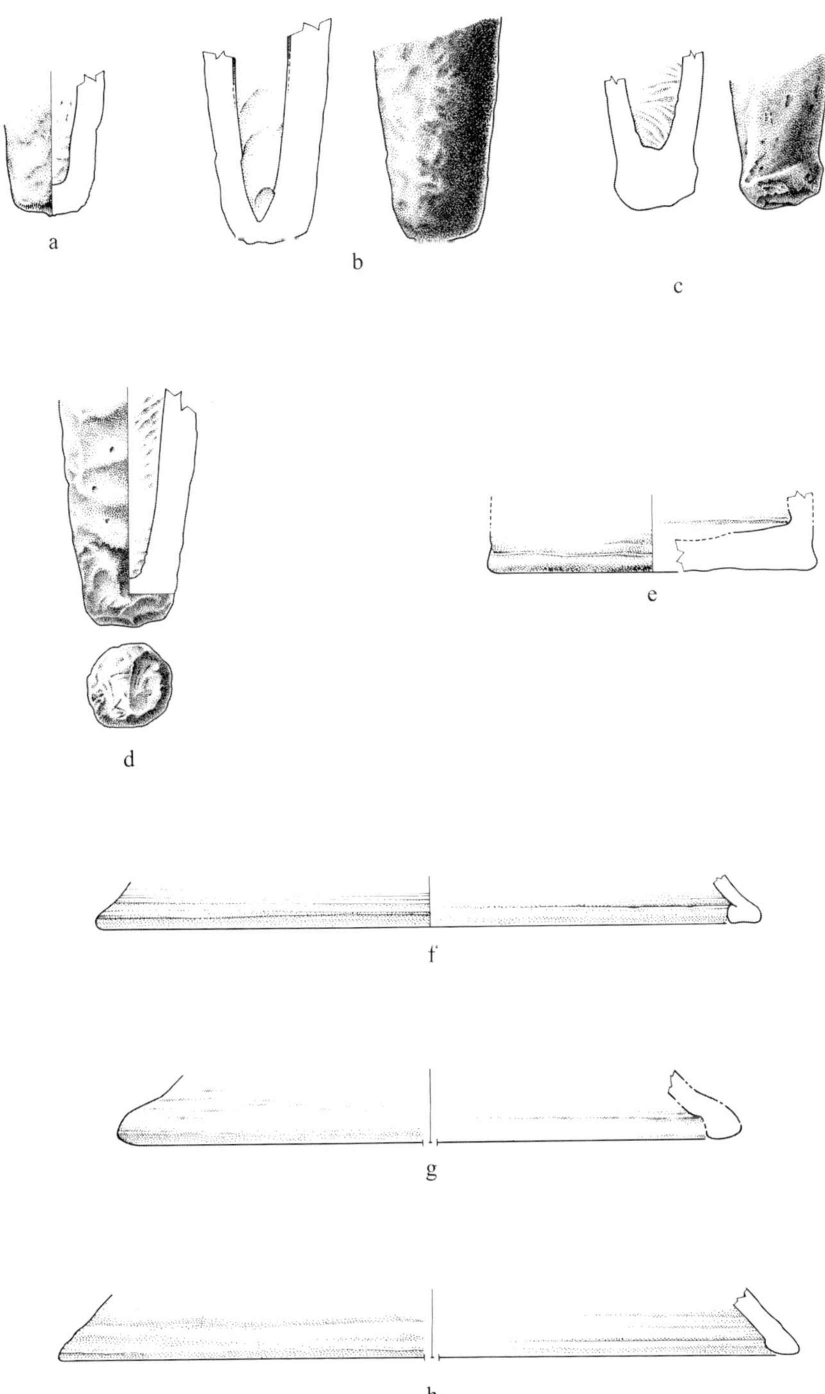

Figure 56. (*a*) **447** AQG **302** (D3-Nile C); (*b*) **447** AJX/AJY/BRS **67** (D3-Nile C); (*c*) **447** BEK **3** (D3-Nile C); (*d*) **447** ATY **217** (D3-Nile C); (*e*) **449** (D4-Nile B2); (*f*) **450** (D4-Nile B2); (*g*) **451** (D4-Nile B2); (*h*) **452** (D4-Nile B2).
1:3

Middle Kingdom and SIP, Marl Fabrics

Figure 57. (*a*) **<u>453</u>** (E1A-Marl C1); (*b*) **<u>454</u>** (E1C-Marl C2); (*c*) **<u>455</u>** (E4-Marl A3); (*d*) **<u>456</u>** (E7-Marl A2); (*e*) **<u>457</u>** (E1A-Marl C1); (*f*) **<u>458</u>** (E1A-Marl C1); (*g*) **<u>459</u>** (E1C-Marl C2); (*h*) **<u>460</u>** (E4-Marl A3); (*i*) **<u>461</u>** (E1A-Marl C1); (*j*) **<u>462</u>** (E1A-Marl C1); (*k*) **<u>463</u>** (E1A-Marl C1); (*l*) **<u>464</u>** (E1B-Marl C Compact); (*m*) **<u>465</u>** (E1A near E1C-Marl C1 near C2). 1:3

Middle Kingdom and SIP, Marl Fabrics

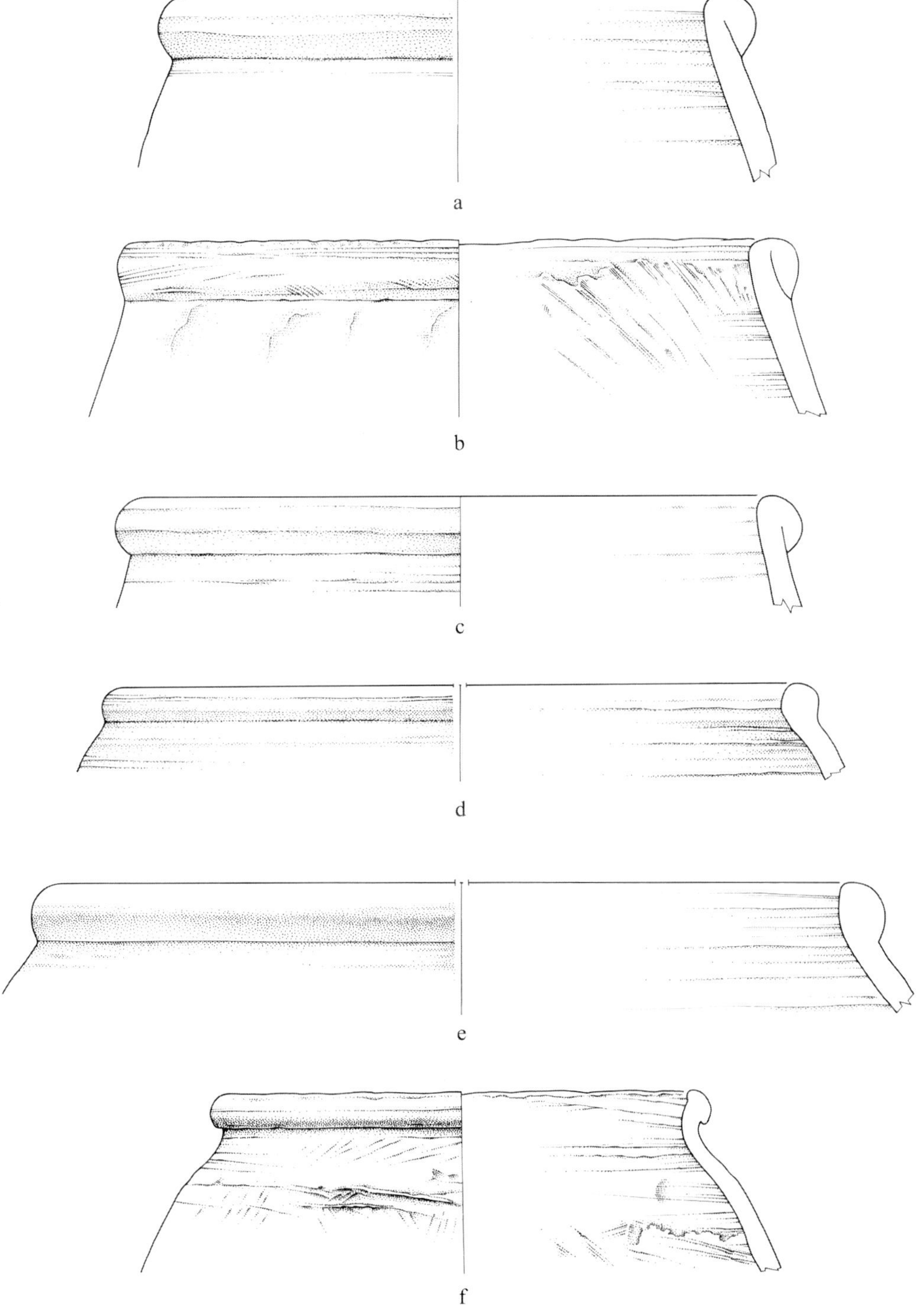

Figure 58. (*a*) 466 (E1A-Marl C1); (*b*) 467 (E1A-Marl C1); (*c*) 468 (E1C-Marl C2); (*d*) 469 (E1A-Marl C1); (*e*) 470 (E1A-Marl C1); (*f*) 471 (E1A-Marl C1). 1:3

Middle Kingdom and SIP, Marl Fabrics

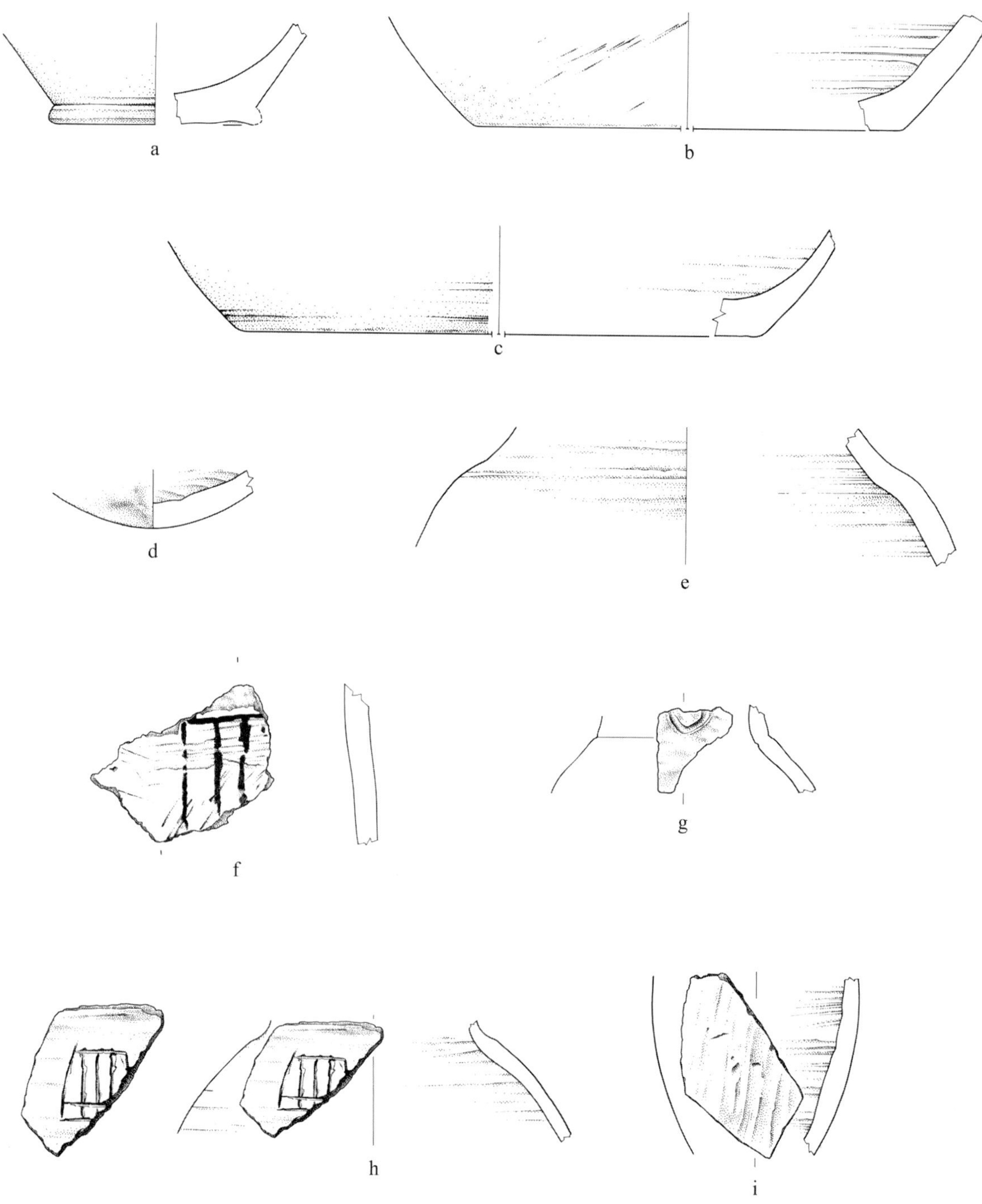

Figure 59. (*a*) **472** (E1C-Marl C2); (*b*) **473** (E1A-Marl C1); (*c*) **474** (E1A-Marl C1); (*d*) **475** (E1A-Marl C1); (*e*) **476** (E1A-Marl C1); (*f*) **477** (E1A-Marl C1); (*g*) **478** AJY/AQH **11** (E1A-Marl C1); (*h*) **478** ATY **199** (E1A-Marl C1); (*i*) **479** ABR North **11** (E1A-Marl C1). 1:3

Middle Kingdom and SIP, Marl Fabrics

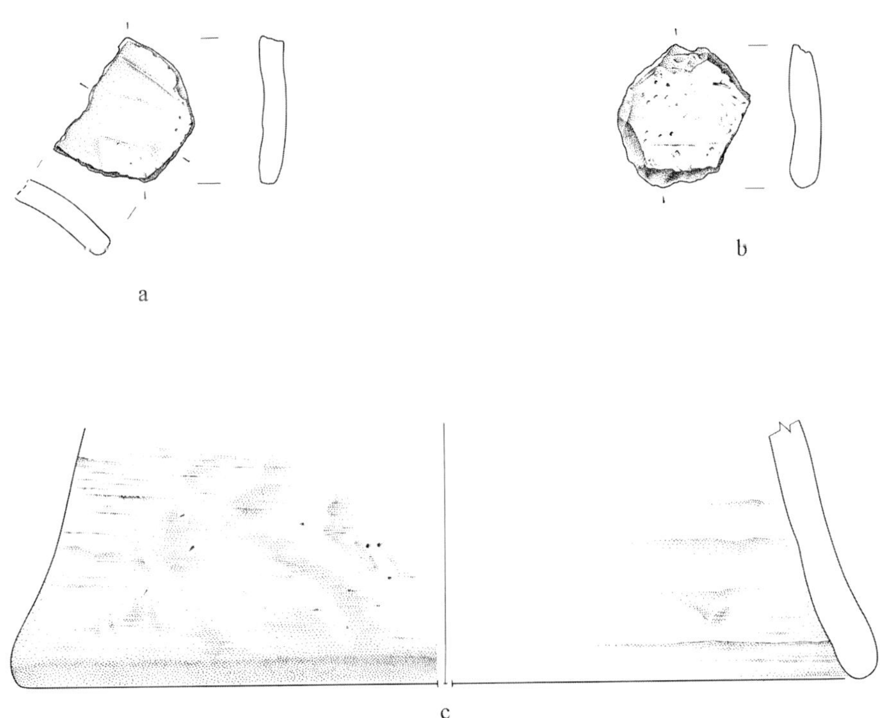

Figure 60. (*a*) **480** AJY **65** (E1A-Marl C1); (*b*) **480** AQE **38** (E1A-Marl C1); (*c*) **482** (E1A-Marl C1). 1:3

New Kingdom and TIP, Nile Fabrics

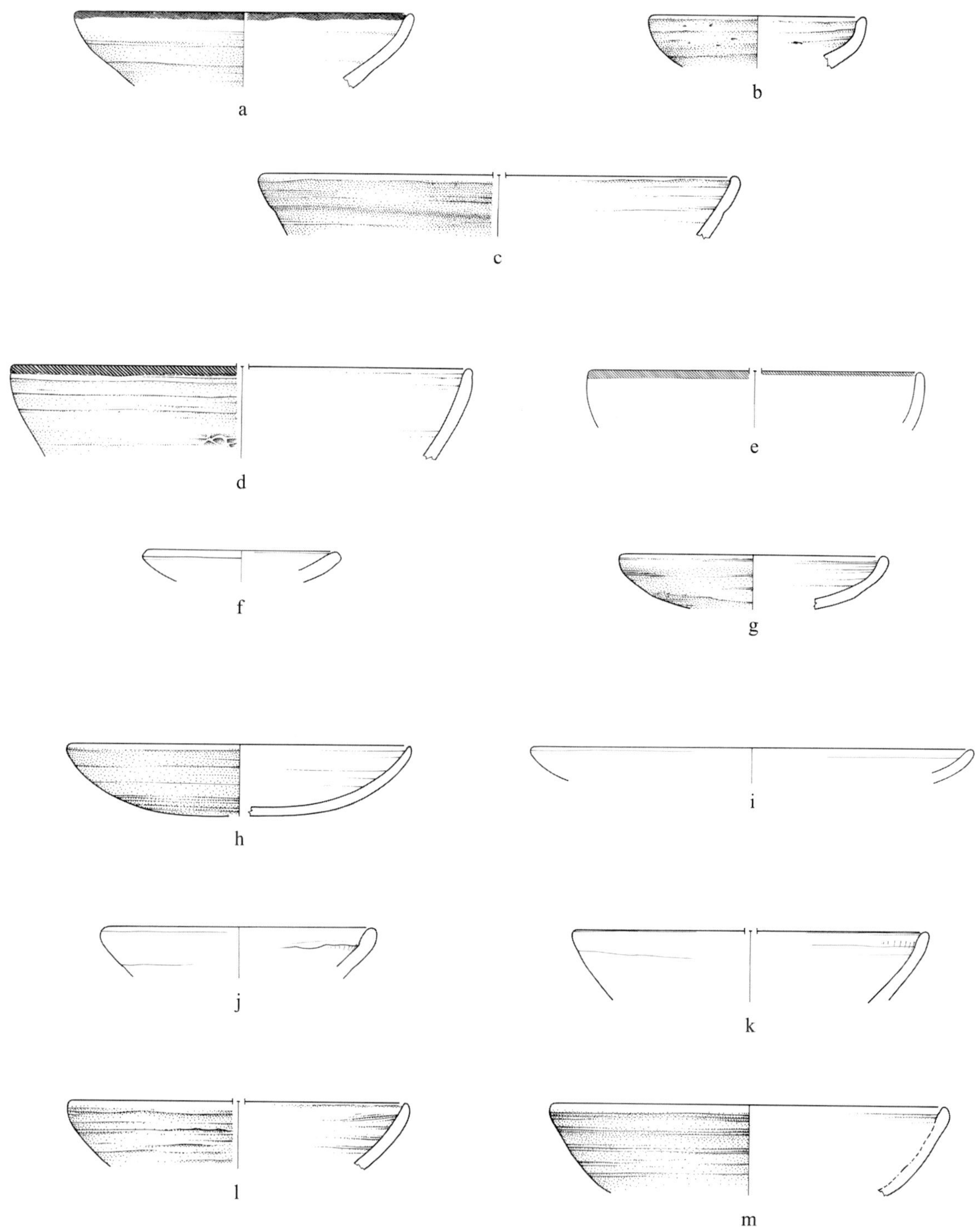

Figure 61. (*a*) **483** (G1-Nile B2); (*b*) **484** (G1-Nile B2); (*c*) **485** (G1-Nile B2); (*d*) **486** (G1-Nile B2); (*e*) **487** (G1-Nile B2); (*f*) **488** (G1-Nile B2); (*g*) **489** (G1-Nile B2); (*h*) **491** AUQ **159+199** (G1-Nile B2); (*i*) **493** ADG **15** (G1-Nile B2); (*j*) **494** (G1-Nile B2); (*k*) **495** (G1-Nile B2); (*l*) **496** (G1-Nile B2); (*m*) **497** (G1-Nile B2). 1:3

New Kingdom and TIP, Nile Fabrics

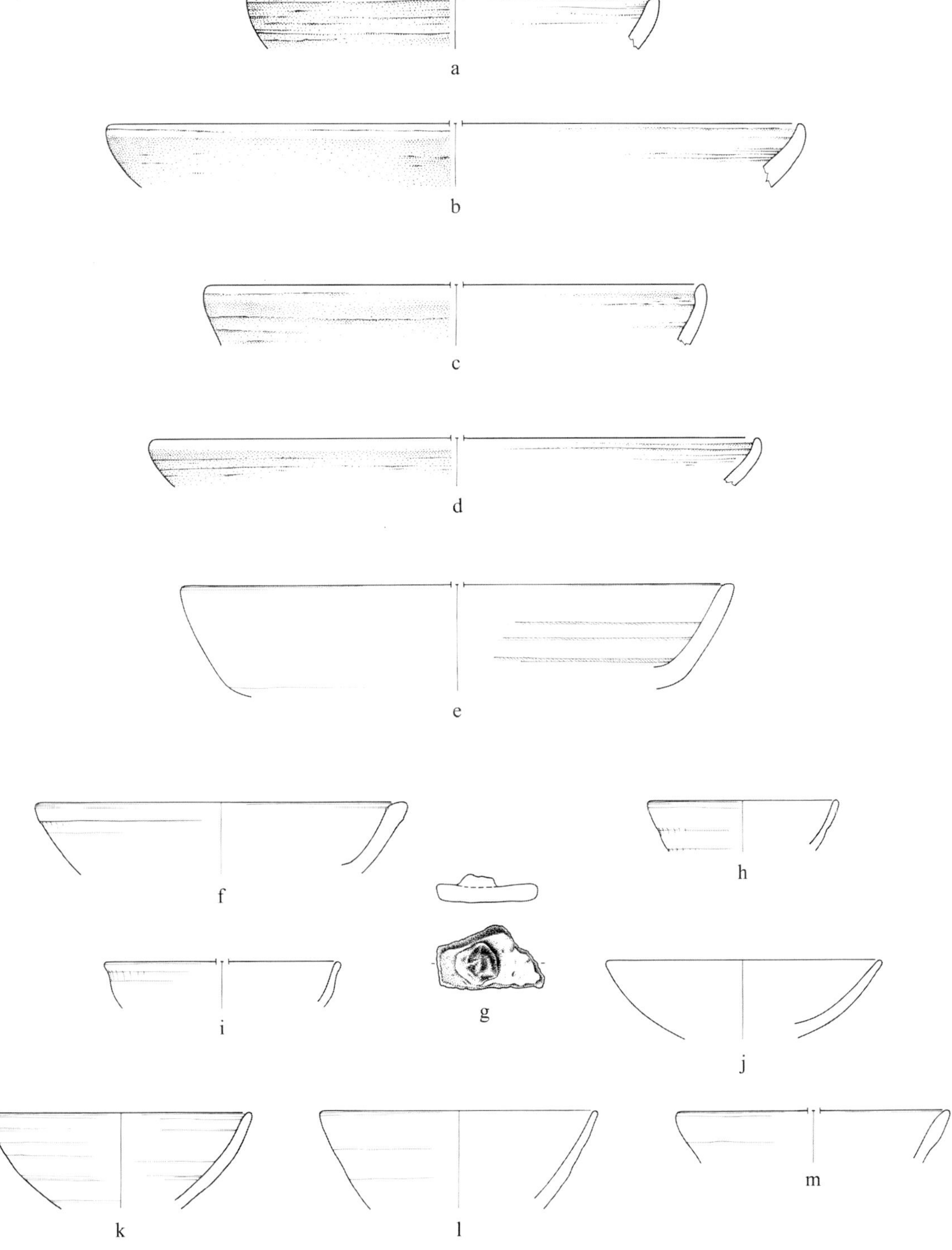

Figure 62. (*a*) **498** (G1-Nile B2); (*b*) **499** (G1-Nile B2); (*c*) **500** (G1-Nile B2); (*d*) **501** BDY/BDX **21** (G1-Nile B2); (*e*) **502** (G1-Nile B2); (*f*) **504** (G1-Nile B2 near G4-Nile C); (*g*) **506** (G1-Nile B2); (*h*) **507** (G1-Nile B2); (*i*) **508** (G1-Nile B2); (*j*) **509** (G1-Nile B2); (*k*) **510** (G1-Nile B2); (*l*) **511** (G1-Nile B2); (*m*) **512** (G1-Nile B2). 1:3

New Kingdom and TIP, Nile Fabrics

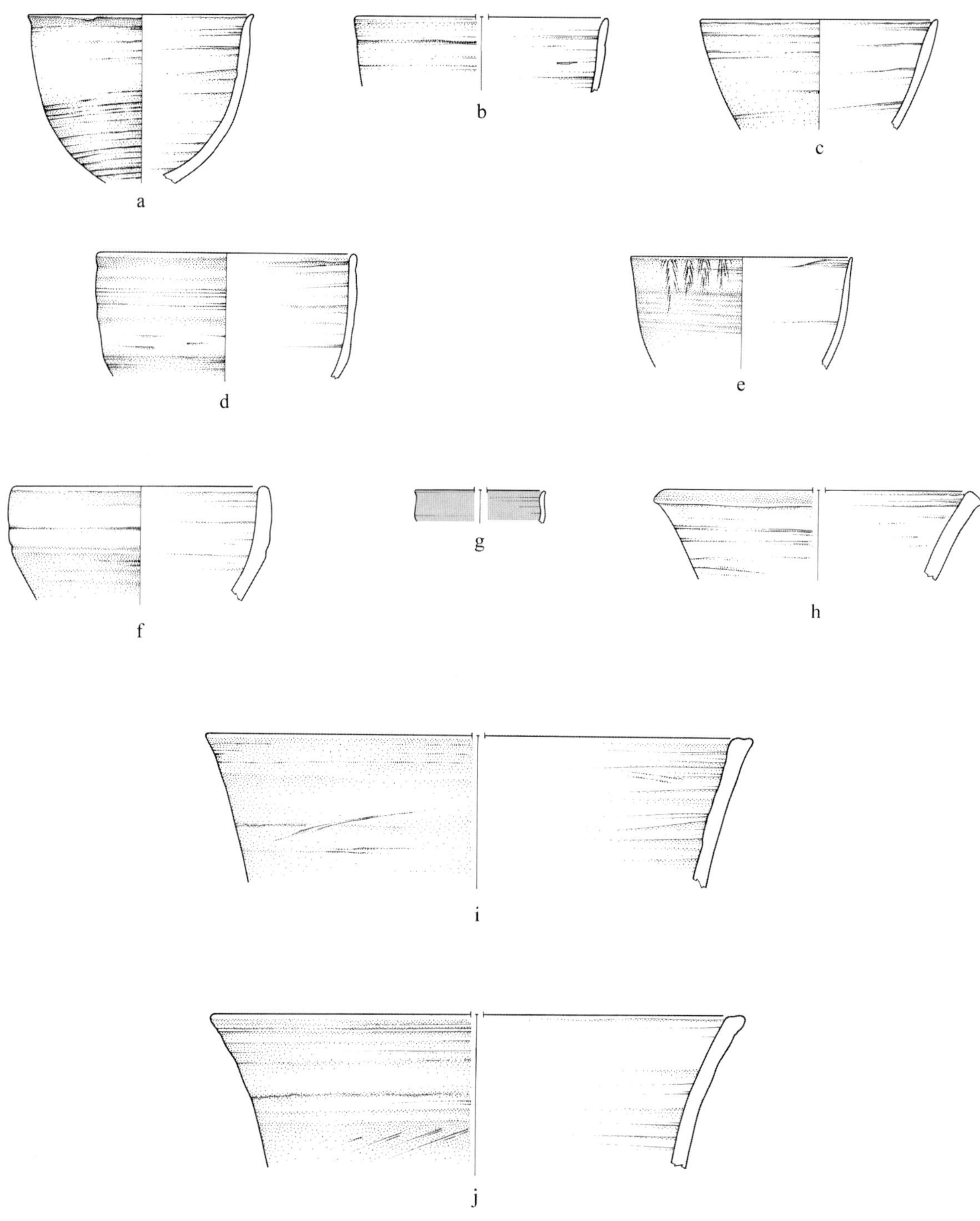

Figure 63. (*a*) **513** AQG/BEO **11** (G1-Nile B2); (*b*) **513** BGG **16** (G1-Nile B2); (*c*) **513** AWG **8** (G1-Nile B2); (*d*) **513** AAA **139** (G1-Nile B2); (*e*) **514** BDR **63** (G1-Nile B2); (*f*) **515** (G1-Nile B2); (*g*) **516** (G1-Nile B2); (*h*) **517** (G1-Nile B2); (*i*) **518** BAC **193** (G1-Nile B2); (*j*) **518** AOM **8** (G1-Nile B2). 1:3

New Kingdom and TIP, Nile Fabrics

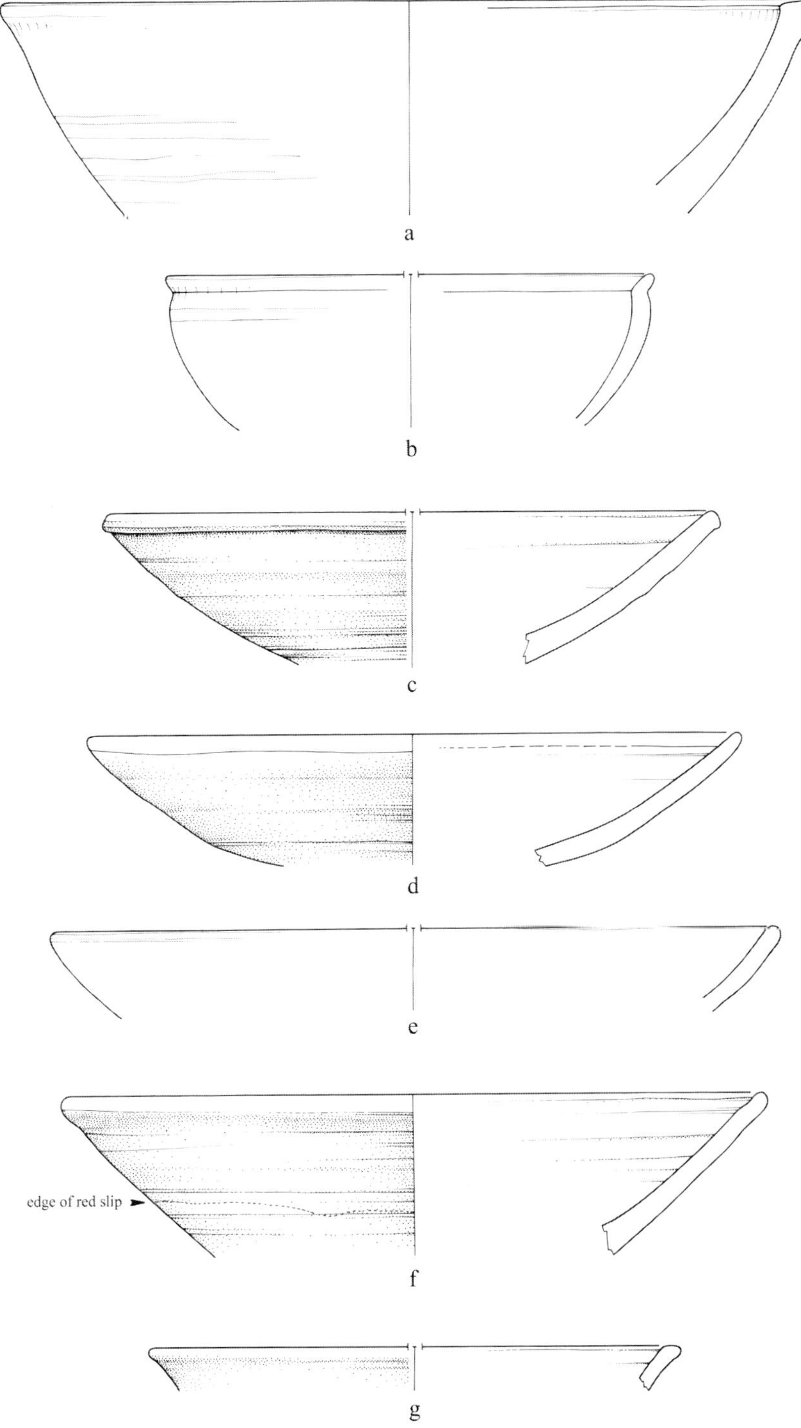

Figure 64. (*a*) **519** (G1-Nile B2); (*b*) **520** (G1-Nile B2); (*c*) **521** (G1-Nile B2); (*d*) **522** CHZ **20** (G1-Nile B2); (*e*) **522** AJY **149** (G1-Nile B2); (*f*) **522** AQG **61** etc (G1-Nile B2); (*g*) **523** (G1-Nile B2). 1:3

New Kingdom and TIP, Nile Fabrics

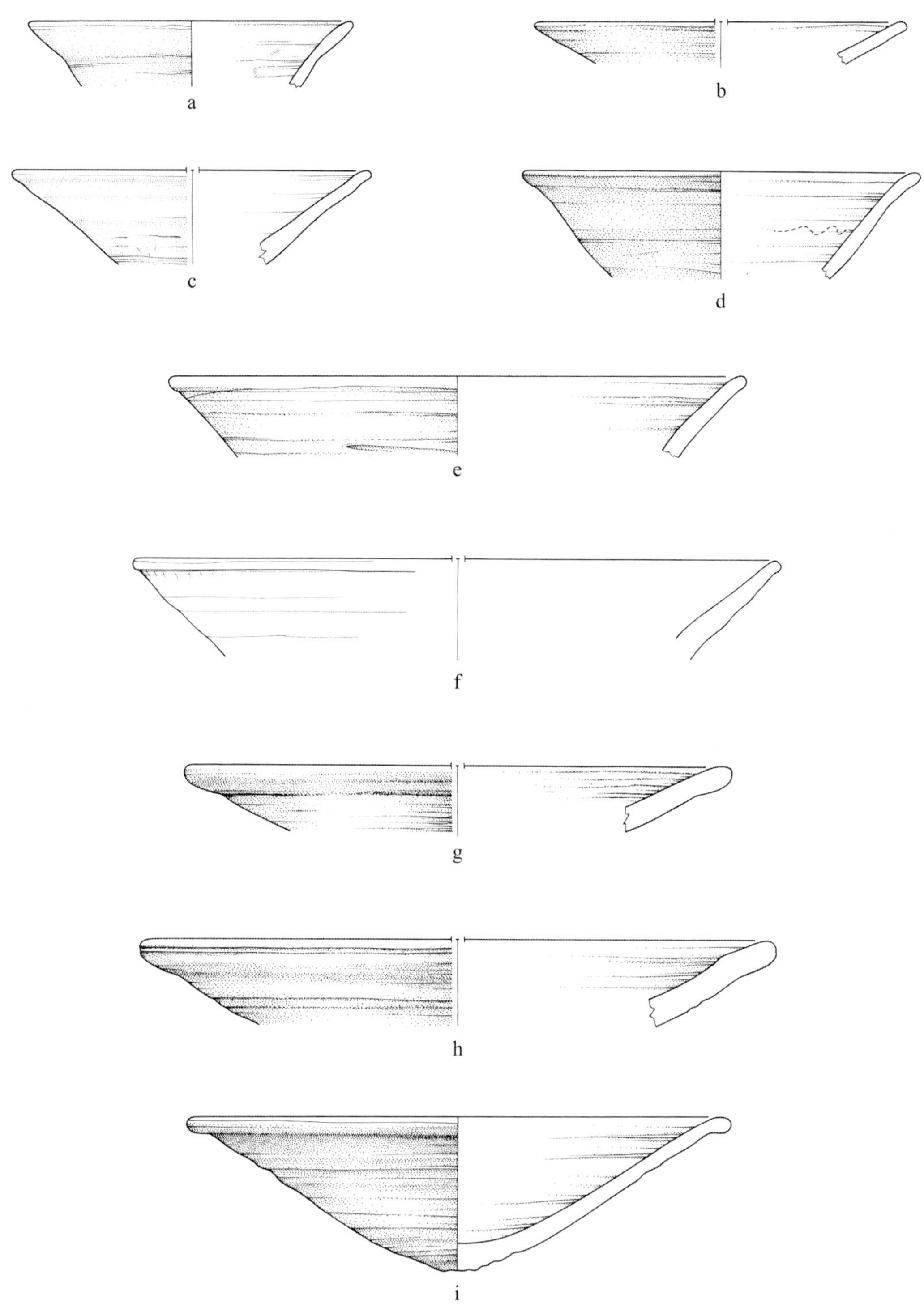

Figure 65. (*a*) 524 (G1-Nile B2); (*b*) 525 CHJ **12** (G1-Nile B2); (*c*) 525 AAA **81** (G1-Nile B2); (*d*) 528 ABI **9** (G1-Nile B2); (*e*) 529 CAA **30** (G1-Nile B2); (*f*) 532 (G1-Nile B2); (*g*) 535 (G1-Nile B2); (*h*) 536 AQG/BEO **19** (G1-Nile B2); (*i*) 536 AQR/AUQ **6**+AON **2** (G1-Nile B2). 1:3

New Kingdom and TIP, Nile Fabrics

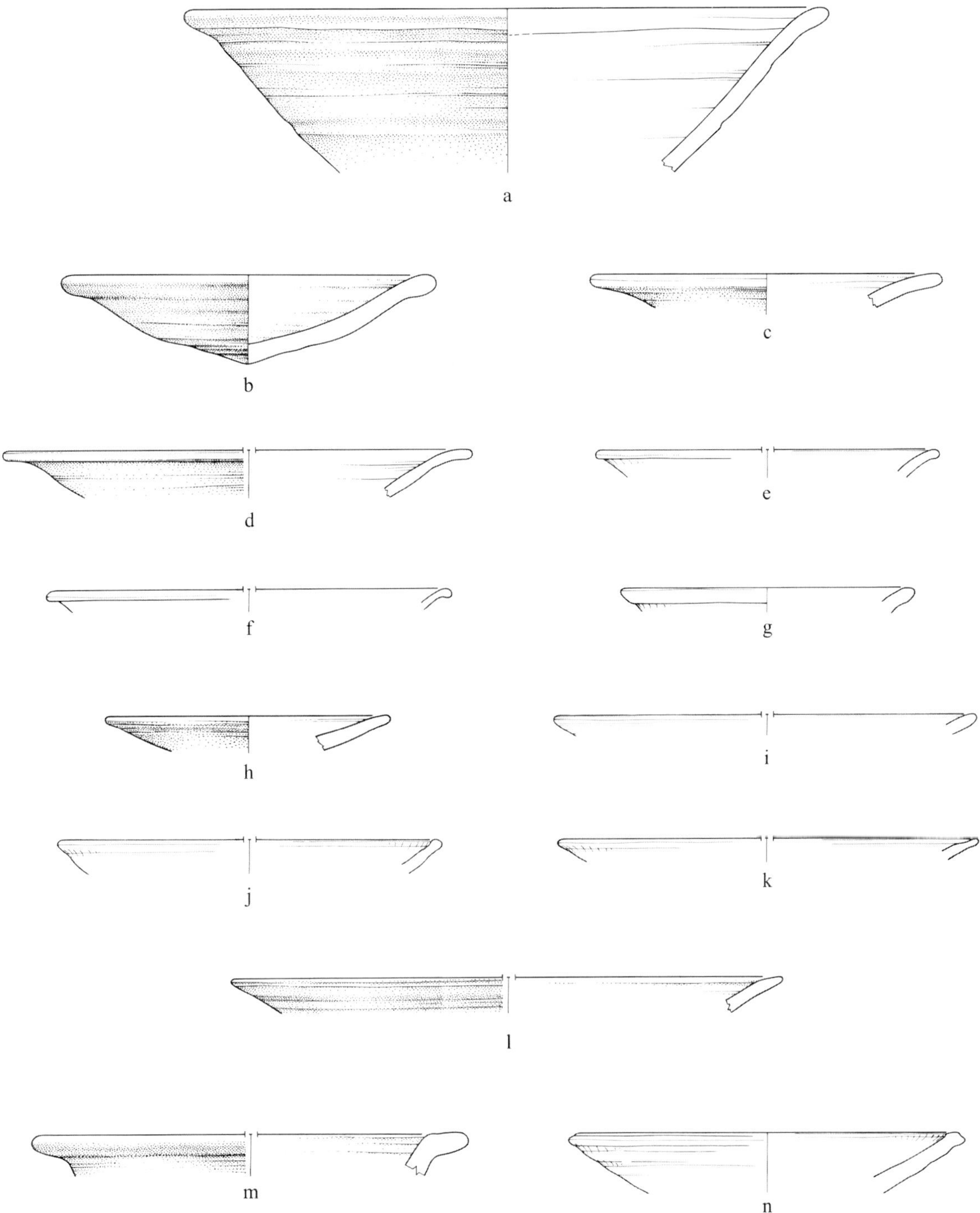

Figure 66. (*a*) **536** BDX **59** (G1-Nile B2); (*b*) **536** AJY/AQH **1+4**+AJY/AVB **52** (G1-Nile B2); (*c*) **536** BJG/BJO(H) **22** (G1-Nile B2); (*d*) **536** AAA **34** (G1-Nile B2); (*e*) **537** ADF **36** (G1-Nile B2); (*f*) **537** ARU=ARZ **36** (G1-Nile B2); (*g*) **537** AHY **86** (G1-Nile B2); (*h*) **538** (G1-Nile B2); (*i*) **539** (G1-Nile B2); (*j*) **540** (G1-Nile B2 near G2-Nile B1); (*k*) **541** (G1-Nile B2); (*l*) **542** (G1-Nile B2); (*m*) **543** (G1-Nile B2); (*n*) **544** AEZ/AFB/AFC/AFD **7** (G1-Nile B2).
1:3

New Kingdom and TIP, Nile Fabrics

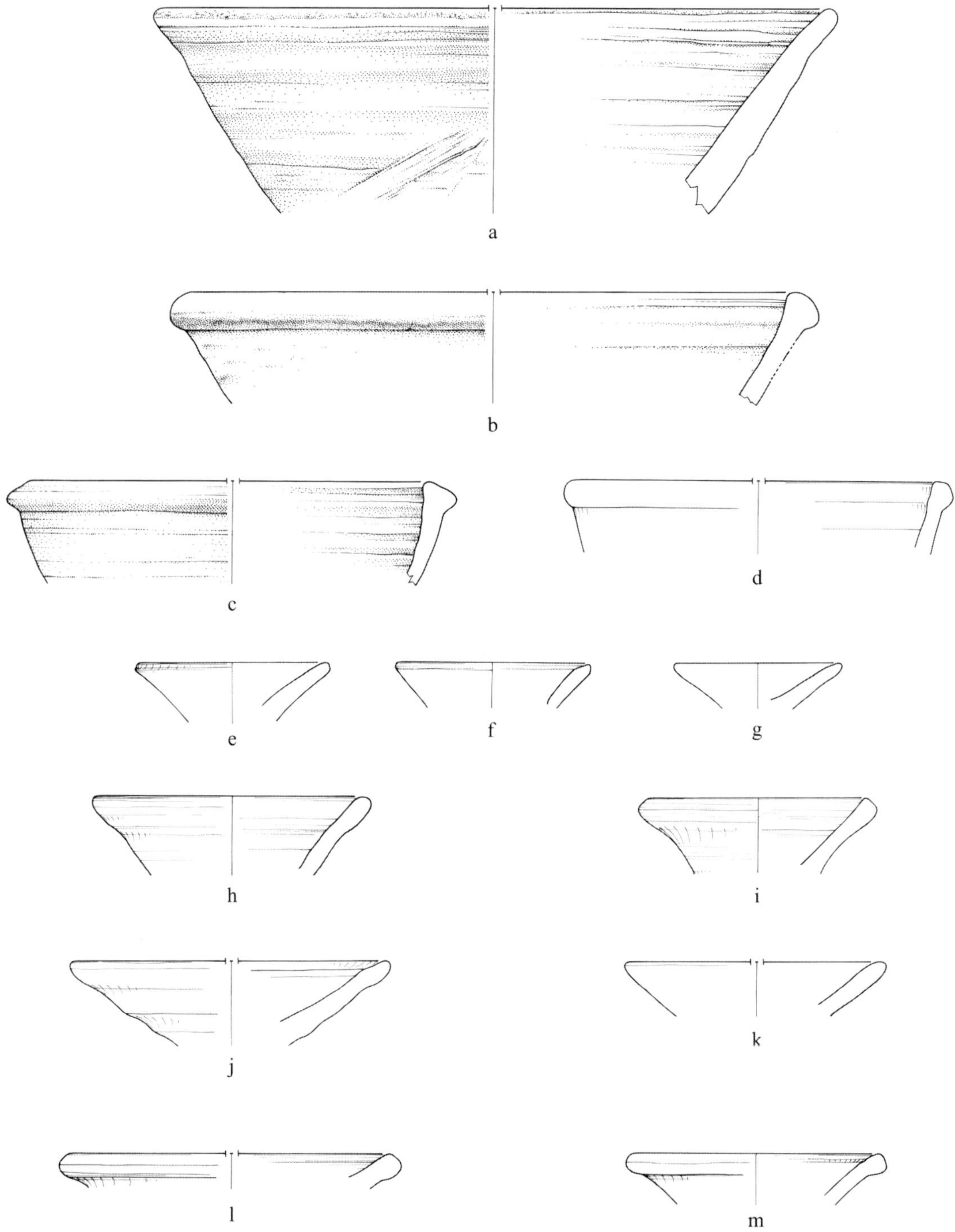

Figure 67. (*a*) **545** (G1-Nile B2); (*b*) **546** (G1-Nile B2); (*c*) **547** (G1-Nile B2); (*d*) **548** AEF **24** (G1-Nile B2); (*e*) **549** BCI **16** (G1-Nile B2); (*f*) **549** BAC/BEI **98** (G1-Nile B2); (*g*) **550** (G1-Nile B2); (*h*) **551** (G1-Nile B2); (*i*) **552** (G1-Nile B2); (*j*) **553** CGV **6** (G1-Nile B2); (*k*) **553** AIIV i/AAT **7** (G1-Nile B2); (*l*) **554** (G1-Nile B2); (*m*) **555** (G1-Nile B2).

1:3

New Kingdom and TIP, Nile Fabrics

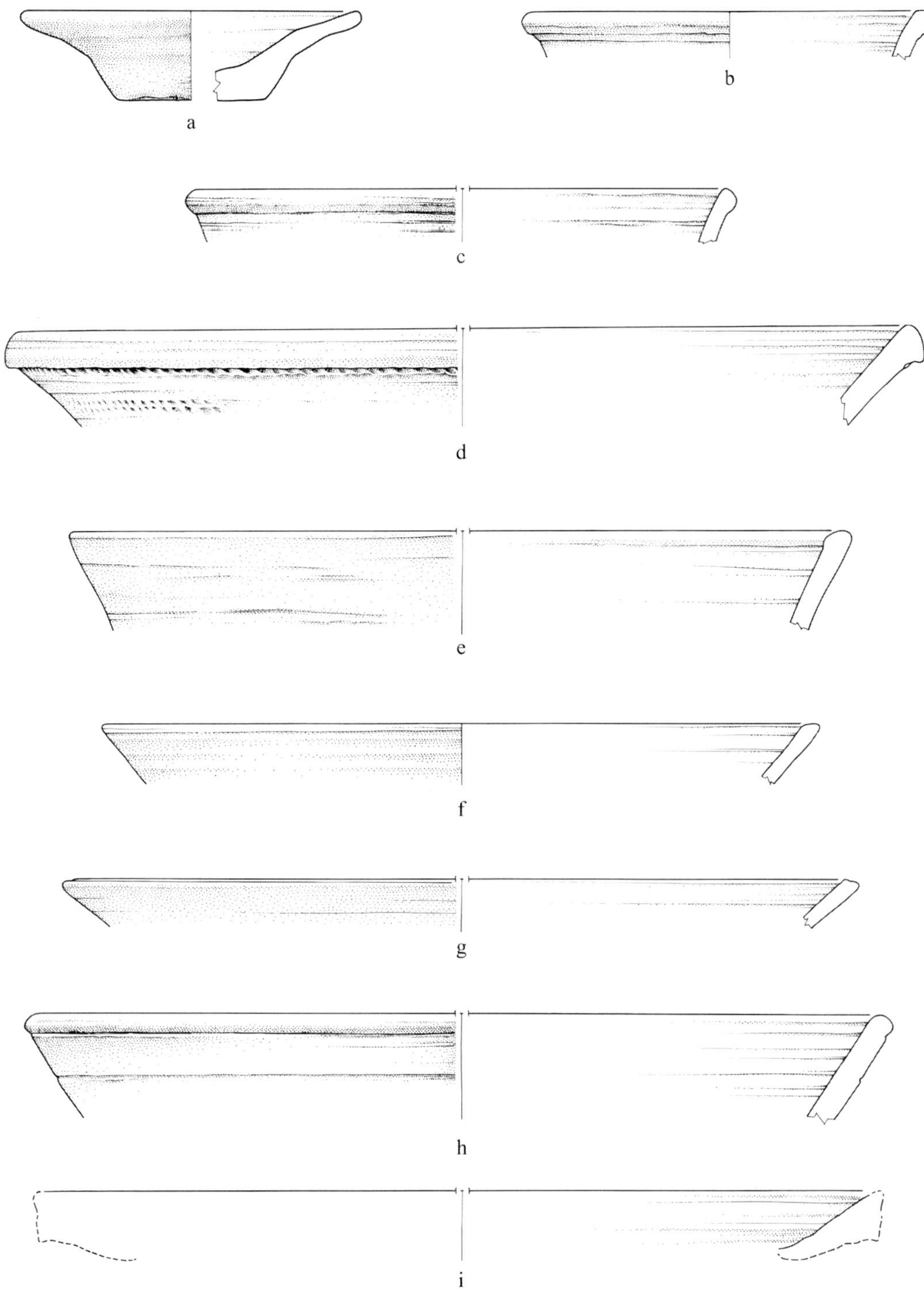

Figure 68. (*a*) 556 AJY **173** (G1-Nile B2); (*b*) 557 (G1-Nile B2); (*c*) 558 (G1-Nile B2); (*d*) 559 (G1-Nile B2); (*e*) 560 ABV/ABY/ABZ **8** (G1-Nile B2); (*f*) 560 ATY **235** (G1-Nile B2); (*g*) 560 AEW **39** (G1-Nile B2); (*h*) 561 (G1-Nile B2 near G4-Nile C); (*i*) 562 (G1-Nile B2). 1:3

New Kingdom and TIP, Nile Fabrics

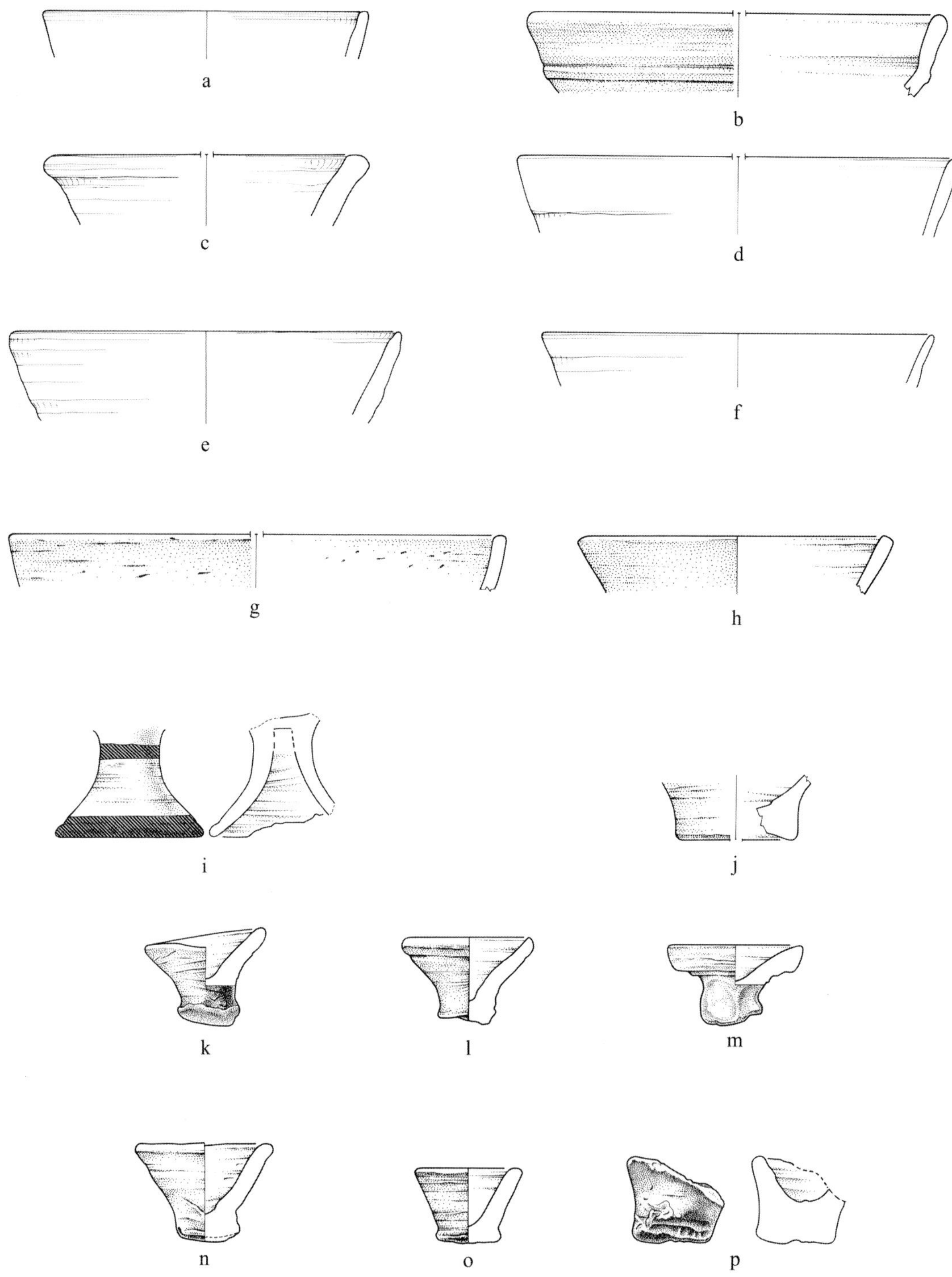

Figure 69. (*a*) **563** (G1-Nile B2); (*b*) **564** (G1-Nile B2); (*c*) **565** (G1-Nile B2); (*d*) **566** BHR **269** (G1-Nile B2); (*e*) **567** AIY **81** (G1-Nile B2); (*f*) **568** (G1-Nile B2); (*g*) **569** (G1-Nile B2); (*h*) **570** (G1-Nile B2); (*i*) **571** (G1-Nile B2); (*j*) **572** (G1-Nile B2); (*k*) **573** AJY **178** (G1-Nile B2); (*l*) **573** BGG **140** (G1-Nile B2); (*m*) **573** AAA **15** (G1-Nile B2); (*n*) **574** (G1-Nile B2); (*o*) **575** (G1-Nile B2); (*p*) **576** (G1-Nile B2). 1:3

New Kingdom and TIP, Nile Fabrics

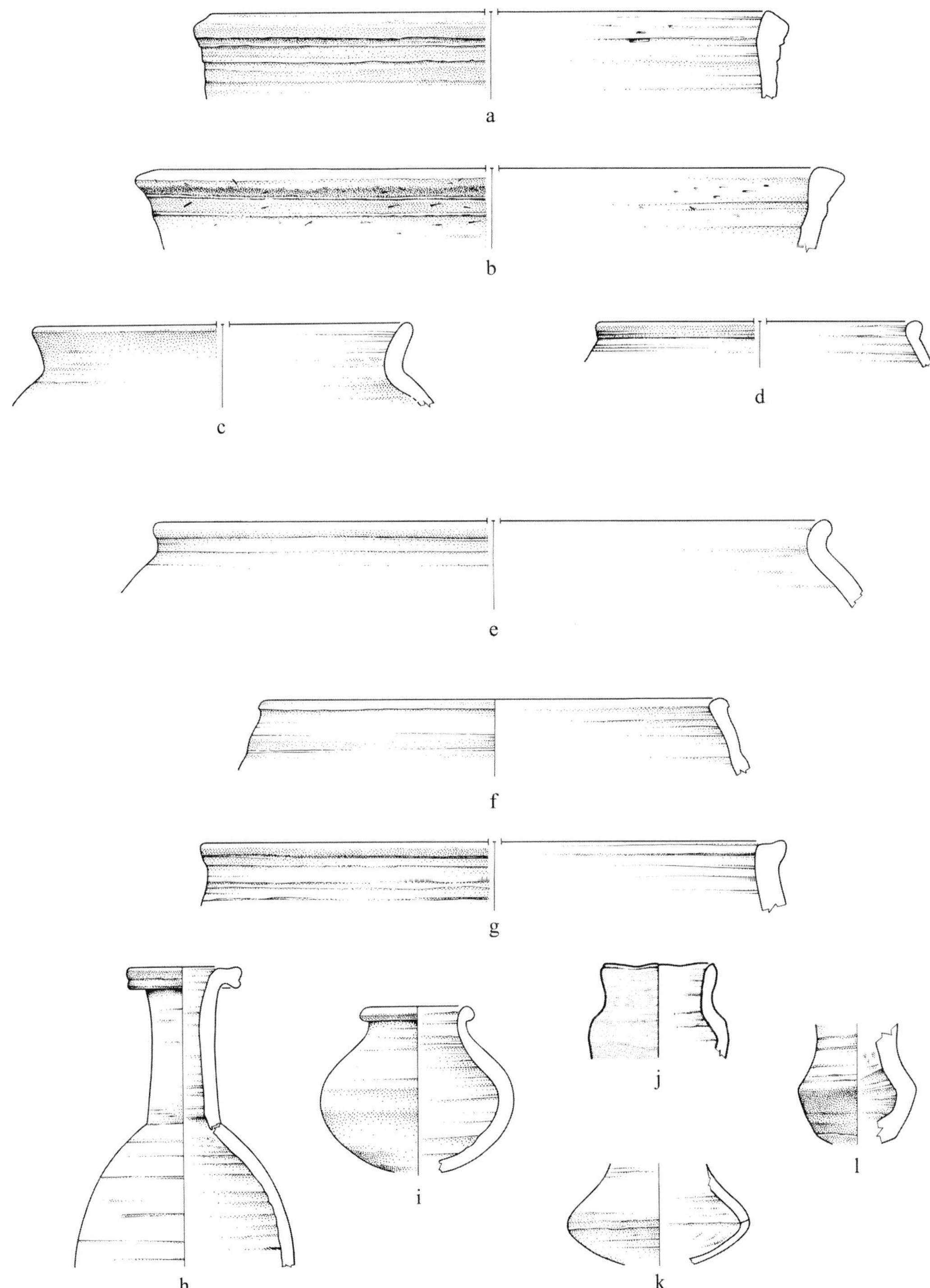

Figure 70. (*a*) **577** (G1-Nile B2); (*b*) **578** (G1-Nile B2); (*c*) **579** (G1-Nile B2); (*d*) **580** (G1-Nile B2); (*e*) **581** (G1-Nile B2); (*f*) **582** (G1-Nile B2); (*g*) **583** (G1-Nile B2 near G4-Nile C); (*h*) **584** BJG/BJO(H) **11**+**12**+**26**+**47** etc (G1-Nile B2); (*i*) **585** (G1-Nile B2); (*j*) **587** (G1-Nile B2); (*k*) **586** (G1-Nile B2); (*l*) **588** (G1-Nile B2). 1:3

New Kingdom and TIP, Nile Fabrics

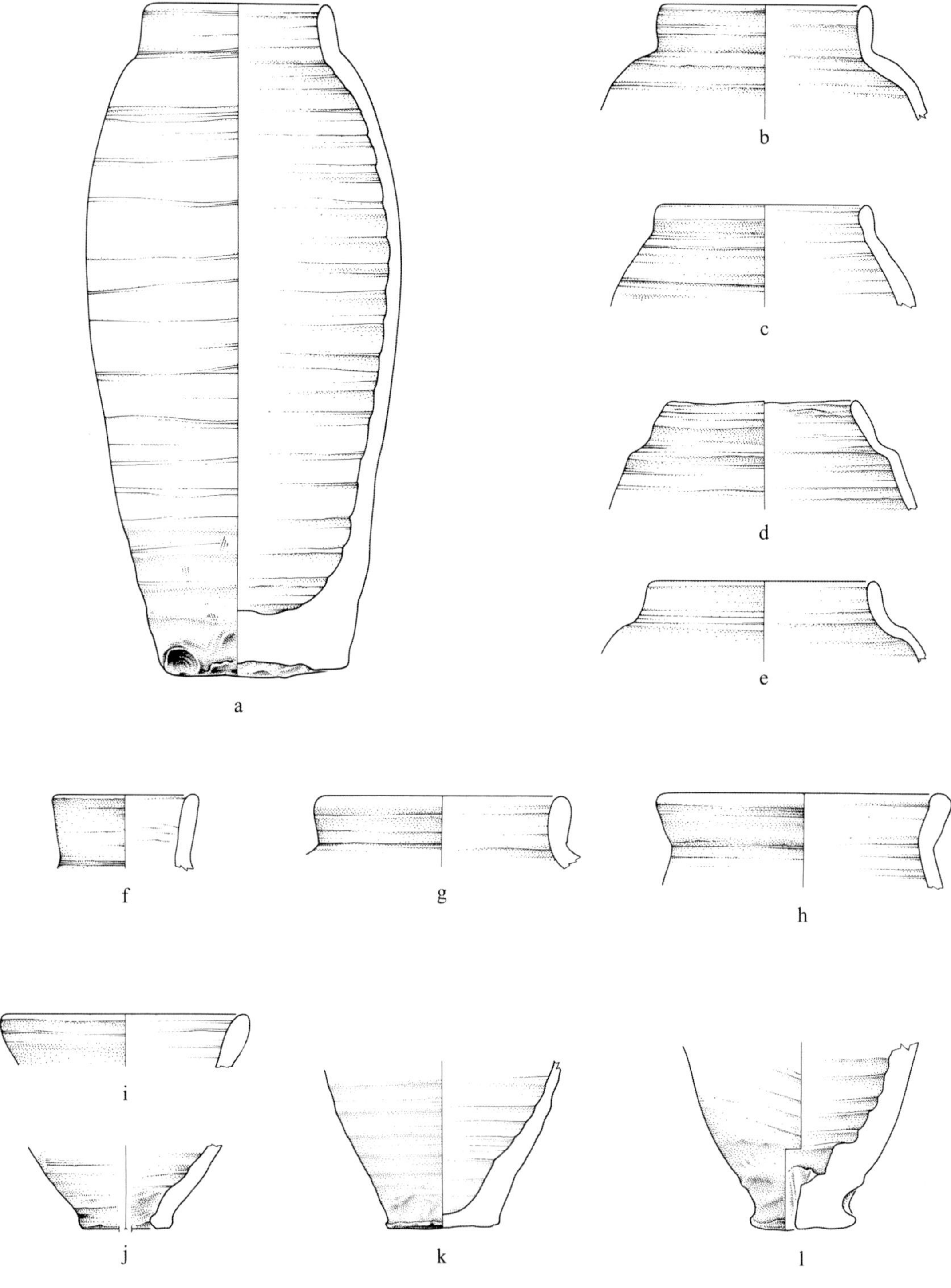

Figure 71. (*a*) 589 (G1-Nile B2); (*b*) 590 ADU **2** (G1-Nile B2); (*c*) 590 ABR North **5** (G1-Nile B2); (*d*) 590 ATY **28** (G1-Nile B2); (*e*) 590 UP 805 **22** (G1-Nile B2); (*f*) 591 CFT **15** (G1-Nile B2); (*g*) 592 (G1-Nile B2); (*h*) 593 (G1-Nile B2); (*i*) 594 (G1-Nile B2); (*j*) 595 (G1-Nile B2); (*k*) 596 (G1-Nile B2); (*l*) 597 ADS/ARP=ARS **3** (G1-Nile B2). 1:3

New Kingdom and TIP, Nile Fabrics

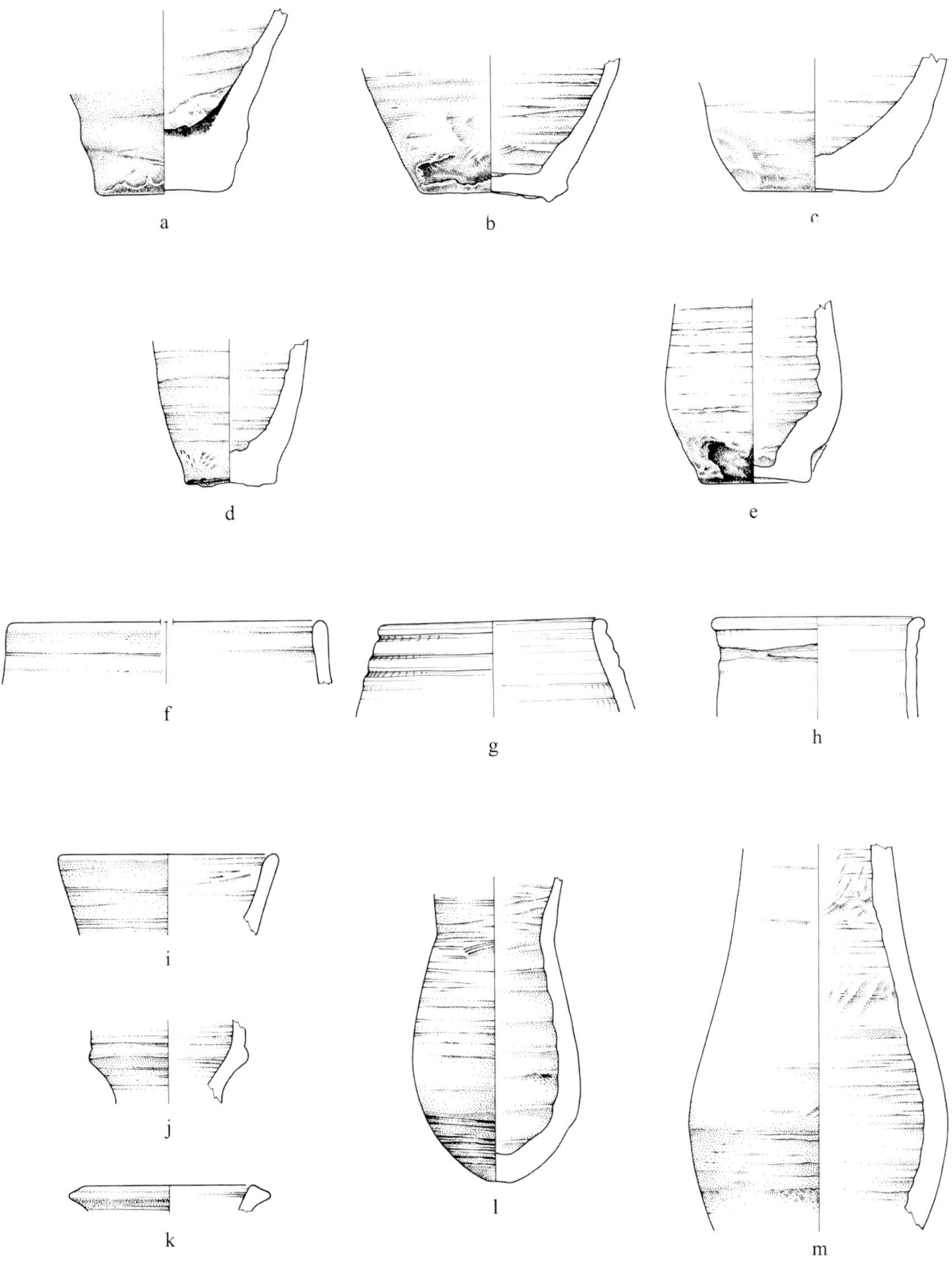

Figure 72. (*a*) **<u>598</u>** BEO **64** (G1-Nile B2); (*b*) **<u>598</u>** AUQ **197** (G1-Nile B2); (*c*) **<u>598</u>** ADG/ADH **13+14** (G1-Nile B2); (*d*) **<u>599</u>** BAC **351** (G1-Nile B2); (*e*) **<u>599</u>** AER **25** (G1-Nile B2); (*f*) **<u>600</u>** (G1-Nile B2); (*g*) **<u>601</u>** (G1-Nile B2); (*h*) **<u>602</u>** (G1-Nile B2); (*i*) **<u>603</u>** (G1-Nile B2); (*j*) **<u>604</u>** (G1-Nile B2); (*k*) **<u>607</u>** (G1-Nile B2); (*l*) **<u>605</u>** (G1-Nile B2); (*m*) **<u>606</u>** (G1-Nile B2).

1:3

New Kingdom and TIP, Nile Fabrics

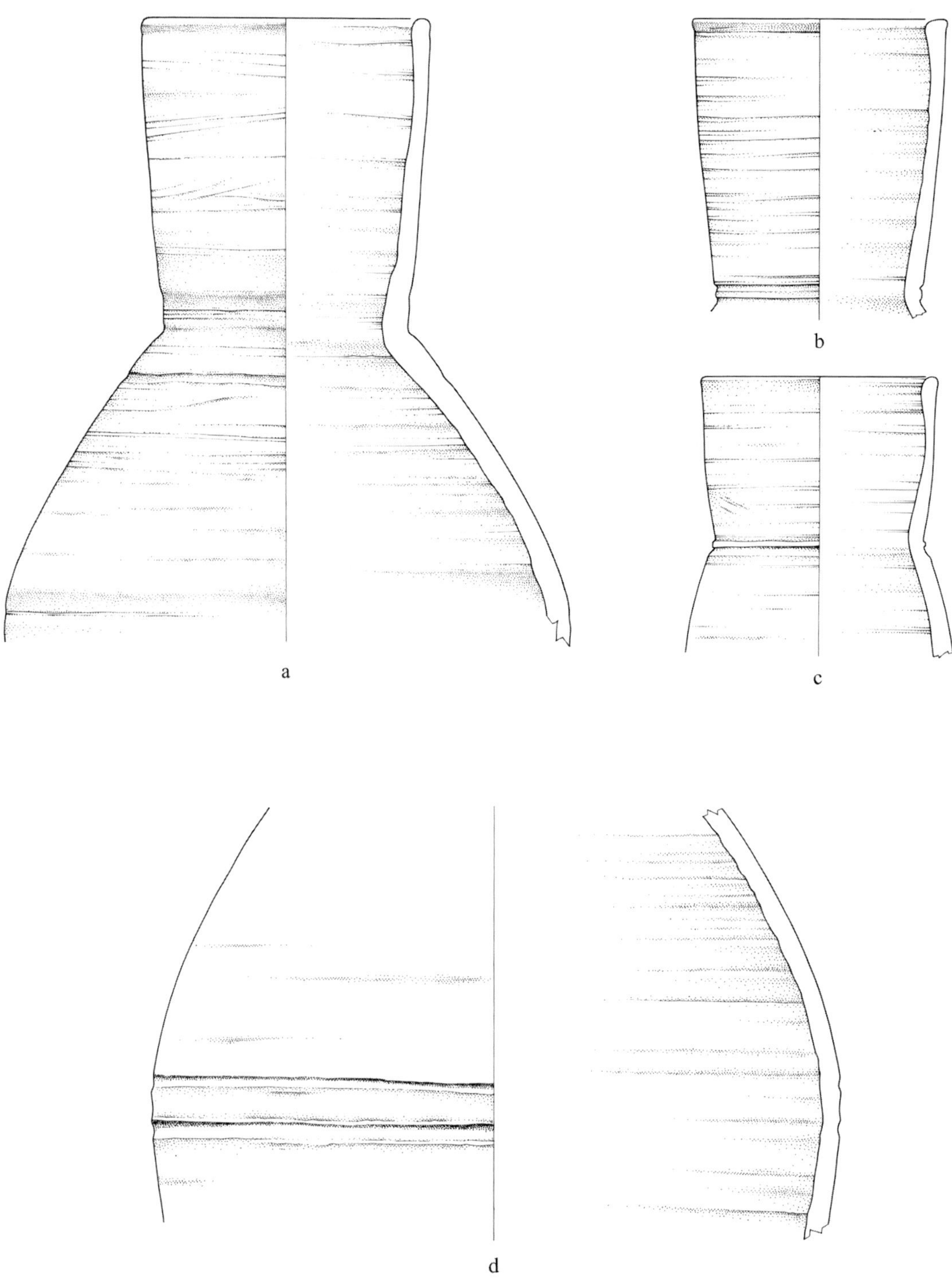

Figure 73. (a) **608** CGQ **68-74** etc (G1-Nile B2); (b) **608** BCQ **5** (G1-Nile B2); (c) **609** AAA **425**+**454**+**455** (G1-Nile B2); (d) **610** BCN **7**+BCC **25** (G1-Nile B2). 1:3

New Kingdom and TIP, Nile Fabrics

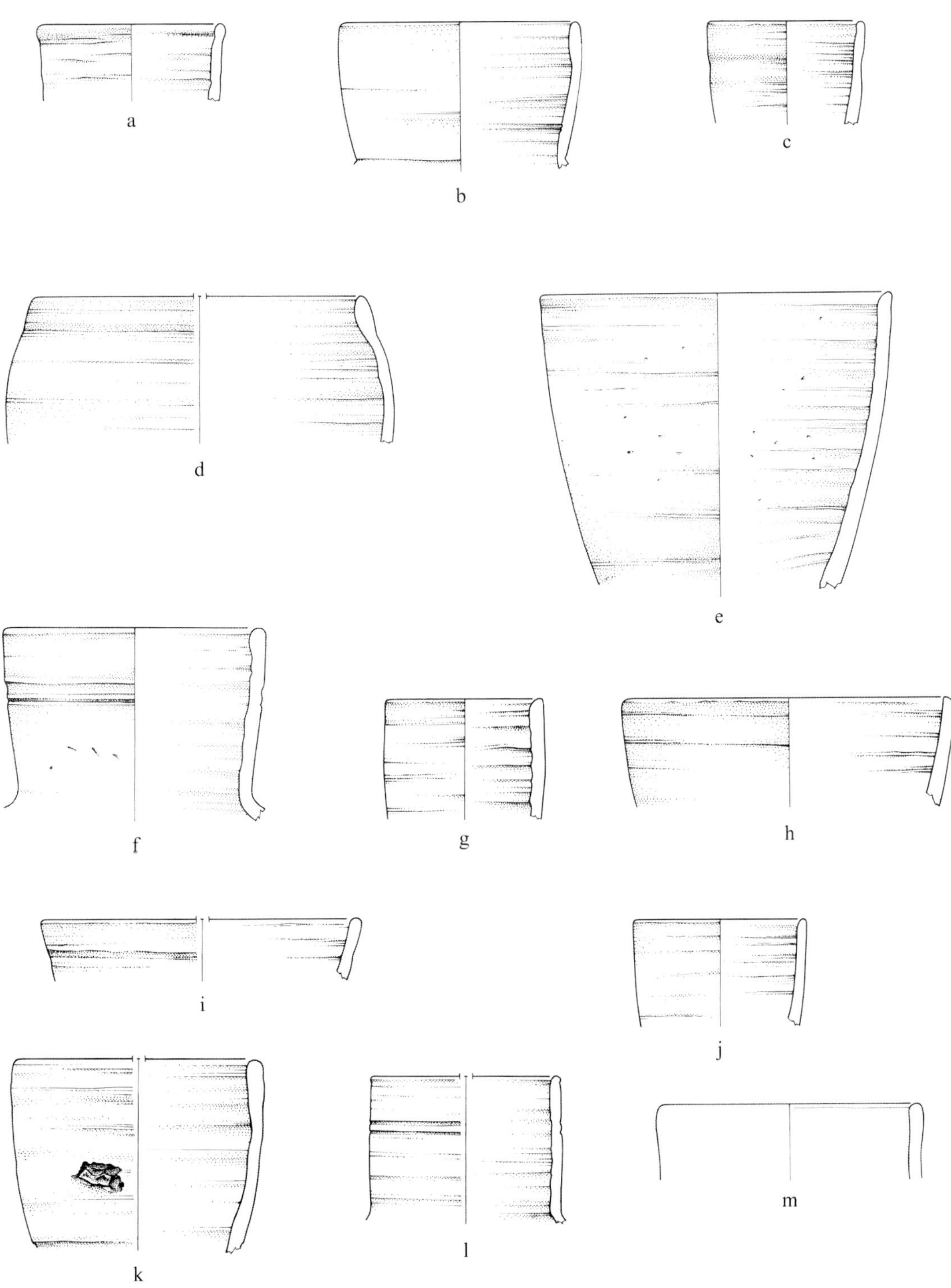

Figure 74. (*a*) **611** AQG **153** (G1-Nile B2); (*b*) **611** BEO **101** (G1-Nile B2); (*c*) **611** AJY **165** (G1-Nile B2; (*d*) **611** AJX/AJY/BRS **63** (G1-Nile B2); (*e*) **611** BJJ **48** (G1-NileB2); (*f*) **611** BKN **35** + BHP **157** (G1-Nile B2); (*g*) **611** AQH **183+185** (G1-Nile B2); (*h*) **611** BHW/BHY **54** (G1-Nile B2); (*i*) **611** BHP **127** (G1-Nile B2); (*j*) **611** BEP **96** (G1-Nile B2); (*k*) **612** (G1-Nile B2); (*l*) **613** (G1-Nile B2); (*m*) **614** (G1-Nile B2). 1:3

New Kingdom and TIP, Nile Fabrics

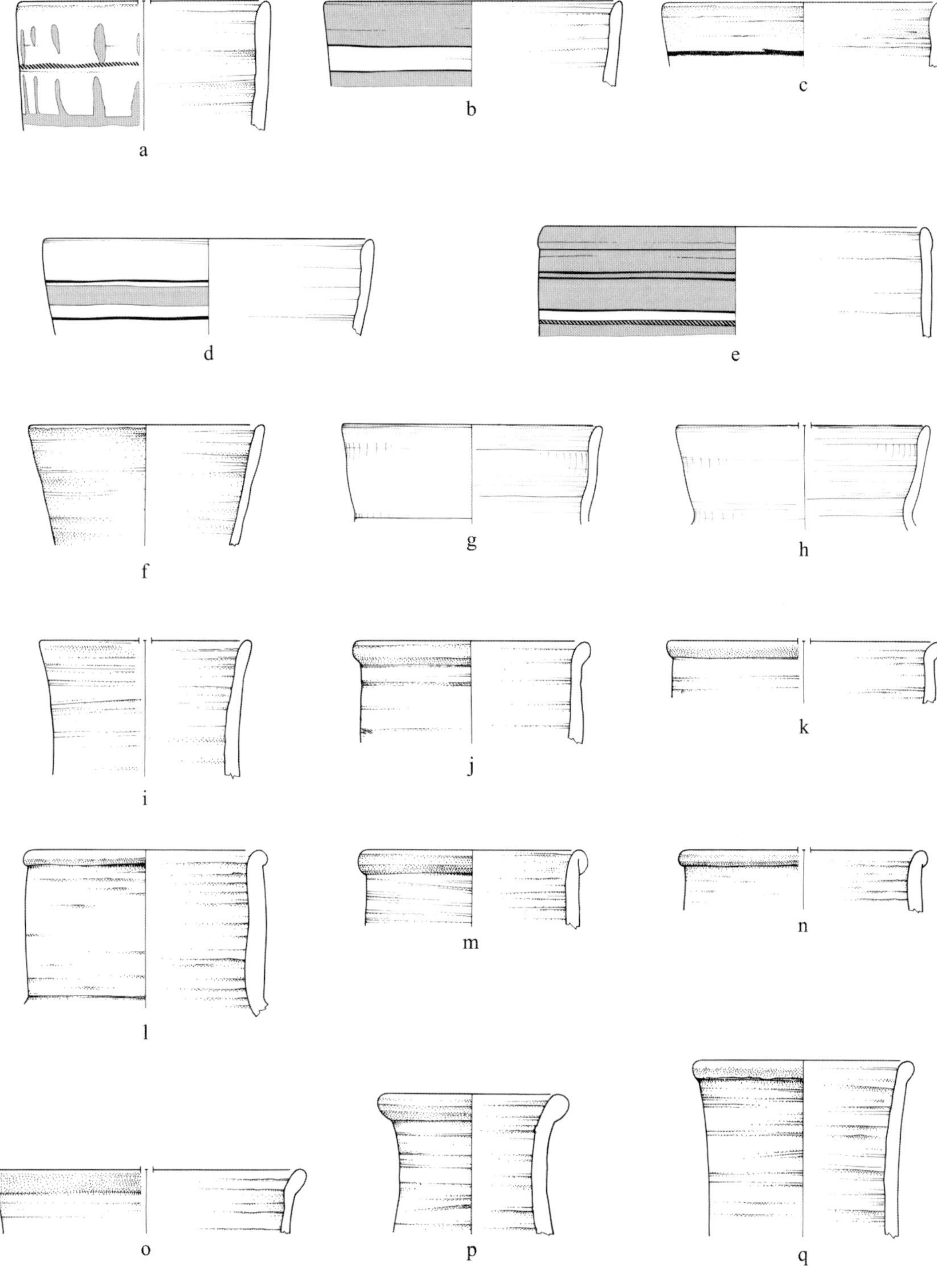

Figure 75. (*a*) **615** BGL **74** (G1-Nile B2); (*b*) **615** AAA **471** (G1-Nile B2); (*c*) **616** (G1-Nile B2); (*d*) **617** (G1-Nile B2); (*e*) **618** (G1-Nile B2); (*f*) **619** AQG **217** etc (G1-Nile B2); (*g*) **619** AQG **249** etc (G1-Nile B2); (*h*) **619** BGG **104** (G1-Nile B2); (*i*) **621** (G1-Nile B2); (*j*) **622** BJG(A) **23** etc (G1-Nile B2); (*k*) **622** BJG/BJO **19** (G1-Nile B2); (*l*) **623** (G1-Nile B2); (*m*) **624** BHR/BTG **109** (G1-Nile B2); (*n*) **624** ABY **59** (G1-Nile B2); (*o*) **625** (G1-Nile B2); (*p*) **626** (G1-Nile B2); (*q*) **627** (G1-Nile B2). 1:3

New Kingdom and TIP, Nile Fabrics

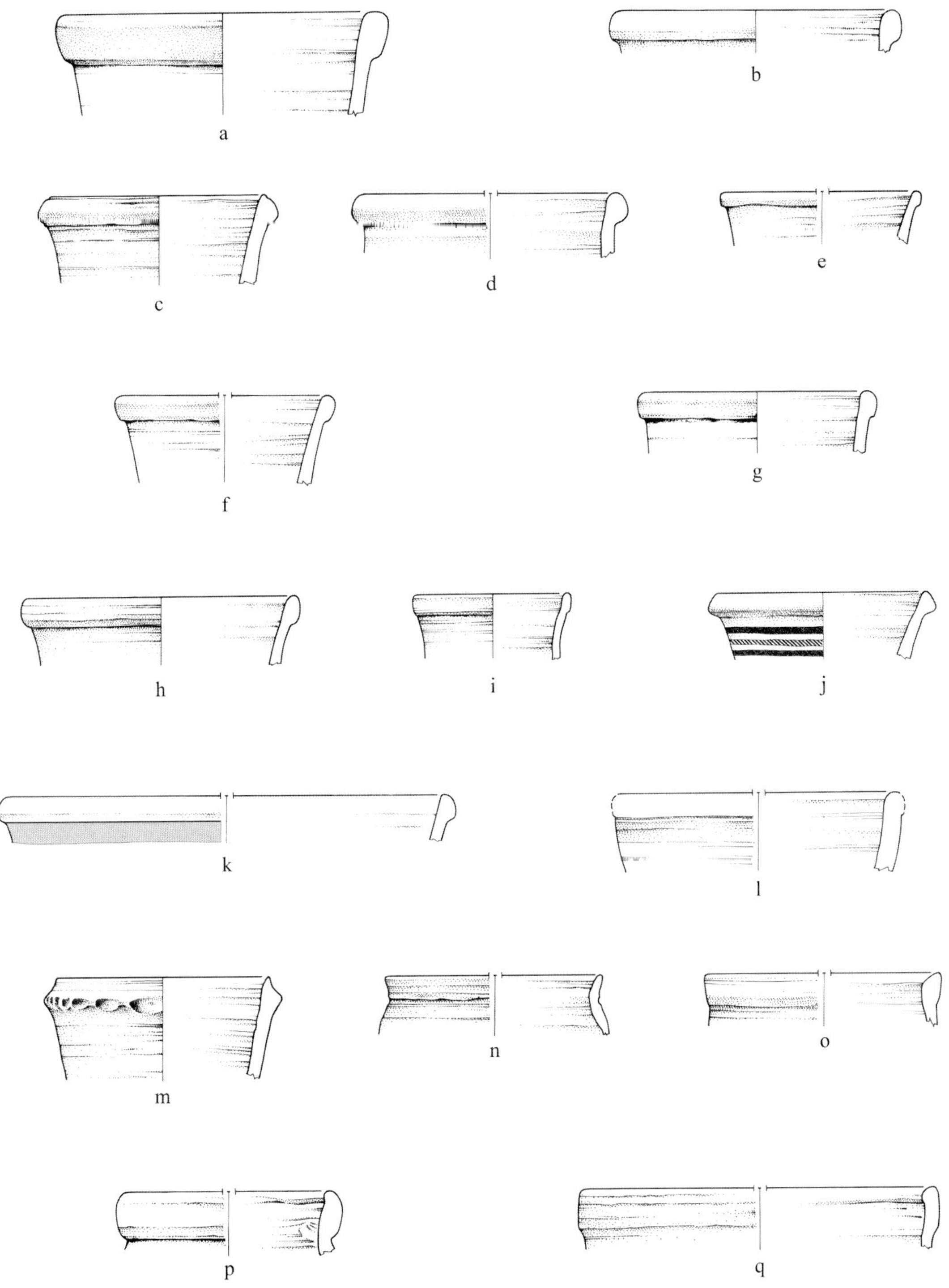

Figure 76. (*a*) **628** (G1-Nile B2); (*b*) **629** (G1-Nile B2); (*c*) **630** (G1-Nile B2); (*d*) **631** (G1-Nile B2); (*e*) **632** (G1-Nile B2); (*f*) **633** AQG/AJY **7** (G1-Nile B2); (*g*) **633** AJY **121** (G1-Nile B2); (*h*) **634** (G1-Nile B2); (*i*) **635** (G1-Nile B2); (*j*) **636** (G1-Nile B2); (*k*) **637** (G1-Nile B2); (*l*) **638** (G1-Nile B2); (*m*) **639** BEN **59** (G1-Nile B2); (*n*) **640** (G1-Nile B2); (*o*) **641** (G1-Nile B2); (*p*) **642** ADC **119** (G1-Nile B2); (*q*) **643** (G1-Nile B2). 1:3

New Kingdom and TIP, Nile Fabrics

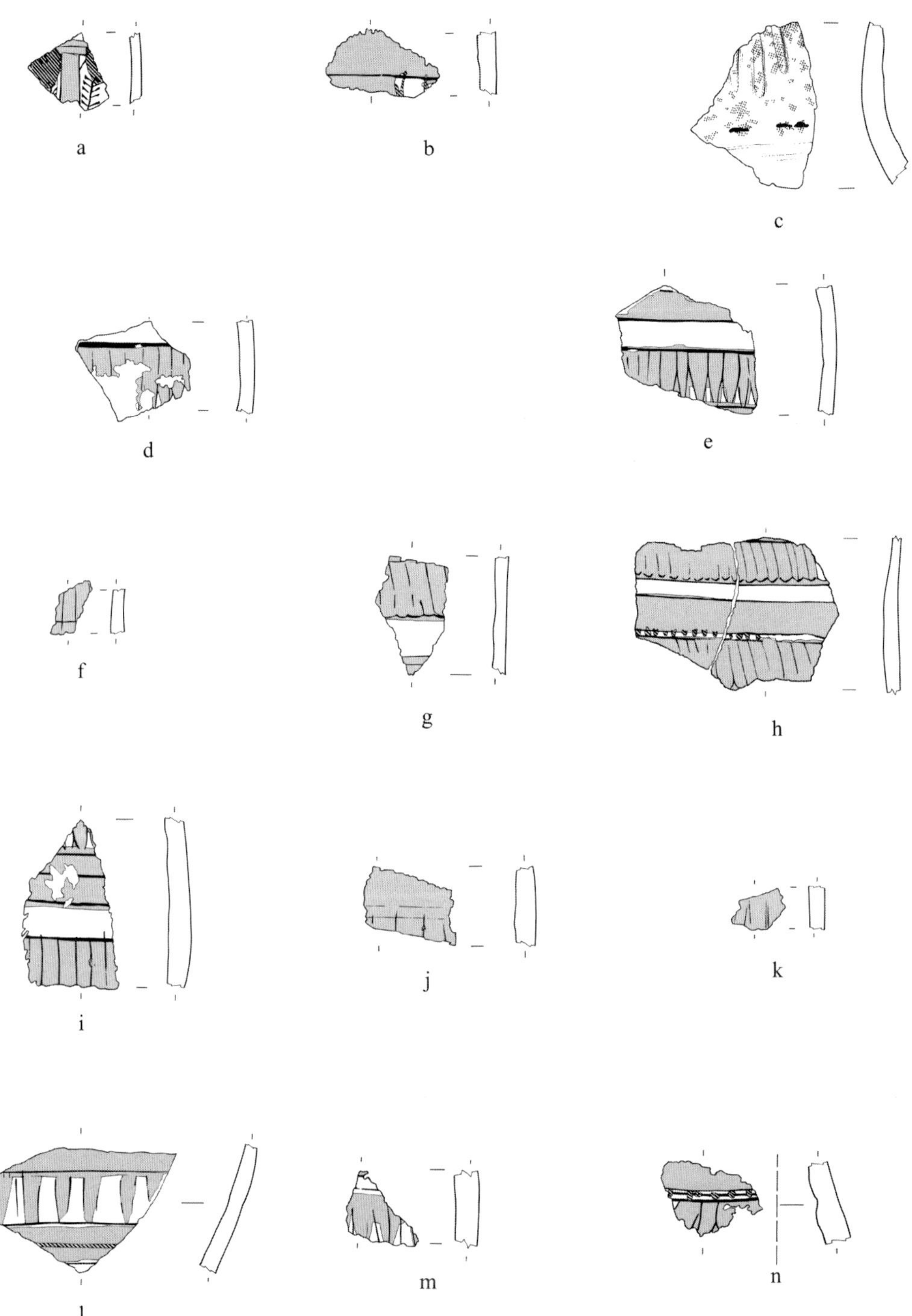

Figure 77. (*a*) **644** (G1-Nile B2); (*b*) **645** (G1-Nile B2); (*c*) **646** (G1-Nile B2); (*d*) **647** AQG/BGU **38** (G1-Nile B2); (*e*) **647** ATY/AAA **7** (G1-Nile B2); (*f*) **647** BAC **267** (G1-Nile B2); (*g*) **647** ABI **12** (G1-Nile B2); (*h*) **647** AAA **429+528** (G1-Nile B2); (*i*) **647** UP 8 **28** (G1-Nile B2); (*j*) **647** AMJ **16** (G1-Nile B2); (*k*) **647** AAA Lower **46** (G1-Nile B2); (*l*) **647** UP 8 **27** (G1-Nile B2); (*m*) **647** AAA **33** (G1-Nile B2); (*n*) **647** AEK **36** (G1-Nile B2). 1:3

New Kingdom and TIP, Nile Fabrics

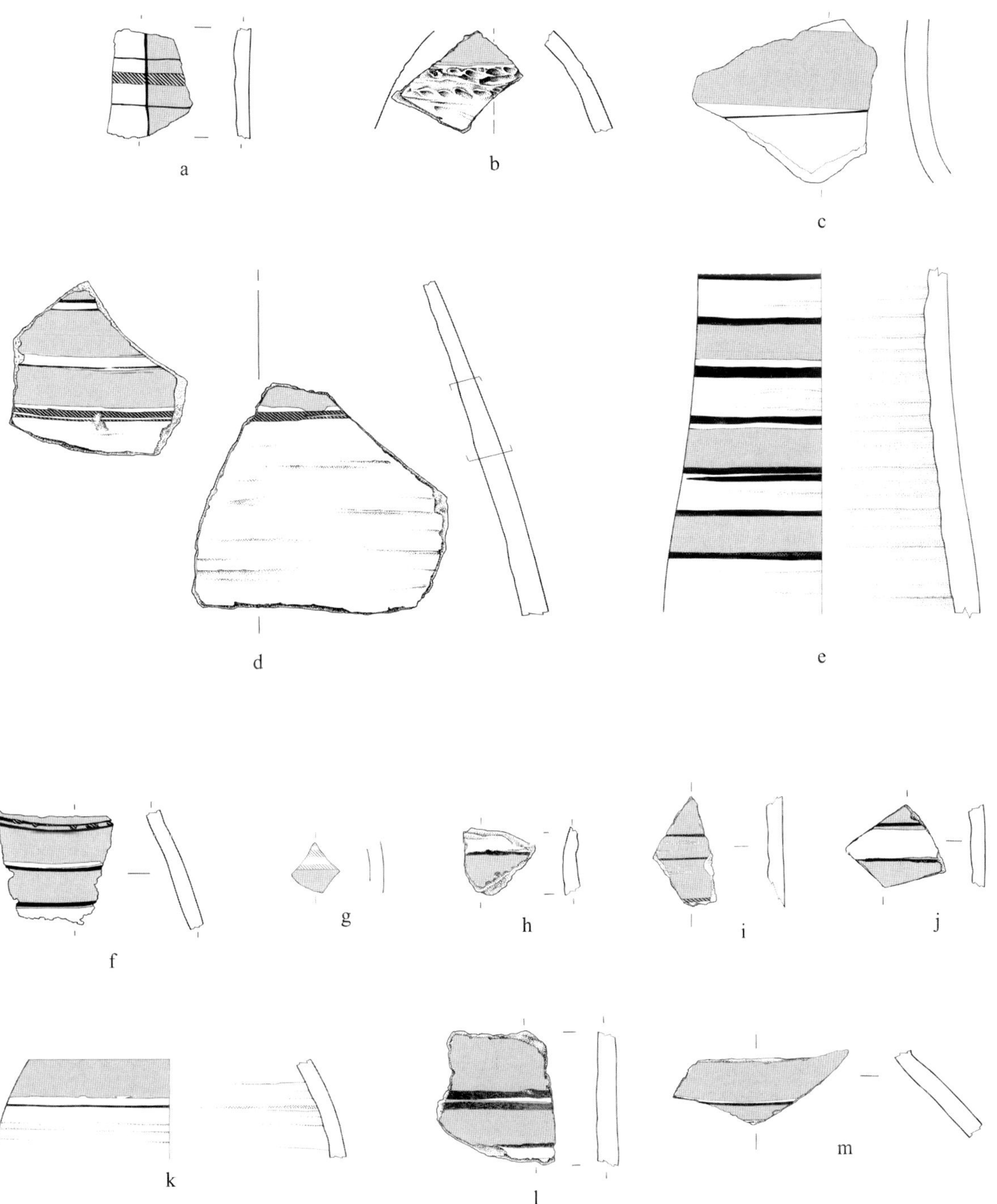

Figure 78. (*a*) **648** (G1-Nile B2); (*b*) **649** CBS **69** (G1-Nile B2); (*c*) **649** AAA **503** (G1-Nile B2); (*d*) **650** BJA/BMW **8** and AIY under Room 10 **153** (G1-Nile B2); (*e*) **650** BAC/BEI **195** (G1-Nile B2); (*f*) **650** BGG **25** (G1-Nile B2); (*g*) **650** BHR **270** (G1-Nile B2); (*h*) **650** AVB **100** (G1-Nile B2); (*i*) **650** AEW **9** (G1-Nile B2); (*j*) **650** AAA **201** (G1-Nile B2); (*k*) **650** AAA **482** (G1-Nile B2); (*l*) **650** AAA **141** (G1-Nile B2); (*m*) **650** BEP **139** (G1-Nile B2). 1:3

New Kingdom and TIP, Nile Fabrics

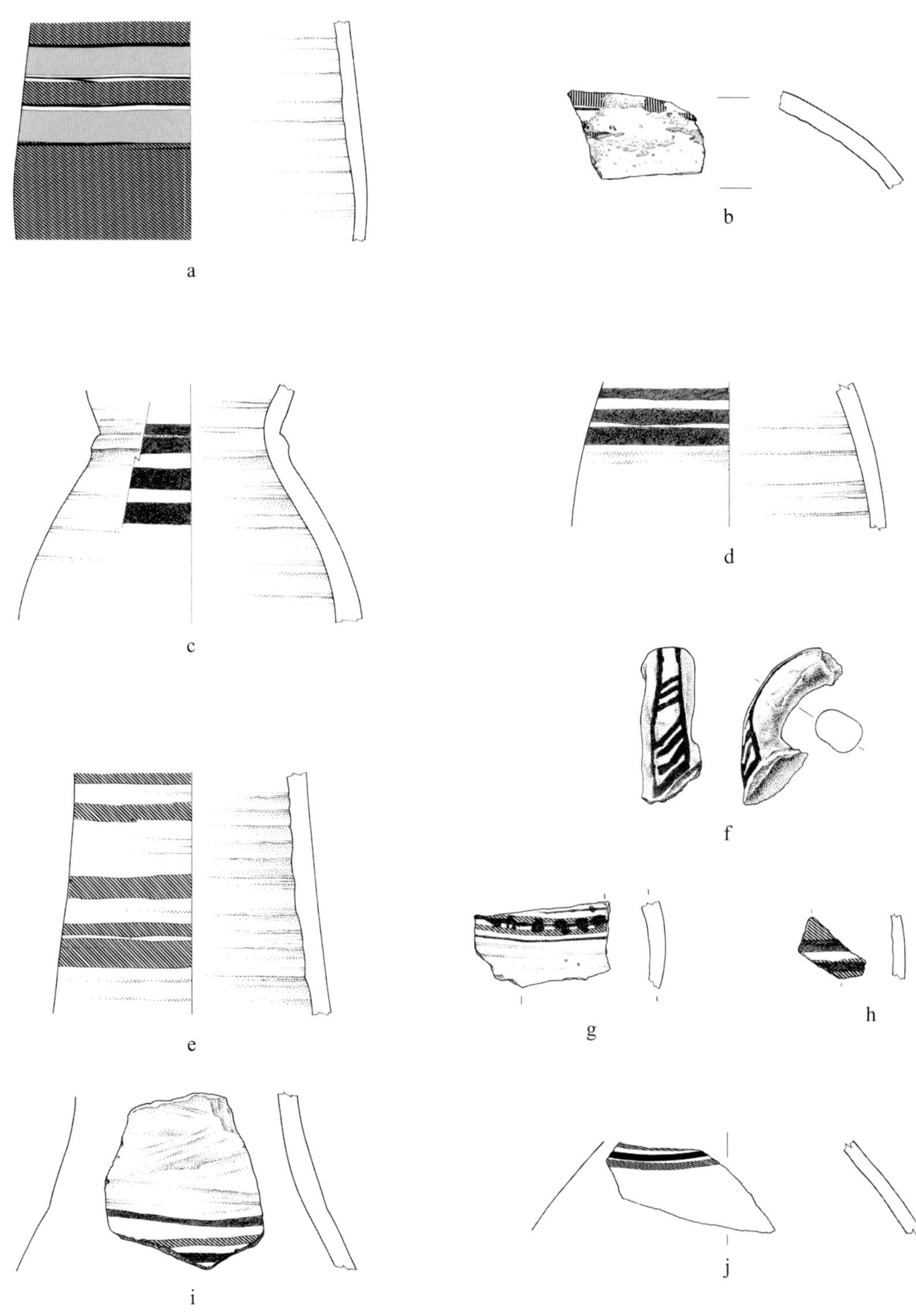

Figure 79. (*a*) **651** BGL **118** (G1-Nile B2); (*b*) **652** (G1-Nile B2); (*c*) **653** (G1-Nile B2); (*d*) **654** UP 8 **11** (G1-Nile B2); (*e*) **655** (G1-Nile B2); (*f*) **656** (G1-Nile B2); (*g*) **657** (G1-Nile B2); (*h*) **658** BTX **195** (G1-Nile B2); (*i*) **658** AAA **32** (G1-Nile B2); (*j*) **658** AAA **57** (G1-Nile B2). 1:3

New Kingdom and TIP, Nile Fabrics

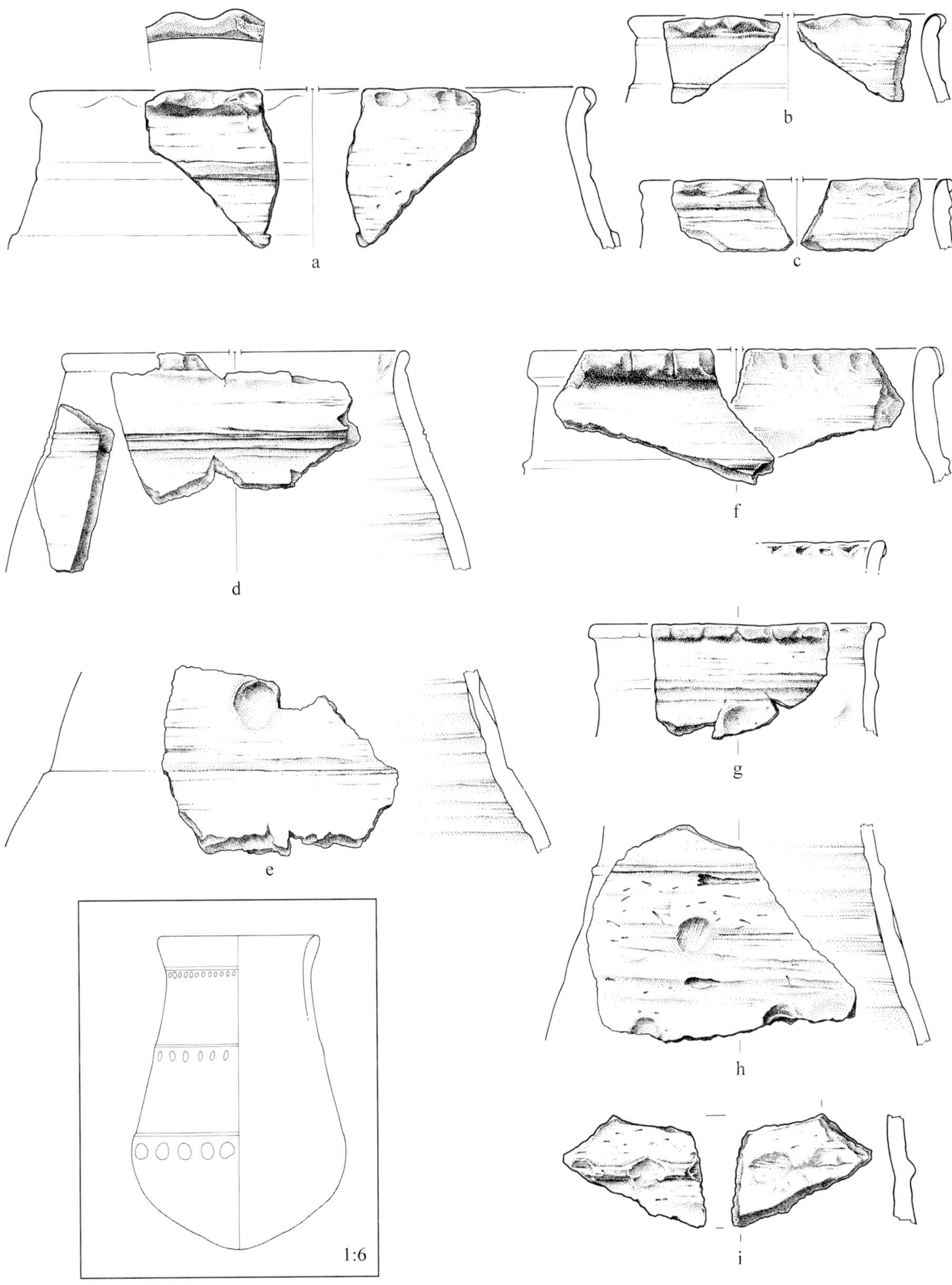

Figure. 80. (*a*) 659 ACE=AJH **39+40** (G1-Nile B2); (*b*) 659 ACE=AJH **38** (G1-Nile B2); (*c*) 659 AJH under AVH **56** (G1-Nile B2); (*d*) 659 AIW **4+6** etc (G1-Nile B2); (*e*) 659 AWD/AVF/AVG/AVJ/AVW/AVZ/AIS **7** etc (G1-Nile B2); (*f*) 659 BDW/ATT **2** (G1-Nile B2); (*g*) 659 AJH **95+132+151** etc (G1-Nile B2); (*h*) 659 AJH Lower **4** + AJH/AWX **40** (G1-Nile B2); (*i*) 659 AOR **3** (G1-Nile B2). (Inset) Vessel A72 from the Sacred Animal Necropolis (G1-Nile B2). 1:3

New Kingdom and TIP, Nile Fabrics

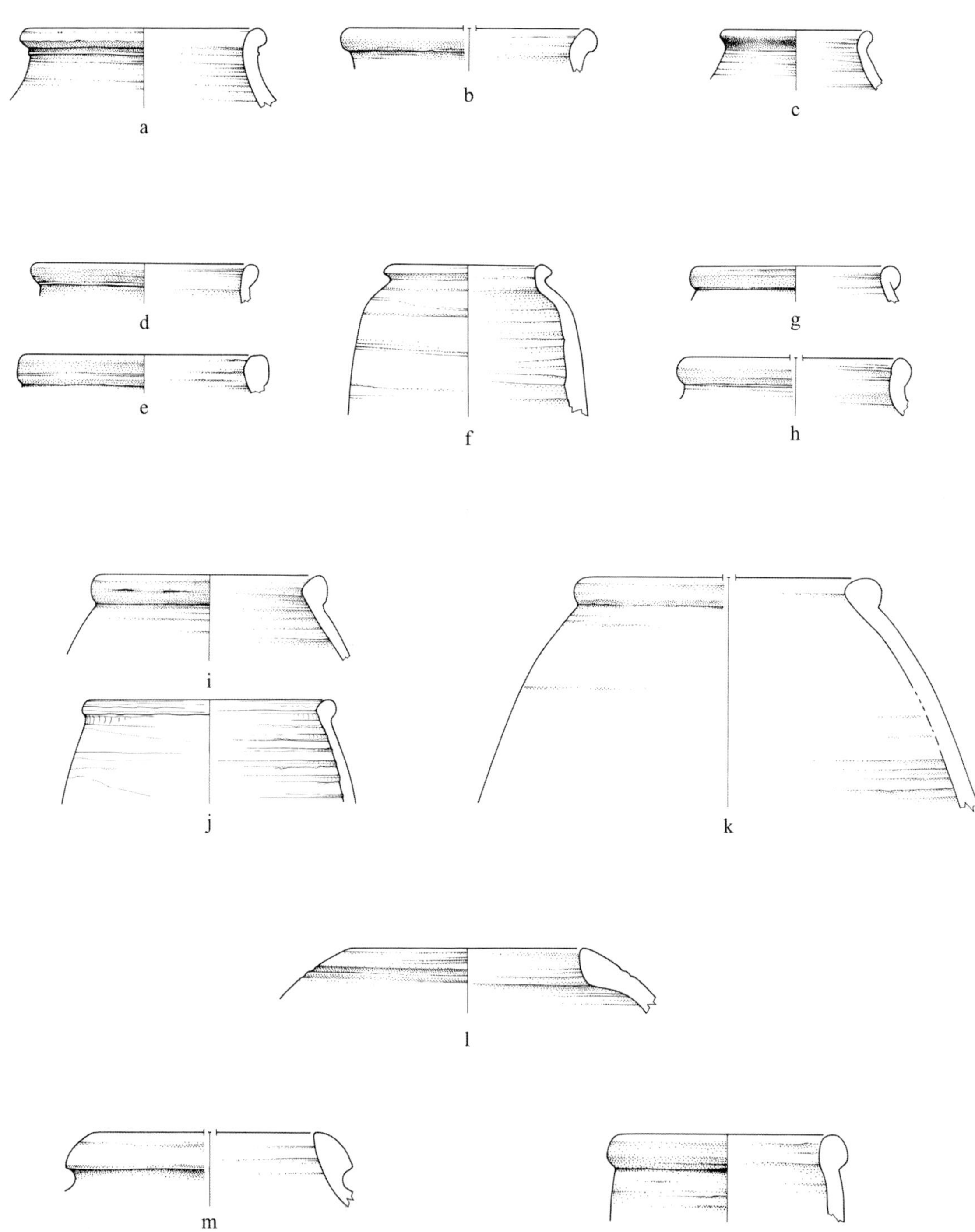

Figure 81. (*a*) **660** (G1-Nile B2); (*b*) **661** (G1-Nile B2); (*c*) **662** (G1-Nile B2); (*d*) **663** (G1-Nile B2); (*e*) **664** (G1-Nile B2); (*f*) **665** AQG **122** etc (G1-Nile B2); (*g*) **666** (G1-Nile B2); (*h*) **667** (G1-Nile B2); (*i*) **668** (G1-Nile B2); (*j*) **669** (G1-Nile B2); (*k*) **670** (G1-Nile B2); (*l*) **671** (G1-Nile B2); (*m*) **672** (G1-Nile B2); (*n*) **673** (G1-Nile B2). 1:3

New Kingdom and TIP, Nile Fabrics

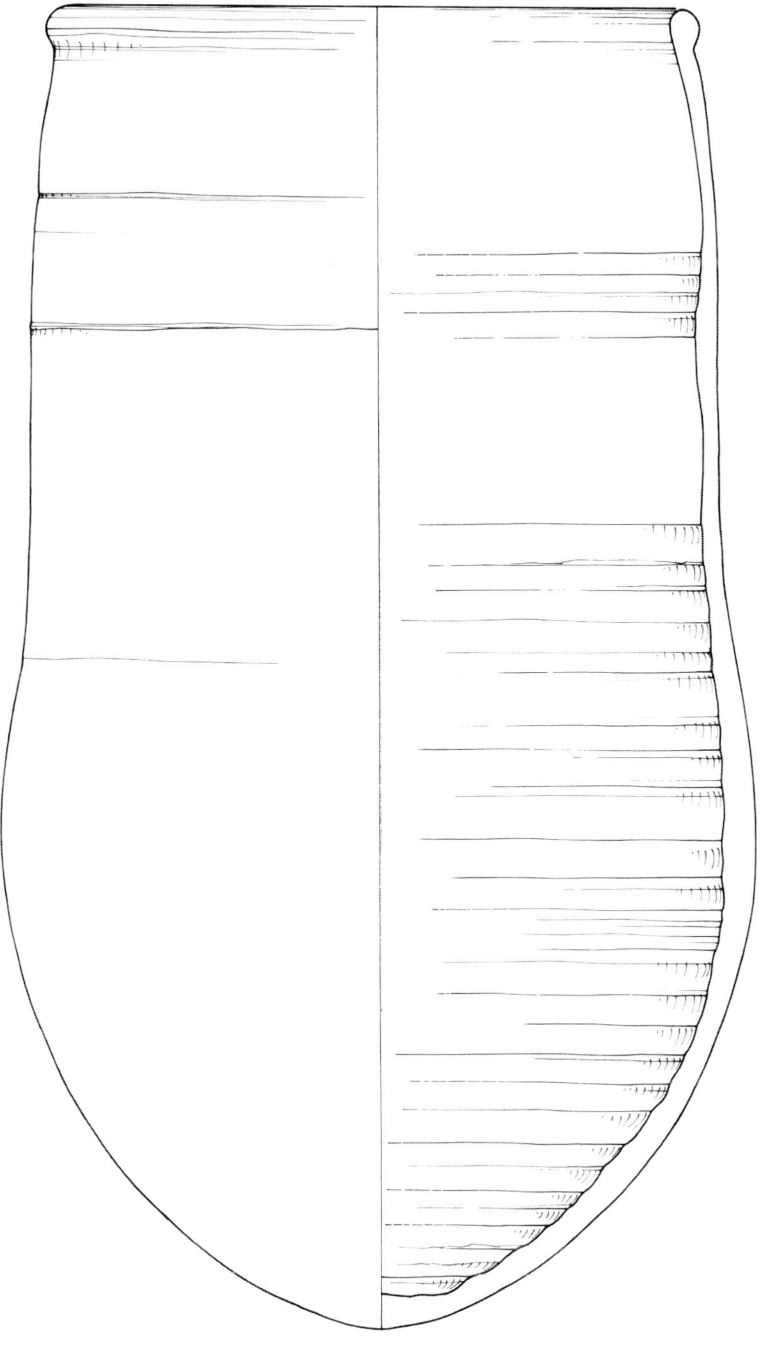

Figure 82. (*a*) **674** BJJ **2+3** etc (G1-Nile B2). 1:4

New Kingdom and TIP, Nile Fabrics

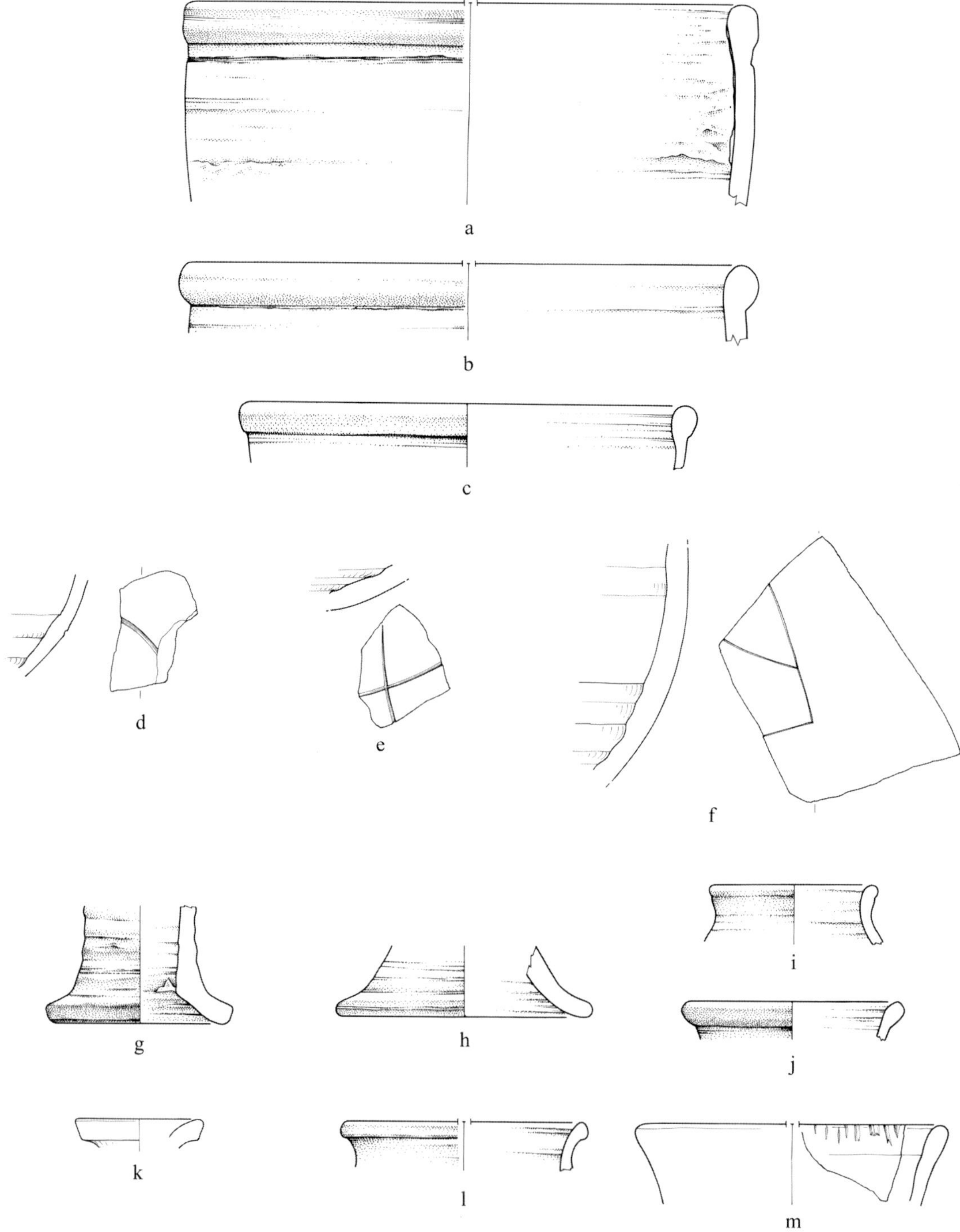

Figure 83. (*a*) **675** DAG **1** (G1-Nile B2 near G4-Nile C); (*b*) **676** (G1-Nile B2); (*c*) **677** (G1-Nile B2); (*d*) **678** (G1-Nile B2); (*e*) **679** AUQ **6** (G1-Nile B2); (*f*) **679** CBU **23** (G1-Nile B2); (*g*) **680** (G1-Nile B2); (*h*) **681** (G1-Nile B2); (*i*) **682** (G1-Nile B2); (*j*) **683** (G1-Nile B2); (*k*) **684** (G1-Nile B2); (*l*) **685** (G1-Nile B2); (*m*) **686** (G1-Nile B2). 1:3

New Kingdom and TIP, Nile Fabrics

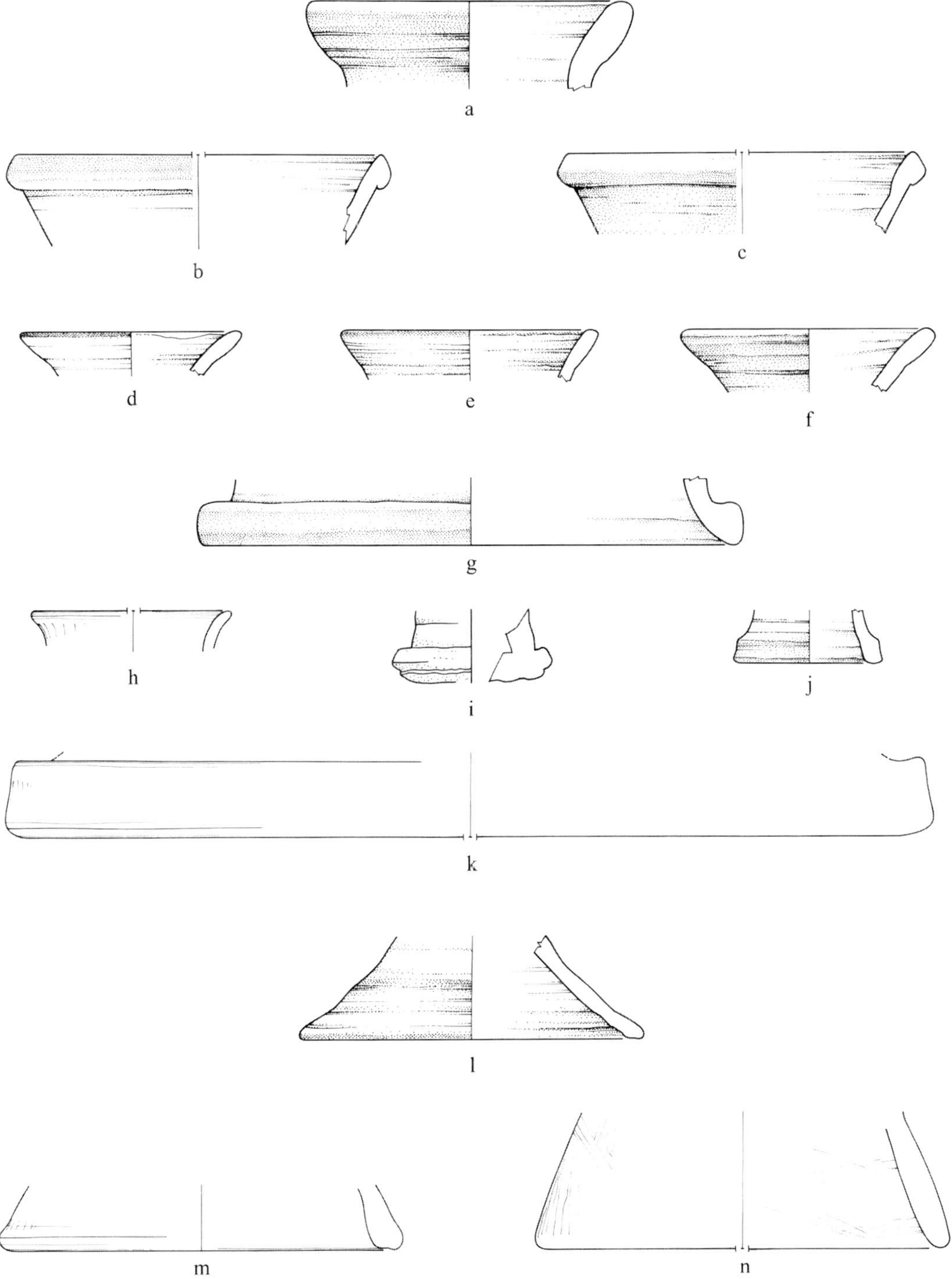

Figure 84. (*a*) **687** (G1-Nile B2); (*b*) **688** ADU **43** (G1-Nile B2); (*c*) **688** ABG **3** (G1-Nile B2); (*d*) **689** AQG/BEO **18** (G1-Nile B2); (*e*) **689** ACE=AJH **59** (G1-Nile B2); (*f*) **690** AUQ **109** (G1-Nile B2); (*g*) **691** (G1-Nile B2); (*h*) **692** (G1-Nile B2); (*i*) **693** (G1-Nile B2); (*j*) **694** (G1-Nile B2); (*k*) **695** (G1-Nile B2); (*l*) **696** (G1-Nile B2); (*m*) **697** (G1-Nile B2); (*n*) **698** (G1-Nile B2). 1:3

New Kingdom and TIP, Nile Fabrics

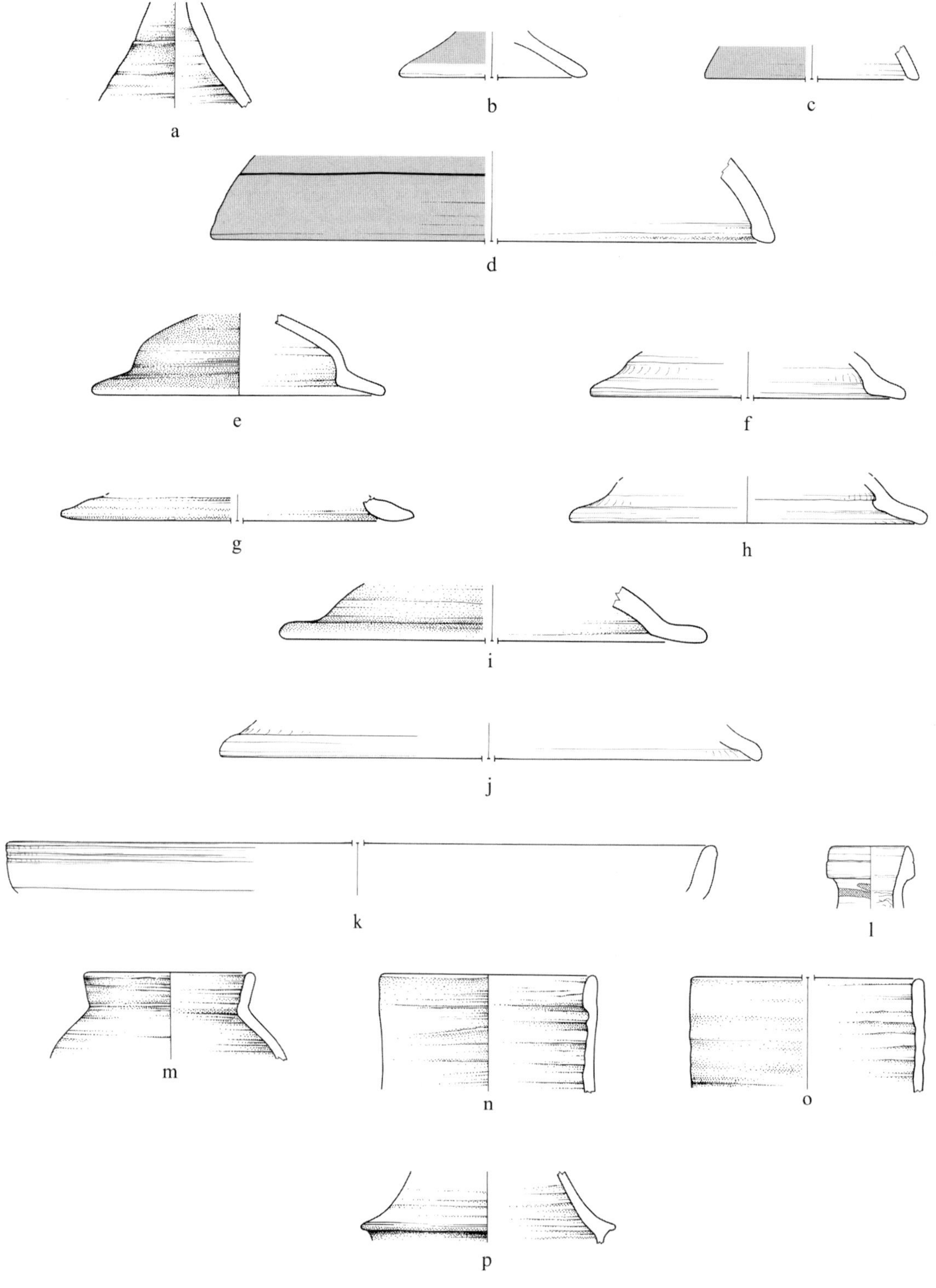

Figure 85. (*a*) **699** (G1-Nile B2); (*b*) **700** (G1-Nile B2); (*c*) **701** (G1-Nile B2); (*d*) **702** AAA **70** (G1-Nile B2); (*e*) **703** (G1-Nile B2); (*f*) **704** (G1-Nile B2); (*g*) **705** (G1-Nile B2); (*h*) **706** AQG **194** (G1-Nile B2); (*i*) **706** AQG/AJY **18** (G1-Nile B2); (*j*) **707** (G1-Nile B2); (*k*) **708** (G2-Nile B1); (*l*) **709** (G2-Nile B1); (*m*) **710** (G2-Nile B1); (*n*) **711** (G2-Nile B1); (*o*) **712** (G2-Nile B1); (*p*) **713** (G2-Nile B1). 1:3

New Kingdom and TIP, Nile Fabrics

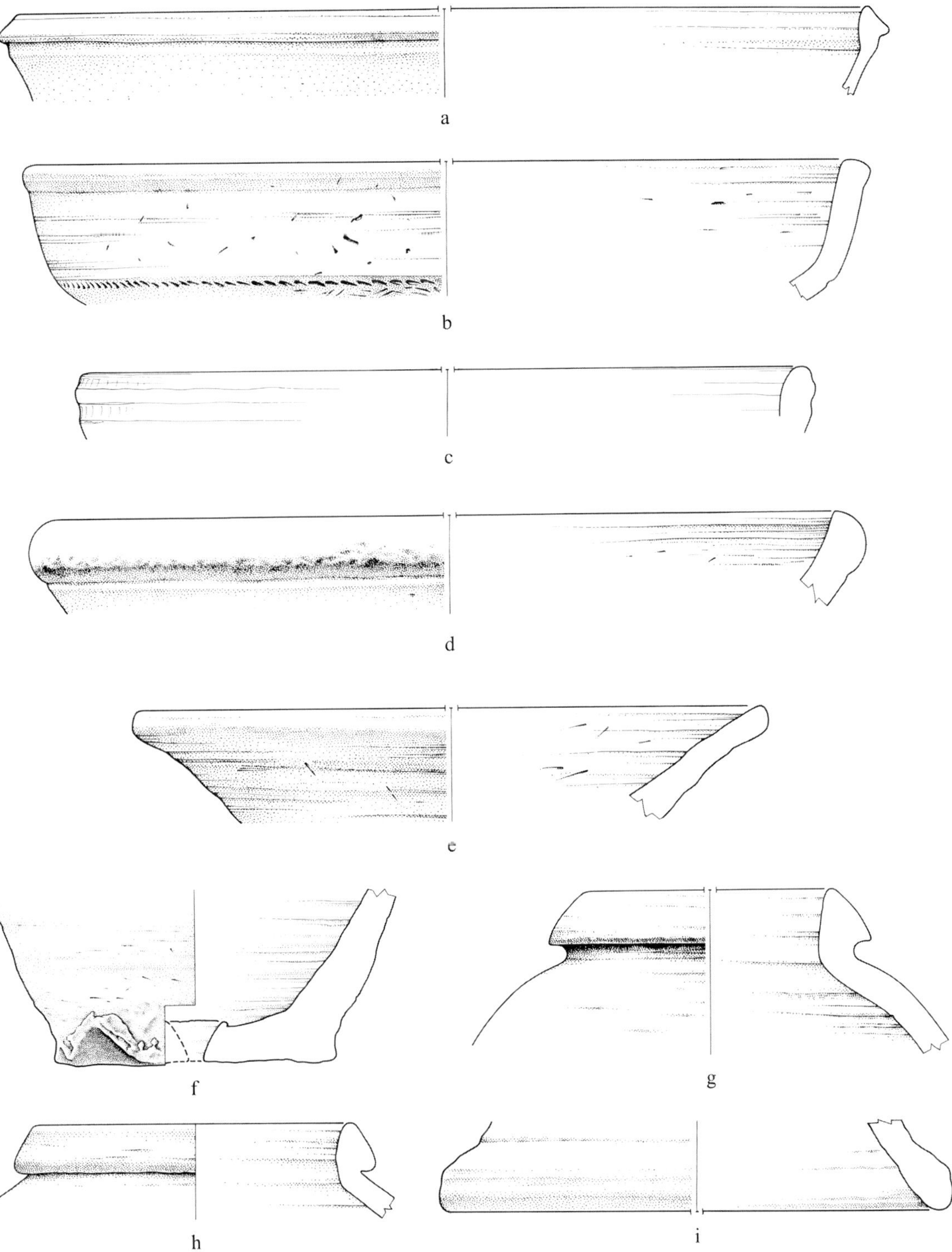

Figure 86. (*a*) 714 (G4-Nile C); (*b*) 715 (G4-Nile C); (*c*) 716 (G4-Nile C); (*d*) 717 (G4-Nile C); (*e*) 718 (G4-Nile C); (*f*) 719 (G4-Nile C); (*g*) 720 BGW **127** (G4-Nile C); (*h*) 720 BQQ **31** (G4-Nile C); (*i*) 721 (G4-Nile C). 1:3

New Kingdom and TIP, Nile Fabrics

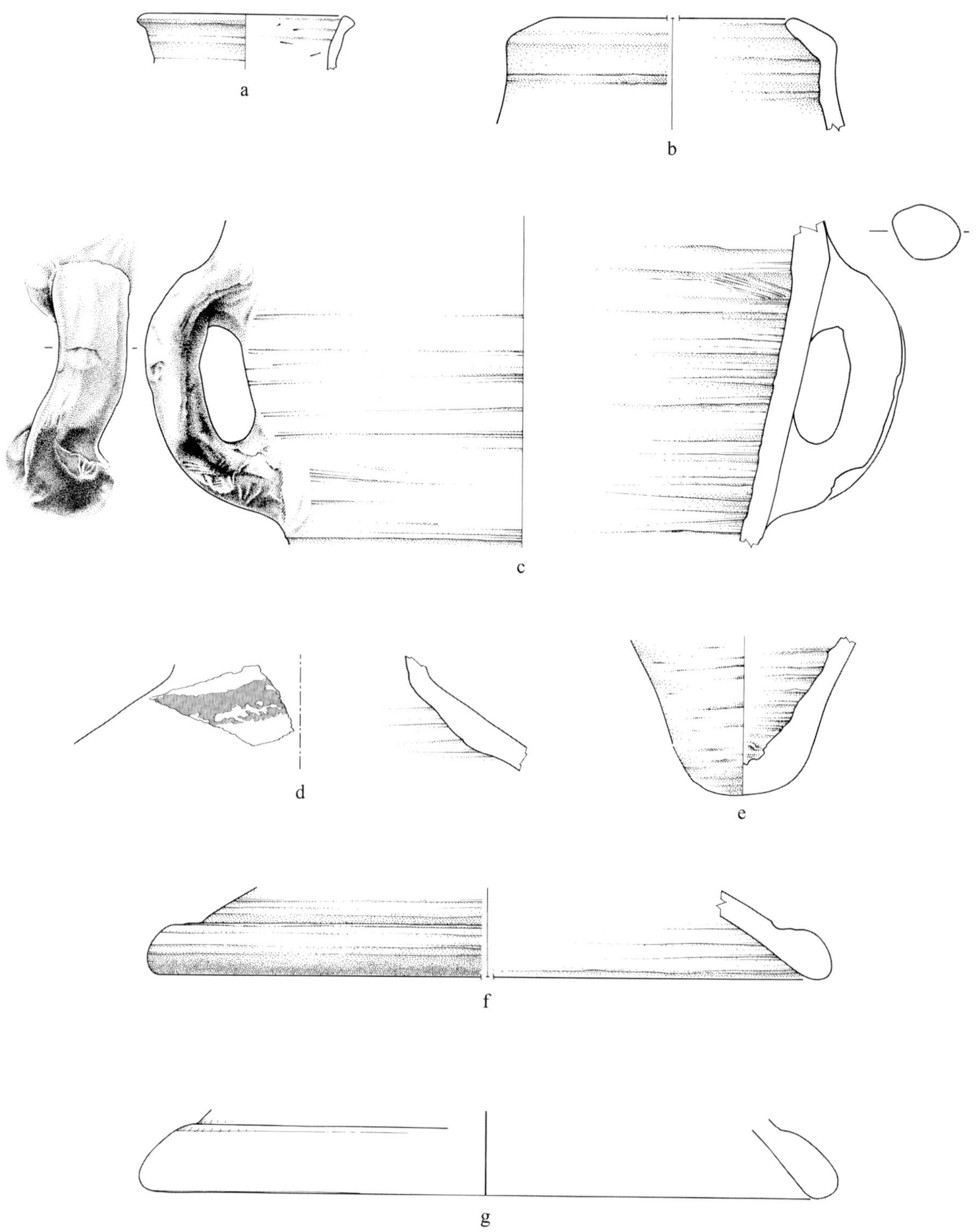

Figure 87. (*a*) **722** (G5-Nile D); (*b*) **723** (G5-Nile D); (*c*) **724** (G5-Nile D); (*d*) **726** (G6a); (*e*) **727** (G6a); (*f*) **730** CEG **50** (G6a); (*g*) **730** ADF North **46** (G6a). 1:3

New Kingdom and TIP, Marl Fabrics

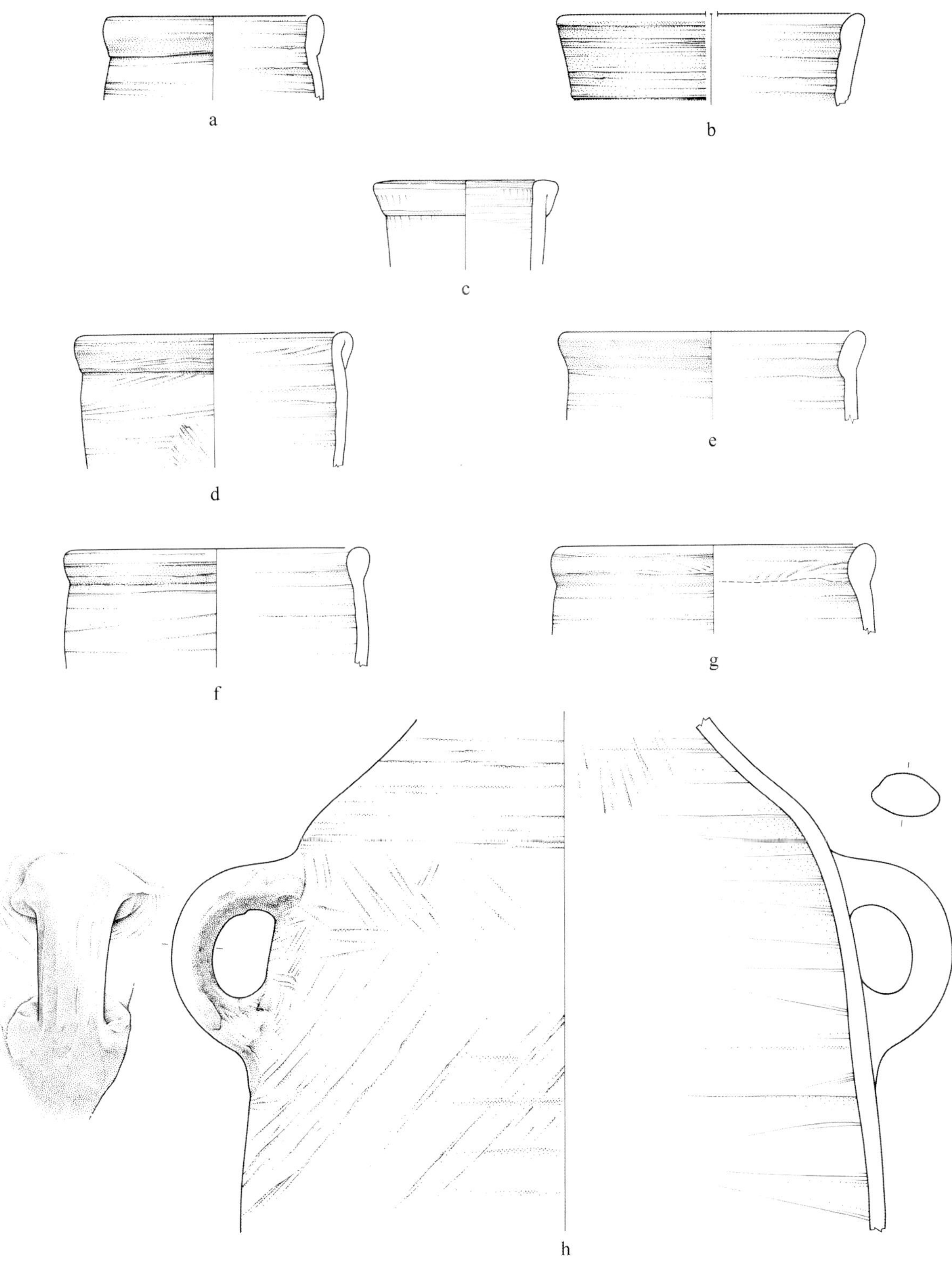

Figure 88. (*a*) 731 (H1-Marl D); (*b*) 732 (H1-Marl D); (*c*) 733 (H1-Marl D); (*d*) 734 ACE **1** (H1-Marl D); (*e*) 734 CBS **55** (H1-Marl D); (*f*) 734 AAA **81** (H1-Marl D); (*g*) 734 AAA **56** (H1-Marl D); (*h*) 735 BJO (A+C) **1** + BJG/BJO (A+C) **7+28** (H1-Marl D). 1:3

New Kingdom and TIP, Marl Fabrics

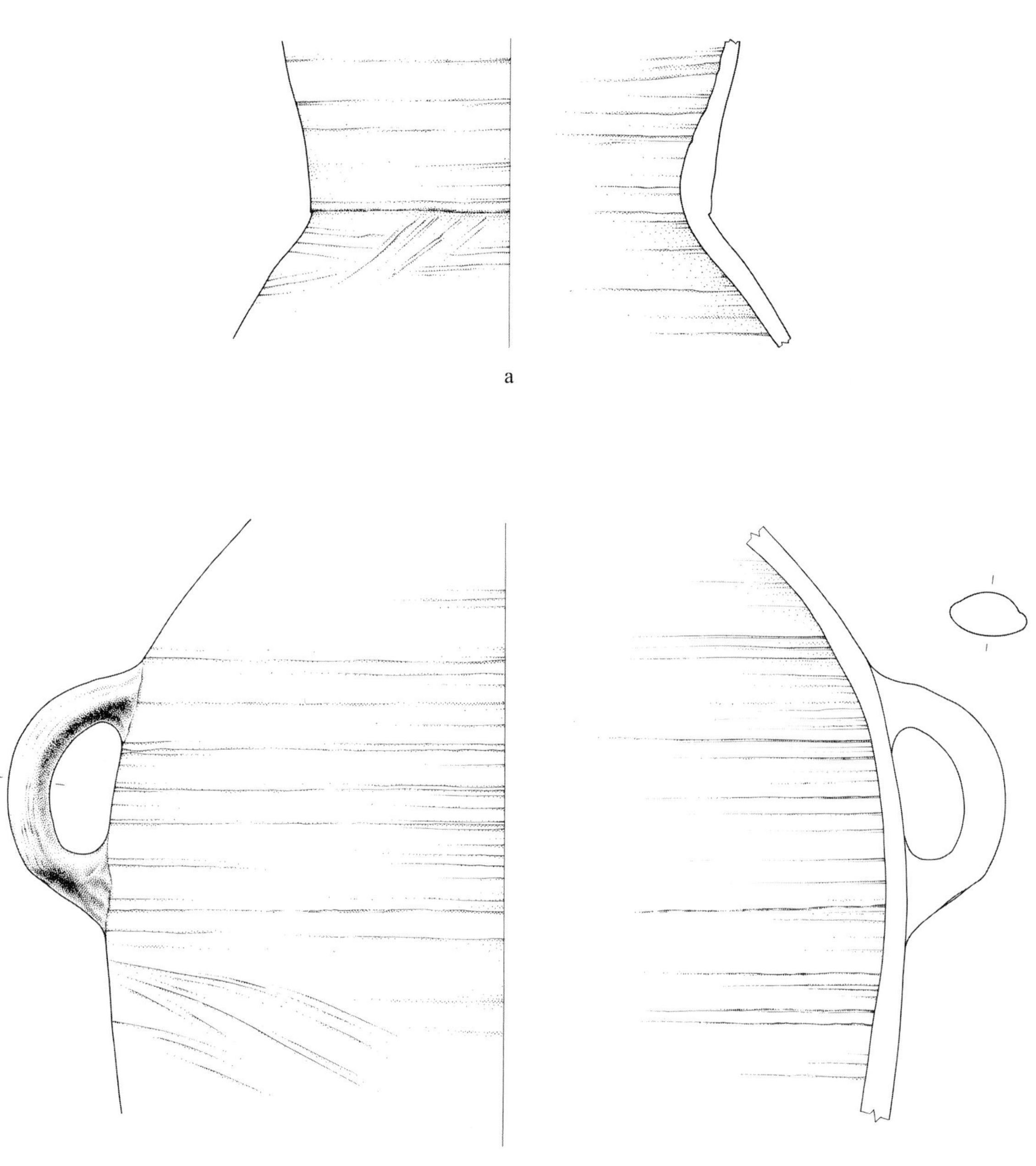

Figure 89. (*a*) 735 BGG **26** + BGH **18** (H1-Marl D); (*b*) 735 BGH **1+9+10+13+16** (H1-Marl D). 1:3

New Kingdom and TIP, Marl Fabrics

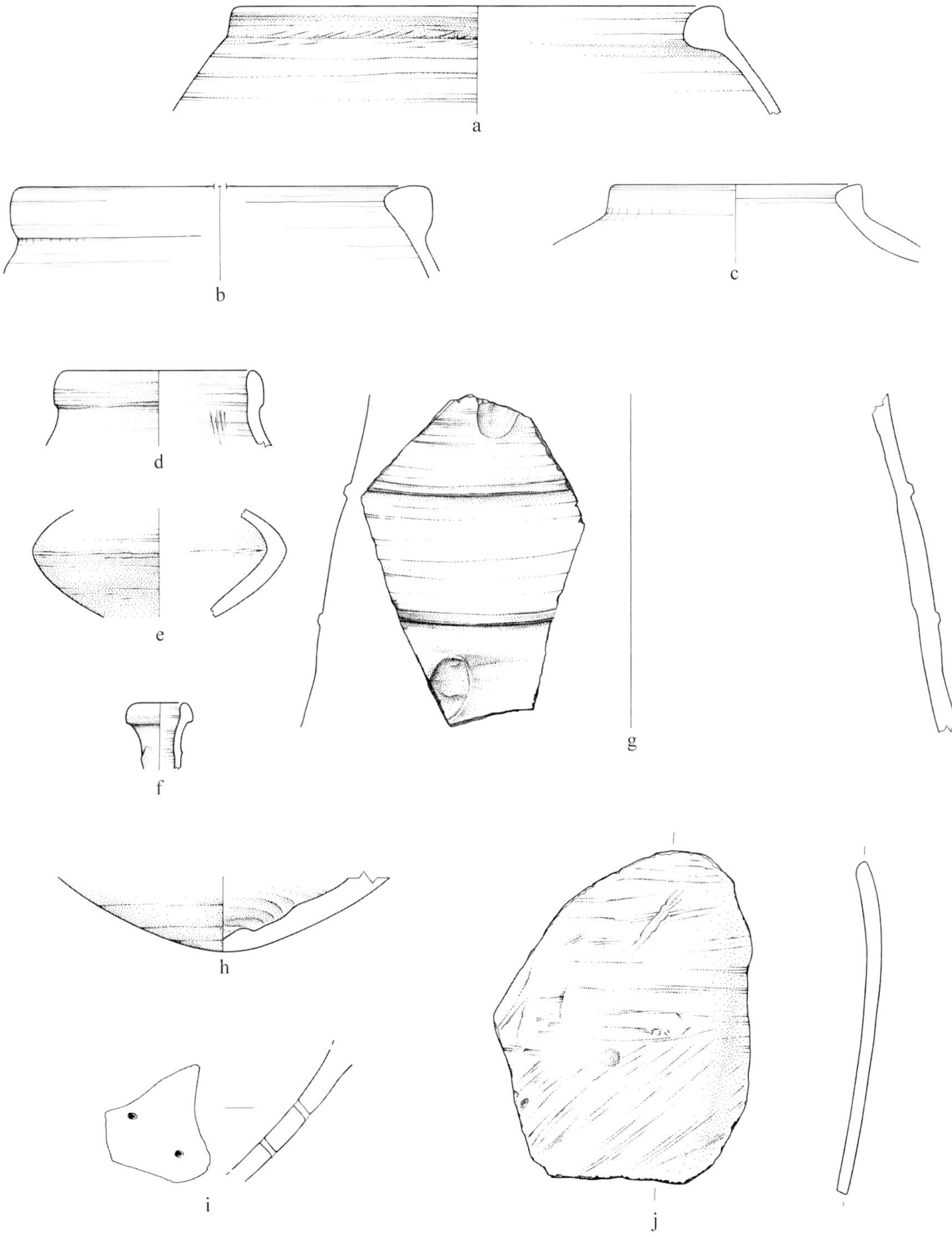

Figure 90. (*a*) **737** (H1-Marl D); (*b*) **738** (H1-Marl D); (*c*) **739** (H1-Marl D); (*d*) **741** (H1-Marl D); (*e*) **742** (H1-Marl D); (*f*) **743** (H1-Marl D); (*g*) **740** AJH **113** etc (H1-Marl D); (*h*) **744** AQG **85+155** (H1-Marl D); (*i*) **754** BQS **6** (H1-Marl D); (*j*) **745** BJG/BJO(H) **42** (H1-Marl D). 1:3

New Kingdom and TIP, Marl Fabrics

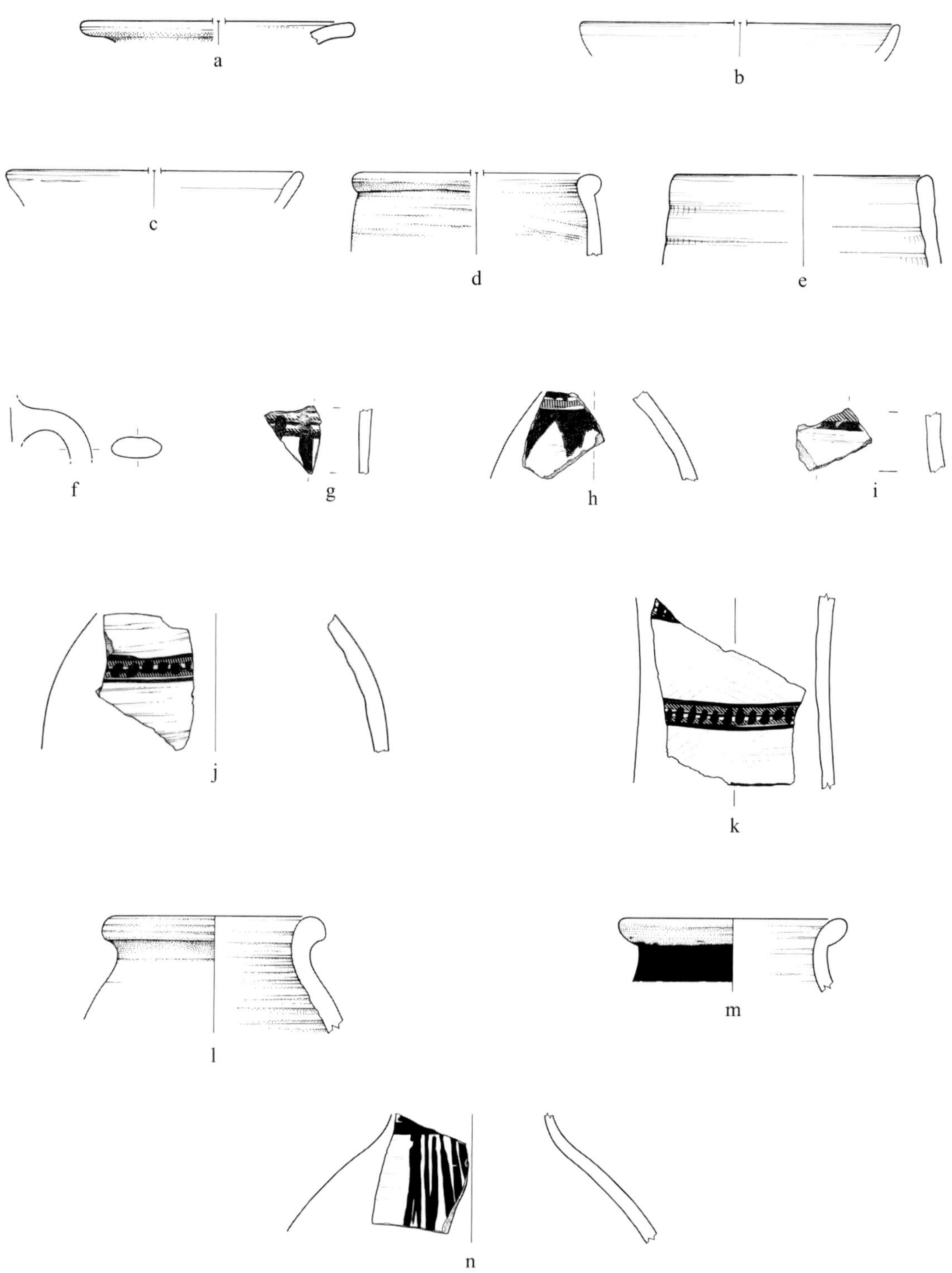

Figure 91. (*a*) **746** (H2-Marl A4); (*b*) **747** (H2-Marl A4); (*c*) **748** (H2-Marl A4); (*d*) **749** (H2-Marl A4); (*e*) **750** (H2-Marl A4); (*f*) **751** (H2-Marl A4); (*g*) **752** BAX **47** (H2-Marl A4); (*h*) **752** BNE **71** (H2-Marl A4); (*i*) **752** AAB Lower **15** (H2-Marl A4); (*j*) **752** DAW **12** (H2-Marl A4); (*k*) **752** DAJ **4** (H2-Marl A4); (*l*) **754** (H4-Marl A4); (*m*) **755** (H4-Marl A4); (*n*) **756** (H4-Marl A4). 1:3

New Kingdom and TIP, Marl Fabrics

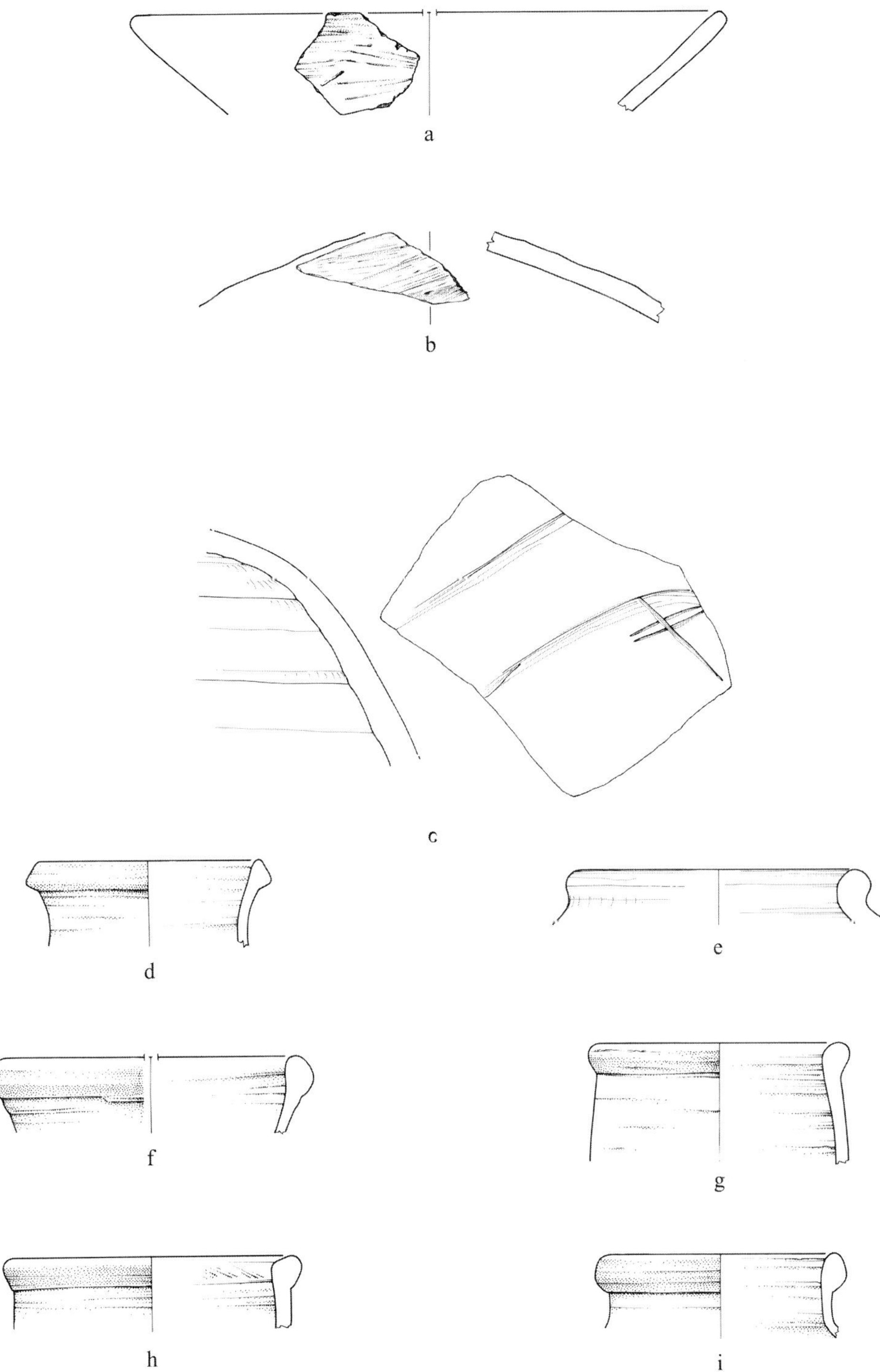

Figure 92. (*a*) 759 (H8-Marl B); (*b*) 761 BDY **3** (H8-Marl B); (*c*) 762 (H8-Marl B); (*d*) 763 (H10-Marl A2); (*e*) 764 (H10-Marl A2); (*f*) 765 (H14-Marl D); (*g*) 766 BHS **235** (H14-Marl D); (*h*) 766 AEP/AEQ/AER **25** (H14-Marl D); (*i*) 768 (H14-Marl D). 1:3

New Kingdom and TIP, Mixed Clay Fabrics

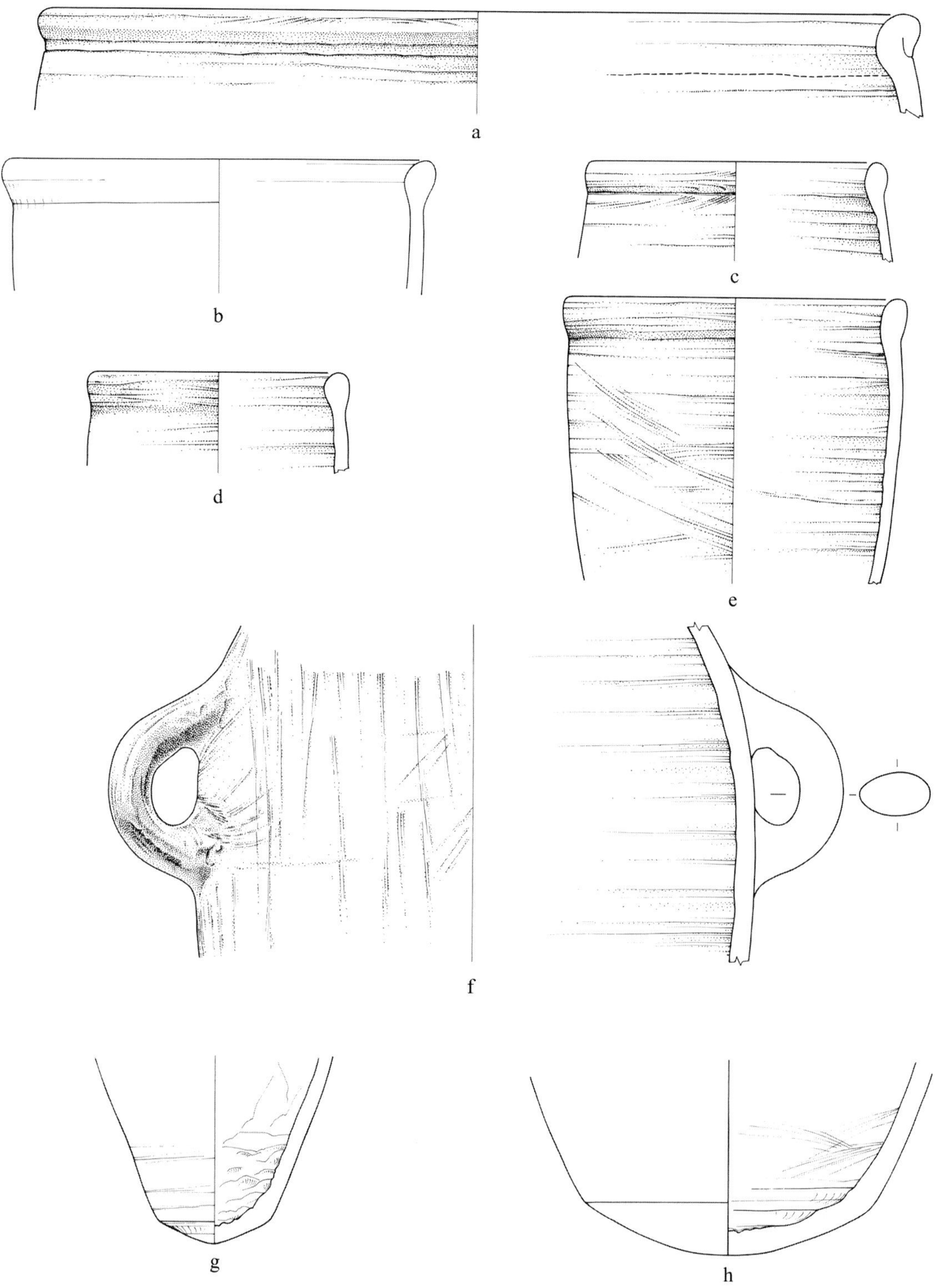

Figure 93. (*a*) 770 (Mixed Clay Fabric 1); (*b*) 771 AEP/AEQ/AER **19** (Mixed Clay Fabric 1); (*c*) 771 AAA **24** (Mixed Clay Fabric 1); (*d*) 771 AAA **135** (Mixed Clay Fabric 1); (*e*) 771 AAA **31** (Mixed Clay Fabric 1); (*f*) 772 AAA **3** (Mixed Clay Fabric 1); (*g*) 773A (Mixed Clay Fabric 1); (*h*) 773B (Mixed Clay Fabric 1). 1:3

New Kingdom and TIP, Mixed Clay Fabrics

Figure 94. (*a*) 774 DAF **3** etc (Mixed Clay Fabric 1); (*b*) 774 AAA **117** + AAA **12** (Mixed Clay Fabric 1); (*c*) 774 AAA **119** + AAA **2** (Mixed Clay Fabric 1).

1:3

New Kingdom and TIP, Mixed Clay Fabrics

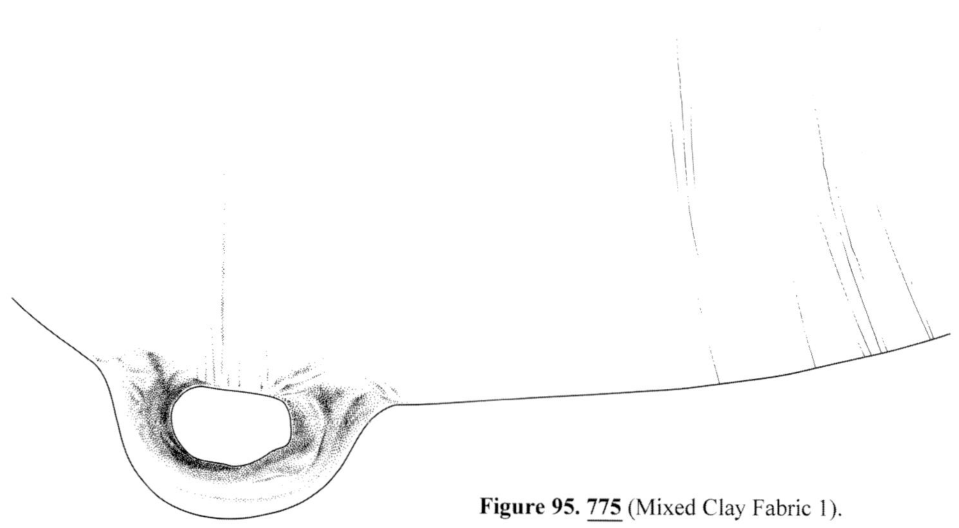

Figure 95. 775 (Mixed Clay Fabric 1). 1:3

New Kingdom and TIP, Mixed Clay and Oasis Fabrics

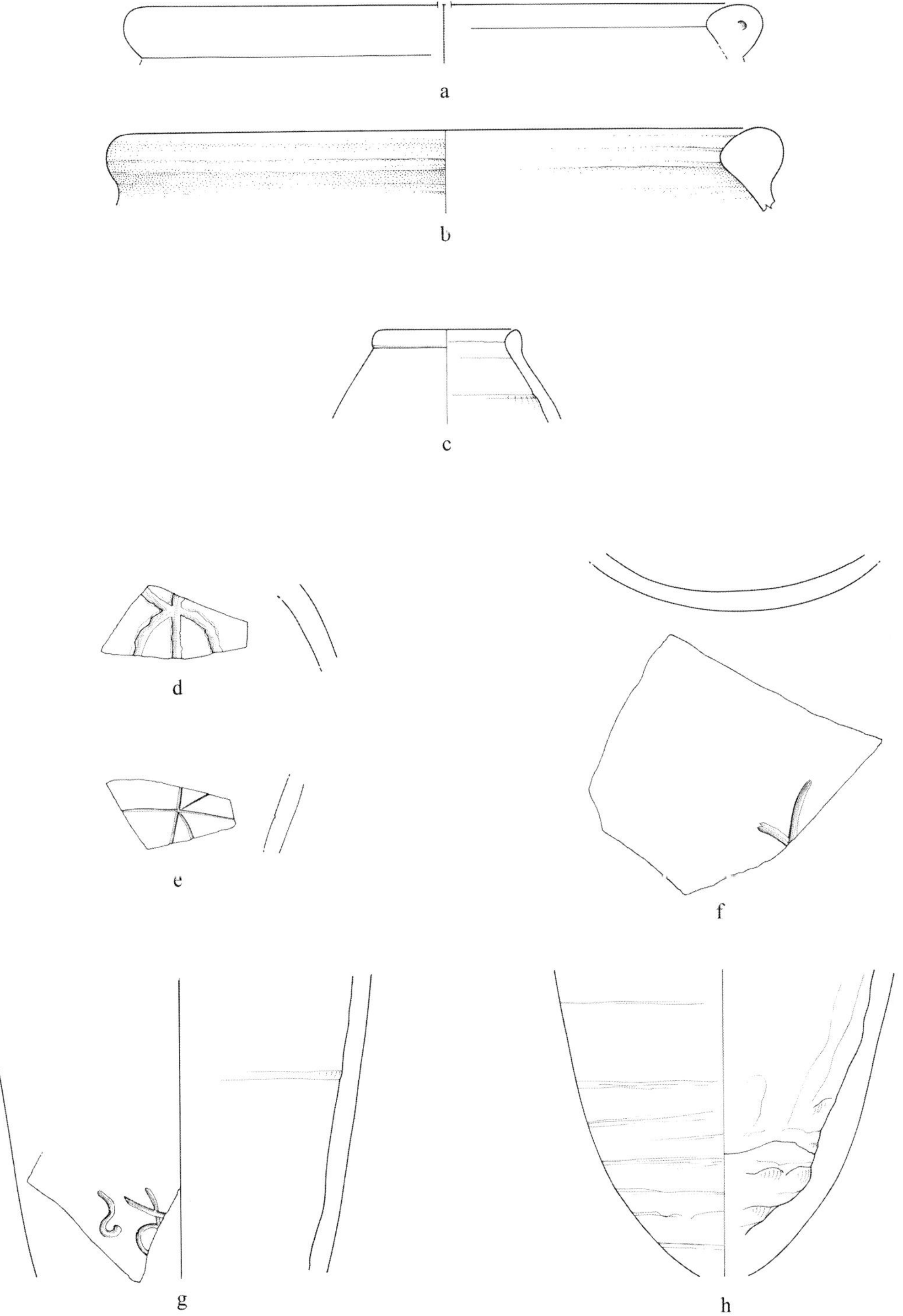

Figure 96. (*a*) 776 BMG **16** (Mixed Clay Fabric 1); (*b*) 776 AAA **144** (Mixed Clay Fabric 1); (*c*) 777 (Mixed Clay Fabric 1); (*d*) 778 ACE **264** (Mixed Clay Fabric 1); (*e*) 778 BAC **361** (Mixed Clay Fabric 1); (*f*) 778 DAC **20** (Mixed Clay Fabric 1); (*g*) 778 UP 8 **49** (Mixed Clay Fabric 1); (*h*) 782 (P44-Oasis Clay). 1:3

New Kingdom and TIP, Imported Fabrics

Figure 97. (*a*) 785 (P30-Canaanite); (*b*) 786 AAA **379** (P30-Canaanite); (*c*) 787 CGN **2** (P31-Canaanite); (*d*) 787 BGI **10** (P31-Canaanite); (*e*) 790 (Canaanite (?) fabric); (*f*) 789 AAA **280** (P40-Canaanite). 1:3

New Kingdom and TIP, Imported Fabrics

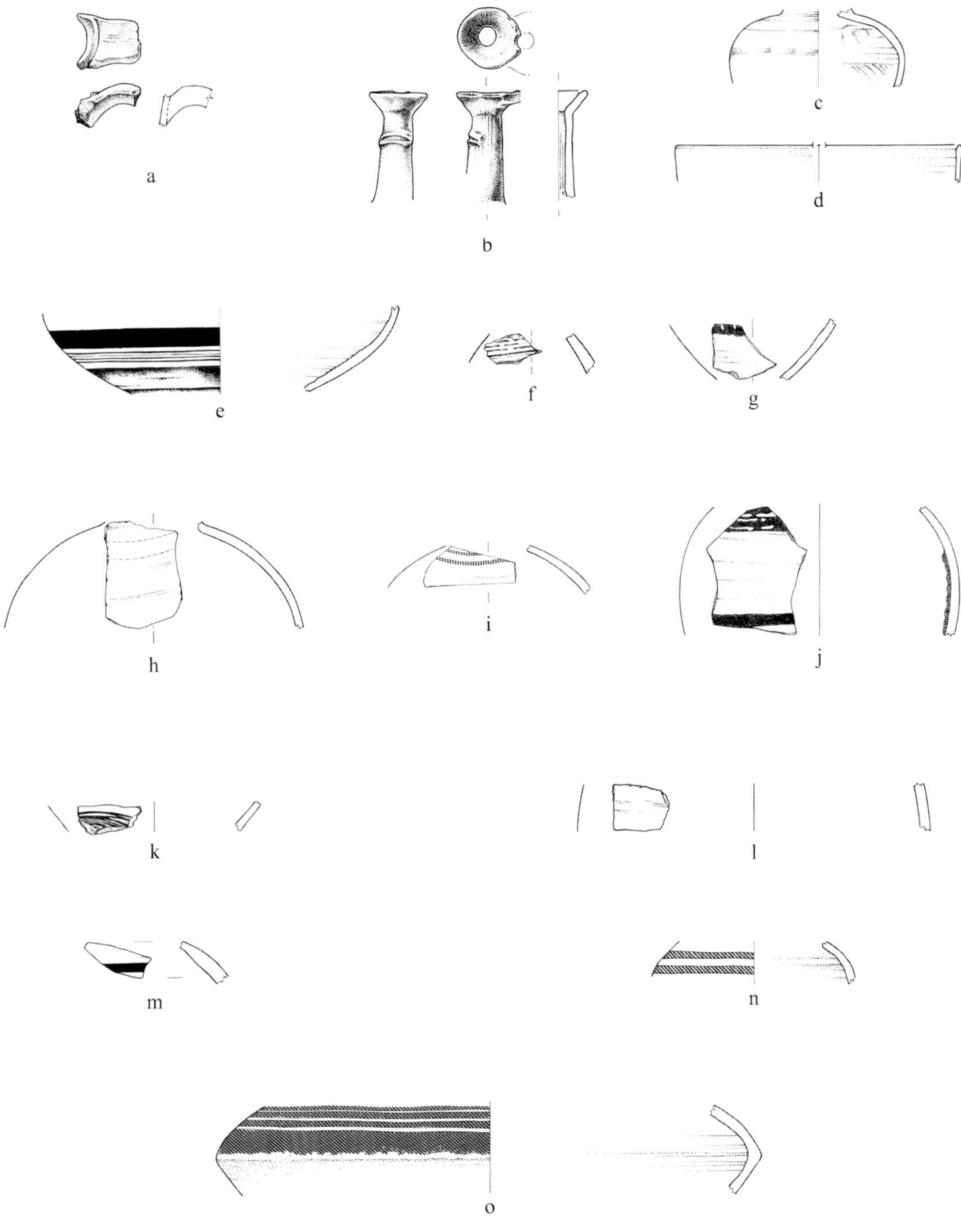

Figure 98. (*a*) 791 (P32-Cypriot); (*b*) 794 (P7-Cypriot); (*c*) 795 (P7-Cypriot); (*d*) 796 (P7-Cypriot); (*e*) 797 (P4-Mycenaean); (*f*) 798 (P4-Mycenaean); (*g*) 799 BDY **19** (P4-Mycenaean); (*h*) 799 ADF **1+2** (P4-Mycenaean); (*i*) 799 ADF **4** (P4-Mycenaean); (*j*) 799 ADF **5** (P4-Mycenaean); (*k*) 800 (P4-Mycenaean); (*l*) 801 (P4-Mycenaean); (*m*) 802 (P4(?)-Mycenaean); (*n*) 803 (Unknown origin); (*o*) 804 (Unknown origin). 1:3